W9-AJO-238

Duane Champagne has been teaching at the University of California, Los Angeles, since 1984. In 1986, he became editor of the *American Indian Culture and Research Journal* and went on to be named associate professor in 1992.

Dr. Champagne received a postdoctoral award from the Rockefeller Foundation in 1982–83 and, during this time, completed fieldwork trips to the Tlingit of southeast Alaska and to the Northern Cheyenne in Montana.

Most of Dr. Champagne's writings focus on issues of social, cultural, and political change in American Indian societies as they adapted to European political, cultural, and economic incorporation. He has published in both the sociology and American Indian studies fields, including his two books *American Indian Societies: Strategies and Conditions of Political and Cultural Survival* (1989) and *Social Order and Political Change: Constitutional Governments Among the Cherokee, the Choctaw, the Chickasaw, and the Creek* (1992).

Dr. Champagne is also the director of the UCLA American Indian Studies Center, which carries out research, conducts a master's degree program in American Indian studies, and publishes books for both academic and Indian communities.

Reference Library of

NATIVE NORTH AMERICA

THE NATIVE NORTH AMERICAN ALMANAC

VOLUME

I

Duane Champagne,
editor

Multiculture In Print

Distributed by Educational Guidance Service,
African American Publications and Proteus Enterprises

The Native North American Almanac
Edited by Duane Champagne
ISBN 0-8103-8865-0

This book is printed on acid-free paper that meets the minimum requirements of American National Standards for Information Sciences –Permanence Paper for Printer Library Materials, ANSI Z39.48-1984.

Printed in the United States of America

10 9 8 7 6 5 4 3 2

Board of Advisors

Editorial Team

Contributing Authors

Frances Abele, *School of Public Administration, Carleton University, Ottawa, Ontario, Canada*
Angela Aleiss, *American Indian Studies Center, University of California, Los Angeles, California*
Gary Anders, *Institute of International Business, Phoenix, Arizona*
Robert Appleford, *Graduate Centre for the Study of Drama, University of Toronto, Toronto, Ontario, Canada*
Russel Barsh, *American Indian Studies, University of Washington, Seattle, Washington*
Janet Berlo, *Department of Art History, Washington University, St. Louis, Missouri*
Ted Binnema, *History Department, University of Alberta, Edmonton, Alberta, Canada*
Daniel Boxberger, *Department of Anthropology, Western Washington University, Bellingham, Washington*
William Bright, *Department of Linguistics, University of Colorado, Boulder, Colorado*
Edward Castillo, *Native American Studies, Sonoma State University, Rohnert Park, California*
Duane Champagne, *American Indian Studies Center, University of California, Los Angeles, California*
Katherine Beaty Chiste, *Department of Social Sciences, University of Lethbridge, Lethbridge, Alberta, Canada*
Richmond Clow, *Native American Studies, University of Montana, Missoula, Montana*
Ken Coates, *Department of History, University of Northern British Columbia, Victoria, British Columbia, Canada*

Margaret Crow, *California Indian Legal Services, Oakland, California*
David de Jong, *Prescott High School, Prescott, Arizona*
Henry Dobyns, *Independent Consultant, Tucson, Arizona*
Leroy Eid, *Department of History, University of Dayton, Dayton, Ohio*
Donald Fixico, *Department of History, Western Michigan University, Kalamazoo, Michigan*
Linda Fritz, *Library, University of Saskatoon, Saskatoon, Saskatchewan, Canada*
Hanay Geiogamah, *Theater Department, University of California, Los Angeles, California*
Ian Getty, *Research Director, Stoney Tribe, Nakota Institute, Calgary, Alberta, Canada*
Carole Goldberg-Ambrose, *School of Law, University of California, Los Angeles, California*
Donald Grinde, *History Department, California Polytechnic State University, San Luis Obispo, California*
Charlotte Heth, *Department of Ethnomusicology, University of California, Los Angeles, California*
Ann Hodes, *Health Services Center, University of Alberta, Edmonton, Alberta, Canada*
Felicia Hodge, *American Indian Cancer Control Project, Berkeley, California*
Cornelius Jaenen, *Department of History, University of Ottawa, Ottawa, Ontario, Canada*
Jennie Joe, *Native American Research and Training Center, University of Arizona, Tucson, Arizona*
Judy Kopp, *School of Social Work, University of Washington, Seattle, Washington*
Daniel Littlefield, *Department of English, University of Arkansas, Little Rock, Arkansas*
John D. Loftin, *Loftin & Loftin, Hillsborough, North Carolina*
J. Anthony Long, *Department of Political Science, University of Lethbridge, Lethbridge, Alberta, Canada*
David C. Mass, *Department of Political Science, University of Alaska, Anchorage, Alaska*
Donald McCaskill, *Department of Native Studies, Trent University, Peterborough, Ontario, Canada*
Alan McMillan, *Department of Archaeology, Simon Frazier College, Port Moody, British Columbia, Canada*
Howard L. Meredith, *Cookson Institute, Oklahoma City, Oklahoma*
Dorothy Lonewolf Miller, *Native American Research and Training Center, University of Arizona, Tucson, Arizona*
Patrick C. Morris, *American Indian Studies, University of Washington, Bothell, Washington*
Ken Morrison, *Religious Studies, Arizona State University, Tempe, Arizona*
Bradford Morse, *Faculty of Law, University of Ottawa, Ottawa, Ontario, Canada*
Joane Nagel, *Department of Sociology, University of Kansas, Lawrence, Kansas*
Sharon O'Brien, *Department of Government, University of Notre Dame, Notre Dame, Indiana*
James O'Donnell III, *Department of History, Marietta College, Marietta, Ohio*
Michael O'Donnell, *Salish Kootenai Community College, Pablo, Montana*
Roxanne Dunbar Ortiz, *Department of History, California State University, Hayward, California*
David Penney, *Detroit Institute of Art, Detroit, Michigan*
Daniel Rogers, *Department of Anthropology, Smithsonian Institution, Washington, D.C.*
Kathryn W. Shanley, *Department of English, Cornell University, Ithaca, New York*
C. Matthew Snipp, *Department of Rural Sociology, University of Wisconsin, Madison, Wisconsin*
Rennard Strickland, *School of Law, University of Oklahoma, Norman, Oklahoma*
Paul Stuart, *School of Social Welfare, University of Alabama, Tuscaloosa, Alabama*
Imre Sutton, *Department of Geography, California State University, Fullerton, California*
Karen Swisher, *College of Education, Arizona State University, Tempe, Arizona*
Steve Talbot, *Department of Sociology and Anthropology, San Joaquin College, Stockton, California*
Clifford Trafzer, *Department of Ethnic Studies, University of California, Riverside,California*
Ronald Trosper, *Department of Forestry, Northern Arizona University, Flagstaff, Arizona*
Daniel Usner, *History Department, Cornell University, Ithaca, New York*
Joan Vastokas, *Department of Anthropology, Trent University, Peterborough, Ontario, Canada*

Brother,

When you first came to this island

you were as children, in need of food and shelter,

and we, a great and mighty nation.

But we took you by the hand

and we planted you and watered you

and you grew to be a great oak,

we a mere sapling in comparison.

Now we are the children

(in need of food and shelter).

An opening speech often used by Northeastern Indian leaders at conferences with Europeans during the early colonial period.

Highlights

Persons interested in a comprehensive reference providing information on all aspects of the Native American and Canadian experience can turn to one accurate source: *The Native North American Almanac.* The first sixteen chapters are composed of signed essays, annotated directory information, and documentary excerpts; the final chapter presents more than 470 concise biographies of prominent Native North Americans. The *Native North American Almanac* covers a broad scope of topics, including:

- History and historical landmarks
- Health
- Law and legislation
- Major culture areas
- Activism
- Environment
- Urbanization and non-reservation populations
- Administration
- Education
- Economy
- Languages
- Demography
- Religion
- Arts
- Literature
- Media

Arrangement Allows for Quick Information Access

The Native North American Almanac provides a wealth of information, and its logical format makes it easy to use. The chapters contain subject-specific bibliographies and are enlivened by 400 photographs, maps, and charts. Other value-added features include:

- Contents section details each chapter's coverage, including directories and bibliographies.
- Alphabetical and geographical lists of tribes
- Multimedia bibliography of sources for further reading and research
- Glossary of Native terms
- A detailed listing of illustrations found in the text
- Comprehensive keyword index listing tribe and band names (with alternate spellings), personal names, important events, and geographic locations
- Detailed occupational index giving insight into Natives who have excelled in their field of endeavor

Contents

Volume I

Volume II

Volume III

Volume IV

Acknowledgments

The undertaking of this volume was a far greater task than originally anticipated, and a great many people contributed to its compilation, writing, editing, and production. I am greatly honored to express my thanks to my fifty-eight colleagues who contributed their manuscripts, and who saw the need and value and provided the inspiration for putting together a reference book about contemporary Native North American peoples. We all share the same vision and the understanding of having put forth our best efforts for a worthy cause. Special thanks must be given to associate editor Troy Johnson, who took on the responsibility of herding in the manuscripts, as well as many thankless tasks that ensured the total production would finally see the light of day. Without Troy's able assistance, the task would have been much more difficult.

Great credit and thanks are due to people at Gale Research Inc. for their vision and support. Chris Nasso deserves special recognition for developing the idea and groundwork for the volume; our readers and the Native peoples are indebted to her for her sympathetic foresight. The Gale editors made workable a long and difficult project. Leslie Joseph started the project, but soon left it in the capable hands of Carol Nagel, to whom we give special thanks for her guidance and understanding. Jane Hoehner also deserves special mention for her willingness to assume a complicated project and guide it to completion.

Special mention must also be made of our advisory board. I fondly remember the two days in early summer 1991 when we hammered out the outline and basic entry assignments for the entire volume. These sessions are a testament that hard work and engaging company need not be separate events. G. Edward Evans, in particular, provided many insights and a guiding hand, and for this we are grateful.

Many of my friends and associates provided valuable contributions, and I take this opportunity to give them thanks. Roselle Kipp provided greatly needed help in preparing manuscripts and securing photographs; Velma Salabiye worked diligently on the bibliographies; Judith St. George, a mainstay for the entire project, took on the burden of typesetting the manuscript, and we all give thanks for her care, understanding, and concern for creating a quality product. Steve Lehmer, our photographic editor, has been an inspiration to us all by tackling new technologies and contributing greatly to enlivening the book with his experience and concern for photography of Native peoples. The book was greatly improved by Steve's contribution. Michael Bogart, our mapmaker, labored hard, and we thank him and appreciate his diligent efforts; Imre Sutton took the time to look over the maps and provide numerous corrections and suggestions for improvement; both Janet Coulon and Linda Jenkins provided valued editorial contributions, and we thank them.

Too numerous to thank are the people who helped collect the many illustrations and photographs. Special thanks to Paula Fleming at the Smithsonian Institution. We also acknowledge Jamie Smith and John Copeland from Rattlesnake Productions, who generously shared their treasure trove of photographs and information.

My family deserves special mention, since this project consumed much of my time, and I could not share with them the time that I wanted. From Demelza, my youngest daughter, I seek forgiveness and understanding. May this book inspire you as it has inspired me.

Duane Champagne
July 1993

Preface

The Native North American Almanac (NNNA) provides historical and contemporary information about the Native peoples of North America. Too often reference books about Native North Americans stop providing information after the 1890s. Consequently, many people cannot find accurate, accessible, and systematic information about contemporary Native culture, art, communities, life, and legal relations. Furthermore, many reference works have given little attention to Canadian Natives, even though Canadian Natives often play a more central role in Canadian constitutional issues and politics than do Native peoples in the United States. In this volume, special efforts were made to gather together experts on many aspects of U.S. and Canadian Native life, as well as to include as many U.S. and Canadian Native authors as possible. This effort paid off greatly, since these authors provided many points of view and information that could only come from individuals continually engaged in Native life and issues. In this way, the book represents an overview of the history of Native peoples in North America and provides new and probing perspectives not found in comparable reference works.

At the turn of the twentieth century, many people believed that Native Americans would disappear and assimilate into Canadian or U.S. society. The experience of the twentieth century, however, has shown that Native communities have survived, and are strongly entrenched in their traditions and institutions. *The NNNA* informs the reader about the struggle of contemporary Native North Americans and gives considerable insight into their present conditions regarding health, education, economy, politics, art, and other areas. This work is devoted to the student who has had little background or knowledge about Native Americans, and we hope will inspire, inform, and educate students and the general public about Native peoples. If this book creates greater understanding and appreciation between the peoples of North America and peoples around the world it will have served one of its primary purposes.

Terminology: Is Indian the Right Name?

Throughout *The NNAA*, a variety of terms are used interchangeably for Native North Americans, such as Indian, American Indian, Native, aborigine, First Nations, First Peoples, and others. The Native peoples of the Americas have the unfortunate distinction of having been given the wrong name, Indians, since the Native people of the Americas were not from the country or civilization of India, the subcontinent in southern Asia. The search for a single name, however, has not been entirely successful. In the United States, Native American has been used but has recently fallen out of favor, and American Indian is now preferred. Nevertheless, American Indian still retains the unfortunate Indian terminology and consequently is not an entirely satisfactory term. Native American also has serious difficulties since anyone born in North or South America may claim to be a "native American."

The Canadians have wrestled with this question of names, and many Native Canadians reject the appellation of Indian. Métis (mixed bloods) and Inuit (often called Eskimos) in Canada will not answer to the name Indian. Similarly, in Alaska the Inuit, Yupik, and Aleut peoples consider themselves distinct from Indian peoples, and do not wish to be called Indian. The

Canadians have developed a range of terms such as Native, aboriginal, First Nations, and First Peoples, which in many ways more accurately describes the Native peoples. Throughout the text, we have tried to respect the Canadian preference for avoiding the inclusive term Indian for denoting all Native peoples. Many Native people in Canada are called Indian, and it is appropriate for most Native peoples below the subarctic region, except for the Métis, who consider themselves a distinct ethnic group from Native as well as non-Native Canadians.

The ultimate problem in these terminological difficulties is that Native peoples in North America do not form a single ethnic group but are better understood as thousands of distinct communities and cultures. Many Native peoples have distinct languages, religious beliefs, ceremonies, and sociopolitical organization. Characterizing this diverse array of cultures and peoples with one inclusive name presents serious difficulties from the start, and no one word can characterize such diversity. The inclusive word Indian must be seen as something akin to European, where there is clear recognition of peoples who occupy a contiguous geographic area but have a wide variety of language, culture, and sociopolitical organization. The same applies in Native North America: the term Indian or other generic terms can denote only the collection of people who occupied the North American continent, but it says little about the diversity and independence of the cultures.

The best way to characterize Native North Americans is by recognizing their specific tribal or community identities, such as Blackfeet, Cherokee, or Cree. Such identifications more accurately capture the unique and varied tribal and cultural distinctions found among Native North American peoples.

Every effort has been made to keep Native tribal and community identities distinct, but when broader tribal designations were appropriate we allowed the many authors to use their own terms. We do not wish to offend anyone, and we offer our apologies to anyone who is offended, but for ease of presentation and because our many authors used a variety of terms, we have decided not to favor one particular term but rather hoped to see that the various terms were used appropriately in all situations.

The Native North American Peoples

Native North Americans occupied their continent for at least the last ten thousand years, if not for a considerably longer period. Unlike all other groups that live in North America, Natives do not have a recent immigrant experience but rather live in cultures that predate the present institutions and societies of Canada and the United States. Native peoples have legal, cultural, and political claims to priority over Canada and the United States for use of the land, for rights to self-government, and for practicing their cultures and religions. Over the past five hundred years Native people have experienced considerable change and dislocation, yet most Native communities have survived and will continue as communities into the next centuries. Native North Americans live in thousands of small communities and exhibit considerable differences in culture, language, religion, and social organization. Perhaps the strongest unifying force among these diverse cultures and communities is the general insistence by U.S. and Canadian societies and governments to treat Natives as a homogeneous ethnic group. Nothing could be further from the truth, but since they are treated as homogeneous, there are many situations in which Natives can act collectively to pursue their economic and political goals. Consequently, Natives have operated in mass North American society in increasingly well-organized national organizations and interest groups. These trends will most likely continue and become a major force in contemporary Native affairs.

Scope and Content

The Native North American Almanac covers the range of Native history and culture in the United States and Canada, providing a chronology, demographic and distribution descriptions and histories, and discussions of religion and religious change, art, music, theater, film, traditional arts, history, economy, administration, and law and legal issues.

Seventeen chapters were written by fifty-eight scholarly contributors while students worked to collect information for wide-ranging directories of Native North American communities, major Native cultural events and major writings, films, and videos produced by Native peoples. The range of topics provides an overview and introduction to the history and present-day life of Native North Americans. Each chapter has an ample bibliography for those users interested in further reading or who wish to conduct more specialized studies. Chapter 17 comprises biographical essays on significant Native North Americans, about one-third of whom are historical figures.

An extensive glossary provides definitions of words and concepts that are commonly used in Native affairs and history.

The index provides a quick means to find information on special topics that are discussed throughout the *Almanac*.

More than four hundred illustrations—including photographs, line drawings, tables, maps, and figures—complement the text. Every effort was made to use

Native photographers and to present views of everyday Native life and scenes.

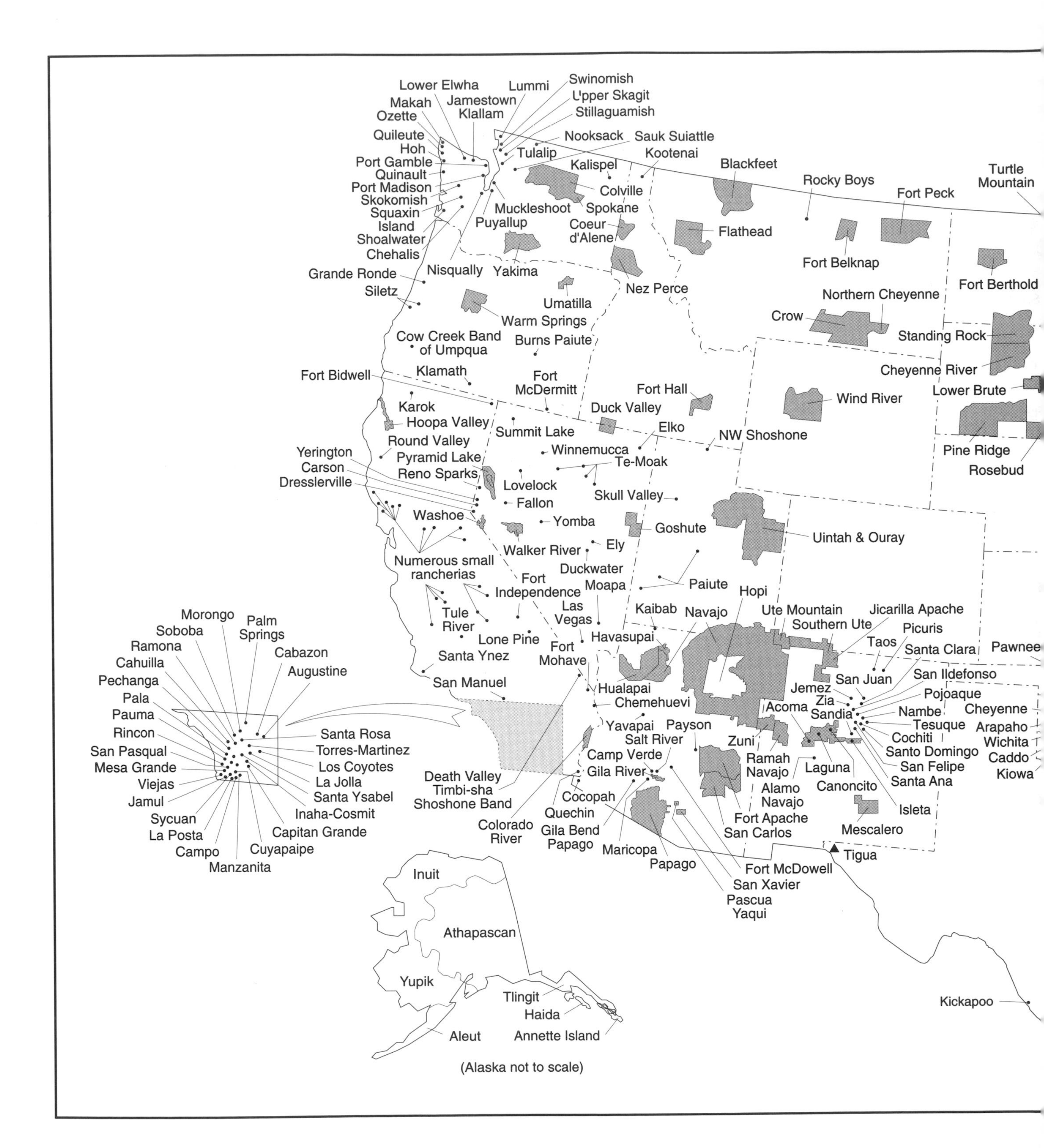

State and Federally Recognized

U.S. Indian Reservations

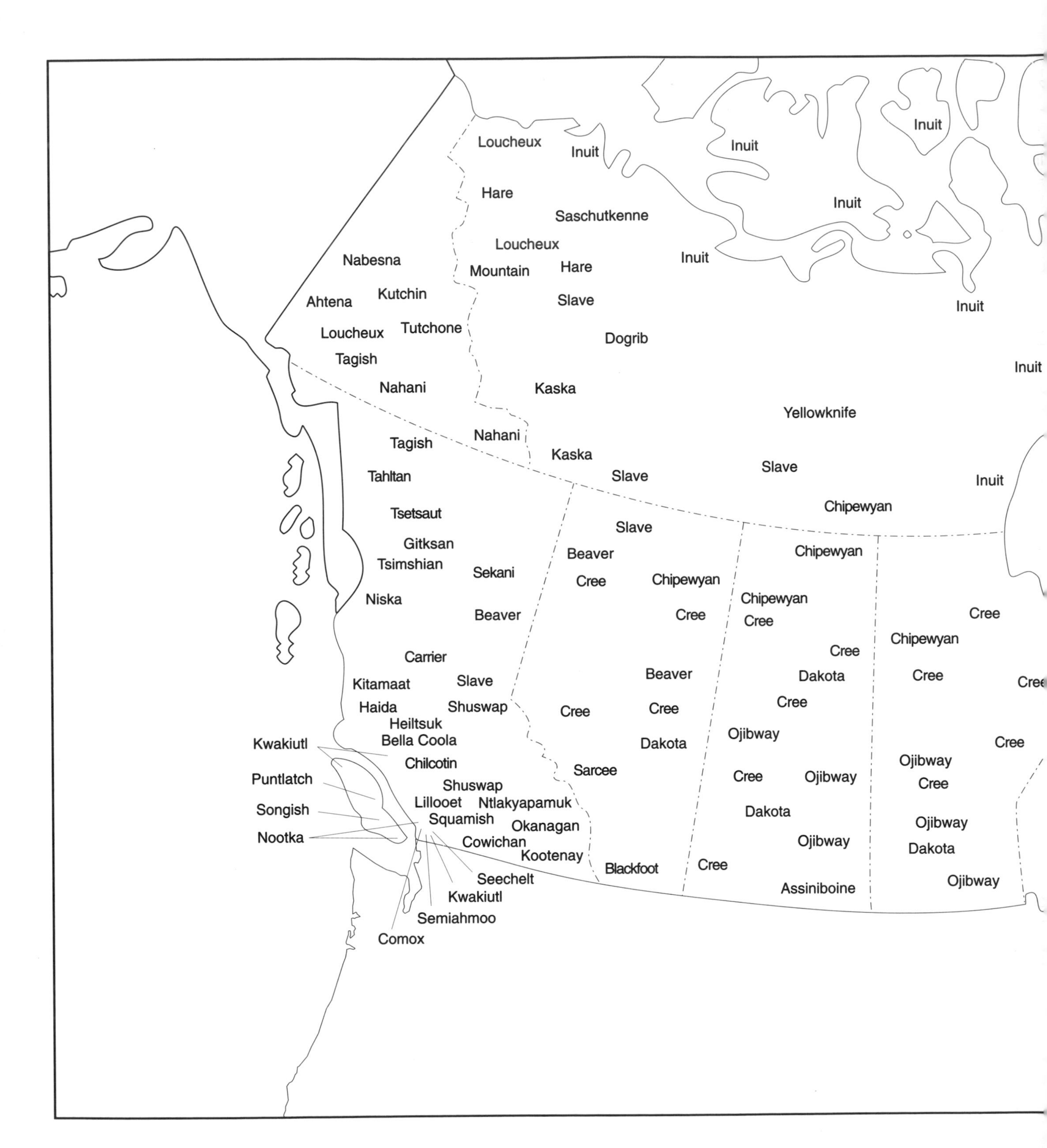

Canadian Native

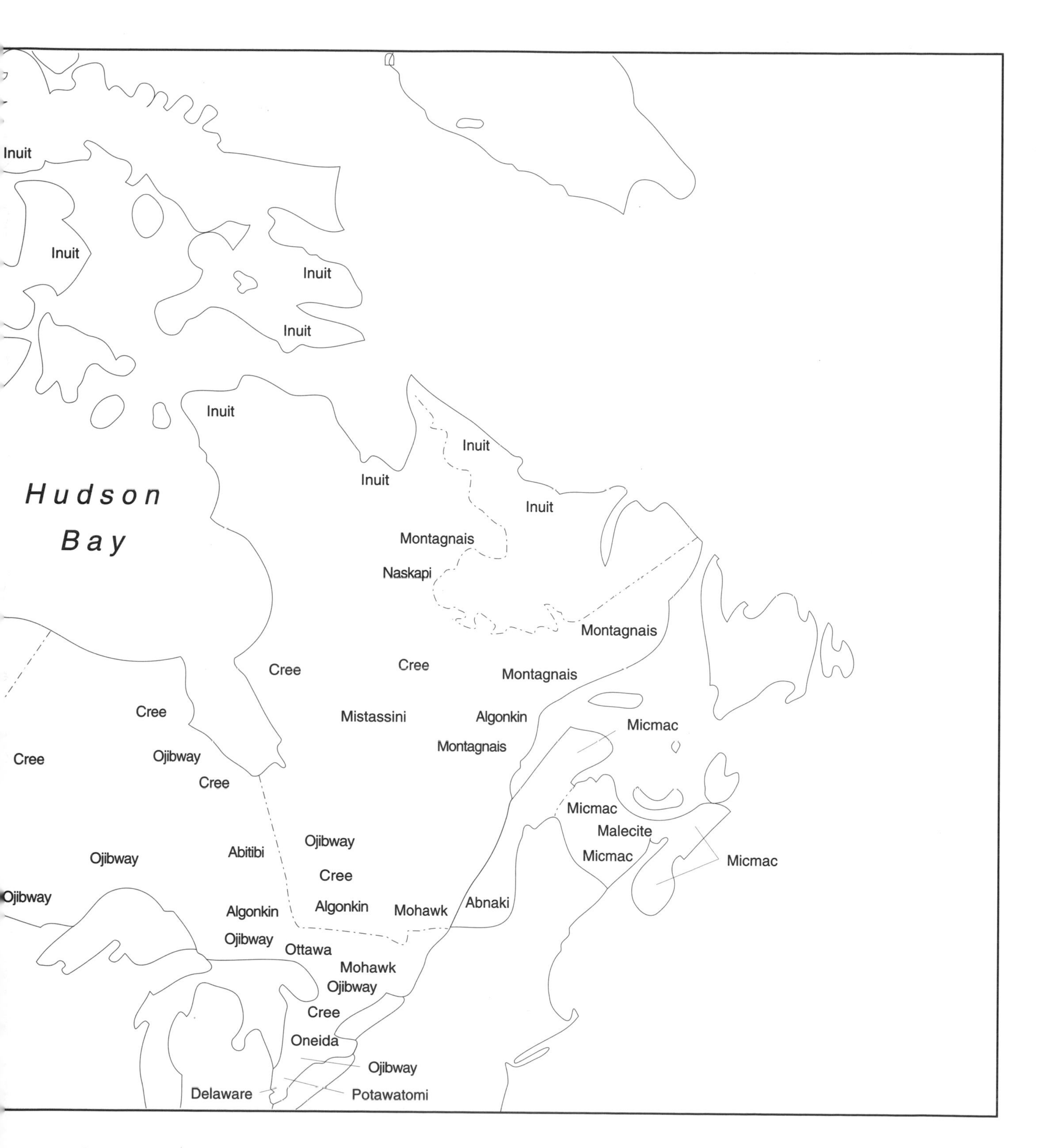

Culture Groups

Major Native Nations

UNITED STATES

♦ Northeast

Abenaki
Brotherton
Cayuga
Chickahominy
Chippewa (Ojibway)
Fox
Huron
Maliseet
Mattaponi
Menominee
Miami
Mohawk
Mohegan
Montauk
Nanticoke
Narragansett
Nipmuc-Hassanamisco
Oneida
Onondaga
Ottawa
Pamunkey
Passamaquoddy
Paugusset
Penobscot
Pequot
Piscataway
Poosepatuck
Potawatomi
Rappahanock
Sauk
Schaghticoke
Seneca
Shawnee
Shinnecock
Sioux
Stockbridge-Munsee
Tuscarora
Wampanoag
Winnebago

♦ Southeast

Alabama
Biloxi
Catawba
Cherokee (Eastern)
Chitimacha
Choctaw (Mississippi)
Coharie
Coushatta
Creek
Edisto
Haliwa
Houma
Lumbee
Miccosukee
Santee
Saponi
Seminole
Texas Kickapoo
Tunica
Waccamaw

♦ Oklahoma

Apache
Caddo
Cherokee
Cheyenne-Arapaho
Chickasaw
Choctaw
Comanche
Creek
Delaware
Iowa
Kaw
Kickapoo
Kiowa

Miami
Modoc
Osage
Otoe-Missouri
Ottawa
Pawnee
Peoria
Ponca
Potawatomi
Quapaw
Sac and Fox
Seminole
Seneca-Cayuga
Shawnee
Tonkawa
Wichita
Wyandotte

♦ Plains

Arikara
Assiniboine
Blackfeet
Cheyenne
Chippewa
Crow
Delaware
Gros Ventre
Hidatsa
Iowa
Kickapoo
Mandan
Omaha
Plains Ojibwa
Potawatomi
Sac and Fox
Sioux
Winnebago
Wyandotte

♦ Rocky Mountain Area

Arapaho
Bannock
Cayuse
Coeur d'Alene
Confederated Tribes of Colville
Flathead
Gosiute
Kalispel
Klamath
Kootenai
Nespelem
Nez Percé
Paiute (Northern)
Sanpoil
Shoshoni (Northern)
Spokane
Umatilla
Ute
Walla Walla
Warm Springs
Wasco
Washo
Yakima

♦ Southwest

Apache
Chemehuevi
Havasupai
Hopi
Hualapai
Mohave
Maricopa
Navajo
Paiute
Pima
Pueblo
Tohono O'Odham (Papago)
Yaqui
Yavapai
Yuma
Zuni

♦ California

Achumawi
Atsugewi
Cahuilla
Cupeño
Diegueño
Gabrieliño
Hupa
Karok
Luiseño
Maidu
Miwok
Mohave
Mono
Ohlone
Paiute
Patwin
Pomo
Serrano
Shasta
Shoshoni (Western)
Tolowa
Washo
Wintu

Wiyot
Yana
Yokuts
Yuki
Yurok

♦ Northwest Coast

Bella Bella
Bella Coola
Chehalis
Chinook
Clallam
Coos
Coquille
Gitksan
Haida
Heiltsuk
Hoh
Kalapuya
Kwakiutl
Lillooet
Lummi
Makah
Molala
Muckleshoot
Nisgha
Nisqually
Nooksack
Nootka
Puyallup
Quileute
Quinault
Rogue River
Sauk-Suiattle
Shasta
Siletz
Siuslaw
Skagit
Skokomish
Snohomish
Squaxin Island
Stillaguamish
Suquamish
Swinomish
Tillamook
Tlingit
Tsimshian
Tulalip
Twana
Umpqua
Wishram

♦ Alaska

Ahtena
Aleut
Athapascan
Eyak
Haida
Inuit
Tlingit
Tsimshian
Yupik

CANADA

Abenaki
Algonquin
Assiniboine
Beaver
Bella Bella
Bella Coola
Blackfoot
Blood
Carrier
Chilcotin
Chipewyan
Chippewa (Ojibway)
Comox
Cowichan
Cree
Dakota
Dogrib
Gitskan
Gitksan
Gros Ventre
Haida
Haisla
Hare
Heiltsuk
Huron
Inuit
Kootenay
Kutchin
Kwakiutl
Lillooet
Loucheux
Maliseet
Micmac
Mohawk
Montagnais
Nahani
Naskapi
Nisgha
Nootka

Ntlakyapamuk
Okanagon
Potawatomi
Sarsi
Sekani
Shuswap
Slave
Songhees
Squamish
Tagish
Tahltan
Tsimshian

1

Chronology

♦ Chronology of Native North American History Before 1500
♦ Chronology of Native North American History, 1500 to 1965
♦ Chronology of Native North American History, 1965 to 1992
♦ Chronology of Canadian Native History, 1500 to 1992

♦ CHRONOLOGY OF NATIVE NORTH AMERICAN HISTORY BEFORE 1500

The ancient history of North America is fascinating for the sheer diversity of cultures that once existed in the lands stretching from the Arctic tundra to the Southwestern deserts and to the coastal marshes of the Southeast. Across the centuries, scores of completely different languages have been spoken across the continent. In many places, cultures developed in a way that maximized the resources of their natural surroundings. Dense populations on the Northwest Coast exploited the plentiful sea mammals and fish of the Pacific Ocean and rivers like the Columbia. In this region, ancestors of the Bella Bella, Haida, and other groups developed elaborate cultures centered around communal longhouses. In the dry lands of the Great Basin, small groups, ancestral to the Paiute, learned to tap every available resource to develop their own distinctive way of life. In other regions people learned to modify their environment through development of agriculture and related water-control strategies. In the deserts of Arizona and New Mexico, groups like the Anasazi developed elaborate apartment-style villages and grew corn in lands where rainfall was scarce. In the Southeast, Mississippian-period farmers cultivated large fields along the major river valleys. Although generally successful, these settlements occasionally faced disasters, of human or natural origin, requiring the inhabitants to abandon a region. Eight hundred years ago major droughts forced many Anasazi peoples to either abandon their homelands or starve. Like people around the world faced with such drastic consequences, they chose to leave.

Because Native American history goes back so many generations before written documents, archaeology is the key to discovering the turning points in this fascinating story. Archaeology is the subfield of anthropology concerned with understanding how past societies survived and developed. Archaeologists study the things people leave behind, and this means carefully excavating places people once lived. The ruins of an ancient house may contain a variety of lost or discarded tools for cutting, grinding, weaving, and many other tasks. The building may also contain a cooking hearth, evidence of sleeping areas, and places for storing supplies. From these bits of evidence archaeologists piece together clues about the kinds of foods eaten, the number of people living in the house, and their activities. By looking at the layout of ceremonial centers, villages, and temporary camps, it is possible to reconstruct the organization of the entire society.

The age of the house or objects in it can be learned by the radiocarbon method and other dating techniques. The radiocarbon method measures extremely low levels of naturally occurring radiation in organic materials like wood or seeds. The radioactive material carbon 14 found in living organisms has a known rate of decay, called its half-life. The half-life is the amount of time it takes for half of the radioactive material to disintegrate. When the plant or animal dies, the carbon 14 begins to decay at a known rate. Once the amount of radioactive material present is determined an approximate date can be assigned for when the organism died. The results of the many kinds of archaeological studies in conjunction with radiocarbon and other dating methods are used to develop chronologies that tell the cultural history of Native Americans.

Archaeologists depend on the methods of science to draw conclusions about when and where cultures originated and developed. But scientific theories are not the only ways of thinking about the past. All cultures around the world have traditions, passed down through the

At Mesa Verde, Colorado, multi-storied pueblos were built to take advantage of the shelter offered by rock overhangs.

generations, that tell how their people came about. Many people rely on these traditional messages as fundamental parts of their religion. Often, scientific theories run counter to the traditional teachings. Probably the most widely discussed set of contradictions resulted from archaeological evidence showing that Native Americans came from Asia across the Bering Sea Land Bridge sometime between twelve and twenty-five thousand years ago. Very few of the traditional teachings held by individual tribal groups support this theory; most point to origins within their traditional homelands. For instance, among a subgroup of the Caddo, who once lived in Texas and Louisiana, the teachings told that their original home was under the earth and that they came out through the mouth of a cave near the confluence of the Red and Mississippi rivers. In the Southwest, the people of Cochiti Pueblo understand their existence on earth began in the north at a place they called "White House," along with all the other peoples of the world. Though this origin story may support the Bering Sea Land Bridge theory, the critical point is that scientific theory and traditional teachings represent different ways of thinking. The beliefs held by many Native Americans should not be discounted because they do not conform to current scientific theory. The oral traditions about where and how different tribal groups originated are fundamental to deeply held religious beliefs.

The Ancient History of North America

Scientists believe that the human history of North America began when the ancestors of contemporary Native Americans started moving from Siberia across the Bering Sea Land Bridge into Alaska. Glaciers covered much of North America, but at key times there were ice-free corridors that allowed relatively easy travel from Alaska into the heart of the continent. The people of this earliest time period are referred to as Paleo-Indians. The general chronology for the Paleo-Indians and subsequent peoples is presented in the following time line. The best known of the early arrivals are described by the name Clovis, dated between 11,200 and 10,900 years ago. These people left remains of their hunting and gathering camps scattered across the continent. They hunted many now-extinct animals such as woolly mammoth, dire wolf, camel, and an ancient species of bison. They also collected a wide variety of wild plant foods. Some archaeologists argue that the

Native American Time Line before 1500

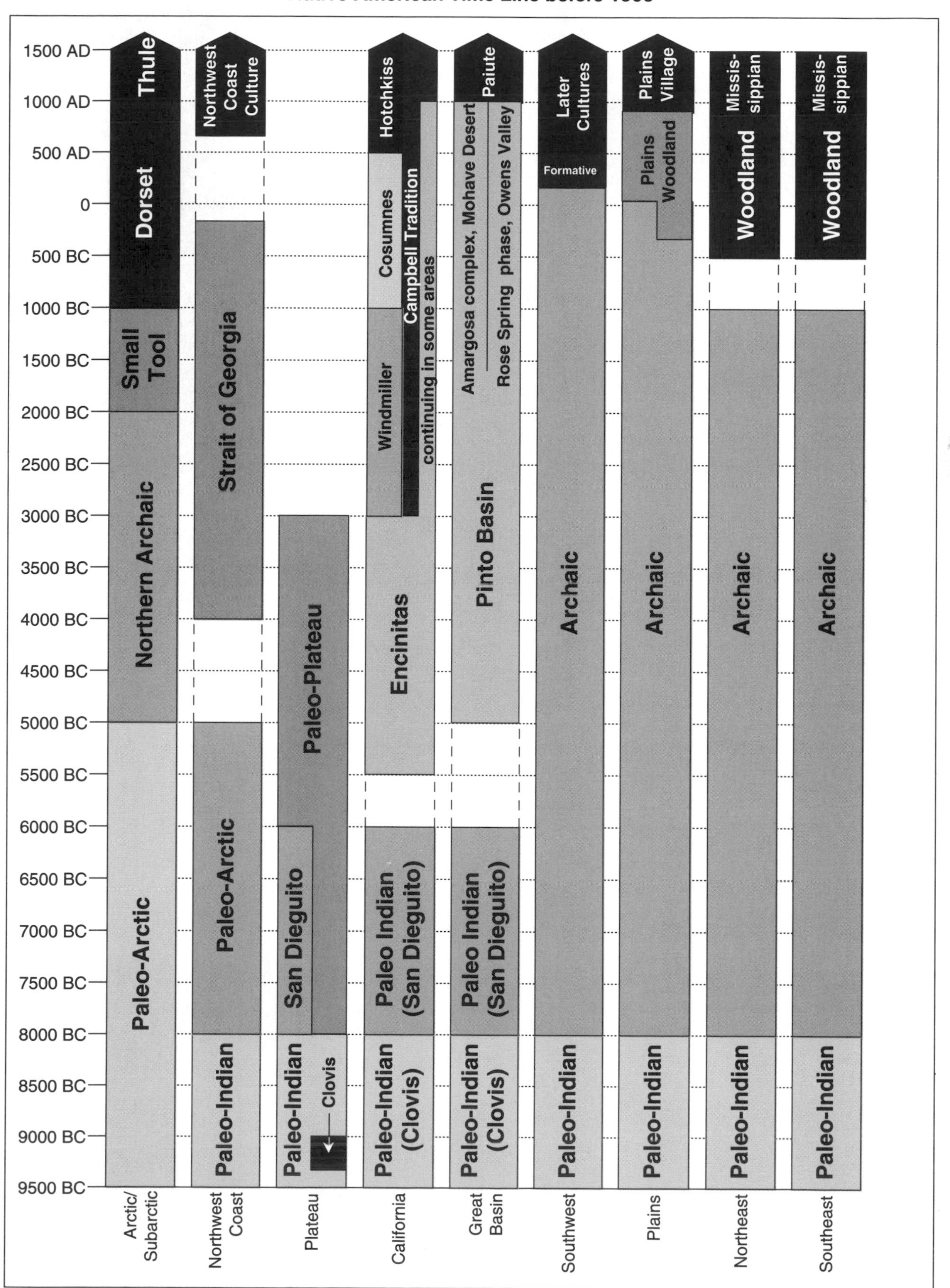

hunting practices of Clovis and other later Paleo-Indian groups were partially responsible for the extinction of the large Pleistocene animals. Although Clovis may be the best known early culture, there is emerging evidence that even older cultures existed before Clovis. Discoveries made at Meadowcroft rock shelter in Pennsylvania and Orogrande cave in New Mexico provide growing evidence for pre-Clovis cultures that may extend back more than 20,000 years. For now, problems with the quality of this early evidence keep it from being widely accepted.

After the end of the Paleo-Indian period, about eight thousand years ago, populations increased and tool types diversified indicating adaptation to more restricted environments. This period, known as the Archaic, stretches from eight thousand to about two to three thousand years ago, depending on the region. At the beginning of the Archaic period climates were changing rapidly. Following the melting of the glacial ice sheets, deciduous forests expanded into the Northeast. Rainfall patterns changed and the climate became more like that of today. The hunting and gathering lifeway of the Paleo-Indian period continued in the Archaic, although a variety of new technologies were developed to allow more efficient exploitation of restricted environments. Late in the Archaic the first pottery in North America was manufactured in the Southeast. In several regions there is also evidence for new forms of social organization and a diversification of belief systems. By the end of the Archaic, people as far north as the Great Lakes had begun to domesticate a variety of native plants eventually leading to intensive agriculture.

Following the Archaic a wide variety of cultures can be defined in different regions. In the Great Plains and present-day eastern United States, the Woodland period dates from about two thousand to eleven hundred years ago. In the Southwest, a similar time range is described as the Formative Period. In the Arctic, Northwest Coast, Plateau, California, and Great Basin, many local traditions took shape. In each of these regions individual cultures dating from about two thousand to one thousand years ago continued to develop and diversify within the longstanding hunting and plant-gathering strategies developed in the Archaic. In the Great Plains, eastern United States, and the Southwest, many cultures moved away from hunting and gathering to the more predictable food supplies available through agriculture. In the Southwest, along rivers like the Rio Grande, Little Colorado, Salt, and Gila, and in less well watered areas, people developed an economy based on cultivation of

A woolly mammoth, one of the late Pleistocene mega-fauna species hunted by the Paleo-Indians.

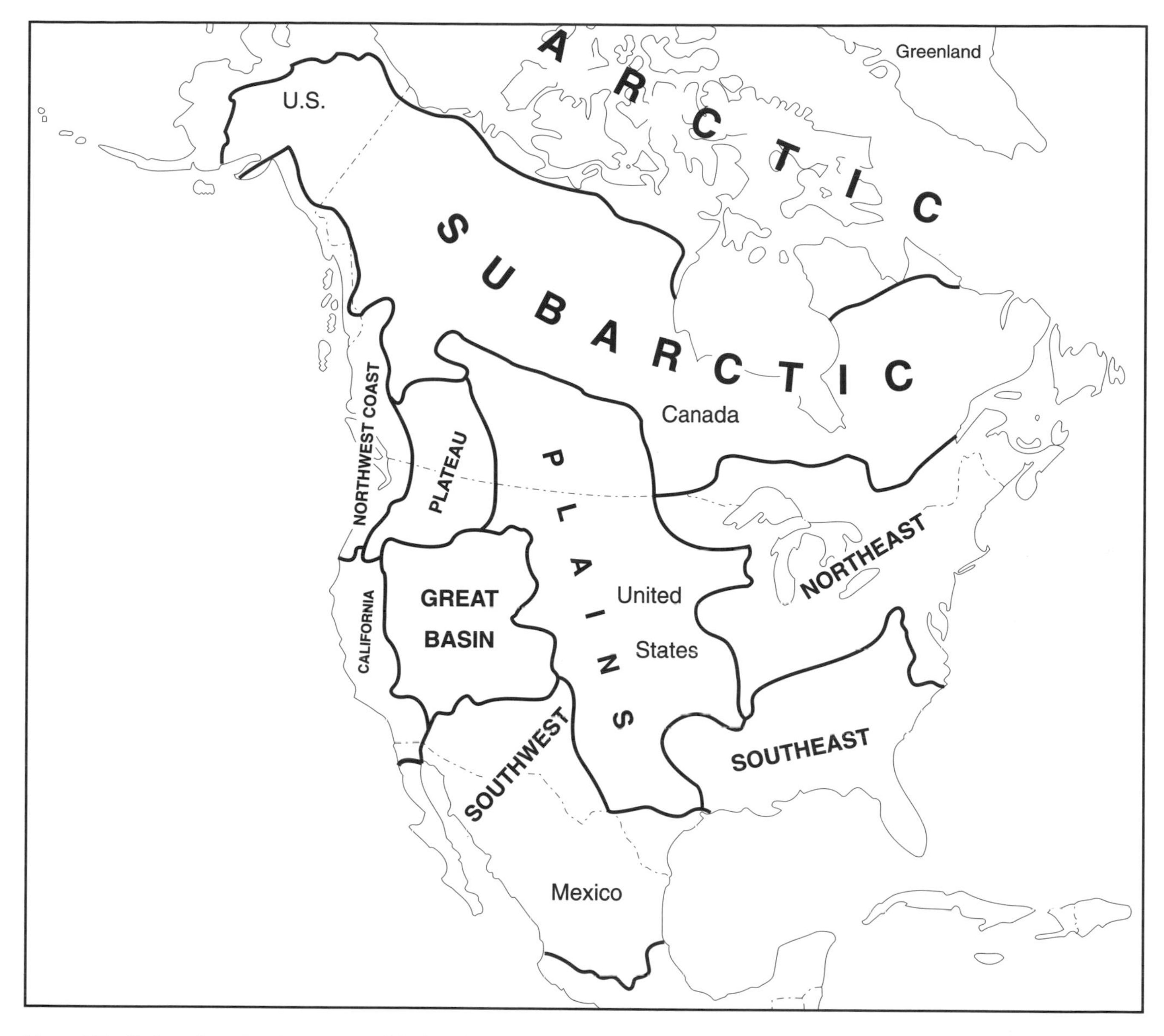

Map of North America showing geographical regions and locations.

corn (maize), beans, squash, cotton, and amaranth, a plant that produces small, highly nutritious seeds that can be ground into flour.

By the time Europeans came to the shores of North America, a mosaic of very different Native American cultures had existed in every region of the continent for thousands of years. North America was not a "vacant" continent or a place untouched by the work of humans as early European explorers believed and as perpetuated by the most recent generation of historians and other scholars. In fact, some of the regions first touched by Europeans were the homelands to the continent's most complex cultures. In the southeastern United States, societies of the Mississippian period developed hereditary leadership, long-distance trading networks, and elaborate systems for obtaining and displaying wealth. In some cases, these societies also made war on their neighbors, forcing other villages and regions to pay tribute or suffer the consequences.

With the arrival of Europeans in North America, many Native American cultures were cut short. European diseases, warfare, and the social disruptions caused by loss of resources forever changed the people of this continent, but it did not destroy them. Native Americans found many ways of adapting to change. The following chronology documents the ancient history of North America, from the earliest foragers through the rise of civilizations, up to the arrival of Europeans.

Before proceeding, a few points about format should be mentioned. First, because the chronology deals with the ancient past most dates are only approximate. The kinds of evidence recovered through archaeological methods rarely give the level of precision available to the historian working in later times with written documents. Second, a chronology such as this tends to obscure long-term processes in favor of discrete events. In many instances the dates listed refer to the beginnings of something, such as the first evidence for a particular culture. The reader should be aware that in many cases the cultures or ways of life being recognized may have continued on for hundreds or even thousands of years from the origin date listed in the chronology. Some of this long-term continuity can be recognized by referring to the time-line chart.

11,000 B.C. Alaska Over a period of years small bands of hunters steadily make their way across the Bering Sea Land Bridge from Siberia. Eventually these people and their descendants spread throughout North and South America to become the ancestors of all subsequent generations of Native Americans. (Some archaeologists believe the first people came across before 18,000 B.C. Although of questionable validity, possible bone artifacts found along the Old Crow River in Canada's Yukon Territory were dated at 24,000 to 27,000 B.C.)

11,000 B.C. Lindenmeier Site, Colorado The Paleo-Indians are the first people to come to the Americas. They live a nomadic life based on hunting many types of animals and collecting wild plants. (Located just south of the Wyoming border in Colorado, the Lindenmeier site was the first Paleo-Indian camp site to be studied. It helped verify the antiquity of humans in the Americas.)

10,200 B.C. North America Dogs have always been with people in North America. Dog remains found at the Jones-Miller site in Colorado and other Paleo-Indian sites in the western United States show animals closely related to wolves, but about three-fourths their size.

10,000 B.C. North America Among the first people to come to the Americas are the Clovis hunters and gatherers. They hunt Pleistocene animals, such as mammoths, horses, camels, and bison, and collect a variety of plants.

Dog pulling travois. Dogs were domesticated by Native people as far back as 10,000 B.C. Paleo-Indians often trained dogs to pull loads during their seasonal migrations.

A monolithic stone axe from Georgia engraved with Southeastern Ceremonial Complex iconography. Courtesy of the National Museum of Natural History.

By this date, Clovis people are spread over most portions of North and South America. Evidence for their distinctive type of tools dies out about 9200 B.C.

9200 B.C. North America Following Clovis a new Paleo-Indian tradition called Folsom emerges across the continent. The Folsom people are hunters and gatherers, like their Clovis ancestors, but they make smaller spear points and focus more attention on hunting the (now-extinct) giant bison called *Bison antiquus*. By the end of the Folsom tradition (8000 B.C.), many of the North American Ice Age mammals, such as the giant ground sloth, woolly mammoth, and dire wolf, are extinct.

9000 B.C. Arctic In areas untouched by glaciers people of the Paleoarctic tradition develop an effective hunting way of life and are the first people in the Americas to find ways of living in the harsh arctic environment. Their tools include scrapers, spear points, and very small, razor-sharp stone tools called microblades. They live in small, highly mobile groups that move over wide territories to take advantage of the best hunting conditions.

9000 B.C. Great Basin Artifacts similar to those found in the San Dieguito complex in California also occur at Danger Cave, west of Salt Lake City, Utah. As defined for California, the San Dieguito complex is a distinctive tradition with a heavy reliance on hunting and no evidence for the use of grinding stones. Some typical San Dieguito artifacts include small, leaf-shaped projectile points and knives, scrapers, and engraving tools. The San Dieguito artifacts may represent a transitional period between the earlier Clovis Paleo-Indians and the later Archaic period cultures in this region.

9000 B.C. Great Plains The species of bison *Bison antiquus* becomes a major food source. Herds increase greatly following the extinction of predators like lions and short-faced bears and climatic changes fostering the expansion of shortgrass prairie.

9000 B.C. Blackwater Draw, New Mexico Early campsites in present-day eastern New Mexico, used by Paleo-Indian groups for more than one thousand years, take advantage of a local environment much wetter than today's. (Remains recovered from the site include those of mammoth and other now-extinct species.)

8500 B.C. Marmes Rockshelter, Washington At Marmes Rockshelter on the lower Snake River in southeast Washington, some of the best early evidence for human habitation of the Plateau region documents hunting of a wide variety of animals.

8500 B.C. Agate Basin Site, Wyoming Located in extreme eastern Wyoming near the Cheyenne River, the Agate Basin site is one of a growing number of places that reveal the hunting strategies of the Paleo-Indians. In this location bison are driven into an arroyo, or gully, where they are surrounded and killed.

8000 B.C. California, Great Basin, and Plateau An artifact complex called San Dieguito forms the last evidence for the Paleo-Indian way of life in these regions.

8000 B.C. Holcombe Site, Western Great Lakes At the Holcombe site, just north of Detroit, early Archaic period foraging peoples develop tools such as gravers, scrapers, and various projectile point forms, replacing earlier styles used by Paleo-Indian groups.

8000 B.C. North America Across the continent people adapt to a new, more diverse, post-Ice Age environment, marking the end of the Paleo-Indian period in most regions.

8000 B.C. Danger Cave, Utah Repeated use by early hunters and gatherers reveals a remarkable record of adaptation to a difficult desert environment.

8000 B.C. Columbia River, Oregon From earliest times to the modern day, people have camped along the Columbia River in a stretch of rapids called the Dalles to take advantage of the rich salmon resources. At sites along the great rapids, on the middle portion of the Columbia River, thousands of salmon bones and a wide variety of tools have been discovered.

8000 B.C. Colorado At the Olson-Chubbuck site, near the Kansas border in east-central Colorado, hunters stampede almost two hundred bison into an arroyo where they kill and butcher them. Bison kill sites like Olson-Chubbuck are known from several places on the Great Plains.

8000 B.C. Bonfire Shelter, Texas At a bison jump site, in Val Verde County, western Texas, Paleo-Indians on at least two separate occasions drive herds of bison over a cliff.

7500 B.C. Southeastern United States Near the end of the Paleo-Indian period a tool complex called Dalton is recognized from such places as the Brand site in Arkansas. The Dalton point style is often used as a projectile as well as a knife and is found in association with stone scrapers and woodworking tools.

7000 B.C. Northwest Coast As the glaciers retreat, hunting and gathering peoples move into the coastal regions from the interior plateau.

6500 B.C. Southeast Freshwater mussels and other river resources become a major part of the diet for Archaic period peoples. Expanding use of these resources probably results from climate change and the beginnings of a lengthy period of river stabilization that increase their availability.

6400 B.C. Hogup Cave, Utah People living along the edges of ancient lakes, in the region west of present-day Salt Lake City, collect pickleweed and hunt many variety of water fowl. The remains of nets and traps also indicate the hunting of rabbits and other small game.

6000 B.C. North America In many regions, groups adapt to smaller ranges as populations begin to increase. Local cultural differences multiply due to decreased interaction.

6000 B.C. Moorehead Cave, Texas At this cave in the Great Bend region of Texas, about 120 miles west of San Antonio, a long history of use associated with the Coahuiltecan cultural tradition verifies a hunting and gathering life-style that exists in this region through to the period of contact with Europeans. The people of the Coahuiltecan culture live in small bands that hunt and collect over a vast region of southwest Texas and northern Mexico. They fish in the Pecos and Rio Grand Rivers and use throwing sticks to hunt rabbits. Because this region is so arid, the Coahuiltecan people never adopt agriculture.

5500 B.C. North America Grinding stones called *manos* and *metates* used for processing seeds and other plant products begin occurring in Archaic period sites.

5500 B.C. Southern California Cultures referred to as the Encinitas tradition develop along the California coast from Paleo-Indian ancestors. Grinding stones and abundant shellfish remains provide evidence for an economy based on collecting marine coastal resources. In the San Diego area, the Encinitas tradition lasts until A.D. 1000.

5000 B.C. Arctic and Subarctic By this time hunting and foraging groups of the Northern Archaic tradition begin exploiting the increasingly ice-free environments. They live in small camps and hunt throughout the tundra and forests. On the northern forest fringes, caribou hunting is a primary occupation. In the dense woodlands slightly farther south, elk, deer, and moose are important.

5000 B.C. Aberdeen Lake, Canadian Subarctic For the next 4000 years, Northern Archaic tradition hunters camp on Aberdeen Lake, about three hundred miles west of Hudson Bay, to intercept the seasonal migrations of vast caribou herds.

5000 B.C. Plateau Region For the next 2000 years there is evidence for increased contact and sharing of ideas between peoples of the Plateau and Great Basin.

5000 B.C. Southern Great Basin For the next 3400 years, Pinto Basin cultures practice a hunting and gathering way of life. (Some evidence for small circular houses indicates they may have been semi-sedentary.)

5000 B.C. Northwestern Great Plains For the next 2500 years, a drier climate prevails, causing reduction in prairie grasses and a dwindling of the bison herds. Fewer archaeological sites for this period indicates that human populations also move out of the region.

4500 B.C. Northeastern California People of the Menlo phase (4500–2500 B.C.) are the first to build sturdy, semi-subterranean earth lodges in this region. From these relatively permanent hamlets they exploit environments ranging from the mountains to the river valleys. Later in time, the climate becomes drier and the people are forced to move more often to find food. They respond by shifting to lighter, easier-to-build dwellings made of brush.

4000 B.C. Ocean Bay, Kodiak Island, Alaska Kodiak Island, about 215 miles south of the modern city of Anchorage, is one of the places where Arctic hunters begin adapting their skills to exploitation of marine resources.

4000 B.C. Onion Portage, Alaska Some of the earliest Northern Archaic tradition artifacts are found at Onion Portage on the Kobuk River in northeast Alaska. They give evidence for increasingly diverse subsistence strategies including a shift to caribou hunting.

4000 B.C. Koster Site, Illinois At least by this date, throughout the Midwest, hunters and gatherers of the Archaic period begin building permanent shelters at base camps. (Some of these camps were discovered in southern Illinois, about seventy miles north of St. Louis, at the Koster site.)

3000 B.C. Umnak Island, Alaska At Umnak and other islands in the Aleutian chain, people skilled at hunting seals, sea lions, and whales build villages with small oval houses, three to five meters in diameter.

3000 B.C. Southern California In some areas along the coast, the Encinitas tradition is replaced by the Campbell tradition, which has a greater orientation toward hunting deer and other game animals, considering the large number of these bones found in the sites. Artifacts of the Campbell tradition include leaf-shaped points and stone mortars and pestles. The Campbell tradition is ancestral to the modern Chumash of the Santa Barbara area.

3000 B.C. Southwest Beginning about this time, favorable conditions for widespread trade and interaction develop, permitting the eventual spread of important domesticated plants from Mexico, especially maize, beans, and squash.

3000 B.C. Southwest Four regional Archaic Period traditions of hunting and gathering peoples, known collectively as the Picosa culture, take shape. In the west is the poorly known San Dieguito-Pinto tradition. The best-known artifact of this tradition is the small Pinto Basin projectile point, but there are a variety of other artifacts, including small grinding slabs and choppers. In the north, the Oshara tradition shows many connections in artifact styles with the western San Dieguito-Pinto tradition. In the east, the Hueco and Coahuiltecan cultural complexes are known to include many wooden and other perishable objects, such as nets and sandals, recovered from dry caves. In the south, during the Chiricahua and San Pedro phases of the Cochise tradition, people use a wide variety of plant processing and hunting tools.

2600 B.C. Southeast Throughout the region there is an expansion of long-distance trade. It is not clear why trade increases at this time, but there is evidence that expanding populations use trade as a means of maintaining good relations with a growing number of neighboring groups. It is also possible that exotic items are becoming important as markers of wealth and status.

2500 B.C. Central California For the next 2000 years people of the Windmiller period (also called the Windmiller pattern) cultures live in permanent villages and practice a wide variety of hunting and gathering activities in California's Central Valley. They bury their dead in small mounds. Among the many objects made by Windmiller people are distinctive, large, obsidian (volcanic glass) projectile points, stone smoking pipes, alabaster charmstones, various types of baskets, and grinding stones.

2500 B.C. Charles River, Massachusetts Several large fish traps, called weirs, are positioned at the mouth of the Charles and other rivers as they feed into the Atlantic Ocean. These types of traps are probably used well before 2500 B.C. and continue in use into the period of European contact.

2500 B.C. Southeast The earliest pottery north of Mexico is made at sites in Georgia and Florida. The simple styles are constructed using plant fibers as tempering material to strengthen the vessels. This and later pottery represent a major technological advance in the preparation and storage of food and other resources.

2000 B.C. Alaska The Arctic Small Tool tradition develops and spreads east as far as Greenland. These hunters and fishers are the first humans to live in the eastern Arctic, other than Antarctica, the last uninhabited region of the world. The people of the Arctic Small Tool tradition are the ancestors of the modern-day Inuit. They are responsible for developing some of the most remarkable technologies for surviving in the world's harshest environment. They develop special harpoons and techniques for hunting seals, walrus, and whales.

2000 B.C. Northwest Coast Beginning as early as 2000 B.C., archaeological remains, designated the Strait of Georgia tradition, point to coastal and interior adaptations that eventually lead to the development of complex societies like the present-day Coast Salish and Bella Bella. Initially, artifact styles are very similar to those from Kodiak Island, Alaska, and include a wide variety of harpoons and fishing equipment. By A.D. 400 distinctive Strait of Georgia tradition artifacts include ground slate spear points, barbed points made of bone, and spindle whorls used to make cloth.

2000 B.C. Labrador Ramah Chalcedony, a translucent type of stone easily worked into a variety of tools, becomes an important trade item after the arrival of Inuit peoples. This stone is traded from Labrador to New England.

2000 B.C. Midwest From about this time into the period of European contact, people mine copper in the Lake Superior area. The copper is obtained in relatively pure chunks and is cold hammered into a variety of tools and ornaments. Over time, copper from this region is traded widely across the eastern woodlands.

2000 B.C. Eastern United States By this date, four native plants are being domesticated in this region. Two of these plants, squash and sunflowers, are still commonly used today. The other two, marsh elder and chenopodium, are now thought of as only weeds.

1500 B.C. Subarctic A period of increasing cold causes the southerly retreat of forests. Northern Archaic tradition hunters, who are adapted to forest environments, also move south. For these hunters the migratory caribou herds are a major food source. Not long after the Northern Archaic tradition hunters move south the vacuum is filled by Inuit (Eskimo) peoples.

1400 B.C. Louisiana By this date, people living along the lower Mississippi River and its tributaries are constructing large mounds and living in planned communities. The best-known example is the Poverty Point site, located 55 miles west of Vicksburg, Mississippi, where a massive semicircle of concentric mounds is constructed. Some archaeologists believe Poverty Point is the first chiefdom north of Mexico. There are approximately one hundred other lesser sites with cultural connections to Poverty Point.

1000 B.C. Southwest The first evidence of the use of maize in the Southwest is documented at Bat Cave and Jemez Cave in southwest New Mexico, north of Silver City.

1000 B.C. Central California Cultures of the Cosumnes period grow out of the earlier Windmiller culture. Artifactual evidence suggests they rely more on harvesting acorns and fishing than their Windmiller culture ancestors, although hunting continues to be important.

1000 B.C. Northeast Vessels carved from a stone called steatite are a common trade item from New England to the southern Appalachian Mountains.

800 B.C. Choris Peninsula, Alaska The first pottery in Alaska appears in this area of Kotzebue Sound about 160 miles north of Nome. Styles and methods of manufacture show recent contact with Asia.

700 B.C. Foxe Basin and Baffin Island, Canada In this vast region north of Hudson Bay, Dorset Inuit culture develops, eventually spreading to many parts of the eastern Arctic. Excavations at the Kapuivik site, near Igloolik, reveal the oldest documented occurrence of Dorset culture. Dwellings used by the Dorset people include skin tents, sod houses, and pit houses.

500 B.C. Eastern Great Plains Throughout the eastern border of the Plains for the next 1500 years, many small mounds are built by people of the Plains Woodland tradition.

500 B.C. Southeast The older practice of using plant fiber as a tempering agent in pottery is replaced by the use of sand and limestone. At about this time, there is a huge increase in the variety of decorations used on pottery throughout the region. This corresponds with expanding cultural diversity and the shift from a hunting and gathering way of life to the establishment of small permanent villages and the cultivation of native plants like sunflower, marsh elder, may grass, and squash. The seeds from the sunflower, marsh elder, and may grass could be collected and ground to produce flour.

500 B.C. Midwest In the Ohio River valley and surrounding regions, an Early Woodland cultural complex, called Adena, develops from late Archaic antecedents. The Adena people build burial mounds and live in small villages of circular semipermanent dwellings.

400 B.C. Ohio People of the Adena Culture build a huge earthwork today called Serpent Mound. The body of the serpent measures 382 meters long. Today its symbolism is unknown.

350 B.C. Southwest Beans and squash, already widely cultivated in Mesoamerica, are introduced and eventually become important food sources.

250 B.C. Eastern United States Peoples begin cultivation of locally domesticated plants.

250 B.C. Eastern Great Plains A variety of cultures referred to as Plains Woodland develop in this region. They differ markedly from earlier cultures; especially noteworthy is their use of pottery, sedentary villages, and mounds as places for a variety of religious purposes, including burial of the dead.

100 B.C. Midwest Centered in Ohio and Illinois, Hopewell societies develop from local roots. The Hopewell people are especially noted for constructing massive, geometric-shaped earthworks and are among the first in North America to develop societies in which people's status is determined by the standing of the family they are born into, rather than by their own personal achievements. Hopewell societies are also known for participating in trade networks extending from the Great Lakes to the Gulf of Mexico. Some of the items traded include conch shell, shark teeth, mica, lead, copper, and various kinds of stone.

A.D. 1 Eastern Kansas For the next 500 years, Hopewellian communities with affinities to the east live in the area of present-day Kansas City. Their semipermanent villages provide evidence for the early cultivation of maize.

A.D. 1 Eastern Woodlands In many parts of the present-day eastern United States, small-scale groups develop more complex social hierarchies with leaders whose authority is derived from group consensus.

A.D. 1 Southeast Throughout the region small oval mounds are built for the burial of important members of society.

A.D. 1 Southwest The roots of the Hohokam cultural tradition emerge in the Sonoran Desert of south-central Arizona and adjacent regions of Chihuahua and Sonora in Mexico. The earlier Hohokam people are hunters and gatherers, but later they develop agriculture and build massive irrigation systems to water their fields. The central Hohokam area is in south-central Arizona around the modern city of Phoenix. The Hohokam tradition continues until after European arrival. The ancient Hohokam may be ancestral to the present-day Pima and Papago.

A.D. 100 Southwest Although maize was known and used in the region at least since 1000 B.C., it does not become significant as a food crop until after A.D. 100.

A.D. 100 Louisiana Sharing similarities with the Hopewellian peoples farther north, the Marksville culture becomes an important regional variant of the Woodland period. The Marksville people develop an economy based on hunting and cultivation of native plants. They also build mounds for ceremonial purposes, including the burial of important individuals.

A.D. 100 Alaska Remains ancestral to modern Inuit peoples have been identified in eastern Siberia and western Alaska. By about A.D. 1000 all northern Native Americans from Alaska to Greenland are part of this same cultural heritage, called the Thule or Northern Maritime tradition. Archaeologically, the Thule tradition is consistently recognized for the use of polished slate and elaborately carved bone, and ivory tools used for hunting sea mammals.

A.D. 200 Southwest Small sedentary villages develop, marking the end of the nomadic hunting and gathering life-style in many parts of the region.

A.D. 200 New Mexico The first evidence for the Mogollon cultural tradition is defined in the mountainous areas of southern New Mexico, eastern Arizona, and adjacent portions of Chihuahua and Sonora, Mexico. Like their neighbors to the north and south, the Mogollon people develop first small villages of earth-covered houses and later multi-storied pueblos and techniques for cultivating crops in a dry environment. Some people of the modern Western Pueblos are believed descended from the Mogollon.

A.D. 200 Southwest The Patayan tradition has its origins in southwestern Arizona, but is primarily associated with the Colorado River region. The Patayan tradition occupies a vast area extending from northern Baja California to northwest Arizona. The Patayan people are among the first pottery producers in the Southwest. Several sites excavated south of the Grand Canyon in Arizona give some information on dwellings and subsistence. Their early dwellings are small and made of wood or masonry, usually with an attached ramada or open-air porch. They probably grow corn and squash and hunt a variety of local animals.

A.D. 300 Central Arizona Construction of what was later to become massive irrigation systems begins in the earliest period of the Hohokam cultural tradition.

A.D. 300 Midwest Around this date Hopewellian societies give way to cultures of the Late Woodland period. The reasons for the decline of Hopewell in the Midwest is not known, but it may be related to the breakup of long-distance trade connections, increased warfare, and climate change.

A.D. 400 Southwest Pottery, used for storage and cooking, comes into wide usage. Most pottery in the Southwest is made by coiling strips of clay to build up the body of the vessel.

A.D. 400 Southwest The Anasazi tradition emerges in the Four Corners region of Arizona, New Mexico, Colorado, and Utah. The Anasazi practice agriculture and through time move from pit-house villages to the construction of large multi-roomed apartment buildings, some with more than twelve hundred rooms. The pueblos in Chaco Canyon in western New Mexico are examples of Anasazi dwellings. The Anasazi produce many distinctive styles of pottery; especially recognizable are the black on white geometric designs. The people of the modern Pueblos of Arizona and New Mexico are descended from the Anasazi.

A.D. 400 North America By this date the bow and arrow are in use in several regions and spread rapidly throughout the continent as a major technological advance for hunting and warfare. Before the bow and arrow, spears and a weapon called the *atlatl* are used widely. The *atlatl* is also called a spear thrower and consists of a spear held on top of a long handle. By holding the handle and propelling the spear forward a lever effect is achieved to add throwing force. Although the bow and arrow become very popular, the spear and *atlatl* still receive some use.

An early colonial drawing of an Indian town in the Southeast.

A.D. 450 Lower Mississippi Valley The people of the Lower Mississippi Valley build conical burial mounds and some of the first flat-top platform mounds in North America. The flat-top platform mounds probably are used as substructures for temples or residences for important people. Platform mounds become a hallmark of the later Mississippian period.

A.D. 500 Eastern Great Basin The Fremont culture develops with a lifeway similar to that of the Puebloan agriculturalists to the south. The Fremont people build pueblo-like dwellings and produce distinctive art styles in pottery. By A.D. 1350, declining rainfall brings an end to widespread agriculture and the Fremont culture.

A.D. 500 Central California Hotchkiss period cultures develop out of the earlier Cosumnes period. Hotchkiss period economy is based heavily on acorn gathering, but also fishing, fowling, and hunting.

A.D. 500 Central Arizona A ball game is played in large oval courts, similar to those found in Mesoamerica at the famous Mayan ceremonial center of Chichén Itzá on the Yucatan Peninsula and the city of Teotihuacán in central Mexico near Mexico City.

A.D. 500 Florida and Georgia Hopewellian cultures along the Gulf Coast continue to thrive after those of the Midwest disintegrate. One of the largest sites is Kolomoki in southern Georgia, with numerous burial mounds and a large rectangular, flat-top mound. The site may have had a population of about one thousand people.

The circular "beehive" house used by ancestors of the modern-day Caddo and Wichita. Dwellings of this type, averaging thirty-five feet in diameter, were ideal for the sedentary Caddo, providing comfortable weatherproof living quarters, warm in the winter and cool in the summer. Courtesy of the Caddoan Mounds State Historic Site.

A.D. 500 Eastern United States Cultures of the Late Woodland period are widespread. Compared to earlier cultures in the eastern woodlands, Late Woodland peoples build very few mounds and participate little in long-distance trade. The Late Woodland groups are organized more simply than their Poverty Point, Adena, or Hopewell ancestors.

A.D. 700 Crenshaw Site, Arkansas This site, near Texarkana, Texas, is the earliest known ceremonial center linked to the modern Caddo people who once occupied the area of western Arkansas, eastern Louisiana, eastern Texas, and eastern Oklahoma, but were removed to lands in western Oklahoma where many of them live today. Between A.D. 900 and 1100, at least six mounds were constructed at the Crenshaw site. One of the mounds contained the remains of more than two thousand deer antlers.

A.D. 750 Eastern United States The simple cultures of the Late Woodland period begin a process of transformation into the more complex societies of the Mississippian period. In some areas there is a dramatic shift in subsistence and social complexity. At about this time, many groups intensify agriculture based on maize cultivation. This is associated with the growth of elaborate status hierarchies and hereditary leadership.

A.D. 750 Range Site, Southern Illinois This site, near East St. Louis, provides some of the first tangible evidence for centralized, large-scale storage of food and settlements planned around a plaza. This may represent evidence for the further development of social hierarchies responsible for the distribution of shared resources.

A.D. 800 Toltec Site, Arkansas The Toltec site, near Little Rock, Arkansas, consists of ten mounds arranged around a plaza, enclosed by a two-meter-high earth embankment. This is the most complex settlement known in the Southeast at this time. Although named for the Toltec people of Mexico, the site is the outgrowth of local social developments and not the result of a migration of people from Mexico.

A.D. 800 Zebree Site, Arkansas At this site, about 55 miles north of Memphis, Tennessee, some of the first evidence for larger storage pits corresponds with the increased importance of maize throughout the region as an easily stored food resource.

A.D. 850 Great Plains Throughout the region, cultures of the Plains Village tradition develop along major and minor river valleys. They practice agriculture in conjunction with bison hunting and wild plant gathering. In the northern and central Plains they build large, well-insulated earth lodges. In the south they construct houses with grass roofs.

A.D. 880 Spiro Site, Oklahoma On the uplands near the Arkansas River, twelve miles west of Fort Smith, Arkansas, Caddoans build a series of large, square ceremonial buildings around a plaza. Over the next 200 years these buildings are periodically destroyed and rebuilt as part of an elaborate ceremonial cycle. By A.D. 1100, Spiro becomes a major ceremonial center known for its extensive trade connections.

A.D. 900 Southwest By this date, agriculture is commonly practiced in most areas. Maize becomes a major crop. Although maize contains less food value than some wild plants, it produces higher and more predictable yields. Southwestern farmers use a variety of irrigation canals, dams, and planting methods to conserve scarce rainfall.

A.D. 900 Alaska Thule Inuit (Eskimo) culture begins to spread east, replacing and acculturating existing Dorset groups.

A.D. 900 Eastern United States In many areas, cultures referred to as Mississippian take shape. These cultures are organized as chiefdoms, with an economy based on maize cultivation and locally domesticated crops. These societies participate in long-distance trade and a widespread religion termed the Southeastern Ceremonial Complex.

A.D. 900 Kincaid Site, Ohio One of the major regional mound centers of the Mississippian period, this site is occupied for five hundred years. The Kincaid Site is located at the confluence of the Ohio, Tennessee, and Cumberland rivers, near the town of Paducah, Kentucky. It contains two mound groups, a large village, and a palisade.

A.D. 950 South Dakota People identified as the Middle Missouri tradition migrate to the Great Plains from Minnesota and Iowa. They bring with them a heritage of farming, so they settle along the fertile bottomlands of the Missouri River in present-day South Dakota where maize, squash, and other crops grow in spite of the cold winters and often dry summers. They are recognized as the ancestors of the modern-day Mandan and Hidatsa.

A.D. 985 Greenland Thule Inuit encounter the first expedition of Norsemen to reach North America.

A.D. 1000 Owens, Panamint, and Death Valleys, Utah By this time, archaeological remains linked with the history of the modern Paiute are identifiable.

A.D. 1000 Central and Southern New Mexico Some of the earliest compact villages, later called pueblos by the Spanish, develop around central plazas in the region of the Mogollon cultural tradition.

A.D. 1000 Kansas and Nebraska Along the major rivers in this region, cultures grouped as the Central Plains tradition develop a farming life-style focusing on maize, beans, squash, tobacco, and sunflowers. They live in large, multi-family, earth-covered houses with extended entryways.

A.D. 1000 New York and St. Lawrence River Valley During the Owasco period (A.D. 1000–1300), people build small villages throughout this region and the first clear evidence for cultivation of maize, beans, and squash occurs. By the end of the Owasco period, dwellings consist of multi-family longhouses, some more than two hundred feet long, and villages are surrounded by fortifications, indicating the prevalence of warfare. People of the Owasco period are the ancestors of the Iroquois.

A.D. 1040 Western New Mexico Over a period of years, several pueblos with hundreds of rooms are constructed near each other. In Chaco Canyon, construction of the huge pueblos, like Pueblo Bonito and Chetro Ketl, reach their maximum extent between A.D. 1040 and 1150. Chaco Canyon is connected throughout a wide region by a road system stretching many miles across the desert.

A.D. 1060 Chihuahua, Mexico At the Casas Grandes site (also called Paquime), 200 miles southwest of El Paso, a large settlement is built with connections probably derived from the west coast of Mexico. It is generally believed that traders from Mexico establish the site to improve trade between the civilizations of Mexico and those of the Southwest. About A.D. 1205 the settlement is destroyed, possibly by a revolt.

The town of Secota, in present-day Beaufort County, North Carolina, was engraved by De Bry in the seventeenth century to illustrate the village life of peoples he met. This drawing and those of other settlements visited by early English observers give a visual idea of the lifeways that developed eight hundred years earlier throughout the Southeast and Midwest at the beginning of the Mississippian period. Courtesy of American Heritage Press.

A.D. 1100 Casa Grande Site, Arizona During the Classic period (A.D. 1100–1450), the Hohokam build a "big house" on the Gila River in the Phoenix Basin. The building is four stories tall and made with caliche-adobe walls. The structure may serve as a chief's house.

A.D. 1100 Eastern United States Overreliance on starchy foods, especially maize, in the diet is linked to the poorer health of Mississippian period populations, especially those living in larger villages.

A.D. 1100 New York Region By this date, the archaeological remains linked to the cultural development of the modern Iroquois can be recognized.

A.D. 1100 Northeast Beginning about this time many groups construct fortifications around their villages, indicating widespread warfare.

A.D. 1100 Cahokia Region, Southern Illinois The Mississippian culture centered at the Cahokia site, near St. Louis, reaches its highest level of complexity. More than one hundred mounds are constructed at Cahokia. The principal mound, Monks Mound, is the largest ancient construction north of Mexico. The town surrounding the mounds hold a population of more than ten thousand people.

Pottery of the Casas Grandes people.

A.D. 1175 Awatovi Site, Arizona Located 75 miles north of Winslow, Arizona, the Hopi call this site "Place of the Bow Clan People." At one point the pueblo consists of thirteen hundred ground-floor rooms with a population of more than one thousand. About A.D. 1450, a large two-story pueblo is built. The Franciscans build a church there in the sixteenth century.

A.D. 1200 Oklahoma In central Oklahoma the people of the Washita River phase (A.D. 1200–1450) develop villages based on an economy of maize cultivation and the hunting of deer and bison.

A.D. 1220 Texas and Oklahoma Panhandles Groups move from New Mexico to take advantage of better agricultural conditions resulting from a moister climate.

A.D. 1300 Eastern United States Common beans were present by at least A.D. 1070, however, they do not come into wide usage until A.D. 1300. Although beans are an important nutritional addition to maize-based diets, they are not adopted in all areas.

A.D. 1350 Eastern Great Basin Hunting and gathering peoples associated with the modern southern Paiute, Ute, and Shoshoni replace the earlier Fremont culture.

A.D. 1350 Moundville, Alabama One of the largest Mississippian period ceremonial centers is located 40 miles south of Tuscaloosa. By this date, the site consists of twenty mounds and an associated village. It is probably the center of a chiefdom that includes a number of other sites situated along the Black Warrior River and adjacent areas in west-central Alabama.

A.D. 1400 Southern California Archaeological remains of the Chumash, a tribe that lived in the vicinity of modern-day Santa Barbara, date through the period of European contact. The Chumash are known archaeologically by the term Canaliño.

A.D. 1400 Midwest Throughout a broad section of Missouri and Illinois, including the once densely populated Cahokia region, an "empty quarter" develops, possibly as a result of a poorer climate for agriculture.

A.D. 1450 Nebraska Groups related to the Pawnee migrate north to the Missouri River in South Dakota. Their descendants are recognized as the present-day

Pueblo Bonito at Chaco Canyon in the present day.

Arikara. Today, the Arikara live in North Dakota and are members of the Three Affiliated Tribes, along with their neighbors, the Mandan and Hidatsa.

A.D. 1492 Caribbean On an island in the Bahamas called Guanahani by Natives and San Salvador by Europeans, the expedition led by Christopher Columbus touches ground.

A.D. 1500 Caribbean Columbus and his successors consolidate Spanish control of the Caribbean and begin a period of exploration in North and Central America with repercussions to the present day.

Daniel Rogers
Smithsonian Institution

♦ CHRONOLOGY OF NATIVE NORTH AMERICAN HISTORY, 1500 TO 1965

By the 1450s, many Native American civilizations had risen and disappeared. In the years before Christopher Columbus's arrival, Native Americans were developing rich and diverse cultures and engaging in agricultural development, cultivating uniquely American crops such as corn, tomatoes, potatoes, green beans, squash, pumpkin, tobacco, and others. They were living in tipis, quonsets, longhouses, A-frames, pueblos (multi-story dwellings), or other types of dwellings. During this time, Native Americans were also gaining considerable knowledge about medicine and astronomy and developing a wide variety of music, art, literature, and writing.

To be sure, what is now the United States was not a garden paradise before the coming of the Europeans. Native Americans fought, enslaved, and exploited one another before 1492. Still, most Indian societies were centered around spiritual beliefs and the family, rather than materialism or economic imperialism. Although a few empires existed, most Indians lived in tribes and bands among people who spoke the same language and shared a common culture.

On October 12, 1492, Columbus sighted land in the Bahamas and stepped ashore to claim the lands. At first the Tieno, or Arawak, Indians, who occupied much of the northern Caribbean Islands, were wary of the Spanish, but soon they communicated, offering the visitors food, water, shelter, and friendship. Columbus wrote that the Tieno "invite you to share anything that they possess, and show as much love as if their hearts went with it." The Arawak did not recognize that their land had been claimed by foreigners. They did not know that their chance meeting with Columbus would begin an era of European conquest, subjugation, and enslavement of Native peoples.

Many Europeans considered all non-Christians to be infidels. Many Europeans believed that as heathens, Indians had few rights such as ownership of land or minerals, and that their diverse cultures, languages, and lifeways should be exchanged for Christian religion and customs. The Spanish and English newcomers enslaved Indians, who in turn frequently died as a result of ill-treatment and contagious diseases brought to the Americas from Europe. Thousands of Indians died of smallpox alone. The number of Native American deaths from disease is unknown—estimates vary from several million to as high as sixty million—but by all accounts it was appalling. The number of deaths had the further result of severely impairing the Indians' ability to resist the European incursions and led to despair among many tribes.

Spanish invaders in particular brought with them military objectives. In their initial settlements on Hispaniola (present-day Haiti and Dominican Republic), Spanish soldiers drove Indians from their lands. According to Bartolome de las Casas, a Spanish clergyman, Spanish soldiers "attacked the towns and spared neither the children nor the aged nor pregnant women in childbed." Spanish generals established presidios, or forts, on Hispaniola and expanded the empire through the conquest of other islands. Within a short time, Spanish soldiers reached the mainland of North,South, and Central America, disrupting Native cultures as they went.

1500 The sixteenth century marks the beginning of a widespread decline in Native population. Over the next four centuries, perhaps as many as sixty million people die primarily of European imported diseases such as smallpox and scarlet fever. In the United States, the population decline continues until about 1900, when Indian populations begin to recover.

1511 Antonio de Montesinos, a Catholic priest, gives a stirring sermon to the Spanish leaders of Hispaniola, condemning them for their treatment of Native Americans. Another priest, Bartolome de las Casas, writes *Destruction of the Indies*, in which he chronicles the Spanish conquistadors' cruelty against Native Americans. These gruesome cruelties include butchering men, women, and children like "sheep in the slaughter house."

1512 De las Casas and others attempt to stop the atrocities and begin a reform movement to alter the Spanish Indian policies. The result is the Laws of Burgos, a series of reforms that outlaws Indian slavery and orders the owners of large tracts of land—taken from the Indians and known as *encomiendas*—to improve the treatment of their Indian laborers. The Spanish conquistadors cannot legally invade, enslave, or exploit Indians without first reading them the *Requerimiento*, a document outlining the Christian interpretation of creation and the hierarchy of the Catholic Church. Indians are told to surrender their hearts, souls, and bodies to the Church and Spanish Crown or face utter devastation. "We ask and require . . . that you acknowledge the Church," the document reads. If Indians did not obey, the Spanish promised to "make war against you . . . subject you to the yoke and obedience of the Church [and Crown] . . . take you, and your wives, and your children, and . . . make slaves of them . . . take away your goods and . . . do you all the harm and damage we can."

The *Requerimiento* is intended to offer Native Americans a chance to surrender and submit peacefully to Spanish rule. But as with the Laws of Burgos, the Spanish ignore the substance as well as the spirit of the Requerimiento. The Laws of Burgos fails to end Spanish abuses, for they continue throughout Latin America for four hundred more years.

1520 The Aztec Empire Falls The Spanish adventurer, Hernando Cortés, accompanied by a few hundred Spaniards and a large number of anti-Aztec Indian allies, defeat the Aztecs at Mexico City. The Spanish thereafter substitute their control over the Indians once subject to Aztec rule.

1535 The Spanish explorer Cabeza de Vaca enters present-day New Mexico and reports on the land, food resources, and people.

1539–43 A Spanish expedition led by Hernando de Soto travels through the present-day southeastern United States. De Soto and his company pillage and fight the

Creek, Hitchiti, Chickasaw, Chakchiuma, Choctaw, Tunica, Alabama, and other indigenous nations. The Spanish find little gold and encounter strong resistance from the southeastern Indian nations.

1540–42 The Spanish explorer Francisco Coronado travels into present-day Arizona and New Mexico, and perhaps as far east as present-day Oklahoma. The expedition meets with several Pueblo peoples, including the Zuni and Hopi. Hostilities develop because of Spanish atrocities; the Zuni and their Indian allies force the Spanish to retreat in 1542.

1540–1600 De Soto and other Spaniards encounter the remnants of the southeastern Mississippian culture, which consists of politically and ceremonially centralized chiefdoms, or small city-states, often managed by priests or sacred chiefs. Diseases transmitted by European explorers, fishermen, and slave raiders decimate Mississippian culture populations. By 1600, most Mississippian ceremonial centers are abandoned and the formerly Mississippian culture groups move up and down the Mississippi Valley and into the present-day southeastern United States, dispersed into decentralized political alliances and confederacies of villages or local kinship groups. By the early 1700s much of the Mississippian culture has disappeared. Some of the remnant Mississippian culture nations are known today as the Creek, Cherokee, Natchez, Chickasaw, Caddo, Pawnee, and Choctaw.

1542–1600 The Iroquoian-speaking nations (Wyandotte, Huron, Five Nations, and others) who live along the St. Lawrence River are invaded and displaced by Algonkian-speaking nations (Montagnais, Ottawa, Algonquin, and others) from the north and west. The Iroquoian-speaking nations retreat south and to the lower Great Lakes area.

1563–65 Protestants known as Huguenots flee Catholic France. They attempt to colonize an area from present-day South Carolina to St. Augustine, in present-day Florida. The colony does not survive because of internal dissension and Spanish attack.

The French artist Jacques le Moyne draws some of the earliest known European representations of Native North Americans.

1565–68 The first permanent European settlement in North America is established at St. Augustine, in present-day Florida. Small posts are established up the Atlantic coastline to present-day Georgia; the area is called Guale. Later, Catholic missions built for the purpose of Christianizing the Natives will be established throughout Guale.

1582–1606 The Spanish Begin Settlement of New Mexico Spanish expeditions begin to enter the southern Plains and Pueblo territory by way of the Rio Grande Valley, in eastern New Mexico. In 1598, a Spanish colony is established at San Juan Pueblo, in present-day northern New Mexico. In 1598 and 1599, Indians at Acoma pueblo revolt against the Spanish, but are put down a year later by a Spanish retaliatory expedition. The Spanish introduce sheep and trade to the Pueblo peoples.

1585–1607 The Spanish are not alone in their desire for lands in North America. In 1585, Sir Walter Raleigh founds an English colony on Roanoke Island, present-day North Carolina, but the settlement does not survive. What happened to the English settlers at the Roanoke colony remains a mystery.

The Rappahannock people of present-day Virginia come into contact with Spanish and English fishermen, slave raiders, and explorers, although many contacts were probably not recorded.

1607 English Settlement in Virginia The British Virginia Company, a monopoly granted by the English King James I, establishes a settlement at Jamestown (present-day Virginia) on the lands of the Pamunkey Indians, a subgroup within the Powhatan Confederacy. Like those from other European nations, English citizens come to America to exploit its resources and get rich. When the colonizers arrive, they spend much of their time exploring the James River and gathering rocks believed to contain gold. The "gold" turns out to be pyrite or "fool's gold," and the English cast about for another resource.

Wahunsonacock, the leader of the Powhatan Confederacy (referred to simply as Powhatan by the English) warmly receives the colonizers. During the first winter, the Indians save the Englishmen from starvation. George Percy, one of the Jamestown settlers, writes that English rations are reduced to "but a small can of barley, sodden in water, to five men a day." Percy praises God who "put the terror into the sauvages' hearts" so that the "wild and cruel pagans" would not destroy the English. Percy proclaims that God sent "those people which were our mortal enemies, to relieve us with victuals, as bread, corn, fish, and flesh in great plenty." Without the help of Powhatan and his people, they would have "all perished."

The English soon repay the Pamunkey by demanding their submission to English rule and the payment of an annual tribute of corn. John Smith, the leader of the Jamestown settlement,advocates an aggressive policy toward the Indians, which causes conflicts between the settlers and the Indians of Chesapeake Bay. At first, Powhatan aids the colonists, but after a few years he becomes disillusioned with the English. He asks, "Why

Proceedings of the Floridians in deliberating on important affairs. Drawing by Le Moyne, from an engraving by T. De Bry, *America,* part II, 1591, plate XXIX. Courtesy of American Heritage Publishing Co.

will you destroy us who supply you with food? What can you get by war?" He cannot understand the English animosity toward the Indians nor can he truly understand the full extent of European desire for material gain.

1609 Henry Hudson, sailing for the Netherlands, opens the lucrative fur trade with the Lenape, Wappinger, Manhattan, Hackensack, Munsee, and Mohican nations of New Netherlands (present-day New York).

John Smith, of Jamestown colony, is captured by members of the Powhatan Confederacy under suspicion that he participated in a raid on one of their villages. Smith is brought to Powhatan's village. Tradition has it that Pocahontas, Powhatan's young daughter, intercedes and prevents Smith's execution. Captain Smith is released and allowed to return to Jamestown.

1613–14 Marriage of Pocahontas and John Rolfe Pocahontas is captured by English settlers and eventually converts to Christianity. In 1614, she marries John Rolfe, the Englishman credited with beginning the European tobacco industry. Pocahontas travels to England, but soon dies of an illness. The marriage further complicates the relationship between Powhatan and the English. Tobacco growing requires new acreage for cultivation every five to seven years; therefore, the colonists seek more land inland in Indian hunting areas or lands that the Indians have already cleared and used for farming. The extension of the tobacco plantations further aggravates relations between colonists and Indians; Powhatan, however, seeks to keep the peace.

1615 The confederacy of Algonkian-speaking nations (Ottawa, Potawatomi, Chippewa, and possibly Cree) continue a migration starting near the Atlantic Coast, then through the St. Lawrence River basin, and finally to the Lake Michigan and Lake Superior area. These nations have a tradition of political and ceremonial unity, although they begin to separate into small bands because of the demands of the fur trade economy. Indians trade furs for European manufactured goods such as rifles, metal hatchets and knives, cloth, beads, alcoholic drinks, and other items. The Indians quickly recognize the value of the manufactured goods and find that the Europeans are willing to trade for skins and furs, most often deerskins and beaver skins, which are made into leather and hats. Indians begin to hunt for fur-bearing animals more often, for longer periods of time, and for the market, instead of for necessity. Consequently, some nations, like the Potawatomi, Ottawa, and Chippewa, migrate into the interior in search of territories that support fur-bearing animals. The fur trade defines the primary economic relation between Europeans and Indians until about 1800.

1615–40s The Wendat (Huron), an Iroquoian-speaking nation of thirty- to thirty-five thousand people living near Lake Huron, in alliance with other Iroquoian-speakers—Tobacco, Attiwandaronk (Neutral Nation), and Erie of present-day Ohio—establish a vast trade network in the eastern interior of North America. Goods are exchanged through trade networks that extend into Mexico, to the Gulf of Mexico, and as far west as present-day Minnesota. By the early 1600s these trade networks are distributing manufactured goods, metal knives, guns, tools, cloth, and others items, which are gained in trade with the French in New France (present-day southeastern Canada). By 1635, beaver supplies in the Huron homeland are depleted owing to European fur demands. The Huron are forced to trade with other nations or hunt on the territories of other Native nations. In the late 1640s the Five Nations (Iroquois of upstate New York), with Dutch supplies of guns, ball, and powder, destroy the Huron and allied nations' trade empire. Under French influence, the Huron and their allies

Pocahontas saving the life of Captain John Smith, from an engraving by T. De Bry, *America,* part XIII, 1634. Courtesy of American Heritage Publishing Co.

Huron dancing ceremony to cure sickness, from Champlain, *Voyages et descouvertures,* Paris, 1620. Courtesy of American Heritage Publishing Co.

refuse to grant the Five Nations trade access to the interior from the early 1620s to 1649.

1616–20 A smallpox epidemic ravages the New England Indians who live along the coast line from present-day Massachusetts to Maine.

1618–31 Powhatan dies in 1618. His brother, Opechancanough, assumes leadership of the tribal confederation. Relations between the colonists and Indians grow more hostile until 1622 when Opechancanough moves against the English, who lose more than one-third of their colony and nearly leave Virginia. The English Crown takes over Jamestown and Virginia, providing aid and protection to the settlers.

Some English feel that the war of 1622 ultimately would be good for the colony. John Smith writes that the conflict "will be good for the Plantation, because we have just cause to destroy them by all meanes possible." Another Englishman writes that the English are "now set at liberty by the treacherous violence of Sauvages." By right of war, the English can now invade Indian lands and thereby "enjoy their cultivated places . . . and possessing the fruits of other labours. Now their cleared grounds in all their villages (which are situated in the fruitfullest places of the land) shall be inhabited by us, whereas heretofore the grubbing of woods was the greatest labour."

The first Virginia War intermittently lasts nearly ten years with many deaths among the Natives and colonists. The territory of the Chickahominy nation, an ally nation within the Powhatan Confederacy, is ravaged by colonial attacks throughout the 1620s. The Native population in Virginia begins to decline significantly, mostly because of disease, warfare, and most likely migration. In 1608, about thirty thousand Natives live on Chesapeake Bay, but by 1669 only two thousand remain.

1620 Arrival of the Pilgrims The Pilgrims arrive aboard the Mayflower at Plymouth, Massachusetts. Before landing, they sign a compact calling for self-rule. The Pilgrims barely survive their first winter in Massachusetts, but are helped by several friendly Indians, one of whom was Tisquantum, more commonly known as Squanto. He is captured sometime between 1605 and 1614, when an English ship abducts several Indians and carries them off for sale in Europe. Tisquantum is brought to Malaga Island, Spain, and sold. He makes his way back home by way of England and Newfoundland, only to find that his home village has been wiped out by disease. Tisquantum lives with the Wampanoag and their chief, Massasoit, who extends authority over much of present-day Massachusetts and Rhode Island. During his travels, Tisquantum learns some English.

Tisquantum, like other Native Americans, aids the colonists, showing them where to hunt and fish, and how to grow and prepare native crops such as squash, corn, and beans. After the disastrous first winter, the Pilgrims learn quickly from the Indians' lessons. In the fall of 1621 they invite Massasoit to a feast to give thanks; he arrives with ninety people. When the Pilgrims do not have sufficient food, Massasoit asks his people to provide food as well.

1626 Manhattan Island Is Sold Peter Minuit, governor of New Netherlands, the Dutch colony in the New World, trades sixty guilders of goods—legend says worth twenty-four dollars—for Manhattan Island, part of present-day New York City. Minuit buys the land from a band of Shinnecock Indians, but later has to buy it again from the Manhattan band, which claims hunting rights to the island.

1629–33 Spanish missionaries establish Catholic churches at Acoma, Hopi, and Zuni pueblos.

1630 The Puritans Arrive Ten years after the Pilgrims' arrival, the Puritans (a Protestant religious sect) led by John Winthrop arrive in Massachusetts. The Puritans believe that they are on a mission from God to establish a "City Upon the Hill," a perfect Christian society in which the Puritans form a covenant among themselves and with God to live a holy life. Outsiders are not invited into the covenant unless they agree to subjugate themselves to the rules of the religious community. Most Native Americans do not want to join this covenant and are considered outside of God's law. In fact, Puritan minister Cotton Mather maintains that Indians are the "accursed seed of Canaan" who have been dispatched by Satan "in hopes that the gospel of Jesus Christ would never come here to destroy or disturb his absolute empire over them." Reverend Mather points to the devastating disease that ravages Native populations to prove English superiority. He called the smallpox epidemic of 1633–35, which kills thousands of Natives, a "remarkable and terrible stroke of God upon the natives." The Puritans argue that God sent the disease to kill Satan's children and to clear the land for his true flock.

1636–37 The Pequot War The Puritans assert their authority over the Pequot, a warlike tribe disliked by many Indians, living in what is now Connecticut. In 1634, Indians kill John Stone and eight companions who are hunting for Native slaves. Puritans use Stone's death to claim jurisdiction over the Pequot and to demand their surrender of land, valuable goods, and Stone's killers. Narragansett, living to the east of the Pequot, are believed to have committed the murders, but the Pequot agree to the Puritan demands. However, they do not abide by the terms of the agreement, and relations with the English grow steadily worse. In 1636, several Narragansett kill an English trader and then flee into Pequot country. When the English demand the return of the Narragansett, the Pequot refuse and a fight ensues. In May 1637, the Massachusetts General Court, the colony's legislature, drafts articles of war, raises an army against the Pequot, and surrounds the Indian village and fort on the Mystic River. Puritans, pilgrims, Mohican, and Narragansett attack and set fire to the Pequot fort, killing as many as seven hundred men, women, and children.

1638 Early Reservations The Puritans establish what would now be called a "reservation" for the Quinnipiac Nation living near present-day New Haven, Connecticut. Under the terms of their agreement, the Quinnipiac retain only twelve hundred acres of their original land on which they are subject to the jurisdiction of an English magistrate or agent. Under English rule, Quinnipiac people cannot sell or leave their lands or receive "foreign" Indians. They cannot buy guns, powder, or whiskey. They must accept Christianity and reject their traditional spiritual beliefs, which Puritans feel are the teachings of Satan.

1640 Five Nations Exhaust Local Beaver Supplies The Five Nations (Iroquois) are no longer able to supply their trade requirements by hunting and trapping on their home territory (present-day upstate New York). The Five Nations have come to depend on trade with the Dutch at Fort Orange (present-day Albany, New York) to supply knives, axes, cloth, beads, and guns and powder. After 1640, the Five Nations look to the interior nations to supply them with trade ties or allow them access to beaver territories. During the 1640s, the Five Nations try to negotiate trade and diplomatic agreements with the Huron, Neutral Nation, Erie, and Wyandotte, but the French move to prevent permanent trade agreements.

1644–46 The Second Virginia War The Powhatan Confederacy stages a second war against Virginia colony. After the war of 1622, the Indians try to live in peace with the settlers, but the English expand onto Indian lands. Some Indians are held as slaves or servants. By 1641, the English have settled in Maryland and south of the James River and covet the land of the Rappahannock, a major Powhatan ally. By 1642, the English are selecting land sites, even some that include Indian villages. The war of 1644–46 temporarily prevents English territorial expansion.

Opechancanough, now old and feeble, is carried to the battlefield where he wants to die a warrior's death rather than submit to the English. After two years of warfare, the Indians and colonists negotiate an agreement defining a boundary between the two. The Treaty of 1646 prohibits English land expansion; however, the Indians are left with only a portion of their former lands. The colonists agree to respect Native rights to these territories. Indians become subject to the rule of the colonial Virginia courts and must provide an annual tribute of beaver pelts. Nevertheless, by 1649 English colonists are already disregarding the treaty and moving farther into Indian territory.

1649–1700 The Beaver Wars After failing to gain a reliable trade agreement with the Huron and their trading allies, the Five Nations, with Dutch support and guns and powder, initiate a series of intermittent wars against the Susquehannock, Huron, Neutral Nation, Erie, Wyandotte, Ottawa, and other French trading nations. By 1650, the Huron trade empire is destroyed by the Five Nations. The Ottawa (whose name means "to trade")

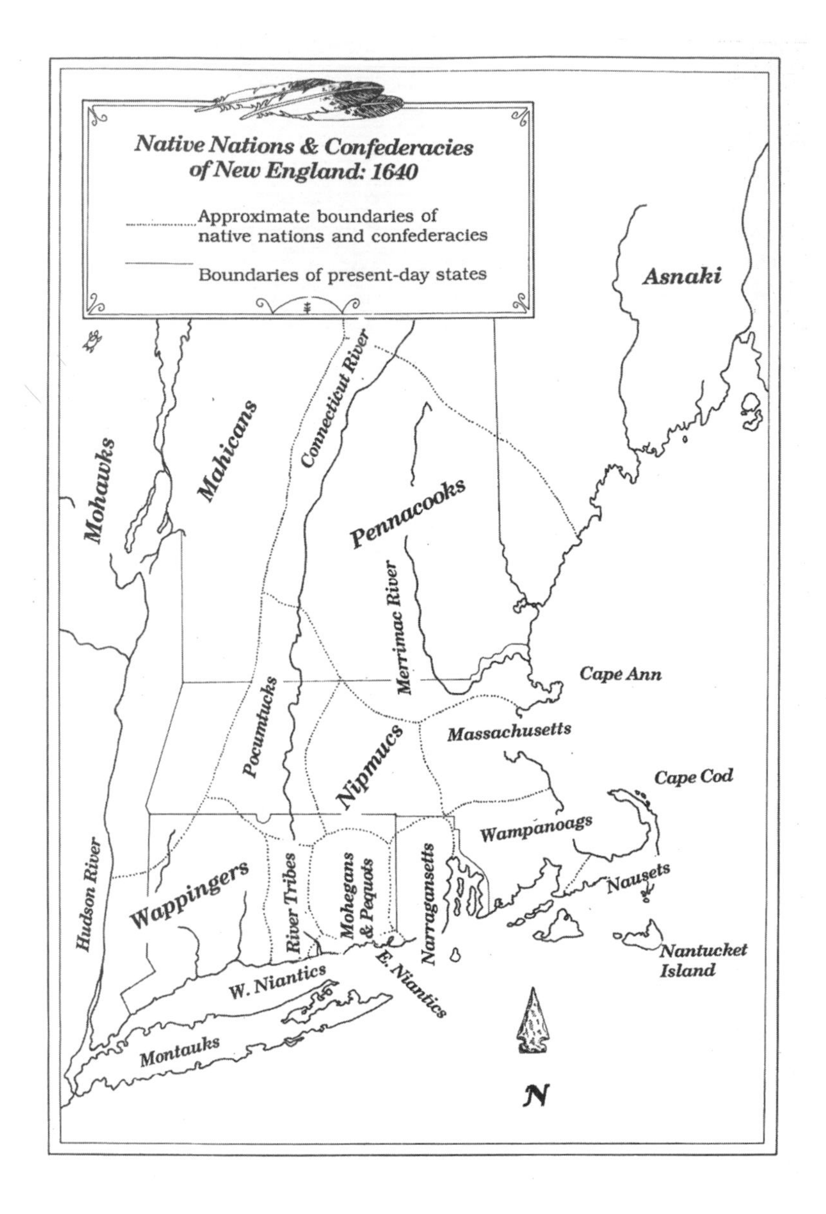

then assume the role of middlemen traders between the interior nations of the Great Lakes area and the French. Thereafter, the Five Nations carry their wars and diplomacy to the Indian nations of the interior, attacking the Chippewa, the Illinois Confederacy, and the Ottawa, and pushing these nations farther into the Great Lakes regions of present-day Michigan and Wisconsin. The Five Nations are generally successful in these wars and are able to supply the Dutch, until 1664, with trade goods. After 1664, the English capture New Netherlands and rename it New York. The English continue the policies of the Dutch traders by supplying the Five Nations with weapons to carry on their trade wars with the interior nations. The French are reluctant to supply their trading partners with guns, and therefore the interior nations are at a disadvantage against the better supplied Five Nations.

1650 Cheyenne Migration Begins Because of the expanding Iroquois trade empire, the Cheyenne, probably living in present-day southern Ontario or Quebec, are forced to migrate westward. By 1775, they reach the Great Plains of present-day Montana and Dakotas, where they adopt Plains culture with buffalo hunting, an original Sun Dance ceremony, and sacred bundles, given to them by the prophetic figure Sweet Medicine.

1660 The Chippewa (Ojibway) living in the upper Great Lakes region start to move west, armed with guns and trade goods. Pushed by colonial and Five Nation expansion, the Chippewa invade Sioux territory in present-day Minnesota. After much fighting with the Chippewa, many Sioux move onto the Plains in the 1700s, where they adopt the buffalo hunting horse culture, for which they are well known in U.S. history. Before this time, the

Sioux were a settled horticultural people living in the woodlands east of the Plains area.

1661 The Chickahominy Are Dispossessed The Chickahominy Nation, part of the Powhatan Confederacy, move from the Pamunkey River to the Mattaponi River. The Chickahominy sell 2,000 acres of land to an Englishman named Hammond. Phillip Mallory buys 743 acres from the Chickahominy, the beginning of the Mallory family's two-century effort to acquire Chickahominy lands in Virginia.

1670–1710 Carolina Colony and Early Southern Indian Slave Trade Charles Town, in present-day South Carolina, is established. Early encounters lead to conflict with the local tribal groups such as the Cusabo and Westo. The English attempt to enslave many Indians for plantation work and enlist other nations such as the Creek and Cherokee to raid interior nations like the Choctaw, living in present-day Mississippi and Louisiana, for slaves. During the 1680s and 1690s, the Choctaw are under considerable pressure and lose many people to slave raids. In 1699, the French establish Louisiana colony, and supply the Choctaw with some weapons, which they use to protect themselves from the English, Creek, and Cherokee slave raids. Some Choctaw regions thereafter are strongly allied to the French in gratitude for their help in preserving the Choctaw nation. By 1710, the Indian slave trade declines; Indians made poor slaves since they knew the local area and escaped often. Thereafter, the fur trade becomes the primary economic relation of the southern Indians to the colonists.

1671–80 Apaches begin migrating to the Southwest from the southern Plains. They raid Spanish settlements and Indian pueblos; sheep, horses, and trade goods are stolen. By this time, the Apache are well equipped with guns and horses and are able to elude and challenge Spanish armed forces.

1675–76 King Philip's War The Puritans proceed to concentrate Indians on reservations and open former Indian lands to Puritan resettlement. By 1671, the Puritans have established fourteen reservations and many Indians have been forced from their homelands. Metacom, the Wampanoag son of Massasoit known to the English as King Philip, protests Puritan policies. He argues that the English set out to destroy Native Ameri-

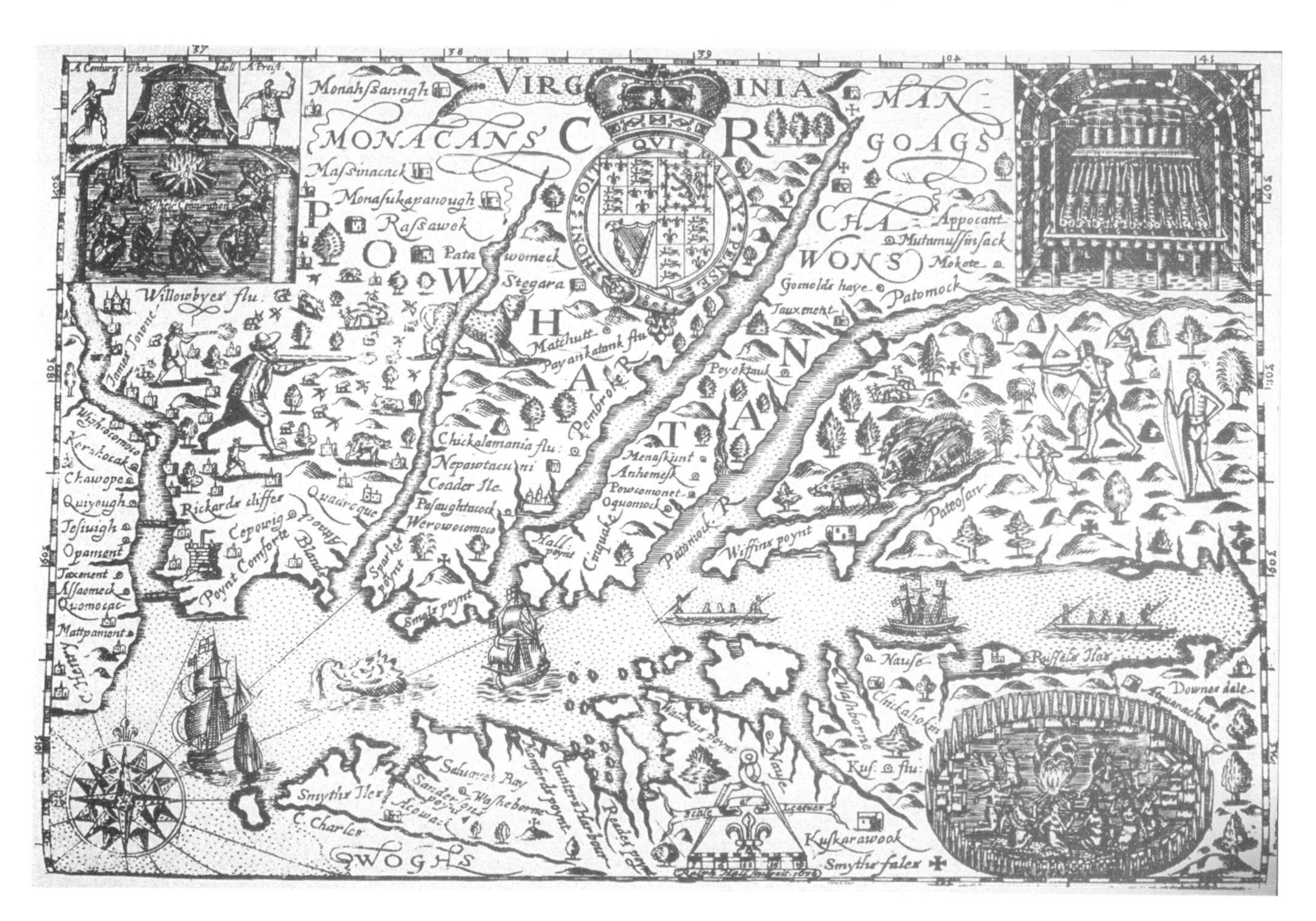

Map of Virginia by Ralph Hall, 1636. Courtesy of American Heritage Publishing Co.

can cultures and steal Indian lands. In 1671, Puritans arrest Metacom, but release him. He continues to move among the tribes, telling them that the settlers are destroying Indian culture and sovereignty. By 1675, Metacom has a sufficient following to launch a war against the English. Abenaki, Nipmuck, Narragansett, and Wampanoag Indians join forces and attack more than half of the ninety English settlements in New England. The Indians, however, do not stand long against the English. Upon conclusion of hostilities, the English General Court decreases the number of reservations from fourteen to five and places all Indians they can find upon these reserves. The Puritan government has Metacom executed and his wife, son, and hundreds of followers sold into slavery. Many of King Philip's allies, such as the Wampanoag, Nipmuck, and Narragansett, are enslaved or flee to the Mahican, a linguistically related group to the Mohican, in New York, or to the Abenaki Confederation in present-day Maine. The remnant northeastern Indian nations settle down to English rule in small communities, and over the next few centuries establish about fifteen "praying towns" of Christian Indians, whose local government is much like the rest of New England. The "praying" Indians become socially and economically marginalized in New England society.

1675–77 Bacon's Rebellion In 1675 and 1676, a third major war erupts between Indians and Virginia settlers. This time, Maryland settlers are involved. The Rappahannock flee their villages, and their land is taken by Virginian settlers. The colonists defeat the Susquehannock, who are pressed in the north by the expanding Iroquois trade empire, and who move into Virginia territory, only to be abused by Virginia traders. The colonists are led by Nathaniel Bacon, who leads a rebellion to free Virginia colony from English rule. The English restore order, but not before Bacon's army kills and enslaves many Susquehannock, Occnaneechi, Appomatuck, Manakin, and members of the Powhatan Confederacy. The Indians lose heavily in the war.

In 1677, a treaty of peace is signed between some Indian nations and Virginia colony. This treaty guarantees the signing Indians at least three miles of land in each direction from each of their villages. This leaves the remainder—most—of the land open to Virginia settlements and plantations. The Indians of Virginia are forced to acknowledge English law and courts, are subject to Virginian rule, and are left without significant land resources.

1677–1731 Shawnee Migrations and Regroupings The Shawnee probably occupy present-day northern Kentucky and southern Ohio before European contact. During the late 1600s Chickasaw and Cherokee slave raiding and fur trading expeditions force the Shawnee to retreat from their homeland. Some Shawnee migrate south to Georgia to live on the Savannah River, which is named after them, while others move to present-day western Virginia and Pennsylvania. Others join the Creek nation, in present-day Alabama, where they establish a permanent village within the Creek nation. By the 1690s many Shawnee are congregating in present-day eastern Pennsylvania, where they are joined by remnant bands of Delaware, Munsee, and Susquehannock. Sometime before 1680 the Five Nations grant the Delaware, Susquehannock, Shawnee, and other remnant coastal nations the right to occupy territory in present-day eastern Pennsylvania, and many locate near what is now Philadelphia. Most of these nations are now landless, and the Iroquois use the landless Indian nations to create a buffer zone between themselves and the English colonies.

1680 The Ottawa now control about two-thirds of the fur trade with the French, while the Chippewa and related groups supply most of the rest. The Iroquois are unsuccessful in persuading or forcing the Algonkian-speaking Indian allies to trade with them or with the English in New York. The Iroquois make greater inroads for hunting and trading south of the Great Lakes area, using both diplomacy and armed forces to attain their commercial ends.

1680–91 The Pueblo Revolt Popé, a Native American visionary from San Juan pueblo, leads an armed revolt against the Spanish. Popé claims he is visited by the spirit world and was given a holy charge to rid his homeland of the Spanish. His message brings about a Native revitalization movement that demands an end to the eighty-year Spanish occupation and a return to traditional life. The Pueblo Revolt begins at Taos pueblo in August 1680 and moves steadily southward, driving the Spanish to El Paso del Norte (El Paso, Texas). The Indian patriots kill more than four hundred people and recover their homelands. Nine years later, a Spanish army returns. More than six hundred Indians are killed in the initial battle for the reconquest of New Mexico. In 1691, the Spanish military commander Diego de Vargas begins the bloody recovery in earnest, ending four years later. Rather than live under Spanish rule, many Pueblos flee to the small Navajo bands in the north, bringing much knowledge of the Pueblo cultural worldview and economic life-style to the Navajo, who until then live mostly by hunting and gathering fruits and nuts.

1682 Pennsylvania Colony and Delaware Treaty William Penn purchases the present site of Philadelphia, Pennsylvania. The treaty is negotiated with a leading Delaware chief, sometimes called Tammany. A long period of peaceful relations begins between Quakers

Walpi, an ancient Hopi Pueblo village.

and the Indians, although relations are not always peaceful with Pennsylvania colony, especially after the 1730s.

1689–97 King William's War King William's War initiates a series of colonial wars that last until the end of the War of 1812. During this time, there is an undeclared war on the frontier, first between the English and French and their respective Indian allies until 1763, or the end of the French and Indian War. Frontier conflict starts again with the Revolutionary War in 1776; war on the borders continues until 1795. The War of 1812 is the last conflict before the United States finally establishes its military control over the eastern coastal states and their frontiers. During this period of more than 125 years of intermittent warfare, Indian nations attempt to maintain trade relations with one or more European colony and to retain their territory and political independence from colonial domination. Since Indian nations cannot produce metal goods or guns and powder, they depend on trade with European powers to supply these and other more domestic economic requirements. This dependency on trade forces the Indian nations to side with one or the other European power in order to have access to trade and weapons, which becomes increasingly important for defense within the climate of almost constant colonial struggle and warfare. Indians nations often sell themselves as mercenaries to one European power as a means of obtaining goods, other than by trapping furs and trading. In the north, the Algonkian-speaking nations often side with the French, until their defeat in 1763, while the Five Nations, especially the Mohawk, often side with the English, at least until 1755, when some Seneca begin to favor the French. After 1763, the western Algonkian-speaking nations (Ottawa, Chippewa, Potawatomi, Miami, and others) side with the British against the United States until the end of the War of 1812. Some nations, like the Five Nations and the Creek in the south, try to balance power diplomatically among the European colonies by not taking sides and by threatening an opponent with defection in order to gain political or trade concessions from the Europeans.

1700 The Missions Native Americans have influenced the Spanish in many areas, particularly with their gifts of foods, natural resources, and architecture. In return, American Indians have acquired horses, cattle, sheep, mules, and other livestock. In California and Texas,

The restored church at San Ildefonso Pueblo.

Iroquois conference, 1753. Drawing by John Kahionhes Fadden.

Indians become skilled cowboys and cowgirls in their own right. They also learn to cultivate wheat, commonly used to make bread, especially fry bread, a traditional bread made by frying wheat dough. Some Indians learn the new religion and Christianity spreads widely among the American tribes. Spanish priests, generally of the Jesuit and Franciscan Orders, establish missions from the Atlantic to the Pacific. The priests oversee Indian life at the missions where Indians supply the labor to build the beautiful structures so admired today.

The mission system is not always a positive influence for most Native Americans. Indians often die from the meager diet and hard work, and sometimes go unattended following injuries or disease. When Indians refuse to work, priests or Christian Indians whip the people, including women and children, into submission. When families flee the missions, presidio soldiers hunt them down and force them to return. Native Americans die in large numbers at the missions from overwork, disease, and unsanitary conditions. Epidemics occur periodically in California under the Spanish occupation, the first recorded one in 1777 at Mission Santa Clara. An epidemic of diphtheria and pneumonia occurs in 1802, ravaging the young from Mission San Carlos to San Luis Obispo. Still another epidemic decimates Native Americans from San Francisco to Santa Barbara with more than sixteen hundred dead due to measles. Children under the age of ten are almost wiped out in this epidemic. The Native American population declines by as much as 45 percent under the Spanish occupation of California as the direct result of introduced sickness and disease.

1701–55 The Iroquois Adopt Neutrality The Iroquois shift their policy from alliance with the English to neutrality between the French (in New France, or present-day Canada) and the English colonies. Late in the 1690s the English begin to occupy Iroquois territory in the Mohawk Valley; this, along with the burden and losses of warfare with the French and their Indian allies, convinces the Iroquois that their English ally is as much a threat to them as were the French. During the 1690s the Iroquois suffered from a series of military setbacks and the new English land threats. In response they slightly centralize the Confederate Council, composed of forty-nine chiefs from the Five Nations, and develop a new policy of a united front against the Europeans. This centralization takes the form of having one chief

Early colonists often observed Native societies. Drawing by John Kahionhes Fadden.

speak for the entire confederacy of Five Nations as if by one voice, rather than five chiefs speaking for their individual nations.

After a treaty of peace with the French in 1701, the Iroquois confederacy negotiates commercial agreements with the Ottawa, Chippewa, Illinois Confederacy, and other interior nations. In exchange for allowing the Iroquois to hunt and trade in the interior and Great Lakes area, the interior nations are allowed to travel to Albany, New York, to trade with the English, who had cheaper, better quality goods and a better selection than the French. This agreement bolsters Iroquois dominance in the region until the 1740s, when Pennsylvania traders follow the retreating Delaware and Shawnee into the Ohio Valley and beyond. The Iroquois restrict English trade to Albany, but the Pennsylvania traders go directly to the interior villages. Thus, the Iroquois lose their strong trade position, and their power and influence decline. The English continue to support the Iroquois Confederacy until the Revolutionary War from 1777 to 1783 as a means to gain trade relations and diplomatic influence over the interior nations. By the 1750s, however, the Iroquois empire is a political puppet for British colonial designs.

1702–1713 Queen Anne's War Queen Anne's War, pitting the English against the French and Spanish, starts in Europe, but is also fought in the American colonies. Between 1702 and 1704, the English and Indian allies (Creek and probably Cherokee) attack the Florida mission Indians of Guale (present-day Georgia) and nearly annihilate the entire population of Appalachee Indians, a remnant of which later joins the Creek. The area from the Savannah River (Georgia) to St. Augustine, Florida, is depopulated of Indian people and the Spanish missions are destroyed. Some Yamasee Indians, many mission Indians in Guale, migrate to Spanish protection in Florida. The Spanish are unable or unwilling to protect them from English expansion into Florida.

1711–22 Tuscarora War and Migration The Tuscarora, an Iroquoian-speaking nation living in present-day North Carolina, become involved in war with the English arising from trade disputes. Many Tuscarora become indebted to English traders, who give them credit in the form of goods in the fall of the year and collected the credit in the spring after the hunt. Many Tuscarora cannot pay back the credit, and some traders confiscate the hunters' children and wives to sell as slaves. This manner of collecting the debts leads to war in 1711, and the Tuscarora are defeated by 1713. Many Tuscarora then decide to migrate out of eastern North Carolina and travel north, where they find, to their surprise, that the Tuscarora and the Iroquois (Five Nations) speak very closely related languages. The Tuscarora are invited by the Oneida, one of the Five Nations of the Iroquois Confederacy, to live with them and join the confederacy. Between 1715 and 1722, many Tuscarora settle in New York with the Iroquois and are adopted into the confederacy. Nevertheless, the forty-nine chiefs do not wish to create new Tuscarora chiefs, which would violate the sacred constitution of the confederacy, and so the Oneida chiefs speak and represent the Tuscarora, at least until the 1800s, when the confederacy was greatly disrupted. After 1715, the Iroquois Five Nations becomes known as the Six Nations.

1715–17 The Yamasee War and Creek Neutrality The Yamasee of present-day Georgia, in alliance with the Creek and other smaller coastal nations such as the Hitchiti, Yuchi, and Mikasuki, rise up against the English because of a series of trade and other abuses. The Yamasee and allies are defeated, and many tribes migrate south into Florida, ultimately forming part of the Seminole, while others join the Creek Confederacy, then occupying what is now central Georgia and Alabama. This defeat convinces the Creek leaders that war against the English is not profitable, and the Creek embark on a policy of neutrality between the English colonies in the Carolinas, the Spanish in Florida and West Florida (now southern Alabama and Mississippi), and the French colony of Louisiana. The Creek play balance of power between the rival European powers and attempt to maximize trade and diplomatic concessions from the colonists.

1716–27 The Creek and Cherokee War In the Yamasee War, the Cherokee side with the English against the Creek and their allies. This leads to bloodshed and several failed attempts to reestablish peace. In 1716, a pro-English faction of Cherokee kills a delegation of visiting Creek and Yamasee emissaries, which initiates the war. Thus, in the period after the end of the Yamasee War, the Creek and Cherokee carry on a low-scale war of raiding parties and revenge attacks against one another.

1720–60 The French Wars on the Chickasaw The Chickasaw are attracted to an English alliance because they are enticed by the low-price, high-quality English trade goods. The English, in turn, seek a Chickasaw alliance because they wish to disrupt the French plan to control the Mississippi Valley by erecting a series of forts and making alliances with the Indian nations along the Mississippi River. In general, the Chickasaw favor the English, although there is a small pro-French faction. Between 1729 and 1752, the French launch four major military expeditions against the Chickasaw villages near the Mississippi in present-day western Kentucky and northwestern Mississippi. The Chickasaw survive all these attacks, although at times are desperate for supplies and ammunition. In 1739, some Chickasaw migrate to South Carolina for English protection, while others, many of whom are survivors of the Natchez Nation who sought Chickasaw protection from the French in 1729, move to live among the western Creeks. The Chickasaw are a major military obstacle to the French plan of enveloping the British colonies and restricting them to the Atlantic seaboard.

1729 Destruction of the Natchez Nation The Natchez nation, a Muskogean-speaking society with a centralized sacred chieftain, "The Great Sun," and a remnant society of the Mississippian culture, rebels against French attempts to impose taxes and confiscate land in their central village, Natchez. The French at Natchez plantation, in the Louisiana colony, are wiped out. The French and their Choctaw allies counterattack and destroy the Natchez villages. The Great Sun is captured, and along with several hundred other captives, is sold into slavery in the Caribbean Islands. The Natchez descendants still live there. Other Natchez escape, some seeking refuge among the Chickasaw, who give them shelter, but this intensifies warring relations between the Natchez and the French and Choctaw.

1739 Arikara Migrate North About this time, the group of Indians known now as the Arikara (a group closely related to the Pawnee) begin to migrate north from the Loup River in present-day Nebraska and travel up the Missouri River to settle eventually in present-day central North Dakota.

1740–1805 Russians Explore the Northwest Coast The first Russian explorers sail over to Alaska and explore the entire Alaska coastline and encounter many Pacific Northwest Coast tribal groups, like the Haida, Tlingit, Aleut, and others. In the 1740s and 1750s, following Vitus Bering who in 1741 sighted the North American continent and explored the Bering Sea and Bering Strait, the Russians open trade with Natives for sea otter pelts. Russian fur traders expand their enterprises in the far

Northwest and by 1805 reach San Francisco, California. French, Dutch, and Russians establish colonies primarily to exploit the rich resource in fur. They trade guns, powder, lead, pots and pans, knives, fishhooks, beads, and cloth for furs. Indians often alter their traditional lives to obtain furs to trade for these items; in doing so, their cultures change and many become dependent on the European supply of manufactured goods.

In the second half of the eighteenth century, the Russian government sends over many Russian Orthodox priests to convert and protect the Natives. Many of these early Russian Orthodox churches and their Native congregations—sometimes singing mass in archaic Russian—can still be found in several places in Alaska.

1744–48 King George's War King George's War was initiated in Europe but also fought by the European colonies in North America. This war pits the French against the English, and each side persuades its Indian allies to fight. It is cheaper and more efficient for colonial governments to hire Indian fighters to engage in war than to import troops from Europe, where they are badly needed. In North America, the war is inconclusive; the Treaty of Aix-la-Chapelle, negotiated in Europe, restores all original boundaries.

1748–51 The Choctaw Civil War The Choctaw Nation is divided during the 1730s and 1740s between loyalty to the French and cheap trade goods given by the English. One region, the central and northeast villages, favors English trade, while the western and southern villages favor French alliance. Civil war erupts between the regions when Red Shoes, the head warrior of the eastern allied towns, is assassinated for a bounty by a pro-French Indian. Both sides rely on their allies to supply weapons and ammunition, but the British fail to provide enough support for their allies and the pro-British eastern villages are defeated by the opposing forces. After 1751, Choctaw political relations are organized into three autonomous political regions: the conservative Six Towns district (or *iksa*, a Choctaw term for a matrilineal descent group) in the south favor the French; the western villages, called "people of the long hair," also favor the French; and the northeastern villages, called the "potato people," favor the British. Each district has a chief and a council, and each decides its own internal matters, rarely meeting with the other two districts to discuss national business. The basic three-district political system lasts among the Choctaw until 1907, when the U.S. government abolishes the government of the Choctaw Nation.

1750–1850 The Chickahominy Nation Disperses The Chickahominy Nation of Virginia break into several smaller communities. Some join the Pamunkey, Mattaponi, and other remaining nations living near the Chesapeake Bay area, while others hang onto their lands, living by hunting and fishing. By the 1760s and later, the Chickahominy people are no longer mentioned in the Virginia records.

1754 The Albany Plan Benjamin Franklin, a prominent citizen and statesmen from Pennsylvania, proposes a plan of union for the British colonies. Franklin has several times visited the Iroquois Confederacy (Six Nations) and suggests their model for unifying the colonies. He remarks that it is strange that the Six Nations could form an apparently indissoluble union, while ten or twelve British colonies could not. The plan fails in 1754—for want of interest by more than a few colonists—but is revived later in the U.S. Articles of Confederation (1777–88), the first laws of U.S. government, and in the U.S. Constitution (implemented in 1789).

1754–63 French and Indian War The French and Indian War begins with the French construction of Fort Duquesne (present-day Pittsburgh, Pennsylvania) on land already claimed by Virginia. The European colonies go to war over lands along the Ohio River. Many Iroquois (Mohawk primarily) reluctantly side with the British, while Seneca favor the French for a time, but many Indians align themselves with the French, including the Wyandotte, Shawnee, Chippewa, Ottawa, Miami, Abenaki, and Lenape. At first the war goes well for the French and their Spanish and Indian allies, but in the end the French lose nearly all of their claims in the Americas, including Canada and the Illinois-Mississippi River valleys. Indians who fought with the French now find themselves without their allies and without suppliers of arms and trade goods.

1760–75 The British in Sole Control of Eastern North America The French defeat by 1760 changes the situation of the eastern Native nations. Since about 1600, there had been at least two or more major European powers fighting for control of trade and land. Now only the British remain, and only one nation controls trade relations, the supplies of goods and of weapons and ammunition. The British try to regulate the distribution of trade and weapons, which makes the formerly French allied Indians suspicious of British intentions. Furthermore, the British intend to occupy the old French forts, such as Detroit and Chicago, in the Great Lakes area, which was territory the Indians claimed and did not grant British occupation. Ottawa, Wyandotte, Miami, Great Lakes nations, and Shawnee Indians living north of the Ohio River fear the British political domination. In the 1760s and early 1770s, the British administration plans to regulate the Indians' trade and activities, but these plans are disrupted by the emergence of the revolutionary war in 1775.

Hendrick, Abraham, and Franklin at the Albany Conference, 1754. Drawing by John Kahionhes Fadden.

1760–63 The Delaware Prophet After the French defeat in the early 1760s, and while the British threaten domination, several prophets emerge among the Delaware people. Two major figures teach very different messages. One brings a militant message, involving borrowed Christian concepts of personal salvation in heaven; the other "domestic" Delaware prophet teaches a message also borrowed from Christian ideas of heaven and a central god, but establishes a new religion designed only for the Delaware, not for any of the other Indian or European nations.

The "militant" prophet emphasizes that the Europeans will have to be driven off the continent and the Indians return to the customs of their ancestors before they can be restored to their former prosperous and happy state. This message greatly influences the Ottawa leader Pontiac, who uses it to mobilize warriors from different nations to strike at the English in 1763. The "domestic" Delaware prophet creates a new national religion, reorganizes the Delawares' disrupted kinship system, and creates new and permanent chiefs for the three reorganized kinship-religious divisions of the religiously-politically unified Delaware Nation.

1763 Pontiac's War Pontiac follows the precepts of the militant Delaware prophet and, through this religious revitalization movement, forms an Indian confederacy of the Ottawa, Lenape (Delaware), Wyandotte, Seneca, Potawatomi, Kickapoo, Shawnee, and Miami tribes. Pontiac leads the confederacy in a short-lived war, which does not prevent the British from occupying the old French forts of the Ohio and Great Lakes area.

1763 The Proclamation of 1763 The British government's proclamation results in the drawing of a boundary, the Proclamation Line of 1763, running along the crest of the Appalachian Mountains. Indian country is west of the line from the Appalachian Mountains to the Mississippi River, while the colonists can settle lands east of the line. This act recognizes Indian rights to land, but many colonists disregard the act and move across the Appalachians, causing conflict with the Indian nations who regard them as intruders.

1763–74 Pre-Revolutionary Policy Between 1763 and 1774, most of the nations in the eastern portion of North America reassess their relationship with the British government and the colonists. Native Americans realize that a rift has developed between the British homeland and the colonists, and many seek positions of neutrality; however, as the British government and the colonists drift closer to war, some of the nations favor alliance with the British. Many Indians believe that in the event of war, the British will win. Many Indians also believe that the colonists, who are interested in acquiring more land, are a greater threat to the Indians than the British government.

1768 Treaty of Fort Stanwix Bowing to British insistence, the Six Nations cede land ranging from south of the Ohio River into present-day northern Kentucky. Most of this land comprises the traditional Shawnee homeland, and the Shawnee recognize no right of the Six Nations to sell it to the British. Thereafter, the Shawnee and their ally, the Delaware, both nations then residing in present-day Ohio, organize a pan-Indian confederacy without the leadership of the Six Nations, now seen as puppets of the British. The Six Nations, since about 1700, have gained informal leadership of a broad coalition of Indian nations, once boasting that they could muster warriors from fifty nations. Now the influence of the Six Nations declines, and the loose confederacy of western Indian nations are led by the Shawnee, Delaware, and Miami. The loose Indian confederation tries to keep settlers out of the Old Northwest, the area west of the Ohio River and including the Great Lakes area. This confederacy defends the Old Northwest until the end of the War of 1812.

1769 Missions Established in California Spanish Franciscan missionaries try to entice Indians to take up residence and Catholic life in mission settings. The Indians are taught to make irrigation networks and to farm and ranch. Mission Indians find life very difficult; many die and others lose much of their traditional culture.

1773–74 Lord Dunmore's War Angry about settlers from Virginia moving onto their lands and sometimes murdering Indians, the Shawnee and their allies move to protect territories in western Virginia and western Pennsylvania. Lord Dunmore, governor of Virginia, musters an army and fights a series of skirmishes with the Indians along the Virginia and Pennsylvania frontier.

1774–75 Formation of the Indian Departments During the First Continental Congress in 1774, the delegates, worried about Indian loyalties, commit $40,000 to Indian affairs and appoint a Committee on Indian Affairs to negotiate terms of neutrality or support from the Indians. In 1775, the First Continental Congress assumes control over Indian affairs, not leaving it to the individual colonies as had the British. Northern, southern, and middle departments are created, with commissioners appointed to the head of each. Indian affairs are considered of such importance at this juncture in U.S. history that Benjamin Franklin, Patrick Henry, and James Wilson, all central leaders in the Revolution, are named the first commissioners of the Indian departments. The commissioners are authorized to make treaties and to arrest British agents. They open negotiations with the Six Nations in order to win their neutrality in the impending war, if not their alliance. The commissioners offer trade goods and blacksmith services as a part of a treaty of alliance, but the Six Nations decline the offer.

1775 The Cheyenne Receive the Sacred Law According to Cheyenne tradition, at about this time the Cheyenne are granted their sacred law and covenant with the Creator through the prophet Sweet Medicine. Sweet Medicine receives the law directly from the Creator on a sacred mountain, present-day Bear Butte in South Dakota. Sweet Medicine then gives the Cheyenne instructions to form a council of forty-four chiefs—forty chiefs elected from the ten traditional Cheyenne bands and four chiefs appointed to represent the four sacred directions. Sweet Medicine also gives the Cheyenne their most sacred bundle, composed of four arrows and their particular version of the Sun Dance. Along with the sacred bundle, Sweet Medicine also teaches the Cheyenne the Sacred Arrow Bundle Dance, which renews the covenant relation between the Cheyenne Nation and the Creator. The covenant relation obliges the Cheyenne people to uphold the sacred law and ceremonies, and in return the Creator preserves the Cheyenne Nation from physical and cultural destruction.

1777–87 Articles of Confederation Under the Articles of Confederation—the first U.S. laws of national government—Native Americans are treated as sovereign nations. Under the terms of the Peace of Paris (1783), the United States receives claim to all the land from the Atlantic to the Mississippi River, and from the Great Lakes to the Florida border. Congress has administrative authority over these lands, but most of them belong to Indians. The British had long followed the precedent that Native Americans had a "natural right" to the land but that they could relinquish title to the lands through agreements. For the most part, the United States follows this principle, although the country will claim vast areas of land from the Indians by right of conquest. In 1779, the Continental Congress passes a law asserting that only the national government can transfer ownership of Indian lands, and, by the Ordinance of 1787, the United States promises that Native Americans' "land and property shall never be taken from them without their consent; and in their property,

On June 11, 1776, an Onondaga sachem gave John Hancock an Iroquois name at Independence Hall. Drawing by John Kahionhes Fadden.

rights and liberty, they shall never be invaded or disturbed, unless in just and lawful wars authorized by Congress."

1777–83 The Iroquois Confederacy Is Dispersed The Revolutionary War permanently disrupts the unity of the Iroquois Confederacy. At the beginning of the war, many Iroquois, especially the Seneca and Onondaga, prefer neutrality and do not wish to join with either of the warring parties. Some Mohawk, led by Joseph Brant, a close family friend to the British agent William Johnson, prefer to fight with the British. The Oneida and Tuscarora, because of local trade and friendship ties with settlers, prefer to side with the United States. This absence of agreement about how to handle the war does not allow the Confederate Council to arrive at a binding plan of action through consensual agreement. (All six nations of the confederacy must agree to all decisions, otherwise each nation acts independently.) Since there is no agreement, the individual nations, villages, even families make their own decisions about alliance or neutrality. This causes a deep rift within the confederacy, which is not effectively restored even after the Revolutionary War. The pro-British Iroquois move to Canada during and after the war and eventually form their own confederacy, and the Iroquois remaining in New York do likewise. Thus, by the early 1800s two independent Iroquois Confederacies emerge.

September 17, 1778 The First U.S.–Indian Treaty Is Signed At Fort Pitt (now Pittsburgh, Pennsylvania), the Delaware, actually primarily the Turtle, one of three Delaware divisions, sign a peace treaty with the United States. The treaty offers the Delawares the right to send representatives to Congress and become part of the U.S. nation. This clause, however, is never implemented. The Delaware Treaty is the first of 370 treaties signed with Indian nations between 1778 and 1871, when Congress passes a law forbidding the government to make treaties with Indians.

1783–95 Intermittent Border Wars After the end of the Revolutionary War in 1783, the political and military situation remains extremely unstable. Between 1783 and 1795 the British continue to occupy the forts of the Old Northwest, at Detroit and Chicago, although by treaty they are to be evacuated. The United States has neither the military strength nor the will to dislodge the

British soldiers. The British occupy the forts and supply their Indian allies west of the Ohio River with goods and weapons, hoping that the Indian nations will create a buffer zone between the United States and Canada. The Indian nations (Delaware, Miami, Shawnee, Ottawa, and others) hope to use British support to keep U.S. settlers from streaming across the Ohio River and taking Indian land.

The U.S. government has little money with which to operate, but it claims all of the Indian land west to the Mississippi River. The new nation makes considerable money by selling western lands in Ohio, Indiana, Kentucky, and Tennessee. In the north, the Wyandotte, Delaware, Shawnee, Miami, Chippewa, Potawatomi, Kickapoo, Ottawa, and some Iroquois warriors join to defy the U.S. invasion of the Old Northwest, bringing war to the settlers in Ohio in their attempt to drive them out. Between 1783 and 1790 perhaps one thousand settlers lose their lives; there are no estimates regarding Indian deaths north of the Ohio River caused by war and disease.

In the 1780s, several unsuccessful treaties are signed between small Indian groups and the U.S. government. The U.S. commissioners negotiate these treaties at Fort Stanwix with the Six Nations (1784); at Fort McIntosh with the Wyandotte, Delaware, Chippewa, and Ottawa (1785); at Fort Finney with the Shawnee (1786); and at Fort Hopewell with the Cherokee, Choctaw, and Chickasaw (1786). The treaties typically contain several articles, including those that cede certain lands to the United States. Not all of the Indian leaders of the various nations agree with or sign the treaties. Trouble results when settlers move onto western lands they purchase from land companies. In Ohio, Kentucky, and Tennessee, settlers often find Native Americans still residing on and laying claim to lands that the settlers have bought. Although some settlers and Indians live peacefully beside one another, there is continued conflict over land ownership.

Land disputes result in intermittent skirmishes along the frontier between 1790 and 1794. President George Washington answers the Indian challenge by directing General Josiah Harmer and fifteen hundred troops to engage the Indians. Kickapoo, Shawnee, and Miami snipers harass the soldiers as they march south of the Maumee River in Ohio. In September 1790 the Indian alliance launches a successful battle that defeats Harmer and provokes Washington into sending Governor Arthur St. Clair and three thousand troops to the Maumee River, in present-day Indiana, to confront the Indians. Once again Native American forces strike hard, killing and wounding more than nine hundred soldiers. Still determined to destroy the Indian alliance in the Old Northwest, Washington orders General Anthony Wayne into Ohio. In August 1794, the confederated nations, led by Little Turtle of the Miami nation, go into battle against Wayne, known to the Indians as "Blacksnake," at the Battle of Fallen Timbers, near present-day Fort Wayne, Indiana. In part, because the British fail to come to the Indians' aid at the battle, the Indians are forced to retreat. The Indians' political position further erodes when, in late 1794, the United States and Britain sign Jay's Treaty; the English depart to Canada and withdraw their military support for their Indian allies. This forces the Indians of the Old Northwest to treat with the United States in 1795 at Fort Greenville, in present-day Indiana. The Indian nations recognize the United States as the primary non-Indian power in the area and cede most of Ohio to the United States for $20,000 worth of goods and an annuity of $10,000. The Indian nations of the Old Northwest—the Wyandotte, Shawnee, Delaware, Potawatomi, Miami, Kickapoo, Ottawa, and Chippewa—lose considerable land and power.

In the South, parts of the Cherokee, Creek, Choctaw, and Chickasaw nations side with the Spanish in order to curtail U.S. settler expansion into their territories. Like the British in the North, the Spanish in Florida and West Florida (present-day Alabama and Mississippi) provide the southern Indians with trade and weapons. This leads to intermittent warfare between the westward-moving settlers and the Indian nations, who are intent on defending their territory. Several of the southern nations form a confederacy against U.S. intrusion and choose Alexander McGillivray to lead them. McGillivray at first sides with the Spanish against the Americans then, after meeting President Washington in New York in 1790, becomes a brigadier general in the U.S. Army; he continues to deal with both the Spanish and U.S. governments until his death in 1793. The loose-knit confederacy McGillivray led did not last long after his death; most Cherokee, Choctaw, and Chickasaw try to live peacefully with the settlers, but some anti-settler Indians, particularly within the Creek Nation and among the Chickamauga Cherokee, maintain their pro-Spanish stance.

Like the British, the Spanish hope to prevent the territorial expansion of the young United States. In 1795, when the Napoleonic Wars begin in Europe, the Spanish turn their attention to Europe and ignore their relatively unprofitable Florida colonies. Thus, the southern Indian nations, in a series of treaties in the middle 1790s, are forced to recognize the United States as the major non-Indian power in the south.

1787–89 Indians and the U.S. Constitution In 1787, delegates come to Philadelphia to frame the Constitution. Some Native Americans and scholars argue that the delegates learned much about representative government from the Iroquois and that the Constitution is patterned after the political ideas of the Iroquois and the political structure of their League. Furthermore, ideas of individual political freedom, free speech, political equality, and political community are recorded in sixteenth- and seventeenth-century encounters with Native societies. Many of these observations are incorporated into the Enlightenment philosophy of the 1700s by such men as Jean-Jacques Rousseau and Voltaire. The Enlightenment philosophy in turn influences contemporary political thought and the organization of democracy in Western nations.

After much debate, the states ratify the Constitution and it becomes the supreme law in the United States. The constitutional delegates want Indian policy to be centralized and determined by Congress. Article 1, Section 8 of the Constitution, often called "the Commerce Clause," empowers Congress to make all laws pertaining to the Indian trade and diplomatic relations. This clause prohibits the original thirteen colonies from negotiating treaties directly with Indian nations and also leaves control over Indian land in federal hands, outside individual state's jurisdiction. Through treaty-making, which requires ratification by the Senate with a two-thirds vote and signature by the president, the Indian nations form a legal relationship with the U.S. government. Treaties end wars and cede to the government millions of acres of land.

1787 The Northwest Ordinances The Northwest Ordinance of 1787 calls for the division of lands north of the Ohio River into territories that can eventually become states. In this way, the Congress establishes the mechanism by which territories and states will be created. In order to open lands for settlement, Congress passes the Ordinance of 1785, which calls for the survey of "Public Land" into townships of 6 miles square divided into 36 sections of 640 acres each, costing $640. This method favors land speculators with money to invest. Real estate companies emerge, buying large tracts of land and subdividing them to make purchases more affordable for smaller farmers. Yet, in order for the two ordinances to work, the United States must secure Indian title to the land. The government establishes this through treaties.

1789 Indian Affairs Moved to War Department Since 1784, Congress has delegated negotiation of treaties to the War Department. In 1786, the Secretary of War assumes management of Indian Affairs, and in 1789, with the creation of the new War Department, Indian Affairs are delegated to the first Secretary of War, Henry Knox. Because many Indian nations on the fron-

On May 2, 1780, Cornplanter addressed Congress in New York City. Drawing by John Kahionhes Fadden.

tier are allied with the British or Spanish and resist U.S. settlement, the War Department is seen as the most appropriate agency to manage Indians relations.

1799 Religious Revitalization and Handsome Lake Handsome Lake, a Seneca clan leader, becomes so ill that his family and friends gather to pay their respects before he dies. Not long after apparently dying, Handsome Lake recovers and tells everyone that his soul left his body and went outside to where he met three Native angels. They told Handsome Lake that he is to end his drinking, live a good life, and follow the teachings of the Creator who would reveal himself in the months ahead. In the fall of 1799, Handsome Lake has a second vision, in which he meets the Creator and learns lessons that become the hallmark of the revitalized Longhouse religion. By the late 1830s, the religion becomes the Handsome Lake Church. His visions and teachings are known as the Gaiwiio—the good word. He teaches that Native Americans should live in peace with the United States, but that they should spiritually or culturally be Iroquois. His doctrines stress peace within the family and among all people.

1803 The Louisiana Purchase The United States buys from France a large portion of land west of the Mississippi River extending in the north to the Pacific Ocean. This land contains large numbers of Indian nations, many of whom have yet to have extended political relations with a European or U.S. government. With the purchase of these western lands, President Thomas Jefferson proposes that many of the Indian nations living east of the Mississippi River be removed west to lands where they would be out of the way of U.S. settlers, and the eastern land would be open to settlement.

1805–1806 Sacajawea Aids Lewis and Clark Expedition While wintering in present-day North Dakota, explorers William Clark and Meriwether Lewis meet Sacajawea, a Shoshoni woman married to a French trader, Toussaint Charbonneau. Charbonneau is hired as an interpreter and guide. Sacajawea proves invaluable to the men's expedition because not only can she speak to Indians encountered along the way, her presence as a female is seen as a peaceful symbol to them. She accompanies the expedition, along with her infant son who is born en route, all the way to the Pacific Ocean and then leaves Lewis and Clark at a Hidatsa village in present-day North Dakota.

1805 The Munsee Prophetess In the early 1800s U.S. officials in present-day Indiana pressure leaders of the Delaware, Shawnee, and other Old Northwest Indian nations into selling significant tracts of land, resulting in considerable tension and dismay among most members of the Indian nations. Between 1803 and 1805, while the Delaware and Munsee are living in the present-day Indianapolis to Munsee, Indiana, area, several Delaware have visions. But in 1805, a female, now known only as the Munsee Prophetess, has a vision and consequently introduces modifications to the Delaware Big House Religion, the Delaware national religion since the Delaware prophet of the 1760s. The Munsee Prophetess teaches that the Indians must retain their traditions and reject farming, Christianity, trade, and European clothing, otherwise the Delaware Nation will continue to decline politically, economically, and spiritually. When Tenskwatawa, the Shawnee prophet who lives in the Delaware and Munsee villages, emerges in February 1806, the prophetess defers to him.

1806–1809 Tecumseh and Tenskwatawa, the Shawnee Prophet In February 1806, while living among the Delaware and Munsee in the present-day Munsee, Indiana, area, Tenskwatawa reportedly dies. While his family prepares him for burial, he regains consciousness, saying that he had died and visited the Master of Life. Tenskwatawa reports that through him, The Open Door, Native Americans can learn "The Way."

Thousands of Indians gravitate toward Tenskwatawa and his teachings, flocking to hear him preach in a village called Prophetstown. So many Native peoples come to the village that resources are depleted, and the prophet is forced to move his town west, settling near the junction of the Tippecanoe and Wabash rivers in eastern Indiana. Through his religious revitalization movement, Tenskwatawa unites many tribes to stand against the United States.

Using his brother's spiritual movement, Tecumseh forges a pan-Indian confederacy that is both political and military. Tecumseh, Tenskwatawa, and their followers reject the Treaty of Fort Wayne (1809), in which some Indian leaders ceded three million acres to the United States. At the treaty council, Tecumseh tells Governor William Henry Harrison (the future U.S. president) that he rejects any agreement with the United States "on the ground that all the land belonged to all the Indians, and that not even the whole membership of a single tribe could alienate the property of the race."

1811 Battle of Tippecanoe With a Creek medicine man named Seekaboo, Tecumseh travels to the southern Indian nations seeking support for his confederacy. Only a portion of the Creek, known as Red Sticks, join the movement. Tecumseh returns to the north to learn that Governor Harrison has led a victorious force of one thousand soldiers against Tenskwatawa at Prophetstown. Tenskwatawa persuades his followers to charge the U.S. soldiers' camp. As a result of the Battle of Tippecanoe, the Indian confederacy is in disarray, and the Shawnee Prophet is no longer held in honor among the Indian nations.

1812–15 The War of 1812 The War of 1812 devastates the land and populations of the Indians of the Old Northwest. At the Treaty of Ghent, which ends the war, the British agree that all the territory south of the Great Lakes belongs to the United States, and the British agree not to give aid to their ally Indians there. This leaves the Indian nations living east of the Mississippi River entirely within the sphere of the U.S. government's influence. The Indians no longer have the supplies or alliance of a rival European power to balance against the United States. By 1819, the Spanish sell Florida and West Florida to the United States, and U.S. claims to the land east of the Mississippi River are undisputed, except by the Indian nations still living there. After 1817 to 1819, however, the political and diplomatic position of the Indian nations rapidly deteriorates, and they have less ability to retain territory and political independence.

1813–14 The Red Stick War Angry over U.S. interference and control within the Creek government and influenced by Tecumseh's message of resistance to the United States, Creek living primarily in present-day Alabama, called Red Stick, attack Creek villages allied with the United States. The Red Stick also attack Fort Mims, killing most of the U.S. citizens there and bringing the United States into the Creek civil war. General Andrew Jackson, with five thousand troops and a number of Indian scouts, marches against the Red Stick at the village of Tohopeka at Horseshoe Bend on the Tallapoosa River. Surrounded and assaulted by cannon, the Creek suffer losses of more than eight hundred men, women, and children. With Red Stick resistance at an end, the Creek Nation is forced to accept the Treaty of Fort Jackson, which cedes twenty-two million acres of Creek land in Georgia and Alabama to the U.S. government.

1817–18 The First Seminole War Some defeated Creek Red Stick join the Seminole in Florida and continue resistance to the United States with the help of English trade companies.

1823 *Johnson v. McIntosh* In *Johnson v. McIntosh,* a case before the U.S. Supreme Court, Justice John Marshall recognizes that Indians have the right to land by their prior use, but rules that Indian tribes cannot sell land to private individuals and must sell only to the federal government. This case curtails Indian control over the use and sale of their own territory.

1823 The Cherokee Syllabary Sequoyah, a Cherokee living in present-day Arkansas, develops the Cherokee syllabary, a writing code using symbols for syllables rather than for sounds as in an alphabet. Many Cherokee quickly learn to read and write in the Cherokee syllabary. Translations of the Bible are made into Cherokee, and Cherokee spiritual leaders and healers record sacred and medicinal knowledge.

1824 The Office of Indian Affairs The Office of Indian Affairs is created within the War Department. The office is formally recognized by Congress in 1831.

1827–28 The Cherokee Republic The Cherokee watch the drift toward a policy of forced removal and decide upon a unique course of action in their attempt to prevent their own removal. In the early 1820s, the Cherokee establish a capital in New Echota, in present-day Georgia. In 1827, they write a constitution calling for three branches of government, in many ways similar to the U.S. federal constitution. In 1828, the Cherokee ratify the new constitution and elect John Ross, a wealthy Cherokee slaveholder, as principal chief. The Cherokee wish to establish their government and right to preserve their homeland in present-day Georgia, Tennessee, and eastern Alabama. The Georgia legislature, wanting to remove the Cherokee from their chartered limits, pass a series of laws that abolish the Cherokee government and appropriate Cherokee territory.

1828–35 *The Cherokee Phoenix* *The Cherokee Phoenix,* a weekly newspaper printed in English and in the Cherokee syllabary, is published. The newspaper's first editor is Elias Boudinot, who was educated in Cornwall, Connecticut, after attending primary school among the Moravian missionaries in Tennessee. The newspaper is discontinued when the U.S. government presses the Cherokee Nation to move west. Boudinot joins a minority group in signing the Treaty of New Echota in 1835, which, according to the U.S. government, obligates the Cherokee to move west to present-day Oklahoma.

1830–60 The Removal Period In 1830, Congress votes in favor of the Indian Removal Act. The removal of Native Americans from their lands becomes an integral element of national Indian policy. During the 1830s and 1840s, the U.S. Army forces thousands of Indian families to leave their belongings and move to lands west of present-day Iowa, Missouri, Kansas, Nebraska, Arkansas, and Oklahoma. The United States forces the Cherokee onto "The Trail of Tears," which directly results in the death of four thousand to eight thousand people. One soldier writes: "I fought through the Civil War and have seen men shot to pieces and slaughtered by thousands, but the Cherokee removal was the cruelest work I ever knew."

The Cherokee is not the only southern nation to suffer removal. The army moves the Choctaw, Chickasaw, Creek, Seminole, and remnants of lesser-known peoples. Northern tribes are also removed, including the Wyandotte, Ottawa, Peoria, Miami, Potawatomi, Sac, Fox, Delaware, and Seneca. The government is ill prepared to handle so many Indians along the trails and in new homes. In 1841, Major Ethan Allan Hitchcock investigates Indian affairs in the West and concludes that the American Indian policy is filled with "bribery, perjury and forgery, short weights, issues of spoiled meat and grain, and every conceivable subterfuge."

1831 *Cherokee Nation v. Georgia* Against Georgia's efforts to remove the Cherokee from their homeland, the Cherokee counter with a law suit in the Supreme Court. *Cherokee Nation v. Georgia* is based on a clause in the Constitution that allows foreign nations to seek redress in the U.S. Supreme Court for damages caused by U.S. citizens. Chief Justice John Marshall rules that the Cherokee Nation is not a foreign but a domestic dependent nation. The Court reasons that Indian nations depend on the United States for legal status. Until now, the United States had treated the tribes as foreign, independent, sovereign nations—on a par with France, England, and Russia.

1832 *Worcester v. Georgia* *Worcester v. Georgia* is brought by Samuel Worcester, a private U.S. citizen convicted and jailed to a four-year prison term for refusing to swear allegiance to Georgia and for speaking out against the Indian policies of the state. In 1829, Georgia extends its laws over the portion of the Cherokee Nation within its chartered limits and demands that all U.S. citizens take an oath of allegiance to Georgia and obey Georgia law. Georgia law prohibits the Cherokee government from meeting and is intended to force the Cherokee to move west. In this case, the Court strikes down the Georgia law arguing that only the federal government has the right to regulate affairs in Indian country, while states cannot extend their laws over Indian governments. The Cherokee are forced to move between 1835 and 1839, but *Worcester v. Georgia* now stands as a major precedent upholding Indian rights to self-government.

1832 The Black Hawk War Remnant bands of the Sauk and Fox tribes attempt to reclaim land in Wisconsin and Illinois but are quickly repressed by U.S. troops. Black Hawk, a keeper of a major medicine bundle among the Sauk and Fox, is strongly opposed to ceding territory in present-day Illinois.

1835–42 The Second U.S. and Seminole War U.S. troops battle in the swamps of Florida, but without conclusive success. The Seminole leader Osceola is deceived and captured and dies in prison in 1838.

1837 Smallpox Epidemic on the Plains The once numerous Mandan and Hidatsa, living in present-day central North Dakota, are decimated. Both tribes lose as much as 90 percent of their population, leaving only a few hundred survivors. Other Plains nations are also hit hard, some left with only about 20 percent of their previous numbers. Between 1837 and 1870, at least four smallpox epidemics kill thousands of people among the Plains Indian nations.

1837–53 Kenekuk, the Kickapoo Prophet After the end of the War of 1812, Kenekuk, a Kickapoo, assumes leadership of a segment of the Kickapoo nation, then living along the Osage River in Illinois. Based on Kenekuk's teachings, these Kickapoo form a community of 350 that turns to agriculture and adopts selected Protestant, Catholic, and traditional religious and moral teachings. While strongly resisting removal from their homeland, they are finally forced to migrate to Missouri in 1833 and to present-day Kansas by 1837. There, the prophet converts a group of Potawatomi, who join the prophet's community in 1851. This community survives to the present. Kenekuk dies in Kansas in 1853, but not before promising his faithful that he will rise again after three days.

1840–60 Indian Territory and the Indian State During the 1840s and 1850s, U.S. officials adhere to a plan of ultimately moving all Indians to Indian Territory, then present-day Kansas and Oklahoma. U.S. officials believe that more land can be opened to settlers, and the Indians can be incorporated into the United States by means of their own state, with elected officials representing Indian interests in Congress. In the post-Civil War period, however, this plan is abandoned because many Indian nations do not want to move to Indian Territory, and most do not want to be incorporated under one Indian political government or be included in the U.S. Congress and government.

1846–48 Mexican-American War Between 1846 and 1848, the United States fights Mexico in a war that ends with the Treaty of Guadalupe Hidalgo. Mexico cedes to the United States any and all claims to California and the Southwest. The U.S. government thus brings American Indian policy to that region of the country and to the Pacific Northwest. As in other parts of the nation, the government considers that Indians have a "natural right" to the land; however, the Indians can also relinquish their lands through treaties. Throughout the West, the

United States commissions agents to extinguish Indian title to millions of acres. Nations such as the Navajo, Sioux, Kiowa, and Modoc fight back against the U.S. Army. Others such as the Crow, Caddo, Blackfeet, Hopi, and Nespelem do not. Regardless of the policies followed by the various nations, the ultimate results are the same; the United States asserts its authority through the army and the Indian administration. Lands are taken from the Indians through treaties or by right of conquest. Western Indians secure for themselves only a minute portion of their former lands and live on lands ruled by Indian agents. Many Indians are relocated to lands controlled by their neighbors. Others are concentrated on reservations with other Indian nations, including former enemies.

1846 Navajo Resistance At the end of the Mexican-American War, U.S. settlers move into California and New Mexico where the *Diné* (Navajo for "the people") face the U.S. Army. The Navajo are one of the first Indian nations in the American Southwest to deal with the United States. Between 1600 and 1846 the Navajo had confronted the *Nakai*, or Spanish, who had moved into the Rio Grande Valley of New Mexico onto lands belonging to Pueblo Indians. The Europeans introduced cattle, sheep, and horses to the Natives, and the Navajo took advantage of the innovations by sweeping down on New Mexican villages to steal stock. Comanche, Kiowa, Apache, Ute, and others followed suit, giving rise to an economy based in part on raiding. By 1846, when the United States enters New Mexico, Navajo people already have extensive holdings of cattle, sheep, and horses.

When Colonel Stephen Watts Kearny enters New Mexico in 1846, he promises to end Navajo raids on New Mexican villages and, to this end, he dispatches Colonel Alexander W. Doniphan to Navajo country. Doniphan meets with a group of Navajo *Naat'aanis* (headmen) at Bear Springs near present-day Gallup, New Mexico. He concludes the first treaty with the Navajo, which is ratified by the Senate and signed by the president. But the treaty means little to the Navajo who attack Doniphan's horse herd shortly after meeting with him.

During the 1850s, a number of Navajo leaders sign treaties with the United States intended to end hostilities and establish trade relations between Indian and non-Indian communities of New Mexico. The agreements fail because the Navajo continue to raid New Mexican villages and because New Mexicans enslave Navajo. The conflict centers on livestock and slaves, not land, since most non-Indians consider Navajo land beautiful but unproductive. In 1860, Colonel Edward R. S. Canby, who had fought the Seminole in Florida, leads a campaign against the Navajo. By sending out small raiding parties and striking purposefully at civilian populations, Canby brings the Navajo to the bargaining table. In the spring of 1861 several Navajo leaders, including Manuelito, Barboncito, Armijo, Herrero, and Ganada Mucho, agree to a peace treaty. Canby's campaign probably would have ended the Navajo wars had it not been for the U.S. Civil War.

1848 The California Gold Rush In 1848, Maidu and other California Indians working for James Marshall, a miller, discover gold on the American River, near Sacramento, California. At first, Native Americans in California work in the gold mines, contributing significantly to their discovery and success. Between 1848 and 1850 California officials estimate that more than one-half of the miners in California were Natives. During the 1850s some California miners abuse and kill many Indian men, women, and children.

1849 The Office of Indian Affairs The Office of Indian Affairs is transferred from the War Department to the newly created Department of the Interior. The new department is created to manage public land, Indian land, and Indian affairs.

1850–60 Nonratification of California Indian Treaties In California, numerous treaties are signed by federal officials with the California Indian nations, but non-Indian Californians prevent their ratification in Congress. Consequently, most California Indians are not recognized by treaty, and many California Indian communities continue to seek official federal recognition.

1850–80 Genocide of California Indians Fearing widespread Indian uprisings, non-Indian Californians kill and terrorize California Indians. The Indian population in California declines from about 100,000 in 1850 to 16,000 in 1880.

1850–1907 Religious Renewal in the Northwest Many Indian peoples turn to their old spiritual beliefs. Indians of the Northwest Plateau (present-day western Washington) join new religious movements like the Indian Shaker Church, or *Waptashi*—the Feather Religion. Some Indians follow the teachings of Smohalla, the Wanapum prophet, who is said to have died on two occasions and traveled to the Sky World to converse with the Creator. Smohalla was given the sacred dance and ceremony known as the Washat and told to return to his people and to remember the ceremonies of thanks for first foods and other gifts of creation. Smohalla leads a fierce resistance to selling land, and provides a new religion that mixes both Christian and traditional northwestern Indian ideas. The new religion helps individual Indians and Indian communities better cope with the

California Paiute Indian family at campfire. Courtesy of the Palmquist Collection.

rapidly changing political, economic, and social conditions in their lives. His church becomes known as the Shaker Church and continues to gather congregations among several northwestern Indian nations such as the Nez Percé.

1853 The Gadsden Purchase The Gadsden Purchase, an agreement between the United States and Mexico, brings to the United States portions of the states of Arizona, California, and New Mexico and fixes the present U.S. boundaries. The purchase brings many Indian nations in these future states under U.S. jurisdiction.

1853–56 A Series of Treaties with Indians During this period many Indian nations are induced to sell most of their remaining land and accept small parcels of land commonly called "reservations." The Chippewa in the 1850s cede most of their lands in Wisconsin and Minnesota and are relegated to small and scattered reservations. The Indian nations of present-day Washington State cede most of their lands and reluctantly settle on small reservations. Between 1853 and 1856 more than fifty-two treaties are made with Indian groups, and the United States acquires 174 million acres of Indian land. In many cases, the Indian communities are economically destitute and Indians are forced to trade land for goods; in some cases, for example in Washington and Wisconsin, Indians retain the right to hunt and fish on their former lands. These hunting and fishing rights are disputed and ignored by U.S. citizens.

1855–1907 The Chickasaw Constitutional Government In 1856, the Chickasaw Nation adopts a constitution, modeled after the U.S. Constitution, with a "governor" as chief executive, a legislature, and a judiciary. In 1834, the Chickasaw sign a removal treaty, but cannot find a new location in the west. In 1838, the Chickasaw agree to join the Choctaw government, then already in Indian Territory (present-day Oklahoma). Between 1840 and 1855, however, most Chickasaw do not wish to live under Choctaw law, feeling they were discriminated against. The Chickasaw appeal to the United States for a return to a independent nationality, and in an 1855 treaty the Chickasaw are granted independence. In 1856, the Chickasaw form a constitutional government, which replaces an older form of government based on clan chiefs and priests. The constitutional government manages Chickasaw affairs until 1907, when the United States abolishes it.

1855–58 The Seminole Form New Government The Seminole in Florida again engage U.S. forces. The army cannot defeat the Seminole and allies, who retreat to the southern Florida swamps. Eventually, the United States has to reconcile itself to leaving the Seminole in Florida. In previous years, in the 1830s, some Seminole were captured and moved to Indian Territory (present-day Oklahoma), where they were joined with the Creek nation. Both nations speak Muskogean languages and have a history of kindred relations. By 1855, the Oklahoma Seminole withdraw from the Creek Nation and create their own government, one that very much resembles traditional Creek government, with about a dozen politically independent villages that meet together to form a national council. The government stays in effect until 1907, when the U.S. government dissolves the major Indian governments in Indian Territory.

1860–1907 The Choctaw Constitutional Government In 1860, after twenty-five years of constitutional change and amendment, the Choctaw residing in Indian Territory (present-day eastern Oklahoma) adopt a centralized constitutional government, with a principal chief, three district chiefs (as was the Choctaw political tradition), a national legislature, and a court system. The government remains in power until 1907, when the U.S. government abolishes the Choctaw government and makes Indian Territory into the state of Oklahoma.

1861–65 The Civil War The Civil War brings Confederate troops under General Henry Hopkins Sibley to New Mexico. Most federal troops are withdrawn, except a contingent at Fort Fauntleroy. During the Civil War the Navajo continue to raid New Mexican villages left undefended when men departed to fight the Confederacy. Federal forces defeat Confederate troops near Pecos, New Mexico, and then move eastward, leaving General James Carleton to administer the New Mexico Department. Colonel Christopher Carson is appointed field commander over an army of volunteers. In weeks, this force defeats the Mescalero Apache and relocates them to the Bosque Redondo of eastern New Mexico onto a bleak, wind-swept reservation on the Llano Estacado, or Staked Plains, near the Pecos River. It was Carleton's plan to gather the Mescalero and Navajo tribes together "little by little onto a Reservation away from the haunts and hills and hiding places of their own country, and there be kind to them: there teach their children how to read and write; teach them the art of peace; teach them the truths of Christianity." Carleton represents liberal reformers who want to place Indians on reservations where they would "acquire new habits, new ideas, new modes of life: the old Indians will die off . . . the

Former California Mission Indians making baskets and hair rope.

young ones will take their places . . . and thus, little by little, they will become a happy and contented people."

Although Carleton wants to "civilize" and Christianize Navajo and Apache on the reservation, he is not adverse to killing them in pursuit of his goal. Under orders from Carleton, Carson pursues Navajo men, women, and children throughout the summer, fall, and winter of 1863–64, causing the deaths of many from hardship, hunger, and exposure. Those Navajo who are captured afford Carson the opportunity to inform the tribe of the removal plans and his correspondence suggests that he does. Navajo oral history, however, indicates that they are unaware of the plans. Approximately ten thousand Navajo surrender, while an equal number flee west to escape the army. The U.S. government forcefully removes these Navajo in its jurisdiction 350 miles to the Bosque Redondo, a place Navajo call *Hweeldi* (prison). There they remain until 1868, when General William Tecumseh Sherman concludes a treaty with the Navajo permitting them to return to a reservation located on a portion of Dinetah.

1862–64 The Minnesota Sioux Uprising Because of Indian agents' corruption and incompetence in their administration of relations with the Minnesota Sioux, the Sioux almost starve from lack of supplies. Under the leadership of Little Crow, they attack Minnesota settlements. The uprising quickly spreads to other Santee Sioux bands living in the eastern Dakotas. Thirty-eight Sioux are sentenced and hanged for their part in the uprising.

1862–65 Kickapoo Migration to Mexico Two bands of Kickapoo, about thirteen hundred people, migrate to Mexico, believing their lands are unfairly treated by the U.S. government and people. Both bands fight battles with Texas troops, who strongly oppose Indians settling or traveling through Texas. Both groups settle in the province of Coahiula, in northern Mexico. Earlier in 1839, a band of Kickapoo had already migrated to Morelos, Mexico, and they were joined by Machemanet, a Kickapoo headman, and six hundred Kickapoo who left Kansas for Mexico, hoping for better treatment at the hands of the Mexican government. By 1865, all Kickapoo, except the band formerly led by the Prophet Kenekuk, leave Kansas because of corrupt handling by U.S. Indian agents and crooked dealings by U.S. citizens. In 1867, about one hundred Kickapoo return from the south and resettle near present-day Leavenworth, Kansas.

1863 The Nez Percé and the "Thief Treaty" Throughout the West Indians attempt to preserve their culture and live a traditional life off the reservation. For example, the Nez Percé Indians of Oregon and Idaho attempt to live in peace with the settlers and remain neutral during the Plateau Indian War of 1855-58. In 1855, the Nez Percé sign a treaty with the United States, securing nearly all of their land, but in 1860 non-Indian "traders" discover gold while prospecting on the Nez Percé reservation in Idaho. Non-Indians flood onto Indian land; the U.S. Army is preoccupied with the Civil War and unable to prevent the invasion. Nez Percé leaders complain to the Indian Service and the government responds in 1863 by writing a new treaty reducing the reservation to one-tenth its original size. When government officials disclose the plan to Nez Percé leaders, almost all of the chiefs leave the council, refusing to accept the new treaty. Only Chief Lawyer, upon whose lands the council is held, agrees to its terms. Lawyer and fifty-one Nez Percé sign the document, and it is ratified by the Senate and signed by the president. According to tribal law, Lawyer could speak only for his small band and not the tribe as a whole. Chief Joseph and the other Nez Percé leaders refuse to adhere to the "Thief Treaty." Chief Joseph objects: "If we ever owned the land we own it still for we never sold it."

1864 The Chivington Massacre On November 29, Colonel John Chivington leads a force from Colorado in an unprovoked attack on a Southern Cheyenne and Arapaho camp, possibly killing up to five hundred men, women, and children. The Sand Creek Massacre, as it becomes known, is one of the bloodiest and cruelest events of the Civil War.

1866 Post-Civil War Indian Reservations In 1853, California Superintendent of Indian Affairs, Edward Fitzgerald Beale, places a number of Indians in the Tejon Valley to become ranchers and farmers. Although this and other reservations meet with only limited success, the system becomes national policy after the Civil War. The Peace Commission meets with many tribes, concluding treaties, and establishing reservations. Some of the tribes, or portions of them, agree to remain on reservations; others do not. In 1867, the commissioners conclude an agreement with some Kiowa and Comanche, creating a reservation in the southwest corner of present-day Oklahoma. At the same time, a portion of Cheyenne and Arapaho country is recognized as a reservation.

1866–74 The Montana Gold Rush By the summer of 1866, non-Indians are flooding into Montana to find gold. Many miners take the Bozeman Trail from Fort Laramie, Wyoming, to the new diggings around Virginia City, Montana. The trail, however, runs though the lands of the Oglala and Brule Sioux, who fight to keep the miners out of the region. The army establishes a series of forts along the trail for the miners' protection, but

Reception of Indians at the White House.

under attack by Sioux and Cheyenne, agrees to abandon them at the Treaty of Fort Laramie in 1868. Under this agreement, some Sioux and Cheyenne leaders agree to move to the reservations in Montana, Wyoming, and the Dakotas. Indians secure for themselves much of the hunting grounds along the Big Horn and Powder rivers (present-day Montana). The treaty does not end U.S. incursion into Indian land, and miners, buffalo hunters, and railroad men continue to trespass on Sioux and Cheyenne country.

In 1874, Colonel George Armstrong Custer leads an expedition to the *Paha Sapa*, the Sioux word for "black hills," of South Dakota where geologists and journalists confirm the presence of gold. A new rush commences, and the Northern Pacific Railroad moves closer to Sioux land.

1867 The U.S. Buys Alaska The U.S. government purchases Alaska from the Russian government. The purchase does not change the situation of the Aleuts, Eskimos, and Indians living in Alaska. No treaties are signed, and no land ownership is determined by Alaska Natives in the sale between the United States and Alaska.

1867–1907 The Creek Constitutional Government In 1867, the Creek nation, now living in Indian Territory, adopts a constitutional government. The first elections in 1867 are controversial, and a small majority of conservatives demand a return to the traditional Creek government based on central villages and a council composed of village leaders. The U.S. supports the constitutional government and, on various occasions, uses marshals and troops to defend it against conservative Creek. Compared to the constitutional governments of the Cherokee, Choctaw, and Chickasaw, the Creek constitutional government is fraught with rebellion and political instability. In 1907, the Creek government is abolished over the protests of the conservative Creek who do not wish to join U.S. society or renounce their treaty and land rights.

1869–71 The First Indian Commissioner of Indian Affairs Is Appointed Brigadier General Ely Parker, a Seneca Indian and personal friend to President Ulysses S. Grant, is appointed commissioner of Indian affairs. Parker helps initiate a policy of providing Indians with food and clothing in exchange for reconciling themselves to life on small, economically marginal reservations of land.

1870–90 The Peyote Road For centuries Indians in northern Mexico have used the peyote plant in religious ceremonies. Peyote induces a mild hallucinatory state, which brings the user closer to the spirit world. In the late nineteenth century the Peyote religion spreads among the Kiowa, Comanche, Cheyenne, and Arapaho. Tribal members develop their own ceremonies, songs, and symbolism and dreams, visions, and prayers become a part of the Peyote religion. Peyote is ingested as a sacrament and followers vow to follow the Peyote Road. They promise to be trustworthy, honorable, and community-oriented. Family, children, and cultural survival become a major emphasis of this movement. Elements of Christianity become a part of the worship service, and in 1918 the membership organize themselves into the Native American church.

The Office of Indian Affairs attempts to extinguish the religion but does not succeed. In the twentieth century Indians introduce the church to Native peoples throughout the United States. The Native American church has survived but continues to face legal attacks during the last decade of the twentieth century.

1870 The First Ghost Dance Movement Perhaps the best known of the Native American religious revitalization movements is the Ghost Dance. Wodziwob, a Paiute Indian living on the California/Nevada border, is credited with beginning this religion in 1870. Wodziwob was informed by the Creator that non-Ghost Dancers would be swallowed up by a great earthquake. Indians would be spared or resurrected in three days so that they might live much as they had before European contact.

March 3, 1871 The End of Treaty Making Congress passes an act that it will no longer negotiate treaties with Indian nations. All treaties signed between 1778 and 1871 are not invalidated, but are to be upheld by the federal government. After this act, agreements with Indian groups are made by congressional acts and executive orders, which are agreements made by the president or designated official, usually by the secretary of the interior.

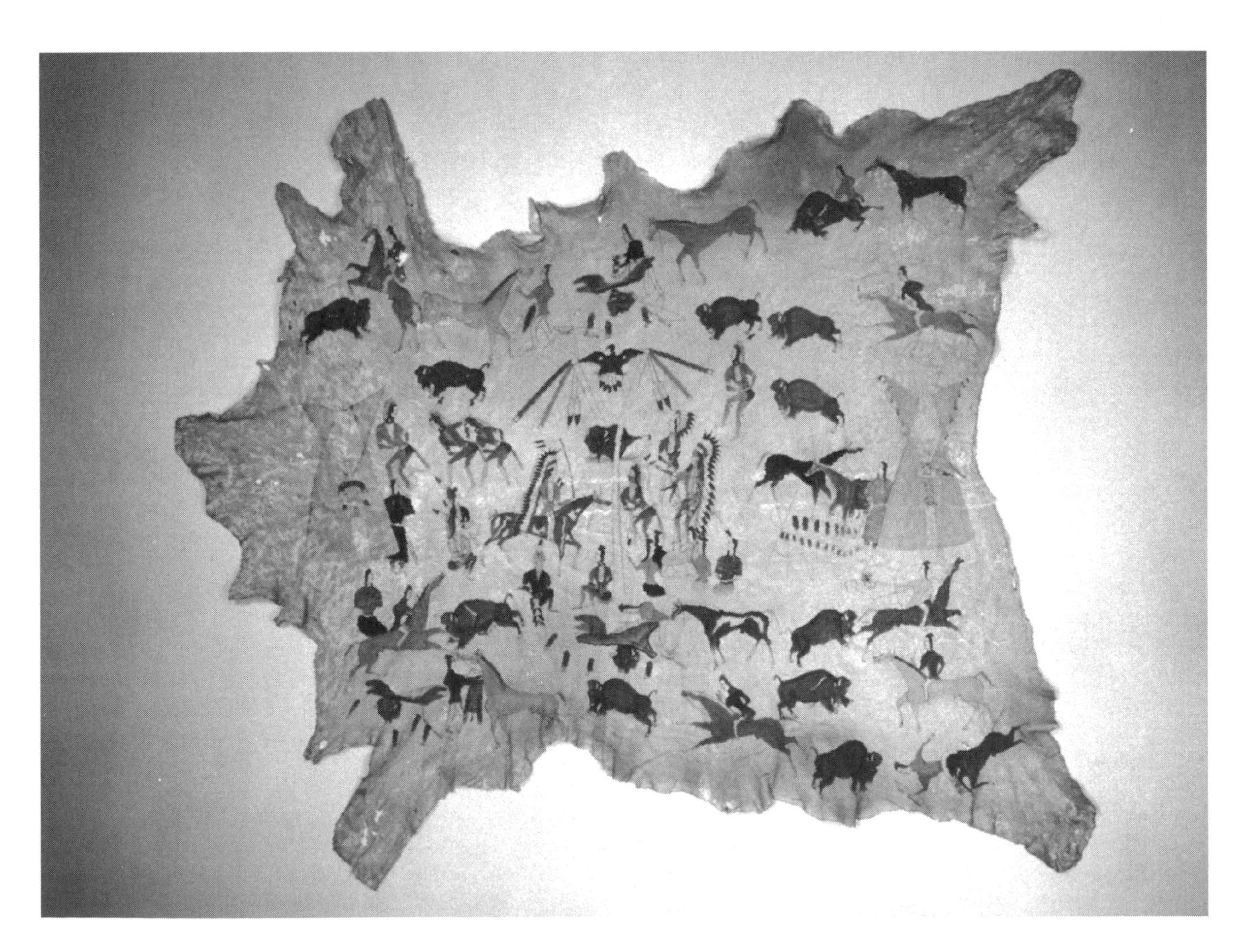

Scene of Indians hunting buffalo, painted on buffalo skin. Courtesy of the National Museum of the American Indian.

Sioux women cutting buffalo meat in hunting camp. Courtesy of the National Park Service.

1871–90 Extermination of the Buffalo on the Plains As early as 1871 U.S. hunters and traders begin a systematic killing of buffalo on the Plains. Hundreds of thousands are killed for their tongue meat and their hides. By the late 1880s there are only about one thousand buffalo left—not enough for the subsistence requirements of the Plains Indians. With their economic base destroyed, the Plains Indians are destitute and eventually forced onto small reservations, where they are dependent on the United States for food and supplies, and, consequently, fall under U.S. political and administrative control.

1876–81 Custer and the End of Sioux Resistance After gold miners start working in the Black Hills, which is sacred land for the Sioux, several bands of Sioux leave their reservations to protect the Black Hills from sacrilege. Led by Crazy Horse of the Oglala Sioux and Sitting Bull of the Hunkpapa band of Teton Sioux, the Indians gather to face the army, which is protecting the miners. Three columns converge on the Sioux and their Cheyenne and Arapaho allies. One of the columns, led by General Alfred Terry, includes the Seventh Cavalry commanded by Colonel George Armstrong Custer. Terry sent Custer to the southern end of Little Big Horn Valley (present-day eastern Montana) where the colonel and his Crow and Arikara scouts locate a large Indian encampment. On June 25, 1876, Custer divides his force for tactical purposes, and with a command of 225 men advances on the Indian camp. Sioux and Cheyenne meet his advance and kill every man, including Custer, and are only prevented from doing likewise to the other forces because they are rescued by General Terry's command. The army pursues the Sioux and in 1877 shoot down Crazy Horse in what the soldiers described as an escape attempt. Sitting Bull and remnants of the Sioux flee to Canada and do not return to the Dakotas until 1881.

1877 The Nez Percé War Between 1863 and 1876 the non-treaty Nez Percé continue to reject the Thief Treaty of 1763. After the defeat of Custer at Little Big Horn, the army orders that all non-reservation Nez Percé be placed on reservations. In 1877, General Oliver O. Howard, commander of the Northwestern Department, meets with Nez Percé chiefs Hinmahtooyahlatkekt (Thunder Coming From Water Over Land, or Joseph), Ollikut, Looking Glass, Rainbow, White Bird, and Toohoolhoolzote. Howard asks each non-treaty leader if he would move. Every one agrees to relocate to the reservation.

On the way to their new home, a skirmish involving young Nez Percé warriors results in the Nez Percé War. The Nez Percé and their Palouse allies fight several running battles with the army as they move from their homelands to Montana. After a defeat at Big Hole, a sacred site in Montana, the Indians move into Wyoming, hoping to settle with the Crow and live like buffalo-hunting Plains people. But they are rejected by the Crow and so move farther north. When they are but forty miles from Canada, they are attacked again by the army. After days of fighting, Joseph concludes a conditional surrender whereby the Nez Percé will not be punished for their resistance but will be allowed to settle on the reservation in Idaho. General Howard and Colonel Nelson A. Miles agree to these conditions, but they are reversed by General William Tecumseh Sherman. Sherman exiles the Nez Percé and Palouse to Fort Leavenworth, Kansas, as prisoners-of-war, before moving them to the Quapaw Agency in northeastern Indian Territory (present-day Oklahoma) and then to the Ponca Agency.

1877–79 The Nez Percé Exiled and Returned Throughout the exile, Joseph presses the government to live up to the terms of the conditional surrender. In 1879, he takes his case to Washington, D.C. More importantly, he gives an interview to the editor of the *North American Review*. The resulting essay clearly reflects his feelings about the injustice of the Nez Percé exile to *Eekish Pah*, the Hot Place, and stirs many people to demand the Nez Percés' return to the northwest. In 1885, the U.S. government agrees to permit the Nez Percé to return. Some Nez Percé relocate to the reservation in Idaho, but Joseph is forced to move to the Colville Reservation in north-central Washington. For years he

Arapaho family cooking dinner.

tries to buy a portion of his homeland, the *Wakllowa*, the Place of Winding Waters, but settlers living there refuse to sell him any land and he dies on the Colville reservation in 1904.

1877–83 The Northern Cheyenne Flee Indian Territory In 1877, the Northern Cheyenne tribe, then living in present-day Montana and the western Dakotas, surrenders to U.S. troops and reluctantly agrees to migrate to Indian Territory. In 1877, Chief Dull Knife, of the Northern Cheyenne, refuses to remain in Indian Territory and leads an escape of his people to return to their homeland in the northern plains. This dramatic escape captures the imagination of the American people through the press and convinces U.S. officials that it would be extremely difficult to detain unwilling Indian nations in Indian Territory. In 1883, the Northern Cheyenne are granted a reservation in eastern Montana. U.S. Indian policy makers abandon the attempt to relocate Indians nations in Indian Territory and allow them to take reservations within their home territories.

1879–90 Civilization and Christianization In 1879, the Carlisle Indian School in Pennsylvania is founded in an effort to show that Indians can be educated in the ways of American culture. Other schools are founded in California, Oregon, Oklahoma, New Mexico, and Arizona, as well as on the individual reservations. U.S. reformers take Indian children from their homes and communities in the belief that it would be in the interest of the children to destroy their Native culture. Government teachers force Indian children to learn English and punish them with whippings and food deprivation when they break the rules and use the Native language. Curriculums are established for vocational education—since Indians are not considered to be intelligent enough to learn the professions—but children are taught some academic skills. When the children reach first grade, government agents routinely take them from their families and send them to Indian boarding schools.

1881–84 *A Century of Dishonor* Published Helen Hunt Jackson, in *A Century of Dishonor* (1881), writes an indictment of U.S. Indian policy and the treatment of American Indians in U.S. society. Because of her work Congress forms a special commission to investigate and suggest reforms of Indian affairs. Jackson's research on the special commission provides her with material to write a biographical novel, *Ramona*, about the life of a California Indian woman. The romanticized biography stimulates considerable interest in the United States about the plight and life of Indians.

1887 The General Allotment Act Congress passes the General Allotment Act, also known as the Dawes Act, dividing reservation land into individual parcels. The act is intended to safeguard the Indians on the land and, to this end, allotments are to be protected for twenty-five years. The Burke Act (1906) amends the Allotment Act of 1887, extending the original twenty-five year trust period for another twenty-five years. Surplus land is purchased by the U.S. government and then opened to settlement, thus making thousands of acres available. Between 1887 and 1934, when the Allotment Act is repealed, the U.S. government divests Native Americans of about ninety million acres.

1889–90 The Second Ghost Dance Religion Wovoka becomes the second Ghost Dance Prophet. He is the son of Tavibo, a Paiute shaman in western Nevada. In 1889, Wovoka reportedly speaks with the Creator, who advises Native Americans to live peacefully with all peoples. The Creator instructs Indians to work hard in this life and pray for an apocalypse that will restore the world to its aboriginal state. If the Indians follow the Ghost Dance path, their dead relatives will rise up, and the game and plants will return.

The Ghost Dance religion spreads to many tribes throughout the West. Some Sioux, devastated by war, reservations, poverty, and disease, turn Wovoka's teachings into a movement advocating violence. Soldiers, settlers, government agents, and missionaries fear for their lives as rumors spread that the Ghost Dance will inspire the Sioux to fight again for their rights and freedom. In 1890, the Office of Indian Affairs outlaws the Ghost Dance, and the U.S. government agents and military strengthens its command on the northern Plains. A group of Sioux Ghost Dancers, led by Big Foot, retreats to a site known as Wounded Knee. They are pursued by the Seventh Cavalry, Custer's old unit. After some misunderstandings about the Ghost Dancers' intentions, the army fires on the Sioux and kills more than three hundred Indian men, women, and children. This incident is known as the Wounded Knee Massacre.

1890–1900 The "Vanishing Americans" At the turn of the twentieth century, most non-Indians believe that the Native peoples are the "Vanishing Americans" and will not long survive. The American Indian population declines to a low point of 237,196 in the 1900 U.S. Census. After 1900, however, the Indian population slowly recovers. In 1920, the Census Bureau records

Scene shortly after Wounded Knee Massacre, 1890. Courtesy of the National Museum of Natural History.

244,437 Native Americans. This number increases to 357,499 in 1950, 1,366,676 in 1980, and 1,959,234 in 1990.

1890–1934 The Assimilationist Policy After 1890 most Indian nations are located on reservations or are not recognized by the federal government. Reservation Indians come under direct administrative control from U.S. Indian agents. Since most reservation economies cannot support their Indian populations, Indian reservation residents become economically and politically dependent on the Office of Indian Affairs and its field agents. Food, clothing, medicine, education, and ceremonial life come under strict regulations. Traditional tribal governments are inhibited from operating and ceremonies, like the Plains Sun Dances, are prohibited. Children are sent to boarding schools, where they cannot speak their native language. Federal policy makers hope to reeducate Indian children and incorporate them into U.S. society, and then abolish the reservations. This policy of assimilation is not successful. Traditional government, traditional ceremonial life, and Indian language and life-style persist, despite the efforts to force Indians into U.S. economic and social life.

1900s Struggle and Change in the Twentieth Century The early years of the twentieth century are difficult times for Native Americans who continue to feel the disastrous effects of the General Allotment Act of 1887. Federal, state, and county officials often work together with the private sector to divest the American Indian of his estate. Railroad, cattle, mining, timber, and oil companies take every opportunity to liquidate Indian title to lands and resources.

Indians living on tribal lands are required to be versatile. Hunting, fishing, gathering, and farming continue and at times government rations are received, but these are not sufficient for survival. For this reason, many Native Americans become wage earners. Indians work as migrant workers, moving from one labor camp to the next during harvests. Indians also work on ranches, performing a variety of menial jobs, while others find

Cartoon criticizing mismanagement of Indian affairs by politically appointed Indian agents. Courtesy of Media Projects.

employment on the reservations themselves. Sometimes the Office of Indian Affairs hires reservation Indians as police officers and judges. And some Indians receive an income from leasing their allotments to non-Indian farmers and ranchers.

1902 *Lone Wolf v. Hitchcock* In 1902, Lone Wolf, a Kiowa leader, files a lawsuit to prevent the Interior Department from expropriating tribal land for public use. The Supreme Court rules against him in *Lone Wolf v. Hitchcock*, giving Congress the authority to decide how to deal with and dispose of all Indian lands. This decision creates the doctrine that Congress has plenary powers in Indian affairs, meaning that there is no higher authority in deciding issues in Indian affairs. The Lone Wolf decision affirms the policy that it is within Congress's power to abrogate, or ignore or change, Indian treaties. This decision is a major blow to Indian treaty rights.

November 16, 1907 Indian Territory Is Formed into Oklahoma The state of Oklahoma is admitted to the Union. Most Indian governments in the former Indian Territory have been abolished, including the constitutional governments of the Cherokee, Choctaw, Chickasaw, Seminole, and Creek nations. Most Indian land is allotted to individuals, sometimes forcibly to conservative Indians who do not recognize U.S. rights to abolish their government or to take their land. In the late 1890s and early 1900s, the Creek Snake Indians under Chitto Harjo and Red Bird Smith among the Nighthawk Keetoowah society, as well as less well known movements among the Seminole, Choctaw, and Chickasaw, try to resist allotment and dissolution of their national governments and land, but without success. Oklahoma citizens urge that the remaining Indian lands be put on the market and that Indian landholdings be taxed. Over the next thirty years, many Indians given allotments lose their land owing to debt, legal fraud, and inability to pay taxes. The tribal governments of the former Indian Territory nations are kept up informally, and some are revived starting in the late 1930s. The Choctaw, Cherokee, Chickasaw, Creek, and Seminole regain the right to elect their own governments in the early 1970s, but the governments are now under the jurisdiction of the Bureau of Indian Affairs.

1908 Winter's Doctrine The Supreme Court decides that Indians on reservation lands retain the right to sufficient access to water to provide for agriculture. This doctrine is designed to preserve water and is a decision in favor of conservationists, who think Indians would not use as much water as free market users. The doctrine, however, guarantees Indian reservations rights to water for economic and agricultural use. This doctrine becomes very important after the 1960s, when Colorado, Arizona, New Mexico, and California start to divide scarce water resources among themselves. Indian reservations in the area are guaranteed access to water for reservation development, because the western states cannot entirely ignore the Winter's Doctrine.

Cartoon criticizing Department of Interior management of Indian affairs. Courtesy of Media Projects.

1911 Ishi, the Last Yahi Indian After years of hiding from California settlers, a Yahi Indian known as Ishi allows himself to be captured. He creates a sensation in the newspapers, which refer to him as the "last wild Indian in North America." Ishi survives for five years, living at a museum in San Francisco and providing much ethnographic and linguistic material to the famous anthropologist Alfred Kroeber.

1912 Founding of the Alaska Native Brotherhood Modeled after religious organizations of the Russian Orthodox and Protestant churches, the Alaska Native Brotherhood is formed in 1912 at Juneau, Alaska, by eleven Tlingits and one Tsimpshian, all strong Presbyterians, who attended the Presbyterian-administered boarding school at Sitka, Alaska, an old Tlingit village. In 1915, an auxiliary organization, the Alaska Native Sisterhood, follows the same path at the Brotherhood. The Brotherhood promotes civil rights issues such as the right to vote, access to public education for Native children, and civil rights in public places such as the right to attend movie theaters. It defends Native workers in the Alaskan canneries, defends the rights of Native fishermen, and fights a major land case for the taking of the Tongass Forest from the Tlingit and Haida tribes of panhandle Alaska. The Brotherhood wins the Tongass Forest case in the 1950s and receives payment of $7.5 million after a struggle that starts in 1929. The Brotherhood continues to the present day as an active political force in Alaska Native issues.

1912 Jim Thorpe, from the Sauk and Fox nation, wins the decathlon in the 1912 Olympic games held in Norway. Thorpe's medal is taken away from him, however, because he played semi-professional baseball; it is formally reinstated in 1978. Thorpe goes on to star in professional football during its early days.

1918 Establishment of the Native American Church U.S. courts and law officers persecute Indian peyote users. Indians argue that the peyote is used to enhance religious experience, but they are denied the right to worship with peyote because the worshipers do not have a church organization. Consequently, the Native American church is incorporated into the state of Oklahoma by members of several Oklahoma nations (Kiowa, Comanche, Apache, Cheyenne, Ponca, and Oto). Since the late 1800s the peyote religion has spread quickly across the Plains tribes and reservation communities, where the old forms of religion and culture no longer sustain the Indians under the new conditions of economic poverty and political and cultural suppression.

1921 Snyder Act Congress passes the Snyder Act, which makes the Department of the Interior responsible for Indian education, health, and social services.

1923 The Committee of One Hundred Reformers begin pressing the government to improve Indian living conditions, and in 1923 Secretary of Interior Hubert Work appoints the Committee of One Hundred to survey American Indian policies and to make recommendations. The committee recommends increasing funds for health care, public education, scholarships, claims courts, and a scientific investigation into the effects of peyote usage.

June 2, 1924 Indians Are Granted U.S. Citizenship Because of the services Indian soldiers performed during the World War I and lobbying by the Alaska Native Brotherhood, Congress grants all Indians the rights of U.S. citizenship. The act, however, does not take away rights that Indians have by treaty or by the Constitution. It allows Indians to vote in federal elections, but some states, such as New Mexico, prohibit Indians from voting in state elections.

1928 The Meriam Report Secretary of Interior Hubert Work also asks the Board of Indian Commissioners to make a study of Indian living conditions, but they provide little help. With a grant from John D. Rockefeller, Jr., the Brookings Institute hires Lewis Meriam and nine scholars to investigate the status of Indian economies, health, education, and the federal administration of Indian affairs.

In 1928, Meriam and his committee publish a significant volume, *The Problem of Indian Administration*, commonly known as the Meriam Report. The study describes the conditions of Indian people as "deplorable," particularly because of high infant mortality and deaths at all ages from tuberculosis, pneumonia, and measles. Navajo, Apache, Pima, and other Arizona nations have death rates from tuberculosis seventeen times the national average. The report details the educational failures and poor living conditions found at the boarding schools, and Meriam's committee recommends increased funding for Indian health and education. It also details the incidence of malnutrition, poverty, and marginal land tenure among American Indians. The Meriam Report urges Congress to appropriate money to fulfill its treaty obligations to the tribes in terms of health, education, and subsistence. It urges the president, secretary of the interior, and commissioner of Indian affairs to reform the Office of Indian Affairs.

1934 The Indian Reorganization Act The Great Depression slows the prospects for Indian reform during President Herbert Hoover's administration. Franklin Roosevelt's administration, however, implements a program of reform. Secretary of Interior Harold Ickes and Commissioner of Indian Affairs John Collier work closely to create an Indian New Deal. The Indian Reorganization Act, or the Wheeler-Howard Act, is passed to fulfill the recommendations of the Meriam Report and to promote the well-being of Native Americans by recognizing the value of their diverse cultures, religions, languages, and economies. Indian tribal governments are allowed to establish their own constitutions, laws, and memberships and are encouraged to form economic business corporations.

1934 The Johnson-O'Malley Act Congress repeals the General Allotment Act, replacing it with the Johnson-O'Malley Act, which allows the federal government to contract with states and territories to provide services for the Indians, including health, social welfare, and education. As another part of the Indian New Deal, the commissioner of Indian affairs orders the Indian Service to hire more Indians and to cease interference with Native American spiritual beliefs, ceremonies, and traditions. Indians join the Works Project Administration (WPA), the Public Works Administration (PWA), and the Civilian Conservation Corps (CCC). While participating in such programs as the CCC, Indian families are introduced to modern farming, ranching, and forestry techniques and are taught English and basic mathematics. Opinions vary about the effect of the Indian New Deal, but the 1930s would prove to be a watershed in American Indian history and a step toward Native American self-determination.

1941–45 World War II On December 7, 1941, the United States enters World War II. More than twenty-five thousand Indian men and women join the services, and those who remain home participate in the war effort through work, buying of war bonds, blood drives, and collecting rubber, paper, and metal. A group of Navajo serve as code talkers in the South Pacific, devising a code based on the Navajo language but constructed in such a way that even a Navajo speaker could not decipher it without the key. The Japanese were never able to break the code. The Navajo Code Talkers most likely saved the lives of thousands of U.S. soldiers.

Indian airmen performing a mock Indian dance for their fellow servicemen during World War II. Courtesy of the Archives Trust Fund.

1944 The National Congress of American Indians The Second World War develops a new leadership of Native Americans who are not satisfied with the status quo. In 1944, tribal leaders meet in Denver, Colorado, to form the National Congress of American Indians, a group dedicated to guarding Indian rights and preserving Native culture, reservations, and tribal lands.

1946–49 Reorganization of the Bureau of Indian Affairs A special congressional commission investigates the Bureau of Indian Affairs (BIA) and recommends reform. For years, the BIA administration has suffered from overcentralization at the Washington, D.C., office. All local agency offices send their requests directly to Washington, and it often takes months to get responses. The new BIA organization creates twelve area offices among the ninety agency offices on the reservations and the Washington office. Much of the day-to-day administrative power of the commissioner of Indian affairs is delegated to the twelve area offices.

1946–78 The Indian Claims Commission Even as Native Americans began to organize, a conservative movement is growing in the national capitol calling for a renunciation of New Deal era politics. In 1946, Congress creates the Indian Claims Commission, enabling tribes to sue the federal government for past wrongs. This bill overcomes conservative opposition to become the last piece of Indian New Deal legislation. The claims cases take years to resolve and are a major cost. Although the commission makes several awards to Native Americans, no land is returned and very meager monetary rewards are given to Indian claimants.

1949 The Hoover Commission In 1949, the Hoover Commission, under former president Herbert Hoover, recommends that Native Americans be "integrated, economically and politically, as well as culturally." Hoover's report suggests that "when the trust status of Indian lands has ended, thus permitting taxation, and surplus Indian families have established themselves off the reservations, special aid to the state and local governments for Indian programs should end." The commission recommends that the federal government remove itself from regulation of and responsibility for Indian affairs. This program gathers considerable support from congressional leaders. Many reservations contain timber, oil, gas, coal, uranium, water, and other natural resources coveted by non-Indians and major corporations.

1952 Relocation During the 1950s, the government begins the relocation program, which assists Indian families to move to urban areas. Administrators argue that with housing and employment in urban areas, Indians will find new lives away from their old lands and become integrated into mainstream America. In 1952, the Bureau of Indians Affairs establishes the Voluntary Relocation Program (also known as the Employment Assistance Program), which pays for training, travel, moving, and assistance in finding urban work. The bureau also provides a strong vocational and academic training program for Indians who relocate. By 1960, approximately thirty-five thousand Native Americans have relocated, but one-third of these return home to the reservations.

1953 The Termination Resolution House Concurrent Resolution 108 is passed. It calls for the end of the special legal relation between Indian governments and the federal government. This legal relation is created by the commerce clause in the Constitution and recognized by a series of court decisions starting in the 1820s and 1830s. The House Resolution sets the tone of Indian Affairs policy by indicating its desire to end the reservation system and to assimilate Indians into U.S. society by terminating Indian treaty rights and legal status as historical nationalities and independent cultural communities.

In the same year, Congress passes Public Law 280, which empowers certain states (California, Wisconsin, Nebraska, Minnesota, Oregon, and, in 1959, Alaska) to assume management over criminal justice on Indian reservations. This law opens the possibility of state jurisdiction over reservation courts. Previously, federal law and courts had upheld the separation of state and Indian government relations because this separation is explicitly written out in the commerce clause of the Constitution.

1954–62 Termination Congress adopts the policy often called termination, a plan to end tribal sovereignty, health care, and most federal obligations to Indians as specified in past treaties or acts of Congress. Responsive to the national conservative swing in the 1950s, Congress passes a series of laws implementing the termination of Indian reservations. Between 1954 and 1962 more than one hundred bands, communities, and rancherias are terminated or severed from direct relations with the federal government. As a result, the terminated Indian communities lose protections and services formerly provided by the national government. The National Congress of American Indians fights against termination and by the late 1950s the movement has lost its momentum. Termination ends during President John F. Kennedy's administration because of opposition by Indians and state governments, who think the policy will result in higher state service costs to Indians.

1959–71 Alaska Native Land Claims Alaska becomes a state in 1959; the federal government grants the new state the right to select 102 million acres of land. Indian title in Alaska, however, has not been settled, and Alaska Native villages protest state land selections by making claims to land with the Bureau of Land Management. By 1964, Alaska Natives claim more than 300 million acres, and the secretary of the interior, Stewart Udall, prohibits the state from selecting land until Indian title is clarified. Alaska Natives mobilize around the land claims issue and other issues like education, health, and jobs. They form local and regional associations of villages. In 1965 and 1966, Alaska Natives create the Alaska Federated Natives (AFN), a statewide organization empowered to pursue land claims and other community interests. The AFN leads Alaska Natives to a Congressional settlement in 1971, called the Alaska Native Claims Settlement Act, which preserves for the Natives 44 million acres and $962 million for giving up claims to the rest of Alaska.

1961 The Chicago Indian Conference After mobilizing against the threat of termination in the late 1950s, representatives from ninety tribes meet in Chicago and set out a policy agenda. The new agenda emphasizes greater academic training for Indian children, increased job training, improved housing on reservations, better medical facilities, access to loans for economic development, and increased emphasis on industrial development and employment on the reservations.

1961 The National Indian Youth Council An activist organization, the National Indian Youth Council, is formed. This organization challenges the approaches of traditional advocate groups such as Christian churches, the National Congress of American Indians, and the Indian Rights Association. The National Indian Youth Council presents a more activist and nationalist orientation to solving Indian problems.

1962 Indian Voting Rights Indians became U.S. citizens in 1924, but many states refuse to allow Indians to vote in state and local elections (although Congress ensures Indians the right to vote in federal elections). This year, the federal government forces New Mexico to grant its large Indian population the right to vote in state and local elections.

1964 The American Indian Historical Society Rupert Costo and Jeanette Henry Costo organize the American Indian Historical Society, dedicated to historical re-

Myra Dorothy Brown (Arapaho) died in 1991 at the age of 89. Her name as a young woman was Yeiy, or Otter.

search and teaching about Native Americans. The society begins publishing *The Indian Historian*, a journal that presents articles on Indian history primarily from an Indian perspective.

1964–66 Indian Community Action Programs President Lyndon B. Johnson's Great Society legislation for alleviating poverty is implemented by creation of the Office of Economic Opportunity (OEO). The OEO organizes an Indian Desk for managing antipoverty programs on Indian reservations. The Bureau of Indian Affairs (BIA) insists on administering Indian antipoverty funds, but the OEO, suspicious of paternalistic BIA management of Indian affairs, delivers antipoverty funds directly to the tribal governments. For the first time, most Indian tribal governments gain direct access to federal funds that are not administered by BIA officials. Community Action Programs (CAP) become the primary funding source and administrative organization for managing Indian antipoverty funds. During the late 1960s and 1970s many tribal governments rapidly expand in personnel, budget, and programs administered. The method of granting funds directly to tribal government control becomes the model for the Self-Determination Policy starting in the early 1970s and for the Self-Determination and Education Assistance Act of 1975.

1964–74 Fishing Rights in Washington State Treaties dating from the 1850s give many Washington Indian tribes the right to fish at their traditional fishing places and rights to half the fish in the rivers. Over the years, state laws and court decisions increasingly excluded Indians from fishing with traps and with certain kinds of fishing nets. Washington Indians become increasingly active in asserting their treaty rights to take fish at their traditional fishing camps and with traditional fishing methods. Eventually, the issue is sent before state and federal courts and is partially settled in 1974 by a federal court ruling, often called the Boldt decision. The decision affirms Indian treaty rights to at least half the fish in many western Washington State rivers.

Clifford E. Trafzer,
University of California, Riverside

Duane Champagne,
University of California, Los Angeles

Nooksack tribal gathering and salmon bake to discuss fishing rights, Deming, Washington, 1970.

♦ CHRONOLOGY OF NATIVE NORTH AMERICAN HISTORY, 1966 TO 1992

The middle 1960s marked a major turning point in U.S. Indian policy. By the middle 1960s, the threat of termination of Indian reservations had subsided, and the new democratic administration introduced government programs aimed at eliminating poverty in the United States. Many Indian reservations and tribal governments benefited from the new programs, and government policy became redirected toward allowing reservation tribal government more control over local administration of government programs. Local management of community reservations, since the 1880s largely managed by the Bureau of Indian Affairs (BIA), became the theme in the new U.S. Indian policy called the Self-Determination Policy, which characterized most of the 1965–1992 period and was the policy for Indian affairs for the foreseeable future. Through the 1960s and 1970s, reservation tribal governments received considerable federal funding in the range of 2 to 3 billion dollars from a variety of federal agencies that service such reservation needs as housing, health, community action, education, and other areas. During the 1980s, federal funding available to Indians declined and inflation made the smaller level of funding worth even less. The 1980s, however, increasingly saw Indian communities work to gain more control over reservation governments, over reservation industry and mineral resources, and over education and other reservation institutions that were generally managed by the BIA. In the future, most Indian reservation communities will search for ways to express, maintain, and live their culture, and will work to develop more meaningful and culturally agreeable ways to eventually realize the goals of cultural and political self-determination.

April 7, 1965 American Indian National Congress executive director and tribal representatives testify before U.S. Senate subcommission against the termination of the Colville tribe of Washington, D.C. The Congressional termination policy began in 1953 with the passage of House Concurrent Resolution 108, whose objective was to solve "the Indian problem" by assimilating Indian people into the American mainstream. This process was to be accomplished by ending the government's relationship with 109 tribes and bands that were considered to have reached a satisfactory level of economic and social achievement. Among the first tribes whose relationship with the federal government was terminated were the Klamath of Oregon and the Menominee of Wisconsin. Many other smaller groups around the nation were also terminated.

By 1965, it becomes increasingly clear that the effects of the termination policy on Indian communities is disastrous. The termination process leaves Indian people in a psychological and legal limbo: one day they are Indian, according to the government, and the following day they are not. Many tribal members, accustomed to the Bureau of Indian Affairs' (BIA) paternalism, are unprepared for the changes thrust upon them. Increases in alcoholism and poverty and the disintegration of the tribal unit follow. The dissolution of the reservations and reservation services mean a larger population of people dependent on state assistance.

May 26, 1965 The House of Representatives approves a $4.7 million award by the Indian Claims Commission to the Miami Indians of Indiana and Oklahoma for the loss of their lands in the nineteenth century.

February 15, 1966 Comedian Dick Gregory and his wife are arrested for illegal net-fishing, which they engage in with members of the Nisqually tribe in a protest "fish-in." The tribe, arguing that they had reserved the right to fish according to their own laws in their 1856 treaty with the federal government, is protesting the application of state game laws that dictate hook-and-line fishing, thereby preventing the tribe from fishing according to their traditional ways.

April 14–16, 1966 Approximately eighty tribal leaders representing sixty-two tribes attend an "emergency conference" called by the National Congress of American Indians to protest their not being included in a congressionally sponsored conference. The conference was called by the chairman of the House Commission on Interior and Insular Affairs, Morris Udall, to discuss the reorganization of the Bureau of Indian Affairs. Representative Udall announces the admittance of representatives to the BIA's conference and confirms that the House commission will establish a tribally comprised group to advise him on the BIA's reorganization.

April 30, 1966 The Senate confirms the appointment of Robert LaFollette Bennett (Oneida) as the BIA commissioner, succeeding Phileo Nash. Bennett is only the second Indian appointed commissioner, following in the footsteps of Ely Parker, a Seneca, appointed by Ulysses S. Grant in 1869.

April 30, 1966 The three hundred members of the Havasupai tribe,who live at the base of the Grand Canyon, reject a Bureau of Indian Affairs proposal to modernize their village, Supai. Each year, one to two thousand visitors make the rough eight-mile trek by horseback to the only village on the 518-acre reservation. The council votes against the BIA's goals to link the reservation by roads, chair lifts, and helicopters.

Spring 1966 The Navajo contract with the BIA to establish the Rough Rock Demonstration School. The school is the first in modern times to be completely administered and controlled by a tribe. Impetus for the school's creation comes from the realization that more than half of all reservation school students fail to complete their high school education. Studies suggest that the high dropout rate results from the teachers' lack of knowledge about Indian culture and behavior and from discriminatory treatment. The Navajo hope that by running their own school, they will be able to reverse the dropout rate and improve the education of their children.

October 1966 The Alaska Federation of Natives (AFN) meets in Anchorage, Alaska. Originally organized by Emil Notti, president of the Cook Inlet Native Association, the three hundred members discuss resolutions and strategies for the preservation of their land base. The organization is particularly concerned with the halting of further state land claims until the issue of Native land rights in Alaska is resolved.

Alaska Natives, who never signed treaties with the U.S. government, are recognized by the government as possessing an aboriginal title to their lands. The exact meaning of aboriginal title, beyond a recognition that Alaska Natives had lived on their lands for thousands of years, however, is unclear. The Alaskan Statehood Act of 1958 guarantees the Natives' hunting and fishing rights, but also gives the state of Alaska the right to appropriate 102 million acres of land for its own use. As economic development and tourism in Alaska increase, the Natives' subsistence living based on hunting, fishing, and trapping becomes increasingly endangered.

November 1966 The forty-four-year-old Association of American Indian Affairs holds a two-day conference on the dismal record of educating American Indian youths. Attended by thirty-five specialists, including the recently appointed chief of education in the Bureau of Indian Affairs, the group hears grim statistics concerning the lack of educational success achieved by Indian children. Coming under particular attack are the eighty-one boarding schools operated by the Bureau of Indian Affairs for some thirty thousand students. In many instances, very young children, having no local schools, are forced to attend boarding schools six hundred miles from their homes and families. Both the boarding school children and the ninety-one thousand other Indian students who attend regular public, church, or private schools face serious problems of adjustment and discrimination, leading to a 50 percent dropout rate among Indian students.

January 10, 1967 President Lyndon B. Johnson, in his State of the Union message, urges, "We should embark upon a major effort to provide self-help assistance to the forgotten in our midst—the American Indians."

January 16, 1967 The Bureau of Indian Affairs announces the formation of a National Indian Education Advisory Committee to assist in the improvement of educational services to Indian students.

February 5, 1967 The Iowa Senate approves the repeal of one of the last examples of discriminatory legislation against Indians, a law that prohibits the sale of liquor to Indians. Congress repealed federal prohibitions against the sale of liquor to Indians in 1954.

March 20–21, 1967 The U.S. Senate and House of Representatives approve a bill to extend the life of the Indian Claims Commission to 1972 and to expand its membership to five. The commission, first established in 1946, still has 347 unadjudicated cases on its dockets.

Congress passed the original legislation to provide Indian tribes with an avenue for settling their land claims against the federal government, enabling tribes to bring suits against the United States for the illegal taking of their lands through error, duress, fraud, or other dishonorable dealings. Although the act provide Indians with their "day in court," criticisms against the act's implementation are many. Tribes are compensated for the value of their lands at the time of taking (in many instances only a dollar or two an acre), not at the land's current value. Funds expended by the government on behalf of the tribe over the years are deducted from the final judgment. Most importantly, however, the act does not provide for the return of land to tribes, but only for a belated, and to many, inadequate, payment for the land.

June 10, 1967 The U.S. Claims Court upholds a 1964 decision by the Indian Claims Commission finding that the Seminole of Florida and Oklahoma have claims to 32 million acres of Florida lands under the terms of the Seminole nation's 1823 treaty with the federal government.

August 6, 1967 The Indian Claims Commission awards $12.2 million to eight Sioux tribes for the compensation of 29 million acres taken in fraudulent treaties during the 1800s. The illegally taken lands include half of Minnesota and parts of Iowa, North and South Dakota, and Wisconsin.

September 11, 1967 The New York Division of National Association for the Advancement of Colored People (NAACP) announces the preparation of a report detailing the United States' genocide of American Indians. The report is to be submitted to the United Nations.

March 6, 1968 Johnson delivers his "Special Message to Congress on the Problem of the American Indian: 'The Forgotten American.'" In announcing his request for a 10 percent increase in federal funding for Indian programs, Johnson outlines three goals in his message: (1) "A standard of living for the Indian equal to that of the country as a whole"; (2) "Freedom of choice: an opportunity to remain in their homelands, if they choose, without surrendering their dignity; and opportunity to move to towns and cities of America, if they choose, equipped with the skills to live in equality and dignity"; and (3) "Full participation in the life of modern America, with a full share of economic opportunity and social justice." The new federal objective, according to Johnson, is "a goal that ends the old debate about 'termination' of Indian programs and stresses self-determination."

March 6, 1968 Johnson signs an executive order establishing the National Council on Indian Opportunity. Chaired by the vice president and comprised of six Indian leaders and the heads of the departments of Interior, Agriculture, Commerce, Labor, Health, Education, and Welfare, and Housing and Urban Affairs and the Office of Economic Opportunity, the council is charged with coordinating efforts to improve programs for Indians.

Although President Johnson's programs constitute one of the first efforts by the federal government to involve Indians in decision making, the tribes continue to voice suspicion and concern that all federal programs ultimately lead to the termination of the government protection of Indian lands and the provisions of federal services—guarantees that the tribes believe Congress obligated itself to provide in return for the taking of Indian lands.

April 11, 1968 Congress passes the American Indian Civil Rights Act, which guarantees to reservation residents many of the same civil rights and liberties in relation to tribal authorities that the U.S. Constitution guarantees to all persons in relation to federal and state authorities. The act is introduced by Senator Sam Ervin after seven years of investigations into rights denied to individual Indians by tribal and state governments and the federal government.

The act is not fully supported by all tribes, especially the Pueblos, who fear that the act will alter their traditional forms of governments and culture. The act also limits the rights of tribes to levy penalties over crimes committed on their reservations to $1000 in fines or six months in jail.

Tribal leaders are supportive of other provisions of the legislation. Title IV of the act, for example, repeals Public Law 280, an act passed by Congress in 1953 that gives states the authority to extend criminal and civil jurisdiction over reservations. The act also allows states to retrocede, or give back, criminal and civil jurisdiction to the tribes. Other parts of the law direct the secretary of the interior to publish updated versions of Charles Kappler's *Indian Affairs: Laws and Treaties*, and Felix Cohen's *Handbook of Federal Indian Law.*

May 8, 1968 John Collier, former U.S. commissioner of Indian affairs from 1935 until 1945 and proponent of tribal rights, dies in Taos, New Mexico. Collier was responsible for the reaffirmation of tribal authority and the strengthening of tribal governments. He sincerely believed in the values of Indian cultures and that Indian problems were best solved by Indian people. He successfully stopped the sale of further Indian allotments, established the Indian Arts and Crafts Board, and oversaw the passage of the 1934 Indian Reorganization Act (IRA). Although the act was not as strong as Collier had hoped, the IRA did revitalize tribal governments, setting the stage for tribes to reassume control over the administration of federal programs that controlled their lives.

May 18, 1968 President Lyndon Johnson signs a bill commemorating the centennial of the federal government's peace treaty with the Navajo. The Navajo nation, the largest in the United States, inhabits a sixteen-million-acre reservation located in Arizona, New Mexico, and Utah. In terms of population and acreage, the Navajo Nation is larger than twenty-six independent countries in the world.

May 19, 1968 The National Congress of American Indians sponsors a tour by forty-nine Indian leaders from fifteen western tribes. The group, which visits New York City and other cities, is designed to encourage companies to establish businesses on reservations.

May 27, 1968 A unanimous Supreme Court upholds in *Puyallup Tribe v. Department of Game* the right of Washington State to prohibit Indian net fishing for salmon in the interest of conservation. The case is an important departure from previous holdings, because it allows state regulation of some treaty fishing rights.

May 30, 1968 One hundred fifty Indians march outside the plaza of the Supreme Court building in protest of the Supreme Court's decision in the Puyallup case.

June 7–July 16, 1968 Comedian Dick Gregory is released from jail in Olympia, Washington, after fasting for six weeks to call attention to the violation of Indian treaty rights.

June 21, 1968 The Poor People's Campaign, in which approximately one hundred Indians take part, marches on the Bureau of Indian Affairs in Washington, D.C.

July 1968 The American Indian Movement (AIM) is founded by Dennis Banks, a member of the Ojibway or Chippewa Nation, and Russell Means, a member of the Lakota or Sioux Nation, in Minneapolis, Minnesota. Founded during a period of general civil unrest and protests by African-Americans and Mexican-Americans, the movement is organized to improve federal, state, and local social services to urban neighborhoods and to prevent the harassment of Indians by the local police. Increasingly confrontational, AIM members form patrols to monitor police activity and to demonstrate against Indian mistreatment.

October 21, 1968 Congress enacts the Supplemental Appropriations Act of 1969, which includes an appropriation for $100,000 to implement the National Council on Indian Opportunity, established by Executive Order 11399 on March 6, 1968. An important piece of President Johnson's efforts to improve the plight of Indians, the council is given the following purposes: (1) to encourage the complete application of federal programs designed to aid Indians; (2) to encourage interagency cooperation in the implementation of these programs; (3) to assess the effect of these programs; and (4) and to suggest ways in which these programs can be improved.

October 24, 1968 The Yavapai tribe of Arizona and the federal government agree to a $5 million settlement for the loss of over 9 million acres illegally taken from the tribe by the federal government in 1874.

January 21, 1969 The Navajo Community College opens at Many Farms, Arizona. The college is the first tribally established and controlled community college in modern times.

March 5, 1969 President Richard Nixon signs an executive order establishing the Office of Minority Business Enterprise. It is the office's function to ensure that a fair proportion of the total government purchases and contracts are awarded to businesses that are owned wholly or in part by minorities and women. Indian tribes, acting in their commercial capacity, are expressly included in the act's provisions. The act's objective is to assist tribes in the economic development of their reservations, where more than half of all families live below the poverty level and unemployment on some reservations is as high as 90 percent.

March 23, 1969 The Indian Health Service reports that the life expectancy for Indians is 64 years of age, compared with an average life expectancy of 70.5 for non-Indians. Despite the continuing gap in life expectancy, the new statistics reveal a major improvement in Indian health care. Twenty years previously, the average life expectancy for an Indian male was only 44 years.

March 23, 1969 The trial of seven Mohawks begins on charges stemming from demonstrations on the International Bridge between the United States and Canada. The bridge is located on the Akwesasne reservation that straddles Canada and the United States. Demonstrators were protesting the imposition of Canadian custom duties on their goods. The Indians argue that the 1794 Jay Treaty signed between the United States and Great Britain on behalf of Canada guaranteed to the border tribes free passage and freedom from import and export taxes on goods traversing the border. Because of the failure of Canada and the United States to recognize the tribes' right to freely export and import goods, Indian families must pay taxes on goods that are only carried from one family members' house to another.

May 5, 1969 N. Scott Momaday (Kiowa) is awarded the Pulitzer Prize for his book *House Made of Dawn*. The book details the life of a young Indian man who leaves the reservation and his subsequent difficulties in adjusting to the outside world. Momaday is the first American Indian awarded a Pulitzer since the prize's inception in 1917.

May 18, 1969 The Klamath tribe of Oregon wins a judgment of $4.1 million from the Indian Claims Commission for the loss of lands resulting from faulty surveys conducted by the government of their reservation in 1871 and 1888.

June 19, 1969 The National Congress of American Indians (NCAI) hosts an exhibition and briefing sessions in New York City in an effort to attract private businesses to reservations. NCAI president Wendall Chino announces that 159 new enterprises have been started on reservations in the previous five years, with a total investment of more than $100 million.

August 7, 1969 President Richard Nixon appoints Louis R. Bruce, a Mohawk-Oglala Sioux and one of the founders of the National Congress of American Indians, as the new commissioner of Indian affairs.

August 19–21, 1969 In what some have termed as the first all-Indian called and attended study group, forty Indians, many of whom are progressives, meet in Denver, Colorado, to plan strategies for dealing with the problems of reservations and with the federal government.

August 23, 1969 Representatives of forty-six North American Indian nations meet at the Onondaga Reser-

Members of the Iroquois League protesting for their rights to cross U.S.–Canadian border in accordance with the 1794 Jay Treaty, July 1969. Courtesy of the Buffalo and Erie County Historical Society.

vation in New York. Representing traditional peoples, the conference passes a resolution calling for the immediate ouster of Interior Secretary Walter Hickel. Hickel, they charge, has not been protective of Indian resources nor sensitive to the needs of Indian peoples.

August 26, 1969 The Quinault tribe of Washington announces the closure of reservation beaches to non-Indians, citing thefts of Indian fishing gear, littering, and defacement. The state responds that the ownership of the beaches remains in question.

October 12, 1969 Dartmouth College, located in New Hampshire and initially established in 1769 to educate Indians, announces that it is dropping its use of an Indian mascot in response to demands by the undergraduate body. Many students support the Indian students' views that the use of an Indian mascot degraded Indian people.

October 13, 1969 The Ford Foundation announces the establishment of a Minority Fellowship Program for minority students, including American Indians. The program's objective is to increase the number of minority scholars obtaining doctorates. The need is particularly acute in Indian Country, where few Indians enter and complete college, much less graduate schools. Without appropriate role models, educators recognize that it will be difficult to improve educational services to Indian students.

November 1969 The National Indian Education Association (NIEA) is organized in Minneapolis, Minnesota, to improve the quality of Indian education. The organization is established specifically to improve communications on Indian educational issues through national conventions and workshops; to advocate for increased funding and creative programs for the education of Indian children; and to provide technical assistance to educators in the field.

November 3, 1969 The Senate Subcommittee on Indian Education issues its final report following a two-year investigation. Chaired by Senator Edward Kennedy, who took over following the death of his brother, Robert Kennedy, the committee spent two years reviewing all areas of Indian education. The report concludes that "our national policies for educating American Indians are a failure of major proportions." In comparing statistics in all aspects of education, the committee states its disbelief with "the low quality of virtually every aspect of schooling available to Indian children." The report spells out sixty recommendations to improve Indian education, headed by the strongest urging that Indian people be given greater control over the schooling of their children.

November 20, 1969 Indian activists occupy Alcatraz Island in San Francisco Bay. The protesters offer to purchase the island from the federal government for $24 worth of beads.

January 17, 1970 A Senate and House of Representative subcommittee publishes a two-volume report on economic conditions on reservations. Detailed in the report are charges by Bureau of Indian Affairs official William Veeder, a water resources expert, that the government has caused "irreparable damage" to the Indians and to the economic development of Indian reservations. Veeder asserts that the basic problem results from an inherent conflict of interest between the Interior and Justice Departments, which are responsible for protecting public lands and streams as well assuring Indian property rights. Veeder suggests that Congress create an independent governmental agency for the protection of Indian water rights.

Desirae Caldwell writing on chalkboard.

March 8, 1970 Actress Jane Fonda and thirteen Indians are arrested following an attempt by a large group of Indians to take over Fort Lawton, Washington, near Seattle. The group demands the base for use as an Indian cultural center.

March 15, 1970 The U.S. Army takes seventy-eight Indians into custody following the group's second attempt to take over Fort Lawton for use as an Indian cultural center.

March 22–23, 1970 Nine Indians are arrested near Denver, Colorado, and twenty-three are arrested at the Bureau of Indian Affair's offices in Chicago, Illinois, for sit-in protests against the BIA's employment policies. Similar protests are held in Cleveland, Ohio; Minneapolis, Minnesota; Sacramento, California; and Santa Fe, New Mexico.

April 11, 1970 The government enacts legislation to provide for loans to federally recognized tribes or tribal corporations from the Farmers Home Administration for the purpose of acquiring lands or interest to lands within reservation boundaries. The act is an extension of the 1934 Indian Reorganization Act, which sought to prevent the further erosion of the tribal land base and to assist tribes in the consolidation of their lands.

April 18–23, 1970 Indians hold sit-ins in several BIA offices throughout the country.

April 27, 1970 In the case of the *Choctaw Nation et al. v. Oklahoma et al.*, the Choctaw, Chickasaw, and Cherokee nations of Oklahoma win control of the lower Arkansas River, by a vote of four to three. The Supreme Court finds that the government had ceded the riverbed and oil and mineral resources beneath the land to the tribes in the 1830 Treaty of Dancing Rabbit Creek and the 1835 Treaty of New Echota.

May 5, 1970 A tribal election at the Isleta Pueblo, located outside Albuquerque, New Mexico, grants women the right to vote.

May 14, 1970 The Indian Claims Commission awards $12.2 million to the Seminole tribe for the government's illegal taking of lands in Florida. The money is to be distributed among the 1,500 Seminole in Florida and the 3,500 Seminole living in Oklahoma. The Seminole, who fought three successive wars with the federal government resisting forced relocation to Oklahoma, success-

Alcatraz Island declaration by Indians of All Tribes.

fully argued to the court that the government had taken title to their lands in Florida under duress.

July 8, 1970 President Richard Nixon delivers a special message to Congress dealing exclusively with American Indians and Alaska Natives, setting forth a legislative program that expresses the idea of self-determination without the threat of termination. "The time has come," Nixon states, "to break decisively with the past and to create the conditions for a new era in which the Indian future is determined by Indian acts and Indian decisions." Nixon proposes: the termination act, House Concurrent Resolution 108, be expressly overturned; tribes be given the means to administer programs now operated by the Bureau of Indian Affairs and be given greater control over Indian education; Blue Lake be restored to the Taos pueblo; greater federal funds be allocated to improve Indian health and the status of urban Indians; the position of Assistant Secretary of Indian Affairs be created as a means of elevating the status of the BIA within the Department of the Interior; and an Indian Trust Counsel Authority be established to represent Indians in the protection of their lands and resources.

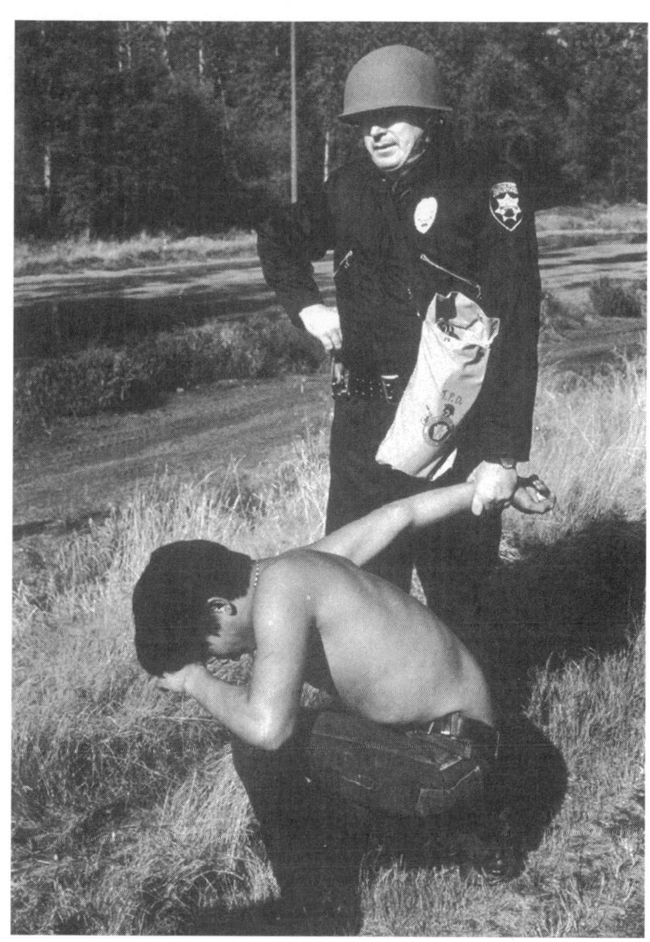

Puyallup Indian arrested for protesting violation of treaty fishing rights.

Powwow singers, Alcatraz Island, 1969.

July 12, 1970 Two hundred members of the Iroquois Confederacy meet in Geneva, New York, to discuss proposals for regaining political power lost to the state and federal governments. The Iroquois Confederacy, or Haudenosaunee, established more than five hundred years ago, is comprised of the Onondaga, the Mohawk, the Seneca, the Oneida, the Cayuga, and the Tuscarora.

July 15, 1970 Members of the Oglala Sioux seize an area on Sheep Mountain, North Dakota, demanding the return of a gunnery range that the military took from the tribe during World War II.

August 1, 1970 Puyallup Indians set up a camp on the Puyallup River in Washington State and begin fishing to reestablish their tribal fishing rights.

September 1, 1970 The Tuscarora Indians successfully obtain a court order allowing for the eviction of some forty non-Indian families from the Tuscarora reservation. The court order follows a series of demonstra-

Indians protesting discrimination in hiring at the Bureau of Indian Affairs office in Denver, Colorado, 1970.

tions staged by the Tuscarora and their supporters since August 20.

September 20, 1970 The Justice Department announces a $13.2 million settlement with the Osage Indian Nation of Oklahoma for 28 million acres of lands purchased by the federal government in Arkansas, Kansas, Missouri, and Oklahoma between 1803 and 1819.

November 8, 1970 Approximately seventy-five Indians seize an abandoned army communications center in Davis, California. The Indians demand that the center be turned over to them for use as an Indian cultural center.

December 15, 1970 President Richard Nixon signs the Taos Land Bill. The legislation returns forty-eight thousand acres of land, including Blue Lake, to the Taos Pueblo. This bill, the first legislation to restore a sizable piece of land to an Indian tribe, acknowledges that the Taos Pueblo Indians had practiced their religion at this sacred site for over seven hundred years. The Pueblo lost the lands in 1906 when President Theodore Roosevelt added the area to the Carson National Forest and lobbied for sixty years for the return of their sacred lands.

December 15, 1970 Nixon signs legislation authorizing the payment of $1.1 million to the Nez Percé tribe of Idaho and the Confederated tribe of Colville of Washington State. The funds were awarded to the tribes by the Indian Claims Commission for the illegal loss of tribal lands to the federal government in the nineteenth century.

1971 The Bureau of Indian Affairs establishes regulations allowing for the direct election of the chiefs of the Five Civilized Tribes. The Five Civilized Tribes—the Cherokee, Creek, Seminole, Choctaw, and Chickasaw, along with more than thirty other tribes, were relocated in the 1800s to what was then Indian Territory and is today Oklahoma. Promising that the territory would always remain in Indian control, Congress reversed this guarantee in the 1890s. Tribes had their lands allotted and their governments, for the most part, dissolved. The BIA was given the authority to appoint a chief for each of the Five Civilized Tribes. The tribes view the return of control over their own electoral system as an important step in the revitalization of their government.

1971 The Native American Rights Fund (NARF) is created with its central office located in Boulder, Colorado, and a branch office in Washington, D.C. NARF was established in 1970 as a special pilot project of the California Indian Legal Services. Funded by the Ford Foundation, the organization's objectives are to pursue the legal protection of Indian lands, treaty rights, individual rights, and the development of tribal law.

January 13, 1971 The NAACP Legal Defense and Education Fund and Harvard University's Center for Law and Education release a 162-page report charging state and local officials with a gross misuse of funds appropriated under the Elementary and Secondary Education Act and the 1934 Johnson-O'Malley Act. Funds, the report charges, which are to be used for the benefit and education of Indian children, are frequently used for non-Indian educational purposes. Some 250 examples of alleged impropriety are provided, such as buying expensive equipment for non-Indian schools and reducing non-Indian property taxes. "By every standard," the report emphasizes, "Indians receive the worst education of any children in the community."

January 14, 1971 The San Francisco regional office of the Health, Education, and Welfare Department gives custody of a 640-acre army communications center in Davis, California, to local Indians. The Indians who received the "care, custody, protection and maintenance" of the base, occupied the deserted base in November 1970. A spokesman for the group, Jack Forbes, announces plans to establish a college for American Indians and Mexican-Americans on the site.

February 19–20, 1971 Tribal leaders from fifty reservations in twelve states meet in Billings, Montana, to discuss the establishment of a national association of tribal council leaders. The decision to establish the National Tribal Chairmen's Association stems from a concern by tribal reservation leaders that national Indian policy is being made in response to the actions of urban Indians and young militant reservation Indians.

April 25, 1971 The U.S. Census Bureau reports that the 1970 census counted 791,839 Indians, an increase of more than 50 percent from the 1960 census. The increase in population is primarily due to a declining death rate and a high birth rate.

Taos Pueblo. Courtesy of Mark Nohl, New Mexico Economic and Tourism Department.

Title VII (Indian Education) Gifted and Talented program provides an electronic video microscope for 3–6 classes. Patricia C'Hair and Franklin Martel show how the TV monitor can display microscopic views to large groups.

May 15, 1971 The Native American Rights Fund files suit in federal court on behalf of sixty-two members of the Hopi tribe to stop strip-mining on 100 square miles of the Hopi reservation. The religious leaders contend that Black Mesa is an area of sacred relevance within Hopi religion and culture. The suit is part of a larger effort by other Indians and conservationists to stop the development of a major power grid in the Four Corners area. The Hopi traditionalists' objective is to prevent mining of the coal by the Peabody Company for use in the six proposed power plants.

May 21, 1971 Members of the American Indian Movement (AIM) occupy a naval air station in Milwaukee, Wisconsin. The group argues that under the terms of the 1868 treaty between the federal government and the Lakota, all abandoned federal property should revert to Indians.

May 26, 1971 The director of the Office of Economic Opportunity (OEO) announces the provision of $880,000 in grants to establish a Model Urban Indian Center program. The funds are to be used to establish Indian centers in Los Angeles, California; Minneapolis, Minnesota; Gallup, New Mexico; and Fairbanks, Alaska. The program's objective is to provide models for the improvements of services in the forty other existing urban Indian service centers.

According to the 1970 census, 44.5 percent of the total Native population lives in urban areas, an increase of almost 15 percent during the last ten years. Much of the movement to the cities stems from the Bureau of Indian Affair's relocation program. In an effort to assimilate Indians into the mainstream, tribal members have been encouraged to move to the urban areas to find work. Others move on their own, forced to leave their reservation homes in search of jobs.

June 6, 1971 Yvonne Knight, a member of the Ponca tribe of Oklahoma, is the first known Indian woman to receive a jurist doctorate (J.D.) degree. She graduates from the University of New Mexico Indian Law Program, established in 1967 to increase the number of Indian lawyers.

June 6–7, 1971 Forty Indians, demanding that the federal government honor its commitments in its 1868

Hopi elder with woman and child outside of Hopi pueblo.

treaty with the Sioux Nation that all lands west of the Missouri River would belong forever to the Sioux nation, establish a camp on the top of the Mount Rushmore National Memorial. Police arrest twenty protesters twelve hours later for climbing the monument.

June 11, 1971 The nineteen-month takeover of Alcatraz Island ends with the removal by federal marshals of the last fifteen Indians occupying the prison. Averaging one hundred protesters from fifty different tribes, the activists had announced plans to turn Alcatraz into a Center for Native American Studies, an Indian Center of Ecology, an American Indian Museum, a Great Indian Training School, and an Indian Center of Ecology.

June 14–17, 1971 Indian leader, John Trudell (Lakota) and fifty Indians occupy a deserted army missile site near Richmond, California. One hundred police remove the protesters three days later.

June 14–July 1, 1971 One hundred Indians occupy an abandoned Nike missile site outside of Chicago, protesting the lack of housing for Indians in Chicago.

July 17, 1971 The Choctaw Indian Nation of Oklahoma is the first Indian tribe to vote to lower their voting age to eighteen in tribal elections.

July 30, 1971 Seventy-five Indians occupy a former Nike site on the grounds of the Argonne National Laboratories in Hinsdale, Illinois.

August 13, 1971 The Inter-Tribal Indian Ceremonial holds its fiftieth-year anniversary celebration in Gallup, New Mexico.

August 14, 1971 Members of the Milwaukee chapter of the American Indian Movement seize an abandoned Coast Guard station.

August 15, 1971 The Taos Pueblo hold a two-day celebration marking the return of their sacred lands, including Blue Lake. Interior Secretary Rogers Morton attends the event.

August 26–September 1, 1971 The Office of Civil Rights of the Health, Education and Welfare Department reports that twenty-nine thousand American Indians are enrolled in colleges and universities.

September 16, 1971 Assistant Secretary of the Interior Harrison Loesch participates in the dedication of the new $13 million Southwestern Indian Polytechnic Institute in Albuquerque, New Mexico. The school will serve seven hundred Indian students from sixty-four tribes. The 164-acre campus will offer training in business management, clerical work, drafting, radio, electronics, commercial food preparation, telecommunications, television, engineering, and optical technology.

October 5, 1971 The Arctic Slope Native Association files suit against the state of Alaska, claiming the seventy-six thousand acre North Slope of Alaska. The suit claims that the state's selection of this oil rich area in 1964 violated Native land rights in that the "Eskimo people have occupied, used and exercised dominion" over the area. The region is currently under lease to private oil companies for approximately $1 billion.

October 9, 1971 The Senate passes a $390.3 million education bill designed to give greater control to tribes over the education of their children.

October 13-15, 1971 The American Indian Movement holds its first national convention. Approximately one hundred delegates representing eighteen chapters attend the conference at Camp Owendigo, Minnesota.

December 15, 1971 The Navajo Community College Act provides $5.5 million for the construction and operation of a new facility for the Navajo Community College.

December 18, 1971 President Richard Nixon signs the Alaska Native Claims Settlement Act (ANSCA) into law. The act extinguishes Alaska Native title to nine-tenths of Alaska in return for 44 million acres and almost $1 billion. The House had passed the vote on December 14 by a vote of 307–60 and the Senate by a voice vote. The legislation provides for the creation of villages and regional corporations under state law for the management of the lands and funds provided to the villages and corporations.

Although the Alaska Federation of Natives approved the bill by a vote of 511–56, the act remains controversial among Alaska Natives who fear that the act will destroy their traditional life-style, which is centered on hunting and fishing.

February 19, 1972 A federal court order takes effect protecting the Chippewas' right to hunt, fish, trap, and gather wild rice according to tribal laws on their Leech Lake reservation. The Leech Lake Band of Chippewa Indians won their suit against the state of Minnesota in December 1971, successfully proving that their 1855 treaty with the United States guaranteed their right to hunt, fish, trap, and gather wild rice on the reservation.

March 2, 1972 Bowing to pressures by Indian students on campus, Stanford University in Palo Alto, California,

Inuit blanket toss, Barrow, Alaska.

ends a forty-year tradition of using an American Indian symbol for its athletic teams.

March 4, 1972 Five persons are charged in Gordon, Nebraska, with manslaughter and false imprisonment in the death of R. Yellow Thunder, a forty-one-year-old Oglala Sioux Indian. Three weeks previously, R. Yellow Thunder had been stripped of his clothes and forced into an American Legion Hall where a dance was in progress.

March 7, 1972 Urban Indians hold a conference in Omaha, Nebraska, forming the National American Indian Council. The council is committed to working on behalf of urban Indians nationwide.

April 23, 1972 Thirty Lakota and Chippewa American Indian Movement members stage a peaceful protest on the Fort Totten Indian Reservation in North Dakota. The sit-in's purpose is to call attention to police brutality on the reservation. According to the protesters, three Indians have died in jail in the last few months.

May 20, 1972 Congress passes the Indian Education Act of 1972, creating a BIA-level Office of Indian Education as well as a National Advisory Council on Indian Education designed to improve the quality of public education for Indian students through grants and contracts for teachers of Indian students.

May 20, 1972 President Richard Nixon signs an order restoring twenty-one thousand acres in Gifford Pinchot National Forest to the Yakima Indians of Washington.

June 1972 Lumbee students at Pembroke State University strive to prevent the destruction of a historic Indian building on the campus. In 1885, the state of North Carolina permitted the Lumbees to operate their own school systems. The state's fifty-year-old constitution recognized the Lumbees as "free people of color," but barred then from attending white schools, permitting them to operate their own schools proved to be an important step in the Lumbee's advancement. The school, started in 1887, became a four-year college in 1935. Old Main, as the building is known, served for many years as the only building on campus. With a current enrollment of twenty-five hundred, 92 percent of whom are white, the mostly white campus administration finds itself pitted against the Lumbees who are determined to save the historic building.

July 21, 1972 The U.S. government announces that it will officially recognize the Shinnecock Indians of Southampton, New York, through their inclusion on an official Bureau of Indian Affairs map showing the location of federally recognized Indian reservations and tribes.

August 24, 1972 The General Accounting Office (GAO) issues a report charging that the Department of Interior has failed to enforce the Environmental Policy Act in its regulation of strip coal mining on Indian and federal lands.

September 13, 1972 Approximately forty Indians seize control of the Bureau of Indian Affairs in Pawnee, Oklahoma, protesting the use of federal funds and presenting a list of demands to federal and state authorities.

November 2–8, 1972 Five hundred Indians arrive in Washington, D.C., with the Trail of Broken Treaties to protest the government's policies toward Indians. The leaders, mostly members of the American Indian Movement, bring with them a twenty-point program, which they plan to present to the administration. Among their demands are that treaty relations be reestablished between the federal government and the Indian nations; that termination policies be repealed, including Public Law 280; that the Indian land base be doubled; that tribes be given criminal jurisdiction over non-Indians on reservations; and that cultural and economic conditions for Indians be improved.

Umiaq frame, Point Hope, Alaska.

The twenty-point program is quickly forgotten in the wake of a disagreement over housing and food provisions during the march in Washington. In protest, members of the Trail of Broken Treaties occupy the Bureau of Indian Affairs building in Washington, D.C.

After almost a week of occupation, in which activists destroy files, furniture, and Indian art, the government agrees to pay for the protesters' return trip home.

November 9, 1972 The Paiute tribe of Nevada wins its suit against the Department of Interior for the department's management of Pyramid Lake. The court agrees that the Interior Department had violated its trust responsibility by allowing water diversion from the lake, thereby threatening the economic and spiritual existence of the tribe.

November 14, 1972 The U.S. Commission on Civil Rights hears testimony from American Indian witnesses that the agency has directed its attention to the needs of African- and Hispanic-Americans and overlooked the needs of American Indians.

January 9, 1973 The administration officially rejects the demands received from the leaders of the Trail of Broken Treaties.

February 6–8, 1973 Two hundred American Indian Movement (AIM) protesters clash with police in Custer, South Dakota. Thirty-seven Indians are arrested during a melee with police over a judge's decision to grant bail to the white man charged with the stabbing death of Wesley Bad Heart.

February 12, 1973 Two hundred-fifty Indians gather in Sturgis, South Dakota, to witness the setting of bond for Harold Withhorn, whom police have charged with the murder of a non-Indian.

February 27-May 8, 1973 Two hundred Indians under AIM leadership occupy Wounded Knee, on the Pine Ridge Reservation in South Dakota. American Indian Movement leaders are asked to the reservation by traditionalists to assist them in their struggle against the elected chairman Richard Wilson, whose administration, they charge, is rife with corruption and nepotism, and silences its critics through intimidation and violence.

Federal marshals and Federal Bureau Investigation (FBI) officers immediately surround the hamlet, creating a standoff that draws national and world-wide media attention. The Indian militants, who are well armed, make clear their intention to fight rather than to surrender to outside forces. The impasse finally ends with a negotiated settlement and the withdrawal of both sides.

March 1973 Clashes occur between Hopi and Navajo over the disposition of the Joint Use Area.

March 27, 1973 The Supreme Court rules in *Mescalero Apache Tribe v. Jones, Commissioner, Board of Revenue of New Mexico, et al.* that Indians are exempt from state taxation on incomes earned within reservation boundaries.

March 31, 1973 The Northern Cheyenne Tribal Council of Montana votes to instruct the Bureau of Indian Affairs to cancel strip mining leases worth millions of dollars negotiated by the BIA on reservation lands. Lawyers for the Cheyenne tribe found thirty-six illegal sections in the leases that the BIA had negotiated on behalf of the tribe.

April 8, 1973 A poll conducted by Louis Harris reports that 51 percent of those polled side with the Indians, while 21 percent side with the federal government in the Wounded Knee standoff.

June 14, 1973 The Federal Trade Commission issues a report charging that a number of non-Indian traders, licensed by the Bureau of Indian Affairs, are engaged in unfair trading practices leading to a worsening of economic conditions for the inhabitants of the Navajo reservation. The report finds that prices charged by the trading posts exceeded off-reservation stores by 16.6 percent and exceeded the national average by 27 percent.

July 16, 1973 The Census Bureau reports that the median income for Indian families in 1969 was $5,832 compared to a national average of $9,590. Forty percent of Indian families live below the poverty level, compared to 14 percent of all families and 32 percent of black families. Education statistics indicate the greatest degree of increase since the last census. One third of all Indians over twenty-five have completed high school, with a median number of 9.8 years of school for all Indians. The number of Indian students in college has doubled since 1960.

August 13, 1973 An Office of Indian Rights is created within the Civil Rights Division of the Justice Department. The office is established to investigate and to protect individual Indian rights guaranteed under the Indian Civil Rights Act.

November 17, 1973 The grand jury in Sioux Falls, South Dakota, returns four indictments against Indians in the Wounded Knee standoff.

November 19, 1973 The Supreme Court, in a unanimous decision in *Department of Game of Washington v. Puyallup Tribe et al.*, rules that Washington State had abrogated the Puyallup Indians' treaty rights by prohibiting the tribe from commercial fishing. State law restricted all available fish to sports fishing.

November 22, 1973 Indigenous peoples of the Arctic area—Eskimos, Lapps, and Indians—meet in Copenhagen, Denmark, to formulate demands for self-government and for control over land and resources. Indigenous peoples from Alaska, Canada, Greenland, Norway, and Sweden attend the four-day meeting.

December 22, 1973 President Richard Nixon signs Public Law 93-197 restoring the Menominee Indian tribe of Wisconsin to full federally recognized status.

December 28, 1973 Congress enacts the Comprehensive Employment and Training Act of 1973 or CETA, as it is commonly known. Title III of the act, Special Federal Responsibilities, Indian Manpower Programs, is designed to assist unemployed and economically disadvantaged Indians.

January 21, 1974 The Supreme Court reverses a lower court decision that barred the Oneida Indian Nation from suing the State of New York for rental on 5 million acres of land the tribe claims was taken in illegal state treaties in 1788 and 1795.

February 7, 1974 Russell Means, leader of the American Indian Movement, is defeated by incumbent Richard Wilson in a run-off election for chairman of the Oglala Sioux Tribal Council. Means had led in a field of twelve nominees by a small margin in the initial vote on January 22. Means, a traditionalist who lost 1,709 to 1,530, vowed to destroy the "white man's tribal government" and to reestablish "a type of government where all Indians would have a voice." Wilson, representing the more assimilationist forces on the reservation, had pledged to continue full cooperation with the federal government. Charges of corruption and illegal vote counting followed the final outcome of the election.

February 12, 1974 U.S. District Court Judge Boldt rules in *United States v. State of Washington* that the

1854 and 1855 treaties signed by the tribes of northwestern Washington, in which they reserved "the right of taking fish, at all usual and accustomed grounds and stations . . . in common with all citizens of the Territory," entitle the tribes to 50 percent of the allowable salmon catch.

February 16, 1974 Russell Means and Dennis Banks, co-founders of the American Indian Movement, are brought to trial for charges stemming from the 1973 occupation of Wounded Knee, South Dakota.

February 20, 1974 The Supreme Court, in *Morton v. Ruiz*, unanimously upholds the right of Indians living off reservation to receive general welfare payments from the Bureau of Indian Affairs.

April 12, 1974 Congress passes the Indian Financing Act, making available $250 million in credits and grants up to $50,000 to facilitate financing the economic development of Indians and Indian organizations.

June 4, 1974 Secretary of Interior Rogers C. B. Morton announces that the Bureau of Indian Affairs was acceding to the request of the Northern Cheyenne tribe in Montana that coal lease terms be renegotiated. The BIA had negotiated the leases on behalf of the tribe beginning in 1969. The tribe had sought cancellation of the leases, which provided for strip mining on the reservation, on the grounds that the terms were not favorable to the tribe. The new guidelines require that all leases meet federal environmental protection standards and a revised royalty schedule, and have obtained the joint approval of both the tribe and the company.

June 17, 1974 The Supreme Court refuses to review a lower court decision upholding the election of an Arizona county supervisor who is a member of the Navajo nation. Non-Indian voters had challenged his eligibility for office on the grounds that his status as a reservation Indian made him immune from state taxes and the normal legal process.

June 17, 1974 The Supreme Court, in *Morton v. Mancari*, upholds the preferential hiring of American Indians within the Bureau of Indian Affairs. The suit, which had been brought by non-Indian BIA employees, argued that preferential hiring of Indians violated the equal protection clause of the Constitution and constituted racial discrimination. The Court denies the claim, pointing out that the federal government has a special obligation to Indians. Special preferences are given to Indians in BIA employment, the Court said, not because of their membership in a racial group, but because of their membership in quasi-sovereign nations that have entered into a special relationship with the federal government.

August 28–30, 1974 The New Mexico Advisory Committee of the U.S. Civil Rights Commission holds three days of hearings near Farmington, New Mexico. The hearings are prompted by the beating death of three Navajo men by three white teenagers who had found the men drunk. The teenagers, according to the terms of state juvenile laws, were sentenced to two to three years in a reformatory. Navajo leaders testified to a variety of abuses ranging from commercial cheating to murder suffered by Navajo in off reservation towns located in Colorado, Utah, and New Mexico. Several Navajo leaders request support in obtaining the closure of off-reservation taverns.

September 16, 1974 Russell Means and Dennis Banks, American Indian Movement founders, are freed following a six-month trial on charges arising from the 1973 occupation of Wounded Knee, South Dakota.

November 1974 Chippewa-Ottawa members of the Bay Mills Indian community are arrested in Petoskey, Michigan, for illegally fishing in Lake Michigan.

December 22, 1974 Congress passes the Hopi and Navajo Relocation Act providing for negotiations between the two tribes over their dispute concerning the Joint Use Area. The bill provides for the partition of the 1.8 million-acre Joint Use Area between the Hopi and Navajo and for $16 million to compensate eight hundred Navajo families who will be required to relocate as a result of the partition.

This legislation is the latest attempt by Congress to deal with the longstanding Navajo-Hopi land dispute. The conflict between the Hopi and the Navajo is complex. The Hopi have never signed a treaty with the United States, largely due to the fact that there has never been open fighting between the tribe and the United States. Hence, the tribe possessed no legal document proving their title to their aboriginal lands. In contrast, the Navajo entered into a treaty with the United States in 1868, following years of hostility and relocations. The treaty established the Navajo reservation in northwestern New Mexico and northeastern Arizona. Previous to the adoption of this treaty, a number of Navajo families had already made their homes in areas claimed by the Hopi.

In 1882, in response to Hopi complaints about Navajo encroachment on their lands, the president issued an executive order establishing the Hopi reservation. Hopi lands continued to be settled by Navajo families as well as Mormon settlers.

In an effort to solve the growing conflict between the two tribes, Congress authorized the courts to make a determination as to the competing land claims. In response, the courts created the Joint Use area, composed of 1.8 million acres, while allotting only 650,000 acres of the 1882 reservation for the exclusive use of the Hopi.

January 1–February 4, 1975 Forty-five Indians of the Menominee Warrior Society seize a Catholic novitiate in Gresham, Wisconsin. The Warrior Society demands that the Alexian Brothers give the 225-acre complex to the tribe for use as a hospital. The compound, comprised of a twenty-room mansion and another sixty-four room building, is currently unused by the religious order.

January 2, 1975 Congress, pursuant to a joint resolution of both houses, agrees to review the government's historical and special legal relationship with the Indian people. The American Indian Policy Review Commission is chaired by Senator James Abourezk of South Dakota. The task force includes three senators, three representatives, and five tribal representatives.

January 4, 1975 Congress passes the Indian Self-Determination and Education Assistance Act, expanding tribal control over reservation programs and authorizing federal funds to build needed public school facilities on or near Indian reservations. Hailed as the most important piece of legislation passed since the 1934 Indian Reorganization Act, the Self-Determination Act's goal is to give governing authority over federal programs to the tribes and to inhibit the pattern of further federal dependency and paternalism.

Wyoming Indian High School students Yvonda Hubbard and Marla Jimerson.

Hopi Bureau of Indian Affairs police officers and a tribal ranger place an elderly Navajo man in custody for allegedly trespassing and interfering with the Hopi BIA fencing crew in the Hopi partitioned lands. The incident is about the ongoing Navajo and Hopi land dispute.

January 8, 1975 The U.S. Commission on Civil Rights issues a report in which the results of the election for tribal chairman on the Oglala Sioux Tribal Council are termed invalid and recommends the calling of a new election. After reviewing the ballots, the commission reports, "almost one-third of all votes cast appear to have been in some manner improper.... The procedures for ensuring the security of the election were so inadequate that actual fraud or wrongdoing could easily have gone undetected."

March 13, 1975 The Fairchild Camera and Instrument Corporation announces that it will close its Shiprock, New Mexico, electronic plant on the Navajo reservation. The plant was occupied by armed members of the American Indian Movement (AIM) for eight days in protest of the plants lay-off of 140 Indian employees. The company, which produces semiconductors and integrated circuits for computers, employed approximately 600 Navajos before the lay-offs took effect in February. In assessing the damage of the takeover, which ended March 3, a Fairchild spokesperson stated, "Fairchild has concluded that it couldn't be reasonably assured that future disruptions wouldn't occur."

April 22, 1975 A story in the *New York Times* reports that violence on the Pine Ridge Reservation has continued since the end of the Wounded Knee seizure. According to an FBI report, six people have been killed and sixty-seven assaulted since January 1. The violence, according to the story, is the legacy of the 1973 takeover, which has divided the reservation into two opposing factions.

June 16, 1975 The American Indian Movement (AIM) ends its national convention in Farmington, New Mexico, with a statement declaring that the U.S. government, religion, and education are the most potent enemies of Indian people.

June 26, 1975 Two FBI officers are killed on the Pine Ridge Reservation in South Dakota.

July 10, 1975 The Alexian Brothers Roman Catholic order rescinds its offer to deed to the Menominee tribe of Wisconsin its novitiate in Gresham, Wisconsin, for use as a tribal hospital.

August 6, 1975 President Gerald Ford signs into law the Voting Rights Act Amendments of 1975. The act, which is designed to protect the voting rights of non-English speaking citizens by permitting voting in more than one language, specifically includes the rights of American Indians.

August 13, 1975 The New Mexico advisory committee to the U.S.Civil Rights Commission issues "The Farmington Report: A Conflict of Cultures." The study concludes that Navajo in San Juan County, New Mexico, which includes Farmington, are subjected to a wide range of injustices and mistreatment. Discrimination, according to the report, is intensified by poverty, severe alcoholism, and substandard health care. The county, the committee points out, has no detoxification or rehabilitation centers, despite the fact that 85 percent of the twenty-one thousand Navajo arrested between 1969 and 1973 were arrested on alcohol-related offenses. The report also took note of the inadequately staffed and funded Indian Health Service Hospital in Shiprock, and the lack of cooperation and commitment evidenced by local doctors responsible for the care of the Navajo population.

October 23, 1975 The Federal Trade Commission issues a report criticizing the Bureau of Indian Affairs' failure to adequately live up to its trust responsibility when negotiating with energy companies on behalf of tribes.

November 25, 1975 A federal grand jury indicts four Indians, Leonard Peltier, Robert Eugene Robideau, Darrelle Dean Butler, and James Theodore Eagle, on charges of the premeditated death of two FBI officers. The officers were killed on July 26 in a gun battle on the Oglala Sioux Indian Reservation near Pine Ridge, South Dakota.

December 23, 1975 The U.S. Court of Appeals, First Circuit, upholds Judge Edward Gignoux's decision in *Passamaquoddy Tribe v. Morton*. The Passamaquoddy and Penobscot of Maine, two non-federally recognized tribes, successfully argue that the 1790 Trade and Non-Intercourse Act established a trust relationship between them and the federal government. The 1790 act forbade the sale of Indian lands without the approval of the federal government. The colony of Massachusetts (which later divided into Massachusetts and Maine) had purchased land from the Passamaquoddy and Penobscot tribes in an illegal colonial treaty. The federal government argued that it was not obligated to represent the tribes in their suit against the state of Maine because the tribes were not federally recognized. Judge Gignoux's decision upholds the principle that the federal government has an obligation to protect the land rights of all tribes, whether recognized or not.

February 24, 1976 City police in Madison, Wisconsin, remove 175 protesters who are demanding the firing of the Menominee tribal police chief for the killing of two tribal members in a shootout.

March 2, 1976 The Supreme Court rules in *Fisher v. District Court* that the Northern Cheyenne tribe of Montana has exclusive authority over adoption proceedings in which the participants are all tribal members and residents of the reservation.

April 27, 1976 The Supreme Court, in *Moe v. Salish and Kootenai Tribes*, rules that the states may not tax either personal property on the reservation or cigarette sales by Indians to Indians on the reservation. In a blow to tribal economic development, however, the Court rules that tribes must collect cigarette sales tax on the reservation on sales by Indians to non-Indians.

May 29, 1976 Congress passes the Indian Crimes Act of 1976. The act ensures that all individuals, Indian and non-Indian alike, will receive equitable treatment for violating crimes in all territories under federal supervision, including Indian reservations, military installations, and national parks.

June 8, 1976 American Indian Movement members Robert Robideau and Darrelle Butler go on trial for the murder of two FBI agents on Pine Ridge Reservation in South Dakota on June 25, 1975.

June 15, 1976 The U.S. Supreme Court, in a victory for tribes, rules in *Bryan v. Itasca* that Public Law 280, a statute giving six states criminal and civil jurisdiction over Indian reservations, does not give states the authority to levy state property tax on Indians living within their reservation boundaries.

September 1, 1976 The All Indian Pueblo Cultural Center opens in Albuquerque, New Mexico. The $2.3 million Indian Cultural Center is a joint effort of the nineteen pueblos that lie along the Rio Grande. The complex houses a museum, a restaurant, and a gift shop.

September 16, 1976 Congress passes the Indian Health Care Improvement Act, authorizing seven years of increased appropriations in an effort to improve Indian health care. The bill provides $480 million in funds for recruiting and training Indian health professionals; providing health services, including patient, dental, and alcoholism care; constructing and renovating health facilities; and providing services to urban Indians.

October 8, 1976 President Gerald Ford signs a bill to terminate the Indian Claims Commission on December 31, 1978. Unresolved cases are to be forwarded to the U.S. Court of Claims for final resolution.

October 10, 1976 President Gerald Ford proclaims the week of October 10 as Native American Awareness Week.

October 13, 1976 The federal government awards $6.6 million to the Mesquakie tribe for lands taken in Iowa, Missouri, Illinois, and Kansas in ten treaties signed between the federal government and the tribe between 1804 and 1867.

October 31, 1976 Approximately sixty members of the Puyallup tribe, including members of the tribal council, occupy the Cascadia Juvenile Diagnostic Center in Tacoma, Washington. After a week-long occupation,

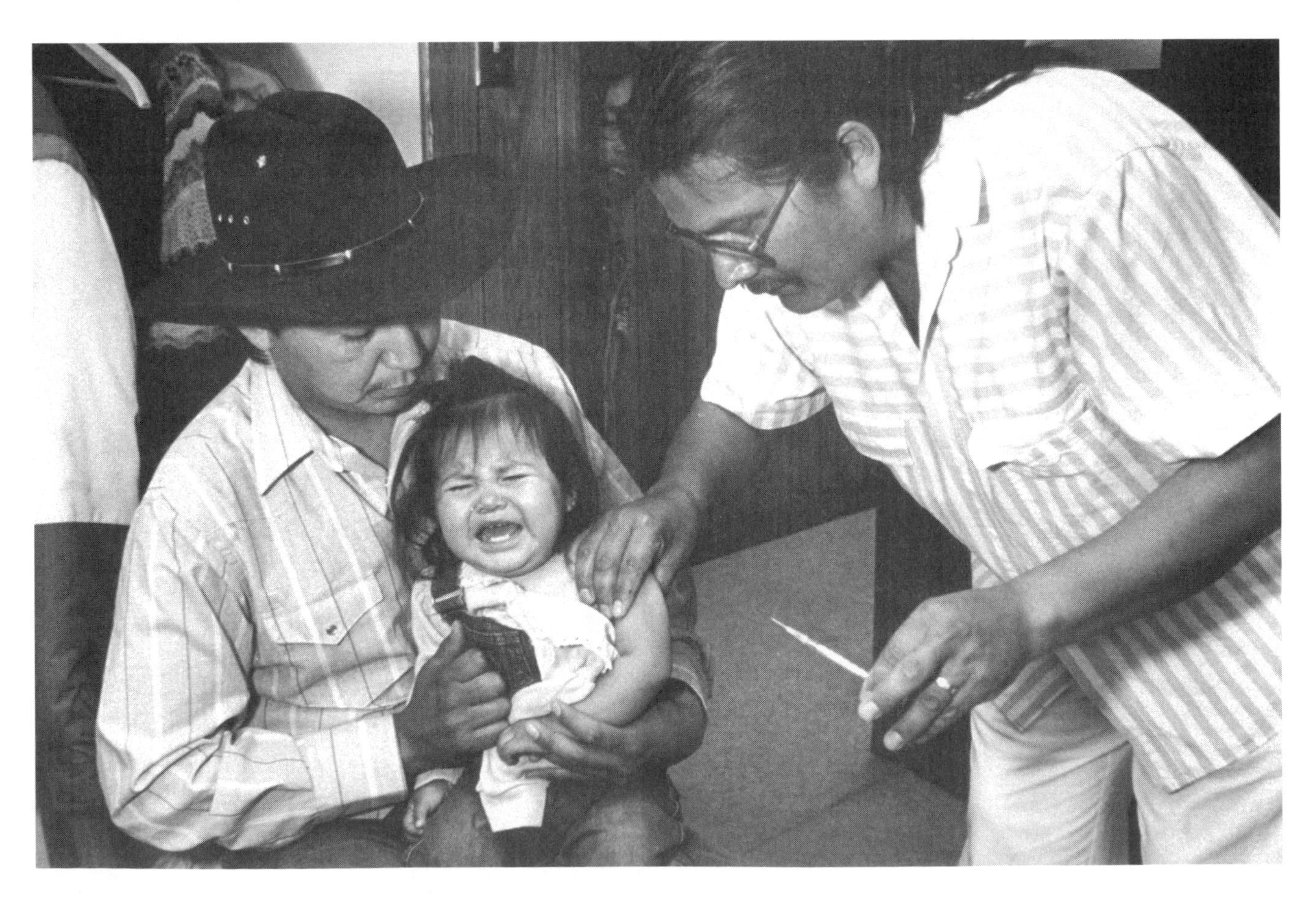

Albert Begay holds his daughter, 15-month-old Devona, after she was given a measles injection by nurse Ron Garnanez at the Shiprock (NM) Indian Hospital.

during which time the tribe claimed title to the building, the governor of Washington announces an agreement to give six acres of land to the tribe.

December 13, 1976 The Navajo radio network broadcasts its first day of news and public interest programming on the reservation in the Navajo language.

January 13, 1977 Secretary of Interior Thomas S. Kleppe rescinds a number of coal leases and lease options on coal reserves on the Crow reservations. The strip-mining agreements, which provided for a royalty payment of 17.5 cents per ton on subtracted coal, had come under attack by Crow tribal members. Tribal members had filed suit to have leases held by Shell Oil, AMAX Inc., Peabody, and Gulf companies revoked.

March 21, 1977 Members of the Menominee Warrior Society take over the courthouse in Keshena, Wisconsin, demanding that authorities charge those responsible for the beating of two women.

April 4, 1977 The Catawba Indians of South Carolina vote 101 to 2 in a tribal council meeting to ask Congress to settle their claims to 144,000 acres in York and Lancaster counties. The tribe, which is requesting recognition of a reservation within their former lands, argues that their 1763 treaty with Great Britain guarantees their ownership of the land. Barring Congressional relief, the tribe agrees to take their suit to court.

April 5, 1977 The Supreme Court, in the *Rosebud Sioux Tribe v. Kneip* case, rules that the congressional legislation, which opened surplus reservation lands to white settlers in the nineteenth century, diminished the size of the reservation and thereby the tribe's jurisdictional authority over that area.

April 18, 1977 American Indian Movement leader Leonard Peltier, 32, is found guilty of two charges of first-degree murde in the shooting deaths of two FBI agents on the Pine Ridge Reservation in 1975. Despite objections by the defense that Peltier is entitled to a public trial, the court is closed to the public for the reading of the verdict by a jury of nine women and three men. Two men, previously charged with Peltier, had been acquitted of the charges on July 16, 1976.

May 13, 1977 Militant Mohawk who for three years have occupied a 612-acre campsite in the Adirondack Mountains reach an agreement with the state of New York. In return for a grant of two separate sites, the Mohawk agree to vacate within the next five months the site they have renamed *Ganienkeh* or "Land of the Flint." The larger area of land, consisting of five thousand acres, is located within the Macomb State Park. A smaller parcel of seven hundred acres lies near the town of Altona, New York. The Mohawk claimed the area as part of the land guaranteed to the tribe in an eighteenth-century treaty.

May 18, 1977 Congress releases its multi-volume American Indian Policy Review Commission Report. Eleven study groups, comprised of thirty-three members, thirty-one of whom were Indian, worked for two years to produce the report. The study recommends that tribes be recognized as sovereign entities with the right to maintain their own judicial systems, to tax, and to control their own resources. The report further recommends that the Bureau of Indian Affairs be abolished and that the government establish a new agency to better represent tribes, to be a liaison between tribes and all federal programs, and to allow tribes to become self-governing.

Representative Lloyd Meeds, Democrat of Washington, formerly an Indian supporter, but now concerned about his reelection with voters angry over Indian fishing rights, issues a minority report. It states that the task force was calling for an "unwarranted extension of the concept of sovereignty which Indians have been trying to forward for some time, and some of its suggestions are so unrealistic as to subject it to ridicule."

June 2, 1977 Leonard Peltier is sentenced by a Fargo, North Dakota, court to two consective life terms for the killings of two FBI agents.

June 13–17, 1977 Two hundred indigenous peoples from Alaska, Canada, and Greenland, convene the first Inuit Circumpolar Conference in Barrows, Alaska. The conference is the first attempt to organize the one hundred thousand Inuits who inhabit the North Pole region. Delegates adopt resolutions concerning the preservation of their cultures, recognition of political rights to self-rule, environmental protections, and the banning of all weapons testing and disposal in the Arctic.

June 17, 1977 The *New York Times* reports that the International Indian Treaty Council, which represents ninety-seven tribes, announces its intention to provide the Soviet Union with a list of human rights abuses by the United States against tribes. The list, which includes treaty violations, the destruction of Native cultures and religions, and the interference in tribal economic and social life, would be provided for Soviet use at the upcoming meetings on the Helsinki Accords in Belgrade, Yugoslavia. The Helsinki Accords, signed by thirty-five nations in 1975, pledge signatory states to respect the self-determination and human rights of all peoples.

July 24, 1977 The Ute and Comanche nations meet to formally end a 200-year-old dispute over hunting rights in jointly claimed territory. More than two thousand members from both tribes attend the traditional ceremony, which includes the exchange of buckskin scrolls, the smoking of a peace pipe, and the shaking of hands.

August 1, 1977 The Seneca Nation holds an opening ceremony for its new $265,000 museum in Salamanca, New York. The museum, designed and constructed by the tribe from federal grants, houses artifacts from the Seneca Nation and the Iroquois confederacy, as well as Indian art work.

August 1, 1977 Congress amends the Public Health Services Act to provide for special scholarship benefits to Indians entering the health professions.

September 1977 The Alaskan Eskimo Whaling Commission is founded to fight the International Whaling Commission's ban against the hunting of all bowhead whale. Culturally and economically dependent on the hunting of bowhead, the Alaskan Eskimo Whaling Commission commits itself to ensure that all hunts are conducted in a traditional and non-wasteful manner to educate non-Native Alaskans about the cultural importance of whaling and to promote scientific research to ensure the bowhead's continued existence.

October 13, 1977 Forrest J. Gerard (Blackfeet) is appointed by President Jimmy Carter as the first assistant secretary of Indian affairs. First proposed by President Richard Nixon, the creation of the assistant secretary of Indian affairs position elevates the Bureau of Indian Affairs administration to an equitable level with other agencies within the Interior Department.

January 2, 1978 The Bureau of Indian Affairs reports that the federal government has reached an out-of-court settlement with the Devils Lake Sioux Indian tribe for the illegal taking of one hundred thousand acres of land between 1880 and 1890. The tribe will receive $8.5 million for land taken from the Fort Totten Indian reservation.

February 1978 Negotiations open among the federal government, New York State, and the Onondaga and Cayuga nations over the tribes' claims to 275,000 acres in New York State.

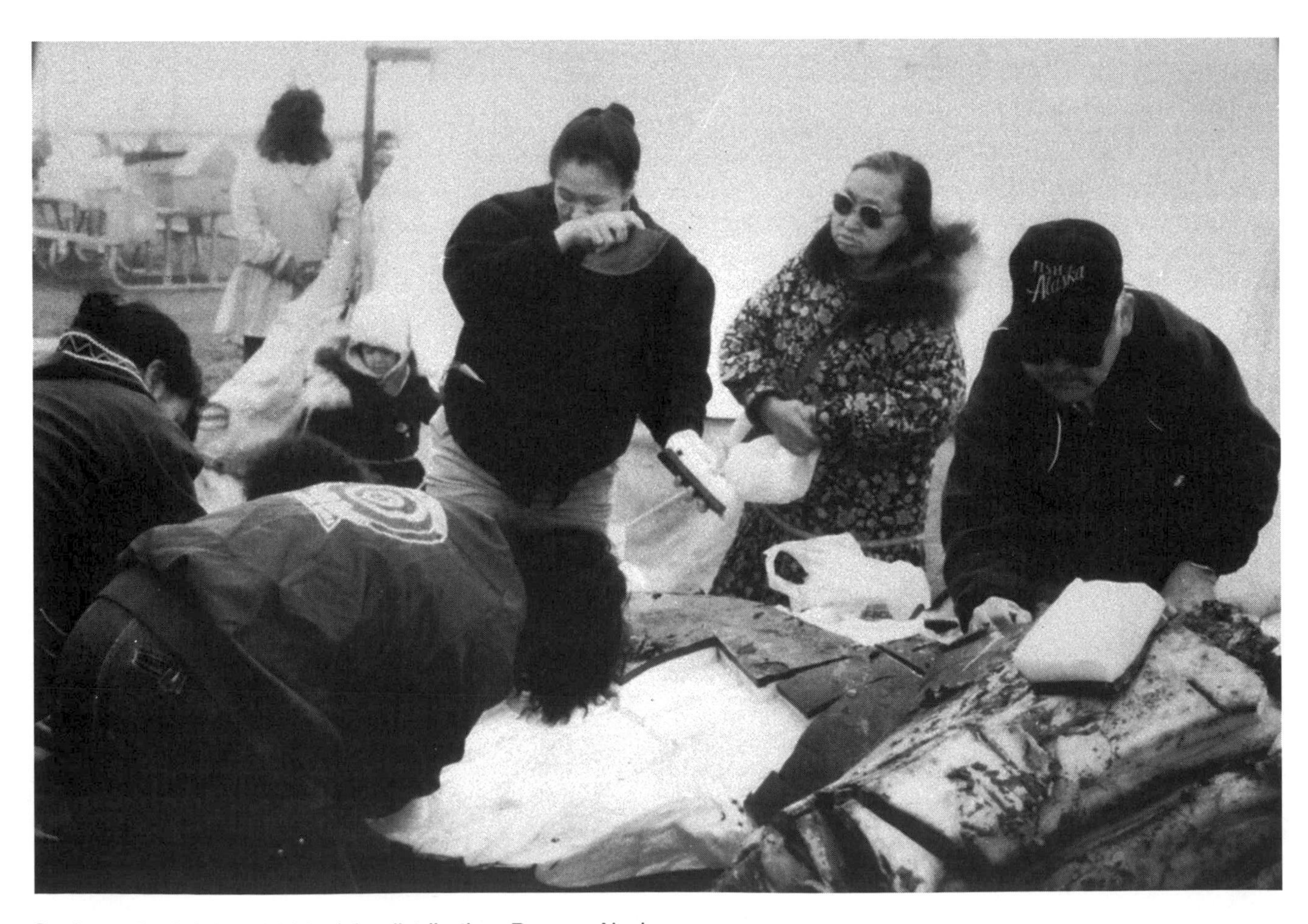

Cutting maktak (whale blubber) for distribution, Barrow, Alaska.

Indians participate in the Longest Walk, a protest to bring attention to broken treaties and ill treatment of Indian people, 1978. Courtesy of Random House Inc.

February 11–July 15, 1978 Indian participants begin the Longest Walk at Alcatraz Island, California, in protest of the government's ill treatment of Indians. The walk concludes with thirty thousand marchers in Washington, D.C.

March 2, 1978 The Narragansett Indians of Rhode Island receive 1,800 acres in what is the first negotiated settlement between state officials and an eastern tribe. The tribe filed suit against Rhode Island for the taking of 3,500 acres in violation of the 1790 Trade and Non-Intercourse Act. Eastern tribes have filed fourteen land claims against the former thirteen colonies.

March 6, 1978 The Supreme Court rules in *Oliphant v. Suquamish Indian Tribe* that tribal courts do not possess jurisdiction over crimes committed by non-Indians on reservations. The case is brought by two white men who had been arrested by the Suquamish tribal police for disturbing the peace and resisting arrest during the tribe's annual Chief Seattle Days. The men argue that tribal governments do not have the inherent authority to exercise criminal jurisdiction over non-Indians. Previously, the courts had invoked a principle of federal Indian law that tribal governments retained all inherent rights of government unless ceded by them in a treaty or expressly extinguished by the federal government in legislation.

In this case, the Supreme Court rules that tribes may not exercise authority that is inconsistent with their status as a domestic dependent nation. The decision represents a major blow to tribes in the protection of their inherent sovereignty. The ruling also presents tribes with the practical problem of how to protect their lands and citizens from criminal actions by non-Indians. For the most part, state police officers do not have the authority to maintain law and order on Indian reservations.

March 22, 1978 The Supreme Court rules unanimously in *United States v. Wheeler* that the United States did not violate a Navajo Indian man's protection against double jeopardy by trying him for rape in a federal court when he had been convicted on a lesser charge arising from the same incident in the Navajo tribal courts. In a victory for tribal sovereignty, the Court underscores that tribal governments are not creations of the federal government, but are separate sovereigns. As separate sovereigns, they have the authority to make and to adjudicate their own laws within limits established by Congress.

March 24, 1978 The Wampanoag claim to 11,000 acres in the Cape Cod area of Massachusetts is dismissed by the U.S. District Court in Boston. The tribe, which had initiated its suit three years earlier, had suffered a defeat on January 6, when an all-white jury ruled that although the Wampanoag constituted a tribe in 1834 and 1842, they had lost their tribal status by 1869, when the land passed into non-Indian hands. Because of the tribe's failure to meet the definitions of a tribe during 1869 and today, the courts refused to acknowledge their claim to 13,700 acres in Mashpee, Massachusetts.

April 17, 1978 An agreement between four oil companies and the Navajo Nation is reached, ending a seventeen-day occupation of an Aneth, Utah, oilfield. The four companies, Conoco, Phillips, Superior Oil, and Texaco, agree to institute a code of conduct for their oil workers and to establish a hiring preference program for Indian employees. The protesters had demanded the code of conduct because of the oil workers' use of alcohol on the reservation and their harassment of Navajo women.

April 19, 1978 Governor Edmund G. Brown of California refuses an official request from Governor Richard F. Kneip of South Dakota to extradite Dennis Banks to stand trial in South Dakota. Banks, an Ojibway and a leader in the American Indian Movement, was convicted by a South Dakota court in 1975 of assault with a deadly weapon without intent to kill and riot while armed. The conviction arose out of the ninety-day seizure of Wounded Knee in 1973. Jumping bail, Banks, 45, first fled to Oregon and then to California, where he has been teaching at a Mexican-American and Indian college near Sacramento. In his letter to the South Dakota governor, Brown referred to "the strong hostility there against the American Indian Movement as well as its leaders." Brown's refusal to extradite Banks to South Dakota was upheld by the California Supreme Court.

April 22, 1978 The Fort Hall Indian reservation's business council votes to deny access of non-Indians to the reservation for all purposes, including hunting and fishing in the Snake River basin. The action is taken in reaction to the Supreme Court's decision in the *Oliphant* case that tribal governments do not possess criminal jurisdiction over non-Indians.

April 30, 1978 The Senate passes a bill to establish a new cabinet level agency, the Department of Education. A provision is included to transfer Indian education programs from the Department of the Interior to the newly established Department of Education.

May 13, 1978 The General Accounting Office reports that substandard housing for reservation families increased from 63,000 in June 1970 to 86,500 in a six-year period. New housing construction on reservations also dropped from 5,000 units to 3,500 units during the same time period. The number of Indian families increased from 46,000 in 1970 to 141,147 in 1976.

May 15, 1978 The Supreme Court rules in *Santa Clara Pueblo v. Martinez* that the Indian Civil Rights Act provides only for review of tribal habeas corpus cases. The case stems from a request by Mrs. Martinez of the Santa Clara Pueblo tribe that the Pueblo's tribal membership law be overturned to allow her children's enrollment. Current tribal law states that the children of enrolled women who married outside the tribe would be ineligible for membership. The ordinance extended membership to the children of men who married outside the tribe. Mrs. Martinez charged that the tribal ordinance constituted a denial of equal protection under federal law. In a victory for tribal sovereignty and culture, the Supreme Court held that the Indian Civil Rights Act does not abrogate tribal sovereignty and allowed the federal courts to intervene in tribal issues beyond that of habeas corpus cases.

May 15, 1978 Congress reinstates its terminated relations with the approximately 1,500 members of the Modoc, Wyandotte, Peoria, and Ottawa Indian tribes of Oklahoma.

May 21, 1978 Approximately twenty-five Chumash Indians agree to end their three-day protest at the site of an ancient burial ground at Little Cohu Bay, Pt. Conception, California, one of the proposed locations for a billion-dollar coast site for the importation of liquefied natural gas. Under the terms of an agreement worked out between the tribe and the utility companies, the tribe will be allowed to have access to the area for religious practices, to protect all ruins and artifacts, and to have six tribal members monitor future excavations.

May 24, 1978 Two Indian activists, Paul Skyhorse and Richard Mohawk, are found innocent of murder and robbery in the death of a taxi driver. The driver's body had been found October 10, 1974, near an American Indian Movement campsite north of Los Angeles. In the courts for three-and-one-half years, the case took thirteen months to try and cost $1.25 million to prosecute. Both men, whom supporters argued were framed for their AIM activities, remained in jail during the entire three-and-one-half years.

June 8, 1978 Tribal leaders from twenty-five reservations containing energy resources agree to establish the Council of Energy Resources Tribes. The organization, to be known as CERT, will have its headquarters in Denver, Colorado. Its primary function will be to assist tribes in the development of their energy and mineral resources.

June 21, 1978 The *Tundra Times* reports the award of $11.2 million by the Indian Claims Commission to the Aleuts of Pribilof Islands for mistreatment by the federal government in the fur seal monopoly from 1870 to 1946. The award settles a twenty-seven-year struggle by the Aleuts for recompense from the federal government.

July 18, 1978 Twenty-five religious Indian leaders and traditional leaders, who are taking part in the "Longest Walk," meet with Vice President Walter Mondale and Secretary of Interior Cecil Andrus for three hours. The leaders' request to meet with President Carter is denied.

August 13, 1978 President Jimmy Carter signs the American Indian Religious Freedom Act (AIRFA) in which Congress recognizes its obligation to "protect and preserve for American Indians their inherent right of freedom to believe, express and exercise their traditional religions." The act directs all federal agencies to examine their regulations and practices for any inherent conflict with the practice of Indian religious rights. The drafters of the legislation intend that the act will reverse a long history of governmental actions designed to suppress and destroy tribal religions. Until 1924, for example, the Bureau of Indian Affairs had regulations prohibiting the practice of Indian religion. Violators, if caught, could receive ten days in jail. In more recent times, Indians have been prohibited from entering sacred areas, from gathering and transporting sacred herbs, and from obtaining eagle feathers and meats necessary for the conduct of ceremonies.

September 5, 1978 The Bureau of Indian Affairs publishes regulations for the newly organized Federal Acknowledgment Program. The BIA estimates that more than 250 tribes are unrecognized in thirty-eight states. Unrecognized tribes generally do not have a land base

A Sun Dance at Pine Ridge, a Sioux reservation in southern South Dakota.

The sacred pole is the center of all Sun Dances. Crow Sun Dancers are preparing to approach the sacred center.

and are ineligible for federal services, such as education, housing, and health benefits. The regulations create a Federal Acknowledgement Branch, comprised of a historian, an anthropologist, a sociologist, and a genealogist, which will be responsible for deciding if tribal petitions for recognition meet the stated requirements.

To gain recognition, tribes must prove the following: (1) continuous existence as an aboriginal tribe; (2) that they live in a geographically contiguous area; (3) that the group has been under the recognized authority of a governing body from historical times to the present; (4) that they are currently governed by a constitution or other document; (5) that they have developed membership criteria; (6) that they possess a list of current members; and (7) that the federal government has not previously terminated its relationship with the tribe.

The 1977 Final Report of the American Indian Policy Review Task Force, created in 1975 to recommend changes in the administration of Indian affairs, strongly urged the establishment of a Federal Acknowledgement Process. Hence, while the creation of the process is hailed as a victory for tribes, the specific requirements are perceived by many Indian people as unduly complicated and unattainable. It is feared that those tribes who have maintained a peaceful existence and have gone virtually unnoticed by their non-Indian neighbors will have a difficult time proving their existence. Similarly, tribes, while operating according to their own understood governing rules, frequently do not possess written documents to prove their continued political existence.

September 11, 1978 Secretary of Interior Cecil Andrus agrees to personally mediate a dispute between the Yurok Indians and federal officials over a federal and state imposed two-week-old ban on salmon fishing, imposed in response to a noticeable drop in salmon returning to the Klamath River to spawn. The ban resulted in a violent confrontation between the tribe and game wardens on the Klamath River in northern California, with the tribe arguing that the ban violates their religious rights given the spiritual importance placed upon fishing in Yurok culture. The reduction in the salmon runs is attributed to heavy fishing by all involved in the fishing industry and to the polluting effects of heavy logging in the area.

Indian maiden, Lame Deer, Montana. Northern Cheyenne Indian Reservation.

October 17, 1978 Congress enacts the Tribally Controlled Community Colleges Act. The legislation provides for grants to tribally controlled colleges, including Alaska Native villages and corporations.

November 1978 The Oglala Sioux tribe announces plans to construct the first Indian-owned and operated television station. The station will serve fourteen thousand people who live on the Pine Ridge Reservation in South Dakota.

November 1, 1978 Congress passes the Education Amendment Act of 1978, giving substantial control of education programs to local Indian communities.

November 8, 1978 Congress passes the Indian Child Welfare Act, establishing a federal policy to promote the stability and security of Indian tribes and families by giving tribal courts jurisdiction over foster care and the adoption of their children. Tribal leaders lobbied extensively for passage of the act. Recent surveys conducted by the Association on American Indian Affairs reported that 25 to 35 percent of all Indian children were being raised in non-Indian foster and adoptive homes or institutions.

CONFERENCE
The Indian Child Welfare Act:
The Next Ten Years
"Indian Homes for Indian Children"

Poster for Indian Child Welfare conference at the University of California, Los Angeles.

May 20, 1979 An uneasy peace follows a weekend of violence on the Red Lake Chippewa Reservation in Minnesota. Fighting between two political factions resulted in the death of two youths, the wounding of three men, and the burning of a number of stores, tribal buildings, homes, and vehicles. The dispute is between the followers of Roger Jordain, tribal chairman for twenty-one years, and his critics who charge that his rule has been characterized by misrule, misappropriation of funds, and nepotism.

May 29, 1979 A nine-hour takeover of the Akwesasne police station ends peacefully. The protest, which stemmed from the arrest of a traditionalist chief over a property dispute, is part of a longstanding feud between traditionalists and those tribal members who support the elected form of government. The traditionalists do not recognize the authority of either the state police or the Franklin County Sheriff's Department, despite it being composed of sixteen Indian officers.

June 13, 1979 The U.S. Court of Claims awards the Lakota Nation $122.5 million for the federal government's illegal taking of the Black Hills in South Dakota.

July 21, 1979 Jay Silverheels, who played Tonto in the television series "The Lone Ranger" is the first Indian actor to have a star placed in the Hollywood Walk of Fame. Silverheels, a member of the Mohawk tribe and an actor for more than thirty-five years, is the founder of the Indian Actors Workshop.

July 27, 1979 The Supreme Court upholds the Boldt decision, affirming the right of Washington tribes to one-half the salmon catch.

August 19, 1979 The 800-member Narragansett Indian tribe of Rhode Island, is the first of the eastern tribes to settle its land claim against the federal and state governments. Filing suit in 1975 for ownership to 3,500 acres, the tribe will receive 1,800 acres. The tribe will purchase 900 acres with federal funds and receive the other 900 acres from public state lands. While hailed as a victory by some tribal members, others express dissatisfaction with the agreement, expressing frustration that the agreement is inadequate for the loss of thousands of acres of land and 300 years of mistreatment.

October 5, 1979 Two thousand Indian activists and supporters demonstrate against the development of uranium mines in the Black Hills of South Dakota.

October 31, 1979 Congress enacts the Archaeological Resources Protection Act of 1979, which provides protection for all important archeological sites on federal public lands and Indian lands. It further requires that scientists or lay personnel must obtain a special permit before excavation will be allowed. Indians are exempt from obtaining federal permits for excavations on Indian lands.

November 1979 The Ottawa and Ojibwa, or Chippewa, Indians are subjected to racist and violent actions as they exercise their inherent right to fish as guaranteed in their treaties with the United States. Indian fishers experience shootings, tire slashings, and the smashing of their boats. Bumper stickers also begin to appear containing derogatory sayings, such as "Spear an Indian—Save a Fish."

November 11, 1979 Reporters from six papers investigate the expenditure of funds on seven South Dakota Indian reservations and find that millions of dollars are unaccounted for or misspent. The FBI begins an investigation on the Rosebud reservation.

November 23, 1979 The Onondaga Indian Nation claims victory in its dispute against New York State for jurisdictional sovereignty. The dispute arises from the nation's forcible eviction in 1974 of eighteen non-Indians living on the reservation. In response to the nation's action, the county indicted six Indians on charges of felony coercion. Tribal leaders hailed the county's request for a dismissal of the charges against the tribal members as acknowledgement of the tribe's jurisdictional authority within its reservation boundaries as defined by the 1794 Canandaigua Treaty between the United States and the Haudenosaunee or Six Nation's confederacy (Iroquois).

December 8, 1979 The Oneida Indian Nation files a class-action suit against New York State, local governments, farmers, and cooperatives in an effort to regain control of 3 million acres illegally taken by the state in violation of the 1790 Trade and Intercourse Act.

December 9, 1979 The Navajo and Hopi tribes agree to a settlement of a one hundred-year-old dispute over control of the Joint Use Area. The dispute involves the ownership and use of 1.8 million acres of land within the Navajo reservation. The dispute between the two tribes stems from an 1882 executive order by President Arthur assigning the land to both tribes for their joint use.

December 9, 1979 Tribal leaders whose reservations contain energy resources and the governors of the western states of Alaska, Arizona, Colorado, Montana, Nebraska, New Mexico, North Dakota, South Dakota, Utah, and Wyoming sign an agreement to ensure that tribal concerns will be considered in any national effort to achieve energy independence. Fearing that the more populous eastern portion of the country will enact an energy policy to the detriment of the West, the agreement's objective is to protect western energy resources for the economic benefit of the areas in which they are located. Tribal and state lands in the West contain an estimated 50 percent of the nation's coal, 33 percent of the oil, 22 percent of the natural gas, 92 percent of the uranium, and 100 percent of the most easily developed oil shale.

January 17, 1980 The U.S. Court of Appeals sides with the Omaha tribe in their claim to 2,900 acres of land on the Iowa side of the Missouri River. The land, originally on the Nebraska side of the river, initially belonged to the tribe, as recognized in their 1854 treaty with the federal government.

January 23, 1980 Leonard Peltier, the American Indian Movement activist serving two life terms in prison, is sentenced to an additional seven years for escaping from a federal prison. Peltier, considered by many Indian supporters to be a political prisoner, was convicted of killing two FBI agents on the Pine Ridge reservation in June 1975. Peltier had escaped, with another inmate, from the Federal Correctional Institution in Lompoc, California, in July 1979.

February 18, 1980 The Italian representative to the European Parliament, Mario Capanna, holds a meeting with the Grand Council of Six Nation Iroquois Confederation on the Onondaga reservation. Capanna is one of twenty-two European Parliament members who introduced a resolution in January calling for the Parliament's condemnation of the state's sending of state troopers into the Mohawk reservation.

March 13, 1980 Five members of the Iroquois and Lakota tribes take their case to the European Parliament, requesting the body's support for their efforts at the international and national levels to gain recognition for their rights.

April 1980 The Indian Health Service issues a report stating that tuberculosis and gastroenteritis are no longer the most important problems facing Indians. Indian health priorities now include "accidents, alcoholism, diabetes, mental health, suicides and homicides," which stem from "changes in their traditional life-styles and values, and from deprivation."

April 3, 1980 Congress passes legislation to fully restore its trust relationship with the 501 members of the Shvwits, Kanosh, Koosharem, and Indian Peaks bands and Cedar City bands of Paiute Indians of Utah. The tribes, whose relationship with Congress was terminated twenty-seven years earlier, will acquire the rights to approximately fifteen thousand acres in southwestern Utah and access to badly needed educational, employment training, and health benefits. An estimated 60 percent of the adults are unemployed, and 40 percent of the children do not attend school regularly.

April 13, 1980 The Washoe Indians win a victory in federal court with the decision that the tribe can enforce its own hunting laws on sixty thousand acres of land owned by the tribe, but never recognized as a reservation, in the Pine Nut Mountains of Nevada.

April 13, 1980 The Citizen's Party selects environmentalist Barry Commoner as its nominee for president and LaDonna Harris, a Comanche Indian activist from Oklahoma and former wife of Senator Fred Harris, as his vice-presidential running mate.

April 15, 1980 The U.S. Court of Appeals for the Sixth Circuit dismisses a suit brought by members of the Eastern Cherokee who are seeking to prevent the construction of the Tellico Dam in eastern Tennessee. Tribal members argue that the dam, a project of the Tennessee Valley Authority, would flood ancestral lands sacred to the Cherokee and thus violate their right to freely practice their religion as protected under the free exercise clause of the First Amendment. The Appeals Court, affirming a lower court decision, rules that the plaintiffs are unable to demonstrate that the land in question is indispensable to the practice of the tribe's religion.

April 20, 1980 St. Regis Mohawk tribe (in New York State) and the federal government reach a tentative agreement on the disposition of tribally claimed land near the St. Lawrence Seaway. According to the terms of the agreement, the Mohawk of Akwesasne will receive 9,750 acres south of the reservation and $6 million in federal funds.

June 14, 1980 New York State sends seventy police to Akwesasne, the St. Regis Mohawk Indian reservation that straddles the Canadian-United States border. The police serve as a barrier between two armed and hostile factions on the reservation. The rift, which has been in existence for more than one hundred years, has grown to the point of civil war in the last year. The dispute is between traditionalists who argue that the reservation is under the governing authority of the traditional leaders recognized by the Haudenosaunee, or Iroquois confederacy. The opposing faction supports the elected tribal government, which was originally appointed in the 1880s by the state of New York and is recognized by the federal and state governments as the legitimate governing authority. At issue is political control of the ten thousand members and economic development of the reservation and the administration of federal grants.

For the previous ten months, in an effort to prevent the arrest of several traditional leaders involved in the 1979 takeover of the Akwesasne police station, approximately seventy traditionalists have maintained an armed camp on twenty acres along the St. Lawrence.

June 17, 1980 Congress passes legislation to regularize and protect Indian tribes in their commercial dealings with federally licensed Indian traders.

June 22, 1980 The Vatican beatifies Kateri Tekakwitha, a Mohawk-Algonquin Indian who died three hundred years previously at the age of twenty-four. The beatification process is the last step before achieving sainthood in the eyes of the Church. She is the first American Indian to be beatified by the Catholic Church. Renamed Kateri at her baptism at the age of twenty (her Indian name being Ioragode or Sunshine), she suffered ridicule by her family, friends, and tribe, actions that ultimately forced her to move two hundred miles away from her family and tribe.

June 30, 1980 The Supreme Court in *U.S. v. Sioux Nation* upholds the $122 million judgment against the United States by the Court of Claims for the illegal taking of the Sioux nation's Black Hills. The Sioux's treaty with the United States in 1868 had clearly guaranteed the Black Hills, or *Paha Sapa*, an area of sacred significance to the tribe. The discovery of gold in 1874, however, brought a flood of settlers to the area. After enduring years of war and the intentional killing off of the buffalo, the tribe's staple food, the Sioux, or Lakota, signed an agreement in 1876 ceding the Black Hills to the United States.

July 8, 1980 Congress enacts the Navajo-Hopi Relocation Act, which requires the relocation of certain Navajo and Hopi families in an effort to settle the Joint Use land dispute. The legislation provides for funds to assist in the purchase of additional lands for the Navajo tribe.

July 18, 1980 The Oglala Sioux file a class-action suit against the federal government and the state of South Dakota for $11 billion, seeking $10 billion for the loss of nonrenewable resources from the Black Hills and $1 billion for "hunger, malnutrition, disease and death" incurred by the Sioux resulting from the loss of their traditional lands. The Oglala Sioux contend that they are not the beneficiaries of the award decided by the Supreme Court the previous month. The Oglala argue that the lawyer's contract with the tribe in the previous case had expired three years previously and had not been renewed by the tribe.

July 20, 1980 Maria Martinez, 95, dies at San Ildefonso Pueblo, New Mexico. A world renowned potter, Martinez, working with her husband, had revived the traditional black pottery of the Pueblos. Her pottery was perfectly crafted and shaped, even though she worked without the use of a potter's wheel. Her pots appear in collections throughout the world.

August 18, 1980 The Creek Nation east of the Mississippi, or Alabama Creek as they are called locally, regains ownership to a thirty-three-acre site known as the "Hickory Grounds." The area, once the headquarters of the entire Creek Nation before its forced removal from the Southeast in the 1830s, was purchased with the proceeds of a $165,000 federal grant.

September 4, 1980 Congress establishes a reservation of 3,663 acres for the Confederated Tribes of Siletz Indians of Oregon. Congress had terminated its relationship with the confederation of twenty-four tribes and bands in 1956. The Confederated Tribes, with approximately nine hundred members, were restored to full federal recognition in 1977.

October 12, 1980 President Jimmy Carter, using a symbolic feather pen, signs legislation settling the claim of the Passamaquoddy, Penobscot, and Maliseet to two-thirds of Maine. The settlement provides for an $81.5 million settlement to the tribes. The money includes a $27 million trust fund and $54.5 million to purchase three hundred thousand acres of illegally taken former tribal lands. The agreement followed the tribes' successful claim that Massachusetts colony (later the state of Maine) had taken their aboriginal homeland, the northern two-thirds of Maine, in violation of the 1790 Trade and Intercourse Act. The Trade and Intercourse Act granted authority only to the federal government to purchase land from the tribes.

November 8, 1980 The U.S. representatives provide the Helsinki conference, meeting in Madrid, Spain, with a federal study on the United States's compliance with the 1975 Helsinki Accords in its treatment of American Indians. The report concludes that the United States's record is "neither as deplorable as sometimes alleged nor as successful as one might hope."

November 23, 1980 The Cayuga Indian Nation files suit against New York State for the taking of former Cayuga lands located in the Finger Lakes region. The tribe is demanding the return of 100 square miles, payment of $350 million in damages, and the relocation of seven thousand property owners.

November 29, 1980 The flood gates of the Tellico Dam on the Little Tennessee River begin to flood the sixteen-thousand-acre reservoir. Several traditional Cherokee had attempted to prevent the flooding of their aboriginal lands on the grounds of religious protection.

December 2, 1980 The Russell Tribunal, an international human rights body located in the Netherlands, finds the United States, Canada, and several countries in Latin America guilty of cultural and physical genocide and of the unlawful seizure of land in their treatment of their Indian populations. The verdict comes following an eight-day hearing, during which the human rights activists heard testimony from fourteen Indian communities. The "judges," many of whom are lawyers, base their decision, which has no legal authority, on the protections afforded to Indian people in the 1975 Helsinki Accords, the International Covenant on Civil and Political Rights, and the Universal Declaration of Human Rights.

December 22, 1980 Congress, primarily in response to the tribes' victories in the *U.S. v. Washington* and *Sohappy v. Smith* cases, passes the Salmon and Steelhead Conservation Act of 1980. The bill, designed in part to meet the guarantees promised by the federal government in treaties signed with the tribes in the 1800s, provides for the conservation and enhancement of the salmon and steelhead runs.

March 3, 1981 Navajo and Hopi religious leaders request the federal district court to halt the construction of a ski resort in the San Francisco Peaks mountains. Arguing that the First Amendment protects their right to religious freedom, the tribal leaders' suit states that construction would destroy sacred sites and that the desecration would anger their gods.

April 18, 1981 A federal court, acting under congressional approval, officially partitions the 1.8 million-acre Joint Use Area equally between the Navajo and Hopi. The division forces the relocation of three thousand to six thousand Navajo and one hundred Hopi tribal members. Four days later, Bureau of Indian Affairs officials began seizing Navajo livestock for removal.

May 8, 1981 One hundred fifty tribal leaders, attending the National Tribal Government Conference in Washington, D.C., send a letter to President Ronald Reagan demanding the immediate resignation of Secretary of Interior James G. Watt. Citing Watt's unwillingness to consult with tribes as dictated by law, the leaders write: "We find this callous disregard of his lawful function and responsibility as the Federal official with general statutory-delegated authority in Indian matters completely intolerable." Elmer Savilla, spokesperson for the group, called further attention to Reagan's proposal to cut Indian funds by consolidating the financing of ten Bureau of Indian Affairs programs into one block grant, thereby reducing the allocation of funds by 26 percent. Other administration proposals call for the reduction of adult and child education, housing, employment, assistance, and vocational training programs.

May 29, 1981 The Supreme Court rules in *Montana v. U.S.* that the state of Montana has the authority to regulate hunting and fishing on the Bighorn River flowing through the Crow Indian reservation. The Court rules that the state had assumed title to the riverbed upon its entrance into the Union in 1889. The case is a blow to tribal authority and its efforts to regulate hunting and fishing within its own boundaries.

June 11, 1981 The U.S. Civil Rights Commission issues a major report on the federal government's treatment of American Indians. Commission Chairman Arthur Flemming sums up the government's policy toward American Indians as one of "inaction and missed opportunities." The commission, after a decade of research, proposes several changes in federal policy toward tribes. One of its primary recommendations is that Congress apportion, as in the case of states, federal funds to tribes as block grants. The commission also recommends the establishment of an Office of Indian Rights within the Civil Rights Division of the Justice Department. The study further urges the government to act expeditiously and fairly in the resolution of fishing rights disputes and the eastern land claims, and that Congress pass legislation allowing tribes that so chose to assume criminal jurisdiction over all peoples within their reservation boundaries.

July 10, 1981 The Bay Mills and Sault Ste. Marie Chippewa and Grand Traverse tribe of Ottawa Indians win a nine-year court battle in the U.S. Court of Appeals for the Sixth Circuit, recognizing their fishing rights in Lakes Michigan, Superior, and Huron. The federal court lets stand a district court decision in which tribes successfully proved that the treaties of 1836 and 1855

Crow Indians protesting state fish and game regulations.

guaranteed their right to fish in the Great Lakes. In addition to acknowledging their fishing rights, the courts rule that tribes may continue to use their traditional gill nets, an apparatus banned under state law. The next step is for the tribes to enter into negotiations with the federal government and the state of Michigan for the development of a fishing management plan.

August 13, 1981 Through the enactment of the "Omnibus Budget Reconciliation Act of 1981," Congress allows the Secretary of Health and Human Services to make community block grants to Indian tribes. The legislation also provides for the establishment of Head Start Programs on Indian reservations and for improvements in the loan process to small, tribe-owned businesses.

August 20, 1981 The state of Montana orders the Crow tribe to open access to fishing on the Bighorn River. In response, members of the Crow tribe barricade a highway bridge over the river near Hardin, Montana. The tribe, which claims ownership of the river, had closed the river to fishing by non-Indians in 1975. In March, the Supreme Court ruled that the state of Montana owned title to the fifty-mile section of the river under dispute. The blockade of both lanes of Highway 313, consisting of approximately fifteen cars, campers, and pick-ups, was lifted fourteen hours later when federal marshals served notice on the tribe that the blockade was illegal.

October 14, 1981 Amnesty International, in a 144-page report, charges the U.S. government with retaining as political prisoners Richard Marshall of the American Indian Movement and Elmer Pratt of the Black Panther Movement. The report alleges official misconduct in the investigations and trials of both leaders.

November 16, 1981 Congressional legislation prohibits the export, import, selling, receiving, acquiring, or purchasing of wildlife in violation of federal law or Indian tribal law.

January 21, 1982 In response to a special commission's sharp criticisms of the Interior Department's collection of royalty money, Secretary of Interior James G. Watt announces a revision in the department's policy for obtaining royalties on oil and natural gas on federal lands.

January 25, 1982 The Supreme Court rules in the *Merrion v. Jicarilla Apache Tribe* that Indian tribes have the authority to levy severance taxes on the extraction of minerals from tribal lands.

June 11, 1982 Tlingit Indians arrive in Washington, D.C., seeking an official apology from the navy for its shelling of their village in the Admiralty Islands in 1882. The navy's actions were undertaken as a means of forcing the Alaskan Indians to return to work for private whalers.

August 14, 1982 President Ronald Reagan declares August 14 as National Navajo Code Talkers Day, commemorating the cadre of Navajo servicemen who sent messages in their tribal language during World War II. The system was never cracked by the Germans or Japanese.

October 13, 1982 The International Olympic Committee announces that it will restore to Jim Thorpe's family the two gold medals Thorpe won in the 1912 Olympic games for the decathlon and the pentathlon. Thorpe was stripped of his medals for having played minor league baseball for $2 a game.

November 2, 1982 The Navajo Nation elects a new tribal chairman, Peterson Zah. Zah, 44, defeats Peter MacDonald, 53, chairman of the tribal council for the last twelve years, by a vote of 29,208 to 24,665. Zah, the

Medals won by Jim Thorpe in the 1912 Olympic Games were returned to the Thorpe family in 1982.

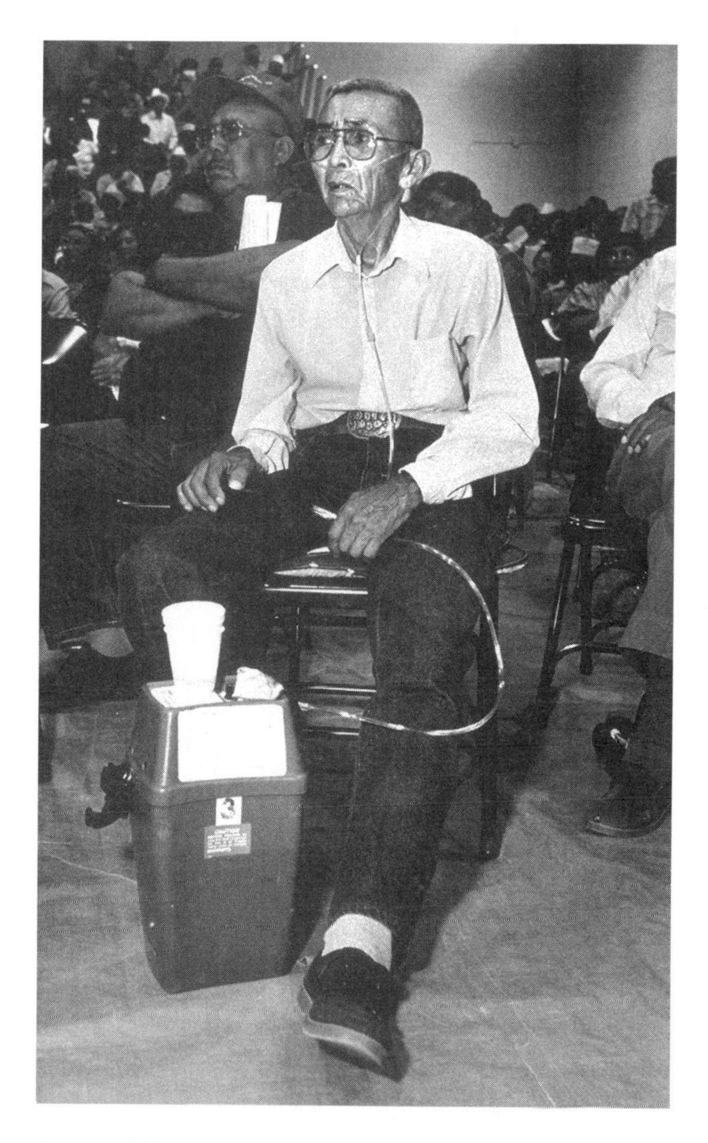

George Kelly, Sr. of Beclabito, New Mexico, was among hundreds of Navajo who converged at the Shiprock High School gymnasium to hear attorney Stewart Udall explain the recently approved U.S. Congress Radiation Exposure Compensation Act. Kelly, who uses an oxygen tank twenty-four hours a day to help him breathe, was diagnosed as having a lung disease due to working in the unventilated uranium mines for thirty years.

founder of the reservation's legal aid organization, pledges to stop further exploitation of energy, minerals, timber, and water resources on reservation lands by non-Indians. Zah's platform also includes a proposal that the Navajo and Hopi seek to mediate their dispute over the Joint Use Area without the interference of the federal government.

December 22, 1982 Passage of the "Indian Mineral Development Act of 1982" confirms and provides federal support for tribes to enter into commercial ventures for the development of their tribal resources.

December 30, 1982 President Ronald Reagan signs legislation extending federal recognition to approximately three hundred members of the Cow Creek Band of Umpqua tribe in Oregon.

January 7, 1983 Congressional passage of the Nuclear Waste Policy Act of 1982 draws considerable criticism from several tribes who interpret the act as a federal attempt to desecrate Indian lands. The act grants authority to the administrator of the Environmental Protection Agency to allow repositories for high-level radioactive waste and spent nuclear fuel to be developed on Indian lands. Although the act requires that permission be received from appropriate government tribal officials, concern is expressed that tribal officials may not convey the opinion or wishes of the tribal majority.

January 8, 1983 Congress passes legislation to allow the Texas Kickapoo to apply for U.S. citizenship and for federal services. The Texas, or Mexican, Kickapoos, as they are called, were part of the larger Kickapoo Nation pushed out of their aboriginal homelands in northern Illinois and southern Wisconsin in the early 1800s. As hostilities continued, one band fled to Mexico, settling near Nacimiento Kikapoo, eighty miles from the Texas border. Today, the six hundred members of the tribe spend their summers in or near Eagle Pass, Texas, working as migrant laborers. In the winters, they return to their home in Mexico for the tribe's sacred winter ceremonial.

January 12, 1983 Passage of the Federal Oil and Gas Royalty Management Act of 1982 provides for cooperative agreements among the secretary of the interior, Indian tribes, and states for the sharing of oil- and gas-royalty management information.

January 12, 1983 Congress passes the Indian Land Consolidation Act to assist tribes in the enormous problems created by fractional interests in many reservation lands. Tribes whose reservation lands were allotted under the terms of the 1887 General Allotment Act now possess, in some cases, allotments owned by over two hundred individuals. The original allotments of 80 to 160 acres, were, by federal regulations, divided equally among allottee heirs. Passage of this act allows for tribes to purchase and consolidate these lands in an effort to make them more economically productive.

January 14, 1983 Passage of the Indian Tribal Tax Status Act of 1982 confirms that tribes possess many of the federal tax advantages enjoyed by states. Like states, tribes are acknowledged to have the power to issue tax-exempt bonds to enable tribal governments to fund economic development projects.

January 19, 1983 Secretary of Interior James Watt states during a television interview that Indian reservations are "examples of the failures of socialism." "If you want an example of the failures of socialism, don't go to Russia. Come to America, and see the American Indian reservations . . . . Socialism toward the American Indian," Watt said, "had led to alcoholism, unemployment, venereal disease, and drug addiction." Watt's remarks provoked an outcry across Indian Country demanding his resignation.

January 24, 1983 President Reagan issues the first Indian policy statement since 1975. The address, which promotes economic development on reservations, states the government's support for industrial development of resources on Indian lands. Tribes and the American society "stand to gain from the prudent development and management of the vast coal, oil, gas, uranium and other resources found on Indian lands." The address is met with skepticism by many Indian leaders who fear the underlying message is terminationist in disguise.

January 25, 1983 The U.S. Court of Appeals for the Seventh Circuit affirms in *Lac Courte Oreilles Band of Lake Superior Chippewa Indians v. Voigt* that the Chippewas' treaties with the United States in 1837 and 1842 preserved the rights of six Chippewa bands to hunt, fish, and cut timber in lands they had ceded to the federal government.

January 31, 1983 President Ronald Reagan sends his first budget to Congress. Proposals include a one-third cut in the total budget for Indians.

March 15, 1983 Congressional passage of the Pacific Salmon Treaty Act of 1984 clarifies and protects tribal fishing rights as provided in executive orders and Indian treaties as they relate to the United States treaty with Canada over Pacific salmon fishing, passed in January.

March 23, 1983 The Onondaga nation, located south of Syracuse, New York, agrees to grant asylum to American Indian Movement leader Dennis Banks, who is fleeing charges in South Dakota arising from the takeover of Wounded Knee.

March 30, 1983 The Supreme Court rejects in *Arizona v. California* a federally appointed factfinder's report that five Indian tribes are entitled to receive a larger share of water allocation in the lower basin of the Colorado River. The five tribes, the Cocopah, Ft. Mohave, Ft. Yuma, Colorado River, and the Chemehuevi, had requested an enlargement of their water rights formerly allocated in 1964 on the basis of an increase in their reservations' sizes.

By the 1970s, the protection of Indian water rights has become one of the most important issues facing Indian Country. Seventy-five percent of all Indians live in the arid West. As reservation populations boom and tribes seek to improve their economic status, the questions whether the tribes or the states possess the right to the precious water supply, and in what amounts, and for what purposes, become critical.

Water rights experts express public concern as early as 1970 over the Bureau of Indian Affair's inadequate protection of Indian water rights. Another government report issued in 1973 by the National Water Commission, created by Congress in 1968, criticizes the federal government for its failure to protect Indian water rights. The commission's report, pointing out a conflict of interest in the Department of Interior, details how Interior supported the construction of irrigation projects on or near reservations, which served to diminish the amount of water available to tribes for their own needs. "In the history of the United States Government's treatment of Indian tribes, its failure to protect Indian water rights for use on the Reservations it set aside for them is one of the sorrier chapters."

June 2, 1983 The National Indian Tribal Chairman's Association holds a news conference to criticize President Ronald Reagan for his failure to uphold his pledge to free tribes of federal regulations and to provide them with greater self-determination over their lives.

June 13, 1983 The Supreme Court rules in *New Mexico v. Mescalero Apache Tribe* that the state of New Mexico cannot enforce state laws against non-Indians hunting and fishing on tribal lands within reservation boundaries. The imposition of state laws in this instance, the Court stated, would interfere with "Congress' overriding objective of encouraging tribal self-government and economic development."

June 24, 1983 The Supreme Court in *Nevada v. U.S.* unanimously upholds a lower court ruling affirming the allocation of water rights to the Pyramid Lake reservation in western Nevada.

July 1, 1983 The Supreme Court rules 6–3 in *Rice v. Rehner* that states have the authority to enforce liquor laws on reservations. Tribes, according to the opinion written by Justice Sandra Day O'Connor, are required to obtain state licenses before selling liquor on the reservation.

July 15, 1983 The Supreme Court rules in *Arizona v. San Carlos Apache Tribe* that the state courts have the authority to decide water rights disputes involving Indians. The decision is another blow to tribes in their quest

Coolidge Dam on San Carlos Apache Reservation, Arizona.

to preserve their water rights. Tribes had attempted to prove that water rights disputes must be settled in the federal courts. Tribes feared that the state courts, under pressure to protect the progress and development of major cities and areas throughout the West, would not provide tribes with a fair hearing.

July 30, 1983 Fifteen hundred Seminole tribal members, who occupy five reservations in southern Florida, recently approve a referendum to establish a judicial system reflecting traditional values and principles. Tribal leaders, who are in the process of developing the new judicial system, are giving careful examination to the neighboring system of the Miccosukee tribe, which operates with two judges, one schooled in modern law and the other in traditional law.

September 13, 1983 American Indian Movement cofounder, Dennis Banks, surrenders to state authorities in Rapid City, South Dakota, following nine years as a fugitive. Banks's surrender allows the state to prosecute him for assault and rioting charges stemming from the 1973 Wounded Knee takeover and flight to avoid prosecution. Banks, who states that he feared for his life, explains that he had given himself up for the sake of his family. Banks had spent six years in California, under the protection of Governor Jerry Brown, before fleeing to the Onondaga Reservation in New York when Brown's successor, Governor George Deukmejian, indicated his willingness to extradite Banks to South Dakota. New York governor Mario Cuomo had agreed to return Banks to South Dakota but had forbidden marshals from entering the Onondaga reservation near Syracuse, New York.

October 20, 1983 President Ronald Reagan signs legislation acknowledging the Mashantucket Pequot Indians of Connecticut as a federally recognized tribe with all powers of self-government. The legislation also provides for a $900,000 appropriation to the Pequots for the purchase of land near their reservation. President Reagan had vetoed a similar bill on April 10, 1983.

March 25, 1984 Members of the Eastern Band of Cherokee and the Cherokee Nation of Oklahoma hold their first joint council meeting in 146 years. An estimated ten thousand tribal members attend the historic meeting held at the Cherokees' sacred ground in Red Clay, Tennessee.

A Cherokee woman puts the finishing touches on a basket at the Oconaluftee Living Village, where tourists may view traditional Cherokee life.

Sixteen thousand Cherokee were forcibly removed from their ancestral lands in Tennessee, North Carolina, Georgia, and Alabama by Andrew Jackson's army in the late 1830s and early 1840s. One-fourth of those forced to relocate died along the route, known as the Trail of Tears. The descendants of those who completed the trip now live around Tahlequah, Oklahoma. A few hundred Cherokee successfully eluded removal by hiding in the hills of western North Carolina. Their descendants now form the Eastern Band of Cherokee.

The two tribes, who confirmed their permanent split, agree to meet annually in the Council of Cherokees to discuss issues and needs of common concern.

June 8, 1984 The United States Senate agrees to make the Senate Select Committee on Indian Affairs a permanent body. The body, which is responsible for the consideration of Indian affairs and oversight, was established on a temporary basis in 1977.

July 5, 1984 The Cayuga Indian Nation agrees to accept approximately 8,500 acres of land in Cayuga and Seneca counties of New York State as a final settlement against the state for the illegal taking of 64,000 acres.

July 22, 1984 Three of the five Indian tribes located in Connecticut protest the state's assumption of police jurisdiction on the reservations.

September 2, 1984 The Mashantucket Pequot Indians from eastern Connecticut take possession of 650 acres of land. Tribal title to the land ends an eight-year struggle by the tribe to regain former reservations lands.

September 23, 1984 The Santa Fe *New Mexican* apologizes to the Santo Domingo Indian community for the publication of two photos of sacred dances. The community has a posted policy of forbidding the taking of photographs at sacred ceremonies.

October 8, 1984 Dennis Banks is sentenced in Custer, South Dakota, to three years in prison for his part in the Custer courthouse riot in 1975.

November 30, 1984 The Presidential Commission on Indian Reservation Economies presents its report to President Ronald Reagan. Characterizing the Bureau of Indian Affair's organization and administration as "byzantine," and "incompetent," the report called for the BIA's replacement with an Indian Trust Services Administration. As an illustration of the BIA's top heavy administration and over-regulation, the report points out that two-thirds of the BIA's budget goes into administration; less than one-third of the federal funds reach the reservation.

Other recommendations in the report include: the placement of tribal businesses in individual hands, the subordination of tribal courts to federal courts in interpreting law, the reduction of tribal immunity, and the allowance of tribal taxation only after the vote of all Indian and non-Indian residents on the reservation. The report further recommends that tribal leaders and federal officials tackle the issue of tribal self-determination through private economic development. The report immediately draws a cool reception from many tribes.

January 9, 1985 Charitable contributions provide for the purchase of a 125-acre parcel of land on the Rio Grande near Eagle Pass, Texas, for the resettlement of the Kickapoo tribe.

January 11, 1985 The National Tribal Council Association, a national group comprised of tribal political leaders, votes 84–18 to reject a proposed program for the development of private enterprises on Indian reservations. As explained by Elmer Savilla, the association's executive director, the program's philosophy is in opposition to the "Indian way," which is "to go into business to provide income for tribal members, to provide employment for as many tribal members as you can."

February 11, 1985 The federal government agrees to pay $5.5 million to Wyandotte Indians in Kansas and Oklahoma for forcing their ancestors to sell their aboriginal lands in 1842 for less than fair market value.

February 20, 1985 In *Dann et al. v. United States*, the Supreme Court rejects a suit by two Shoshoni Indians claiming ownership of 5,100 acres of the tribe's aboriginal homeland. In 1951, the Shoshoni tribe had sought compensation for the loss of their aboriginal homeland and were awarded $26 million by the Indian Claims Commission. The tribe refused to accept payment of the funds, requesting instead the return of their lands. The courts ruled that once the funds were placed in an interest-bearing account, the tribe's claim to the lands were extinguished.

March 4, 1985 The Supreme Court, in *County of Oneida v. Oneida Nation*, upholds the right of the Oneida Nation of New York State to sue for lands illegally taken in 1795.

March 5, 1985 The *Journal of the Society for American Archeology* reports that scientists, through the analysis of Winnebago calendar sticks, have the first evidence that tribes, through systematic astronomical observations, had developed advanced full-year calendars.

March 15, 1985 After a thirteen-year effort, Congress passes the Pacific Salmon Treaty Act of 1985. The act, which many legislators and biologists hail as the most important key to saving the salmon runs from extinction, was passed following the intervention and support of the northwestern tribes who depend on fishing for cultural and economic survival.

April 16, 1985 The Supreme Court, in *Kerr-McGee Corp. v. Navajo Tribe*, upholds unanimously the right of the Navajo Nation to tax business on the reservation without first obtaining federal approval. The decision allows for the Navajos' continued taxation of mineral leases on reservation lands.

May 16, 1985 Montana Governor Ted Schwinden signs an agreement with the Sioux and Assiniboine tribes guaranteeing water allocations between the tribes and their neighbors.

June 3, 1985 The Supreme Court, in *Montana v. Blackfeet Tribe*, upholds a Court of Appeals ruling that Montana could not tax the royalty interests earned by the Blackfeet from leases issued in accordance with the Indian Mineral Leasing Act of 1938. At issue was the legal status of state taxation of oil, gas, and minerals from Indian lands.

July 2, 1985 The Jicarilla Apache tribe of New Mexico is the first tribe to offer tax-exempt municipal bonds to institutional investors issuing $30.2 million in revenue bonds.

October 2, 1985 News services report that nine young Arapaho and Shoshoni Indians on the Wind River Reservation in Wyoming have hanged themselves in the last two months. The reservation, which has a population of six thousand people and an unemployment rate of 80 percent, reported forty-eight suicide attempts in 1985. The National Center of Health has reported that the suicide rate at the Wind River Reservation, 233 suicides per 100,000, is almost twenty times higher than the national average, 12 per 100,000.

November 22, 1985 One hundred forty-three members of the Kickapoo of Texas and Mexico are issued citizenship cards acknowledging their status as a "subgroup" of the Kickapoo tribe of Oklahoma.

November 22, 1985 American Indian Movement leader Dennis Banks is granted parole from the South Dakota Penitentiary. He served approximately one year of a three-year prison term, which arose from a 1973 disturbance at Custer County Courthouse in South Dakota.

December 13, 1985 Ross Swimmer, Cherokee and former Principal Chief of the Cherokee Nation of Oklahoma, is sworn in as assistant secretary of the interior for Indian affairs in Washington, D.C.

December 14, 1985 Wilma Mankiller is sworn in as Principal Chief of the Cherokee Nation of Oklahoma. The nation, the largest Indian tribe in the country after the Navajo, is headed by a fifteen-member council. Mankiller, 40, becomes the first woman to lead a large tribe in modern history.

February 14, 1986 The Smithsonian's Museum of Natural History agrees to return skeletal remains to tribal leaders for reburial when a clear biological or cultural link can be established. Several Indian organizations, while applauding the museum's decision, have requested that all Indian remains be returned for reburial, as required by Indian spiritual beliefs. Studies have estimated that more than one million Indian remains are in the hands of museums and universities.

May 15, 1986 The Lummi Indian tribe of western Washington is fighting a demand from the Internal Revenue Service that Indian fishers pay an income tax on the sale of salmon caught by the tribe in Puget Sound. The tribe argues that their natural resources, as guaranteed to the tribe by treaty, are immune from taxation.

June 3, 1986 The Catawbas lose a major case before the Supreme Court in their quest to reclaim 144,000 acres of aboriginal lands now in private hands. The Court rules that the tribe lost the opportunity to bring a suit due to a statute of limitations.

August 18, 1986 Congress officially passes legislation to settle the land claims of the Wampanoag Tribal Council of Gay Head, Massachusetts. In exchange for relinquishing further land claims, the state of Massachusetts will pay $225 million to the tribe for the purchase of tribal trust lands.

August 27, 1986 Congress reinstates its federal relationship with the Klamath, Modoc, and the Yahuskin band of Snake Indians of Oregon. The approximately three thousand-member tribe was one of the first terminated by Congress in the 1950s. The Klamaths, Modocs, and Snakes, along with the Menominees of Wisconsin, were the largest tribes to be terminated.

September 7, 1986 New Hampshire announces the designation of an official site for the reburial of repatriated Indian remains and artifacts.

October 17, 1986 Legislative approval is granted for the establishment of an Institute of American Indian and Alaska Native Culture and Arts Development. The institute, to be administered by a board of trustees, is charged with acknowledging and promoting the contributions of Native arts to American society.

October 27, 1986 Congress revises the Indian Civil Rights Act to allow tribal courts to impose fines of $5,000 and one year in jail for violating tribal criminal offenses.

October 27, 1986 Recognizing that alcoholism and alcohol and substance abuse is currently the most severe social and health problem facing Indian people, Congress passes the Indian Alcohol and Substance Abuse Prevention and Treatment Act of 1986. When adjusted for age, Indians are four times more likely to die from alcoholism than the general population. Four of the top ten causes of death among Indians are alcohol related. Indians between the ages of 15 and 24 years are twice as likely to die from vehicular accidents, 75 percent of which are alcohol related.

November 4, 1986 Peter MacDonald regains his elected position as the tribal chairman of the Navajo nation, the largest Indian group in the United States. MacDonald, chairman from 1970 to 1982, defeated the incumbent, Peterson Zah.

November 6, 1986 Ben Nighthorse Campbell, a member of the Northern Cheyenne tribe of Montana, is elected to the U.S. House of Representatives from the third district of Colorado. Campbell is only the second Indian elected to the U.S. House of Representative in recent times. Ben Reifel, a Sioux from South Dakota, served in the House from 1961 to 1971.

November 19, 1986 The Grandfather Plaque or Amerind Vietnam Plaque is dedicated at Arlington National Cemetery in Virginia. The plaque commemorates the service of approximately forty-three thousand indigenous combatants who served in Vietnam. An estimated one out of every four eligible Indian males served in Vietnam.

January 1, 1987 Isleta Pueblo, located near Albuquerque, New Mexico, elects its first woman governor.

August 23, 1987 President Ronald Reagan signs a bill ceding to the Wampanoag more than four hundred acres of undeveloped land located on Martha's Vineyard, Massachusetts. The Bureau of Indian Affairs extended federal recognition to the Wampanoag Indians of Gay Head, Massachusetts, on March 8.

September 18, 1987 Pope John Paul II speaks to a group of sixteen hundred American Indian leaders in Phoenix, Arizona, urging them to forget the past and to focus on the church's current support of Indian rights. An American Indian Catholic attendee responds that the church still has much to accomplish in the United States.

October 9, 1987 The U.S. Justice Department announces the dropping of all charges against Seminole Indian Chief James E. Billie. Billie, who had killed a rare species of Florida panther, was arrested for violating the Endangered Species Act. Billie admitted killing the panther in December 1983, but argued that his right to hunt panthers was part of his right of religious freedom and, further, was protected by the Seminoles' treaty of 1842 with the United States. Billie's first trial ended in a mistrial on August 27, 1987, when the jury could not agree on how Billie could identify the panther when the hunting occurred at night. Billie's second trial ended in an acquittal October 8.

December 2, 1987 The U.S. House of Representatives passes a bill commemorating the centennial anniversary of the army's forcible removal of the Cherokees from the southeastern portion of the United States to northeastern Oklahoma.

January 11, 1988 The Northern Cheyenne tribe in Montana proposes to exercise its inherent right to tax by levying a tax on BIA contractors operating within reservation boundaries.

February 1, 1988 Two Tuscarora Indian men seize the newspaper office of the *Robesonian* in Lumberton, North Carolina. They hold seventeen of the newspaper's employees hostage for ten hours, demanding that the paper investigate corruption and discrimination by the police against the African-Americans and Indians of the area. The standoff ends with an agreement by the governor of North Carolina to investigate the charges. This hostage crisis is only one of the many incidents manifesting the rising racial tensions in Robeson County, which is composed of 40 percent white residents, with the remaining 60 percent divided evenly between Blacks and Indians.

February 6, 1988 President Ronald Reagan signs into law a set of amendments to the 1971 Alaska Native Claims Settlement Act, which had extinguished the Natives' title to their lands in exchange for 44 million

Returning from seal hunt, Barrow, Alaska.

Boy's Mother (played by Sherice Guina) sings to Boy after Lord of the Sun sent a spark of life to earth (where the boy was conceived). Pueblo Indian tale, "Arrow to the Sun," is portrayed by Wyoming Indian Elementary School students in class play.

acres and one billion dollars. The lands and money were distributed among over two hundred village corporations and several regional corporations. According to the 1971 act, individuals would have been free to sell their shares in the corporations, a move which many Alaska Natives feared would result in the loss of Native lands and rights in Alaska. According to the 1991 amendments, corporations may only sell their stock if a majority of the shareholders support the sale.

March 17, 1988 The Warm Springs tribe of Oregon hosts a conference on suicide among Indians. The conference follows a rash of suicides on the reservation inhabited by 2,800 members of the Wascoe, Paiute, and Warm Springs tribes. Six young people have killed themselves and sixteen others have tried in the last two months. Nationwide, young Indian men kill themselves at a rate more than twice the national average.

The conference, which is attended by Indian leaders and families as well as psychologists and social workers, seeks in part to find the answer to the recent epidemics by returning to traditional practices and methods of counseling for young people.

April 19, 1988 The Supreme Court, in a 5–3 decision, rules in *Lyng v. Northwest Indian Cemetery Protective Association* that the Forest Service is free to build a five-mile logging road through the sacred lands of the Yurok, Karok, and Tolowa tribes of California. Three justices, William T. Brennan, Jr., Thurgood Marshall, and Harry Blackmun, dissent, arguing against the majority's "surreal" logic that "governmental action that will virtually destroy a religion is nevertheless deemed not to 'burden' that religion."

April 28, 1988 As part of the Elementary and Secondary Education Act, H.R. 5, Title V, Congress passes legislation to repeal the termination policy established by House Concurrent Resolution 108, passed in 1953. Without tribal approval or input, the resolution provided for the termination of 108 tribes and bands over the following ten years.

The act also prohibited the BIA from terminating, consolidating, or transferring BIA-administered schools without the consent of the affected tribes.

June 29, 1988 Indians and Alaska Natives are finally brought under the United States Housing Act of 1937 with the provision of an amendment establishing a separate program under the supervision of the Secretary of Housing and Urban Development.

July 8, 1988 The Absentee Shawnee and the Citizen Band of Potawatomi, both of Shawnee, the Iowa of Oklahoma in Perkins, the Sac and Fox of Oklahoma in Stroud, and the Kickapoo of Oklahoma in McLoud announce plans to contract with the BIA for all services currently provided by the Shawnee Agency.

July 8, 1988 In *Oklahoma Tax Commission v. Muscogee (Creek) Nation*, the Supreme Court refuses to overturn a lower court ruling that exempted the Creek Nation from paying a state sales tax on their bingo operations. The gaming operation, located in Tulsa, is built on Creek tribal trust lands.

August 10, 1988 In a White House ceremony, President Ronald Reagan signs into law a reparations bill for Japanese-Americans interned during World War II. Included in the bill are an apology and $12,000 in reparations for the survivors of the several hundred Aleut who were forcibly relocated from their native villages on the island of Attu in 1942. Although they were removed for fear of a Japanese attack, the government admitted that the relocation "resulted in widespread illness, disease and death among the residents of the camps."

September 17, 1988 A ceremony is held to commemorate the origin of the Iroquois Confederacy. The confederacy was organized by the Mohawk, Seneca, Oneida, Cayuga, and Onondaga tribes in the mid-1600s. The government, in existence since that time, is based on a constitution marked by separation of powers and a system of checks and balances.

October 5, 1988 President Reagan signs Public Law 100-472 into law. Popularly referred to as the 638 amendments, the bill provides for an overhaul of the contracting process between the BIA and Indian tribal governments.

October 17, 1988 It is estimated that by the late 1980s close to one hundred tribes, acting on their inherent sovereignty and freedom from state laws, have established some form of gaming facilities as a means of improving tribal economies and providing employment for tribal members. Pursuant to concerns expressed by non-Indian neighbors, federal officials, and some tribal officials, Congress passes the Indian Gaming Regulatory Act, Public Law 100-497. The legislation provides for the establishment of federal regulations and standards for the conduct of gaming on Indian lands. The act has two basic purposes: to strengthen tribal governments and promote economic self-sufficiency through gaming, and to provide regulation of tribal gaming thereby allaying fears of criminal influences in gaming operations. In order to ensure the effective regulation of gaming operations, the act establishes the National Indian Gaming Commission with the authority to monitor class II gaming on Indian lands.

November 1, 1988 Congress updates the review procedures, as originally outlined in the Indian Reorganization Act of 1934, of tribal constitutions, bylaws, and amendments.

December 12, 1988 President Ronald Reagan holds a meeting at the White House with sixteen Indian leaders. Billed as a "meeting among friends," it is the first held at the White House between Indian leaders and the president of the United States in modern history. The meeting is an attempt to smooth over the controversy caused by the president's remarks to Russian students in the Soviet Union in May. While speaking at Moscow University, Reagan stated: "Maybe we made a mistake. Maybe we should not have humored them [the Indians] in wanting to stay in that kind of primitive life style. Maybe we should have said: 'No come join us. Be citizens along with the rest of us.'" President Reagan also made reference to the fact that a large number of Indians had become very wealthy due to oil money. Both remarks, which Indians leaders quickly pointed out as incorrect, raised considerable concern within Indian Country as to the level of knowledge possessed by the administration regarding the current state of Indian affairs.

The twenty-minute meeting was viewed as successful by the participants. The vice chairman of the Navajo nation, Johnny Thompson, stated that "there was a spirit of forgiveness by all of us."

1989 Harper and Row publishing company publishes *The Broken Cord* by Michael Dorris. The book details the struggle of a father with his adopted Indian child, whom he later finds to be afflicted with Fetal Alcohol Syndrome. The book brings to light the increasing and devastating impact of alcohol use on reservations, especially the effect of alcohol use on the unborn.

January 19, 1989 The Seneca Indians of New York agree to the settlement of a dispute with outside local governments and with the state of New York over taxes. The tribe, standing on its sovereign authority to levy taxes, had established stores selling non-taxed goods on the reservation. In response to pressures by outside competitors, the tribe agrees to levy its own tribal tax on goods, thereby making products comparable in price. In return, the state agrees to allow the tribe to keep all tax revenues for tribal programs and to dismiss its suit against the tribe for $10 million in state sales tax for goods sold to non-Indians.

March 3, 1989 In the case of the *Lac Courte Oreilles Band of Lake Superior Chippewa Indians et al. v. State of Wisconsin,* several Chippewa Indian tribes seek to clarify their rights, based on the treaties of 1837 and 1842, to hunt, fish, and gather on off-reservation lands. Judge Barbara Crabb, presiding over the U.S. District Court for the western district of Wisconsin, rules that the Chippewas are not obligated to negotiate with the state concerning the length of their spearfishing season, the number of lakes to be fished, or the size of the catch. Furthermore, the court rules that the usufructuary rights of the Chippewa Indians, their rights to use the resources of their lands, may only be regulated if it is shown that such regulation is both reasonable and necessary for public health or the conservation of natural resources. Moreover, it must be shown that such regulation does not discriminate against the Chippewa.

April 3, 1989 In *Mississippi Choctaw Band v. Holyfield,* the Supreme Court upholds the jurisdictional rights of tribal courts under the Indian Child Welfare Act of 1978. The Indian Child Welfare Act was enacted in an attempt to address the problems that resulted from the separation of large numbers of Indian children from their families and their subsequent placement in non-Indian homes. The 1978 act gave sole jurisdiction in custody proceedings to tribal courts. This case involves an attempt by the Mississippi Choctaw band to negate an adoption decree that had been signed by the parents. The Supreme Court of Mississippi originally ruled that the adoption decree was binding in part because the twins were born off-reservation and had never been "domiciled" there and, thus, the decree did not come under the tribal court's jurisdiction. The Supreme Court overturns the lower court's decision and rules that the twins were domiciled on the Mississippi Choctaw Band's reservation and, therefore, that the tribal court has exclusive jurisdiction.

April 23–May 7, 1989 More than one hundred people are arrested in protests against the rights of northern Wisconsin tribes to fish as guaranteed by their treaties of 1837 and 1842. Almost nine hundred individuals assembled to protest the Indian's fishing rights, while more than one hundred people gathered in support of the Indians.

June 24, 1989 Stanford University agrees to repatriate for reburial the remains of 550 Ohlone Indians to descendant tribes in northern California. Stanford is one of the first universities to agree to a repatriation request by tribal leaders.

June 28, 1989 The Coquille Tribe of Indians Trust Relationship Act restores Congress' federal relationship with the Coquille Indians of Oregon, which was canceled by the Termination Act of 1954 in an attempt to facilitate the assimilation of the Coquille into American society. In light of the failure of this integration strategy, Congress began to reestablish federal recognition of Indian tribes in the 1970s.

July 7, 1989 Eddie Brown, an enrolled member of the Pasqua Yaqui of Arizona, takes the oath of office as Assistant Secretary for Indian Affairs.

July 21, 1989 The Supreme Court rules in *Brendale v. Confederated Tribes and Bands of the Yakima Indian Council* that tribal zoning laws do not apply to non-Indian-owned lands within reservation boundaries where that land is surrounded by other non-Indian-owned lands. Non-Indian-owned land surrounded by tribally owned lands is subject to tribal zoning laws.

July 21, 1989 Approximately 225 state troopers and FBI agents sweep into the part of the St. Regis Reservation (Akwesasne) located in the United States around Hogansburg, New York, closing down seven suspected casinos and arresting eight people.

July 22, 1989 Two individuals are killed and nine injured in a clash in Window Rock, Arizona, between police and the supporters of ousted Navajo Chairman Peter MacDonald. The tribal council had voted on February 17 to place MacDonald on involuntary leave in the wake of bribery accusations.

July 27, 1989 New York State police close all roads to the New York portion of the St. Regis Mohawk Reservation. Tribal factions dispute the legality of gambling on the reservation and whether the traditional Mohawk Sovereignty Security Force or the state police properly exercises jurisdiction over the reservation.

August 4, 1989 Tohono O'Odham tribal leaders request Mexican government officials in Mexico City to return thousands of acres of indigenously owned lands to the tribe. The Tohono O'Odham Nation argues that the

Gadsden Treaty of 1853 illegally divided its tribal lands by the establishment of the international boundary.

August 10, 1989 State and federally recognized tribal officials report that the St. Regis Mohawk Reservation has voted to allow gambling on the United States side within reservation boundaries.

August 11, 1989 Washington Governor Booth Gardner and the state's twenty-six federally recognized tribes sign the Centennial Accord. In the historic agreement, the state recognizes the sovereignty of Washington tribes and agrees to a government-to-government process for solving problems of mutual concern between the two governmental entities.

August 11, 1989 Secretary of Interior Manuel Lujan announces the formation of the Working Group on Indian Water Settlements. The group, which will report to the Interior's Water Policy Council, is charged with: establishing principles to guide Indian water settlements; assisting in negotiations with tribes; and reporting to the council on the progress of such negotiations.

August 13, 1989 New York State agrees to the return of twelve wampum belts to the Onondaga Nation of New York. The wampum belts, woven of shells and beads, signify important historical and cultural events in Onondaga and the Iroquois confederacy history. The New York Senate and Assembly had passed legislation in 1971 requiring the return of five wampum belts to the nation.

August 21, 1989 The Peabody Museum at Harvard University returns a sacred pole to the Omaha tribe. The pole, which has a human scalp on top and is estimated to be three hundred years old, is a symbol of unity to the tribe. The sacred object was placed in the museum's care 101 years ago by Yellow Smoke, the last keeper.

October 8, 1989 The Inspector General issues a report detailing the Bureau of Indian Affairs' irresponsible management of Indian trust funds. Trust funds of twenty tribes and two hundred individuals totaling $1.8 billion are administered by the BIA under its obligation of trustee for Indian moneys. The report states that some $17 million is missing as a result of sloppy bookkeeping.

November 17, 1989 A specially convened Senate panel issues its report following a two-year investigation into the corruption and mismanagement of American Indian lands and money. The report, the first study of its kind in more than a decade, uncovers corruption in the administration of tribal governments and a failure of the federal trust responsibility. Specifically cited as a violation of the trust obligation is Bureau of Indian Affairs management that allowed oil companies to rob tribes of oil proceeds and inadequate monitoring of teachers in BIA boarding schools found guilty of sexually molesting Indian children. The report's major recommendation is that tribes be given greater control over federal funds and programs. In particular, the panel proposes that a new executive agency be given responsibility for providing the more than five hundred Indian tribes and Alaska Native groups with block grants to administer their own programs.

November 28, 1989 Congress approves a bill to establish a National Museum of the American Indian under the administration of the Smithsonian Institution. The museum, which will be devoted to Indian culture and history, will be located in Washington, D.C.

February 27, 1990 Leaders of several North American tribes enter into an agreement to collectively defend rights granted by their treaties with the government of the United States. In accordance with the agreement, several tribes from both the United States and Canada will assist each other with legal services and lobbying and law-enforcement aid. The tribes also agree to work together in attempting to educate the non-Indian public about federal treaties with Indians.

March 25, 1990 The Puyallup tribe of Washington ends a longstanding land dispute with the city of Tacoma and the state. In return for extinguishing its land claims, the tribe agrees to a $162 million package settlement comprised of money, jobs, and education guarantees, and title to a section of the Tacoma waterfront.

April 17, 1990 The Supreme Court rules, 6-3, in *Oregon v. Smith* that a state ban against the use of peyote by American Indians did not violate the plaintiffs' First Amendment rights. The decision represents another blow to tribes in their efforts to protect their religious freedoms. The case involved the firing of two Indian drug counselors after testing positive for drug use. As members of the Native American church, the two men had ingested peyote as part of the church's ritual. Founded in 1918, the church's beliefs are a mixture of traditional beliefs and Christianity. Members believe that the taking of peyote allows them to communicate more closely with God.

April 30–May 3, 1990 A factional dispute between those in favor of gambling and those opposed on Akwesasne Reservation results in the killing of two men on the Canadian side of the reservation. Hundreds of New York and Canadian police are sent to seal off the reservation, while negotiators sent by Governor Mario Cuomo attempt to settle the dispute.

May 22, 1990 The Seneca nation, local leaders of Salamanca, New York, and state and federal officials reach an agreement on the land rented by the city of Salamanca from the tribe. Under the terms of the first lease, negotiated in 1892, the town paid the nation $17,000 annually. Ninety percent of the town of 6,600 lies within the boundaries of the Allegany reservation. According to the terms of the new lease, the town, which is the only city in the United States built on leased Indian land, will pay the tribe $800,000 a year. In addition, state and federal officials will reimburse the tribe $60 million for the inequities of the previous lease.

May 29, 1990 The Supreme Court rules in *Duro v. Reina* that tribes do not possess the authority to exercise criminal jurisdiction over non-member Indians on the reservation. The decision is a major legal and political blow to tribes in their struggle to regain and protect their inherent right of self-determination. The decision also creates a very difficult situation on reservations, where many non-enrolled tribal members have married within the tribe or are working on the reservation. According to the Court's decision, no governmental body currently possesses criminal jurisdiction over these individuals.

July 2–3, 1990 Assistant Secretary of the Interior Eddie Brown signs historic agreements with six tribes: Quinault Indian nation, Tahola, Washington; Lummi Indian nation, Bellingham, Washington; Jamestown Klallam Indian tribe, Sequim, Washington; Hoopa Valley Indian tribe, Hoopa, California; Cherokee nation, Tahlequah, Oklahoma; and Mille Lacs Band of Chippewa Indians, Onamia, Minnesota. The tribes are part of a Self-Governance Pilot Program that will ultimately allow up to twenty tribes the authority to administer and set priorities for federal funds received directly from the government.

August 1990 Congress passes legislation to convene the White House Conference on Indian Education. The

Martin Gutierrez, 12, looks on as Baudelio Gutierrez, 13, shows their grandfather, Thomas Brown, Sr., 78, some of the math textbooks during Grandparent's Day activities at Wyoming Indian Middle School.

Indian students march during "American Indian Heritage Month."

conference is charged with examining the feasibility of establishing an independent Indian Board of Education, which would oversee all federal programs directed at Indian education and recommend improvements to current educational programs.

The Bureau of Indian Affairs currently funds 182 schools, attended by thirty-nine thousand Indian children. Of these 182, 70 are contracted by tribal education committees. Another four hundred thousand Indian children attend public schools operated by the states.

August 3, 1990 Congress declares November as "American Indian Heritage Month."

September 25, 1990 Congress enacts the Tribally Controlled Vocational Institutional Support Act of 1990. The legislation provides for grants to operate and improve tribally controlled post-secondary vocational institutions.

September 28, 1990 Secretary of Interior Manuel Lujan and Assistant Secretary Eddie Brown call the Indian Tribal Leaders Conference in Albuquerque, New Mexico, to discuss proposals to reorganize the Bureau of Indian Affairs. More than one thousand Indian tribal leaders attend the first such meeting since 1976.

October 4, 1990 Congress passes the Indian Environmental Regulatory Act. The act serves to reinforce and clarify the authority of Interior officials to protect areas of environmental concern in Indian Country.

October 30, 1990 Congress enacts the Native American Languages Act which is designed to preserve, protect, and promote the practice and development of Indian languages. The act is important given the government's historic efforts, especially in the nineteenth century, to eradicate Indian languages. It is estimated that more than half of all Indian languages are now extinct. Approximately 250 Indian languages remain in existence, although some are spoken by only a few individuals.

October 31, 1990 Congress passes the Ponca Restoration Act to reestablish all formal ties and services to the Ponca tribe of Nebraska. Federal recognition of the tribe had been taken away in 1962. As with other Indian tribes, the termination policy had negative ramifications for the Poncas both economically and culturally.

November 6, 1990 President George Bush signs a defense appropriations bill that includes an amendment to delay enforcement of the *Duro* decision until September 30, 1991. The amendment, according to the bill's authors, filled the vacuum created by "an emergency situation": "Throughout the history of this country, the Congress has never questioned the power of tribal governments to exercise misdemeanor jurisdiction over non-tribal member Indians in the same manner that such courts exercise misdemeanor jurisdiction over tribal members."

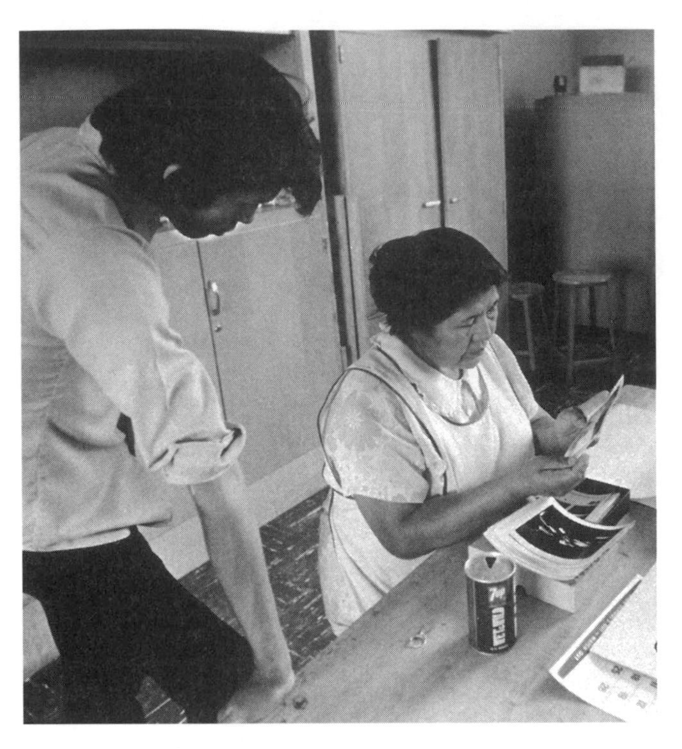

Daisy Hooee, Hopi potter and educator, passes knowledge on to the next generation.

November 16, 1990 Bowing to intense lobbying efforts by individual tribes and national and local Indian organization, Congress enacts the Native American Graves Protection and Repatriation Act. The act provides for the protection of American Indian grave sites and the repatriation of Indian remains and cultural artifacts to tribes.

November 20, 1990 The Navajo Nation elects Peterson Zah as tribal president. Zah takes over leadership of the tribe from Peter MacDonald, Sr., who was convicted of taking bribes by the Navajo tribal court in October.

November 28, 1990 Historically a rare problem, child abuse is being experienced increasingly on tribal reservations. Now, under the terms of the Indian Child Protection and Family Abuse Prevention Act, tribes are required to report abusive situations and to establish tribal programs to treat and prevent future abuse.

The passage of the National Indian Forest Resources Management Act provides for improved protection and coordination between the Department of Interior and Indian tribes in the management of Indian forest lands.

November 29, 1990 With the increase in value of tribal art work and jewelry, tribal artists have faced competition from non-Indian, machine-manufactured art works. Now, under the terms of the Indian Arts and Crafts Act of 1990, Congress gives the Indian Arts and Crafts Board, first established by the 1935 Indian Arts and Crafts Act, expanded powers to bring civil and criminal jurisdiction over counterfeit Indian arts and crafts.

December 1990 Secretary of Interior Manuel Lujan announces the formation of a forty-three-member advisory task force to recommend reorganization plans for the Bureau of Indian Affairs. The task force is composed of thirty-six Indian tribal leaders and seven Department of Interior and Bureau of Interior representatives.

Although the BIA reports that tribes have contracted to administer approximately one-third of all BIA programs, the secretary of the interior has urged the reorganization so that less funding be used for administering tribal programs. By contracting with the BIA, tribes are free to operate and manage federal programs, some $415 million annually, as they perceive to be in the tribe's best interest.

December 29, 1990 Approximately four hundred people attended the centennial of the Wounded Knee massacre. On October 19, the House of Representatives provided the final approval needed for a resolution expressing "deep regret" over the Seventh Cavalry's massacre on the Pine Ridge reservation. The Seventh

Cavalry rounded up and killed more than three hundred women, men, and children at Wounded Knee, South Dakota, in 1890.

January 29, 1991 Peter MacDonald, Sr., the former Navajo Nation chairman, is convicted by a tribal court on charges of conspiracy, fraud, and ethics violations. The tribal court had previously convicted him and his son of accepting bribes and violating the tribe's ethics code. At that time, the tribal court suspended MacDonald from tribal office and forbade him from holding a leadership position in the tribe for four years. In addition, he was sentenced to almost six years in prison and fined $11,000. His son was sentenced to eighteen months in prison and was fined $2,500.

March 5, 1991 The new National Museum of the American Indian, under the auspices of the Smithsonian Institution, announces its policy for the return of Indian artifacts. Tribes may formally request the return of all sacred objects, funerary artifacts, communally owned tribal property, and illegally obtained objects.

April 4, 1991 The Census Bureau announces that 1,959,234 American Indians and Alaska Natives live in the United States. Of these numbers, 1,878,285 are American Indian, 57,152 are Eskimo, and 23,797 are Aleut. These figures represent a total increase in population since 1980 of almost 40 percent. The increase is attributed to improved census taking and a greater

The Navajo Nation officially welcomed home all war veterans and Navajo service men and women who served in the Persian Gulf War during Operation Desert Storm. Approximately 450 Navajo service personnel served in the Gulf.

willingness on the part of individuals to be identified as American Indian.

Included in these numbers are 510 federally recognized tribes in the United States and approximately 200 Alaska Native villages and communities.

May 20, 1991 Members of the Chippewa tribes of Wisconsin and the state of Wisconsin announce an agreement which ends a seventeen-year dispute over treaty fishing rights in Wisconsin. Based on previous court decisions, the tribes and the state agree to compromise on a number of issues that had divided them for more than a decade. Under the terms of the agreement, tribes will continue to spearfish in Wisconsin lakes, but only according to strictly held conservation limits. The Chippewas also agree not to appeal a ruling that prevents them from harvesting timber in off-reservation areas.

May 24, 1991 Secretary of Interior Manuel Lujan approves a request from the Mashantucket Pequot to operate a gambling casino on tribal lands. Permission is granted under the terms of the 1988 Indian Gaming Regulatory Act, which permits Indian gaming if generally legal under state law. Connecticut state officials had sought to block approval. The Pequot casino becomes the only casino on the East Coast besides the operations in Atlantic City, New Jersey.

June 14, 1991 President George Bush issues his policy statement on American Indians in which he reaffirms the government's commitment to the government-to-government relationship between the federal government and the Indian nations.

November 26, 1991 Congress passed a bill, after considerable debate, renaming the Custer Battlefield National Monument in eastern Montana as the Little Bighorn Battlefield Monument. At the Little Bighorn site in 1876, Colonel George Armstrong Custer and more than 250 soldiers of the Sevententh Cavalry lost a battle against allied groups of Sioux and Cheyenne. This well publicized battle is often known as "Custer's Last Stand."

December 1991 According to *American Indians Today,* a publication by the Bureau of Indian Affairs issued in the winter of 1991, the BIA is responsible in its trusteeship capacity for 278 reservations, comprising some 56.2 million acres. (The term *reservation* includes reservations, pueblos, rancherias, communities, etc.)

The federal government's trusteeship responsibility currently extends to 510 federally recognized tribes, including approximately 200 village groups in Alaska.

Window Rock Elementary School students perform a Navajo Gourd Dance as part of their demonstration and skill in traditional and culture category during Native American Indian Day.

Since the establishment of the Federal Acknowledgment Program in 1978, the BIA has received 126 petitions for federal recognition; it has extended recognition to 8 tribal petitions and denied recognition to 12. The U.S. Congress during this time has legislatively recognized twelve groups.

The same publication reports that the Bureau of Indian Affairs currently provides grants for the operation of twenty-two tribally controlled community colleges, enrolling approximately seven thousand students. The BIA further estimates that more than seventy thousand Indian students are attending colleges and universities. More than four hundred Indian students are known to be pursuing graduate or law degrees.

December 4, 1991 Congress passes legislation to amend the Indian Self-Determination and Education Assistance Act. Entitled the Tribal Self-Governance Demonstration Project, the act extends the number of tribes taking part in the tribal self-governance pilot project from twenty to thirty.

Sharon O'Brien
University of Notre Dame

♦ CHRONOLOGY OF CANADIAN NATIVE HISTORY, 1500 TO 1992

The Canadian Native experience has been considerably different from U.S. Native history. Canadian Native groups were smaller and more decentralized than many U.S. Indian nations, and the Canadian Natives did not engage in protracted open conflict with Canadian society similar to the experience of many U.S. Indian nations. By 1867, however, the Canadian government extended powerful controls and limitations over Native civil rights. Powerful provincial law courts and political interests generally ruled against Canadian Native land claims and Native assertions of self-government. Nevertheless, the latter half of the twentieth century has seen a major revival among Canadian Natives, with the formation of numerous national and provincial political interest organizations and direct attempts by Canadian Natives to gain acceptance of Native rights to land and recognition of rights to Native self-government within the scope of Canada's attempts to write a national constitution and agree upon a Charter of Rights, similar to the U.S. Bill of Rights or the first several amendments to the Constitution. In late 1992, the Canadian people voted against a proposed constitution, which included recognition of many Native civil and political rights. Natives in Canada are actively engaged in national discussions to develop a workable constitutional government for Canada, and Canadian Natives are working to see that their rights to self-government, cultural freedom, and claims to land will be recognized within any new national government that is established by Canada in the future.

1503 Indigenous peoples along the east coast of Canada begin irregular trade with groups of European fishermen and whalers. The Natives give up furs in exchange for metal goods.

Near Chaleur Bay, in the Gulf of St. Lawrence along North America's east coast, Jacques Cartier trades with a group of Indians who have obviously traded with Europeans before. Near Gaspé, at the end of the Gaspé Peninsula in the Gulf of St. Lawrence, he kidnaps two sons of the Iroquois chief, Donnacona. In France, the youths tell stories of the Kingdom of Saguenay, a fictitious kingdom rich in precious metals.

1535–36 Donnacona's two sons guide Cartier, who is searching for the Kingdom of Saguenay, to their Iroquois village of Stadacona (Quebec City). The Stadaconans trade with Cartier, but are angered when his party sails farther upriver to trade at Hochelega (Montreal). Stadaconans claim the right to control traffic traveling up the St. Lawrence River. The party winters near Stadacona, depending on Indian help to survive. In spring, Cartier kidnaps ten Iroquois, including Donnacona. All eventually die in France.

1541–43 Jacques Cartier and Sieur de Roberval, the newly commissioned lieutenant-general in Canada, establish a settlement near Stadacona. The settlement fails largely as a result of Indian hostility.

1543–88 Instead of establishing permanent settlements, Europeans embark for important Indian coastal trade centers each year. The Montagnais, nomadic hunter-gatherers of the area north of the St. Lawrence River and the major Indian traders, greatly improve their returns by trading only when at least two competing ships are on hand.

1576–78 A party of Inuit (Native inhabitants of northern regions of North America) has a hostile encounter with English mariner Martin Frobisher on Baffin Island, in the northeastern arctic. Frobisher kidnaps one Inuk man, who causes a stir in London.

1588 King Henry III of France grants a fur trade monopoly to nephews of Jacques Cartier. During the following decades monopolies are granted and revoked as monopoly holders fail to force interlopers to honor the monopoly. Indians find increased demand for *castor gras* (greasy beaver), beaver skins that have shed their guard hairs and absorbed perspiration and body oils after being used as clothing for a season or two. Europeans seek *castor gras* to make felt.

1604–1607 Sieur de Monts, the current French monopoly holder, and French mariner, Samuel Champlain, establish Port Royal, a year-round trading base on the Bay of Fundy, a large bay separating today's provinces of Nova Scotia and New Brunswick. Micmac chief Membertou concludes an agreement with the French that gives the Micmac access to European weapons in exchange for food and furs. The Micmac were the Native inhabitants of most of Acadia, France's possessions southeast of the St. Lawrence River. Port Royal is abandoned in 1607 because of its poor location.

1608 Champlain establishes Quebec City (New France) as the new French trading base. Since 1544, the agricultural, Iroquoian inhabitants have been displaced by nomadic Algonkian-speaking peoples. The Algonkian language family is the largest in Canada. Algonkian languages are spoken by many Indian groups from the Atlantic to the Rocky Mountains. Iroquoian languages dominate only in the southern Great Lakes-St. Lawrence River region.

1609 A group of Huron led by Chief Ochasteguin and Algonquin led by Chief Iroquet visit Quebec to negotiate a trade alliance. The Huron were Iroquoian, agricultural peoples of the area just east of Lake Huron. The Algonquin were hunter-gatherers of the regions north of the St. Lawrence River. They induce Champlain to join them on a raid against the Iroquois Five Nations Confederacy tribes (Cayuga, Mohawk, Oneida, Onondaga, and Seneca), who reside southeast of Quebec. The battle initiates almost two centuries of enmity between the Five Nations and the French. Following Indian customs, French and Indians intermarry and Indians accept French emissaries, including missionaries. Some of these emissaries provide valuable information to the French about the area around the Great Lakes.

1610 A lone Cree man trades with Henry Hudson's party on the shores of Hudson Bay. Hudson was exploring the region for the English. The Cree are Algonkian-speaking Indians who today live in areas from Quebec to Alberta.

1611 The Iroquois acquire firearms from Dutch traders on the Hudson River. The Iroquois-Huron trade rivalry intensifies. The French are reluctant to trade guns with Indians.

1615–49 Champlain visits Huron lands southeast of Lake Huron to conclude a trade alliance with the Huron. Already central to a web of trade relations to the north and west, the Huron become important middlemen, carrying furs and European goods between New France and various Indian peoples to the north and west as far away as Hudson Bay and Lake Michigan. (By essentially demanding payment for delivery of goods, Indian middlemen acquired European goods without having to trap themselves.) In order to protect their middleman role, the Huron prevent direct trade between the French and neighboring Indians. Increased wealth allows for increasingly elaborate celebrations of such Huron rituals as the Feast of the Dead, an important Huron burial ceremony held every ten to fifteen years.

1615 Roman Catholic Récollet missionaries arrive in New France. Indian groups accept missionaries as emissaries from their French trading partners. The Ottawa, Algonkian hunters living east of Lake Huron's Georgian Bay, conduct Champlain as far as Lake Huron.

In order to cement a trade alliance, Champlain joined a Huron and Algonquin raid on the Iroquois in 1609. This was the most successful of several raids that Champlain joined. Courtesy of the National Library of Canada.

In almost every region in Canada, early Native-Euro-Canadian interaction was based on the mutually beneficial fur trade. In this eighteenth-century engraving, an Indian examines a gun he is about to buy. Natives proved to be skillful traders throughout the fur trade area. *Indians Trading Furs, 1785,* by C. W. Jefferys. Courtesy of the National Archives of Canada.

1617 An epidemic kills many Micmac in Acadia.

1623 The French government grants its first seigneury (feudal land grant) in New France. Indians do not acknowledge French sovereignty to any land, just as the French do not recognize aboriginal rights to the land. Thus, Indians and the French do not negotiate any land cession treaties (treaties in which one party surrenders its land rights to another).

1624 The Huron and Iroquois negotiate a truce in their longstanding warfare. The French try to prevent the peace because they fear that the Iroquois will allow the Hurons access to Hudson River trading posts.

1629 English buccaneers take New France and Acadia for England.

1632 The Treaty of St. Germain returns Acadia and New France to France. The Jesuits, members of a Roman Catholic religious order also known as the Society of Jesus, begin an intensive missionary effort among the Huron and Algonquin.

1634 A Huron guide takes French interpreter Jean Nicollet as far west as Lake Michigan.

1634 Smallpox strikes the Montagnais.

1635 Residential schools for Indians are established by Jesuits in New France.

1636 Renewed warfare breaks out between the Huron and Iroquois as their trade rivalry intensifies. The Iroquois have exhausted fur supplies in their territory and are struggling to capture the Huron trade network.

1637 Feeling that nomadic hunters must be settled in order to be Christianized, Jesuits establish an Algonquin agricultural settlement at Sillery, near Quebec City.

1639 The Jesuits establish a mission settlement at Sainte-Marie-among-the-Huron (Midland, Ontario).

1635–40 Several smallpox epidemics reduce Huron population from about twenty thousand to ten thousand.

1641 The French begin selling guns to Huron who profess to be Christian. The Iroquois begin unlimited warfare on the French.

1642 Ville Maric (Montreal) is established as a missionary outpost. It soon develops into a trade center.

1649–50 In a concerted effort to seize the middleman role in the French fur trade, the Iroquois crush the Huron. Some Huron are integrated into the Five Nations and other peoples, some are established at Lorette near Quebec City, and some scatter throughout the Great Lakes region where they become known as Wyandotte. The Ottawa assume the main middleman role. *Coureurs de bois* (traveling French fur traders who spend most of their time among the Indians) also assume an important role in trading with interior Indians. This increases Indian contact and intermarriage with the French.

1666–67 With the two thousand colonists of New France threatened by continual Iroquois attack, French troops attack Iroquois villages. The expedition kills few Indians but destroys Iroquois villages and crops. As a result, the Iroquois and French conclude a truce that lasts ten years.

1667 Iroquois converts are established at La Prairie (Caughnawaga) near Montreal. They become allies of the French. Missionaries seek to isolate Indian settlements because they believe Europeans are a corrupting influence on the Indians.

1668 Three hundred Cree trade with traders on a British ship at the mouth of the Rupert River along the coast of James Bay, a large bay in Hudson Bay. French fur traders, Pierre Esprit Radisson and Médard Chouart des Grosseliers, realized the value of the Hudson Bay as a fur-trading base after a foray to the James Bay hinterland earlier in the decade.

1670 Cree and Ojibway (Ojibwa, Chippewa), Algonkian hunters centered along the eastern and northern shores of Lake Superior, begin traveling to the Hudson's Bay Company (HBC) posts at mouths of the Rupert, Moose, and Albany rivers on James Bay in present-day northern Quebec and Ontario. The HBC sends no missionaries to the Indians.

1671–73 The French establish forts on the Great Lakes as far northwest as Sault Ste. Marie, at the "Sault" (Falls) on the St. Marys River, which joins Lakes Superior and Huron, for the purpose of defense, trade, missions, and diplomacy. Competition with the Hudson's Bay Company induces the French to dramatically increase their trade in firearms. Ojibway ceremonial life becomes more elaborate as they become important traders around the Sault. Some Indian bands near French and HBC posts serve as Home Guard bands—bands with a significantly more intense relationship with traders. Frequent intermarriage follows Indian customs, and mixed-blood children are usually raised by the Indians.

1680 Renewed Iroquois attacks force French *coureurs de bois* to replace retreating Ottawa middlemen in the fur trade.

1682–1774 The Hudson's Bay Company establishes York Factory at the mouth of the Nelson and Hayes Rivers on the western shores of Hudson Bay in present-day Manitoba. The rivers drain a vast territory as far west as the Rocky Mountains. Cree and Assiniboine become middlemen, trading European goods with Plains Indians as far west and south as the Rocky Mountains and the Missouri River Basin before 1750. Access to European goods, particularly weaponry, increases the wealth and power of Cree and Assiniboine bands. Cree bands living near Hudson Bay become Home Guard Indians at the post. The Assiniboine are Siouan-speaking, a group that inhabited areas south and southeast of Lake Winnipeg (in today's Manitoba) at that time.

1700–1750 The Shoshoni in today's southwestern Alberta become the first Indians residing in present-day Canada to acquire horses. Horses spread to most Plains Indians by 1750, bringing significant changes in lifestyles and diplomacy.

1701 The Iroquois and French conclude a peace agreement, ending a century of hostilities. Iroquois power and population has been significantly reduced by years of warfare. The Mississauga (Ojibway) have expanded from the north to occupy most of the former Huron lands.

1701–38 The Fox Indians, occupying the area of present-day northeastern Wisconsin, slow French westward expansion. The Fox were enemies of the French and many of their Indian allies.

1713 By the Treaty of Utrecht, France cedes Acadia (renamed Nova Scotia) to England and relinquishes claims to Newfoundland and Hudson Bay. France also recognizes the Iroquois as English subjects. The Micmac and the Maliseet (Malecite), who occupy lands west of the St. John River (in today's New Brunswick), begin opposing the English, and the Iroquois continue to see themselves as subject to no foreign power.

1713–53 The French traders establish fur trade posts as far west as Lake Winnipeg and the Saskatchewan River. The Ojibwa, originally centered near Sault Ste. Marie, just east of Lake Superior, spread as far west as the prairies.

1717 The Hudson's Bay Company establishes Fort Prince of Wales (Churchill) on the western shores of Hudson Bay (in present-day Manitoba) allowing bands of Chipewyan to establish themselves as middlemen. The Chipewyan were Athapaskan-speaking hunter-gatherers centered in the region of today's northern Manitoba and Saskatchewan and southern Northwest Territories. They guard their role by preventing Yellowknife and Dogrib, both Athapaskan hunters of the Great Bear Lake and Great Slave Lake area (in today's Northwest Territories) from reaching the post. Secure access to European goods allows them to expand against other Indians and Inuit, leading to acrimonious relations between the Chipewyan and these other Indians. Most Indians in northwestern Canada speak an Athapaskan language.

1729 Four hundred Iroquois of Caughnawaga settle at a mission at Lake of Two Mountains (Oka), just west of Montreal.

1750 Around this time, the Sarcee, Athapaskan-speaking hunters from the forested Lesser Slave Lake region (in today's northern Alberta), migrate to the southern prairies and adopt a Plains Indian way of life.

1752 Moravian missionaries (Protestant missionaries from Germany) and traders arrive among the Inuit in Labrador.

1752 The Subenacadie band of Micmac sign the Halifax Treaty with the British, easing hostility between the Micmac and the British in Nova Scotia. The British deny that the Indians hold any rights to land in Nova Scotia.

1755 Father Gordon, a Roman Catholic missionary, establishes an Iroquois settlement at St. Regis (Akwesasne). Today Akwesasne straddles the Ontario-Quebec-New York State borders near Montreal.

1760 New France falls to the British. The British agree to respect land granted to Indians by the French, but anger Indians by ending the French practice of giving gifts to Indians to cement alliances.

1763–66 Pontiac, a chief of the Ottawa tribe, leads Indian resistance to the British. In 1763, Indian forces capture all British forts west of Niagara Falls except Fort Detroit and Fort Pitt (Pittsburgh). Detroit is besieged for five months.

February 1763 By the Treaty of Paris, France cedes all North American possessions, except two small islands, to Great Britain. The Indian inhabitants reject the treaty as an infringement on their rights.

October 7, 1763 The British Royal Proclamation of 1763 recognizes the possessory right of North American Indians to all land in British territories outside established colonies (Hudson's Bay Company land is exempt), but claims underlying title for the King. The Crown claims the exclusive right to negotiate land surrender and peace treaties with the Indians and prohibits settlement in areas not covered by land cession treaties. (The proclamation has been enshrined in Canada's 1982 Constitution.)

1767 Newly surveyed land in Prince Edward Island in the Gulf of St. Lawrence is granted to British proprietors. No land is set aside for indigenous peoples.

1769–72 Matonabbee, a Chipewyan-Cree, guides Hudson's Bay Company employee Samuel Hearne, to the Slave and Coppermine Rivers in the southwestern interior of today's Northwest Territories and as far as the Arctic Coast.

1774 The Hudson's Bay Company establishes Cumberland House on the Saskatchewan River (near today's The Pas, Manitoba) as its first inland trading post after learning that Cree and Assiniboine are trading many of their highest quality furs to Canadian traders who have infiltrated the area around Lake Winnipeg (in today's Manitoba).

1774–1800 The Hudson's Bay Company and Canadian traders (Nor'Westers) establish competing fur-trade posts throughout the northern prairies, dramatically reducing the cost of European goods to Plains Indians, who can now trade directly with Euro-Canadians. These Indians are able displace Indian groups with poor access to trading posts. Former Cree and Assiniboine middlemen assume roles as Home Guard Indians and provisioners at North West Company and HBC posts. Intermarriage between Indians and fur traders produces a sizable mixed-blood population.

1774 Nootka (Nuu-chah-nulth), coastal Indians of Vancouver Island, trade with Spanish explorer Juan Perez. West Coast Indians have already begun trading with Russians. The Indians of the northwest coast of North America live in substantial villages and rely heavily on abundant supplies of salmon. Coastal Indians' highly structured, hierarchical societies are unique among Native groups of northern North America.

1775–83 Britain's Indian allies take a prominent role in the American War of Independence. They believe the British best represent their interests.

1779–1821 The North West Company, operating from Montreal, becomes the dominant force in the fur trade and in exploration of the northwest, allowing many northern Indian groups to trade directly with Euro-Canadian traders. This alters interethnic relations in the region. Natives on the prairies supply large amounts of pemmican, a preserved meat usually produced from buffalo and used to feed traders in the north.

1780–82 Smallpox kills up to half of the Plains Indians and up to nine-tenths of the Chipewyan.

1783 By the Treaty of Versailles, the British cede land south of the Great Lakes angering their Indian allies who still control the area.

1784 The British negotiate land purchases from Mississauga (Ojibway) Indians and grant the land to "loyalist" Indians who had found their land turned over to the United States. Iroquois Captain Joseph Brant (Thyendanega) and more than 1,550 Iroquois are given a tract of land on the Grand River (Six Nations Reserve near Brantford, Ontario), and Captain John Deseronto's Mohawk are given land near the Bay of Quinte on the north shore of Lake Ontario.

Interior of an Inuit house. Courtesy of American Heritage Press.

1784 New Brunswick is formed as a separate province as loyalists settle there. Maliseet and Micmac begin to suffer gradual encroachment on their lands.

1785 The Indians of the west coast begin regular trade with shipborne traders, increasing their returns by trading only when competing ships are at hand. Coastal middlemen trade with Indians well inland. Sea otter pelts and blankets become trade staples, with blankets forming a kind of currency.

1793 With Indian guidance, North West Company employee Alexander Mackenzie becomes the first white man to cross North America by land.

1794 The Jay Treaty establishes the border between the United States and British North America beyond the Great Lakes. Britain agrees to withdraw troops and traders from land ceded to the United States in 1783. The British had kept troops posted there to appease their Indian allies in the region. Indians are guaranteed unhindered travel across the border.

1795 Around this time, the first of several hundred Iroquois migrate to the prairies where they become important trappers.

1812 The Hudson's Bay Company establishes the Red River Colony (Selkirk Settlement) near today's Winnipeg. Chief Peguis's band of Saulteaux (Ojibway) provides important help to the settlers in their first difficult years.

1812–14 Tecumseh (Shawnee) leads Britain's Indian allies in their important role in the War of 1812. Many Indian groups ally with Britain in the hope that the British will able to create a buffer state for them.

1814 The Treaty of Ghent, ending the War of 1812, ends Indian hopes of a buffer state.

1816 At the Battle of Seven Oaks (Red River), twenty-one Red River settlers and one Métis die in a skirmish. The battle fosters an increased sense of nationhood among the Métis. The Métis, of mixed Indian-European

Inuit man ice fishing.

descent, have developed a unique society and culture based on farming and buffalo hunting.

1817 The Saulteaux and Cree sign a land cession treaty for land occupied by the Red River Colony. They are promised a yearly annuity.

1818 The British Government begins its practice of acquiring Indian land in exchange for annuities (yearly payments) rather than lump-sum payments.

1820 John West of the Anglican Church Missionary Society (C.M.S.) arrives to serve the English speaking, non-Catholic population at the Red River Colony. The C.M.S. and the Roman Catholic Oblates of Mary Immaculate become the major missionary groups in the Northwest.

1821 The North West Company and the Hudson's Bay Company merge, retaining the name of the HBC. The HBC reduces employment and opportunities for Indians and mixed-blood inhabitants throughout the northwest. It also reduces trade in alcohol. Many mixed-blood move to the Red River settlement where a large Métis community develops.

1827 With the establishment of Fort Langley on the Fraser River (in the southwestern corner of today's British Columbia), land-based trade in southwest British Columbia begins. The region was the home of Coast Salish, who lived in villages and depended heavily on salmon.

1829 Shanawdithit, the last Beothuk, dies. The reclusive Beothuk, the Native inhabitants of Newfoundland, were gradually killed by non-Indians, enemy Indians, and disease.

1830 Responsibility for Indian affairs in Upper Canada is transferred from the military secretary to civilian administrators, reflecting the waning importance of Indians as military allies and a growing emphasis on assimilation of Indians into non-Indian society.

1830 An attempt by Methodist missionaries to settle Ojibway Indians as farmers on the southeast corner of Lake Huron's Georgian Bay (the Coldwater Experiment) begins. The project is abandoned in 1837.

1834 The establishment of Fort Simpson, along the north coast of today's British Columbia, begins the land-based trade in the Pacific Northwest. Coastal Indian bands gather near posts to protect their role as middlemen.

1835 The Aborigines Protection Society is founded in Great Britain.

1836 A plan to relocate Upper Canada's Indians to the Manitoulin Islands (in Lake Huron) is abandoned after humanitarian groups committed to the assimilation of Indians oppose the plan.

1835–40 Smallpox kills up to one-third of some British Columbia coastal Indians.

1837–38 Smallpox kills up to three-quarters of the Plains Indians. Hudson's Bay Company traders vaccinate the Cree, preventing the spread of the disease to the Cree and their northern neighbors.

1840s Roman Catholic missionaries (Oblates of Mary Immaculate) arrive in British Columbia. They employ the "Durieu System," named after French Oblate Pierre Paul Durieu, in order to transform Native cultures.

1841 Methodist missionary James Evans prints a hymnal using the Cree syllabics that he devised. The written Cree language, adapted to Athapaskan and Inuit languages, stimulates the growth of literacy among northern Natives.

1842 The first significant attempt to establish reserves for Indians in Nova Scotia begins.

1844 The New Brunswick government passes legislation restricting Indian reserves to twenty hectares per family.

1844 The Bagot Commission Report on Indian Affairs in the Canadas (present-day Ontario and Quebec) recommends an Indian affairs policy with the aim of the complete assimilation of Indians into Canadian society. The Bagot Commission was commissioned to recommend a new Indian policy because the current policy of the 1830s, which emphasized the creation of Indian settlements, was questioned.

1846 The Treaty of Washington extends the boundary between the United States and British North America to the Pacific.

1850 In a law designed to protect Indians lands, the government claims, for the first time, the right to define who is an Indian.

1850 The Ojibway sign the Robinson Treaties covering land north of Lake Superior. These treaties, covering twice as much land as all earlier treaties in Upper Canada combined, are the first treaties signed to clear the way for mineral exploration rather than settlement.

1851 Coast Salish Indians of Vancouver Island and James Douglas, governor of the Hudson's Bay Company colony on Vancouver Island, conclude the first of fourteen land cession treaties covering small areas of the island.

1857 Captain John Palliser leads a British scientific expedition to study the agricultural potential of the western prairies. Its report includes information about the Indians of the area.

1857 The Imperial (British) Government passes the Gradual Civilization Act, which makes Canadian Indians non-citizens, but creates a process by which Indians are expected to seek "enfranchisement"—the acceptance of citizenship and renunciation of any legal distinction as an Indian. Adult male Indians seeking enfranchisement for themselves and their families will need to demonstrate that they are educated, debt free, capable of managing their own affairs, and of "good moral character." Enfranchised individuals will be granted their share of band funds and ownership of twenty hectares of reserve land and will lose their Indian status. In order to acquaint unenfranchised Indians with the Canadian political system, the act encourages the formation of elected band councils (to replace traditional leaders) by offering such councils limited powers over reserve affairs.

1858 Thousands of gold seekers come to the lower Fraser River Valley (in the southwestern corner of present-day British Columbia) and clash with resident Coast Salish Indians.

1860 The Imperial Government transfers control of Indian affairs to the Province of Canada.

1862 William Duncan of the Anglican's Church Missionary Society establishes an isolated missionary settlement for Tsimshian Indians at Metlakatla, near Port Simpson, British Columbia. Tsimshian are coastal Indians of the Skeena River Region of British Columbia's north coast. In British Columbia, Anglicans and Roman Catholics focus their efforts in separate regions. As a result, Indian groups there overwhelmingly become either Catholic or Protestant.

1862 Indians of the interior of British Columbia clash with thousands of gold seekers rushing to the Cariboo region. Smallpox decimates Indians in the interior and coast of British Columbia.

1862 A number of Dakota (Sioux), Siouan Indians of the northern U.S. plains, flee north after attacking settlements in Minnesota. Many eventually settle in Canada.

1864 James Douglas retires as governor of Vancouver Island. Joseph Trutch, the new chief commissioner of lands and works in the colony, initiates British Columbia's policy of refusing to negotiate land surrender agreements with Indians.

July 1, 1867 The British North America Act, recognizing Canadian Confederation, grants legislative responsibility for Indian affairs to the new federal government, but gives control of land and natural resources to the provincial governments, thus giving both levels of government an interest in future land-claims negotiations. The new federal government adopts the established British policy toward the Indians as administered in Canada West (Ontario). Land cession treaties have been negotiated only in Ontario, although reserves have been granted in the other provinces.

1868 The Canadian government's first Indian Act adopts pre-Confederation Indian policy. It also introduces "location tickets," a means by which provisional individual title to reserve lands can be given to those seeking enfranchisement. Responsibility for Indian affairs is given to the Secretary of State.

1869–74 The whiskey trade on the southwestern prairies brings serious social problems to the Blackfoot Confederacy. The Blackfoot Confederacy is composed of the Blackfoot, Blood, and Peigan, Plains Indians who inhabit the southwestern plains of Canada and the northwestern plains of the United States.

1869 The Canadian government lays out the method by which it seeks to assimilate Indians in the Gradual Enfranchisement Act. Responding to Indian resistance to the establishment of elected band councils, agents are given power to depose traditional leaders for "dishonesty, intemperance and immorality," and to impose elected band councils. This act also stipulates that Indian women and their children will lose their Indian status when they marry non-Indians.

1870 Cree and Blackfoot fight the last plains war in Canada near Fort Whoop-up (at today's Lethbridge, Alberta). During the 1860s, the Cree had followed the diminishing buffalo herds toward the southwest, increasing their conflicts with the Blackfoot.

1870 Canada acquires Hudson's Bay Company lands from the British government with the provision that it will negotiate land cession treaties with the Indians. Most of the area becomes the Northwest Territories, administered by the federal government. As a result of negotiations with a provisional government established by Métis leader Louis Riel, a small area becomes the province of Manitoba. The federal government recognizes Métis land title in the province. The federal government retains control of land and natural resources in the entire area.

1871 British Columbia enters the Confederation. It retains control of land and natural resources, but agrees to transfer land to the federal government for use as Indian reserves.

1871 The first of eleven numbered treaties covering former Hudson's Bay Company lands is signed. Treaty 1, covering Manitoba (including the area of the Selkirk treaty of 1817) and areas of the Northwest Territories (today's southern Manitoba), is signed by the Saulteaux (Ojibway) and Swampy Cree. Treaty 2, covering areas of the Northwest Territories (today's central and southwest Manitoba, and southeast Saskatchewan) is signed by the Ojibway. Both treaties promise land and farm implements and seed, but make no mention of hunting, fishing, or trapping rights.

1873 The province of Prince Edward Island enters the Confederation having signed no land cession treaties with Indian groups.

1873 The Department of the Interior is given responsibility over Indian affairs.

1873 Ten Americans and Canadians kill up to thirty Assiniboine in the Cypress Hills Massacre. The Cypress Hills are in Canada's southwestern prairies.

1873 The Saulteaux sign Treaty 3 covering today's western Ontario and southeastern Manitoba. The treaty promises land and livestock, but also includes hunting, fishing, and trapping rights.

1874 The Plains Cree, Assiniboine, and Saulteaux tribes sign Treaty 4, covering areas of the Northwest Territories (now southern Saskatchewan).

1874 The North West Mounted Police are sent to the Canadian prairies to stop the whisky trade, prevent such violence as the Cypress Hills massacre (1873), and prepare the west for peaceful settlement.

1875 The Saulteaux and Swampy Cree sign Treaty 5 covering land in today's northern Manitoba and western Ontario. Treaties 1 and 2 are revised to increase land allotments.

1876 A new Indian Act makes elected band councils voluntary. It also gives such councils wider powers. Location tickets, re-introduced in eastern Canada, are part of a plan to lead Indians to abandon the practice of holding land in common. Location tickets give individuals rights to twenty hectares of reserve land. Indians who farm their allotment over a period of three years are to be enfranchised and receive absolute title to the land. Only one Indian was enfranchised between 1857 and 1876. The act forbids the sale of alcohol to Indians and bars non-Indians from reserves after nightfall.

1876 Plains Cree, Woodland Cree, and Assiniboine tribes sign Treaty 6, covering areas of the Northwest Territories (today's central Alberta and Saskatchewan). The treaty includes famine relief provisions and a "medicine chest" provision, which becomes the basis of free health care for all Indians. Big Bear, chief of the Saskatchewan River Cree, assembles a band that renounces the treaty.

1876 Canadian governor-general Lord Dufferin protests the British Columbia government's refusal to acknowledge Indian land rights.

1877 Sitting Bull, a chief of the Dakota, and hundreds of his Dakota followers flee to Canada after Sitting Bull led resistance to U.S. forces. The U.S. army burns the prairies near the Canadian border, preventing many buffalo from migrating north into Canada. Most of these Indians eventually return to the United States.

1877 The Blackfoot Confederacy, Sarcee, and Stoney (Assiniboine) tribes sign Treaty 7, covering areas of the Northwest Territories (today's southern Alberta).

1879–85 Plains Indian groups gradually settle on reserves in western Canada.

1879 The Canadian government removes the power to grant reserve lands to individuals from band councils and grants it to the superintendent-general of Indian affairs.

1879 Buffalo disappear from the Canadian prairies, forcing Indian bands to follow herds into the United States or face famine. The government rejects a demand by Cree bands led by Piapot, Little Pine, and Big Bear for contiguous reserves in the Cypress Hills.

1880 The federal government revises the 1876 Indian Act to empower it to impose elected band councils east of Lake Superior. The Department of Indian Affairs is created as a separate government department.

1882 Cree bands seeking contiguous reserves abandon the Cypress Hills after being told they will not be given food aid there.

1883 The Canadian government begins establishing residential schools for Indians in the west. Most Indians seek education for their children but resist the assimilationist aims of government schools.

1884 The Indian Advancement Act (applied to Indians east of Lake Superior) extends the powers of elected band councils but authorizes the superintendent-general (minister) of Indian Affairs to depose Indian chiefs he deems to be unfit to lead. The amendment is made after Indian bands elect band councils which had earlier been chosen by traditional means.

1884 Indian bands meet near Battleford, Northwest Territories (now in Saskatchewan) to unite western Indians in efforts to improve their treaty terms. Another council is scheduled for 1885.

1885 Amendments to the Indian Act prohibit Indians from traveling off their reserves without a pass from an Indian Affairs agent, prohibit the reelection of deposed Indian leaders, and prohibit Sun Dances, annual midsummer Plains Indian ceremonies, and potlatches, elaborate ceremonies held among coastal Indians. Agricultural instructors are sent to Indian reserves in western Canada.

1885 At Batoche, Northwest Territories (now in Saskatchewan), federal government forces crush a Métis uprising led by Louis Riel. After his execution for treason in November, Riel becomes a powerful symbol for the Métis.

1885 Members of Big Bear's Cree band kill nine people at Frog Lake and members of Cree chief Poundmaker's

LOUIS RIEL,
CHEF METIS,
Exécuté le 16 Novembre 1885.
MARTYR POLITIQUE!
Coupable d'avoir aimé ses compatriotes opprimés,
Victime du fanatisme orangiste, auquel l'ont sacrifié des politiciens sans âme et sans cœur.

QUE LES VRAIS PATRIOTES S'EN SOUVIENNENT!!

Louis Riel's execution in 1885 vaulted him to the status of martyr for the Métis cause. He remains one of the most controversial figures in Canadian history. Courtesy of the National Archives of Canada.

band raid homesteads near Duck Lake, Northwest Territories (now in Saskatchewan). Big Bear, Poundmaker, and forty-two other Indians are jailed.

1889 In the *St. Catharine's Milling and Lumber Company* case, the Privy Council, the highest court in the British Empire until 1949, rules that aboriginal land rights were created by the Royal Proclamation of 1763 and can be abolished by unilateral legislative action.

1894 Federal legislation empowers the superintendent-general of Indian Affairs to depose Indian leaders in the west.

1895 An amendment to the Indian Act authorizes the Department of Indian Affairs to rent out reserve lands at the request of an individual Indian without the band's permission.

1897–99 Thousands of gold seekers disrupt the lives of Indians in the Yukon, in northwestern Canada. Yukon is created as a separate territory.

1898 Quebec boundaries are extended to the north. No mention is made of how Indian land rights in the area are to be dealt with.

1899 The Cree of present-day northern Alberta; the Beaver, Athapaskan hunters of the Peace River region of today's northern Alberta; the Sekani, Athapaskan hunters of the Finlay and Parsnip River region of northeastern British Columbia; and the Chipewyan of today's northern Alberta and the Northwest Territories south of Great Slave Lake, sign Treaty 8. The Indians demanded the treaty as the number of non-Indians in the area increased during the Yukon gold rush.

1905 The Cree and Ojibway of northern Ontario sign Treaty 9.

1905 The provinces of Alberta and Saskatchewan are created from areas of the Northwest Territories but are not given control of land or resources.

1906 Joe Capilano, chief of the Squamish band near Vancouver, petitions the British Crown to help British Columbia Indians gain redress of their grievances.

1906 The Chipewyan and Cree of northern Ontario sign Treaty 10.

1909 The Indian Tribes of the Province of British Columbia, an alliance of twenty Indian nations, appeals to the British throne for help in settling their land claims.

1911 About this time, the Canadian Indian population reaches its lowest level (under 110,000 persons). This is approximately half the number of Indians that lived in the same territory in 1500.

1912 Quebec is granted territory as far north as Hudson Strait on the condition it will negotiate land surrender agreements with Natives.

1912–16 A Royal Commission on Indian Affairs in British Columbia (the McKenna-McBride Commission) meets to determine the appropriate size for each British Columbia reserve. Its final report recommends adding land to some reserves and cutting off land (of considerably greater value) from others. The recommendations are rejected by the Allied Tribes of British Columbia.

1913 The Privy Council refuses to rule on a Nishga (Nisga'a) land claim because the Canadian government will not sponsor the appeal. The Nishga are Indians of the Nass River Valley in northwestern British Columbia.

1914–18 Up to four thousand Indians, approximately 35 percent of those eligible, fight for Canada in World War I.

1915 Opposition to the conduct of the McKenna-McBride Commission (1912-16) spurs Rev. Peter Kelly (Haida) and Andrew Paull (Squamish) to organize the Allied Tribes of British Columbia. It appeals to the federal government for help in settling Nishga and Salish land claims. British Columbia has the longest history of pan-tribal organization in Canada.

1919 The League of Indians of Canada becomes the first attempt to organize Indians nationally. Government resistance to the organization contributes to its eventual collapse.

1919–20 Following recommendations of the McKenna-McBride Commission, the British Columbia government begins adjusting the size of reserves.

1920 The federal government amends the Indian Act to allow for compulsory enfranchisement. Only 250 Indians have opted for enfranchisement between 1857 and 1920.

1921 The Slave, Dogrib, and Hare tribes, all Athapaskan hunters of western Northwest Territories, sign Treaty 11, covering land north and west of Great Slave Lake, Northwest Territories. The Canadian government sought the treaty after oil was discovered at Norman Wells, along the Mackenzie River in the Northwest Territories.

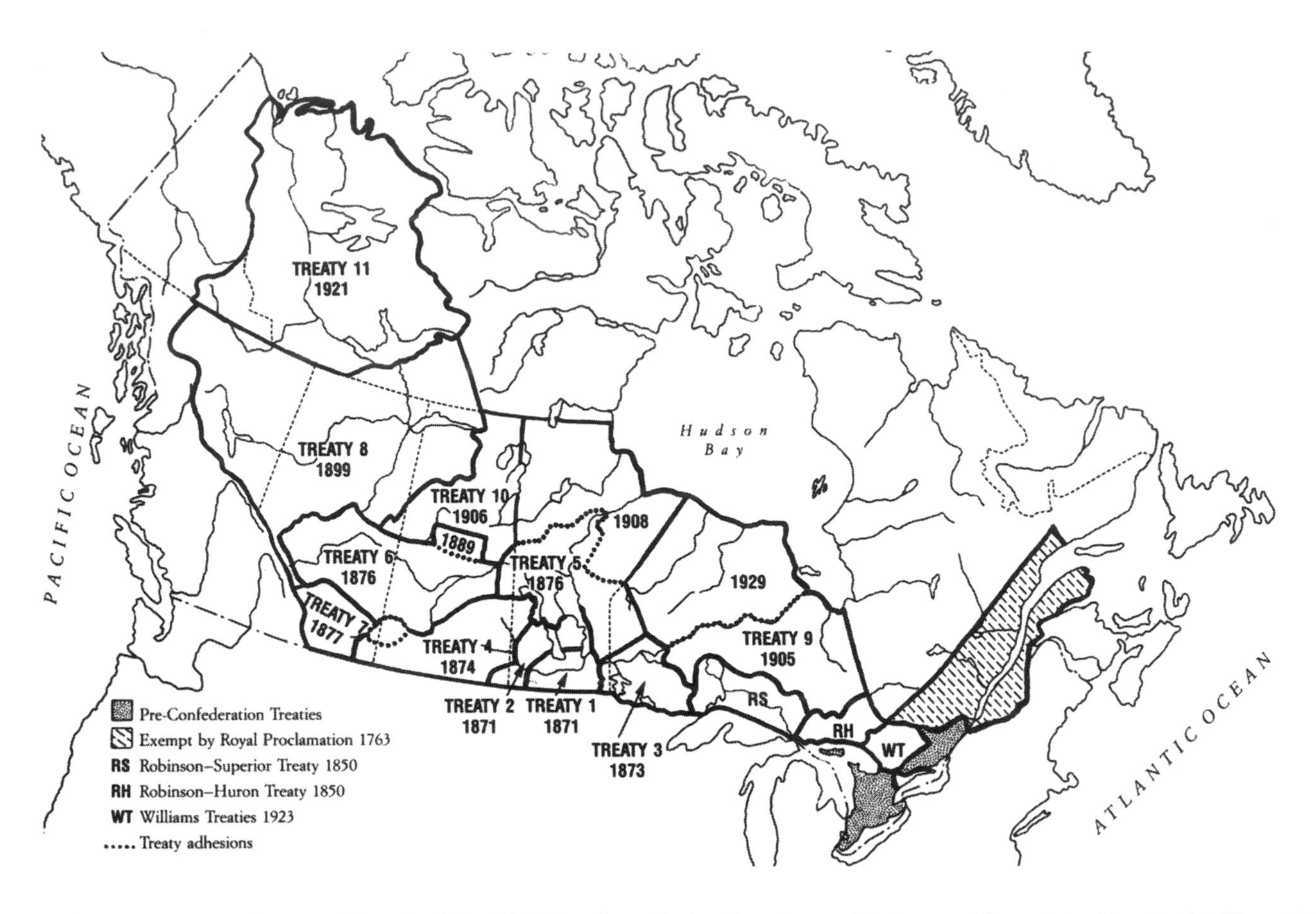

Indian treaty area in Canada. Maps by Brian McMillan from *Native Peoples and Cultures of Canada* by Alan D. McMillan, 1988, published by Douglas & McIntyre. Reprinted by permission.

1923 Several disputed pre-confederation treaties in Southern Ontario are resolved several decades after the government acknowledged that, because of missing papers, unclear agreements, or misunderstandings, the Indians had legitimate claims. These claims cover some of the most valuable real estate in Canada.

1927 A joint Parliamentary Committee decides that British Columbia Indians have established no legal claim to land. In place of treaty money, British Columbia Indians will get $100,000 annually. The Allied Tribes of British Columbia collapses soon after the ruling.

1927 An amendment to the Indian Act makes it illegal to raise funds or donate funds for the prosecution of any Indian land claims. The law remains in force until 1951.

1930 Control of natural resources is passed from the federal government to the prairie provinces on the condition that the provincial governments will transfer "unoccupied" land to the federal government for Indian reserves in order to meet the outstanding treaty obligations.

1931 The Native Brotherhood of British Columbia is formed by Haida Alfred Adams.

1936 Kwakiutl (Kwagiulth, Kwak waka'wakw) fishermen along the central coast of British Columbia establish the Pacific Coast Native Fisherman's Association.

1936 Responsibility for Indian affairs is transferred to the Department of Mines and Resources.

1938 Alberta passes the Métis Population Betterment Act, establishing eight Métis settlements in the province.

1939 Eugene Steinhauer spearheads the formation of the Indian Association of Alberta.

1939 The Supreme Court of Canada rules that Eskimo (Inuit) are to be legally regarded as Indians. This makes them the responsibility of the federal government.

1941 A census shows that the Indian population is growing steadily. Indian populations stopped their decline between 1911 and 1921.

1939–45 Up to six thousand Indians volunteer for service in World War II. Their status as non-citizens makes them ineligible for conscription or for certain veterans' benefits.

1942 The Pacific Coast Native Fisherman's Association merges with the Native Brotherhood of British Columbia (NBBC), which consists of Protestant British Columbia Indians.

1942–43 Andrew Paull leads the organization of the North American Indian Brotherhood, an attempt to establish a national Indian organization. It becomes dominated by British Columbia Roman Catholics.

1942–43 The Alaska Highway is built from Dawson Creek, British Columbia, to Alaska, bringing dramatic social change and new diseases to Indians in the region.

1944 Cree John Tootoosis spearheads the formation of the Saskatchewan Indian Association.

1945 Jurisdiction of Indian Affairs is transferred to the Department of Health and Welfare.

1946–48 A Joint Senate and House of Commons committee meets to consider changes to the Indian Act. For the first time, such a committee consults with Indian groups. Its report supports the aim of complete assimilation of Indian peoples but recommends that the Indian Act be revised to eliminate its coercive elements and that a commission be established to settle Indian land claims. Indian organizations reject the aim of assimilation.

1948 The last Sadliq Inuit dies. These Inuit of Southampton Island, in Hudson Bay, have gradually been wiped out by foreign diseases.

1949 The Indian Affairs Branch becomes the responsibility of the Minister of Citizenship and Immigration.

1949 British Columbia Indians vote in a provincial election for the first time. Only Nova Scotia Indians already have the franchise. Nishga Frank Calder becomes the first Indian elected to a provincial legislature.

1949 Newfoundland enters the Confederation without having negotiated land surrenders with Natives.

1950 The North American Indian Brotherhood and Native Brotherhood of British Columbia dissolve.

1951 The federal government passes a new Indian Act, which adopts the main thrust of the Joint Senate and House of Commons Committee report of 1948, significantly reducing the powers of the Indian Affairs Department but retaining the assimilative aim of the Indian Act. The government rejects the establishment of a land claims commission. The new act makes it easier for Indians to be enfranchised and to acquire location tickets. It also makes provisions allowing Indian children to be placed in integrated provincial schools.

1952 Indians in Manitoba receive the provincial franchise.

1953 Inuit families from Port Harrison, on the eastern shore of Hudson Bay, and Pond Inlet on Baffin Island, in Canada's arctic, are moved north to new communities at Resolute Bay (Cornwallis Island) and Grise Fiord (Ellesmere Island), both in the high arctic. Hundreds of Inuit were relocated in government-sponsored relocations beginning in the 1930s.

1955 The construction of the Distant Early Warning (DEW) line (a line of radar stations intended to warn of Soviet attack) in Canada's Arctic increases the presence of non-indigens in northern Canada and increases cross-cultural contact. Increased interest in the resources of the north also increases the non-aboriginal population of the north.

1955 Ontario Indians are given the provincial franchise. Some Indians boycott the polls claiming that the extension of the franchise threatens recognition of Indians as separate nations.

1958 Alberta Blood James Gladstone (Many Guns) becomes Canada's first Indian senator.

1958 Cree William Wuttunee spearheads the organization of the Federation of Saskatchewan Indians.

1959 The Union of Ontario Indians is formed as the first provincial Indian organization east of the prairies. Its membership is predominantly Ojibwa.

1960 Indians are given the national franchise.

1961 The National Indian Council is formed as the first truly national Indian organization. William Wuttunee and the Federation of Saskatchewan Indians lead in its founding. Though it seeks to represent status and non-status Indians, most of its members are non-status Indians and Métis.

1964 The Ojibway of Grassy Narrows in northern Ontario are moved from their island homes to a new mainland reserve. The move brings about significant social and economic dislocation.

Two Inuit fishing in a traditional manner.

1965 The Department of Northern Affairs and Natural Resources is given charge of Indian affairs.

1966 The Department of Indian Affairs and Northern Development is created.

1966–68 *A Survey of the Contemporary Indians of Canada* (Hawthorn Report) criticizes Canadian Indian policy, noting that Natives are an economically, socially, and politically disadvantaged group. The report, noting that Indians have been treated as "citizens minus," calls for a new Indian policy that would treat them as "citizens plus." Indian leaders endorse the report.

1967 The National Indian Council plans, and the federal government funds, the Canadian Indian Pavilion at Expo '67 in Montreal. The Indians use the opportunity to express their grievances.

August 1967 *Indians and the Law*, a study commissioned by the Department of Indian Affairs and conducted by the Canadian Corrections Association, issues its report. The report, the first in-depth study of the extent of Natives' problems with the law, criticizes the impact of police and legal services on Indians.

February 1968 The National Indian Council separates into the National Indian Brotherhood (NIB) and the Canadian Métis Society. The NIB will seek to protect benefits status Indians enjoy under treaties and the Indian Act. Walter Deiter, from Saskatchewan, becomes its first president (1968–70). The Canadian Métis Society will seek to protect the aboriginal rights of Métis and non-status Indians. (The Canadian Métis Society evolved into the Native Council of Canada in 1971.)

June 25, 1968 Leonard Marchand (Liberal), an Okanagan Indian (Interior Salish) from British Columbia, becomes the first Indian elected to the House of Commons. He later becomes a member of the cabinet.

July 25, 1968 The federal government begins consultations with Indian groups toward establishing a new Indian policy.

December 18, 1968 Mohawk from the Akwesasne Reserve block a bridge connecting New York State with Ontario in order to protest duties charged on goods imported by the Indians. The Mohawk claim the Jay Treaty of 1794 gives them the right to bring goods across the border duty-free.

March 1969 Quebec Indians become the last Indians in Canada to be given the provincial franchise.

June 25, 1969 Jean Cretien, minister of Indian Affairs, releases the federal government's White Paper (policy paper) *Statement of the Government of Canada on Indian Policy, 1969*. The discussion paper rejects the Hawthorn Report's recommendation that Indians be treated as "citizens plus," arguing instead that Indians' special legal status has hindered their social, economic, and political development. Thus, the policy paper proposes legislation to end all legal and constitutional distinctions relating to Indians. The Indian Act and the Indian Affairs Department would be abolished in about five years, and reserves, held in trust by the government since before confederation, would pass to Indian ownership. The provinces would assume the same jurisdiction over Indians as they do over other Canadians. During a transition period, Indians would be given aid to alleviate social and economic problems on reserves. The policy paper dismisses aboriginal land claims as too general and vague to be remedied.

June–December 1969 Indians and Indian organizations begin to unite in opposition to the government's White Paper. As early as June 26, Walter Deiter, leader of the National Indian Brotherhood rejects the White Paper, saying that it ignores both the views Indians expressed during the government's consultations and the special status for Indians as guaranteed by treaties. In the following months most aboriginal organizations fight the government's policy. Late in the year, Harold Cardinal, Cree leader of the Indian Association of Alberta, publishes *Unjust Society*, a vociferous denunciation of the White Paper.

September 1969 Trent University in Peterborough, Ontario, begins the first Native studies program in Canada.

November 20, 1969 In the *Drybones* case, the Supreme Court strikes down sections of the Indian Act that restrict liquor sales to Indians because they contravene sections of the 1960 Bill of Rights guaranteeing all Canadians equality before the law. This, the first ruling on the Bill of Rights, finds that the Bill of Rights prevails over other legislation.

December 19, 1969 Dr. Lloyd Barber, vice president of the University of Saskatchewan, is appointed land claims commissioner according to guidelines set out in June's White Paper. The appointment is denounced by Indian groups because the commissioner has no power to negotiate settlements.

1970 The Reed Paper Company in Dryden, Ontario, is found to have dumped mercury into the English-Wabigoon river system between 1962 and 1970, causing mercury poisoning on the Grassy Narrows Indian Reserve 120 kilometers downstream.

1970 George Manuel, a Shuswap Indian (Interior Salish) from British Columbia, is chosen as the new president of the National Indian Brotherhood. He serves until 1976.

1970 William Wuttunee, a Cree lawyer and former leader of the National Indian Council writes *Ruffled Feathers*, an attack on Harold Cardinal's *Unjust Society* and a defense of the government's White Paper. Several bands, including his own Red Pheasant band, respond by banning him from their reserves. Wuttunee, Blood Indian senator James Gladstone, and a small number of other leaders support the White Paper.

1970 The Canadian government begins funding various Indian organizations, thus marking the reversal of its 1927 law repressing Indian political organizations. Funding helps further strengthen organizations established or united by opposition to the White Paper.

June 4, 1970 Two hundred Indians from across Canada present *Citizens Plus* (the "Red Paper") to Minister of Indian Affairs Jean Cretien and Prime Minister Pierre Trudeau. The Red Paper was written as the Indian Association of Alberta's response to the government's White Paper. Following some revisions on June 3, Indian organizations from across Canada adopt it as the official Indian response to the White Paper. Taking its title from the Hawthorn Report of 1968, *Citizens Plus* condemns the government's proposal to remove Indians' special status and to transfer responsibility for Indians to the provinces. The Red Paper demands that the special legal status of Indians be retained and that treaty obligations be kept. It also calls for a reorganization of the federal Indian Affairs Department in order to make it more responsive to the needs and desires of Indian peoples. The Red Paper also calls for the creation of an Indian Claims Commission with the power to settle the claims. Upon receiving the submission, Trudeau implies that the government is willing to withdraw the White Paper.

September 1, 1970 A Cree band in northeastern Alberta takes over control of the Blue Quills school from the federal government, thus becoming the first Indian band in Canada to control its own school.

1971 The Inuit Tapirisat (Inuit Brotherhood) of Canada is formed as a national alliance of Inuit organizations to protect Inuit interests.

1971 A Canadian government census reveals that only 57 percent of the Indian labor force worked forty weeks or more in 1970. Of those that did, 62 percent earned less than $6,000. Of the total Canadian labor force that worked forty weeks or more, 33 percent earned less than $6,000.

1971 The government adopts a policy of multi-culturalism under which grants will be given to ethnic minorities, including aboriginals, to help preserve their cultural identities.

March 3, 1971 Dorion Commission Report (Quebec) notes that aboriginals have land rights in most of Quebec and that they deserve compensation for the loss of these rights. It recommends that the province seek to assume responsibility for Indian and Eskimo (Inuit) affairs in the province.

March 17, 1971 Jean Cretien, minister of Indian affairs, formally announces the retraction of the White Paper.

April 30, 1971 The Quebec government announces the James Bay Hydroelectric Project in northern Quebec. Construction on Phase One of the project, which would flood about 10,500 square kilometers (4000 square miles) and divert several rivers, is scheduled to begin immediately. The Cree and Inuit tribes of the region, who view the project as a threat to their way of life, have not been consulted before this announcement. Quebec has not negotiated land surrender agreements with the Natives of the region despite a 1912 agreement to do so.

June 30, 1971 A House of Commons committee on Indian Affairs recommends that control of education

A women's sewing group in a village in the Northwest Territory.

Coppermine kids, Northwest Territory, winter celebrations.

should be turned over to Indians rather than to the provinces. Since 1951 an increasing number of Indians are being educated in provincial schools.

October 1971 Manitoba Indians release *Wahbung: Our Tomorrows*, their rejection of the federal government's White Paper.

October 28, 1971 Alberta Indians begin a sit-in at the Indian Affairs office in Edmonton to protest conditions at reserve schools.

November 1971 The Association of Iroquois and Allied Indians releases its "Position Paper," a rejection of the government's White Paper.

November 17, 1971 The Union of British Columbia Indian Chiefs releases "A Declaration of Indian Rights—The British Columbia Indian Position Paper," usually known as the Brown Paper. It rejects the White Paper along similar lines as the Red Paper, but puts more emphasis on land claims issues.

April 21, 1972 Alberta Indians end a six-month sit-in at the Indian Affairs offices in Edmonton.

May 3, 1972 The Cree and Inuit tribes of northern Quebec file for a permanent injunction to halt construction of the James Bay Hydroelectric Project. This is their first court action to stop the development announced in April 1971.

December 1972 The National Indian Brotherhood (NIB) presents "Indian Control of Indian Education," which calls for greater band control of Indian education. The NIB statement calls attention to the fact that Indians do not enjoy parental or local control over education—rights taken for granted by most Canadians. The Department of Indian Affairs endorses the statement.

January 31, 1973 The Supreme Court rules in the *Calder* case that aboriginal rights to land exist in law, but that the rights of British Columbia Indians and of Nishga claimants specifically have been extinguished by government legislation. On this basis the court rejects the claim of the Nishga of the Nass River Valley in West Central British Columbia but greatly strengthens the case for Indian land claims.

February 14, 1973 The Yukon Indian Brotherhood presents the first northern land claim, *Together Today For Our Children Tomorrow*, on behalf of the twelve Indian bands of the Yukon Territory. Prime Minister Trudeau announces that a federal committee will negotiate the claim.

May 24, 1973 The federal government announces that Indians will be given greater control of their education and that responsibility for Indian education will not be transferred to the provinces without consultation with Natives. The National Indian Brotherhood welcomes the announcement.

August 8, 1973 The Canadian government announces that it will establish an Office of Native Claims, a branch of the Department of Indian Affairs and Northern Development. It will negotiate "comprehensive claims," claims for land not covered by treaty, and "specific claims," claims based on treaties, the Indian Act, or other legislation. The office will deal with only six comprehensive claims at a time. Indian Affairs Minister Jean Cretien cites the *Calder* ruling as influencing this complete reversal of the White Paper's land claims proposals. The Inuit Tapirisat welcomes the announcement. George Manuel, leader of the National Indian Brotherhood, expresses cautious approval.

August 27, 1973 In the *Lavell* case, the Supreme Court decides that provisions in the Indian Act that remove Indian status from Indian women who marry non-Indians are an excusable violation of the Bill of Right's equality guarantees. Most treaty Indian organizations welcome the ruling because they fear that the Bill of Rights could be used to strike down the entire Indian Act.

September 6, 1973 In the *Paulette* case, the Supreme Court of the Northwest Territories rules that Northwest Territories Indians have the right to file a caveat (notice of claim) on approximately one-third of the Northwest Territories, because there is significant doubt about whether Treaties 8 and 11 are legitimate land cession treaties. The case is appealed to a higher court.

November 1973 The Quebec Superior Court grants the Cree and Inuit of northern Quebec an injunction halting development of the James Bay Hydroelectric Project in northern Quebec on the grounds that Quebec has not kept provisions of the Proclamation of 1763 or its 1912 agreement with the federal government. The Quebec Court of Appeal overturns the injunction a week later, but the Quebec government begins negotiating the Indian and Inuit claims immediately.

April 1974 Indian bands in northern Manitoba form the Northern Flood Committee to represent them in negotiations with the Manitoba government. The government promises to compensate them for any damage caused by hydroelectric developments planned for the province.

July 1974 The federal government establishes the Office of Native Claims to evaluate and negotiate Indian land claims.

August 28, 1974 Ojibway Indians end a five-week occupation of the Anicinibe Park in Kenora (in northwestern Ontario) after reaching a tentative agreement with authorities. The Ojibway claim the fourteen-acre park occupies land taken from their reserve without their permission in 1959. The confrontation had become an armed siege on August 13.

September 20, 1974 Five Indians are arrested for assaulting and obstructing police officers as two hundred Indians, trying to storm the Parliament buildings in Ottawa, battle with police and the military. The protest started September 15 when the "Native Caravan" began traveling from Vancouver to Ottawa to demand settlement of their land claims and to protest the poor housing conditions and social services on their reserves.

November 15, 1974 The Indians and Inuit of northern Quebec sign an agreement-in-principle with the Quebec and Canadian governments to settle their land claim in northern Quebec. Cree Chief Billy Diamond and Inuit Charlie Watt lead the negotiations for the Natives.

1975 Uranium mining begins near Wollaston Lake in northeastern Saskatchewan bringing disruption to the hunting and trapping way of life of the Chipewyan residents. The Chipewyan had not been informed of the development, and few find employment in the mines.

1975 The Union of British Columbia Indian Chiefs and the British Columbia Association of Non-Status Indians collapse (although both organizations are later revived). Both organizations were formed in 1969 to lead opposition to the White Paper. A trend of forming organizations to represent status and non-status Indians of specific tribes lines gains strength. This trend is unique to British Columbia.

1975 George Manuel, president of the National Indian Brotherhood, is selected to head the World Council of

Indigenous People at its creation at a conference in Port Alberni, British Columbia.

April 1975 The federal government creates a Joint Cabinet-National Indian Brotherhood Committee and a Cabinet-Native Council of Canada Committee to improve communication between the government and Native organizations.

June 24, 1975 The British Columbia government and the Indians of British Columbia agree to settle the issue of "cut-off" reserve lands. Following the recommendations of the McKenna-McBride Commission the British Columbia government "cut off" (removed) land from twenty-two British Columbia bands in 1919 and 1920, but they did not get the Indians' consent to do so.

July 19, 1975 The Indian Brotherhood of the Northwest Territories and the Métis Association of the Northwest Territories issue the "Dene Declaration," declaring that the aboriginal peoples of the Northwest Territories form a nation with the right to self-government. Dene means "people" in most Athapaskan dialects.

September 10, 1975 Indian Affairs minister Judd Buchanan rejects the concept of a separate Native government in the Northwest Territories. He describes the Dene Declaration as "gobbledygook" and compares the position taken by the Dene to that of Quebec separatists. Indian leaders respond by calling for Buchanan's resignation, saying that he does not understand the declaration.

October 27, 1975 Seven Indian bands, including the Lubicon Cree band, submit a caveat on land in northern Alberta. A ruling on a similar caveat filed in the Northwest Territories suggests that such a caveat would be accepted in an Alberta court.

November 11, 1975 The East Main Cree, Montagnais, Naskapi (6,500 people), and Inuit (4,200 people) bands of northern Quebec sign the James Bay and Northern Quebec Agreement with the federal and Quebec governments and three Quebec Crown Corporations. In this way, Quebec finally keeps its 1912 agreement with the federal government to negotiate land surrender agreements with Natives. According to the agreement, the Natives surrender their claims to 1,062,000 square kilometers (410,000 square miles) of land for a cash settlement ($225 million over twenty years) and surrender their aboriginal rights in exchange for rights granted them in the agreement. These rights include significant control over their political, economic, and social affairs. The agreement creates three land categories in northern Quebec—Natives will own 14,000 square kilometers (5,408 square miles) and will enjoy exclusive hunting, fishing, and trapping rights on an additional 62,160 square kilometers (24,000 square miles). The general public will have equal access to the rest of the land. The agreement also includes income security for Cree hunters and trappers. Some Natives criticize the deal, claiming it compares poorly with a land claims settlement in Alaska (the Alaska Native Claims Settlement Act) in 1971, which gave the Alaska Natives 44 million acres of land and $962.5 million.

1976 A hydroelectric development on the Churchill River in northern Manitoba floods half the Cree community of South Indian Lake, causing significant damage to fishing, hunting, and trapping in the region. Indians affected by diversions and flooding were promised compensation in 1974. The flooding follows relocation of Indians from Chemanwawin, on Cedar Lake in central Manitoba, to nearby Easterville in 1965 to make way for another hydroelectric project. That relocation coincided with significant social and economic dislocation among the Indians.

February 27, 1976 The Inuit Tapirisat of Canada presents its claim to an immense area in Canada's Arctic. The claim, on behalf of all the Inuit of the Northwest Territories, follows a unique federally funded study of Inuit land use and occupancy in the Northwest Territories. It proposes to establish Nunavut ("our land"), as a new territory covering most of Canada north of the treeline. The territory, which would be taken from the Northwest Territories, would be controlled by the Inuit who comprise over 80 percent of the population of that region.

May 1976 The Yukon Indians (status and non-status) reach an agreement-in-principle with the Canadian government to settle their land claim. Under the agreement the Indians would retain title to 52 hectares (128 acres) per person and exclusive hunting, trapping, and fishing rights on an additional 44,000 square kilometers (17,000 square miles). The agreement would have them surrender subsurface rights to all the land. The membership of the organization rejects the deal because they believe it compares poorly to a settlement in Alaska in 1971.

May 1976 The Saskatchewan Indian Federated College, an independent college integrated with the University of Regina, is organized as the first college under Native control. Intended to encourage Native socioeconomic development and contribute to the general academic community, it will accept aboriginal and non-aboriginal students.

June 22, 1976 A team of doctors recommends closing the English/Wabigoon river systems in northern Ontario to all fishing because of mercury pollution. The Ojibway of Grassy Narrows have been told not to eat fish from the rivers, but they continue to eat them because the rivers remain open to sport fishermen. Experts have found evidence of Minimata disease (mercury poisoning) among the Indians.

September 1976 Noel Starblanket, a Cree from Saskatchewan, becomes the president of the National Indian Brotherhood. He serves until 1980.

September 17, 1976 The chief of Correctional Services in the Northwest Territories resigns after a racist prison manual is made public in Yellowknife.

October 26, 1976 The Dene of the Northwest Territories present their claim to much of the land in the western Northwest Territories. The claim includes a proposal for an Indian government for the Northwest Territories with powers like that of a province. Major centers of population would not be included in the territory of the new government. The Métis Association does not support this claim and instead is asking for separate funds from the federal government in order to fund their own claims research.

October 29, 1976 Thomas Berger, justice of the Supreme Court of British Columbia, issues a draft report of the Mackenzie Valley Pipeline Inquiry (Berger Inquiry) recommending a ten- to fifteen-year delay in the construction of a pipeline from Prudhoe Bay (Alaska) and the Mackenzie Delta to southern markets via the Mackenzie River Valley. Oil was discovered in Prudhoe Bay in 1968.

November 3, 1976 Indian Affairs minister Warren Allmand says that as long as Yukon Indians do not take a meaningful role in Yukon politics, the territory will not be given provincial status. Aboriginals account for half the population of the Yukon but have no representatives in the territorial legislature.

November 19, 1976 The Berger Inquiry on the Mackenzie Valley pipeline concludes its hearings. Televised hearings in the Northwest Territories have increased public awareness of the concerns of northern aboriginals about development on their traditional lands.

December 20, 1976 On a technicality, the Supreme Court of Canada rules against the Indians of the Northwest Territories for the right to file a caveat. The ruling does not alter the lower court's finding, which casts doubt on the legality of Treaties 8 and 11 as land cession treaties. On this basis, the federal government has already accepted the Dene claim as a comprehensive claim. The proposed Mackenzie Valley Pipeline would pass through part of the area in question.

1977 The Labrador Inuit Association releases "Our Footprints are Everywhere," a land use study similar to that done in the Northwest Territories. Later in the year, it presents the claim of the Labrador Inuit to land and sea-ice in northern Labrador.

1977 The Conseil Attikamek/Montagnais, an alliance of Attikamek (Tête-de-Boule) and Montagnais-Naskapi Indians of northern Quebec and Labrador, presents its claim to land in Quebec and Labrador.

1977 The Northern Flood Agreement establishes a process by which the Manitoba government agrees to compensate northern Manitoba Indians whose reserve lands were flooded by hydroelectric projects in the 1960s and early 1970s.

1977 The Federation of Saskatchewan Indian Nations and the federal and Saskatchewan governments reach preliminary agreement on a formula by which the Indians will receive land promised in treaties. The Saskatchewan Formula will calculate the land still due Indians by using 1976 population figures rather than population figures from when the treaties were signed.

February 1, 1977 A United States Federal Power Commission Report recommends approval of a proposed Mackenzie Valley Pipeline. The report suggests that land claims should not cause a long delay to the project.

March 1977 The Committee for Original People's Entitlement (COPE), established in 1969, presents *Inuvialuit Nunangat*, a land claim on behalf of twenty-five hundred Inuit in the western arctic. COPE was originally part of the Inuit Tapirisat of Canada claim presented in February 1976 but, because of differences of opinion, withdrew in order to present its own claim.

March 17, 1977 The Canadian government and the National Indian Brotherhood establish the Canadian Indian Rights Commission to replace the federal government's Indian Claims Commission established in 1969.

April 15, 1977 The Mackenzie Valley Pipeline Inquiry (Berger Inquiry) calls for a ten-year moratorium on construction of any pipeline in the Mackenzie Valley to allow time for the Indians and Inuit to settle their land claims with the government and for the residents to prepare for changes the development would bring. The report points out that residents fear the development and that aboriginals have not benefitted from northern developments in the past. The Indian Brotherhood of the Northwest Territories, the Native Council of Canada and the National Indian Brotherhood endorse the report, but the Northwest Territories Métis Association, which supports the principle of the development, expresses disappointment with the report.

May 1977 The Alberta government passes a law that makes it impossible to file a caveat on unpatented Crown land. The law is to be applied retroactively, effectively killing an attempt by several Alberta Indian bands to file such a caveat. The provincial government has been fighting the caveat since October 1975.

May 31, 1977 The Supreme Court of Canada upholds a federal order to establish an elected system of government at the Six Nations Reserve near Brantford, Ontario.

July 4, 1977 The National Energy Board endorses the Alaska Highway route for a pipeline from Alaska to the south.

July 29, 1977 Kenneth Lysyk, the chair of the Alaska Highway Pipeline Inquiry, recommends approval-in-principle of the Alaska Highway Pipeline but recommends that construction be delayed by two years in order that Indian land claims can be settled before construction begins. The report also recommends that $50 million in advance payments be given to help Indians prepare their claims.

August 3, 1977 The federal government rejects the proposals for separate Dene and Inuit governments in the Northwest Territories. These proposals are stalling negotiations on northern land claims.

September 28, 1977 The Métis and non-status Indians of the Northwest Territories present their claim to land in the Mackenzie Valley in the Northwest Territories to the federal government. This group had been part of the Dene claim of October 1976, but withdrew to present its own claim.

October 31, 1977 The James Bay Settlement Acts are passed by the Quebec and Canadian governments. This gives the James Bay Agreement greater legal force than former Indian treaties.

November 1977 The Naskapi-Montagnais Innu Association of Labrador presents a claim on behalf of the Naskapi and Montagnais tribes in northern Labrador. The claim includes a declaration of sovereignty similar to the 1975 Dene Declaration.

November 22, 1977 Harold Cardinal, former president of the Indian Association of Alberta, leaves his position as director-general of Indian Affairs in Alberta seven months after being hired. Indian bands had called for his resignation.

December 1977 The Inuit Tapirisat of Canada presents a revised claim to land in the central and eastern arctic. The revised claim was made necessary by the withdrawal of the Inuit of the western arctic from the original ITC claim.

December 8, 1977 A special Native commission created by the Native Council of Canada condemns the effects of the Canadian justice system on Natives. It associates the large number of Indians in jails with high unemployment, little education, pervasive poverty, and lack of opportunities among Natives. It also associates a tendency for Natives to become repeat offenders with the lack of adequate rehabilitation programs in correctional facilities.

1978 The Department of National Health and Welfare announces cuts in some free medical services to Indians. Some Indian groups denounce the move as an attempt to implement the policies of the White Paper of 1969.

January 12, 1978 The Naskapi and Inuit of northeastern Quebec sign an agreement parallel to the James Bay and Northern Quebec Agreement of 1975.

March 30, 1978 The Indian Brotherhood of the Northwest Territories changes its name to the Dene Nation and opens membership not only to treaty Indians but all Native people, including Métis. The Dene and Métis have claims to the same regions of the Northwest Territories, and differences between the two have complicated negotiations with the federal government since 1976.

April 13, 1978 The National Indian Brotherhood (NIB) pulls out of a joint Cabinet-National Indian Brotherhood Committee formed in 1975. Noel Starblanket, president of the NIB, cites lack of progress in issues important to his group and the NIB belief that the government is attempting to implement its 1969 White Paper.

June 1978 The federal government's discussion paper *A Time For Action* calls for Native constitutional issues to be addressed and identified in the upcoming constitutional reform process. Constitutional reform became a prominent issue after Quebec elected a separatist government in 1976.

September 28, 1978 The federal and Ontario governments, together with the Chiefs of Ontario establish the

Indian Commission of Ontario to help resolve land claims and other disputes in Ontario. The organization began after the Canadian Indian Rights Commission dissolved.

October 31, 1978 The Committee for Original People's Entitlement signs an agreement-in-principle with the Canadian government to settle the Inuvialuit (Inuit of the western arctic) land claim in the western arctic.

1979 The Inuit Tapirisat of Canada forms the Inuit Committee on National Issues to represent it on constitutional matters.

1979 The Native Council of Canada issues its *Declaration of Métis and Indian Rights*. The document claims Natives have rights to self-determination, to representation in legislatures and in the constitutional reform process, and to recognition of special status in confederation.

1979 Peter Freuchen Ittinuar is elected as the first Inuk member of Parliament.

January 1979 The Canadian Indian Rights Commission (a joint federal government-National Indian Brotherhood commission) is officially dissolved because of dissatisfaction on the part of the NIB.

February 5–6, 1979 Canada's first ministers (prime minister and premiers) meet to discuss constitutional reform. Indian groups are offered observer status at the talks, but boycott the meeting to underscore their demands for direct participation in the talks.

July 1, 1979 Three hundred Indian chiefs of the National Indian Brotherhood visit London, England, to press British politicians to block any change to the British North America Act unless Indians are given a greater role in constitutional reform discussions. The Indians are fighting the government's proposed constitutional amendment that would recognize the existence of two founding nations (English and French) in Canada, but would give no special recognition to aboriginals. Aboriginals demand direct participation in constitutional talks.

1980 The Tungavik Federation of Nunavut, formed by the Inuit Tapirisat of Canada in 1979 to negotiate its claim in the central and eastern arctic, agrees to set aside demands for the Nunavut Territory in order to get negotiations on its land claim started. The federal government refuses to negotiate demands for the territory.

1980 Negotiations resume between the Council of Yukon Indians and the federal and Yukon governments. Negotiations broke off after the Yukon Indians rejected a tentative agreement in May 1976.

1980 The Dene and Métis of the Northwest Territories approve the laying of a pipeline from Norman Wells, along the Mackenzie River, to the south.

1980 In the *Baker Lake* case, the federal court rules that the aboriginal inhabitants of the Northwest Territories have hunting, trapping, and fishing rights to the land based on occupancy, not based on the Royal Proclamation of 1763. The court, however, also finds that governments can extinguish aboriginal title unilaterally. The ruling includes criteria by which the court can determine whether a group has proven to have aboriginal rights to land. According to these criteria, members of an organized society have a legitimate claim if they can prove that their ancestors belonged to an organized society that occupied the claimed land to the exclusion of other societies at the time the government asserted its sovereignty over the area. Notwithstanding the ruling, the Indians of Baker Lake lose this case because the court finds that aboriginal rights do not allow them to prevent mining in the area.

June 9, 1980 At constitutional talks among Canada's first ministers (prime minister and provincial premiers), the premiers decide that Indian groups will be invited to participate only in discussions that directly affect them.

June 24, 1980 A federal report says alcoholism, unemployment, and poor living conditions are leading to family breakdown on Indian reserves.

June 24, 1980 The federal government announces that Alberta Indians will be given control over their own health care.

July 12, 1980 The Cree of northern Quebec file suit against the government of Quebec, claiming that the government has failed to live up to the James Bay and Northern Quebec agreement.

July 17, 1980 Twenty-eight female members of Parliament from all political parties announce that they will fight for the repeal of a section of the Indian Act that denies Indian status to Indian women (and their children) when they marry non-Indians.

September 8–12, 1980 The first ministers meet to discuss constitutional reform. Representatives of Native organizations attend as observers.

September 25, 1980 Indian groups file application in federal court to prevent the patriation of the British North America Act without Indian consent.

October 13, 1980 Seven hundred British Columbia Indians protest the number of Native children placed in non-Native foster homes in the 1960s and 1970s. As a result, the government begins to increase band control of child welfare services, a trend that also begins in other provinces.

November 7, 1980 Indian leaders hold a press conference in London, England, to explain why they feel threatened by Canada's constitutional proposals. Prime Minister Trudeau announces that he is willing to include a provision to protect aboriginal rights in the Constitution if such an amendment would be accepted by the premiers.

December 17, 1980 National Indian Brotherhood president Del Riley appearing before a Joint Parliamentary Committee on constitutional reform protests the lack of Native involvement in the reform process. He says aboriginal peoples want a third level of government that would allow them to control their own land, resources, and people. He also calls for the entrenchment of the Proclamation of 1763 in the new constitution.

Indians gather at the home of Grace McCarthy, Human Resources Minister, to protest the British Columbia government's child welfare policies. During the 1980s, Indians fought to take control of a wide range of government services as part of their claim to their right to self-government. Courtesy of *Vancouver Sun*–Ken Oakes, October 1980 (appeared in *Handbook of North American Indians*, vol. 7).

1981 The Stony Rapids band in Saskatchewan becomes the first band to receive its outstanding treaty entitlement according to the Saskatchewan Formula of 1977.

1981 In the *Taylor and Williams* case, the Supreme Court of Ontario finds that the terms of a cession treaty (a treaty in which Natives surrender their land rights in exchange for other rights) must be kept even if they do not appear in the treaty document.

January 30, 1981 The federal government accepts a constitutional amendment that would entrench the provisions of the Proclamation of 1763. Another amendment would read: "The aboriginal and treaty rights of the aboriginal peoples of Canada are hereby recognized and affirmed." Del Riley, president of the National Indian Brotherhood, endorses the amendments.

April 11, 1981 Ontario Indians present "A New Proposal for Claims Resolution in Ontario" to the federal and Ontario governments.

April 24, 1981 The Federation of Saskatchewan Indians and the Association of Métis and Non-Status Indians of Saskatchewan reject the proposed new constitution, saying that it does not go far enough in protecting Indian rights.

September 2, 1981 The United Nations Human Rights Commission rules that Canada's Indian Act violates international human rights because it discriminates on the basis of sex. The ruling was made in regard to Sandra Lovelace, a Maliseet, who had lost her Indian status and right to live on her tribal reserve because she married a non-Indian.

November 2–5, 1981 Nine of ten provinces accept an amending formula for the Constitution and a Charter of Rights only after amendments guaranteeing aboriginal rights (January 30, 1981) are deleted from the package. Several premiers oppose the provisions because they find them too poorly defined. The agreement meets with immediate angry denunciation by Indian leaders across Canada.

November 26, 1981 The House of Commons reinstates a reworded version of a constitutional provision agreed upon on January 30, 1981. The new amendment recognized "existing aboriginal and treaty rights." Indian groups demanded the removal of the word "existing" despite assurances that the word would not alter the intended meaning of the section. The House of Commons also adds a provision that guarantees a federal-provincial conference, with Native participation, to define these existing rights.

December 16, 1981 John Munro, minister of Indian Affairs, releases "In All Fairness," a new comprehensive Native claims policy, which implies acceptance of aboriginal land title in areas not covered by treaties and announces the government's intention to negotiate fair and equitable settlements that would allow Native people to live the way they wish. It also promises that the land claims process will be speeded up.

1982 The Penticton band becomes the first in British Columbia to settle its claim for compensation for land "cut-off" its reserve following the McKenna-McBride Commission report in 1916. The band will receive $14.2 million and 4,855 hectares of land. Twenty-one other bands await compensation.

January 29, 1982 The British Court of Appeal rules that Britain no longer has any responsibility for the protection of Indian rights in Canada. Indian groups made the appeal to the British court in an attempt to convince the British government to block patriation (transfer to Canada) of the Constitution.

March 27, 1982 The Wagnatcook Micmac band becomes the first band in Atlantic Canada to settle its specific claim. The Nova Scotia band will receive $1.2 million in compensation for land improperly taken from its reserve.

April 14, 1982 The people of the Northwest Territories vote to approve the division of the Northwest Territories into Denendeh and Nunavut as proposed in Dene and Inuit claims.

April 17, 1982 Canada's new Constitution and Charter of Rights and Freedoms is proclaimed by the British government despite opposition by Canadian Indian groups. Section 25 of the Charter says that its equality guarantees do not affect aboriginal treaty rights or rights recognized by the Proclamation of 1763. Section 35 of the Constitution recognizes "existing aboriginal and treaty rights of the aboriginal peoples." (Indians, Inuit, and Métis are explicitly identified as aboriginal peoples.) The Constitution also guarantees aboriginal participation at a conference to define what these existing rights are. Indian groups boycott celebrations and denounce the new Constitution.

April 21, 1982 David Ahenakew, a Cree from Saskatchewan, is elected to replace Del Riley as the new president of the National Indian Brotherhood. The National Indian Brotherhood announces its reorganization as the Assembly of First Nations (AFN), an association of chiefs rather than an alliance of bands.

May 13, 1982 The federal government releases "Outstanding Business," which clarifies its policy on specific claims. The statement expresses the government's aim to meet its legal obligations as set out in post-confederation treaties and the Indian Act.

July 1982 The federal government announces it will inject $61.4 million to deal with problems with the James Bay Agreement. The announcement follows reviews by the Indian Affairs Department and the Justice Department that found that the federal government is keeping the letter but not the spirit of the 1975 agreement.

September 22, 1982 The Parliamentary Sub-Committee on Indian Women and the Indian Act releases its report calling for an end to gender discrimination in the Indian Act. The Supreme Court upheld the discriminatory section in 1973 but the passage of the Charter of Rights, which guarantees gender equality, has once again put the law in question.

March 1983 Alberta, Saskatchewan, and Manitoba associations of the Native Council of Canada withdraw to form the Métis National Council, over differences on the constitutional negotiation process.

March 15–16, 1983 At a conference guaranteed by the 1982 constitution, representatives of aboriginal peoples, the first ministers, and the elected governments of Yukon and Northwest Territories agree to alter Section 25 of the Charter of Rights to recognize all aboriginal rights acquired in past and future land claims settlements. Section 35 of the Constitution will be amended to guarantee gender equality in the enjoyment of treaty rights. Native groups are also guaranteed participation at two more conferences to define the nature and extent of "existing" aboriginal and treaty rights enshrined in Section 35 of the Constitution. This is the first constitutional conference in which Native groups have full participation. Indian leaders endorse the amendments but express frustration at the slow progress being made on central issues.

November 3, 1983 The Report of the Special Parliamentary Committee on Indian Self-Government (the Penner Report) unanimously agrees that the aboriginal right to self-government should be entrenched in the

Indian chiefs open the first ministers' conference on aboriginal issues, March 1983. This conference, guaranteed by the 1982 Constitution, marked the first time that aboriginals were given full participation at constitutional conferences. Courtesy of Canadian Press (*Globe and Mail,* March 17, 1983).

Constitution. It suggests that Indian governments should be formed as a distinct order of government, with authority to control reserve land and resources. It suggests that present reserves are too small. The commission also recommends abolishing the Indian Act and the Indian Affairs Department. The report receives unanimous support in the House of Commons.

1984 A new government in Saskatchewan announces that it will not negotiate land transfers according to the Saskatchewan Formula of 1977, but according to population figures from when treaties were signed. This will reduce potential land transfers by about 155,000 acres.

1984 The Canadian Education Association reports that Indian bands that have taken over control of Indian education have witnessed marked improvement in student achievement. Since 1970, increasing numbers of Indian bands have taken over control of Indian education.

January 26, 1984 The Council of Yukon Indians sign an agreement-in-principle to settle their land claim with the federal government. The Indians would retain title to twenty thousand square kilometers of land and would get $540 million over twenty years to surrender their aboriginal land rights. National Native groups condemn this last provision.

March 8–9, 1984 The second first ministers' constitutional conference on aboriginal issues ends with an agreement to amend the Indian Act to guarantee gender equality but without agreement on the major aim of defining aboriginal rights. Six premiers reject a proposed amendment that would recognize the right to aboriginal self-government complaining that it was too vague.

May 17, 1984 Alberta Indians walk out of an Assembly of First Nations (AFN) meeting because of disagreement over the gender equality amendment. The Indian Association of Alberta then withdraws from the AFN for a time.

June 5, 1984 The final agreement is reached on the comprehensive claim of the Committee of Original People's Entitlement (COPE) on behalf of the 2,500 Inuvialuits of the Mackenzie Valley. This is the first comprehensive land claims settlement north of the 60th parallel. The agreement calls for the Inuvialuit to surrender their aboriginal rights in return for the rights and benefits provided in the agreement, which include a cash settlement and provisions regarding wildlife, the environment, and economic development. The agreement is unique in that it gives the Inuvialuits outright ownership of 82,880 square kilometers (32,000 square miles) including subsurface rights in 13,000 square kilometers (5,000 square miles). It also allows the Inuvialuit to participate in wildlife management decisions. The federal government also agrees to establish a 13,000 square-kilometer (5,000 square-mile) National Wilderness Area in which the Inuit will enjoy hunting, trapping, and fishing rights. Native leaders criticized the provisions that would have the Inuit give up their aboriginal rights in exchange for the rights specified by the agreement. COPE was formed in 1969 to represent the claims of all the aboriginals of the Mackenzie Valley, but by 1984 represented only the Inuvialuit.

June 12, 1984 The Micmac of Conne River, Newfoundland, are recognized as an Indian band under the Indian Act. They settled at Conne River in 1870.

June 21, 1984 The first amendments to the Canadian Constitution are proclaimed. The two amendments are provisions agreed upon at the first ministers' conference in March 1983.

July 3, 1984 The Canadian Government proclaims the Cree-Naskapi (of Quebec) Act according to a provision in the James Bay and Northern Quebec Agreement of 1975. The act gives the Natives of northern Quebec a type of self-government. The Indians no longer fall under the jurisdiction of the Indian Act.

September 9–20, 1984 Pope John Paul II visits Canada, but fog forces him to cancel a planned visit to Fort Simpson, Northwest Territories, where he intended to deliver a speech sympathetic to aboriginal peoples' demands for self-government. He promises to return to Fort Simpson at a future date.

October 23, 1984 The Gitksan and Wet'suwet'en (Carrier) Indians of the Skeena and Bulkley River Valleys of northern British Columbia initiate a court action to claim over fifty-seven thousand square kilometers of northwestern and north central British Columbia.

November 1984 In the *Guerin* case, the Supreme Court rules that the Canadian government must pay the Musqueam band (Vancouver) $10 million for violating its legal obligations to the band. The Court rules that aboriginal rights were not created by law.

December 17–18, 1984 Federal, provincial, and territorial leaders meet with Native leaders to discuss Native constitutional issues in preparation for a conference in March. They make little progress.

December 20, 1984 The federal government announces that the Yukon land-claims agreement has collapsed because several Indian bands want to renegotiate the deal.

February 26, 1985 Inuits from Grise Fiord, Ellesmere Island, in Canada's high arctic, meet with Indian Affairs Minister John Crosbie to seek help to move south. The Inuit were relocated from Port Harrison (Inoucdjuac), Quebec, in 1953. The government claims that the relocation was made in the best interests of the Inuit, but the Inuit claim the government moved them to assert its sovereignty over northern arctic islands.

April 2–3, 1985 At a constitutional conference on aboriginal issues, four premiers refuse to approve a constitutional amendment that would entrench the Indian right to self-government without a clear definition of such a right. The Assembly of First Nations refuses an amendment that would entrench the principle of self-rule for aboriginals but would not guarantee a process for defining such powers. The participants agree to meet again in June.

May 7, 1985 There is a second leak of contents of a preliminary report of the Nielson Task Force, conducted by Member of Parliament Erik Nielson, less than a month after the first leak. The report recommends the dissolution of the Department of Indian Affairs and the transfer of responsibility for Indian programs to the provinces. It also urges the government to stop negotiating comprehensive land claims and to cut funding to Indian organizations. It explains how the government can save $312.3 million by cutting funding to Native housing, education, medical, economic, and land-claims programs. Indian organizations condemn the report, comparing it to the White Paper of 1969. Prime Minister Mulroney says the report is not government policy. The task force had been commissioned to find ways to reduce government spending.

June 5–6, 1985 Constitutional talks with first ministers and aboriginal organizations fail to make progress in defining Indian rights to self-government. The federal government announces that it will begin negotiating self-government agreements with individual groups of Indians.

June 28, 1985 Passage of Bill C-31 removes sections of the Indian Act that discriminate against women in order to harmonize the Indian Act with the Charter of Rights and Freedoms. Some Indians protest that the federal government has no right to define who is or is not an Indian. Many Indian bands are also concerned about the effect of a sudden influx of new status Indians on reserve life and band funds.

July 29–31, 1985 The Prairie Treaty Nations Alliance, accounting for approximately one-third of the membership of the Assembly of First Nations, walks out of an Assembly of First Nations convention in Vancouver over disagreements arising out of the AFN's negotiating strategy with the government. The defection follows earlier defections by Alberta and Atlantic organizations. Incumbent AFN leader, David Ahenakew from Saskatchewan, facing questions about the AFN's $3.6 million debt, becomes leader of the PTNA. Dene Georges Erasmus from the Northwest Territories is chosen president of the AFN. Under Erasmus, the Indian Association of Alberta and Atlantic Indians return, and the debt is eliminated.

September 19–21, 1985 The Inuit Circumpolar Conference (ICC) meets in Montreal. Participants from Canada, the United States, Greenland, and Scandinavia discuss issues of mutual concern. The conference calls for the Canadian government to pay more attention to issues important to the Inuit. The ICC, first organized in Alaska in 1977, aims to promote Inuit unity, dignity, political rights, and economic self-sufficiency.

October 3, 1985 Indian Affairs Minister David Crombie announces a reorganization of the department in order to reduce manpower and move toward Indian self-government. He says money saved will be used to the benefit of Indians.

October 9, 1985 Leaders of the Roman Catholic, Anglican, Evangelical Lutheran, and United Churches issue a call for the governments to recognize aboriginal rights, including their right to self-government. They also criticize British Columbia's policy of refusing to recognize aboriginal title.

November 1985 Seventy-two Haida and their supporters are arrested while trying to prevent logging on Lyell Island (Queen Charlotte Islands, British Columbia). The Haida, who have protested logging in the area since 1974, filed a claim in 1983 and set up a blockade on October 30 after the British Columbia government approved logging on the island. The federal government and environmentalists have expressed interest in establishing a national park in the region.

December 1985 Minister of Indian Affairs David Crombie issues *Living Treaties: Lasting Agreements* (the Coolican Report), a revision of the government's comprehensive land claims policy. The new policy notes that little progress has been made in settling land claims. It announces the government's commitment to settling claims through negotiation rather than litigation. The new policy announces that land claims agreements would not necessarily require Natives to surrender their aboriginal rights and would be viewed as flexible over time. The policy also calls for agreements that will allow Native peoples to share in the financial rewards of development in their territories. Native organizations welcome the new policy as a breakthrough.

December 1985 The Ojibway of the Grassy Narrows Band and nearby Whitedog Reserve in northwestern Ontario accept an offer of $16.7 million from the federal and Ontario governments for compensation for mercury poisoning on both reserves and for land on the Whitedog Reserve flooded by a hydroelectric project in 1958.

October 9, 1986 Legislation giving the Sechelt band of Salish Indians in British Columbia self-government is passed. The band has agreed to a form of self-government akin to a municipal government.

December 1986 Indian Affairs Minister Bill McKnight unveils a new comprehensive land claims policy, which announces the government's intention to restrict land claims negotiations to land issues. The government will seek to make one-time settlements with Indians.

March 26–27, 1987 The final constitutional conference on aboriginal issues guaranteed by amendments to the Constitution of 1982 ends with no agreement on how to define Indian rights to self-government, and no agreement to meet again. Differences center around the concept of the "inherent" aboriginal right to self-government. Aboriginal groups argue that the right to self-government is an inherent one, one they have held since before Europeans came to North America, and one which they never relinquished. Several provincial governments and the federal government are willing to recognize a delegated and well-defined right to self-government.

April 30, 1987 The prime minister and the premiers unanimously agree on a constitutional reform package, which becomes known as the Meech Lake Accord. The first ministers formulate the new package because Quebec refused to sign the Constitution of 1982. This reform package makes no reference to aboriginal issues.

May 28, 1987 Native leaders hold a press conference to accuse the first ministers of holding a double standard in the Meech Lake Accord. They accuse the governments of being willing to enshrine an undefined recognition of Quebec as a distinct society after rejecting amendments guaranteeing aboriginal rights to self-government because they are undefined. They also protest that they were shut out of these constitutional talks.

July 1, 1987 The federal government announces an agreement with the British Columbia government to establish a national park in the South Moresby region of the Queen Charlotte Islands. The Haida have been protesting logging operations in the area.

September 20, 1987 Pope John Paul II visits Fort Simpson, Northwest Territories, thus keeping a promise made after fog prevented him from making a planned visit in 1984. The Pope expresses sympathy with Native desires for self-government and a hope that Canada will become a model in the way it treats it Natives.

October 1987 Negotiations resume between the Lubicon Lake Cree band in northern Alberta and the federal government regarding the band's claim. The Lubicon Lake band was missed when the government and northern Alberta Indians signed Treaty 8 in 1899. The band launched a claim in 1933 and were promised a reserve in 1940. However, no reserve was ever given to them. In 1980 an access road was built to their settlement area and about four hundred oil wells were drilled, seriously disrupting the band's traditional self-sufficient dependence on hunting and trapping. Most of the band turned to welfare. Negotiations with the government broke down in July 1986.

1988 The Canadian Bar Association issues a report denouncing the impact of Canada's justice system on Natives. It calls for reform that would allow for self-administered aboriginal justice system.

May 31, 1988 Georges Erasmus is elected to a second term as national chief of the Assembly of First Nations. He warns Canadians that the present generation of aboriginal people in Canada may be the last that is willing to deal peacefully with the government.

June 2, 1988 The federal government amends the Indian Act to clarify and expand band councils' powers to levy taxes. This is the first amendment to the Indian Act launched by Indians.

June 2, 1988 Mohawks at Kahnawake, a reserve on the south shore of the St. Lawrence River, block two highways and the Mercier bridge (which connect Montreal with its southern suburbs) for thirty hours to protest a June 1 police raid in which seventeen Mohawks were charged with smuggling cigarettes from the United States.

September 5, 1988 Representatives of thirteen thousand Dene and Métis of the Mackenzie River Valley reach an agreement-in-principle with the federal government to settle their land claim.

October 14, 1988 Mohawk Indians from the Akwesasne Reserve block the Seaway International bridge between New York and Ontario to protest an October 13 police raid in which seven were arrested on smuggling and weapons charges. The Indians claim that provisions of the 1794 Jay Treaty exempt them from customs regulations and their status as a sovereign nation does not make them subject to Canadian or American law.

October 22, 1988 Chief Bernard Ominayak of the Lubicon Lake Cree band reaches a preliminary agreement with Alberta Premier Don Getty on terms to settle the band's long-standing land claim. The agreement would provide the band with a 250 square kilometer (95 square mile) reserve. On October 15, the Lubicon set up a blockade on the road leading to their community after negotiations with the federal government broke down. On October 20, twenty-seven Indians were arrested when the Royal Canadian Mounted Police removed the blockade. The Lubicon gained international attention by organizing a boycott of "The Spirit Sings," an exposition of Native artifacts held during the Calgary Olympics in February 1988.

November 1988 Wilton Littlechild (from the Progressive Conservative Party), an Alberta Cree, becomes the first treaty Indian elected to the House of Commons. Ethel Blondin (Liberal Party) becomes the first Native woman member of Parliament.

November 1988 The Yukon Council of Indians (6,500 people) reach an agreement-in-principle to settle their land claim with the federal and Yukon governments.

September 11, 1988 The Innu of North West River in Labrador begin protesting low-altitude training at a NATO training base near Goose Bay, which began in 1980 by camping at the end of a runway at the base. The Innu claim that the flights are causing reduction of wildlife populations, particularly of the George River Caribou herd upon which they depend, and is causing distress to the Indians themselves.

January 1989 The federal government halts negotiations with the Lubicon Lake band after submitting a final offer of $45 million.

Dene girl at Blanchford Lake Lodge Springs Camp. Quinzee buildings and snowshoes.

February 27, 1989 The Ontario Court of Appeal upholds a 1984 finding that the Teme-Augama Anishnabai (Bear Island People) band of Ojibway had lost title to its land in 1850 even though they had not signed the treaty. The federal government had granted the Indians a reserve at the south end of Lake Temagami, in east-central Ontario, in 1885, but the Ontario government refused to transfer the land in the agreement. The Indians began their latest negotiations in 1973, with litigation in 1982.

March 1989 The federal government announces a ceiling on funding for Indian students attending post-secondary institutions. Indians protest with sit-ins and hunger strikes in Thunder Bay (western Ontario), claiming that the funding is a treaty right. Special funding for Indians in post-secondary education began in 1968 with the number of Indians in post-secondary institutions increasing dramatically since then.

May 10, 1989 Cree of northern Quebec file suit to stop construction of the $7.5 billion Great Whale Project (Phase II of the James Bay Hydroelectric Project) in northern Quebec. Studies by Hydro-Quebec confirmed that mercury levels in reservoirs created by the first phase of the James Bay project increased to up to nine times the federal government's guidelines for safety. The 1975 James Bay and Northern Quebec Agreement made provisions for this second phase, even bigger than the first, but the Quebec government elected to begin construction without the project undergoing the environmental review process established by the agreement.

August 28, 1989 The federal government announces that it will settle with a band (the Woodland Cree) composed of Indians which it claims have defected from the Lubicon Lake band in northern Alberta. This follows the federal government's rejection of an agreement reached between Chief Bernard Ominayak of the Lubicon Lake band and the Alberta premier in October 1988, and the Lubicon's rejection of the Government's offer of January 1989.

September 1989 The Nisga'a (Nishga) tribe signs a framework agreement with the federal government toward resolving their claim to land in west central British Columbia, but the British Columbia government refuses to recognize the legitimacy of the claim.

November 11, 1989 The Teme-Augama Anishnabai tribe sets up roadblocks on a logging road being built to give access to lands they claim near Lake Temagami in northern Ontario. The action follows an Ontario Supreme Court decision not to order a halt to road construction until the Supreme Court hears rules on their land claim. The Teme-Augama lost their case in the Ontario Supreme Court in February 1989.

1990 After reaching a framework agreement, the Labrador Inuit Association, representing sixteen hundred Inuits, begins negotiations with the federal and Newfoundland governments toward an agreement-in-principle to settle its claim.

1990 The Conseil Attikamek/Montagnais, an alliance of twelve Indian bands in Quebec, reaches a framework agreement with the federal government for their claim submitted in 1977.

January 26, 1990 An inquiry in Nova Scotia finds that, because of racism and incompetence in the police force and legal community, Donald Marshall, a Micmac, had been wrongfully convicted of murder in 1972 and spent the next eleven years in prison. The report recommends that the government establish a cabinet committee on race relations and a Native criminal justice system.

February 7, 1990 The Nova Scotia government issues an apology to Donald Marshall. The government announces that it will establish a cabinet committee on race relations and establish a Native criminal court as a pilot project.

February 20, 1990 The new federal budget places new limits on spending by the Indian Affairs Department.

March 7, 1990 The Nova Scotia Court of Appeal rules that provisions in the Constitution Act of 1982 give Micmac Indians the constitutional right to fish for food and give them some immunity from government regulations.

March 31, 1990 The Council of Yukon Indians, representing 6,500 Indians, and the federal government and Yukon governments reach an umbrella final agreement to settle their 1973 land claim. This agreement is designed to serve as the blueprint for negotiations between the government and the fourteen First Nations of the Council. It is unique in that it offers the Indians a share of federal royalties from mining and exemption from some forms of taxation, although the status Indians will give up their rights under the Indian Act in exchange for rights specified in the agreement. The Indians will retain title to 41,440 square kilometers (8.6 percent of the land in the Yukon) and will receive $242.7 million over fifteen years.

April 4, 1990 The New York State legislature passes a law that will require an environmental assessment of the Great Whale Project before it signs a contract to buy the power from the project. The legislation followed lobbying by the Cree of northern Quebec who oppose the project. The Cree began fighting the project immediately after the government's 1989 announcement that it would begin construction.

April 9, 1990 The thirteen thousand Dene and Métis of the Northwest Territories sign a land-claim agreement for the Mackenzie Valley in the western arctic. The agreement would give the claimants title to 180,000 square kilometers of land. Issues of treaty rights and self-government remain to be negotiated.

April 23, 1990 The Teme-Augama Anishnabai Indian band is granted a veto over logging on a tract of land, which they claim as theirs.

April 30, 1990 The Tungavik Federation of Nunavut, established to negotiate the claim of seventeen thousand Inuits in northern Canada, reaches an agreement-in-principle with the federal government in its claim for an immense area of the central and eastern arctic. Under the agreement, the Inuit will own 350,000 square kilometers of land and their corporations will be given $580 million for the surrendered land. It also includes provisions for the creation of the territory of Nunavut. Still to be negotiated are provisions concerning the extinguishment of aboriginal rights and conflicting claims of the Dene and Métis of surrounding areas in the Northwest Territories and the northern prairie provinces.

May 1, 1990 Two Mohawks die in gun battles at the Akwesasne (St. Regis) Reserve. Conflict centers around gambling casinos in the U.S. part of the reserve.

May 24, 1990 In the *Siuoi* case, the Supreme Court rules that a 230-year-old treaty signed by the Huron Indians of Quebec supersedes later legislation that contradicts it. The ruling is based upon Section 35 of the Constitution of 1982, which guarantees aboriginal treaty rights.

May 31, 1990 The Supreme Court of Canada orders a retrial for Ronald Sparrow, from the Musqueam band

Charlie Ugyuk, an Inuit carver, carving soapstone, Northwest Territory.

(Vancouver), who had been convicted of violating federal fishing regulations. The Court rules that Section 35 of the Charter supersedes wildlife regulations.

June 22, 1990 Elijah Harper, a Cree-Ojibway member of the provincial legislature in Manitoba, is able to use procedural rules to prevent the passage of the Meech Lake Accord in the Manitoba legislature. This effectively kills the constitutional reform package that aboriginals have been opposing since its inception in 1987.

July 11, 1990 A police officer is killed after Quebec police storm a barricade on the Mohawk reserve at Kanesatake (Oka), near Montreal. The Mohawk set up the blockade in March to prevent construction of a golf course on land they claim. After their failed attempt to storm the barricades on July 11, police surround Kanesatake. In sympathy with the Mohawk at Kanesatake, members of the Mohawk Warrior Society at Kahnawake (Caughnawaga), south of Montreal, block access to the Mercier Bridge, a bridge linking the southern suburbs of Montreal with the city. The actions initiate a seventy-eight-day standoff between the police and military and the Mohawk Warriors of Kahnawake and Kanesatake, a conflict that draws worldwide attention.

July 19, 1990 The Dene and Métis reject their comprehensive land claim settlement with the federal government because of concern over the provision that would have them surrender their aboriginal rights.

August 1990 Black South African Anglican Archbishop Desmond Tutu visits the Osnaburgh Ojibway Reserve in northwestern Ontario. He says Canada's treatment of its indigenous peoples is reminiscent of treatment of blacks under apartheid in South Africa.

August 9, 1990 The British Columbia government announces that it is willing to join Indians and the federal government in land claims negotiations based on the legitimacy of aboriginal title. The policy reverses the position held by every British Columbia government since 1864. The promise is made after Indians bands blocked rail lines and roads in the province.

August 20, 1990 Twenty-five hundred Canadian soldiers replace provincial police at Mohawk blockades at Kanesatake and Kahnawake. Since the conflict began, Indians in several places across the country have dem-

Inuit hunters in the Canadian North.

Repulse Bay, Inuit street scene.

onstrated and blocked roads and railways to express sympathy with the Mohawks and present their own grievances.

August 29, 1990 A report recommends the slaughter of a herd of wood buffalo in northern Alberta because they risk transmitting tuberculosis and brucellosis to cattle. Indians and Métis who depend on the herd for food reject the plan.

September 7, 1990 The Royal Canadian Mounted Police move in on the Peigan Lonefighters (a revived warrior society) camp, ending a month-long attempt by the Lonefighters to divert the Oldman River around the site of a partially completed dam. The leader of the Lonefighters, Milton Born With A Tooth, is arrested on weapons charges. The Lonefighters oppose the dam because it would flood land they consider sacred and because they fear its environmental effects.

September 25, 1990 Prime Minister Brian Mulroney announces a new government agenda to meet aboriginal grievances. He commits the government to speeding up settlement of all land claims and meeting all its outstanding treaty obligations. For the first time, the government will begin negotiating more than six comprehensive claims at a time. He also announces a commitment to improve housing, sewage treatment, and water facilities on reserves, and to increase aboriginal control over their own affairs.

September 26, 1990 The warriors at Kahnawake and Kanesatake surrender after an eleven-week standoff with police and soldiers. The seventy-eight day armed standoff attracted international attention and made Canadians more aware of the depth of frustration among many Native Canadians. The federal government refused to negotiate with the Indians as long as the standoff continued.

October 11, 1990 The British Columbia government signs an agreement to join the federal government in land claims negotiations with the Nisga'a (Nishga) Tribal Council.

November 1990 Thirteen Lubicon Lake Cree are arrested after logging equipment is damaged. The provincial government has approved logging on land which the Lubicon Cree claim as theirs.

November 7, 1990 The federal government announces that as a result of the rejection by the Dene and Métis of their land claims settlement in July, the government will begin negotiating with individual Indian groups in the western arctic, saying that such groups had indicated their desire to negotiate separately. Indian leaders accuse the government of adopting a "divide and conquer" strategy.

November 21, 1990 The Canadian Human Rights Commission condemns the Indians Act and the Indian Affairs Department. It calls for a new land claims policy to speed up the process and for a royal commission on Native issues. Indian Affairs Minister Tom Siddon rejects the recommendations.

November 30, 1990 The Naskapi-Montagnais Innu Association signs a framework agreement with the federal and Labrador/Newfoundland governments toward settlement of its land claim in Labrador. The claim was submitted in 1977. Negotiations were slowed by the group's claim to sovereignty, acrimonious relations between the Quebec and Newfoundland governments, and Innu protests of low-level flights at a NATO base at Goose Bay in 1989. Work begins on an agreement-in-principle.

December 19, 1990 The federal and Alberta governments reach an agreement with a band known as the Woodland Cree, formed in 1989 as a breakaway band of the Lubicon Lake band, which has been seeking a settlement since the 1930s. They also reach agreement with a band of Stoney Indians for compensation for land flooded by the Bighorn Dam on the North Saskatchewan River. Stoney Indians are Assiniboine Indians who live near the Rocky Mountains.

January 31, 1991 The British Columbia government releases its new guidelines for negotiating land claims.

March 1991 The federal and British Columbia governments reach a new framework agreement with the Nisga'a. The agreement follows British Columbia's decision to negotiate with its Indians.

March 8, 1991 The British Columbia Supreme Court rules in *Delgamuukw v. Attorney-General* that the Gitksan-Wet'suwet'ens of west central British Columbia do not hold aboriginal title to fifty-seven thousand square kilometers they claim, because such title was extinguished by British Columbia before it entered Confederation and because the Proclamation of 1763 does not apply to British Columbia. The Indians announce that they will appeal the decision. The British Columbia government announces that the decision will not change its policy of negotiating with Indian claimants. The Gitksan-Wet'suwet'en submitted its formal claim in 1977 and began litigation in 1984.

March 25, 1991 A federal-Alberta task force finds that Indians suffer racist treatment in the justice system. It recommends the establishment of Native courts and police forces.

April 1991 Indian Affairs Minister Tom Siddon announces changes to the federal government's policy of dealing with specific land claims. The new policy would accept some pre-Confederation claims and would inject more money and personnel into the process in order to speed it up.

May 1991 Ontario Premier Bob Rae announces that the Indians of Ontario will be given immunity from provincial wildlife laws.

May 24, 1991 The Nova Scotia legislature endorses the concept to creating a special seat in the provincial legislature reserved for Micmac Indians.

May 31, 1991 The residents of the Kanesatake Mohawk Reserve vote in plebiscite to hold direct band council elections rather than hold the traditional selection of leaders by hereditary clan mothers. The federal government ordered the plebiscite saying that negotiations on Mohawk claims following the conflicts of the summer of 1990 could not be successful until it could negotiate with one group that had the support of the community. The traditional leadership unsuccessfully tried to block the plebiscite through court action.

June 1991 The Department of Indian Affairs acknowledges responsibility for abuses incurred on Native children in residential schools. It promises to fund programs to help victims deal with lasting problems caused by the abuse.

June 12, 1991 Ovide Mercredi, a Cree lawyer from Manitoba, is elected as the new president of the Assembly of First Nations. He promises to take a tough stand with the government in his calls for a constitutionally entrenched recognition of the inherent aboriginal right to self-government.

June 26, 1991 Indian Affairs Minister Tom Siddon announces that the government will seek to ameliorate damage done to Indian societies by residential schools. Evidence of physical and sexual abuse at residential schools has been revealed in the past few years. Native leaders say that high rates of family breakdown, physical and sexual abuse, depression, alcoholism, and suicide are related to damage done by residential schools.

July 5, 1991 Constitutional Affairs Minister Joe Clark and Ovide Mercredi agree that the Assembly of First Nations (AFN) should hold its own hearings and constituent assemblies in an effort to reform Canada's constitution. The AFN would then share its information and proposals with the federal government. The constitutional reform process was prolonged after Manitoba Indians engineered the failure of the Meech Lake Accord in June 1990.

July 6, 1991 The Woodland Cree band, a band created by the federal government in 1989, votes to accept the government's offer to settle its land claim.

July 10, 1991 The federal government decides to hold its own full environmental review of the Great Whale Project in northern Quebec according to the Environmental Assessment Review Process (EARP), a process established to study the environmental impact of resource development projects. The federal government announces its own assessment because it cannot agree with the Quebec government on a joint review process. Native groups denounce federal review as a betrayal because it allows construction on the project to continue while the review is being done. The federal government claims that its EARP guidelines do not give it power to halt the project. The Natives of northern Quebec are pushing for a review based on the more rigorous guidelines of the James Bay and Northern Quebec Agreement of 1975.

July 13, 1991 The Gwich'in (Kutchin) tribe, Athapaskan Indians of the Mackenzie delta, reaches a land claims settlement with the federal government based on the agreement rejected by the Dene and Métis of Northwest Territories in April 1990. The agreement gives the Indians fifteen thousand square kilometers in the Northwest Territories and the Yukon. Negotiations began in November 1990 when the government announced that it would no longer negotiate with the Dene and Métis Association of the Northwest Territories.

July 24, 1991 Rev. Douglas Crosby, president the Oblate Conference of Canada, the largest Roman Catholic missionary order in Canada, asks Natives to forgive the order for the abuses Indians suffered at its residential schools. The apology follows allegations that Indians had suffered physical and sexual abuse at many residential schools.

July 30, 1991 Quebec Natives announce that they will determine their own course if Quebec separates from the rest of Canada.

August 6, 1991 Bob Rae, premier of Ontario, signs an agreement with Indian chiefs committing Ontario to push for the entrenchment of the aboriginal right to self-government in the constitution.

August 12, 1991 The report of the Manitoba Aboriginal Justice Inquiry finds that aboriginal peoples suffer discrimination in the justice system. It recommends the establishment of a separate aboriginal justice system that would give the aboriginal people the right to enact and enforce laws in their own communities. The inquiry finds that racism played an important part in the deaths of Helen Betty Osborne, a Cree woman murdered by non-Natives in The Pas, in northern Manitoba, and J. J. Harper, a Cree man killed by a Winnipeg police officer.

August 15, 1991 The Supreme Court of Canada rules that the Teme-Augama Anishnabai tribe does not hold aboriginal title to land it claims near Lake Temagami in Ontario. The court rules that aboriginal rights do exist in law but that because these Ojibwas had accepted treaty rights, they had become party to the Robinson-Huron Treaty (1850), which they had not actually signed.

August 27, 1991 The Quebec government announces that construction of the Great Whale Project (Phase II of the James Bay Hydroelectric Project) will be delayed one year. The announcement follows a negotiations between Quebec and New York State. The Quebec government hopes to sell most of the electricity to the northern states of the United States. The Cree of northern Quebec have lobbied New York legislators to refuse to buy the power.

September 7, 1991 Federal Justice Minister Kim Campbell announces that she is willing to consider fundamental changes in Canada's justice system in an effort to solve the problems that aboriginals face in the justice system. Campbell, however, rejects the concept of a separate Native justice system. The comment follows several provincial and federal reports calling for a separate Native justice system.

September 10, 1991 A federal court judge orders Ottawa to carry out an environmental review of the Great Whale Project according to the guidelines set down in the 1975 James Bay and Northern Quebec Agreement, not those set down in the government's

Environmental Assessment Review Process. The terms of the James Bay Agreement, unlike the EARP guidelines, would allow the federal government to halt the development until the review was finished. The federal government indicates that it will appeal the ruling.

September 18, 1991 A royal commission on electoral reform recommends the establishment of separate seats reserved for aboriginal peoples.

September 24, 1991 The federal government releases *Shaping Canada's Future Together*, its first constitutional proposal since the Meech Lake Accord collapsed in June 1990. The document proposes to entrench the aboriginal right to self-government within ten years. Leaders of Canada's treaty Indians denounce the proposals because the government refuses to recognize this right as an inherent right. Ovide Mercredi says the AFN will consider boycotting the parliamentary committee that will seek input. Métis leaders respond more positively to the proposal.

December 7, 1991 The Council of Yukon Indians votes to accept their umbrella final agreement on their land claim with the federal government. The agreement was reached in March 1990. The agreement establishes guidelines for settlements with the each of Yukon's fourteen First Nations. The Indians will receive title to 41,440 square kilometers (8.6 percent of the Yukon) and $257 million. The agreement includes provisions for self-government for the Indians.

December 11, 1991 The Law Reform Commission of Canada recommends the establishment of a separate Native justice system in Canada.

December 16, 1991 Indian Affairs Minister Tom Siddon announces that the government has reached a final agreement with the Inuit (Tungavik Federation of Nunavut) of the eastern Arctic. The agreement follows fifteen years of negotiations. The agreement would create a new territory of Nunavut in the eastern arctic. The new territory would be publicly governed although Inuit presently account for 80 percent of the area's population. The provision resembles part of the Inuits' original claim, but had been rejected earlier by the federal government. The agreement also calls for the Inuit to surrender their aboriginal rights. They would be given cash ($580 million over fourteen years) in exchange for title to most of the land, but would retain 350,000 square kilometers of land (approximately 17.5 percent of the territory). Dene in the western arctic and in Manitoba and Saskatchewan challenge the agreement because it covers land they claim as theirs. Other aboriginal leaders call for the Inuit to reject the deal because it requires the Inuits to surrender their aboriginal rights. The settlement includes provisions that would give the Inuits a voice in wildlife management. The agreement will be the subject of a plebiscite in July 1992.

January 24, 1992 The federal and Quebec governments, together with the Crees and Inuits of northern Quebec, agree on a environmental review process for the Great Whale Project in northern Quebec. The agreement follows Cree litigation and a delay in the start of construction.

January 28, 1992 Responding to the report of the Manitoba Justice Inquiry, the Manitoba government announces that it will hire more Native judges and improve legal services to Indians in the provinces, but rejects the suggestion that a separate justice system be established in Manitoba.

February 1992 The Cree of South Indian Lake, Manitoba, vote to accept a tentative settlement of $18 million in compensation for land flooded by a hydroelectric project in the 1970s. Critics call the offer inadequate.

February 14, 1992 Following a meeting with Ovide Mercredi, leader of the Assembly of First Nations, Constitutional Affairs Minister Joe Clark suggests that the government may be prepared to consider recognizing a limited inherent aboriginal right to self-government. In turn, Mercredi says the AFN would consider dropping demands that aboriginals be recognized as a distinct society. Two days earlier Clark had suggested that inflexibility of Indian leaders could lead the government to make a constitutional deal without them.

February 15, 1992 The Micmac of Cape Breton agree with the federal and Nova Scotia governments to establish an all-Native police force for Micmac on the island.

March 9, 1992 The Alberta Court of Appeal orders a retrial for Alberta Cree Wilson Nepoose who has spent five-and-one-half years in jail after being convicted of murder. The court rules that his conviction may have been a miscarriage of justice. Nepoose's family calls for a public inquiry, claiming that he was framed by police. The Crown announces that they will probably not retry Nepoose, and the provincial government rejects calls for an inquiry.

March 12–13, 1992 At a constitutional conference sponsored by the federal government, participants agree that aboriginal self-government should be entrenched in the constitution, but differed on the issue of what powers such a government should have. Representatives of federal and provincial governments and Native organizations participated in the conference.

March 26, 1992 The Canadian Human Rights Commission's annual report lists the injustices which aboriginals face as the most important human rights issue in Canada for the third year in a row. The commission recommends that the inherent right of aboriginal self-government be entrenched in the federal constitution.

March 31, 1992 The Quebec government blames the Cree of northern Quebec for New York State's decision to cancel a contract to buy power from the Great Whale Project, putting the project in jeopardy. The Cree have lobbied against the project.

April 1992 Representatives of the federal government, nine provincial provinces, two territories, and four aboriginal groups unanimously agree that the Constitution should recognize the inherent aboriginal right to self-government. The exact powers of Indian governments that would form a third level of government has not been negotiated, but aboriginal leaders and governments hail the agreement as the beginning of a new era for Canada's Natives. The Assembly of First Nations announces the creation of a women's committee on constitutional matters to meet criticism that it is ignoring the concerns of Native women. The Native Women's Association of Canada has argued that Native governments must be bound by the Charter of Rights to protect aboriginal women.

April 21, 1992 The Assembly of First Nations advisory body on the Constitution labels constitutional recognition of the inherent aboriginal right to self-government as its key demand. Other demands include the recognition of aboriginal societies as distinct societies and increased Native control over resources on and off reserves.

April 21, 1992 Georges Erasmus, former head of the Assembly of First Nations, and Rene Dussault, Quebec judge, co-chairs of the Royal Commission on Aboriginal Peoples, begin their work. The royal commission has a broad mandate to deal with issues affecting aboriginal peoples, including self-government, land claims, justice, and education. The work will take several years.

May 4, 1992 Residents of the Northwest Territories narrowly approve the creation of Nunavut in a plebiscite.

Ted Binnema
University of Alberta

Sites and Landmarks

UNITED STATES

♦ ALABAMA

MOUNDVILLE STATE MONUMENT
P.O. Box 66
Moundville, AL 35474
(205)371-2572

RUSSELL CAVE NATIONAL MONUMENT
Rte. 1, Box 175
Bridgeport, AL 35740
(205)495-2672
Archaic, Woodland, and Mississippian periods.

♦ ALASKA

ETOLIN CANOE
Tongass National Forest
Wrangell, AK 99929
No phone number available.
(On the National Register of Historical Places, 1/30/92)

♦ ARIZONA

AWATOVI RUINS
Keams Canyon, AZ 86034
No phone number available.
(On the National Register of Historical Places, 1/30/92)

CANYON DE CHELLY NATIONAL MONUMENT
P.O. Box 588
Chinle, AZ 86503
(602)674-5436

CASA GRANDE RUINS NATIONAL MONUMENT
1100 Ruins Dr.
Coolidge, AZ 85228
(602)723-3172
Hohokam village site, A.D. 500–1450.

CHIRICAHUA NATIONAL MONUMENT MUSEUM
Dos Cabezas Route, Box 5600
Wilcox, AZ 85643
(602)824-3560

GUEVAVI MISSION RUINS
Nogales, AZ 85621
No phone number available.
(On the National Register of Historical Places, 1/30/92)

HUBBELL TRADING POST NATIONAL HISTORIC SITE
P.O. Box 150
Ganado, AZ 86505
(602)755-3475
Oldest continually operating Indian trading post.

MISSION SAN XAVIER DEL BAC
1950 West San Xavier
Tucson, AZ 85746
(602)294-2624
Spanish colonial Indian mission.

MONTEZUMA CASTLE MUSEUM
P.O. Box 219
Camp Verde, AZ 86322
(602)567-3322

NAVAJO NATIONAL MONUMENT
HC 71, Box 3
Tonalea, AZ 86044-9704
(602)672-2366
Site of three cliff villages, of the Kayenta, Anasazi, and Navajo cultures.

OLD ORAIBI
Hopi Indian Reservation
Oraibi, AZ 86039
No phone number available.
(On the National Register of Historical Places, 1/30/92)

PUEBLO GRANDE MUSEUM
4619 East Washington St.
Phoenix, AZ 85034
(602)495-0901
Hohokam site, 300 B.C.–A.D. 1450

TONTO NATIONAL MONUMENT MUSEUM
HC 02, Box 4602
Roosevelt, AZ 85545
(602)467-2241
Prehistoric Salado Indian cliff dwellings.

TUMACACORI NATIONAL HISTORICAL PARK
P.O. Box 67
Tumacacori, AZ 85640
(602)398-2341

TUZIGOOT NATIONAL MONUMENT
P.O. Box 68
Clarkdale, AZ 86324
(602)634-5564

WALNUT CANYON NATIONAL MONUMENT
Walnut Canyon Rd.
Flagstaff, AZ 86004-9705
(602)526-3367
Sinagua Indian ruins site, A.D. 110–1270

WUPATKI AND SUNSET CRATER NATIONAL MONUMENT
HC 33, Box 444A
Flagstaff, AZ 86001
(602)556-7152
Ruins of the Lomaki, Nalakihum-Citadel, Wuwoki, and Wupatki.

YAVAPAI MUSEUM
Grand Canyon National Park
P.O. Box 129
Grand Canyon, AZ 86023
(602)638-7890
Tusayan ruins.

♦ ARKANSAS

KA-DO-HA INDIAN VILLAGE
P.O. Box 669
Murfreesboro, AR 71958
(501)285-3736
Caddo (mound builders) grounds; site excavation.

PIONEER WASHINGTON RESTORATION FOUNDATION
P.O. Box 127
Washington, AR 71862
(501)983-2828

♦ CALIFORNIA

DEATH VALLEY MUSEUM
Death Valley National Monument
Death Valley, CA 92328
(619)786-2331
Exhibits of local basketry; archaeological artifacts.

LA PURISIMA MISSION STATE HISTORIC PARK
2295 Purisima Rd.
Lompoc, CA 93436
(805)733-3713

LAVA BEDS NATIONAL MONUMENT
P.O. Box 867
Tulelake, CA 96134
(916)667-2282
Modoc Indian war (1872–73) museum.

♦ COLORADO

BENT'S OLD FORT NATIONAL HISTORIC SITE
35110 Highway 194 E.
La Junta, CO 81050
(719)384-2596
Adobe trading post built in 1833.

GREAT SAND DUNES NATIONAL MONUMENT
11500 Highway 150
Mosca, CO 81146
(719)378-2312

HOVENWEEP NATIONAL MONUMENT
Mesa Verde National Park
Mesa Verde, CO 81330
(303)529-4461

MESA VERDE NATIONAL PARK MUSEUM
Mesa Verde, CO 81330
(303)529-4475
Prehistoric Pueblo dwellings, with museums of Anasazi remains, A.D. 500–1330

♦ FLORIDA

TEMPLE MOUND MUSEUM
139 Miracle Strip Pkwy.
Fort Walton Beach, FL 32548
(904)243-6521
The largest Mississippian temple mound on the Gulf Coast.

♦ GEORGIA

ETOWAH MOUNDS HISTORIC SITE
813 Indian Mounds Rd. S.W.
Cartersville, GA 30120
(706)387-3747
Seven mounds; excavations.

KOLOMOKI MOUNDS MUSEUM
Rte. 1, Box 114
Blakely, GA 31723
(912)723-3398
Indian burial mound and village, c. A.D. 1250

NEW ECHOTA HISTORIC SITE
1211 Chatsworth Hwy. N.E.
Calhoun, GA 30701
(404)629-8151
1825 capital of the Cherokee Nation; a Preservation Project.

OCMULGEE NATIONAL MONUMENT
1207 Emery Hwy.
Macon, GA 31201
(912)752-8257
Seven mounds, c. A.D. 900

♦ IDAHO

NEZ PERCÉ NATIONAL HISTORICAL PARK MUSEUM
P.O. Box 93
Spalding, ID 83551
(208)843-2261
Early mission site.

♦ ILLINOIS

CAHOKIA MOUNDS STATE HISTORIC SITE AND MUSEUM
P.O. Box 681
Collinsville, IL 62234
(618)346-5160

DICKSON MOUNDS MUSEUM
Rtes. 97 and 78
Lewiston, IL 61542
(309)547-3721

STARVED ROCK STATE PARK AND MUSEUM
P.O. Box 116
Utica, IL 61373
(815)667-4726
Site of village occupied first by Illinois Indians, then Ottawa and Potawatomi.

♦ INDIANA

ANGEL MOUNDS STATE HISTORIC SITE
8215 Pollack Ave.
Evansville, IN 47715
(812)853-3956
Mississippian archaeological site; ten mounds, A.D. 1250–1450 Reconstructed structures.

CHIEF RICHARDSVILLE HOUSE AND MIAMI TREATY GROUNDS
Huntington, IN 46750
No phone number available.
(On the National Registry of Historic Places, 1/30/92)

SONOTABAC PREHISTORIC INDIAN MOUND AND MUSEUM
P.O. Box 1979
2401 Wabash Ave.
Vincennes, IN 47591
(812)885-4330
Largest ceremonial mound in Indiana.

♦ IOWA

CHIEF WAPELLO'S MEMORIAL PARK
Agency, IA 52530
No phone number available.
(On the National Register of Historic Places, 1/30/92)

EFFIGY MOUNDS NATIONAL MONUMENT
R.R. 1, Box 25A
Harpers Ferry, IA 52146
(319)873-3491
Burial mounds.

SPIRIT LAKE MASSACRE LOG CABIN
Arnolds Park, IA 51331
No phone number available.
(On the National Register of Historic Places, 1/30/92)

♦ KANSAS

FORT LARNED NATIONAL HISTORIC SITE
R.R. 3
Larned, KS 67550
(316)285-6911

PAWNEE INDIAN VILLAGE MUSEUM
Box 475, R.R. 1
Republic, KS 66964
(913)361-2255
Best preserved Pawnee earth lodge site on the Plains.

PAWNEE ROCK
Pawnee Rock, KS 67567
No phone number available.
(On the National Register of Historic Places, 1/30/92)

♦ MASSACHUSETTS

WAMPANOAG INDIAN PROGRAM OF PLYMOUTH PLANTATION
P.O. Box 1620
Plymouth, MA 02362
(508)746-1622
Outdoor living history museum of colonial period.

♦ MINNESOTA

GRAND PORTAGE NATIONAL MONUMENT
P.O. Box 668
Grand Marais, MN 55064
(218)387-2788

LOWER SIOUX AGENCY HISTORY CENTER
R.R. 1, Box 125
Morton, MN 56270
(507)697-6321
1835 Indian mission.

PIPESTONE NATIONAL MONUMENT
P.O. Box 727
Pipestone, MN 56164
(507)825-5464
Original Dakota pipestone quarry for ceremonial pipes.

♦ MISSISSIPPI

THE GRAND VILLAGE OF THE NATCHEZ INDIANS
400 Jefferson Davis Blvd.
Natchez, MS 39120
(601)446-6502
Ceremonial mound center for the Natchez Tribe, 1682–1730.

WINTERVILLE INDIAN MOUNDS
State Park
Rte. 3, Box 600
Greenville, MS 38703
(601)334-4684
Mounds, A.D. 1441

♦ MONTANA

BIG HOLE NATIONAL BATTLEFIELD
P.O. Box 237
Wisdom, MT 59761
(406)689-3155
Preserves scene of battle between Nez Percé and the Seventh U.S. Infantry, 1877.

CHIEF PLENTY COUPS STATE MONUMENT
P.O. Box 100
Pryor, MT 59066
(406)252-1289
Crow Indian Museum.

LITTLE BIG HORN BATTLEFIELD NATIONAL MONUMENT AND MUSEUM
P.O. Box 39
Crow Agency, MT 59022
(406)638-2621
Commemorates the Battle of the Little Big Horn and Indian wars on the Northern Plains (1865–91).

MADISON BUFFALO JUMP STATE MONUMENT
Logan, MT 59741
No phone number available.
(On the National Register of Historic Places, 1/30/92)

♦ NEBRASKA

OREGON TRAIL MUSEUM
P.O. Box 27
Gering, NB 69341-0027
(308)436-5794

♦ NEVADA

GATECLIFF ROCKSHELTER
Austin, NV 89310
No phone number available.
(On the National Register of Historic Places, 1/30/92)

♦ NEW MEXICO

AZTEC RUINS NATIONAL MONUMENT
P.O. Box 640
Aztec, NM 87410
(505)334-6174
Pueblo ruins at Chaco Canyon and Mesa Verde.

BANDELIER NATIONAL MONUMENT
HCR 1, Box 1, Suite 15
Los Alamos, NM 87544
(505)672-3861
Anasazi ruins, A.D. 1200–1600

CHACO CULTURE NATIONAL HISTORICAL PARK
Star Rte. 4, Box 6500
Bloomfield, NM 87413
(505)786-7014
Thirteen major Anasazi sites; more than 400 smaller village sites.

CORONADO STATE MONUMENT
P.O. Box 95
Bernalillo, NM 87004
(505)867-5351
Pueblo ruin, A.D. 1300–1600 ; reconstructed kiva.

EL MORRO NATIONAL MONUMENT
Rte. 2, Box 43
Ramah, NM 87321
(505)783-4226
Archaeological site of Inscription Rock; Pueblo ruins.

PECOS NATIONAL HISTORICAL PARK
P.O. Drawer 418
Pecos, NM 87552
(505)757-6414
Pueblo ruins; Spanish church ruins.

SALINAS NATIONAL MONUMENT
P.O. Box 496
Mountainair, NM 87036
(505)847-2585
Prehistoric pithouses, A.D. 800, ruins, A.D. 1100–1670; Spanish mission ruins, A.D.1627–72.

SALMON RUIN
San Juan County Museum Association
975 U.S. Highway 64
Farmington, NM 87401
(505)632-2013
Anasazi ruin.

♦ NEW YORK

MOHAWK-CAUGHNAWAGA MUSEUM
Rte. 5, Box 55
Fonda, NY 12068
No phone number available; located near Tekakwitha Shrine (see next entry).
Excavated Caughnawaga Indian village.

TEKAKWITHA SHRINE
P.O. Box 629
Fonda, NY 12068
(518)853-3646
Mohawk Indian castle; residence of Kateri Tekakwitha. Religious shrine and historic archaeological site, 1666–93.

♦ NORTH CAROLINA

MUSEUM OF THE CHEROKEE INDIAN
P.O. Box 1599
Cherokee, NC 28719
(704)492-3481

OCONALUFTEE INDIAN VILLAGE
P.O. Box 398
Cherokee, NC 28719
(704)497-2315
A replica of a 1750 Cherokee village.

TOWN CREEK INDIAN MOUND STATE HISTORIC SITE
Rte. 3, Box 50
Mt. Gilead, NC 27306
(919)439-6802
Reconstructed sixteenth-century Indian ceremonial center.

♦ NORTH DAKOTA

BIG HIDATSA VILLAGE SITE
Stanton, ND 58571
No phone number available.
(On the National Register of Historic Places, 1/30/92)

♦ OHIO

FORT ANCIENT MUSEUM
Fort Ancient State Memorial
6123 State Route 350
Oregonia, OH 45054

HOPEWELL CULTURE NATIONAL HISTORICAL PARK
16062 Route 104
Chillecothe, OH 45601
(614)774-1126
Twenty-three Hopewell culture burial mounds.

MOUNDBUILDERS STATE MEMORIAL AND MUSEUM
99 Cooper Ave.
Newark, OH 43055
(614)344-1920
The Great Circle Earthworks: Ceremonial grounds of Hopewell culture, 1000 B.C.–A.D. 700.

PIQUA HISTORICAL MUSEUM
509 North Main
Piqua, OH 45356
(513)773-2307
Collection of pre-contact tools and weapons from the Adena, Hopewell, and Fort Ancient cultures.

SERPENT MOUND MUSEUM
3850 Rte. 73, Box 234
Peebles, OH 45660
(513)587-2796
Adena culture.

♦ OKLAHOMA

CREEK INDIAN COUNCIL HOUSE
Council House Square
Okmulgee, OK 74447
(918)756-2324

SEQUOYAH HOME SITE
Rte. 1, Box 141
Sallisaw, OK 74955
(918)775-2413
1829 log cabin of Cherokee leader Sequoyah.

♦ PENNSYLVANIA

BUSHY RUN BATTLEFIELD PARK
P.O. Box 468
Harrison City, PA 15636-0468
(412)527-5584
Site of Chief Pontiac's rebellion, 1763.

♦ SOUTH DAKOTA

BEAR BUTTE STATE PARK
P.O. Box 688
Sturgis, SD 57785
(605)347-5240
Native American traditional religious site.

INDIAN MUSEUM OF NORTH AMERICA
Crazy Horse Memorial Foundation
Avenue of the Chiefs
Crazy Horse, SD 57730-9506
(605)673-4681
Crazy Horse Memorial project in the Black Hills.

THE HERITAGE CENTER
Red Cloud Indian School
P.O. Box 100
Pine Ridge, SD 57770
(605)867-5491
Art museum near scene of Wounded Knee Massacre.

♦ TENNESSEE

CHUCALISSA INDIAN VILLAGE
1987 Indian Village Dr.
Memphis, TN 38109
(901)785-3160
Museum and rebuilt Indian village.

PINSON MOUNDS STATE ARCHAEOLOGICAL AREA
460 Ozier Rd.
Pinson, TN 38366
(901)988-5614
Middle Woodland Period ceremonial site; mounds and earthworks.

RED CLAY STATE HISTORICAL PARK
1140 Red Clay State Park Rd.
Cleveland, TN 37311
(615)478-0339
Cherokee government seat, 1832–38; Cherokee Council site.

♦ TEXAS

CADDOAN MOUNDS STATE HISTORIC SITE
Rte. 2, Box 85-C
Alto, TX 75925
(409)858-3218
Caddoan village and ceremonial center with three mounds, A.D. 750–1300

♦ UTAH

ANASAZI INDIAN VILLAGE STATE HISTORICAL MONUMENT
P.O. Box 1329
Boulder, UT 84716
(801)335-7308
Excavated Anasazi Indian village, A.D. 1050–1200

EDGE OF THE CEDARS STATE HISTORICAL MONUMENT AND MUSEUM
P.O. Box 788, 660 West, 400 North
Blanding, UT 84511
(801)678-2238
Anasazi ruins, A.D. 700–1200

INDIAN CREEK STATE PARK
Monticello, UT 84535
No phone number available.
(On the National Register of Historic Places, 1/30/92)

♦ VIRGINIA

HISTORIC CRAB ORCHARD MUSEUM
Rte. 1, Box 194
Tazewell, VA 24651
(703)988-6755
Big Crab Orchard Archaeological and Historic Site.

PAMUNKEY CULTURAL CENTER MUSEUM
Rte. 1, Box 787
King William, VA 23086
(804)843-4792

WOODLAWN HISTORIC AND ARCHEOLOGICAL DISTRICT
Port Conway, VA
No phone number available.
(On the National Register of Historic Places, 1/30/92)

♦ WEST VIRGINIA

MOUND MUSEUM
801 Jefferson Ave.
Moundsville, WV 26041
(304)843-1410

♦ WISCONSIN

BARRON COUNTY PIPESTONE QUARRY
Rice Lake, WI 54868
No phone number available.
(On the National Register of Historic Places, 1/30/92)

OLD INDIAN AGENCY HOUSE
Portage, WI 53901
No phone number available.
(On the National Register of Historic Places, 1/30/92)

RICE LAKE MOUNDS
Rice Lake, WI 54868
No phone number available.
(On the National Register of Historic Places, 1/30/92)

WAUKESHA COUNTY HISTORICAL MUSEUM
101 West Main St.
Waukesha, WI 53186
(414)548-7186
Located on prehistoric burial mound of the Turtle.

CANADA

♦ ALBERTA

WRITING-ON-STONE PROVISIONAL PARK
P.O. Box 297
Milk River, AL T0K 1M0
(403)647-2364

♦ NEWFOUNDLAND

CASTLE HILL NATIONAL HISTORIC PARK
P.O. Box 10
Jersey Side
Placentia Bay, NF A0B 2G0
(709)227-2401

SIGNAL HILL NATIONAL HISTORIC PARK
P.O. Box 5879
St. John's, NF A1C 5X4
(709)772-5367

♦ ONTARIO

CHAMPLAIN TRAIL MUSEUM
1035 Pembroke St. E.
Pembroke, ON K8A 6Z2
(613)735-0517
Agricultural artifacts of the 1840s.

LONDON MUSEUM OF ARCHAEOLOGY
1600 Attawandaron Rd.
London, ON N6G 3M6
(519)473-1360
Archaeological site of a reconstructed 500-year-old Iroquoian village; prehistory of Ontario.

OLD FORT WILLIAM
Vickers Heights Post Office
Thunder Bay, ON P0T 2Z0
(807)577-8461
Reconstruction of the nineteenth-century inland headquarters of the North West Company, including a living history program reenacting the fur trade activities of Scottish Partners, French-Canadian voyageurs, and native Ojibwa.

SERPENT MOUNDS PROVINCIAL PARK
R.R. 3
Keene, ON K0L 2G0
(705)295-6879
Walking path to Indian burial mounds.

SKA-NAH-DOHT INDIAN VILLAGE
Longwoods Rd. Conservation Area, R.R. 1
Mt. Brydges, ON N0L 1W0
(519)264-2420
A recreated Iroquoian village of about one thousand years ago. *Ska-Nah-Doht* means "A village stands again" (Oneida).

Native American Place Names

UNITED STATES

♦ ALABAMA

Alabama: Name of state and river; meaning "clearers of thickets" (Choctaw)

Autauga: Name of county and creek; meaning "border" (Creek)

Chickasaw: Name of town; derived from tribal name (Chickasaw)

Choctaw: Name of city and county; derived from tribal name (Choctaw)

Conecuh: Name of county, river, and national forest; probably meaning "land of cane" (Creek)

Eufaula: Name of city and wildlife refuge; derived from former village name (Creek)

Mobile: Name of city, county, and river; derived from tribal name, probably meaning "the rowers" (Choctaw)

Natchez: Name of town; derived from tribal name, probably meaning "timber land" (Muskogean)

Sipsey: Name of town and river; meaning "poplar tree" (Chickasaw-Choctaw)

Talladega: Name of city, county, and national forest; derived from village name, meaning "town on the border" (Creek)

Tuscaloosa: Name of city and county; named after chief whose name means "Black warrior" (Choctaw)

Tuscumbia: Name of city; named after chief whose name means "warrior rain maker" (Cherokee)

Tuskegee: Name of town, institute, and national forest; derived from tribal name, meaning "warrior" (probably Creek)

♦ ALASKA

Alaska: Name of state, gulf, and peninsula; meaning "a great country or continent" (Aleut)

Anaktuvuk: Name of river and pass; meaning "dung everywhere" (Inupiat)

Iditarod: Name of river; derived from a former Indian village (Ingalik)

Kenai: Name of lake, mountains, and peninsula; derived from tribal name (Kenai)

Ketchikan: Name of city and lake; meaning "eagle wing river" or "city under the eagle" (probably Tlingit or Haida)

Kodiak: Name of town, island, and national wildlife refuge; meaning "island" (probably Eskimo)

Metlakatla: Name of town; derived from former village name (Tsimshian)

Nunivak: Name of island and national wildlife refuge; probably meaning "big land" (Eskimo)

Sitka: Name of town, national monument, and sound; probably meaning "by the sea" (Tlingit)

Skagway: Name of village and river; probably meaning "home of the north wind" (Tlingit)

Stikine: Name of river and strait; meaning "great river" (Tlingit)

Tanana: Name of village, river, and island; derived from tribal name, meaning "mountain river" (Athapascan)

Unalaska: Name of village, island, bay, and lake; meaning "dwelling together harmoniously" (Aleut)

Yukon: Name of river; meaning "big river" (Yupik Eskimo)

♦ ARIZONA

Ajo: Name of town and mountains; meaning "paint" (Tohono O'Odham, also known as Papago)

Apache: Name of town, county, lake, pass, and peak; derived from tribal name, meaning "enemy" (Yuma or Zuni)

Arizona: Name of state; meaning "small place of the spring" (Tohono O'Odham)

Chinle: Name of town and trading center; meaning "mouth of canyon" (Navajo)

Chiricahua: Name of mountains, peak, and national monument; derived from tribal name, meaning "great mountain" (Apache)

Chuska: Name of mountains; meaning "white spruce" (probably Navajo)

Cochise: Name of county; named after famous chief (Chiricahua Apache)

Coconino: Name of county, plateau, and national forest; derived from tribal name, meaning "pinyon people" (Zuni) or "little water" (Havasupai)

Hopi: Name of Indian reservation; derived from tribal name, meaning "the peaceful ones" (Hopi)

Kaibab: Name of town, plateau, and national forest; meaning "a mountain lying down" (Paiute)

Kayenta: Name of town; meaning "where they fell into a creek" (Navajo)

Maricopa: Name of town and county; derived from tribal name (Pima)

Mohave: Name of county, mountains, and lake; derived from tribal name, meaning "three mountains" (Mohave)

Navajo: Name of Indian reservation and county; derived from tribal name, probably meaning "large area of cultivated lands" (Spanish)

Paria: Name of river and plateau; meaning "elk water" (Paiute)

Pima: Name of town and county; derived from tribal name, meaning "no" (probably Spanish)

Yavapai: Name of county; derived from tribal name, meaning "people of the sun" (Yuman)

Yuma: Name of town, county, and desert; derived from tribal name, probably meaning "sons of the river" (Hokan)

♦ ARKANSAS

Ponca: Name of town; derived from tribal name, meaning "sacred head" (Siouan)

♦ CALIFORNIA

Azusa: Name of town; meaning "skunk hill" (Gabrieliño)

Cahuilla: Name of town and valley; derived from tribal name, probably meaning "master" (Cahuilla)

Chemehuevi: Name of valley; derived from tribal name (Chemehuevi)

Chowchilla: Name of town; derived from tribal name, meaning "to kill" (Yokuts)

Cucamonga: Name of town; meaning "sandy place" (probably Gabrieliño)

Gualala: Name of town; derived from village name, meaning "river mouth" (Kashaya Pomo)

Inyo: Name of mountains, county, and national forest; meaning "dwelling place of a great spirit" (probably Paiute)

Lompoc: Name of town; probably meaning "where the waters break through" (Chumash)

Malibu: Name of city; probably derived from former village name (Chumash)

Marin: Name of county and peninsula; named after a leader (Coast Miwok)

Napa: Name of town and county; meaning "house" or "fish" (probably Patwin)

Ojai: Name of town; meaning "moon" (Chumash)

Otay: Name of town; meaning "brushy" (Diegueño)

Pala: Name of town; probably meaning "water" (Luiseño)

Petaluma: Name of town; derived from village and tribal name, meaning "flat" (Coast Miwok)

Simi: Name of valley; probably meaning "valley of the wind" or "village" (Chumash)

Sonoma: Name of town and county; derived from village name (Coast Miwok)

Tahoe: Name of city, lake, and national forest; meaning "big water" (Washo)

♦ COLORADO

Apishapa: Name of river; meaning "standing water" (Ute)

Kiowa: Name of town and county; derived from tribal name, meaning "principal people" (Shoshonean and Tanoan)

Montezuma: Name of town and county; named after the ruler of Mexico (Aztec)

Uncompahgre: Name of mountains, peak, plateau, river, and national forest; meaning "red water canyon" (Ute)

Yampa: Name of town and river; derived from name of band and name of edible root (Ute)

♦ CONNECTICUT

Connecticut: Name of state and river; meaning "the long river" (Mohican)

Mystic: Name of town; meaning "great tidal river" (Algonkian)

Naugatuck: Name of town and river; meaning "long tree" (Algonkian)

Niantic: Name of town and river; derived from tribal name, meaning "at the point of land on a tidal river" (Algonkian)

Ouray: Name of town, county, and peak; named after chief, probably meaning "the arrow" (probably Algonkian)

Saugatuck: Name of town, river, and reservoir; meaning "tidal outlet" (Paugusett)

Taconic: Name of town and mountain; probably meaning "forest" (Algonkian)

Willimantic: Name of river and reservoir; meaning "good cedar swamp" (Nipmuc)

Yantic: Name of town and river; meaning "tidal limit" (Mohegan)

♦ DELAWARE

Minquadale: Name of town; derived from Iroquorian tribe also known as Susquehanna (Iroquois)

♦ FLORIDA

Alachua: Name of town and county; meaning "grassy, marshy plain" (probably Creek)

Apalachicola: Name of town, river, bay, and national forest; meaning "people on the other side" (Hitchiti)

Chokoloskee: Name of town; meaning "old house" (Seminole)

Chuluota: Name of town; meaning "fox den" (probably Seminole)

Loxahatchee: Name of town and river; meaning "turtle river" (Seminole)

Miami: Name of city; meaning "people of the peninsula" (Ojibway)

Micanopy: Name of town; meaning "head chief" (Seminole)

Miccosukee: Name of town and lake; derived from tribal name (probably Muskogean)

Myakka: Name of town and river; derived from former village name (Timucuan)

Ocala: Name of town and national forest; derived from former village name (Timucuan)

Ochlockonee: Name of river; meaning "yellow water" (Hitchiti)

Okaloosa: Name of county; meaning "black water" (Choctaw)

Okeechobee: Name of town, county, and lake; meaning "big water" (Hitchiti)

Pensacola: Name of town and river; derived from tribal name, meaning "long-haired people" (Choctaw)

Seminole: Name of town, county, and lake; derived from tribal name, meaning "runaway" or "pioneer" (Muskogean)

Steinhatchee: Name of town and river; meaning "man-his-river" (Seminole)

Suwannee: Name of town, county, sound, and river; meaning "echo" (probably Algonkian)

Tallahassee: Name of city and bay; derived from village name, meaning "old town" (Creek)

Tampa: Name of city and bay; derived from village name, meaning "near it" (probably Muskogean)

Wakulla: Name of town, county, river, and springs; meaning "loon" (Seminole)

♦ GEORGIA

Alapaha: Name of town; derived from former village name (Seminole)

Canoochee: Name of town and river; derived from name of an ancient Indian region (Creek)

Catoosa: Name of county; named after chief whose name means "high place" (probably Cherokee)

Chickamauga: Name of town and river; derived from tribal name, meaning "sluggish water" (Cherokee)

Coosa: Name of town; derived from tribal name, meaning "reed" (Creek)

Ellijay: Name of town; derived from former village name (Cherokee)

Hiawassee: Name of town; meaning "meadow" (Cherokee)

Muscogee: Name of county; derived from tribal name (Muskogean)

Ocmulgee: Name of river and national monument; derived from tribal name, meaning "where the water bubbles up" (Hitchiti)

Oconee: Name of town, county, river, and national forest; meaning "water" (Muskogean)

Okefenokee: Name of swamp and national wildlife refuge; meaning "trembling water" (Hitchiti)

Satolah: Name of town and battlefield; meaning "six" (Cherokee)

Savannah: Name of river; meaning "southerner" (Shawnee)

Withlacoochie: Name of river; meaning "little creek" (Creek)

♦ IDAHO

Bannock: Name of county, river, mountain and peak; derived from tribal name, meaning "hair in backward motion" (Shoshonean)

Blackfoot: Name of river and reservoir; derived from tribal name referring to their dyeing their moccasins black (Algonkian)

Kootenai: Name of county, river and national wildlife refuge; derived from tribal name, meaning "water people" (Algonkian)

Lochsa: Name of river; meaning "rough water" (Flathead)

Minidoka: Name of town, county, national wildlife refuge; meaning "broad expanse" (probably Shoshonean)

Nez Percé: Name of town, county, and national forest; derived from tribal name, meaning "pierced nose" (French version of Indian word)

Pocatello: Name of city; named after Bannock chief, probably meaning "the wayward one" (Shoshonean)

Potlatch: Name of town; meaning "giveaway," a type of public event (Chinook)

Shoshone: Name of town, county, and falls; derived from tribal name (Shoshonean)

Targhee: Name of pass and national forest; probably named after Shoshoni chief (Bannock)

♦ ILLINOIS

Aptakisic: Name of town; named after chief whose name means "halfday" (Potawatomi)

Cahokia: Name of town; derived from tribal name (Cahokia)

Chicago: Name of city and river; meaning "onion place" (Algonkian)

Chillicothe: Name of town; derived from tribal name, meaning "village" (probably Shawnee)

Illinois: Name of state and river; derived from tribal name, meaning "men" (Algonkian)

Iroquois: Name of city, county, and river; derived from tribal name, meaning "real adders" (Algonkian, with French spelling)

Kankakee: Name of town, county, and river; meaning "wolf land" (Mohegan)

Kaskaskia: Name of river; derived from tribal name (Kaskaskia)

Macoupin: Name of county; meaning "potato" (Algonkian)

Ottawa: Name of city; derived from tribal name, meaning "to trade" (Algonkian)

Peoria: Name of town and county; derived from tribal name, meaning "carriers" (Peoria)

Prophetstown: Name of town; named after medicine man, White Cloud (English version of Winnebago word)

Sangamon: Name of county and river; probably meaning "outlet" (Ojibway)

Sauk: Name of town; derived from tribal name, meaning "people of the yellow earth" (Algonkian)

Skokie: Name of town and river; meaning "marsh" (Potawatomi)

Spoon: Name of river; meaning "mussel shell" (Algonkian)

Waukegan: Name of town; meaning "trading post" (Algonkian)

♦ INDIANA

Genesee: Name of city; meaning "beautiful valley" (Algonkian)

Indiana: Name of state and county; derived from the Latinized form of Indian

Kokomo: Name of city; named after chief whose name means "black walnut" (Miami)

Muncie: Name of city; derived from tribal name, meaning "people of the stone country" (Algonkian)

Muscatatuck: Name of river and national wildlife refuge; meaning "clear river" (Delaware)

Wabash: Name of county and river; meaning "white water" (Miami)

♦ IOWA

Black Hawk: Name of city, county, and lake; named after chief of Sauk and Fox tribes

Iowa: Name of state, county, river, and falls; derived from tribal name, meaning "sleepy ones" (Siouan)

Keokuk: Name of town and county; named after Fox chief whose name means "he who moves around alert" (Algonkian)

Lakota: Name of city; derived from tribal name (often called Sioux), meaning "allies" (Siouan)

Maquoketa: Name of town and river; meaning "bear river" (Algonkian)

Muscatine: Name of town, county, and island; derived from tribal name (Muscatine)

Oskaloosa: Name of town; named after one of Osceola's wives whose name means "black water" (Choctaw)

Oto: Name of town; derived from tribal name, meaning "lovers" or "lechers" (Siouan)

Pocahontas: Name of city and county; named after the Indian princess whose name means "radiant" or "playful" (Algonkian)

Poweshiek: Name of county; named after chief whose name means "he who shakes something off" (Fox)

Sac: Name of city and county; derived from tribal name (same as Sauk), meaning "people of the yellow earth" (Algonkian)

Sioux: Name of city, county, and river; derived from Ojibway word, meaning "snakes" or "enemies" (French version of Ojibway word for Dakota)

Wapello: Name of town and county; named after Fox chief whose name means "he, of the morning" (Algonkian)

Wapsipinicon: Name of river; meaning "white potato" (Algonkian)

Winneshiek: Name of county; named after chief (Winnebago)

♦ KANSAS

Comanche: Name of county; derived from tribal name, meaning "always ready to fight" (Shoshonean)

Kansas: Name of state, city, and river; derived from tribal name, meaning "people of the south wind" (Siouan)

Kiowa: Name of county; derived from tribal name, meaning "principal people" (Shoshonean and Tanoan)

Osage: Name of city, county, and river; derived from tribal name, probably meaning "people" (Siouan)

Potawatomi: Name of county; derived from tribal name, meaning "people of the place of fire" (Algonkian)

Satanta: Name of city; named after chief (Kiowa)

Shawnee: Name of city and county; derived from tribal name, meaning "southerner" (Algonkian)

Topeka: Name of city; meaning "good potato place" (Kansa)

Wabaunsee: Name of county; named after Potawatomi chief (Algonkian)

Wichita: Name of city and county; derived from tribal name, meaning "man" (Caddoan)

♦ KENTUCKY

Kentucky: Name of state, lake, and river; meaning "land of tomorrow" (Wyandotte) or "meadow land" (Iroquoian)

Paducah: Name of town; named after chief and derived from tribal name (Chickasaw)

♦ LOUISIANA

Atchafalaya: Name of bay and river; meaning "long river" (Choctaw)

Bogalusa: Name of town; meaning "large stream" (Choctaw)

Caddo: Name of parish and lake; derived from tribal name, meaning "chief" (Caddoan)

Coushatta: Name of town; derived from tribal name, meaning "white canebreak" (Choctaw)

Houma: Name of town; derived from tribal name, meaning "red" (Choctaw)

Kisatchie: Name of town and national forest; meaning "reed river" (Choctaw)

Natchez: Name of city; derived from tribal name, probably meaning "timber land" (Muskogean)

Natchitoches: Name of town and parish; derived from tribal name, meaning "chestnut eaters" (Caddoan)

Tichfaw: Name of town and river; probably meaning "pine rest" (Choctaw)

Tunica: Name of town; derived from tribal name, meaning "the people" (Tunican)

♦ MAINE

Allagash: Name of river; meaning "bark shelter" (Abnaki)

Androscoggin: Name of county, river, and lake; derived from tribal name, meaning "fish spearing" (probably Algonkian)

Aroostook: Name of county and river; meaning "good, beautiful, or clear river" (Algonkian)

Kennebec: Name of county and river; meaning "long lake" (Algonkian)

Kennebunk: Name of town and river; meaning "long cut bank" (Algonkian)

Passadumkeag: Name of town and mountains; meaning "rapids over sandy places" (Abnaki)

Penobscot: Name of county, bay, lake, and river; derived from tribal name, meaning "rocky place" (Algonkian)

Piscataquis: Name of county and river; meaning "at the fork of the river" (Abnaki)

Saco: Name of town and river (Algonkian)

Sagadahoc: Name of county; meaning "mouth of river" (Algonkian)

Sebec: Name of town and lake; meaning "big lake" (Algonkian)

Seboeis: Name of town, lake, and river; meaning "small lake" (Algonkian)

Tulamdie: Name of river; meaning "canoe sandbar" (Algonkian)

♦ MARYLAND

Nanticoke: Name of town and river; derived from tribal name, meaning "tidewater people" (Delaware)

Pocomoke: Name of town and sound; meaning "small field" (Algonkian)

Potomac: Name of city and river; derived from tribal name, meaning "where the goods are brought in" (probably Algonkian)

Wicomico: Name of county and river; derived from tribal name, meaning "pleasant village" (Delaware)

♦ MASSACHUSETTS

Chappaquiddick: Name of island; meaning "separated island" (Wampanoag)

Chicopee: Name of town and river; meaning "swift water" (Algonkian)

Housatonic: Name of town and river; meaning "at the place beyond the mountain" (Mahican)

Massachusetts: Name of state and bay; meaning "great hill" (Algonkian)

Muskegel: Name of channel and island; meaning "grassy place" (Wampanoag)

Nantucket: Name of county, island, and sound; meaning "narrow tidal river at" (Algonkian)

Natick: Name of town; derived from tribal name, meaning "a place of hills" (Algonkian)

Weweantic: Name of river; meaning "crooked river" (Algonkian)

♦ MICHIGAN

Cheboygan: Name of town, county, and river; probably meaning "pipe" (Algonkian)

Chippewa: Name of county and river; derived from tribal name, meaning "voice" and "gathering up" (Ojibway)

Gogebic: Name of county and lake; meaning "high lake" (Ojibway)

Kalamazoo: Name of town and county; meaning "it smokes" (Algonkian)

Mackinaw: Name of town, county, island, and straits; meaning "island of the large turtle" (Ojibway)

Manistee: Name of town, county, river, and national forest; meaning "crooked river" (Ojibway)

Manitou: Name of islands; meaning "spirit" (Algonkian)

Mecosta: Name of county; named after chief whose name means "bear cub" (Potawatomi)

Menominee: Name of town, county, river, and mountains; derived from tribal name, meaning "wild rice people" (Algonkian)

Michigan: Name of state and one of the Great Lakes; meaning "big lake" (Ojibway)

Missaukee: Name of county and lake; after Ottowa chief whose name means "big outlet at" (probably Algonkian)

Munuscong: Name of lake and river; meaning "the place of the reeds" (Algonkian)

Muskegon: Name of town, county, and river; meaning "swampy" (Ojibway)

Ontonagon: Name of town, county, and river; meaning "a place where game was shot by luck" (Ojibway)

Otsego: Name of town, county, and lake; meaning "rock place" (Iroquoian)

Pontiac: Name of city; named after Ottawa chief (probably Algonkian)

Sanilac: Name of county; named after Wyandotte chief (probably Iroquoian)

Shiawassee: Name of county and national wildlife refuge; meaning "straight ahead water" (Algonkian)

Tahquamenon: Name of river and falls; meaning "dark-colored water" (Ojibway)

Tecumseh: Name of town; named after chief whose name means "a panther crouching for its prey" (Shawnee)

Tittabawassee: Name of river; probably meaning "river following the line of the shore" (Algonkian)

Washtenaw: Name of county; meaning "on the river" (Ojibway)

♦ MINNESOTA

Anoka: Name of town and county; meaning "on both sides" (Siouan)

Bemidji: Name of town and lake; named after chief whose name probably means "river crossing lake" (probably Algonkian)

Chanhassen: Name of town and river; meaning "tree with sweet juice" (Siouan)

Chaska: Name of town, lake, and creek; meaning "first-born son" (Siouan)

Chisago: Name of county; meaning "large and beautiful" (Ojibway)

Isanti: Name of town and county; derived from tribal name (probably Siouan)

Kanabec: Name of county; meaning "snake" (Ojibway)

Kandiyohi: Name of county; meaning "buffalo fish come" (Siouan)

Koochiching: Name of county; probably meaning "rainy lake" (Cree)

Mahnomen: Name of town and county; meaning "wild rice" (Ojibway)

Mesabi: Name of mountains; meaning "giant" (Ojibway)

Minneapolis: Name of city; meaning "waterfall" (Siouan) and "city" (Greek)

Minnesota: Name of state, lake, and river; probably meaning "land of many lakes" (Siouan)

Minnetonka: Name of town and lake; meaning "big water" (Siouan)

Wabasha: Name of town and county; a personal name for hereditary chiefs, meaning "red leaf" or "red battle-standard" (Siouan)

Wadena: Name of town and county; meaning "little round hill" (Ojibway)

Waseca: Name of town and county; meaning "fertile" (Siouan)

Watonwan: Name of county and river; meaning "where fish bait can be found" (probably Siouan)

♦ MISSISSIPPI

Biloxi: Name of town, bay, and river; derived from tribal name, meaning "broken pot" (probably Muskogean)

Chickasawhay: Name of river; derived from village name, meaning "potato" (Choctaw)

Escatawpa: Name of town and river; meaning "cane cut there" (Choctaw)

Hatchie: Name of river and natural wildlife refuge; meaning "stream" (Choctaw)

Homochitto: Name of river and national forest; meaning "red chief" (Choctaw)

Issaquena: Name of county; meaning "deer's head" (Choctaw)

Mississippi: Name of state and river; meaning "big river" (Algonkian)

Neshoba: Name of town and county; probably meaning "wolf" (Choctaw)

Noxubee: Name of county and river; meaning "stinking water" (Choctaw)

Oktibbeha: Name of county; meaning "pure water" (Choctaw)

Pascagoula: Name of town and river; derived from tribal name, meaning "bread people" (probably Muskogean)

Pontotoc: Name of town and county; meaning "cattails on the prairie" (Chickasaw)

Tallahatchie: Name of county and river; meaning "town" and "river" (Creek)

Tishomingo: Name of town and county; after chief whose name means "assistant chief" (Chickasaw)

Tombigbee: Name of river and national forest; meaning "coffin makers" (Choctaw)

Tougaloo: Name of city; meaning "fork of a stream" (Cherokee)

Tunica: Name of county; derived from tribal name, meaning "the people" (Tunica)

Yalobusha: Name of county and river; meaning "little tadpole" (Choctaw)

Yazoo: Name of town, county, and river; derived from tribal name, probably meaning "those who are the people" (Tunican)

♦ MISSOURI

Meramec: Name of river; derived from tribal name, meaning "catfish" (Meramec)

Missouri: Name of state and river; derived from tribal name, meaning "muddy water" (probably Siouan)

Neosho: Name of town; meaning "cold, clear water" (Osage)

Pemiscot: Name of county; meaning "place of the long rock" (possibly Fox)

Wyaconda: Name of town and river; meaning "spirit" (Siouan)

♦ MONTANA

Chinook: Name of town; derived from tribal name (Chinookan)

Flathead: Name of county, river, lake, and national forest; derived from tribal name (Flathead)

Kootenai: Name of river and mountains; derived from tribal name, meaning "water people" (Kootenai)

Mackinac: Name of town; meaning "island of the large turtle" (Ojibway)

Missoula: Name of town and county; meaning "feared water" (Flathead)

Tepee: Name of mountains and Indian tent (Siouan)

♦ NEBRASKA

Arapaho: Name of town; derived from tribal name, meaning "he who trades" (Pawnee)

Nebraska: Name of state and national forest; meaning "wide water" (probably Siouan)

Niobrara: Name of river; meaning "spreading water river" (unknown)

Ogallala: Name of city; derived from tribal name, meaning "to scatter one's own" (Siouan)

Omaha: Name of city; derived from tribal name, meaning "those who live upstream beyond others" (probably Siouan)

Pawnee: Name of county; derived from tribal name, meaning "horn," "hunter," or "braid" (Caddoan)

Red Cloud: Name of town; named after chief (Siouan)

Santee: Name of town; derived from tribal name, meaning "knife" (Dakota)

♦ NEVADA

Beowawe: Name of pass to canyon; meaning "an open gate" (Shoshonean)

Hiko: Name of mountain range; meaning "white people" (Southern Paiute)

Pahranagat: Name of valley and mountain range; derived from tribal name, meaning "people of the marshy spring" (Pauite)

Pequop: Name of mountain; derived from tribal name (Algonkian)

Timpahute: Name of mountain range; derived from tribal name, meaning "rock spring people" (Pauite)

Toana: Name of mountain range; meaning "black hill" (Shoshonean)

Toquima: Name of mountain range; derived from tribal name, meaning "black backs" (Shoshonean)

Washoe: Name of town, county, lake, valley, and mountain range; derived from tribal name, meaning "person" (Hokan)

Winnemucca: Name of lake; meaning "bread giver" (Paiute)

♦ NEW HAMPSHIRE

Coos: Name of county; meaning "pine tree" (Pennacook)

Merrimack: Name of town, county, and river; probably meaning "deep place" (Algonkian)

Nashua: Name of town and river; derived from tribal name, meaning "beautiful river with pebbly bottom" (probably Algonkian)

Ossipee: Name of town, lake, river, and mountains; meaning "beyond the water" (Abnaki)

Suncook: Name of town, river, and lakes; meaning "at the rocks" (Algonkian)

Winnisquam: Name of lake; meaning "salmon" (Algonkian)

♦ NEW JERSEY

Hackensack: Name of city and river; derived from tribal name, probably meaning "hook mouth" or "big snake land" (Algonkian)

Hoboken: Name of city; meaning "land of the tobacco pipe" (Delaware)

Hopatcong: Name of city and lake; probably meaning "hill above a body of still water having an outlet" (Algonkian)

Navesink: Name of town and river; meaning "point at" (Algonkian)

Parsippany: Name of town; probably derived from tribal name (probably Algonkian)

Passaic: Name of city, county, and river; probably meaning "valley" or "peace" (Delaware)

Pequannock: Name of city and river; meaning "open field" (Algonkian)

Raritan: Name of city, river, and bay; derived from tribal name, probably meaning "stream overflows" or "forked river" (Algonkian)

Wanaque: Name of city and reservoir; probably meaning "sassafras place" (Algonkian)

Whippany: Name of city and river; probably meaning "arrow stream" (Delaware)

♦ NEW MEXICO

Abiquiu: Name of city and reservoir; probably derived from village name, meaning "chokecherry" (Tewa)

Acomita: Name of city; named after Indian pueblo and people, meaning "whiterock people" (Pueblo)

Aztec: Name of town; derived from tribal name, meaning "place of the heron" or "land of flamingos" (Aztec)

Mescalero: Name of city; derived from a Spanish word for an Apache tribe, referring to their practice of preparing a food called mescal (Spanish)

Mexico: Name of state and gulf; meaning "place of the war god" (Aztec)

Taos: Name of city and county; probably meaning "red willow place" or "at the village" (Tewa)

Tucumcari: Name of city and mountain; meaning "to lie in ambush" (Comanche)

Ute: Name of city and park; derived from tribal name (Uto-Aztecan)

Zuni: Name of city, river, and mountains; derived from village and tribal names (Zuni)

♦ NEW YORK

Adirondacks: Name of town, park, and mountain range; derived from tribal name, meaning "bark eaters" (Iroquoian)

Allegheny: Name of plateau and reservoir; probably from the name for Allegheny and Ohio rivers (Delaware)

Canadaigua: Name of town and lake; meaning "town set off" (Iroquoian)

Cassadaga: Name of town, creek, and lakes; meaning "under the rocks" (Iroquoian)

Cattaraugus: Name of town, county, and creek; meaning "bad smelling shore" (Iroquoian)

Cayuga: Name of town, county, canal, and lake; derived from tribal name, meaning "where they take the boats out" (probably Iroquoian)

Chemung: Name of town, county, and river; meaning "big horn" (Seneca)

Chenango: Name of county and river; meaning "bull thistle" (Onondaga)

Manhasset: Name of town; derived from tribal name (Algonkian)

Manhattan: Name of island and borough; derived from tribal name, probably meaning "island-mountain" (Algonkian)

Mohawk: Name of town and river; derived from a name used by their Algonkian enemies, meaning "man eaters" (Algonkian)

Niagara: Name of town, county, river, and falls; meaning "point of land cut in two" (Iroquoian)

Oneida: Name of town, county, and lake; derived from tribal name, meaning "stone people" (Iroquoian)

Onondaga: Name of county; derived from tribal name, meaning "hill people" (Iroquoian)

Oswego: Name of town, county, river, and lake; probably meaning "the outpouring" or "the place where the valley widens" (Iroquoian)

Poughkeepsie: Name of town; meaning "little rock at water" (Algonkian)

Saratoga: Name of town, county, and lake; meaning "springs from the hillside" (probably Mohawk)

Seneca: Name of county, river, lake, and falls; derived from tribal name, probably meaning "people of the stone" (Mohegan)

Susquehanna: Name of river; derived from tribal name (Iroquoian)

Tuscarora: Name of town; derived from tribal name, meaning "hemp gatherers" (Iroquoian)

♦ NORTH CAROLINA

Alamance: Name of county and creek; meaning "noisy stream" (probably Siouan)

Catawba: Name of town, county, and river; derived from tribal name (probably Siouan)

Cherokee: Name of town, county, and national forest; derived from tribal name, meaning "people of a different speech" (probably Algonkian)

Chowan: Name of county and river; derived from tribal name (probably Algonkian)

Croatoan: Name of city and national forest; probably meaning "talk town" (probably Algonkian)

Currituck: Name of town, county, and sound; derived from tribal name, probably meaning "wild geese" (probably Algonkian)

Nantahala: Name of mountains, gorge, lake, river, and national forest; meaning "place of the middle sun" (Cherokee)

Pasquotank: Name of county; derived from tribal name, probably meaning "divided tidal river" (Weapemeoc)

Perquimans: Name of county and river; derived from tribal name (Weapemeoc)

Tuckaseigee: Name of river; derived from village name, probably meaning "crawling turtle" (Cherokee)

Waccamaw: Name of lake and river; derived from tribal name (probably Siouan)

♦ NORTH DAKOTA

Dakota: Name of states and river; derived from tribal name of people also known as Sioux, meaning "allies" (Siouan)

Mandan: Name of city; derived from tribal name, meaning "those who live along the bank of the river" (Dakota)

Minnewaukan: Name of city; meaning "water of the bad spirit" (Siouan)

Pembina: Name of town, county, and river; meaning "summer berry" (Ojibway)

Wahpeton: Name of town; derived from one of the seven divisions of the Dakotas, meaning "dwellers among the leaves" (Siouan)

♦ OHIO

Cuyahoga: Name of county, river, and falls; meaning "important river" (probably Iroquoian)

Mahoning: Name of county; meaning "salt lick" (Delaware)

Maumee: Name of town and river; derived from tribal name, meaning "people of the peninsula" (Ojibway)

Mississinewa: Name of river; meaning "river of big stones" (Algonkian)

Muskingum: Name of county and river; derived from village name, meaning "at the river" (Algonkian)

Newcomerstown: Name of town; named after chief Netawatwees, whose name means "beaver" (Delaware)

Ohio: Name of state and river; meaning "beautiful" (Iroquoian)

Sandusky: Name of town, county, bay, and river; meaning "source of pure water" (Wyandotte)

Tippecanoe: Name of city; meaning "buffalo fish" (Potawatomi)

Wyandotte: Name of county; derived from tribal name, meaning "islanders" or "peninsula dwellers" (Iroquoian)

♦ OKLAHOMA

Atoka: Name of town and county; named after the Choctaw athlete, Captain Atoka, whose name means "ball ground" (Choctaw)

Broken Arrow: Name of city; derived from a Creek village name (translated from Muskogean)

Cheyenne: Name of city; derived from tribal name, meaning "red talkers" (Algonkian)

Coweta: Name of town; derived from a Creek town name (Muskogean)

Creek: Name of county; derived from tribal name given by the English to the Muskogee tribe (English)

Kiamichi: Name of river; derived from village name (Caddoan)

Muskogee: Name of town and county; derived from tribal name (Muskogean)

Nowata: Name of town and county; meaning "welcome" (Delaware)

Okfuskee: Name of county; meaning "promontory" (Muskogean)

Oklahoma: Name of city, county, and state; meaning "red people" (Muskogean)

Okmulgee: Name of town and county; derived from tribal name, meaning "where water boils up" (Hitchiti)

Oologah: Name of town and reservoir; named after chief whose name means "dark cloud"

Pushmataha: Name of county; named after chief (Choctaw)

Sequoyah: Name of county; named after a Cherokee who devised a written language (Cherokee)

Tonkawa: Name of city; derived from tribal name, meaning "they all stay together" (probably Waco)

Tulsa: Name of city and county; derived from a Creek village name, meaning "old town" (Muskogean)

Wewoka: Name of town and creek; derived from a Creek village name, meaning "water roaring" (Muskogean)

Wichita: Name of mountains; derived from tribal name, meaning "man" (Caddoan)

♦ OREGON

Clackamas: Name of county and river; derived from name of a subtribe (Chinookan)

Clatsop: Name of county; derived from name of a subtribe (Chinookan)

Klamath: Name of county, lake, and river; derived from a tribal name (Chinook)

Metolius: Name of town and river; meaning "light-colored fish"

Multnomah: Name of county and falls; derived from tribal name (Multnomah)

Nehalem: Name of river; derived from a tribal name (Chinook)

Oregon: Name of state; probably meaning "place of plenty" or "river of the west" (Shoshonean)

Sacajawea: Name of peak; named after the Shoshoni woman who was part of the Lewis and Clark Expedition, meaning "bird woman" (Shoshonean)

Siskiyou: Name of town, national forest and mountains; meaning "bobtail horse" (probably Cree)

Siuslaw: Name of river and national forest; derived from tribal name, meaning "people of Nehalem" (Chinook)

Tillamook: Name of county, bay, and cape; derived from tribal name (Tillamook)

Umatilla: Name of town, county, river, and dam; derived from tribal name, probably meaning "water rippling over sand" (Umatilla)

Umpqua: Name of town and river; derived from tribal name, meaning "thunder" or "high and low water" (Athapascan)

Wallowa: Name of town, county, lake, river, national forest, and mountains; meaning "triangular stakes," a type of fish trap (Nez Percé)

♦ PENNSYLVANIA

Aliquippa: Name of borough; named after a Seneca matron (Iroquoian)

Lenape: Name of town; derived from tribal name, meaning "men of our nation" or "real people" (Delaware)

Lycoming: Name of county; meaning "sandy creek" (Delaware)

Monongahela: Name of town and river; meaning "river with the sliding banks" (Delaware)

Pocono: Name of lake, creek, and mountains; probably meaning "valley stream" (Delaware)

Shenango: Name of river and reservoir; derived from village name, meaning "beautiful one" (probably Algonkian)

Susquehanna: Name of county and river; derived from tribal name (Iroquoian)

Tioga: Name of town, county, and river; meaning "at the forks" (Iroquoian)

♦ RHODE ISLAND

Narragansett: Name of city and bay; derived from tribal name, meaning "people of the small point" (Algonkian)

Pascoag: Name of town and reservoir; meaning "forking place" (Algonkian)

Pawtucket: Name of city; meaning "at the falls in the river" (Algonkian)

Wallum: Name of town and lake; meaning "dog" (Nipmuc)

Woonsocket: Name of city; probably meaning "at a steep spot" (Algonkian)

♦ SOUTH CAROLINA

Congaree: Name of river; derived from tribal name (Congaree)

Coosawhatchie: Name of town and river; meaning "stream with cane" (Muskogean)

Edisto: Name of island and river; derived from tribal name (probably Muskogean)

Pacolet: Name of town and river; derived from tribal name (Pacolet)

Wateree: Name of river and lake; derived from a subtribe (Catawba)

♦ SOUTH DAKOTA

Dakota: Name of states; derived from tribal name of people also known as Sioux, meaning "allies" (Siouan)

Wakpala: Name of town; meaning "creek" (Siouan)

Waubay: Name of town and lake; meaning "nesting place for wild fowl" (Siouan)

Wetonka: Name of town; meaning "big" (probably Siouan)

Wewela: Name of town; meaning "small spring" (probably Siouan)

Yankton: Name of town and county; derived from tribal village, meaning "end village" (Siouan)

♦ TENNESSEE

Chattanooga: Name of city; meaning "rock rising to a point" (Creek)

Obion: Name of town, county and river; probably meaning "many forks" (unknown)

Sequatchie: Name of county and river; named after a chief whose name means "hog river" (Cherokee)

Telico: Name of town; derived from village name, probably meaning "place of refuge" (Cherokee)

Tennessee: Name of state and river; derived from village name (Cherokee)

Unicoi: Name of town, county, and pass; meaning "white" (Cherokee)

♦ TEXAS

Anahuac: Name of national wildlife refuge; meaning "plain near the water" (Aztec)

Miami: Name of town; derived from tribal name, meaning "people of the peninsula" (Ojibway)

Nacogdoches: Name of county; derived from tribal name (Caddoan)

Neches: Name of river; derived from tribal name, meaning "snow river" (Hasinai)

Pecos: Name of county and river; meaning "watering place" (Keresan)

Quanah: Name of town; named after chief, meaning "better flowers" (Comanche)

Tehuacana: Name of town; meaning "the three canes" (Wichita)

Waco: Name of lake; derived from tribal name, meaning "heron" (probably Caddoan)

Waxahachie: Name of town; meaning "cow stream" (Tonkawa)

♦ UTAH

Goshute: Name of town; derived from tribal name, meaning "dust people" (probably Shoshonean)

Juab: Name of county; meaning "valley" (Gosiute)

Paiute: Name of county; derived from tribal name, meaning "Ute of the water" (Paiute)

Panguitch: Name of town and lake; derived from tribal name, meaning "fish people" (Paiute)

Parowan: Name of town; derived from tribal name, meaning "marsh people" (Parowan)

Sanpete: Name of county; meaning "homelands" (Ute)

Uinta: Name of river, national forest, and mountains; derived from tribal name, meaning "pineland" (Shoshonean)

Utah: Name of state, county, and lake; derived from tribal name, meaning "high up" or "the land of the sun" (Ute)

Wah Wah: Name of mountains; probably meaning "juniper" (Paiute)

♦ VERMONT

Missisquoi: Name of river; meaning "much water fowl" (Algonkian)

Winooski: Name of town and river; meaning "onion land" (Abnaki)

♦ VIRGINIA

Accomac: Name of town and county; derived from tribal name, meaning "the other side" (probably Algonkian)

Alleghany: Name of town and county; named for Allegheny and Ohio Rivers (Delaware)

Appomattox: Name of town, county, and river; derived from tribal name, probably meaning "tobacco plant country" or "curving tidal estuary" (Algonkian)

Chesapeake: Name of city and bay; probably meaning "on the big bay" (Algonkian)

Nansemond: Name of county; derived from tribal name, meaning "whence we were driven off" (Nansemond)

Nottoway: Name of town, county, and river; derived from tribal name, meaning "rattlesnake" (Algonkian)

Powhatan: Name of city and county; named after chief, probably meaning "falls in a current of water" (Algonkian)

Rappahannock: Name of county and river; derived from tribal name, meaning "back-and-forth stream" (Algonkian)

Roanoke: Name of town, county, and river; probably meaning "white-shell place" (Algonkian)

♦ WASHINGTON

Chehalis: Name of city, county, river, and Indian reservation; derived from tribal name, meaning "shining sands" (Salishan)

Clallam: Name of county, river, and bay; derived from tribal name, meaning "big brave nation" (Clallam)

Cowlitz: Name of county and river; derived from tribal name, meaning "capturing the medicine spirit" (Cowlitz)

Duwamish: Name of river; derived from tribal name, meaning "the people living on the river" (Duwamish)

Hoh: Name of river and Indian reservation; derived from tribal name (Hoh)

Kitsap: Name of county and lake; named after chief, meaning "brave" (Kitsap)

Kittitas: Name of town and county; probably derived from tribal name, meaning "shoal people" (Kittitas)

Klickitat: Name of county and river; derived from tribal name, meaning "beyond" (Klickitat)

Lummi: Name of river, island, and Indian reservation; derived from tribal name (Lummi)

Nespelem: Name of town; derived from tribal name, meaning "large, open meadow" (Nespelem)

Okanogan: Name of county, river, and national forest; derived from tribal name, probably meaning "meeting place" (Okanogan)

Puyallup: Name of city and river; derived from tribal name, meaning "generous people" (Puyallup)

Seattle: Name of city; named after chief (Salishan)

Skagit: Name of county, river, and bay; derived from tribal name (Skagit)

Snoqualmie: Name of river, pass, and national forest; derived from tribal name, meaning "moon" (Snoqualmie)

Spokane: Name of city, county, river, and mountain; derived from tribal name, meaning "chief of the sun" (Spokane)

Tulalip: Name of bay and Indian reservation; meaning "bay with a small mouth" (Tulalip)

Walla Walla: Name of city, county, valley, and river; derived from tribal name, meaning "little swift river" (Walla Walla)

Wenatchee: Name of city, lake, national forest, and mountains; derived from tribal name, meaning "river issuing from canyon" (Wenatchee)

Yakima: Name of city, county, and river; derived from tribal name, probably meaning "runaway" (Yakima)

♦ WEST VIRGINIA

Chattaroy: Name of town; derived from tribal name (probably Algonkian)

Kanawha: Name of county and river; derived from tribal name, probably meaning "hurricane" (Kanawha)

Mingo: Name of county; meaning "stealthy" or "treacherous" (Algonkian)

♦ WISCONSIN

Horicon: Name of town and national wildlife refuge; derived from tribal name, probably meaning "silver water" (Horicon)

Kenosha: Name of town and county; meaning "pickerel" (Potawatomi)

Kickapoo: Name of river; derived from tribal name, meaning "he moves about" (Algonkian)

Manitowoc: Name of town and county; meaning "land of the spirit" (Algonkian)

Milwaukee: Name of city, county, river, and bay; probably meaning "good land" (Algonkian)

Monona: Name of town and lake; named after either an Indian divinity or a legendary Indian girl who jumped into the Mississippi River when she thought her lover had been killed (Algonkian)

Namekagon: Name of town, lake, and river; meaning "place for sturgeon" (Ojibway)

Necedah: Name of town and national wildlife refuge; meaning "yellow" (Winnebago)

Oconto: Name of town, county, river, and falls; meaning "pickerel place" (Menominee)

Ojibway: Name of town; derived from tribal name, meaning "puckered up," referring to a style of moccasin (Ojibway)

Ozaukee: Name of county; derived from tribal name, meaning "river-mouth people" or "yellow earth" (Ozaukee)

Waukesha: Name of town and county; derived from tribal name (Potawatomi)

Winnebago: Name of town, county, and lake; derived from tribal name, probably meaning "people of the filthy waters" (Algonkian)

Wisconsin: Name of state, river, lake, and rapids; meaning "the gathering of the waters" or "grassy place" (French version of Ojibway word)

♦ WYOMING

Absaroka: Name of mountains; named after a bird, meaning "crow" (Siouan)

Sundance: Name of town and mountain; named after annual purification or world renewal ceremony (English)

Washakie: Name of town, county, lake, mountain, creek, and national forest; named after Snake chief (unknown)

Wyoming: Name of state, range, and peak; meaning "large meadows" (Delaware)

CANADA

♦ ALBERTA

Athabaska: Name of river and mountain; meaning "where there are needs" (Cree)

Chipewyan: Name of lakes, river, and Hudson's Bay Company post; derived from tribal name, meaning "pointed skins" (Cree)

Okotoks: Name of town and mountains; meaning "big rock" (Blackfoot)

Ponoka: Name of town; meaning "black elk" (Blackfoot)

Wetaskiwin: Name of city; meaning "hills of peace" (Cree)

♦ BRITISH COLUMBIA

Chilliwack: Name of city; derived from tribal name, meaning "valley of many waters" (Halkomelem)

Coquitlam: Name of river and mountain; derived from tribal name, meaning "stinking of fish slime" (Halkomelem)

Cowichan: Name of village, river, and lake; derived from tribal name, meaning "warm country" (Halkomelem)

Illecillewaet: Name of river, glacier, and mining district; meaning "end of water" (Okanagon)

Kelowna: Name of city; meaning "female grizzly bear" (Okanagon)

Kootenay: Name of river and national park; derived from tribal name, meaning "water people" (Kutenai)

Lillooet: Name of town, district, and river; derived from tribal name, meaning "wild onion" (Lillooet)

Naas: Name of river and bay; meaning "satisfier of the stomach" (Tlingit)

Nanaimo: Name of city, river, and harbor; meaning "strong, strong water" (Halkomelem)

Okanagan: Name of town, valley, and lake; derived from tribal name, meaning "place of water" (Straits Salish)

Skeena: Name of river; meaning "out of the clouds" (Tsimshian)

Stikine: Name of river; meaning "great river" (Tlingit)

♦ MANITOBA

Manitoba: Name of province and lake; meaning "the strait of the spirit" (Cree)

Minnedosa: Name of town and river; meaning "swift water" (Siouan)

Pembina: Name of county, river, and mountains; meaning "summer berry" (Cree)

Tadoule: Name of lake; meaning "floating charcoal" (Chipewyan)

Winnipeg: Name of city, river, and lake; probably meaning "murky water" (Cree)

♦ NEW BRUNSWICK

Great Manan: Name of island; meaning "the island" (Malecite-Passamaquoddy)

Kennebecasis: Name of island, river, and bay; meaning "little, long bay place" (Malecite)

Miramichi: Name of river; meaning "the land of the Micmacs" (Algonkian)

Oromocto: Name of island, village, river, and lake; meaning "good river" (Micmac and Malecite)

Petitcodiac: Name of village and river; meaning "river that bends in a bow fitted to an arrow" (Micmac)

Shippigan: Name of island, village, and harbor; meaning "a small passage through which ducks fly" (Micmac)

♦ NORTHWEST TERRITORIES

Akimiski: Name of island; meaning "the land across" (Cree)

Aklavik: Name of town; meaning "place of the barrenland grizzly" (Inuit)

Akpatok: Name of island; meaning "place of birds" (Inuit)

Auyuittuq: Name of national park; meaning "the place where ice does not melt" (Inuit)

Inuvik: Name of locality; meaning "the place of man" (Inuit)

Keewatin: Name of district; meaning "north wind" (Cree)

♦ NOVA SCOTIA

Antigonish: Name of county and harbor; meaning "broken branches" (Micmac)

Arichat: Name of island; meaning "the camping ground" (Micmac)

Chignecto: Name of bay; meaning "foot cloth" (Micmac)

Maccan: Name of settlement; meaning "fishing place" (Micmac)

Missinaibi: Name of lake and river; meaning "pictures on the water" (Micmac)

Pugwash: Name of river and bay; meaning "a bank of sand " or "shallow water" (Micmac)

Scubenacadie: Name of village, river, and lake; meaning "where nuts grow in abundance" (Micmac)

♦ ONTARIO

Abitibi: Name of lake and river; derived from tribal name, meaning "halfway water" (Algonkian)

Brant/Brantford: Name of city and county; named after chief Joseph Brant (Mohawk)

Cataraqui: Name of river; meaning "where river and lake meet" (Iroquoian)

Cayuga: Name of town and county; derived from tribal name, meaning "here they take the boats out" (Iroquoian)

Iroquois: Name of town; derived from tribal name, meaning "real adders" (Algonkian word with French spelling)

Muskota: Name of district, lake, river, and bay; probably named after a chief (Ojibway)

Niagara: Name of township, river, and falls; probably meaning "thunderer of waters" or "resounding with great noise" (Iroquoian)

Oneida: Name of township; derived from tribal name, meaning "people of the upright stone" (Iroquoian)

Ottawa: Name of city and river; derived from tribal name, probably meaning "to trade" (Algonkian)

Petawawa: Name of township, village, and river; meaning "where one hears the noise of water far away" (probably Algonkian)

Saugeen: Name of township and river; meaning "river mouth" (Huron)

Tecumseh: Name of township; named after chief whose name means "a panther crouching for its prey" (Shawnee)

Toronto: Name of city; probably meaning "fallen trees in the water" or "a place of meeting" (Huron)

♦ QUEBEC

Arthabaska: Name of county and cantons; meaning "a place obstructed by reeds and grass" (Cree)

Chibougamau: Name of settlement, river, and lake; meaning "the water is stopped" (Algonkian)

Chicoutimi: Name of city, county, and river; meaning "end of the deep water" (Montagnais)

Matane: Name of town, county, river, and lakes; meaning "beaver ponds" (Micmac)

Pontiac: Name of county; named after Ottawa chief (probably Algonkian)

Quebec: Name of city, county, and province; meaning "where the river narrows" (Algonkian)

Shawinigan: Name of lake, river, and falls; meaning "a portage shaped like a beech-nut" (probably Cree)

Temiscouata: Name of county and lake; meaning "deep lake" (Cree)

Ungava: Name of bay; meaning "an unknown, faraway land" (Inuit)

♦ SASKATCHEWAN

Assiniboine: Name of river; derived from a word for a Sioux tribe, meaning "he who cooks with stones" (Ojibway)

Saskatchewan: Name of province and river; meaning "swift-flowing river" (Cree)

Saskatoon: Name of city; named for edible red berry (Cree)

Wakaw: Name of lake; meaning "crooked lake" (Cree)

♦ YUKON TERRITORY

Dezadeash: Name of lake; meaning "a native fishing method" (Athapascan)

Itsi: Name of lake and mountains; meaning "wind" (Athapascan)

Klondike: Name of village and river; meaning "river full of fish"

Teslin: Name of town, lake, and river; meaning "long waters" (Athapascan)

Ulu: Name of mountain; named for a knife with a crescent-shaped blade and a handle of bone or wood (Inuit)

Yukon: Name of river and mountain; meaning "great river" (probably Athapascan)

Tribal Collections

UNITED STATES

♦ ALASKA

ALASKA INDIAN ARTS, INC.
P.O. Box 271
23 Fort Seward Dr.
Haines, AK 99827
(907)766-2160
Tlingit and Chilkat.

ALASKA NATIVE VILLAGE MUSEUM
Athapascan Alaska Inc.
P.O. Box 75001
Fairbanks, AK 99707-5001
(907)456-3851

SEALASKA HERITAGE FOUNDATION
Sealaska Plaza Bldg. No. 201
Juneau, AK 99801
(907)586-9265

♦ ARIZONA

COLORADO RIVER INDIAN TRIBES MUSEUM
Rte. 1, Box 23-B
Parker, AZ 85344
(602)669-9211
Mohave, Chemehuevi, Navajo, and Hopi.

HOPI TRIBAL MUSEUM
P.O. Box 7
Second Mesa, AZ 86035
(602)734-6650

NAVAJO NATION TRIBAL MUSEUM
P.O. Box 308, Highway 264
Window Rock, AZ 86515
(602)871-6673

♦ CALIFORNIA

CUPA CULTURAL CENTER
Temecula Rd., Box I
Pala, CA 92059
(619)742-1590
Pala Indian Reservation museum.

HOOPA TRIBAL MUSEUM
P.O. Box 1348
Hoopa, CA 95546
(916)625-4110
Hupa, Yurok, and Karuk.

MALKI MUSEUM
Morongo Reservation
11-795 Fields Rd.
Banning, CA 92220
(714)849-7289
Cahuilla, Serrano, Luiseño, and other California tribal groups.

♦ COLORADO

UTE INDIAN MUSEUM
Box 1736, Chipeta Dr.
Montrose, CO 81402
(303)249-3098

UTE MOUNTAIN TRIBAL PARK
General Delivery
Towaoc, CO 81334
(303)565-3751

♦ CONNECTICUT

TANTAQUIDGEON INDIAN MUSEUM
Rte. 32, Norwich-New London Rd.
Uncasville, CT 06382
(203) 848-9145
Built and maintained by descendants of Uncas, chief of the Mohegans.

♦ DELAWARE

NANTICOKE INDIAN ASSOCIATION MUSEUM
Rte. 4, Box 107A
Millsboro, DE 19966
(302)945-7022

♦ FLORIDA

BOBBY'S SEMINOLE INDIAN VILLAGE
5221 North Orient Rd.
Tampa, FL 33610
(813)620-3077

MICCOUSUKEE CULTURAL CENTER
P.O. Box 440021
Miami, FL 33143
(305)223-8380

♦ IDAHO

SHOSHONE-BANNOCK TRIBAL MUSEUM
I-15, Exit 80
Fort Hall, ID 83203
(208)237-9791

♦ KANSAS

THE INDIAN MUSEUM
Mid-America All-Indian Center
650 North Seneca
Wichita, KS 67203
(316)262-5221

♦ MAINE

MAINE TRIBAL UNITY MUSEUM
Quaker Hill Rd.
Unity, ME 04988
(207)948-3131

♦ MISSISSIPPI

THE CHOCTAW MUSEUM OF THE SOUTHERN INDIAN
Mississippi Band of Choctaw Indians
P.O. Box 6010
Philadelphia, MS 39350
(601)656-5251

♦ MONTANA

CROW TRIBE HISTORICAL AND CULTURAL COMMISSION
P.O. Box 173
Crow Agency, MT 59022
(406)638-2601

FLATHEAD INDIAN MUSEUM
Flathead Indian Reservation
1 Museum Ln.
St. Ignatius, MT 59865
(406)745-2951

FORT PECK TRIBAL MUSEUM
Assiniboine Sioux Tribes
Fort Peck Indian Reservation
P.O. Box 1566
Poplar, MT 59255
(406)768-5155

♦ NEW MEXICO

ACOMA MUSEUM
P.O. Box 309
Pueblo of Acoma
Acomita, NM 87034
(800)747-0181
Photo archives and documents relating to the history of Acoma.

MESCALERO CULTURAL CENTER
P.O. Box 176
Mescalero, NM 88340
(505)671-4495

PICURIS PUEBLO MUSEUM
P.O. Box 487
Penasco, NM 87553
(505)587-2957

SAN ILDEFONSO PUEBLO MUSEUM
Rte. 5, Box 315-A
Santa Fe, NM 87501
(505)455-2424

♦ NEW YORK

AKWESASNE MUSEUM
Akwesasne Cultural Center
R.R. 1, Box 14CAk
Hogansburg, NY 13655
(518)358-2461
Mohawk culture.

IROQUOIS INDIAN MUSEUM
P.O. Box 7
Howes Cave, NY 12092
(518)296-8949
Iroquois people and culture.

SENECA-IROQUOIS NATIONAL MUSEUM
Allegany Indian Reservation
P.O. Box 442, Broad St. Extension
Salamanca, NY 14779
(716)945-1738

TONAWANDA-SENECA MUSEUM
Tonawanda-Seneca Reservation
Basom, NY 14013
(716)542-4244

♦ NORTH CAROLINA

MUSEUM OF THE CHEROKEE INDIAN
P.O. Box 1599
Cherokee, NC 28719
(704)497-3481

♦ OKLAHOMA

CHEROKEE NATIONAL MUSEUM (TSA-LA-GI)
Cherokee Heritage Center
P.O. Box 515
Tahlequah, OK 74464
(918)456-6007

CHICKASAW COUNCIL HOUSE MUSEUM
P.O. Box 717
Tishomingo, OK 73460
(405)371-3351

CHOCTAW NATION HISTORICAL MUSEUM
Rte. 1, Box 105AAA
Tuskahoma, OK 74574
(405)569-4465

CREEK COUNCIL HOUSE MUSEUM
Town Square
Okmulgee, OK 74447
(918)756-2324

DELAWARE TRIBAL MUSEUM
c/o Delaware Executive Board
P.O. Box 825
Anadarko, OK 73005
(405)247-2448

OSAGE TRIBAL MUSEUM
Osage Agency Reserve
Pawhuska, OK 74056
(918)287-2495

POTAWATOMI INDIAN NATION ARCHIVES AND MUSEUM
1901 South Gordon Cooper Dr.
Shawnee, OK 74801
(405)275-3121

SEMINOLE NATION MUSEUM
524 South Wewoka, Box 1532
Wewoka, OK 74884
(405)257-5580

TONKAWA TRIBAL MUSEUM
P.O. Box 70
Tonkawa, OK 74653
(405)628-5301

WICHITA MEMORY EXHIBIT MUSEUM
Wichita Tribal Cultural Center
P.O. Box 729
Anadarko, OK 73005
(405)247-2425

♦ PENNSYLVANIA

LENNI LENAPE HISTORICAL SOCIETY OF PENNSYLVANIA
R.D. 2, Fish Hatchery Rd.
Allentown, PA 18103
(215)797-2121
Lenni Lenape (Delaware) museum and traditional village.

♦ RHODE ISLAND

TOMAQUAG INDIAN MEMORIAL MUSEUM
386 Summit Rd.
Exeter, RI 02822
(401)596-2446

♦ SOUTH DAKOTA

H. V. JOHNSTON AMERICAN INDIAN CULTURAL CENTER
Cheyenne River Reservation
P.O. Box 857
Eagle Butte, SD 57625
(605)964-2542

♦ TEXAS

ALABAMA-COUSHATTA INDIAN MUSEUM
Rte. 3, Box 640, Highway 190
Livingston, TX 77351
(409)563-4391

TIGUA PUEBLO CULTURAL CENTER
Tigua Arts and Crafts Center
Texas Indian Reservation
El Paso, TX 79907
(915)859-3916

♦ UTAH

UTE TRIBAL MUSEUM
P.O. Box 190, Highway 40
Fort Duchesne, UT 84026
(801)722-4992

♦ VIRGINIA

MATTAPONI INDIAN MUSEUM AND TRADING POST
Mattaponi Indian Reservation
Rte. 2, Box 255
West Point, VA 23181
(804)769-2194

♦ WASHINGTON

COLVILLE CONFEDERATED TRIBES MUSEUM
P.O. Box 233
Coulee Dam, WA 99116
(509)634-4711

MAKAH CULTURAL RESEARCH CENTER
P.O. Box 160, Bayview Ave.
Neah, WA 98357
(206)645-2711

PUYALLUP TRIBE MUSEUM
2215 East 22nd St.
Tacoma, WA 98404
(206)597-6200

STEILACOOM CULTURAL CENTER
P.O. Box 88419
Steilacoom, WA 98388
(206)584-6308

SUQUAMISH MUSEUM
15838 Sandy Hook N.E.
P.O. Box 498
Suquamish, WA 98392
(206)598-3311

YAKIMA NATION MUSEUM
Yakima Nation Cultural Center
P.O. Box 151
Toppenish, WA 98948
(509)865-2800

♦ WISCONSIN

LAC DU FLAMBEAU CHIPPEWA CULTURAL CENTER
P.O. Box 804
Lac du Flambeau, WI 54538
(715)588-3333

ONEIDA NATION MUSEUM
Oneida Nation Cultural Center
P.O. Box 365
Oneida, WI 54155
(414)869-2768

STOCKBRIDGE-MUNSEE HISTORICAL LIBRARY AND MUSEUM
Rte. 1, Box 300
Bowler, WI 54416
(715)793-4270

WINNEBAGO INDIAN MUSEUM
3889 North River Rd.
P.O. Box 441
Wisconsin Dells, WI 53965
(608)254-2268

♦ WYOMING

ARAPAHO CULTURAL MUSEUM
P.O. Box 8066
Ethete, WY 82520
(307)332-2660

CANADA

♦ ALBERTA

ANDERSON NATIVE HERITAGE AND CULTURAL CENTRE
13140 St. Albert Tr.
Edmonton, AB T5L 4R8
(401)455-2200

NINASTAKO CULTURAL CENTRE
P.O. Box 1299
Cardston, AB T0K 0K0
(403)737-3774

TSUT'INA K'OSA (SARCEE)
3700 Anderson Rd. S.W.
Box 67
Calgary, AB T2W 3T0
(403)238-2677

♦ BRITISH COLUMBIA

SECWEPEMC MUSEUM
Kamloops Indian Reserve
345 Yellowhead Hwy.
Kamloops, BC V6H 1H1
(604)828-9801

SHESHAHT CULTURAL CENTRE
5211 Wilkinson Rd.
Port Alberni, BC V9Y 7B2
(604)723-5421

U'MISTA CULTURAL CENTRE
P.O. Box 253
Alert Bay, BC V0N 1A0
(604)974-5403

♦ MANITOBA

BROKENHEAD CULTURAL CENTRE
Scanterbury, MB R0E 1W0
(204)766-2494

♦ ONTARIO

WOODLANDS INDIAN MUSEUM
184 Mohawk St.
Brantford, ON N3S 2X2
(519)759-2650

♦ SASKATCHEWAN

SASKATCHEWAN INDIAN CULTURAL CENTRE
120 33rd St. E.
Saskatoon, SK S7K 0S2
(306)244-1146

Major Museums

UNITED STATES

♦ ALABAMA

BIRMINGHAM MUSEUM OF ART
2000 Eighth Ave. N.
Birmingham, AL 35203-2278
(205)254-2566
North, Central, and South American Indian art.

♦ ALASKA

ALASKA STATE MUSEUM
395 Whittier St.
Juneau, AK 99801-1718
(907)465-2901
Alaskan Native Gallery (companion museum to Sheldon Jackson Museum).

ANCHORAGE MUSEUM OF HISTORY AND ART
121 West Seventh Ave.
Anchorage, AK 99501
(907)343-4326
Alaskan tribes, Plains; Cook Inlet Region, Inc., Community Collection (CIRI).

SHELDON JACKSON MUSEUM
104 College Dr.
Sitka, AK 99835-7657
(907)747-8981
Alaskan Native Gallery (companion museum to Alaska State Museum).

♦ ARIZONA

THE AMERIND FOUNDATION MUSEUM
P.O. Box 400
Dragoon, AZ 85609
(602)586-3666
North America; emphasis on regional prehistory.

THE HEARD MUSEUM OF ANTHROPOLOGY AND PRIMITIVE ART
22 East Monte Vista Rd.
Phoenix, AZ 85004
(602)252-8848
Southwestern Native American Artists Resource Collection contains documentation of individual artists' achievements.

♦ ARKANSAS

ARKANSAS STATE UNIVERSITY MUSEUM
P.O. Box 490
State University, AR 72467
(501)972-2074
Northeast Arkansas regional emphasis.

♦ CALIFORNIA

PHOEBE HEARST MUSEUM OF ANTHROPOLOGY
103 Kroeber Hall
University of California
Berkeley, CA 94720
(510)642-3681
North America, especially California.

SOUTHWEST MUSEUM
234 Museum Dr.
Los Angeles, CA 90065
(213)221-2164
Native people of the Americas, especially California and the Southwest.

♦ COLORADO

DENVER MUSEUM OF NATURAL HISTORY
2001 South Colorado Blvd.
Denver, CO 80205
(303)322-7009
Emphasis on regional, including the original Folsom point (found at Folsom site, New Mexico, between the ribs of an extinct buffalo).

UNIVERSITY OF COLORADO MUSEUM
Henderson Bldg., Campus Box 218
Boulder, CO 80309-0218
(303)492-6165
North American prehistory, especially the Plains and the Southwest.

♦ CONNECTICUT

AMERICAN INDIAN ARCHAEOLOGICAL INSTITUTE
P.O. Box 1260
Off Route 199, 38 Curtis Rd.
Washington, CT 06793-0260
(203)868-0518
Primarily Northeast Woodlands, including Indian village.

PEABODY MUSEUM OF NATURAL HISTORY
Yale University
170 Whitney Ave.
New Haven, CT 06511-8161
(203)432-5050
Extensive archaeological collection, especially regional.

♦ DELAWARE

DELAWARE STATE MUSEUM
316 South Governors Ave.
Dover, DE 19901
(302)739-3260
Regional emphasis.

♦ DISTRICT OF COLUMBIA

NATIONAL MUSEUM OF THE AMERICAN INDIAN
National Mall
Washington, DC
(202)357-1300
By 2000, the new building for this collection will be constructed.

NATIONAL MUSEUM OF NATURAL HISTORY
NATIONAL MUSEUM OF MAN
Department of Anthropology/American Indian Program
NHB 112, Smithsonian Institution
Washington, DC 20560
(202)357-4760
Indians of the Americas (nearly two million objects); film archives; internships and fellowships.

♦ FLORIDA

LOWE ART MUSEUM (BARTON WING COLLECTION)
University of Miami
1301 Stanford Dr.
Coral Gables, FL 33124-6310
(305)284-3535
North American, especially Southwestern.

♦ GEORGIA

COLUMBUS MUSEUM
1251 Wynnton Rd.
Columbus, GA 31906
(706)649-0713
Artifacts from Paleo through Mississippian cultures, especially Yuchi.

♦ IDAHO

IDAHO STATE HISTORICAL MUSEUM
610 North Julia Davis Dr.
Boise, ID 83702
(208)334-2120
Northwest Coast, Alaskan, and Plains, especially Upper Great Basin.

♦ ILLINOIS

FIELD MUSEUM OF NATURAL HISTORY
Roosevelt Rd. at Lake Shore Dr.
Chicago, IL 60605
(312)922-9410
North and South America, diverse and extensive; Pawnee earth lodge.

ILLINOIS STATE MUSEUM
Corner of Spring and Edwards Streets
Springfield, IL 62706
(217)782-7386
Paleo into historic. Archaeological site branch: Dickson Mounds Museum, Lewistown, IL 61542; phone: (309)547-3721.

♦ INDIANA

EITELJORG MUSEUM OF AMERICAN INDIAN AND WESTERN ART
500 West Washington St.
Indianapolis, IN 46204
(317)636-9378
Primarily North American, especially Northeast Woodlands, Great Plains, and Southwest.

MATHERS MUSEUM
Indiana University
601 East Eighth St.
Bloomington, IN 47405
(812)855-MUSE
North America, especially Plains and Alaskan Eskimo; Wanamaker Collection of American Indian Photographs.

♦ IOWA

STATE HISTORICAL SOCIETY OF IOWA
Capitol Complex
600 East Locust St.
Des Moines, IA 50319
(515)281-5111
Emphasis on Western Great Lakes and Plains.

♦ KANSAS

MUSEUM OF ANTHROPOLOGY
University of Kansas
Lawrence, KS 66045
(913)864-4245
North America, especially regional, Southwest, and Northwest Coast.

♦ KENTUCKY

J. B. SPEED ART MUSEUM
2035 South Third St., Box 2600
Louisville, KY 40201-2600
(502)636-2893
Primarily Plains.

MUSEUM OF ANTHROPOLOGY
Department of Anthropology
University of Kentucky
211 Lafferty Hall
Lexington, KY 40506-0024
(606)257-2710

♦ LOUISIANA

LOUISIANA ARTS AND SCIENCE CENTER
P.O. Box 3373
Baton Rouge, LA 70821
(504)344-5272
North America.

♦ MAINE

THE ABBE MUSEUM
P.O. Box 286
Bar Harbor, ME 04609
(207)288-3519
Primarily Maine and Maritime Provinces (Canada), prehistoric and historic.

THE PEARY-MACMILLAN ARCTIC MUSEUM AND ARCTIC STUDIES CENTER
Hubbard Hall
Bowdoin College
Brunswick, ME 04011
(207)725-3416
Labrador, Baffin, and Greenland Inuit and Indian.

♦ MASSACHUSETTS

PEABODY MUSEUM OF ARCHAEOLOGY AND ETHNOLOGY
Harvard University
11 Divinity Ave.
Cambridge, MA 02138
(617)495-2248
North America, especially dynamics of interactions between Indians and whites over past 500 years.

♦ MICHIGAN

CRANBROOK INSTITUTE OF SCIENCE
500 Lone Pine Rd., Box 801
Bloomfield Hills, MI 48303-0801
(313)645-3230
North America, especially Woodlands and Plains.

MUSEUM OF ANTHROPOLOGY
University of Michigan
4009 Museum Bldg.
1109 Geddes Ave.
Ann Arbor, MI 48109-1079
(313)764-0485
North America.

♦ MINNESOTA

MINNESOTA HISTORICAL SOCIETY
345 Kellogg Blvd. W.
St. Paul, MN 55102-1906
(612)296-8071
Minnesota emphasis, especially Dakota (Sioux) and Ojibwa (Chippewa).

♦ MISSOURI

KANSAS CITY MUSEUM
3218 Gladstone Blvd.
Kansas City, MO 64123
(816)483-8300
Southern and Central Plains, Eastern Woodlands, Southwest, Northwest Coast; extensive.

ST. LOUIS SCIENCE CENTER
5050 Oakland Ave.
St. Louis, MO 63110
(314)289-4400
Emphasis on midwestern cultures, especially Mississippian.

♦ MONTANA

MUSEUM OF THE PLAINS INDIAN
Box 400, Highway 89
Browning, MT 59417
(406)338-2230
Northern Plains; administered by the Indian Arts and Crafts Board (see Bureau of Indian Affairs agencies, p. 553).

♦ NEBRASKA

MUSEUM OF THE FUR TRADE
HC 74, Box 18
Chadron, NE 69337
(308)432-3843
North American Indian cultures; influence of fur trade on cultures.

MUSEUM OF NEBRASKA HISTORY
15th and P Sts.
131 Centennial Mall North
Lincoln, NE 68508
(402)471-4754
Emphasis on Nebraska and Central Plains.

♦ NEVADA

NEVADA HISTORICAL SOCIETY MUSEUM
1650 North Virginia St.
Reno, NV 89503
(702)688-1190
Emphasis on Washo, Northern Paiute, Southern Paiute, and Western Shoshoni.

STEWART INDIAN MUSEUM
5366 Snyder Ave.
Carson City, NV 89701
(702)882-1808
North America, especially regional.

♦ NEW HAMPSHIRE

DARTMOUTH COLLEGE MUSEUM
East Wheelock St.
Hanover, NH 03755
(603)646-2808
North, Central, and South America, especially Southwestern and New England.

♦ NEW JERSEY

MORRIS MUSEUM OF ARTS AND SCIENCES
6 Normandy Heights Rd.
Morristown, NJ 07961
(201)538-0454
Woodlands, Northwest Coast, Southwest, and Plains.

NEW JERSEY STATE MUSEUM
205 West State St.
Trenton, NJ 08625
(609)292-6308

♦ NEW MEXICO

INSTITUTE OF AMERICAN INDIAN ARTS MUSEUM
108 Cathedral Place
Santa Fe, NM 87501
(505)988-6281
Paintings, graphics, sculpture, ceramics, textiles, costumes, jewelry, and ethnographic material, primarily by Native American students.

MAXWELL MUSEUM OF ANTHROPOLOGY
University of New Mexico
Albuquerque, NM 87131-1201
(505)277-4404
Archaeology and ethnography, especially the Southwest.

MUSEUM OF INDIAN ARTS AND CULTURE
Laboratory of Anthropology
P.O. Box 2087
Santa Fe, NM 87504-2087
(505)827-6344
Primarily Southwest; emphasis on Pueblo, Navajo, and Apache.

THE WHEELWRIGHT MUSEUM OF THE AMERICAN INDIAN
P.O. Box 5153
Santa Fe, NM 87502
(505)982-4636
North America, especially Southwest; emphasis on Navajo.

♦ NEW YORK

AMERICAN MUSEUM OF NATURAL HISTORY
79th St. and Central Park West
New York, NY 10024-5192
(212)769-5000
Extensive and diverse.

NATIONAL MUSEUM OF THE AMERICAN INDIAN
George Gustav Heye Center
Alexander Hamilton Custom House
New York, NY
One of the world's finest and most comprehensive collections of artifacts and contemporary art from North, Central, and South American cultures. By 2000, the primary collection will be housed in a new building constructed at the National Mall in Washington, DC. The Heye Center in New York will be a significant exhibition and education facility. An additional storage, research, and conservation facility for the museum will be located in Suitland, Maryland.

♦ NORTH CAROLINA

INDIAN MUSEUM OF THE CAROLINAS
607 Turnpike Rd.
Laurinburg, NC 28352
(919)276-5880
Southeast, primarily North and South Carolina.

NATIVE AMERICAN RESOURCE CENTER
Pembroke State University
Old Main Bldg.
Pembroke, NC 28372
(919)521-6282
North and South America, especially Eastern Woodlands.

SCHIELE MUSEUM REFERENCE LIBRARY AND CENTER FOR SOUTHEASTERN NATIVE AMERICAN STUDIES
P.O. Box 953
Gastonia, NC 28053-0953
(704)866-6916
Extensive collection from twelve cultural areas, especially the Southeast and North Carolina.

♦ NORTH DAKOTA

BUFFALO TRAILS MUSEUM
P.O. Box 22
Epping, ND 58843
(701)859-3512
Upper Missouri area.

STATE HISTORICAL SOCIETY OF NORTH DAKOTA
North Dakota Heritage Center
Capitol Grounds
612 East Blvd.
Bismarck, ND 58505
(701)224-2666
Primarily northern Great Plains.

♦ OHIO

CLEVELAND MUSEUM OF NATURAL HISTORY
1 Wade Oval Dr., University Cir.
Cleveland, OH 44106-1767
(216)231-4600
North America, especially Ohio.

OHIO HISTORICAL CENTER
1982 Velma Ave.
Columbus, OH 43211-2497
(614)297-2439
Emphasis on regional prehistory.

♦ OKLAHOMA

GILCREASE MUSEUM
1400 Gilcrease Museum Rd.
Tulsa, OK 74127-9990
(918)582-3122
North America, prehistory to present; extensive. World's largest collection of art of the American West.

OKLAHOMA MUSEUM OF NATURAL HISTORY
University of Oklahoma
1335 Asp Ave.
Norman, OK 73019-0616
(405)325-4712
North America, especially Southern Plains, Southwest, Northwest Coast, and Spiro Mounds.

SOUTHERN PLAINS INDIAN MUSEUM
Box 749, Highway 62 E.
Anadarko, OK 73005
(405)247-6221
Tribes of western Oklahoma: Kiowa, Comanche, Kiowa-Apache, Southern Cheyenne, Southern Arapaho, Wichita, Caddo, Delaware, and Fort Sill Apache. Administered by the Indian Arts and Crafts Board (see Bureau of Indian Affairs agencies, p. 553).

♦ OREGON

MUSEUM OF NATURAL HISTORY
University of Oregon
1680 East 15th Ave.
Eugene, OR 97403
(503)346-3024
North America, especially Northwest Coast and Pacific Rim.

PORTLAND ART MUSEUM
OREGON ART INSTITUTE
1219 Southwest Park Ave.
Portland, OR 97205
(503)226-2811
North and Middle America, especially Northwest Coast.

♦ PENNSYLVANIA

THE CARNEGIE MUSEUM OF NATURAL HISTORY
4400 Forbes Ave.
Pittsburgh, PA 15213-4080
(412)622-3131
North and South America, especially Upper Ohio Valley. New permanent hall of Native Americans planned for 1996.

♦ RHODE ISLAND

THE HAFFENREFFER MUSEUM OF ANTHROPOLOGY
Brown University
Mount Hope Grant
Bristol, RI 02809
(401)253-8388
The Americas, especially Arctic and Red Paint (Maine).

♦ SOUTH CAROLINA

CHESTER COUNTY HISTORICAL SOCIETY MUSEUM
P.O. Box 811
Chester, SC 29706
(803)385-2330
Regional; over 30,000 Catawba Indian artifacts.

♦ SOUTH DAKOTA

SIOUX INDIAN MUSEUM
515 West Blvd.
Box 1504
Rapid City, SD 57709
(605)348-0557
North America, especially Sioux. Administered by the Indian Arts and Crafts Board (see Bureau of Indian Affairs agencies, p. 553).

THE W. H. OVER STATE MUSEUM
414 East Clark
Vermillion, SD 57069-2390
(605)677-5228
Emphasis on South Dakota Sioux.

♦ TENNESSEE

FRANK H. MCCLUNG MUSEUM
University of Tennessee
1327 Circle Park Dr.
Knoxville, TN 37996-3200
(615)974-2144
Regional emphasis.

THE TENNESSEE STATE MUSEUM
505 Deaderick St.
Nashville, TN 37243-1120
(615)741-2692
Regional emphasis; prehistoric Mississippian.

♦ TEXAS

PANHANDLE PLAINS HISTORICAL MUSEUM
2401 Fourth Ave.
Canyon, TX 79016
(806)656-2244
Emphasis on Comanche and Kiowa.

TEXAS MEMORIAL MUSEUM
University of Texas
2400 Trinity
Austin, TX 78705
(512)471-1604
Emphasis on Texas, Southwest, and Latin America.

WITTE MEMORIAL MUSEUM OF HISTORY AND NATURAL SCIENCE
3801 Broadway
San Antonio, TX 78209
(512)829-7262
North America, emphasis on Texas and the Southwest.

♦ UTAH

MUSEUM OF PEOPLES AND CULTURES
Brigham Young University
105 Allen Hall
Provo, UT 84602
(801)378-6112
North America, emphasis on Maya, Anasazi, Fremont, Mogollon, and Casas Grandes.

UTAH MUSEUM OF NATURAL HISTORY
University of Utah
Salt Lake City, UT 84112
(801)581-4303
Regional, Great Basin, and the Southwest.

♦ VERMONT

ROBERT HULL FLEMING MUSEUM
University of Vermont
61 Colchester Ave.
Burlington, VT 05405
(802)656-0750
North America.

♦ VIRGINIA

JAMESTOWN SETTLEMENT
P.O. Drawer JF
Williamsburg, VA 23187
(804)229-1607
Virginia Indian artifacts; reconstruction of Powhatan's lodge.

♦ WASHINGTON

CHENEY COWLES STATE MUSEUM
2316 West First Ave.
Spokane, WA 99204
(509)456-3931
North, Central, and South America.

WASHINGTON STATE MUSEUM
The Burke Museum
DB-10
University of Washington
Seattle, WA 98195
(206)543-5590
Emphasis on Northwest Coast.

♦ WEST VIRGINIA

WEST VIRGINIA GEOLOGICAL SURVEY ARCHEOLOGY MUSEUM
Mineral Industries Bldg.
Willey St.
West Virginia University
Morgantown, WV 26506
(304)293-0111
Regional cultures.

♦ WISCONSIN

MILWAUKEE PUBLIC MUSEUM
800 West Wells St.
Milwaukee, WI 53233
(414)278-2700
North America, especially Midwest archaeology.

MUSEUMS OF BELOIT COLLEGE
LOGAN MUSEUM OF ANTHROPOLOGY
Beloit College
700 College St.
Beloit, WI 53511-5595
(608)363-2677
Regional emphasis; North and South America.

♦ WYOMING

PLAINS INDIAN MUSEUM
Buffalo Bill Historical Center
Box 1000, 720 Sheridan Ave.
Cody, WY 82414
(307)587-4771
Primarily Northern Plains; recreation of 1890 Sioux camp.

WYOMING STATE MUSEUM
Barrett Bldg.
2301 Central
Cheyenne, WY 82002
(307)777-7022
Primarily Northern Plains.

CANADA

♦ ALBERTA

GLENBOW MUSEUM
130 Ninth Ave. S.E.
Calgary, AB T2G 0P3
(403)264-8300

PROVINCIAL MUSEUM OF ALBERTA
12845 102nd Ave.
Edmonton, AB T5N OM6
(403)453-9100
Emphasis on Alberta, Northern Plains, and Inuit.

♦ BRITISH COLUMBIA

ANTHROPOLOGY MUSEUM
University of British Columbia
Vancouver, BC V6T 1Z1
(604)822-3825

BRITISH COLUMBIA PROVINCIAL MUSEUM
675 Belleville St.
Victoria, BC V8V 1X4
(604)387-3701
Regional archaeology; totem pole exhibit in Thunderbird Park.

MUSEUM OF NORTHERN BRITISH COLUMBIA
P.O. Box 669
Prince Rupert, BC V8J 3S1
(604)624-3207
Northwest Coast, especially Tsimshian, Haida, and Tlingit.

♦ MANITOBA

MANITOBA MUSEUM OF MAN AND NATURE
190 Rupert Ave.
Winnipeg, MB R3B ON2
(204)956-2830
Regional; relationship between humans and environment.

♦ NEW BRUNSWICK

NEW BRUNSWICK MUSEUM
277 Douglas Ave.
St. John, NB E2K 1E5
(506)693-1196
Regional pre-Algonkian.

♦ NEWFOUNDLAND

NEWFOUNDLAND MUSEUM
285 Duckworth St.
St. Johns, NF A1C 1G9
(709)729-2329
Regional, especially Beothuck and Nascapi.

♦ NORTHWEST TERRITORIES

DENE CULTURAL INSTITUTE
P.O. Box 207
Yellowknife, NT X1A 2N2
(403)873-6617

NORTHERN LIFE MUSEUM AND NATIONAL EXHIBITION CENTRE
P.O. Box 420
Fort Smith, NT X0E 0P0
(403)872-2859
Regional, especially Athapascan and Inuit.

♦ NOVA SCOTIA

NOVA SCOTIA MUSEUM
1747 Summer St.
Halifax, NS B3H 3A6
(902)424-7353
Regional Paleo-Indian through Woodland cultures, especially Micmac.

♦ ONTARIO

NATIONAL EXHIBIT CENTRE FOR INDIAN ART
Thunder Bay Art Gallery
P.O. Box 1193
Thunder Bay, ON P7C 4X9
(807)577-6427

THE NORTH AMERICAN INDIAN TRAVELING COLLEGE
THE LIVING MUSEUM AND WOODLANDS INDIAN VILLAGE
R.R. 3, Cornwall Island
Cornwall, ON K6H 5R7
(613)932-9452
Eastern Woodlands cultural and educational center; traditional structures and crafts.

ROYAL ONTARIO MUSEUM
100 Queen's Park Crescent
Toronto, ON M5S 2C6
(416)586-5549
North America, especially Canada, Arctic, and regional.

♦ PRINCE EDWARD ISLAND

MICMAC INDIAN VILLAGE
P.O. Box 51
Cornwall, PEI C0A 1H0
16th-century village with artifacts.
(902)675-2971 (winter)
(902)675-3800 (summer)

PRINCE EDWARD ISLAND MUSEUM AND HERITAGE FOUNDATION
Beaconsfield
2 Kent St.
Charlottetown, PEI C1A 1ME
(902)368-3833

♦ QUEBEC

CANADIAN MUSEUM OF CIVILIZATION
100 Laurier St.
Box 3100, Station B
Hull, PQ J8X 4H2
(819)776-7002

♦ SASKATCHEWAN

SASKATCHEWAN MUSEUM OF NATURAL HISTORY
Wascana Park
Regina, SK S4P 3V7
(306)787-2812
Regional, especially Cree, Assiniboin, Saulteaux, Dakota, and Dene.

♦ YUKON TERRITORY

MACBRIDE MUSEUM
P.O. Box 4037
Whitehorse, YT Y1A 3S9
(403)667-2709
Regional, especially Athapascan, Tlingit, and Inuvialuit.

Archives and Special Collections

UNITED STATES

♦ ALABAMA

ALABAMA DEPARTMENT OF ARCHIVES AND HISTORY
624 Washington Ave.
Montgomery, AL 36130
(205)242-4443

♦ ARIZONA

ARIZONA HISTORICAL SOCIETY RESEARCH LIBRARY
949 East Second St.
Tucson, AZ 85719
(602)628-5774
Maps of Indian reservations; manuscripts of teachers, doctors, and agents on their observations of various reservations.

CAPITOL MUSEUM
1700 West Washington St.
Phoenix, AZ 85007-2896
(602)542-4675

MUSEUM OF NORTHERN ARIZONA
Rte. 4, Box 720
Flagstaff, AZ 86001
(602)774-5211
Natural history and Native American museum; one of the largest collections in the country, containing more than two million Native American artifacts.

PUEBLO GRANDE RUINS AND MUSEUM
4619 East Washington St.
Phoenix, AZ 85034
(602)495-0901

♦ ARKANSAS

ARKANSAS STATE UNIVERSITY MUSEUM
Arkansas State University
P.O. Box 490
State University, AR 72467
Quapaw, Osage, and Cherokee mound builders.

♦ CALIFORNIA

AMERICAN INDIAN STUDIES CENTER LIBRARY
University of California
3220 Campbell Hall
Los Angeles, CA 90024-1548
(310)825-7315

BANCROFT LIBRARY
University of California
Berkeley, CA 94720
(510)642-6481
California Indians.

HUNTINGTON LIBRARY
1151 Oxford Rd.
San Marino, CA 91108
(818)405-2191

RANCHO LOS CERRITOS HISTORIC SITE
4600 Virginia Rd.
Long Beach, CA 90807
(310)424-9423
California and Western history.

♦ COLORADO

NATIONAL INDIAN LAW LIBRARY
Native American Rights Fund
1522 Broadway
Boulder, CO 80302
(303)447-8760
Collections exclusively on federal Indian law.

♦ DISTRICT OF COLUMBIA

THE LIBRARY OF CONGRESS
101 Independence Ave. S.E.
Washington, DC 20540
(202)707-5522
Records of tribal council minutes; manuscripts on the relations of tribes with the United States; prints and photographs.

NATIONAL ANTHROPOLOGICAL ARCHIVES
Natural History Museum MRC 152
Smithsonian Institution
Washington, DC 20560
(202)357-1976

NATURAL RESOURCES LIBRARY
United States Department of the Interior
Mail Stop 1151
Washington, DC 20240
(202)208-5815
Manuscripts of treaties between the federal government and Indians; Indian Claims Commission annual reports.

♦ GEORGIA

HARGRETT RARE BOOKS AND MANUSCRIPT LIBRARY
University of Georgia
Athens, GA 30602
(706)542-7123
Rare manuscripts and photographs of the Cherokee and Creek; holdings of the Cherokee *Phoenix* (probably the first American Indian newspaper).

♦ ILLINOIS

MADISON COUNTY HISTORICAL MUSEUM
715 North Main St.
Edwardsville, IL 62025
(618)656-7562
John R. Sutter Collection: regional and Southwest items.

♦ INDIANA

LILLY LIBRARY
Indiana University
Bloomington, IN 47405
(812)855-2452
Collection of folktales of North American Western Indian groups; record of interviews of Indian survivors from Custer's Last Stand.

♦ MASSACHUSETTS

FRUITLANDS MUSEUM
102 Prospect Hill Rd.
Harvard, MA 01451
(508)456-9028

♦ MICHIGAN

FORT ST. JOSEPH MUSEUM
508 East Main St.
Niles, MI 49120
(616)683-4702
Plym/Quimby Collection of Sioux Indian artifacts, 1881–83, including drawings by Sitting Bull and Rain-in-the-Face.

MUSEUMS LIBRARY AT CLEMENTS LIBRARY AND HATCHER GRADUATE LIBRARY
University of Michigan
Ann Arbor, MI
(313)764-2347

♦ MINNESOTA

MINNESOTA HISTORICAL SOCIETY LIBRARY
Research Center
345 Kellogg Blvd. W.
St. Paul, MN 55102-1906
(612)296-2143
Print, sound, and visual collections of Plains Indians, especially the Ojibwa and Dakota.

♦ NEBRASKA

LIBRARY AND STATE ARCHIVES
Nebraska Historical Society
P.O. Box 82554
Lincoln, NE 68501
(402)471-3270
Central Plains Indians.

♦ NEW JERSEY

FIRESTONE LIBRARY
PRINCETON COLLECTIONS OF WESTERN AMERICANA
Princeton University
Princeton, NJ 08544
(609)258-3214

♦ NEW MEXICO

INDIAN PUEBLO CULTURAL CENTER
2401 12th St. N.W.
Albuquerque, NM 87102
(505)843-7270
Archival collection on the Southwest; owned and operated by nineteen pueblos of New Mexico.

LABORATORY OF ANTHROPOLOGY LIBRARY
Museum of New Mexico
P.O. Box 2087
Santa Fe, NM 87504
(505)827-6344

SAN JUAN COUNTY ARCHAEOLOGICAL RESEARCH CENTER AND LIBRARY AT SALMON RUIN
P.O. Box 125
Bloomfield, NM 87413
(505)632-2013
Anasazi artifacts; oral history collection, especially Navajo.

SCHOOL OF AMERICAN RESEARCH
Indian Arts Research Center
P.O. Box 2188
Santa Fe, NM 87501
(505)982-3583
Southwestern American Indian art.

ZUNI ARCHAEOLOGY PROGRAM
P.O. Box 339
Zuni, NM 87327
(505)782-4814
Archaeological site records, maps, air photos of Zuni Reservation; unpublished manuscripts on Zuni.

♦ NEW YORK

HUNTINGTON FREE LIBRARY
9 Westchester Sq.
Bronx, NY 10461
(212)829-7770
Outstanding archival collections on American Indian languages and newspapers; fieldnotes of prominent archaeologists.

NEW YORK PUBLIC LIBRARY
Fifth Ave. and 42nd St.
New York, NY 10018
(212)930-0827

♦ NORTH CAROLINA

HUNTER LIBRARY
Western Carolina University
Cullowhee, NC 28723
(704)227-7307
Collections on the Cherokee.

NORTH CAROLINA STATE ARCHIVES
109 East Jones St.
Raleigh, NC 27601-2807
(919)733-3952
North Carolina Indian records.

♦ OHIO

THE HISTORY LIBRARY OF THE WESTERN RESERVE HISTORICAL SOCIETY
10825 East Blvd.
Cleveland, OH 44106
(216)721-5722

OHIO HISTORICAL SOCIETY ARCHIVES AND LIBRARY DIVISION
1982 Velma Ave.
Columbus, OH 43211
(614)297-2300
Ohio Indians.

♦ OKLAHOMA

ARCHIVES AND MANUSCRIPTS DIVISION, OKLAHOMA HISTORICAL SOCIETY
2100 North Lincoln Blvd.
Oklahoma City, OK 73105
(405)521-2491
Five Civilized Tribes in Oklahoma.

MUSEUM OF THE GREAT PLAINS
P.O. Box 68
Lawton, OK 73502
(405)581-3460
Photograph collections of the Great Plains.

WESTERN HISTORY COLLECTIONS
University of Oklahoma Libraries
630 Parrington Oval, Room 452
Norman, OK 73091
(405)325-3641
One of the largest collections on North American Indians, especially on Southern Plains Indians.

♦ PENNSYLVANIA

AMERICAN PHILOSOPHICAL SOCIETY LIBRARY
105 South Fifth St.
Philadelphia, PA 19106-3386
(215)440-3400
Fieldnotes of prominent anthropologists who worked closely with Indians.

FRIENDS HISTORICAL LIBRARY
500 College Ave.
Swarthmore College
Swarthmore, PA 19081
(215)328-4900

READING PUBLIC MUSEUM AND ART GALLERY
500 Museum Rd.
Reading, PA 19611
(215)371-5850
Special collection of southeastern Pennsylvania lithic objects; Speck Collection of Delaware material; mound pottery.

VAN PELT LIBRARY AND UNIVERSITY MUSEUM LIBRARY
University of Pennsylvania
Philadelphia, PA 19104
(215)898-7091

♦ RHODE ISLAND

JOHN CARTER BROWN LIBRARY
Brown University
P.O. Box 1894
Providence, RI 02912
(401)863-2725
Rare manuscripts; Americana collections from 1492 to 1830.

♦ SOUTH DAKOTA

AGRICULTURAL HERITAGE MUSEUM
South Dakota State University
P.O. Box 2207C
Brookings, SD 57007
(605)688-6226
Indian Agricultural Heritage Collection of South Dakota.

CENTER FOR WESTERN STUDIES
Augustana College
P.O. Box 727
Sioux Falls, SD 57197
(605)336-4007
Native American Historical Research and Archival Agency.

I.D. WEEKS LIBRARY
University of South Dakota
414 East Clark St.
Vermillion, SD 57069
(605)677-5371
Upper Great Plains Sioux Indians.

ROBINSON MUSEUM
900 Governor's Drive
Pierre, SD 57501
(605)773-3797
Special Plains Indian collection.

SIOUXLAND HERITAGE MUSEUM
200 West Sixth St.
Sioux Falls, SD 57102
Pettigrew-Drady Indian Collection, primarily Dakota artifacts, 1870–1920; Photograph Collection, 1870–1900.

♦ TEXAS

CROCKETT COUNTY MUSEUM
P.O. Box 1444
Ozona, TX 76943
(915)392-2837
Frank Mills Indian Collection.

FIKES HALL OF SPECIAL COLLECTIONS
De Golyer Library
P.O. Box 396, SMU Station
Southern Methodist University
Dallas, TX 75275
(214)692-2253
History and archaeology of the American West.

♦ UTAH

FAMILY HISTORY LIBRARY
35 West Temple
Salt Lake City, UT 84150
(801)240-4750
Geneological information on American Indians.

♦ WASHINGTON

SPECIAL COLLECTIONS AND PRESERVATION DIVISION
Allen Library FM-25
University of Washington
Seattle, WA 98195
(206)543-1929
Pacific Northwest region.

♦ WEST VIRGINIA

WEST VIRGINIA STATE MUSEUM
Culture and History
Cultural Center
1900 Kwanall Blvd. E.
Charleston, WV 25305-0300
Migration records of Indian groups.

♦ WISCONSIN

FAIRLAWN HISTORICAL MUSEUM
Harvard View Pkwy.
Superior, WI 54880
(715)394-5712
David F. Barry Collection of Sioux Indian Portraits; Catlin Lithographs of Indians of the Plains.

THE RAHR PUBLIC MUSEUM
610 North Eighth St.
Manitowoc, WI 54220
(414)683-4501
Manitowoc County Indian Artifacts Collection.

♦ WYOMING

AMERICAN HERITAGE CENTER
University of Wyoming
P.O. Box 3924
Laramie, WY 82071
(307)766-4114

CANADA

♦ ALBERTA

BRUCE PEEL LIBRARY
South Rutherford
University of Alberta
Edmonton, AB T6G 2J8
(403)492-5998

CANADIAN CIRCUMPOLAR LIBRARY
University of Alberta
B-03 Cameron
Edmonton, AB T6G 2J8
(403)492-4409

HUMANITIES AND SOCIAL SCIENCES LIBRARY
Rutherford North
University of Alberta
Edmonton, AB T6G 2J8
(403)492-3790

NAKODA LEARNING CENTRE
Stoney Tribal Administration
P.O. Box 120
Morley, AB T0L 1N0
(403)881-3949 or (403)881-3951

UNIVERSITY OF ALBERTA
Bibliotheque Faculte St. Jean Library
8406 91st St.
Edmonton, AB T6C 4G9
(403)465-8711

♦ BRITISH COLUMBIA

BRITISH COLUMBIA ARCHIVES AND RECORDS SERVICE
655 Belleville
Victoria, BC V8V 1X4
(604)387-1952

KAMLOOPS MUSEUM AND ARCHIVES
207 Seymour St.
Kamloops, BC V2C 2E7
(604)828-3576

UNIVERSITY OF BRITISH COLUMBIA LIBRARY
Humanities and Social Sciences Division
1956 Main Mall
Vancouver, BC V6T 1Z1
(604)822-2725

♦ MANITOBA

DEPARTMENT OF INDIAN AFFAIRS—COMMUNICATION SERVICES
275 Portage Avenue, 8th Floor
Winnipeg, MB R3B 3A3
(204)983-4928

NORTHWEST COMPANY LIBRARY
77 Main St.
Winnipeg, MB R3C 2R1
(204)943-0881

MANITOBA INDIAN CULTURE-EDUCATIONAL CENTRE
Peoples Library
119 Sutherland Avenue
Winnipeg, MB R2W 3C9
(204)942-0228

PROVINCIAL ARCHIVES OF MANITOBA
200 Vaughan St.
Winnipeg, MB R3C 1T5
(204)945-3971

♦ NORTHWEST TERRITORIES

ARCTIC COLLEGE
Thebacha Campus Library
Bag Service No. 2
Fort Smith, NWT X0E 0P0
(403)872-7544

♦ ONTARIO

DEPARTMENT OF INDIAN NORTHERN AFFAIRS DEVELOPMENT
Departmental Library
Les Terrasses de la Chaudiere
Ottawa, ON K1A 0H4
(819)997-0811

LAURENTIAN UNIVERSITY
J.N. Desmarais Library
Ramsey Lake Rd.
Sudbury, ON P3E 2C6
(705)675-1151

ASSEMBLY OF FIRST NATIONS
Resource Centre
55 Murray St., Suite 500
Ottawa, ON K1N 5M3
(613)236-0673

THE MOHAWK COUNCIL OF AKWESASNE
Research Archives
P.O. Box 579
Cornwall, ON K6H 5T3
(613)575-2250, ext. 191

OJIBWAY-CREE CULTURAL CENTRE
Resource Centre Library
152 Third Avenue
Timmins, ON P4N 1C5
(705)267-7911, ext. 16

QUEEN'S UNIVERSITY
Douglas Library
Kingston, ON K7L 5C4
(613)545-2528

ROYAL ONTARIO MUSEUM LIBRARY
100 Queen's Park
Toronto, ON M5S 2C6
(416)586-5595

TRENT UNIVERSITY
Thomas J. Bata Library
P.O. Box 4800
Peterborough, ON K9J 7B8
(705)748-1324

♦ QUEBEC

CANADIAN MUSEUM OF CIVILIZATION LIBRARY
100 Laurier Street
Hull, PQ J8X 4H2
(819)776-7173

♦ SASKATCHEWAN

GABRIEL DUMONT INSTITUTE OF NATIVE STUDIES AND APPLIED RESEARCH LIBRARY
121 Broadway Ave. E.
Regina, SK S4N 0Z6
(306)522-5691, ext. 184

NATIVE LAW CENTRE LIBRARY
University of Saskatchewan
150 Diefenbaker Centre, Room 159
Saskatoon, SK S7N 0W0
(306)966-6195

SASKATCHEWAN DEPARTMENT OF SOCIAL WORK SERVICES
Chateau Tower
1920 Broad Street
Regina, SK S4P 3V6
(306)787-3680

SASKATCHEWAN INDIAN CULTURAL CENTRE
Library & Information Services
401 Packham Pl
Saskatoon, SK S7N 2T7
(306)244-1146

SASKATCHEWAN INDIAN FEDERATED COLLEGE LIBRARY
University of Regina
Room 118, College West
Regina, SK S4S 0A2
(306)779-6269

Historical Societies and Organizations

UNITED STATES

♦ ARIZONA

SOCIETY FOR HISTORICAL ARCHAEOLOGY
P.O. Box 30446
Tucson, AZ 85751

♦ ARKANSAS

ARKANSAS HISTORY COMMISSION
1 Capitol Mall
Little Rock, AR 72201
(501)682-6900

ORDER OF THE INDIAN WARS
P.O. Box 7401
Little Rock, AR 72217
(501)225-3996

♦ CALIFORNIA

CALIFORNIA HISTORICAL SOCIETY
2099 Pacific Ave.
San Francisco, CA 94109
(415)567-1848

♦ CONNECTICUT

CONNECTICUT HISTORICAL SOCIETY MUSEUM
1 Elizabeth St.
Hartford, CT 06105
(203)236-5621

♦ DISTRICT OF COLUMBIA

AMERICAN ANTHROPOLOGICAL ASSOCIATION
AMERICAN ETHNOLOGICAL SOCIETY
1703 New Hampshire Ave. N.W.
Washington, DC 20009
(202)232-8800

AMERICAN HISTORICAL ASSOCIATION
400 A St. S.E.
Washington, DC 20003
(202)544-2422

NATIONAL GEOGRAPHIC SOCIETY
Washington, DC 20036
(202)857-7000

♦ ILLINOIS

AMERICAN INDIAN LIBRARY ASSOCIATION (AILA)
American Library Association
Office of Library Outreach Services (OLOS)
50 East Huron St.
Chicago, IL 60611
(800)545-2433 Ext. 4295 or 4296

AMERICAN SOCIETY FOR ETHNOHISTORY
Center for the History of the American Indian
Newberry Library
60 West Walton St.
Chicago, IL 60610
(312)943-9090

♦ INDIANA

SOCIETY FOR ETHNOMUSICOLOGY
Indiana University
Morrison Hall 005
Bloomington, IN 47405
(812)855-6672

♦ KANSAS

KANSAS STATE HISTORICAL SOCIETY MUSEUM
120 West Tenth St.
Topeka, KS 66612-1291
(913)296-3251

♦ MASSACHUSETTS

AMERICAN ANTIQUARIAN SOCIETY
185 Salisbury St.
Worcester, MA 01609
(508)755-5221

ARCHAEOLOGICAL INSTITUTE OF AMERICA
675 Commonwealth Ave.
Boston, MA 02215
(617)353-9361

♦ MICHIGAN

MICHIGAN HISTORICAL MUSEUM
717 West Allegan
Lansing, MI 48918
(517)373-3559

♦ MINNESOTA

MINNESOTA HISTORICAL SOCIETY MUSEUM
345 Kellogg Blvd.
St. Paul, MN 55102-1906
(612)296-8071
Minnesota Indians, especially Dakota (Sioux), and Ojibwa (Chippewa); Oral History Collection Archives.

♦ MISSOURI

MISSOURI HISTORICAL SOCIETY MUSEUM
P.O. Box 11940
St. Louis, MO 63112-0040
(314)746-4599

♦ MONTANA

MONTANA HISTORICAL SOCIETY MUSEUM
225 North Roberts
Helena, MT 59620-9990
(406)444-2694
Primarily regional, especially Blackfeet, Sioux, and northern Plains.

♦ NEBRASKA

FORT ROBINSON MUSEUM
Nebraska State Historical Society
P.O. Box 304
Crawford, NE 69339
(308)665-2852
Microfilm records of Red Cloud and Spotted Tail Agencies.

♦ NEVADA

NEVADA HISTORICAL SOCIETY MUSEUM
1650 North Virginia St.
Reno, NV 89503
(702)688-1190
Emphasis on Washoe, Paiute, and Shoshoni.

♦ NEW MEXICO

AMERICAN SOCIETY FOR CONSERVATION ARCHAEOLOGY
Laboratory of Anthropology
Museum of New Mexico
P.O. Box 2087
Santa Fe, NM 87504-2087
(505)827-6344

ARCHAEOLOGICAL CONSERVANCY
415 Orchard Dr.
Santa Fe, NM 87501
(505)982-3278

♦ NORTH CAROLINA

CHEROKEE HISTORICAL ASSOCIATION
P.O. Box 398
Cherokee, NC 28719
(704)497-2111

♦ NORTH DAKOTA

STATE HISTORICAL SOCIETY OF NORTH DAKOTA
612 East Boulevard Ave.
Bismarck, ND 58505
(701)224-2666

♦ OKLAHOMA

CHEROKEE NATIONAL HISTORICAL SOCIETY
P.O. Box 515
Tahlequah, OK 74465
(918)456-6007

OKLAHOMA HISTORICAL SOCIETY MUSEUM
THE STATE MUSEUM OF OKLAHOMA
2100 North Lincoln Blvd.
Wiley Post Historical Blvd.
Oklahoma City, OK 73105
(405)521-2491
One of the largest collections of Indian historical documents in the world.

♦ RHODE ISLAND

RHODE ISLAND HISTORICAL SOCIETY MUSEUM
110 Benevolent St.
Providence, RI 02906
(401)331-8575
Primarily Narragansett and Wampanoag tribes.

♦ SOUTH CAROLINA

CHESTER COUNTY HISTORICAL SOCIETY MUSEUM
124 Saluda St.
Chester, SC 29706
(803)385-2330
Gatlin Catawba Indian Collection.

♦ SOUTH DAKOTA

SOUTH DAKOTA STATE HISTORICAL MUSEUM
Cultural Heritage Center
900 Governor's Dr.
Pierre, SD 57501-2217
(605)773-3458

♦ VERMONT

VERMONT HISTORICAL SOCIETY
109 State St.
Montpelier, VT 05609-0901
(802)828-2291

♦ VIRGINIA

VIRGINIA HISTORICAL SOCIETY
428 North Blvd.
Richmond, VA 23221
(804)358-4901

♦ WASHINGTON

WASHINGTON STATE HISTORICAL SOCIETY
315 North Stadium Way
Tacoma, WA 98403
(206)593-2830

♦ WISCONSIN

MUSEUM OF THE STATE HISTORICAL SOCIETY OF WISCONSIN
816 State St.
Madison, WI 53706-1488
(608)264-6400

CANADA

♦ ONTARIO

ANTHROPOLOGICAL ASSOCIATION OF CANADA
1575 Forlan Dr.
Ottawa, ON K2C OR8
(613)225-3405

CANADIAN HISTORICAL SOCIETY
395 Wellington St.
Ottawa, ON K1A 0N3
(613)233-7885

References

Before A.D. 1500

Cordell, Linda S. *Prehistory of the Southwest.* Orlando, FL: Academic Press, 1984.

Deetz, James. *Invitation to Archaeology.* Garden City, NY: Published for the American Museum of Natural History by the Natural History Press, 1967.

Jelks, Edward B. and Juliet C. Jelks, eds. *Historical Dictionary of North American Archaeology.* New York: Greenwood Press, 1988.

Jennings, Jesse D., ed. *Ancient Native Americans.* San Francisco: W. H. Freeman, 1978.

Milanich, Jerald T. and Charles H. Fairbanks. *Florida Archaeology.* New York: Academic Press, 1980.

Moratto, Michael J. *California Archaeology.* Orlando, FL: Academic Press, 1984.

Morse, Dan F. and Phyliss A. Morse. *Archaeology of the Central Mississippi Valley.* New York: Academic Press, 1983.

Ritchie, William A. *The Archaeology of New York State.* Rev. edition. Garden City, NY: Published for the American Museum of Natural History by the Natural History Press, 1969.

Smith, Bruce D., ed. *Mississippian Settlement Patterns.* New York: Academic Press, 1978.

Snow, Dean R. *The Archaeology of New England.* New York: Academic Press, 1980.

Taylor, R. E. and Clement W. Meighan, eds. *Chronologies in New World Archaeology.* New York: Academic Press, 1978.

Wedel, Waldo R. *Prehistoric Man on the Great Plains.* Norman: University of Oklahoma Press, 1961.

J. Daniel Rogers

U.S. Indians, 1500 to 1965

Aberle, David. *The Peyote Religion Among the Navaho.* Chicago: Aldine, 1966.

Baird, W. David. *Peter Pitchlynn: Chief of the Choctaws.* Norman: University of Oklahoma Press, 1972.

Bannon, John F. *The Mission Frontier in Sonora, 1620–1687*. Edited by James A. Reynolds. New York: U.S. Catholic Historical Society, 1955.

Berthrong, Donald J. *The Southern Cheyennes*. Norman: University of Oklahoma Press, 1963.

Casas, Bartolome de las. *A Short Account of the Destruction of the Indies*. New York: Penguin, 1992.

Cohen, Felix S. *Handbook of Federal Indian Law*. Albuquerque: University of New Mexico Press, 1971.

Corkran, David H. *The Cherokee Frontier: Conflict and Survival, 1740–62*. Norman: University of Oklahoma Press, 1962.

Debo, Angie. *And Still the Waters Run*. Princeton: Princeton University Press, 1940.

____. *A History of the Indians of the United States*. Norman: University of Oklahoma Press, 1971.

Edmunds, R. David. *The Shawnee Prophet*. Lincoln: University of Nebraska Press, 1983.

____. *Tecumseh and the Quest for Indian Leadership*. Boston: Little, Brown, 1984.

Foreman, Grant. *Indian Removal: The Emigration of the Five Civilized Tribes of Indians*. Norman: University of Oklahoma Press, 1932.

____. *Last Trek of the Indians*. Chicago: University of Chicago Press, 1946.

Gibson, Arrell M. *The American Indian: Prehistory to the Present*. Lexington, MA: D.C. Heath, 1980.

____, ed. *America's Exiles: Indian Colonization in Oklahoma*. Oklahoma City: Oklahoma Historical Society, 1976.

Grinde, Donald A. and Bruce E. Johansen. *Exemplar of Liberty: Native America and the Evolution of Democracy*. Los Angeles: American Indian Studies Center, UCLA, 1991.

Hagan, William T. *Indian Police and Judges: Experiments in Acculturation and Control*. Lincoln: University of Nebraska Press, 1980.

Heizer, Robert A., ed. *The Destruction of California Indians*. Santa Barbara, CA: Peregrine Smith, 1974.

Hertzberg, Hazel. *The Search for an American Indian Identity: Modern Pan-Indian Movements*. Syracuse, NY: Syracuse University Press, 1971.

Hoig, Stan. *The Sand Creek Massacre*. Norman: University of Oklahoma Press, 1961.

The Indian Historian. San Francisco: American Indian Historical Society, 1967–1979.

Jackson, Helen Hunt. *A Century of Dishonor*. New York: Harper & Brothers, 1881.

Jahoda, Gloria. *The Trail of Tears*. New York: Holt, Rinehart and Winston, 1975.

Jane, Cecil, trans. *Select Documents Illustrating the Four Voyages of Columbus*. Vol. 1. London: Hakluyt Society, 1930.

Josephy, Alvin M., Jr. *The Indian Heritage of America*. New York: Knopf, 1968.

____. *Now That the Buffalo's Gone: A Study of Today's American Indians*. New York: Knopf, 1982.

La Barre, Weston. *The Ghost Dance: Origins of Religion*. Garden City, NY: Doubleday, 1970.

Miner, Craig H. *The Corporation and the Indian: Tribal Sovereignty and Industrial Civilization in Indian Territory*. Columbia: University of Missouri Press, 1976.

Otis, Delos S. *The Dawes Act and the Allotment of Indian Lands*. Norman: University of Oklahoma Press, 1973.

Philp, Kenneth R. *John Collier's Crusade for Indian Reform, 1920–1954*. Tucson: University of Arizona Press, 1977.

Ruby, Robert H. and John A. Brown. *Indians of the Pacific Northwest: A History*. Norman: University of Oklahoma Press, 1981.

Satz, Ronald N. *American Indian Policy in the Jacksonian Era*. Lincoln: University of Nebraska Press, 1975.

Szasz, Margaret C. *Education and the American Indian: The Road to Self-Determination, 1928–1973*. Albuquerque: University of New Mexico Press, 1974.

Thompson, Gerald. *The Army and the Navajo: The Bosque Redondo Reservation Experiment, 1863–1868*. Tucson: University of Arizona Press, 1976.

Trafzer, Clifford E. *The Kit Carson Campaign: The Last Great Navajo War*. Norman: University of Oklahoma Press, 1982.

____ and Richard D. Scheuerman. *Renegade Tribe: The Palouse Indians and the Invasion of the Pacific Northwest*. Pullman: Washington State University Press, 1986.

Trennert, Robert A., Jr. *Alternative to Extinction: Federal Indian Policy and the Beginnings of the Reservation System, 1846–51*. Philadelphia: Temple University Press, 1975.

Tyler, S. Lyman. *A History of Indian Policy*. Washington, DC: U.S. Department of the Interior, Bureau of Indian Affairs, 1973.

Unrau, William E. *The Kansa Indians: A History of the Wind People*. Norman: University of Oklahoma Press, 1971.

Utley, Robert M. *Frontier Regulars: The United States Army and the Indian, 1866–1891*. New York: Macmillan, 1974.

Vaughan, Alden T. *New England Frontier: Puritans and Indians, 1620–1675*. Boston: Little, Brown, 1965.

Clifford E. Trafzer and Duane Champagne

U.S. Indians, 1966–91

American Antiquity. Washington, DC, 1935–present.

American Friends Service Committee. *Uncommon Controversy: Fishing Rights of the Muckleshoot, Puyallup and Nisqually Indians*. Seattle: University of Washington Press, 1970.

American Indians Today: Answers to Your Questions. Washington, DC: U.S. Department of the Interior, Bureau of Indian Affairs, 1991.

Cahn, Edgar, ed. *Our Brother's Keeper: The Indian in White America.* Washington, DC: New Community Press, 1969.

Castile, George P. and Robert L. Bee. *State and Reservation: New Perspectives in Federal Indian Policy.* Tucson: University of Arizona Press, 1992.

Cohen, Felix S. *Felix S. Cohen's Handbook of Federal Indian Law.* Charlottesville, VA: Michie: Bobbs-Merrill, 1982.

Deloria, Vine, Jr. *Behind the Trail of Broken Treaties: An Indian Declaration of Independence.* New York: Delacorte Press, 1974.

____. *Custer Died for Your Sins: An Indian Manifesto.* New York: Macmillan, 1969.

____. *We Talk, You Listen: New Tribes, New Turf.* New York: Macmillan, 1970.

Dorris, Michael. *The Broken Cord.* New York: Harper & Row, 1989.

Fixico, Donald L. *Urban Indians.* New York: Chelsea House, 1991.

Gibson, Arrell M. *The American Indian: Prehistory to Present.* Lexington, MA: D.C. Heath, 1980.

Josephy, Alvin, Jr. *Now That the Buffalo's Gone: A Study of Today's American Indians.* Norman: University of Oklahoma Press, 1984.

____. *Red Power: The American Indians' Fight for Freedom.* New York: American Heritage Press, 1971.

Kappler, Charles J., comp. and ed. *Indian Affairs: Laws and Treaties.* Washington, DC: U.S. Government Printing Office, 1903–41.

Messerschmidt, Jim. *The Trial of Leonard Peltier.* Boston: South End Press, 1983.

Momaday, N. Scott. *House Made of Dawn.* New York: Harper & Row, 1968.

O'Brien, Sharon. *American Indian Tribal Governments.* Norman: University of Oklahoma Press, 1989.

Prucha, Francis P. *American Indian Policy.* Norman: University of Oklahoma Press, 1986.

____. *The Great Father: The United States Government and the American Indians.* 2 vols. Lincoln: University of Nebraska Press, 1984.

Steiner, Stan. *The New Indians.* New York: Harper & Row, 1968.

Tundra Times. Anchorage, Alaska, 1962–82.

Sharon O'Brien

Canadian Native History, 1500 to 1992

Adams, Howard. *Prison of Grass: Canada from the Native Point of View.* Toronto: New Press, 1975.

Ahenakew, Edward. *Voices of the Plains Cree.* Toronto: McClelland and Stewart, 1973.

Angus, Murray. *"—And the Last Shall Be First": Native Policy in an Era of Cutbacks.* Rev. edition. Toronto: NC Press, 1991.

Asch, Michael. *Home and Native Land: Aboriginal Rights and the Canadian Constitution.* Toronto: Methuen, 1984.

Bailey, Alfred G. *The Conflict of European and Eastern Algonkian Cultures, 1504–1700: A Study in Canadian Civilization.* 2d edition. Toronto: University of Toronto Press, 1976.

Barman, Jean, Yvonne Hebert, and Don McCaskill, eds. *Indian Education in Canada.* 2 vols. Vancouver: University of British Columbia Press, 1986.

Brown, Jennifer S. H. *Strangers in Blood: Fur Trade Company Families in Indian Country.* Vancouver: University of British Columbia Press, 1980.

Canadian Department of Indian Affairs and Northern Development. *Statement of the Government of Canada on Indian Policy, 1969; Presented to the First Session of the Twenty-Eighth Parliament by the Honourable Jean Chretien, Minister of Indian Affairs and Northern Development.* Ottawa, 1969.

Cardinal, Harold. *The Rebirth of Canada's Indians.* Edmonton: Hurtig, 1977.

____. *The Unjust Society: The Tragedy of Canada's Indians.* Edmonton: Hurtig, 1969.

Crowe, Keith J. *A History of the Original Peoples of Northern Canada.* Rev. edition. Montreal: McGill-Queen's University Press, 1991.

Cumming, Peter A. and Neil H. Mickenberg, eds. *Native Rights in Canada.* 2d ed. Toronto: Indian-Eskimo Association of Canada in association with General Pub. Co., 1972.

Daniel, Richard C. *A History of the Native Claims Process in Canada, 1867–1979.* Ottawa: Research Branch, Department of Indian and Northern Affairs, 1980.

Dickason, Olive P. *Canada's First Nations: A History of Founding Peoples from Earliest Times.* Toronto: McClelland and Stewart, 1992.

Eccles, William J. *The Canadian Frontier: 1534–1760.* New York: Holt, Rinehart and Winston, 1969.

Fisher, Robin. *Contact and Conflict: Indian-European Relations in British Columbia, 1774–1890.* Vancouver: University of British Columbia Press, 1977.

____ and Kenneth Coates, eds. *Out of the Background: Readings on Canadian Native History.* Toronto: Copp Clark Pitman, 1988.

Fumoleau, Rene. *As Long As This Land Shall Last: A History of Treaty 8 and Treaty 11, 1870–1939.* Toronto: McClelland and Stewart, 1975?

Getty, Ian A. L. and Antoine S. Lussier, eds. *As Long as the Sun Shines and Water Flows: A Reader in Canadian Native Studies.* Vancouver: University of British Columbia Press, 1979.

Gifford, Martin, J. R. Aldridge, and Graham W. Allen. *Indians and the Law*. Vancouver: Continuing Legal Education Society of British Columbia, 1982–86.

Grant, John W. *Moon of Wintertime: Missionaries and the Indians of Canada in Encounter since 1534*. Toronto: University of Toronto Press, 1984.

Hawthorn, Harry B., ed. *A Survey of the Contemporary Indians of Canada: A Report on Economic, Political, Educational Needs and Policies*. 2 vols. Ottawa: Queen's Printer, 1966–67.

Indian Association of Alberta. *Citizens Plus*. Edmonton, 1970.

Jenness, Diamond. *The Indians of Canada*. 7th edition. Toronto: University of Toronto Press, 1977.

McCullum, Hugh, Karmel McCullum, and John Olthuis. *Moratorium: Justice, Energy, the North, and the Native People*. Toronto: Anglican Book Centre, 1977.

Miller, J. R. *Skyscrapers Hide the Heavens: A History of Indian-White Relations in Canada*. Rev. ed. Toronto: University of Toronto Press, 1991.

Morse, Bradford W., ed. *Aboriginal Peoples and the Law: Indian, Metis and Inuit Rights in Canada*. Ottawa: Carleton University Press, 1985.

Patterson, E. Palmer III. *The Canadian Indian: A History since 1500*. Don Mills: Collier-Macmillan Canada, 1972.

Ponting, J. Rick and Roger Gibbins. *Out of Irrelevance: A Socio-Political Introduction to Indian Affairs in Canada*. Toronto: Butterworths, 1980.

Price, Richard T. *Legacy: Indian Treaty Relationships*. Edmonton: Plains Publishing, 1991.

Purich, Donald. *Our Land: Native Rights in Canada*. Toronto: J. Lorimer, 1986.

Ray, Arthur J. *Indians in the Fur Trade: Their Role as Trappers, Hunters, and Middlemen in the Lands Southwest of Hudson Bay, 1660–1870*. Toronto: University of Toronto Press, 1974.

Tennant, Paul. *Aboriginal Peoples and Politics: The Indian Land Question in British Columbia, 1849–1984*. Vancouver: University of British Columbia, 1990.

Tobias, John L. "Canada's Subjugation of the Plains Cree, 1879–1885." *Canadian Historical Review* 64: 4 (1983): 519–48.

Trigger, Bruce G. *The Children of Aataentsic: A History of the Huron People to 1660*. Montreal: McGill-Queen's University Press, 1976.

Van Kirk, Sylvia. *"Many Tender Ties": Women in Fur Trade Society in Western Canada, 1670–1870*. Winnipeg: Watson & Dwyer, 1980 or 1981.

Weaver, Sally M. *Making Canadian Indian Policy: The Hidden Agenda 1968–70*. Toronto: University of Toronto Press, 1981.

Wuttunee, William I. C. *Ruffled Feathers: Indians in Canadian Society*. Calgary: Bell Books, 1971.

York, Geoffrey. *The Dispossessed: Life and Death in Native Canada*. Toronto: Lester & Orpen Dennys Publishers, 1989.

Ted Binnema

2

Demography

♦ Native Demography Before 1700
♦ Geographic and Demographic Change During the Eighteenth Century
♦ Indian Geographic Distribution, Habitat, and Demography During the Nineteenth Century
♦ Land Tenure in the Twentieth Century ♦ Canadian Native Distribution, Habitat, and Demography

♦ NATIVE DEMOGRAPHY BEFORE 1700

Indian groups moved from place to place in search of adequate food sources, for protection, or to escape changing climatic conditions, such as long droughts in the region. Many Indian peoples have stories of migrations, which sometimes send the people on religious quests. For example, one Creek story claims that the people migrated east for many years in search of the home of the sun, but upon reaching the Atlantic Ocean, gave up the quest and decided to settle. While there were some migrations prior to 1500, Indian migrations and population changes began to increase rapidly after the arrival of European colonists. The territorial expansion of the European colonies pushed many coastal Indian nations into the interior, where they were incorporated into other Indian nations or where they resettled, far from their original homelands. New trade relations with the Europeans, especially the fur trade, induced many Indian nations to seek new hunting territories, which often expanded into the lands of other nations. Perhaps the greatest change to Indian populations came from the introduction of several European diseases which were unknown previously to Indians, such as smallpox and scarlet fever. These diseases caused many deaths among the Indians, and were possibly responsible for 60 million deaths in North and South America by 1900, when the U.S. Indian population declined to a low point of about a quarter of a million. These events are often referred to as a demographic catastrophe. Native American demography is especially interesting because of the rapid decline and dispersion of the population after colonial contact.

Paleo-Indians

Archeologists, students of ancient cultures, believe that the first human beings entered the Americas by way of a land bridge that connected Siberia and Alaska toward the end of the last glacial period, approximately 15,000 to 25,000 years ago. At this time, huge continental glaciers contained so much frozen water that sea level had fallen below the bottom of what is now the Bering Strait. After crossing, the first Americans spread rapidly beyond present-day Alaska, and by the end of glacial times, about 12,000 years ago, had settled throughout North and South America.

It is important to note that some Native Americans do not believe that their ancestors walked across the Bering Strait. Most Indian cultures have oral traditions that recount the origins of people on earth. Many of these stories are analogous to the stories of Adam and Eve in the Bible. Other Indians have traditions of eastward migrations. For example, the Lenape,or Delaware Indians, who are considered by many Indian nations to be the grandfather of the Algonkian-speaking nations, have a long epic tradition of migration from the northwest to the Atlantic coast in present-day New England. Other nations such as the Cherokee, Choctaw, Chickasaw, and Creek have similar migration stories, where their whole nation was led by the instructions of a sacred pole, which each day pointed in the direction of that day's journey, and finally indicated the end of the march and new homeland by remaining upright. The migration traditions are not inconsistent with the Bering Strait theory of the archeologists; and considering the age of many creation stories, it is possible that these ancient traditions have roots that predate a migration over the Bering Strait.

For a few thousands years after the glacial period, many large game animals, such as woolly mammoths and large bison, roamed North America. These animals died out about 10,000 years ago, probably because of changing climatic conditions caused by the retreat north of the glaciers. Early Paleo-Indian culture revolved around hunting these animals. Paleo-Indians were large game hunting Indian peoples whose cultures predate the adoption of horticulture and the bow and arrow. Because of the large game animals' extinction, for the next seven or eight thousand years, Native Americans hunted smaller game, fished, and foraged for wild plant foods. Sometime around 1500 B.C. Indian groups began to plant crops such as corn, squash, and beans. Particularly in the present-day eastern and southwestern United States, Indian groups became increasingly dependent on horticulture, or farming with hand tools.

Native Americans slowly increased in numbers for several millennia. People acquired and transmitted to their descendants specialized knowledge about the natural resources in different regions and regional culture areas formed. These cultural areas are now known as the Northeast, Southeast, Plains, Southwest, Great Basin, California, Plateau, Pacific Northwest, Subarctic, and Arctic. (See the culture area sections of Chapter 3.)

By A.D. 1500, between seven and fifteen million people inhabited the present-day United States. Many people resided in the Southeast and Mississippi Valley where they dry-farmed or irrigated their crops. In the dry-farming Southeast, large towns grew on the natural levees flood waters formed along the edges of the major rivers. Levees rose high enough to keep settlements safe from most floods and supported a large assortment of plants that attracted game animals, making hunting easy and efficient near the towns. Townspeople depended significantly on fish caught from backwater lakes left by stream channel shifts. This cultural pattern is usually called Mississippian.

In the Southwest sometime after A.D. 1200, the Hohokam, ancestors of the present-day Piman-speaking tribes, began constructing multi-story, earthen-walled buildings. The Hohokam farmed with irrigation methods, and stored their crops within the earthen buildings. Ancestors of the present-day Pueblo began building similar multi-stories as early as A.D. 900. The Spanish

Storing Their Crops in the Public Granary. Many of the islands produce an abundance of fruits. These are gathered twice a year, carried home in canoes, and stored in low and roomy granaries, built of stones and earth and thickly roofed with palm branches and a kind of soft earth. Drawings by John White and Jacques Le Moyne and engraved by Theodore de Bry.

word *pueblo* applied to the compact, multi-storied fortress towns. Pueblo peoples sharing a common culture, despite speaking seven different languages, occupied hundreds of pueblos by A.D. 1500.

The peoples of California, the Pacific Northwest, the Great Basin, and the Subarctic and Arctic by 1500 had not adopted horticulture and continued as hunters and gatherers as they had for thousands of years.

Sixteenth Century

Few records dating from 1500 to 1620 describe the present-day United States. Yet the available documents consistently attest that European diseases rapidly spread throughout the Native American groups. By the time of his second voyage in 1493, Christopher Columbus's crews and colonists had transmitted diseases to the Native Americans. The "Columbian Exchange" of microbes and viruses turned into a demographic catastrophe for the Indians.

The Southeast Some of the earliest contacts of Southeastern Indians were with the Spanish in the early 1500s. One disease of unknown type reached present-day Florida by 1514. In 1528, Spanish castaways transmitted an undiagnosed ailment to their Galveston Island hosts on the modern Texas coast. Although it killed half of the Natives, we do not know how far the disease spread. From 1539 through 1543, Fernando de Soto's Spanish army marauded through the Southeast, slaughtering warriors, kidnapping women, and transmitting diseases to the Natives. Soto found several Indian villages that were already unoccupied owing to diseases that preceded his arrival. Natives probably contracted these diseases from unrecorded Spanish explorations or trading expeditions, and Native travelers and traders most likely transmitted the diseases from one village to another.

In 1559, a Spanish colonizing expedition carried epidemic influenza from Veracruz, Mexico, to Florida's Pensacola Bay. Colonists traveled inland seeking supplies from some of the populous towns Soto had visited. The colonists stayed hungry because the populous and prosperous Southeastern Indian nations that Soto's marauders had seen had dispersed into small village groups between 1543 and 1559. Malaria and stomach disorders probably caused most of the mortality, although the plague might have spread from the Spanish occupation of Mexico. In the Southeast, the diseases caused a significant loss of life as well as the reorganization of Native political and social structures. Many of the southeastern Indians were part of centralized Mississippian culture groups with hierarchal bodies of priests and chiefs. After the population declined, these Mississippian cultures collapsed and the Indians regrouped as egalitarian coalitions of villages. It was these egalitarian Indian nations that the colonists encountered by the 1700s. Known today as the Cherokee, the Catawba, the Creek, and the Choctaw, these groups survived by constantly incorporating remnant peoples.

The Northeast In 1535, Jacques Cartier, a French explorer, and his crews transmitted a lethal disease to the Iroquois who were living along the St. Lawrence River. Before the century ended, the Iroquois abandoned their homeland because Algonkian-speaking nations, the Chippewa, Ottawa and others, invaded the St. Lawrence area. Some Iroquois probably migrated to join the Mohawk in present-day upstate New York. By the end of the 1500s, Chippewa, Ottawa, Potawatomi, and other Algonkian speakers were beginning to migrate from eastern Canada toward the Great Lakes. Iroquois and Algonkian communities were dispersed and forced to migrate inland owing to rampant disease and new colonial occupation.

Southward, in the middle Atlantic area of present-day Virginia, Europeans reported outbreaks of smallpox in 1564 among Indian peoples ranging from the Timucuan in Florida to the Chesapeake Bay people, such as the Powhatan, Pamunkey, and Mattaponi. The virus apparently spread north up the Susquehanna River through present-day Pennsylvania, carried by Native traders and travelers. As a consequence, the Susquehannock lost so many people to disease that by 1580 the entire nation was reduced to a single village.

English colonists carried lethal disease to Roanoke Island Natives in 1585. Viral diseases evidently killed a quarter of North Carolina's Indian population during that same year. In 1586, the English explorer Francis Drake attacked the Spanish at St. Augustine, Florida and transmitted disease to the Timucuan, a major tribe of the region.

The Southwest Because colonists often could not diagnose diseases that struck Natives, it is difficult to estimate how far the diseases spread. As the Native population declined, survivors abandoned some settlements and amalgamated in others. The sequence of abandonment of Hopi pueblos on the Little Colorado River in present-day Arizona provides clues to epidemic disease among all Pueblo peoples. About 1500, the Hopi, a western Pueblo nation, inhabited about ten pueblos. When Spaniards arrived in 1540, seven were still inhabited, indicating perhaps that disease had spread there from New Spain, or present-day Mexico.

In 1583, when the Spaniards next encountered the Hopi, only five pueblos were occupied. This attrition indicates that one or more of the four major epidemics that afflicted Mexico during the interval had spread among the Pueblo, resulting in abandonment and amalgamation. Hopi inhabited four pueblos in 1598, and epidemics of smallpox or measles probably reached them sometime between 1592 and 1593. This epidemic caused significant mortality and abandonment of one pueblo.

After the 1613–20 plague epidemic, the Hopi abandoned the remaining pueblos on the Little Colorado River. The survivors migrated to join five Hopi pueblos at Black Mesa, sixty miles to the north, also in present-day Arizona. Thus, between 1519 and 1650, the ten once-populous Hopi pueblos were decimated and abandoned.

Historic attrition among other Pueblo language groups shows that Hopi depopulation was a typical experience among all pueblos. By 1630, Franciscan missionaries had consolidated 6,000 Piro from fourteen pueblos in three missions and one village, a 71 percent reduction in the number of Piro Pueblo settlements. Southern Tiwa-speakers inhabited sixteen Rio Grande Valley pueblos in 1540; by 1641, only three Tiwa pueblos were left, an 81 percent reduction in settlements. Other Pueblo peoples, such as the Jemez and the Towa-speakers in the Rio Grande Valley, suffered similar declines in population.

Thanks to European records of the 1500s, we know more about the demography of the east and southwest Indian groups than we do about the demography of the Native peoples of the Subarctic, Northeast Coast, California, Plateau, or Great Basin areas during this time. While we know virtually nothing about these groups during the 1500s, there is more information about these peoples from the following century.

Seventeenth Century

As European colonies proliferated, so did records of migrations and of epidemics disastrous to Native Americans. In contrast to the 1500s, which were marked by severe demographic change in the loss of human life to disease, the 1600s are more characterized by the intensification of trade relations, and the expansion of colonial empires. Indian nations came under great pressure to adapt to European trade and political pressures, and many Indian nations were forced to migrate into the interior for relief from colonial expansion, while some remained in their homelands and attempted to accommodate the new laws and political domination of the European colonists. Despite increased pressure to migrate and adapt, disease and death continued as a persistent feature of Indian life during the 1600s.

The Northeast When English colonists came to what became Jamestown in present-day Virginia, they encountered the Powhatan, a confederacy of twenty-seven tribes on the James, York, and Potomac Rivers,

Kiva at San Juan Pueblo.

Taos Pueblo.

with a total population exceeding 10,000. Sixteen other Algonkian-speaking groups, numbering about 15,000 people, also lived in the same coastal area. In 1607, the English colonists invaded the Powhatan territory, causing some deaths among the Powhatan and their neighboring allies. In 1613–17, the Powhatan and allies suffered a plague epidemic that had originated with Florida's Indian population. In an apparent response to the loss of life and continued aggression by the colonists, the Powhatan rose up against the colonists in 1622. The war lasted intermittently for about ten years, causing many deaths on both sides. The surviving Powhatan rose up against the colonists again in 1644–46 but were defeated and forced to cede their lands between the York and Blackwater rivers. By the late 1600s, most of the Indians in the area were dispossessed and made subject to Virginia law.

In 1614, Dutch merchants on the Hudson River in present-day New York established a trading post in Mahican territory, near present-day Albany, New York. The fur trade—the exchange of beaver, deer, and other skins for European manufactured goods (especially metal goods such as guns, hoes, and hatchets)—became the most significant exchange between the early colonists and Indian nations. Indians quickly realized the value of European goods over their own stone tools, and soon found the Europeans willing to trade for furs, which were sold as beaver hats, leather and coats in Europe. After a few years, the Indians began to prefer trade goods, and discontinued producing many traditional arts and crafts. Soon, many Indian nations were not willing or able to reproduce their own material or economic needs, and came to depend on the trade of furs to supply basic economic and manufacturing needs. Thereafter, the Indians were dependent on the Europeans to supply many basic needs, and could no longer live without trade with the colonists.

For three years, from 1614 to 1617, Algonkian-speaking Mahican collected tribute from the Mohawk, the easternmost nation of the Five Nations Iroquois Confederacy, for crossing their territory to trade with the Dutch. In 1624, the Dutch built Fort Orange, now Albany, and a Mahican village moved nearby. From 1624 to 1648, the Mohawk waged war on the Mahican and ousted them from the area around the new European outpost.

Death rates ran high among Natives on New England's frontier. For example, in 1613–17, plague killed half of

Florida's Native population. The plague spread northward along the Atlantic coast, weakening the Powhatan. It killed so many Massachusetts Indians that the Puritans who settled in the area during the 1630s believed that God had cleared away the lands of the infidel Natives, preparing it for the Puritan arrival and settlement. In 1634, the Nipmuck lost 450 of 1,000 inhabitants of one town. Colonists compounded the impact of scarlet fever with the Pequot War in 1637, which started when the Pequot people allowed Dutch traders to establish a post east of the Connecticut River at present-day East Hartford. The English raised an army, including Narragansett and Mohegan allies, and burned down a major Pequot village, killing at least 300 men, women, and children. Two hundred survivors were sold into slavery.

Because the Natives depended on trade, Native peoples began fighting over areas of access to European trading posts and to areas that were endowed with fur-bearing animals that could be traded to Europeans. In 1643, Mahican conquered three Algonkian-speaking tribes and several hundred others fled to Manhattan and Pavoia where the Dutch massacred them, ensuring Mahican dominance. This conflict cost about 1,000 Native lives.

Because of a scarlet fever epidemic in 1638, 600 Wenro, an Iroquoian-speaking nation living along the lower Great Lakes, abandoned their territory and moved in with the Huron, another Iroquoian-speaking group living nearby. Other Wenro found refuge among other Iroquoian-speaking nations.

Epidemics might have motivated the Mascouten, Kickapoo, Fox, Sauk, and Potawatomi to leave the lower peninsula of Michigan about 1641 to migrate to Winnebago territory at Green Bay. The once-powerful Winnebago lost 1,500 men to an epidemic and lost another five hundred men to war with the Fox, which greatly weakened the Winnebago's resistance to prevent other Indian nations from moving into their territory.

By the 1640s, the Iroquois, the Five Nations, had already over-exploited their fur-bearing territories and were looking westward to gain access to trade or hunting territories. Most tribes in the Great Lakes region sided with the French, who wished to prevent Iroquois expansion into the interior, since the Iroquois were Dutch and English trading allies. In the late 1640s,unable to secure trade agreements with the interior nations (the Huron, the Erie, the Petun, the Neutral Nation, and others), the Iroquois initiated military action to secure access to fur-bearing territories. Dutch traders supported the Five Nations by supplying them with guns and powder; this gave the Five Nations an advantage over the French-allied Indians since the French were reluctant to trade weapons with the Indians. Between 1649 and 1700, the Iroquois waged a series of conflicts with interior nations such as the Illinois Confederacy, the Ottawa, the Huron, and others. These wars, called the Beaver Wars, represented a period of almost constant warfare in the northeast region among the Five Nations, the French and their Indian trade allies.

During the winter of 1649–50, an Iroquois army marched west and dispersed the Petun people. A Seneca and Mohawk army, composed of two of the Five Nations of the Iroquois Confederacy, then attacked the Neutral Nation traders and its refugees, dispersing them. The campaign demonstrated that the Seneca and Mohawk were extremely dependent on European goods. In 1652, the Iroquois defeated the Susquehannock people, taking from 500 to 600 prisoners. The Susquehannock population fell to between 3,000 and 2,000. In 1653, the Iroquois waged war on the Erie people and dispersed them. Between 1649 and 1670, most of the Iroquoian-speaking nations of the lower Great Lakes, such as the Huron, the Petun, the Erie, and the Neutral Nation, were either destroyed, dispersed, or adopted by the Five Nations' military expansion.

At the time of the Iroquois expansion, New England's colonists openly waged a genocidal war of territorial conquest against Native peoples in 1675. The Wampanoag of Massachusetts bore the brunt of the assault. The colonists virtually exterminated the Wampanoag in a war the colonists called King Philip's War, after a Wampanoag leader. By this time the Massachusetts Indians had been so reduced by diseases, that the colonists ignored them. Although the Narragansett people of Connecticut and Rhode Island did not participate early in King Philip's War, a colonial army invaded their territory and broke their power. Narragansett people either found refuge with the Niantic people or left New England altogether. The New England Indians were thereafter subject to English law and many lived on the outskirts of English settlements, eking out a marginal existence. About fifteen New England Indian villages adopted Christianity; they became known as Praying Towns, and, to a certain extent, lived in the tradition of New England town government and Puritan religion.

By the late 1600s, the Indian nations of Virginia and Maryland were also subject to colonial law, and were to a large extent dispossessed of their original coastal lands. Disease and war caused their populations to decline significantly, and the colonists already outnumbered them in the colonial territories. By 1700, the colonial governments largely ignored most Indians in the middle Atlantic colonies; the Indian communities persisted, however, and remained targets of land speculators, who often succeeded in purchasing the remnants of their land.

Not all Indian nations were dispossessed of their homeland by the colonists. During most of the 1600s, the

Shawnee lived in northern Kentucky, southern Ohio, and western Virginia. By the late 1690s, however, they were constantly raided for slaves by the Chickasaw and Cherokee, who sold them to the English colonists. The Shawnee abandoned their homeland in the 1690s, some moving to present-day Georgia, others migrating to join the Creek Nation, while others still joined the Delaware in eastern Pennsylvania. There, on land granted by the Five Nations, and under obligation to pay tribute to the Iroquois Empire, the Shawnee joined in alliance with the Delaware, who themselves had retreated from the coastal areas of New York and New Jersey in search of furbearing territories and refuge from the colonial expansion. Both the Shawnee and Delaware nations were buffeted throughout their history by colonial expansion, and were subjected to trade dependency which required them to work as hunters for European traders. Both nations were eventually forced to migrate into Ohio, Indiana, and by the early 1800s to Kansas, and some settled in Indian Territory, or present-day Oklahoma. Many nations of the northeast were also forced to migrate further west, but the Delaware and Shawnee illustrate the fate of a people who were ultimately forced to migrate half-way across the North American continent in an effort to find refuge from colonial expansion.

The Susquehannock, who during the late 1600s lived in southern present-day Pennsylvania, virtually disappeared because of disease and colonial expansion. Although they held their native Susquehanna River against Iroquois assaults until 1675, mortality from epidemic influenza that spread among the Iroquois and New England's Native peoples in 1675 during King Philip's War might have been the decisive factor in the Susquehannock's decline and subjugation. Suffering calamitous losses during the Iroquois wars against the French beginning in 1677, many of the remaining Susquehannock joined the Shawnee and the Delaware who were living near present-day Philadelphia between 1677 and 1700.

Further west, in the Great Lakes area, many of the Algonkian speakers and other nations were also affected by the Beaver Wars and colonial expansion. The Potawatomi who lived between Lake Michigan and Green Bay (Wisconsin), were, by 1670, expanding south along the western shore of the lake, into Winnebago territory. The Winnebago entered the fur trade in 1665, abandoning their former warlike actions against the western migrating Indian nations. Indeed, Winnebago married Ojibwa, Potawatomi, Sauk, and Fox, all of whom were invaders into Winnebago territory.

New fur trade opportunities and rivalries among Indian nations motivated a shift in intergroup alliances and residence. For example, in 1667, traders reached the Menominee living northwest of Green Bay. After the Menominee entered the fur trade, they quickly abandoned their villages and scattered in small bands. And in 1666, the Mascouten, Kickapoo, and Miami shared with some Peoria a large trading village upstream from Green Bay. The fur trade had become so economically important to Native Americans that several tribes who had never lived near each other before came together to live in one trading village.

The nations of the Illinois Confederacy—including the Kaskaskia, the Cahokia, the Peoria, and others—were also displaced as a result of the Beaver Wars and new trade opportunities. According to French reports, the Illinois Confederacy numbered about 100,000 people in the mid-1600s, inhabiting 60 villages in present-day Iowa, Illinois, and Wisconsin. Chequamegon Bay on Lake Superior became a trading center for Illinois trappers, and the Illinois began to migrate further north from their original territories. In 1682, French traders built a post at Starved Rock (northern Illinois) and attracted nearly 18,000 Illinois, Miami, and Shawnee. At about the same time, the nations of the Illinois Confederacy came under attack by the Iroquois who were interested in Illinois fur trading lands. For example, the Espenimkia tribe of the Illinois Confederacy was virtually destroyed by an Iroquois attack. The Iroquois, in search of access to beaver-producing areas, continued to invade and attack the Illinois Confederacy villages until the end of the 1600s. By 1700, there remained only about 6,500 members of the Illinois Confederacy.

Further west, in present-day Minnesota, the Chippewa, who were migrating from the East (in part, because of the Iroquois military expansion for furbearing territories), invaded Dakota (Sioux) lands. The Sioux and the Chippewa would fight over this land for the next century. In the end, the Chippewa forced many of the Sioux to migrate onto the Plains, where they adapted to the horse-riding and buffalo-hunting lifestyle for which they are now well known. The Chippewa ultimately moved into the Minnesota region, where they continued to hunt, trade, and harvest wild rice.

The Southeast Unlike the Northeast, where permanent settlements began in the 1620s, the Southeast did not have permanent European settlements until after 1670. Spanish Florida, established at St. Augustine in 1565, was the exception. The Spanish built a series of Catholic missions for the Indians throughout Florida and present-day Georgia. These missions soon failed because diseases killed the Indians, and English attacks destroyed the remainder in the 1690s. In spite of this initial Spanish settlement, we know less about southeastern Indian demography than we know about the Northeast for most of the 1600s.

In the mid-1660s, yellow fever and smallpox decimated Florida Natives. Measles killed more than 10,000

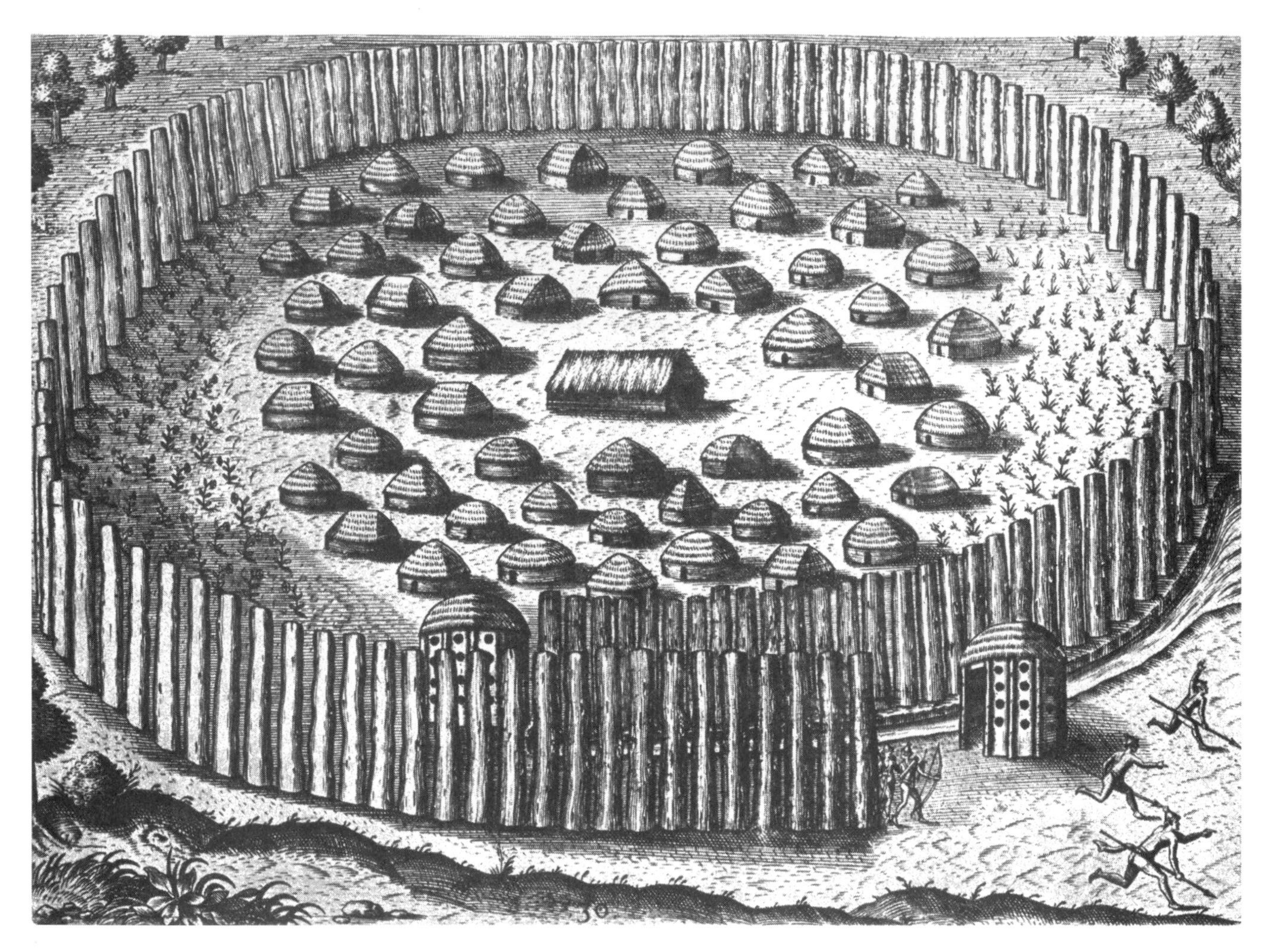

Construction of Fortified Towns among the Floridians. Drawing by Le Moyne, engraving from Theodore de Bry, *America,* Part II, 1591, plate XXX.

Florida Natives in 1658, and a smallpox epidemic between 1665 and 1667 affected Natives from Florida to Virginia, with unknown death tolls. As their numbers declined, Native peoples amalgamated despite traditional animosities and linguistic differences. For example, some Algonkian-speaking Weanock joined the Iroquoian-speaking Nottaway in the Virginia Piedmont region before 1700. The once powerful Natchez ruler gave refuge to remnants of other nations who were abandoning their homelands near the coast of the Gulf of Mexico. By 1700, migrating Tunican tribes joined the Natchez villages on the Mississippi River in present-day west Mississippi.

After the settlement of Charles Town (South Carolina) in 1670, many tribes, such as the Creek and Cherokee, started to trade with the English. During this period, the English were interested in acquiring slaves for their plantations; they traded guns and other manufactured goods to Indians who accompanied them on slave raids in the interior Indian nations. For example, the Shawnee in the 1680s and 1690s suffered severe losses as a result of English, Chickasaw, and Cherokee slave raids. In particular, the Choctaw, a populous nation that once lived in present-day Mississippi and Louisiana, were decimated during the 1680s and 1690s by such slave raids. Some traditional districts of the Choctaw Nation were so depleted by slave raids that it is now virtually impossible to reconstruct their original social and political organization. The beleaguered Choctaw found an ally when the French established the Louisiana Colony in 1699. The French supplied the Choctaw with guns, which they used to withstand the continuing English-supported slave raids.

Between 1670 and 1710, trade relations between Indians and the English were dominated by the capture and sale of Indian slaves. Indians, however, did not make very good slaves. Enslaving people in their homeland was difficult because they knew the land and the people much better than their English captors; the Indian slaves found it relatively easy to escape and hide.

After 1700, the English began to transport Indian slaves to the Caribbean, where escape was more difficult. Thereafter, the English imported slaves from Africa to work the plantations.

The Plains During the 1600s, the people living on the Plains began to be greatly affected by the northward migration of the horse, which the Spanish had brought to the Southeast and Mexico during the middle 1500s. The horse's ability to travel far and fast eventually transformed the grassy Plains from a nearly vacant zone into an overpopulated one. Nearly constant intergroup strife and horse rustling characterized life on the Plains. As was true of the people of the Northeast, the Plains people soon became dependent on trade goods. Plains tribes traded horses, mules, and tanned hides for firearms, axes, knives, and other tools. French and English demand for horses and mules drove the post-horse Plains economy. Because Plains Natives did not breed horses and mules, they rustled them from each other and from Spanish settlements.

By the late 1600s, many formerly horticultural nations began migrating to the Plains area from places farther east. During the 1500s, many of the nations living in the Mississippi Valley had been part of the Mississippi Culture, which built elaborate mounds and ceremonial centers. Some, such as the Caddoan and Siouan nations, had large populations in small towns; they were decimated in the epidemics of the 1500s, however, and by the early 1600s, only small local groups without strong central organization remained. These small tribal groups began feeling the pressure of the expanding eastern trade networks and wars, and encountered the western-moving Indian nations who were forced westward by the colonists and the expansive Iroquois or Five Nations.

Before 1600, most nations in the Plains area lived by horticulture. By the late 1600s, the adoption of horses made it possible to raid corn fields and put pressure on nations who preferred to grow corn and to remain in settled villages. As the horse raids became increasingly effective, more and more of the Indian peoples living on or near the Plains were forced to acquire horses for self defense and for retaliatory raids. This situation led to an intensification of economic raids and revenge attacks among the different nations; peoples with horses had clear advantages in these early skirmishes.

Nevertheless, many nations, such as the Hidatsa, Mandan, and Cheyenne, were reluctant to give up horticulture. While the Cheyenne gradually began to specialize in buffalo hunting and raiding, the Hidatsa and Mandan tried to maintain their villages and horticultural economy, which more reflected the old Indian traditions than did the new culture associated with raiding, buffalo hunting, the Sun Dance (an annual world renewal ceremony), warrior societies, and annual communal tribal hunts, all of which are considered to be representative of the high Plains culture as it developed over the next two centuries. This Plains culture has become the most recognized image of American Indians, even though it does not have a long history, and does not represent a long-standing tradition among any Indian nation.

Many Mississippi Valley Indian nations moved westward in the late 1600s. Native migrations from the Great Lakes area forced several Siouan-speaking nations, including the Iowa and Chiwere, into the Minnesota and Iowa region. By the 1680s, some of the first Sioux, or Teton Dakota, moved onto the Plains, while most Sioux remained and fought with the invading Chippewa. The Osage, Caddoan speakers living in present-day western Missouri, continued to grow corn, squash and pumpkins, but turned to replenishing their horses by raiding other Caddoan-speaking nations in present-day Oklahoma. The Hidatsa and Mandan, also Caddoan speakers from old Mississippian mound-building cultures, migrated up the Missouri River, where, by the late 1600s, they began trading horticultural products for European goods. The Crow people, led by a religious leader who claimed he had visions of a new sacred land, left the Hidatsa to wander northward on the Plains. The religious leader took the Crow people on a pilgrimage into the Canadian plains and finally settled in the 1700s in the western and northern Plains, in what is approximately present-day Montana.

Many of the Indian nations who migrated to the southern Plains were Athapascan—Apache and Navajo—hunters and gatherers who had very different traditions from the horticultural peoples who were moving onto the Plains in the north. The southern Athapascan migrated south from northeastern Canada or Alaska during the thirteenth or fourteenth centuries, and remained big game hunters and collected wild food. They fitted pack dogs to travois, or small sleds, and carried trade goods between the Pueblo villages on the Rio Grande and the Caddoan horticulturalists along the Mississippi Valley.

Southern Athapascan acquired horses from the Spanish, who arrived in 1598. Beginning soon after 1600, Apache, with the aid of horses and Spanish-like lances, dominated the southern Plains. The Apache prospered, grew in number, and divided into several different bands. Jicarilla and Faraon Apache lived on the Canadian River in northeastern New Mexico and the Texas Panhandle. Carlana Apache lived on the Purgatoire River tributary of the Arkansas River (Colorado), and Cuartelejo Apache inhabited the upper Arkansas River Valley. Paloma Apache resided on the upper Republican River (Nebraska) and Lipan Apache migrated over much of what is now Texas. Although they rustled Pueblo and Spanish livestock, Apache peoples traded slaves for stock and other commodities at Taos and Pecos Pueblo where periodic trading took place.

A few southern Athapascan acquired not only horses but also sheep which they learned to pasture and breed. By 1630, the Spanish recognized these Athapascan as "Navajo." With the increase in the standard of living associated with the permanent supply of domesticated mutton, the Navajo population began to increase steadily. The Navajo are now the largest U.S. Indian nation, with approximately 167,000 people.

The Southwest Although the Apache lived primarily on the southern Plains, by the second half of the 1600s, they also traded and raided Pueblo and Spanish settlements in the Southwest. In 1670, a disease killed many of the Apache horses. The Apache subsequently migrated into New Mexico, where they depended on hunting and fighting for their survival, and by 1672, they began to rustle what they could not purchase. Almost overnight, traditional horse traders became horse raiders; when their traditional Apache trading partners turned into rustlers, residents of five pueblos—Tajique, Chililí, Quarai, Abó, and Pueblo de los Jumanos—migrated to Pueblo villages along the Rio Grande.

In 1680, most Pueblo peoples used weapons to force Spanish colonists from Indian lands. The Spaniards, along with Pueblos who were loyal to them, retreated down the Rio Grande to present-day El Paso, Texas, where their descendants still live.

The collapse of the eastern pueblo frontier, coupled with the Spanish retreat, removed a military barrier that, in effect, allowed the Apache to remain on the southern Plains. By 1698, an Apache vanguard migrated westward to the mountains on the present-day Arizona-New Mexico border and would later evolve into eight bands. Meanwhile, Spaniards recolonized Pueblo territory in 1694. In 1696, a smallpox epidemic triggered an abortive revolt. Tewa-Pueblo people, who refused to live under Spanish rule, fled west to Hopi First Mesa. As a minority group, the Tewa-Pueblo learned the Hopi language and served as interpreters and traders, and assisted in Hopi defense.

The Jemez people defended a mesa-top town until 1695, when they submitted to the Spanish by returning to their fields. In the 1696 growing season, the Jemez joined other Pueblo and rebelled against the Spanish in the wake of a smallpox epidemic. After slaying resident Spanish in Jemez pueblo, the Jemez retreated to their mesa-top fortification. After repelling a Spanish attack, they dispersed. Having established close relations with the Navajo between 1680 and 1694, many of the Jemez fled to them. Inasmuch as the Navajo reckon descent through the mother, the children of Jemez women created a new Navajo clan. The refugee Jemez people had great influence on Navajo ceremony, religion, crafts, and horticulture.

Conclusion

Disease and military expansion greatly changed Indian demography and social and political order even before they had direct and sustained contact with Europeans. During the 1600s, the best, although fragmented, evidence of Native Americans is found among the nations of the Plains, Northeast, Southeast, and Southwest. We know very little about the demography of Indian peoples before 1700 in the Great Basin, California, the Pacific Northwest, the Plateau, the Subarctic, and the Arctic regions. In the East, by the late 1600s, very few Native Americans escaped the military turmoil of European expansion. European diseases continued to infect Native Americans and diminished their numbers. By 1700, two centuries of European diseases reduced Native American populations in the Northeast, Southeast, and Southwest to less than one-tenth of what their numbers had been in 1500. Many groups simply disappeared. Those who endured by amalgamating the survivors of villages, towns, and former tribes became much more egalitarian than the populous, socially stratified societies that had thrived prior to 1500. The Mississippi Culture, with its full-time artists and priests, had mostly perished from disease and military turmoil. Between 1500 and 1700, so many Native Americans died that they lost a considerable amount of knowledge about their traditional cultures and political systems; most of what is known about Indian societies is based on documents and knowledge of the post-1700 societies. Because these societies were greatly changed during the period between 1500 and 1700, they only partially reflect the age-old traditions of thousands of years of culture that existed before European arrival.

Henry Dobyns

♦ GEOGRAPHIC AND DEMOGRAPHIC CHANGE DURING THE EIGHTEENTH CENTURY

The eighteenth century brought a wide variety of geographic and demographic changes to the many Native American societies across North America. Numerous diverse cultures had experienced close contact with European colonies since the sixteenth century. Others were just entering into direct relationships with colonial societies, while many more remained distant from the expansion of European empires. The contest over Indian trade and territory among Spain, France, and England affected all Native American societies in some way before the end of the eighteenth century.

At the beginning of the eighteenth century, the French implemented a strategic plan of encircling the English colonies on the Atlantic coast by creating a chain of Indian alliances and forts along the Mississippi River. In the late 1690s, the French created Louisiana Colony and struggled with the English until the end of the French and Indian War in 1760. The period from the 1690s through the end of the eighteenth century was marked by constant warfare in eastern North America with such campaigns as Queen Anne's War, King William's War, the French and Indian War, and the American War of Independence, as well as considerable intermittent border warfare during times of undeclared war. Warfare and trade relations greatly effected the location and political relations of the Native nations, which managed their affairs and interests within the context of increasingly powerful and competitive colonial governments. Many changes in the location of Indian peoples were made on their own initiatives and for their own objectives. As the colonies grew more powerful, some Indians acted to protect their economic and trade interests by establishing neutrality and bargaining relations with the rival European colonists, as was the case of the Iroquois and Creek. Other Indian nations sought close trade and political relations with specific European colonies, as did the Cherokee who often sought trade and diplomatic ties with Carolina Colony, or the Ottawa who had long-standing trade ties with the French in New France. In order to develop greater capacities for managing trade and diplomatic relations with the colonists, some nations, such as the Creek and Iroquois, created confederacies and sought to strengthen political and trade relations between themselves. At times during the 1700s, the Iroquois stated that they commanded the men of fifty nations, although this was a bluff intended to impress English and French diplomats and military officers. Nevertheless, the confederacy of western Indian nations that the Iroquois led was passed onto other nations, especially after the 1750s, when Iroquois power was declining and the British government openly supported the Iroquois in order to gain trade and indirect diplomatic control over the western Indian nations.

During the 1750s, the Delaware and Shawnee increasingly took the initiative in forming a confederacy of Indian nations who fought to prevent westward colonial expansion. During the early 1760s, the Delaware Prophet emerged, preaching that God commanded the Indian nations to unite and drive the Europeans from the continent, since only then would prosperity and happiness be restored to the Indian peoples. Pontiac, the Ottawa leader, used the teachings of the Delaware Prophet to muster attacks on the British forts in the Great Lakes area in 1763. Although Pontiac was not able to drive the British away from Indian land, he temporarily convened a military confederacy of western Indian nations. During the 1780s and early 1790s, the western nations were led by Little Turtle, a Miami war chief. The Indian confederacy resisted U.S. attempts to settle the Ohio and Great Lakes area. After Little Turtle's death, the Shawnee leader, Tecumseh, and his brother, the Shawnee Prophet, revived the confederacy of Indian nations from 1806 to 1813. After the War of 1812, the Indian confederacy of Ohio and Great Lakes Indians disbanded.

While the eighteenth century did not see major demographic movements among Indian nations, political and economic change greatly affected their economies and political relations. By the beginning of the eighteenth century, most eastern Indian nations were engaged in trading furs for European manufactured goods, especially guns, powder, metal goods, textiles, and other goods. Most soon became dependent on trade in order to secure newly desired and needed goods, and hence trade became a new way of life. In the southeast, Indian slaves were sought, but were found difficult to contain; they were exported to the Caribbean Islands, while Black slaves from Africa were imported to the continent to work on tobacco and other plantations. Since interior Indians became victims of slave raids from coastal Indians and their English allies, guns and ammunition soon became necessary items for defense, and hence the eastern nations found that they had to develop trade and diplomatic relations with one or more of the European colonies in order to secure a steady supply of guns, powder, ball, and other trade goods.

Epidemics and wars had traumatically reduced Native American groups along the Atlantic seaboard by 1700, but through coalescence and adaptation many refugees from different tribes reorganized themselves into new communities. In the early eighteenth century, Wampanoag and Pequot in southern New England, Chickahominy and Nanticoke in the Chesapeake Bay region, and Catawba and Apalachee in the lower South managed to maintain a degree of political autonomy while securing stable social and economic relations with neighboring settlements and towns. However, in the southeast, slave raiding starting in the 1680s decimated many nations such as the Shawnee in present-day Kentucky and the Choctaw in present-day Mississippi and Louisiana. The Shawnee Nation was dispersed, with some joining the Delaware near present-day Philadelphia. Others joined the Creek Nation in present-day Alabama, while a third group settled for a while in Georgia, but decided to rejoin the Shawnee in Pennsylvania. The raids on the Choctaw were so severe that the several major groups within their social order were permanently disrupted and Choctaw social and political relations gravitated toward secular, local, and regional organization. Choctaw society was so disrupted by the slave raids that it may be impossible for historians to reconstruct the traditional relations of clans, villages, and government.

The Yamasee War of 1715 and the Natchez War of 1729 were the last major struggles of resistance waged by coastal tribes in the eastern woodlands. The Yamasee War started because many Indians incurred increasing debts to English traders, and the traders employed harsh methods such as taking children as slaves in order to satisfy the debt. The powerful Creek Confederacy sought to aid the coastal Yamasee in the war, but when the war ended badly, the Creek turned to a new strategy of balancing diplomatic and trade relations among the English colonies on the east coast, the Spanish in the Floridas, and the French in Louisiana Colony. The Natchez War (1729) started because the French wished to impose taxes on Natchez fur trade. The Natchez were one of the few remaining Mississippi culture societies still intact in the early 1700s, and their leader was the sacred priest-leader called the Great Sun. The French with their Choctaw allies quickly destroyed the Natchez Nation and captured the Great Sun, who was deported into slavery to the Caribbean Islands with several thousand other Natchez. Some Natchez fled to live with the Chickasaw in present-day northern Louisiana and western Tennessee; others went to live among the Creek in present-day Alabama. The Natchez and Chickasaw thereafter fought a constant war, with several major campaigns waged against the French and Choctaw from 1729 to 1760, when the French were defeated by the English in the French and Indian War.

These wars and slave raids, together with English raids against mission Indians in Spanish Florida in the early 1700s, caused the death of thousands of Indian people and the exportation of thousands more, as slaves, to the West Indies. Some refugees from these southeastern conflicts migrated into the territory of larger Indian nations like the Creek and Chickasaw. After fighting several battles with North Carolina militia in the early 1710s, the Tuscarora fled North Carolina and joined their Iroquoian brethren in New York, becoming the sixth nation of the Iroquois Confederacy.

In the mid-Atlantic region, discontent over settlers' encroachment and traders' abuses drove Delaware, Shawnee, Nanticoke, and smaller groups up the Susquehanna River during the 1720s and 1730s. Eventually, most of these Indian migrants resettled in the Ohio River Valley. The Great Lakes and Ohio River region already had become a dynamic world of pan-tribal migration and mixture. Under the influence of French trade, Wyandot, Miami, Potawatomi, Ottawa, and tribes farther west interacted across a vast and fluid network of villages and posts. Intermarriage with French traders created a Métis population, which grew in close association with Indian villagers. When the Seven Years' War erupted between Great Britain and France in 1754, Native American nations in the Great Lakes area entered a long and difficult period of military resistance against the English and, after 1783, against U.S. expansion, which lasted until the end of the War of 1812.

Most interior tribes of the eastern woodlands experienced a measure of peace and stability during the first half of the eighteenth century. The Iroquois Nations in the Northeast and the Cherokee Nation in the Southeast developed strong trade ties to English colonies, but did not relinquish their avenues to French diplomacy and commerce. During the 1600s, the Iroquois allied themselves to the Dutch and English against the French, but by 1700 the expanding English colonies alerted the Iroquois, who thereafter embarked on policy-neutral diplomatic and trade relations with the French and English colonies. The populous and tribally diverse Creek Confederacy maintained an effective position of neutrality among British, Spanish, and French colonies along its borders. In the lower Mississippi Valley, the powerful Choctaw were highly regarded trade partners and military allies of French Louisiana. The Chickasaw allied themselves with the British and were consequently in continuous conflict with the French and their Indian allies. Even during times of stability and peace, all of these large Native American groups suffered population decline from contagious diseases introduced by European settlers and traders. Their involvement in the Seven Years' War and in the American Revolution, during the second half of the eighteenth century, took an especially heavy toll on the Iroquois and Cherokee peoples.

Geographic and demographic changes occurred in various forms among Native Americans in the eighteenth-century Southwest. By 1696, the Spanish had completed their reconquest of New Mexico, following the Pueblo Revolt of 1680. Pueblo communities worked out a stable social and economic relationship with Hispanic settlements. They accepted missionaries into their towns on the condition that they not meddle with traditional beliefs and rituals. The Hopi maintained the greatest degree of independence among Pueblo peoples, destroying the mission town of Awatowi in 1700. Depopulation slowed down over the eighteenth century, but diseases continued to plague the Native American population of the Southwest. The Pueblo and Hispano developed closer ties to the Navajo, Ute, and Apache occupying territory around New Mexico in scattered, mobile bands. The Navajo incorporated sheep herding into their already diversified livelihood, setting themselves on a course of geographic and demographic expansion. The migration of Comanche onto the southern Plains during the eighteenth century circumscribed colonial expansion in the northern Rio Grande Valley, until peace was established in 1786.

The migration of Native American groups to the Great Plains was perhaps the most significant demographic and geographic movement of the eighteenth century. From the eastern woodlands around Lake Superior, Cheyenne and Lakota Sioux migrated across the

Crow tipis. In the eighteenth century, the Crow were migrating and living throughout the northern Plains area, where they followed the buffalo herds for their sustenance. They had divided into two major groups: the mountain and river Crow.

Missouri River to the northern Plains. The Sioux and Cheyenne were woodland people who farmed corn, collected wild plants, and hunted, but they soon took up the Sun Dance, buffalo hunting, horse riding, and migratory lifeways characteristic of the Plains culture. From the Rocky Mountains came the Kiowa and Comanche, who eventually populated the southern Plains. These emigrants combined uses of the gun and horse to develop a vibrant culture and economy based on buffalo hunting. Meanwhile, the townspeople who had occupied the lower Missouri River and its tributaries for centuries—Pawnee, Oto, and Mandan, among others—suffered a steady decline in population. The Hidatsa, Arikara, and Crow migrated up the Missouri River and eventually settled near present-day Bismarck, North Dakota. These sedentary, horticultural peoples depended heavily on corn production and lived in houses that looked like earthen mounds. Nevertheless, they represented the primary form of social and economic life found on the Plains before the introduction of the horse. The migrant Lakota began to raid the corn fields of the sedentary nations, putting considerable economic pressure on them. By the end of the century, the sedentary Indian nations were facing intensive trade pressures from Europeans along with competitive territorial pressures from Cheyenne and Sioux newcomers.

Throughout most of the eighteenth century, other trans-Mississippi Native Americans experienced little or no direct contact with Europeans. Trade goods from the Hudson's Bay Company's expansive subarctic and northern Plains network began to reach Rocky Mountain and Great Basin societies. Through raiding and trading, these same people also acquired horses. Ute in the southern Rockies and Nez Percé in the Columbia Basin, for example, attained greater mobility in procuring food, fighting enemies, and trading with allies. Contagious diseases introduced by Europeans from different directions undoubtedly affected most Native Americans in the western interior, but migration and intertribal relations were still determined principally by their own design.

During the second half of the eighteenth century, external forces began to reach the Far West from the Pacific Coast. In 1769, Spain established its first mission among California Native Americans at San Diego. Poor living conditions and diseases rapidly took their toll on mission Indians along the California coast, from the Diegueño northward to the Miwok. Expeditions to replace them intimidated interior tribes like the Yokut and Wintun. Throughout the remainder of the eighteenth century, Spanish Franciscan missionaries established missions at locations farther north in California. Thousands of Indians were brought into the missions and induced to become Christians. They worked as laborers to support and build the California missions, and many died from overwork and disease, while many others no longer practiced their traditional cultures.

Russian explorers began sailing along the Alaska coast by 1741, and reported good prospects for trade in seal and sea otter skins. During the 1700s, these skins were in high demand in China, where they were used to make clothing. By the 1760s, Russian traders and Russian Orthodox priests were extending political and cultural control over the Aleutian islands and along the southern coastal regions of Alaska. Russian forts and trading establishments extended as far south as present-day northern California. In particular, the Aleut suffered greatly from Russian colonization, and many were forced to hunt and secure furs. Aleutian culture significantly disintegrated under the force of Russian political and cultural domination. Nevertheless, the Tlingit, living on the Alaska Panhandle, kept their political and cultural independence from the Russians, although the Russian-American Company located its center of operations at New Archangel, present-day Sitka, Alaska, which is near a long-standing Tlingit village. The Tlingit quickly joined in the fur trade with the Russians and added the new-found wealth to their traditional potlatches, where significant quantities of food, tools, art, sacred objects, and symbolic goods were exchanged in ceremonies designed to honor their clan ancestors.

In the Pacific Northwest, British and American merchants began commerce with coastal Native Americans for sea otter pelts and other furs. By the 1790s, the Chinook, Nootka, and Tlingit were trading regularly with ships from New England as well as Europe. The Russian American Company trade settlements along the Gulf of Alaska drew large quantities of seal and sea otter skins from Native American hunters. The vibrant life of this commercial frontier produced a growing number of people of mixed Native American and Russian descent. Many Alaska Natives converted to the

Mandan earth lodge.

Russian Orthodox religion, as missionaries and churches usually accompanied the establishment of major trade posts.

Meanwhile, in the eastern woodlands, Native American societies were facing the aftermath of the American Revolution. The Treaty of Paris (1783) rearranged the geopolitical map of North America more profoundly than any previous agreement made in Europe over the colonial period. The creation along the Atlantic seaboard of a new nation by rebellious English colonies set in motion forces that Native Americans had not experienced before. As the United States asserted power over much of eastern North America and European governments wound down their imperial contest over the continent, Indian nations lost their former allies and found themselves face to face with an ambitious new republic. Military resistance by Ohio Valley and Great Lakes tribes climaxed in costly defeat by 1794. Many of the Indian nations of the Ohio and Great Lakes area, already immigrants from eastern territories, tried to prevent U.S. expansion across the Ohio River, which the Indians considered a border between themselves and the United States. Several battles were fought in the Indiana and Ohio area. Nevertheless, the signing of Jay's Treaty by the United States and England in late 1794 changed the diplomatic situation dramatically, and the Indian nations were forced to recognize the United States as the major power in the region. The British agreed not to support the Indian nations, who wished to prevent U.S. occupation of the forts and towns in the Ohio and Great Lakes area.

In the Southeast, the Creek Confederacy, especially the towns in present-day Alabama, allied themselves to the Spanish colony in Florida and hoped to resist U.S. territorial expansion. A segment of the Cherokee Nation called the Chickamauga also waged a war of resistance against encroaching settlements and began to migrate west of the Mississippi River during the 1790s. As long as the Chickamauga and Creek had military support from the Spanish, they had access to military supplies that enabled them to resist U.S. efforts to occupy their territory. In 1795, however, the Spanish government turned its attention to the wars in Europe and decided to limit investment in Florida Colony. Like the northern Indian nations, after 1795, the southern Indian nations were forced to sign treaties that recognized the United States as the predominant power in the region.

Migration was selected by several Native American societies as a means of preserving their autonomy against U.S. aggression. Following the Revolutionary War, many Iroquois people decided to take permanent refuge in British Canada. Many had joined the British cause during the revolutionary war, and after the war, the British offered their Iroquois allies a relatively small tract of land in southern Ontario, which constitutes the present-day Iroquois reserve. Other Iroquois who fought with the colonists during the war stayed on to live in New York within their traditional homeland. Nevertheless, because of increasing impoverishment and U.S. land pressures, by 1796, the Iroquois land base was reduced to a handful of small tracts of land. The once-influential Iroquois Nation had to reconcile itself to life under the powerful shadow of the United States.

The movement of many Creek Indians into Florida during the late eighteenth century resulted in the formation of a new tribal group called the Seminole. As early as the 1750s, many Creek and Hitchiti Indians migrated into Florida and ceased to communicate with the Creek Nation. The Seminole, who were discontented with English colonial relations, formed a loose confederacy and created a new nation. Sizable groups of Shawnee, Delaware, Peoria, and Piankashaw sought social and economic security by migrating across the Mississippi River into Missouri and Arkansas country, on lands offered them by Spanish Louisiana. Southeastern Indian emigrants, especially Choctaw, Tunica, Biloxi, Apalachee, and Coushatta, began settling parts of Louisiana and east Texas in the 1790s.

Encroachment on Native Americans' territory and disruption of their livelihood escalated significantly in eastern North America by the end of the eighteenth century. Epidemic disease continued to besiege Indian societies at varying rates, but demographic and geographic change became increasingly determined by the expansionist policies of the United States. By 1800, the U.S. government began a policy of assimilating Indians into Christianity and a farming culture. It was reasoned that, if Indians turned to farming, they would no longer need large areas of land to carry on their hunting and fur trade economies. Indians as farmers would be more willing to sell land to the United States and also enter into citizenship. Missionaries were hired to teach school, religion, farming, and homemaking to the Indians. Some of these first missions were to the Seneca reservations in western New York.

With the Louisiana Purchase of 1803, however, Native Americans across western North America began to face unprecedented challenges and threats. Early in the nineteenth century, the prospect of U.S. expansion across the continent,changed early policies of quick assimilation and later focused on removal and reservations. Strategies of adaptation and resistance tested over the eighteenth century, especially migration and consolidation, would serve many of the Native American groups effectively in future struggles for cultural and political survival.

Daniel H. Usner, Jr.
Cornell University

♦ INDIAN GEOGRAPHIC DISTRIBUTION, HABITAT, AND DEMOGRAPHY DURING THE NINETEENTH CENTURY

Indian America after 1800

Indian America after 1800 was soon to become a series of constantly relocated displaced persons camps under military surveillance and located primarily for the benefit of non-Indians. Most of the U.S.-Indian treaties negotiated between 1817 and 1849 dealt with the removal of tribes to the so-called vacant lands in the West. Most surviving tribes of the Northeast woodlands were already in 1800 on the moving escalator that would drop them off on a reservation west of the Mississippi River or push them into the extreme western Great Lakes region. Removing a large percentage of the estimated hundred thousand Indians east of the Mississippi River did not take place all at once, but proceeded in an evolutionary manner reflecting the historical vagaries of the advancing European-American settlement frontier. The Delaware (or Lenni Lenape) Indians, who led a seasonal hunting, fishing, and gathering life, had met William Penn on the Atlantic Coast in the 1680s, but in 1800 were very tentatively living in Indiana. Some Delaware were already living in Missouri, from which they were moved successively to Arkansas, Texas, Kansas, and finally Oklahoma. Tribes regularly splintered. In the 1840s some Kickapoo went to Texas, some to Missouri, and some to Kansas. Very few Northeast groups, such as the remnants of the Five (Six) Nation Iroquois of upstate New York and the Chippewa (Ojibwa) of the lower Great Lakes, remained in part of their homelands. By 1812, Indian title had been lost to much of Ohio, Indiana, and Illinois. By 1840, Michigan, Wisconsin, Iowa, and Minnesota were largely opened to non-Indian exploitation. An 1842 congressional report listed 82,118 Indians on the frontier who had been "removed west by Government."

Most Indians finally wound up in John C. Calhoun's creation, the so-called Indian Territory, which originally included Nebraska and Kansas. When reduced in size to present-day Oklahoma, it came to possess the greatest number of Indians of any state. After the period of forced dislocations, the Indian Territory had nine times as many tribes as before. Indians moving there met a variety of land forms that supported different life-styles. In the east were the Ozark mountains and plateaus; in the southeast were level plains similar to those of Louisiana, Mississippi, and Alabama; in the rest of the state were the gradually rising plains from the Central Lowlands west to the Great Plains and the High Plains of the western half of the Oklahoma Panhandle.

The first Indians to be exiled to Oklahoma were the five nations (Cherokee, Creek, Chickasaw, Choctaw, Seminole) of the Southeast. Their removal has become the symbol of the American attitude toward Indians in general. While the numerous southern coastal tribes had mostly disappeared by 1800, the large and adaptive tribes of the southern Piedmont and mountainous areas approached the new century with some confidence. Nevertheless, an 1802 agreement between the new federal government and the state of Georgia would be used by an aggressive frontier culture as the club for forcing out the five "civilized" tribes of the Southeast by the late 1830s.

In Texas, the Gila and Rio Grande River areas of the Arizona and New Mexico region, and California, the Spanish continued in 1800 to interact with quite disparate Indian societies. The ancient inhabitants of the Southwest had evolved a characteristic city (pueblo) and farm community. On the outskirts of these stable communities were found the Navajo and the even more nomadic Apache and Comanche peoples. In Texas, the nomadic Plains Indians met the wandering gatherers of the deserts of southern Texas. Relying particularly on Pueblo Indian allies, Spanish officials tried restraining the nomadic groups. The marauding nomadic tribes had, for their part, found the Spanish and their Indian allies to be unending sources of revenue. The Pueblo Indians paid lip service to Spanish rule and religion, and then did rather what they pleased.

This was certainly not the case in 1800 for the Indians of California whose lives had long centered on the dependable supply of acorns gathered from groves of oak trees. Starting in 1769, the Spanish had systematically assaulted the peaceful and sedentary California Native peoples along the coast through the founding of church missions and military presidios as far north as the San Francisco area. Friars and soldiers combined to impose a penitentiary-like existence on many of the California Indians. Some interior tribes moved east to avoid both the mission-induced epidemics and the near-slavery of mission life. There were in 1800 indications that their newly acquired equestrian skills and newly found love of horse meat would energize the interior tribes of California to resist further white aggression. However, the northern California gold strike of 1848 doomed the California Indians within a decade.

North of California, the fishing life of the Indians of the Pacific Northwest (Oregon and Washington) was hardly touched in 1800 by any European menace. In 1805 the Lewis and Clark expedition would end Northwest Indian isolation, and by the 1850s survivors of epidemics and wars would already be relegated by the Americans to military supervision on small reservations.

The Lewis and Clark expedition also initiated the U.S. claim to the Plains. For several decades before Americans could appear in force, however, Indian life on the

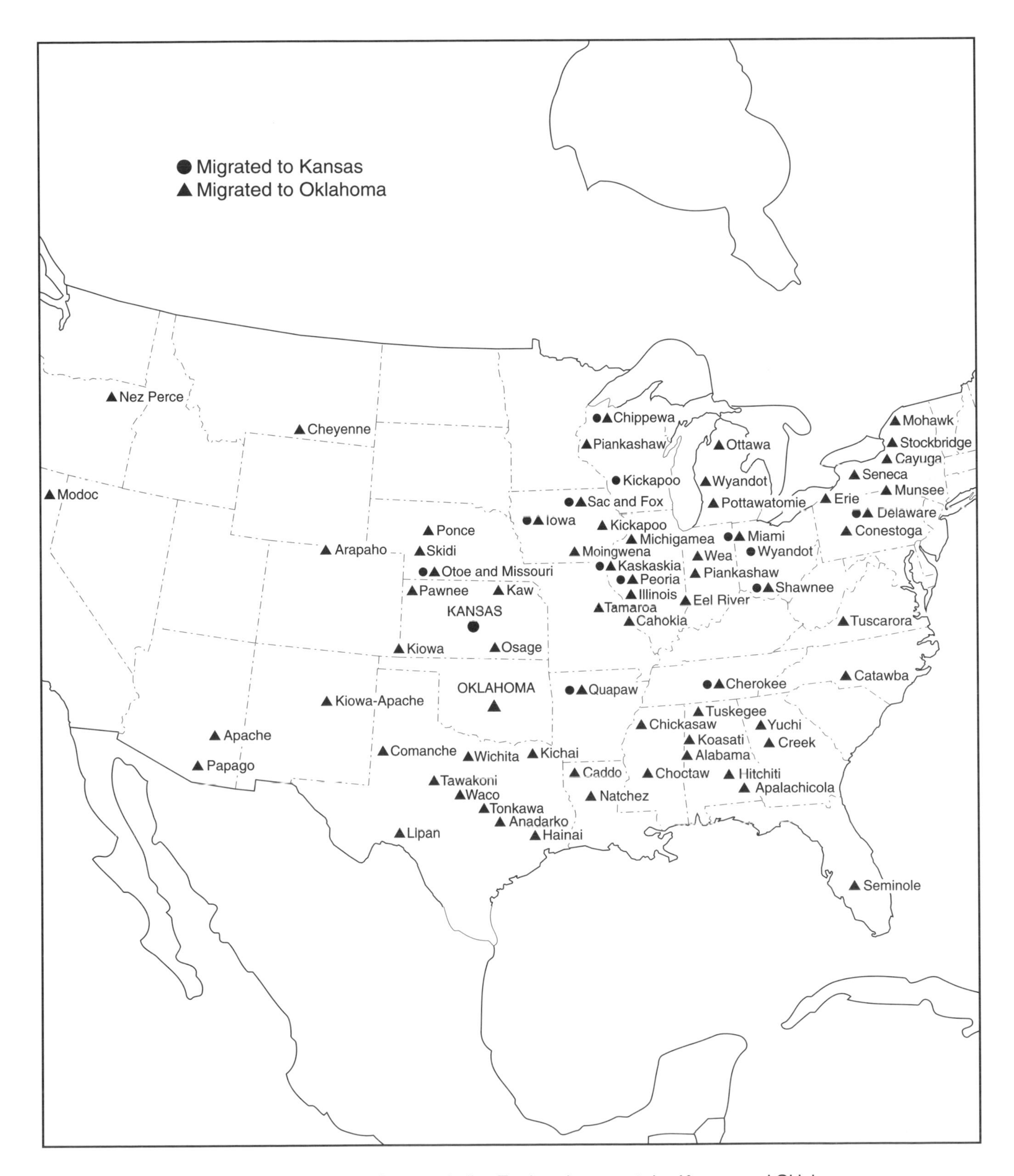

Homelands of Indians who were forced to migrate to Indian Territory in present-day Kansas and Oklahoma.

Plains would be greatly enriched by European artifacts. With horses acquired from the Spanish borderlands in the Southwest and guns gained from Europeans and Americans through the fur trade, the Plains Indians would revel for a full generation as lords of the lands between the Mississippi River and the Rockies. Many Indians (such as the Flathead, Kutenai, or Nez Percé) living in the Plateau area between the Rocky Mountains and the California Mountains also participated with gusto in this Plains life-style. Most of the tribes enjoying this life-style were, it must be stressed, originally immigrants, and some (such as the Dakota and Cheyenne) had fled misery caused ultimately by the westward movement of the Americans. The early nineteenth century for these fugitive groups was simply a period of rest before they would again be uprooted. By the 1870s they would be subjected to American rule, often on reservations quite far from their Plains homelands.

A number of Indians had met very few Europeans by the year 1800. These were the ill-defined groups, such as the Paiute, who lived in the quite inhospitable Great Basin region. That harsh and stingy environment had long forced them to live the simplest of any Indian life-style as they moved constantly in search of food. Additionally, their lot had worsened by 1800 because Plains, Plateau, and Southwest marauder Indians all raided the Great Basin looking for captives to trade for Spanish and American goods. Nevertheless, in 1800 nobody desired their land, and they would not be elbowed aside by covetous Americans for half a century.

In summary, Indian America circa 1800 saw flourishing Native American life-styles in the Southeast, the Plains, the Northwest, and the Plateau areas. In the Southwest and the western part of the Northeast, the Indian life-styles were under attack but still so strong that Spanish and American leaders feared Indian power. In California, Indian life-styles were under heavy assault. East of Ohio, very few Indians could be found in the Northeast.

Population

The most important reason for the success of the continuing assault on Native America, most scholars agree, was the terrible number of disease-inflicted deaths that resulted from the introduction of European diseases. In 1837, the Mandan, who were agriculturalists of the Missouri River, were dramatically reduced by smallpox from 1,600 to 31. The Blackfeet, Comanche, and Kiowa tribes of the Great Plains also suffered similar disastrous epidemics. Seventy-four percent of 220 Hopi who refused Western medicine in an 1898 smallpox epidemic died. Such unbelievably high mortality rates have been verified by comparison with various epidemics striking the Amazon Indians in the twentieth century. This disease-fueled depopulation constitutes the most important part of that seizure of Indian lands in what has been called the European and American conquest of Native America.

Traditionally, scholars estimated that north of the Rio Grande the aboriginal Indian population never exceeded much more than a million. Today, some important scholars argue for a number many times larger than a million. Even so, by 1800 the "widowed" Indian population was seemingly close to the older traditional figures. A conservative estimate by the Office of Indian Affairs (1943) projected an 1800 Indian population of around 600,000. Jedediah Morse, who had been sent by the federal government on a fact-finding tour of the Indian tribes, carefully collected information for his *Report on Indian Affairs* (1822) and estimated the Indian population as slightly over 471,000, not counting California. The vast dislocation of Indians in the East and Plains, the extraordinary decline of California Indians, and the demoralization among all Indians forcibly relocated, initiated a sharp decline in Indian population in the nineteenth century.

Many of the northeastern tribes moved a number of times west of the Mississippi. Kansas, as part of the northern half of Indian Territory, was a temporary home for many displaced Eastern Indians. Although the western two-thirds of Kansas belongs to the Great Plains, the many hills and valleys of the eastern third created a familiar environment for these exiles. Some of the most important of the nearly thirty tribes to settle there were the Wyandot and Shawnee from Ohio, Miami (with the Wea and Piankashaw) from Indiana, Kaskaskia and Peoria from Illinois, Ottawa and Potawatomi from Michigan, Kickapoo, Sauk, and Fox from Wisconsin, and some Cherokee from Tennessee. In the 1850s both the pro- and anti-slavery factions agreed that these Indians must be pushed out of Kansas and Nebraska. By punishing the Five Civilized Tribes (Cherokee, Choctaw, Chickasaw, Creek, and Seminole) for joining the Confederacy in the American Civil War, the U.S. acquired land in Oklahoma to re-locate Kansas tribes. Some of these Indians (Shawnee, Wyandot, and Ottawa) were fortunate in 1867 in finally being placed in the extreme northeast part of Oklahoma where a scenic beauty combines with fertile soil. On the other hand, the numerous members of the Osage, Kansa, and Ottawa tribes were nearly halved as a result of difficulties suffered under this second Trail of Tears.

California Indian population declined from an estimated 300,000 to approximately 20,000—a decline of 90 percent—between 1770 when the Spanish missions started and 1900. Although the Catholic priests in charge of the California missions were often of good intent, living conditions in the missions had caused lethal diseases to flourish. By the end of Mexican occupation (1846–47), the population figure was down to around

150,000. The gold rush decade quickly added to the death toll in a brutal (even genocidal) fashion as the number of Indians quickly dropped to 50,000.

By 1850, the nation's entire Indian population, according to the U.S. Census, had dropped to around 400,000. By 1900, the U.S. Census estimated a further drop in the Indian population to only 237,000 Indians, not counting those in Alaska. In short, there was a marked drop in Indian population in the nineteenth century, and the end of the century marked the Indian population's nadir.

Land Hunger and Racism

Just as certainly as disease and relocation accounted for the decline in Indian population, land hunger and racism were the major reasons for mistreatment of Indians. Americans (and European immigrants) wanted the land Indians had lived on for millennia. Called the "Westward Movement" by historians and rationalized by the participants as "Manifest Destiny," the central thrust of nineteenth-century America was the acquisition of as much land as possible, by any means possible. The federal government revealed an array of techniques for acquiring Indian land: secret payments and gifts to leaders, feting Indian delegates, bringing Indian leaders to Washington, establishing stores with liberal credit that guaranteed Indians going deeply in debt, dealing with minority chiefs, buying land from a group that did not actually control it, deliberately withholding annuity payments to force negotiations or compliance, allowing non-Indians to squat illegally on Indian land and to harass Indian farmers and cattlemen, permitting whites to acquire individually owned Indian land (allotments) by any method, and—behind every other technique—the will to use naked power. In short, Indians might delay the inevitable, as Kenekuk did for the Indiana Kickapoo, but in the end the Indian land disappeared.

Frontier ruffians and entrepreneurs fueled the Jacksonian Indian removal policy. Even a tribe such as the Wyandot (Huron), which contained many white people through marriage, whose people were noted for their long and sincere acceptance of Christianity, who accepted individually held land holdings (allotments), and who often had become American citizens, still suffered inequality, impoverishment, and settler depredations in Kansas. Some tribes driven out of Kansas by such mistreatment, such as the Kickapoo, Wea, and Piankashaw, had already been through a similar process elsewhere!

By 1800, the defeat of Tecumseh, the Shawnee leader, and the Red Stick faction of the Creek Nation in the War of 1812 guaranteed that there would be no permanent Indian barrier to American settler expansion. American frontier pressures splintered tribes into conflicting factions. Some segments would voluntarily move west. Some entire Indian groups would be forced to move because battle-hardened Indian enemies who were better equipped militarily would push them. For example, the Chippewa (Ojibwa) continued successfully to push north, west, and south against Indian enemies in the first half of the nineteenth century. More generally, tribes were simply trying to get out of the way of lawless American frontiersmen.

Any national or individual guilt over how Indians lost their lands was partially assuaged by the fallacious arguments that Indians had only a wasteful hunting idea of land ownership and no concepts of personal property. It was almost universally accepted that Indians must stop roaming over vast territories and settle down on a reasonable number of acres that could be farmed. In fact, many Indians did farm, and indeed, Indian farming before allotment was growing at a substantial rate. Indian farming generally was carried out on individual plots with tribal recognition of each family's plot of ground. Americans assumed, nevertheless, that Indians had to substitute an individualistic concept of property for their ancient communal concept of ownership. In fact, many Indians, particularly with the passage of time, did possess concepts of personal property. The Yakima and Flathead Indians of the Plateau, for example, had a workable system of individual property.

In any case, the argument that Indians could not understand the European concept of private property was a red herring. Mexico in the 1830s believed in private property in the European sense, but that did not keep America from coveting its Texas and California lands. President James Polk almost took all of Mexico. National and individual American land hunger explains in great part the despoliation of Indian lands.

Racism joined with avarice to guarantee that Indians would not be able, in general, to live the lives of frontier farmers. What Chief Justice Taney in the *Dred Scott* decision declared of Blacks was true in practice for Indians: they possessed "no rights which the white man was bound to respect."

The history of many of the Sauk and Fox Indians in Kansas (originally part of the Indian Territory) is typical of Indians pushed out of an area even though they were making efforts to live like typical westerners (see maps of Indian Territory in Oklahoma section of Chapter 3). After the Indians accepted personal allotments of land, speculators defrauded hapless Indians of their property, and many of the successful Indians were coerced into selling and moving to an Indian Territory reservation.

The key legal consideration that forced most Indians to leave Kansas (as well as other states) were the difficulties involved in becoming citizens of an individual state. For example, tribal leaders could suddenly face state laws levying huge fines for anyone function-

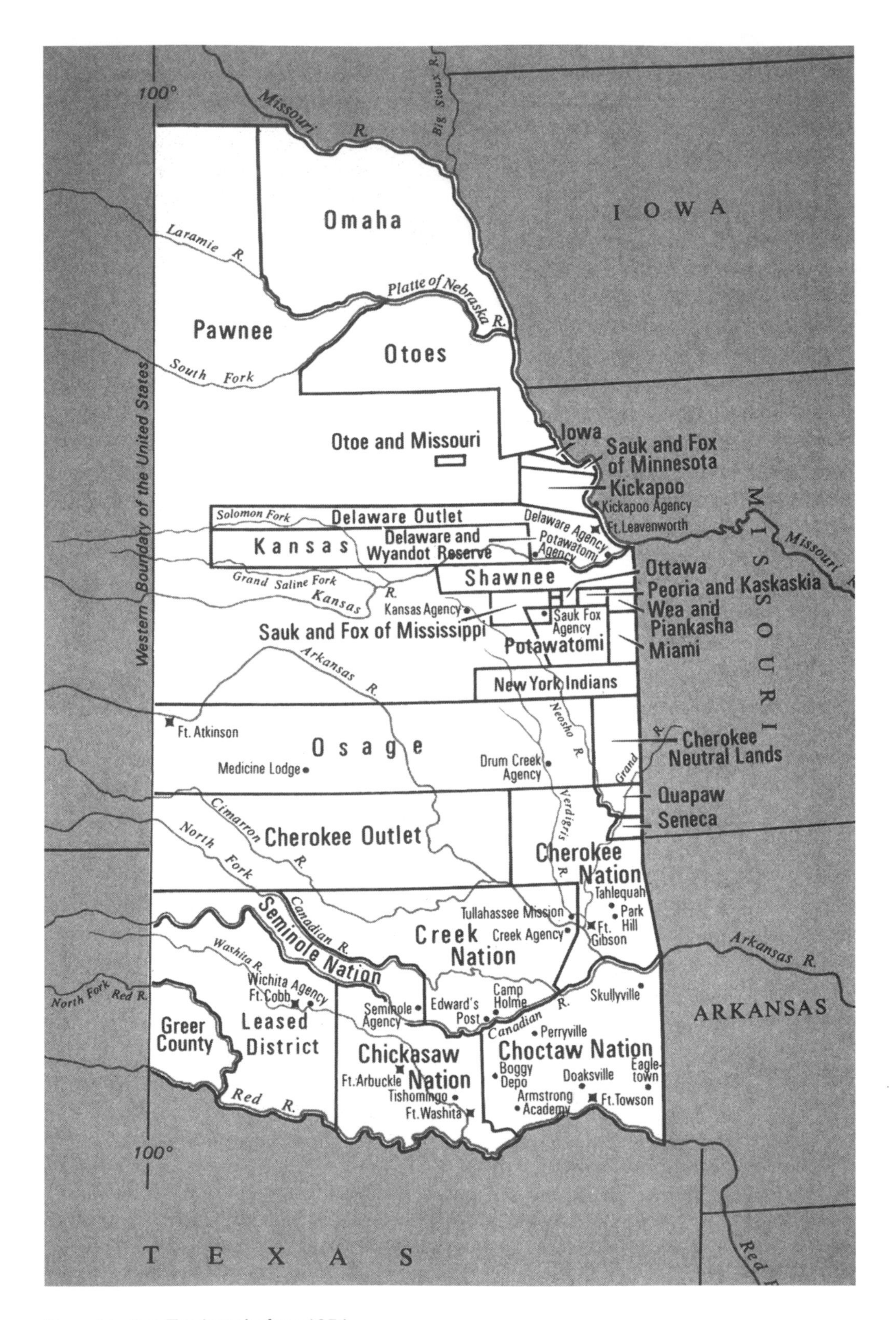

Map of Indian Territory before 1854.

ing as the leader of the tribe. President Andrew Jackson (1828–36) knew what he was doing in 1829 when he gave Indians only two options—move west or become subject to both selective enforcement and discriminatory state laws. Observers knew that Indians believed that no state laws and state courts would place them on an equal footing with U.S. citizens. Georgia, for example, forbade the Cherokee from mining their own gold. Many states refused to allow Indians to testify against non-Indians. As late as 1908, Oklahoma passed a law declaring that all adult Indians were incompetent to manage (legally) their farms. The federal government, for its part, refused to give treaty-guaranteed protection against exploitation and cheating. Indeed, President Jackson had earlier negotiated several questionable Indian treaties, and his refusal to enforce an 1832 ruling of the U.S. Supreme Court (*Worcester v. Georgia*) ensured Georgian domination of the Cherokee.

Inevitably, the American commissioner would appear and make an offer for land that could not be refused. By every method possible, tribes would be forced to cede (or appear to cede) their lands. Chief Spotted Tail of the Sioux is supposed to have tongue-in-cheeked the quip, "Why does not the Great Father put his red children on wheels, so he can move them as he will?" Indians were not just pushed out of one parcel of land; they were forced to relocate on different assigned lands. These reserved lands in time would then be either totally eliminated or taken away piecemeal by new treaties (or by negotiation after 1871), unjust state laws, or individual acts of barbarism. Shortly after the end of the nineteenth century, most of the remaining lands were lost through a process called allotment where Indians were forced to live on small parcels of privately owned land. By 1900, most tribes had lost their communal lands, and most Indian people would soon lose the allotted land given them.

The continuing drop in numbers in the total Indian population and the continuous loss of most of the valuable Indian lands reinforced the idea by 1900 that the Indian was disappearing. Nobody realized that the low point of Indian population figures had been reached and that Indians would multiply dramatically in the twentieth century. No such renaissance was possible in ownership of land—the Indian land heritage was forever gone, and often the old life-style tied to that land was in 1900 only a memory among the elders of the tribe. Of the nearly three billion acres of pre-Columbian Indian America, in 1934 Indians owned only forty-eight million, a great deal of it useless desert land.

Representative Case Studies

The Abenaki (Penobscot and Passamaquoddy) of New England are an example of New England tribe members that barely maintained themselves on small parcels of their old land. In 1786 they refused to sign a treaty with Massachusetts, but in 1794 they ceded the state more than a million acres. By 1820, the Abenaki owned only a few thousand acres. By 1850, they were confined to two separate villages. Some, in fact, were forced out of villages in Vermont by whites and fled to relatives in Canada. It would be 130 years before the federal government paid them $81.5 million for land taken illegally.

The Miami-speaking Indians are an Eastern tribe, most of whose members were forcibly relocated in the West, although a significant number were allowed to stay on allotted land in Indiana. The Piankashaw, a small Miami-speaking tribe, had begun selling their Indian lands as early as 1804 and had been moved as prisoners of war in 1814 to Missouri. In 1832, the Piankashaw had to cede their lands in Missouri and go to Kansas. The tribe then was moved again to the Indian Territory. Another closely related Miami-speaking group, the Wea, ceded their lands in Indiana in 1820 and 1824. The Wea moved then to Missouri and like the Piankashaw were forced to emigrate to Kansas. Large groups of the tribe known as the Miami left Indiana at various times beginning in the early 1830s. After several treaties that failed to convince the remaining Miami to emigrate (and which infuriated President Jackson), their head chief suddenly announced in 1838 that the last part of the tribe was ready to move. The rapid influx of hostile squatters into Miami areas seems to have been the final motivator. Another chief skillfully procrastinated until rather good terms had been negotiated for the removal of the tribe and for the sale of tribal lands. Families and relatives of the principal chiefs, and most of the mixed bloods, were exempted from the movement west by the terms of the treaty. Although only the presence of the army ensured the movement to Kansas of the less-influential Miami, the 1846 exodus was more humane in general than many such forced migrations. The reluctant Miami were also convinced by the fact that government annuities would now be paid only to Indians in the new western lands. A few years later, they were forced to move again, this time to the Oklahoma Indian Territory.

The fate of the Catawba, a Siouan-speaking tribe of the coastal Carolinas, illustrates how some minuscule Indian groups survived in the southern coastal region. Although in 1763 the British Crown had given them 144,000 fertile acres, by 1800 disease had so decimated the tribe that they could offer no resistance to white encroachments. After South Carolina purchased the 144,000 acres in 1840, a number of Catawba moved to the Indian Territory. So many Catawba would not leave the state, or returned after being unpleasantly rejected in North Carolina, that a 630-acre reservation was started by South Carolina in 1841. That miniature Catawba state lasted until 1962. A billion-dollar court claim filed by the

Catawba has kept alive the issue of the treatment of Indians in the Jacksonian Era.

The 1830s Trail of Tears of the Five Tribes of the Southeast Indians is a rather well-known example of the personal and community tragedies that accompanied the many forced deportations of Indians during most of the nineteenth century. By the end of the 1830s, the Southeast had lost sixty to ninety percent of the estimated 150,000 Indian population of 1830. The Southeast represented the most thoroughgoing application of the Jacksonian removal policy.

The Cherokee, whose unhappy relocation from Alabama, Georgia, and Tennessee to the West seems to have been the worst migratory experience, saw the first group leave to present-day Arkansas after an 1808 treaty. Another Cherokee land cession and emigration took place in 1817–19. The state of Georgia increasingly insisted that the federal government live up to the Compact of 1802 in which Georgia gave up the territory that became Alabama and Mississippi in return for the federal government's help in extinguishing Indian title to land within the state. At the same time, Andrew Jackson emphasized the "Indian must move west" policy, which had been enunciated in 1824 by President Monroe and accepted by his successor, John Quincy Adams, as the only solution to the Indian situation. Indeed, as early as 1804, at Thomas Jefferson's request, Congress gave the president the power to exchange lands west of the Mississippi River for ceded Indian lands east of the river.

Faced with this long history of antagonism, a small group of Cherokee signed the Treaty of New Echota in 1835, which exchanged all Southeast Cherokee lands for land in southeast Oklahoma. Although fifteen thousand Cherokee signed a petition denouncing the treaty, the U.S. government proceeded to force the Cherokee out. In the summer of 1838, the U.S. Army rounded up and imprisoned in stockades individual Cherokee, after burning their homes and crops. In the suddenness of the attack, parents and their children often became separated. Water and food were at a premium in the stockades. Leaving late in the fall, some detachments were delayed as much as six months on the eight-hundred-mile journey west. In traveling to their new homes in the winter of 1838–39, between one-fourth and one-third of the main group of thirteen thousand reluctant emigrés died. Meeting the survivors in Indian Territory were the "Old Settlers," who were the 1808 Cherokee group, recently ejected by biased whites from their Arkansas homes.

Only about a thousand Cherokee in western North Carolina—most of whom descended from Cherokee who had accepted American citizenship and 640 acres of land in the 1819 treaty—were not forced west by General Winfield Scott. Along with some who escaped detection and some who returned over the years, this 1819 group became the present Eastern Cherokee of the Great Smokies.

All the other Southeast tribes suffered similar experiences. The Choctaw Nation of southern Mississippi and Alabama was the first to go west, leaving over three years (1831–34) in parties of five hundred to a thousand. Hundreds died from exposure to winter blizzards, cholera epidemics, and lack of necessary supplies. The death rate in the new environment continued to be high for some years.

Two Southeast tribes fought back. In the Creek War of 1836, General Winfield Scott had to capture and shackle the Indian leaders. On the way to Oklahoma, the sinking of a steamboat cost three hundred Creek lives. The usual diseases, hunger, and exposure claimed a large number. Over 20 percent of the fifteen thousand Creek died within a short period as a result of exposure and the unhealthy conditions in the new homeland. Seminole Indians in Florida fought the Second Seminole War (1835–42) as a protest against migration, but 90 to 95 percent of the Seminole were finally removed.

Historians consider the forced migration in 1837–38 of the Chickasaw of northern Mississippi and Alabama as the least lethal among the Southeast tribes. The Chickasaw had made the best financial arrangements concerning the sale of their ancient lands. Even so, they suffered the usual deprivations and epidemics on the journey. For several years, the Chickasaw lived in tents in immigrant camps. They had found that hostile Plains tribes (Kiowa and Comanche) and marauding Shawnee and Kickapoo Indians had made the assigned area nearly uninhabitable for a decade.

Unlike the Five Tribes, the California Indians were often of marked pacifist tendencies. Miwok and Yokut carried on an effective hit-and-run guerrilla war in the 1830s against the Mexicans, but this military expertise was not typical. Thus, California Indians were pushed aside early. In addition, Indians in California lacked any legal control of land; neither Spain nor Mexico had acknowledged Indian ownership of the land. The secularization of the Catholic missions in 1834 benefited the Indians not a whit. When in 1851–52 the Indians' negotiation with the federal government led to treaties promising seven million acres of reservation lands, the Californians responded so violently that Congress rejected the treaties. Nevertheless, the land ceded in those rejected treaties were considered valid cessions! One militarily adept tribe, the Hupa, did indeed gain land in their homeland. However, the participants in the 1870s Modoc War in northern California found themselves exiled to Oklahoma. The Yokayo Pomo found a new secure home only because they paid for it out of their own funds. When reservations began to appear in the 1880s in California, the Mission Indians found that their reservations in southern California were practically worthless because of an inadequate water supply. The Ohlone of the San Francisco Bay area illustrate the severity of Indian decline in California. From a populous group possessing some thirty to forty permanent villages in the years before the Spanish arrival in 1768, by the 1860s the Ohlone could be found only as parts of small multi-Indian nation ghetto-like villages. By 1900, all communal Ohlone life had ceased. (See also the California section of Chapter 3.)

Almost all Great Plains Indians had a history different from such people as the Ohlone, who from time immemorial had lived in just one fixed locale. In the late seventeenth century the Cheyenne, for example, were a farming people in the northeast and north-central parts of Minnesota. By the 1750s, they had moved (under Sioux pressure) both south to the Minnesota River area and west to the Sheyenne River (not the same river as the Cheyenne in South Dakota) of North Dakota. By 1780, they were buffalo hunters in South Dakota. At the beginning of the 1800s, they were on the Cheyenne River at the extreme southwestern corner of South Dakota. Under constant pressure from Indian enemies they moved even further westward to the upper branches of the Platte River. There in the Rocky Mountains they came finally to be completely involved in the nomadic horse culture. By 1851, the Southern Cheyenne lived on the Arkansas River in southern Colorado and the Northern Cheyenne lived at the headwaters of the Platte and Yellowstone rivers. After the Medicine Lodge Council of 1867, the U.S. assigned them a reservation in western Oklahoma. A well-publicized desertion in 1878 of some three hundred Northern Cheyenne under Dull Knife and their continuing escape from some thirteen thousand pursuing U.S. troops caused an embarrassed U.S. government to allow the Northern Cheyenne to settle in Montana, while the Southern Cheyenne continued to stay in Oklahoma. (See also the Plains section of Chapter 3.)

Like the Plains Indians, the dramatically reduced number of Plateau Indians of western Oregon and Washington, Idaho, and Montana struggled in several wars to save their lands, but by the 1850s, they had begun to be placed on reduced portions of their former lands. The Americans by then had succeeded in putting a wall between Indians in the eastern parts of Oregon and Washington and whites in the fertile valleys near the coast. The Cayuse Indians, one prominent Plateau tribe,

Plains Indian squaw dance, 1893.

had first brought on the wrath of the Americans in 1847 by killing a missionary (Marcus Whitman), his wife, and twelve others. A vigilante army wreaked havoc on the Cayuse. A year after the 1855 Walla Walla Treaty council, a general war broke out between most of the Plateau Indians and the United States. In essence, the Indians wanted their lands back, but the Cayuse were unable to keep their Walla Walla Valley and instead had to move to the Umatilla Reservation. Disease and drink continued to undermine the tribe. When settlers noticed the beautiful grazing land on the Umatilla Reservation, the reservation was reduced in 1886 by about one-fourth.

Relatively few readers may know about the Cayuse and their troubles, but many among the reading public know about the 1864 Long Walk of the Navajo, the culmination of a long period of hostility between Navajo and U.S. society. Previously the Navajo had come into constant conflict with Spanish and then Mexican slave catchers. The hostile Hispanic approach was continued by the Americans when they arrived in the late 1840s. In 1858, the Bonneville Treaty reduced drastically the size of the area that the Navajo could consider theirs. In 1860, a thousand Navajo unsuccessfully attacked Fort Defiance, which was located in the heart of their country. In 1862 General Carleton arrived with a column of troops from California, bringing with him the Californian Indian extermination policy. Carleton ordered Kit Carson and the New Mexico Volunteers to move against the Navajo, and in early 1864 Carleton's scorched earth policy caused the surrender of the Navajo bastion of Canyon de Chelly. The Navajo were walked under duress eight hundred miles to a forty-square-mile reserve at Fort Sumner (Bosque Redondo), New Mexico. Ten percent of 2,500 Navajo died in a March 1864 convoy to Fort Sumner. Whites enslaved stragglers and captured their livestock. Absolutely no mercy was shown the trekking Navajo.

Some 9,000 Navajo (and 500 Mescalero Apache) herders and hunters were to be made anew into farmers. At Fort Sumner crops failed because of lack of water, alkaline soil, and hordes of grasshoppers. Available wood was five to eighteen miles away; the local Comanche Indians were hostile; and inadequate government financial support led to starvation and suffering. Conditions were so bad that the Santa Fe, New Mexico newspaper publicized the fort's more inhumane shortcomings. For such reasons, the government in 1868 allowed the Navajo to return to a portion (10 percent) of the hills and mesa of the old homeland. Ten years later, more land was added to the reservation, the first of many additions made to a tribe whose population began to rise dramatically. While the Navajo were quite pleased with these additions, the neighboring Hopi reservation saw with chagrin that they had become completely surrounded by the Navajo and their herds.

Besides the Navajo Apache, most of the other Apache of the Southwest were militarily inclined Indians. Their homeland, "Apacheria," was the last Indian area to lay down its arms. Because the Apachean-speaking tribes of the Southwest were not a centralized group, their history is accordingly complex. The Mescalero Apache of southeastern New Mexico, Texas, and the Chihuahua and Coahuila areas of Mexico were placed first on two tiny reservations in Texas. When vigilante Texans vigorously objected, the Apache were moved to safety in Oklahoma. In 1862, some five hundred Mescalero complied with an order to join the Navajo on the Pecos River wasteland at Bosque Redondo. Most soon deserted. A decade later, they were moved to reservations in south-central New Mexico near Fort Stanton. For a time, the Jicarilla Apache also lived there. In 1922, Congress finally did for the Mescalero Reservation what Spain had never done—it confirmed the Indians' title to the land they lived on.

Through administrative indecision, the Jicarilla Apache of northeastern New Mexico were, in 1873, the only New Mexico tribe not living on a reservation. Only in 1887 did the Jicarilla finally get a reservation that annoyed neither Washington, the local New Mexican whites, nor the Jicarilla. Of course, it was still a most wrenching move, since it was a bit west of the historic Jicarilla home and most of the valuable lands were already owned by non-Indian farmers and ranchers.

The various groups comprising the Western Apache began to receive reservations in 1871–72, although keeping them on the reservations to the east of Phoenix was a constant problem. Discovery of gold in their territory in 1863 had begun the troubles between the Americans and the Tonto Apache. However, the more northerly White Mountain and Cibecue Apache remained, rather uneasily, at peace.

Particularly hard to keep on any reservation were the Chiricahua Apache of southern New Mexico and Arizona, who lived just west of the Mescalero. The Chiricahua first had run into problems when tough silver and gold miners flooded their country in 1852. For a while, the Chiricahua had a reservation in the extreme southeast corner of Arizona abutting the international line. Then the American government tried to move them into the quite different environment of the San Carlos Reservation on the Gila River in Arizona, where the Western Apaches were living. Discovery of coal brought intrusive miners, and water rights on the Gila River were seized by whites. Such difficulties led to more than two decades of war (1860–86) against the Americans under leaders such as Mangas Coloradas, Cochise, and Geronimo. After a final sixteen-month flight (1885–86), they were captured and treated as prisoners of war. They were punished by being sent to Florida, then to Alabama, and finally to Oklahoma. Later, in 1913, most surviving Chiricahua chose to go to the Mescalero reservation rather than become allottees in Oklahoma.

The history of the Yuman (or Quechan) tribe also represents the treatment accorded a hostile military group of the Southwest. In 1884, a reservation (Fort Yuma) of forty-five thousand acres of land on the California side of the Colorado River was established. As usual, the tract included only a small portion of the territory the tribe had previously controlled, and in any case it contained a good portion of land unfit for farming. The reservation was allotted, divided into individual portions, in 1893. The usual governmental mismanagement, Indian hostility to agricultural pursuits, and white cupidity led to many Indians not receiving the ten-acre allotment, at least not in the valuable irrigable area.

By the 1870s, there were no more places to exile Indians when whites wanted their lands. Some principle for concentrating Indians on smaller areas was needed to augment the reservation policy. As seen in the Yuman case, an old technique could be used to separate the Indians from most of their good land. Many of the sixty treaties concluded between 1853 and 1857 had called for the allotment of tribal lands. In 1887, after eight years of congressional debate, President Grover Cleveland signed the Dawes General Allotment Act into law. The president was given the authority to subdivide communal Indian land into private ownership of individual plots, a practice sometimes referred to in legal language as "fee simple ownership." The traditional plot of a homesteader (160 acres) was given to the head of a family and smaller plots were awarded to others. Acreage was doubled on reservations suited only for grazing. A group could be punished as were the recalcitrant Kickapoo in Indian Territory who were only assigned 80 acres each. The land so awarded could not be sold for twenty-five years. In general, only the northern Plains and Southwest Indians escaped allotment.

Allotment was supposed to guarantee the assimilation of Indians into the American mainstream. Instead, it led to permanent underclass status as Indian real estate began to shrivel in three ways during the allotment era. Outside pressures and internal weaknesses combined to encourage tribes to lease out communal tribal lands. For example, in the early 1880s seven cattlemen had leases on the Cheyenne and Arapaho Reservation in Oklahoma ranging in size from 140,000 to 570,000 acres. More ominously, unallocated reservation lands were declared surplus and put up for sale to non-Indians. In addition, laws had been passed that allowed many Indians to sell their land earlier than the original twenty-five year no-sale period. In 1891 alone, one-seventh (17.4 million acres) of all remaining Indian lands was lost. In 1881, 155 million acres were Indian owned, but in 1900, the number had halved to about 78 million! Land ownership figures, however, are misleadingly high. When it was noticed that a large percentage of Indian land was held by women, orphans, children, and incapacitated males, a law was passed in 1891 allowing these groups to lease their allotted land. Thus, quite quickly reservations (such as the Omaha and Winnebago) often had the majority of their acres leased to non-Indians. In the decades after the 1887 allotment law, Indians lost at least two-thirds of all their landholdings. Ninety percent of the acres originally allotted in Oklahoma are no longer owned by Oklahoma Indians.

Originally, intense opposition from the Five Tribes in Indian Territory had allowed them to be exceptions to the Dawes Act. Nevertheless, between 1897 and 1902 the Dawes Commission forced them to accept allotment, and today Oklahoma has no reservations. Congress early began to open up the Indian Territory (Oklahoma) to non-Indian settlers. In fact, a number of trespassers were already "booming" the rich lands while waiting for the federal government to legalize their squatter actions. In 1889, President William Henry Harrison opened up nearly two million acres of land in the "Oklahoma District" in central Oklahoma. On April 22, 1889, the army supervised people recklessly seeking homesteads in an area known for its fertility and which in time produced great petroleum wealth. A hundred thousand non-Indians participated in the 5.7-million-acre Cherokee (plus Pawnee and Tonkawa "surplus" land) Outlet Run on September 16, 1893. The model for these nearly instantaneous transfers of land from Indian to individual non-Indian settler was the earlier opening of the rich Iowa farm lands on May 1, 1843 (with a second run in 1845) of what had once been the domain of the Sauk and Fox Indians. Similar Oklahoma "runs" opened up 868,000 acres of Iowa, Sauk and Fox, Potawatomi-Shawnee lands on September 22, 1891; the 3.5-million-acre Cheyenne-Arapaho areas (April 19, 1892); and the 85,000 acre Kickapoo land in Oklahoma (May 23, 1895). In 1901, the 3.2 million acres of the Kiowa-Comanche and the Wichita-Caddo reservations were opened, and 170,000 persons registered for a drawing of 13,000 quarter-sections.

The imperative to force Indian cession of lands—which lay behind the allotment principle—also led Congress in 1889 to break up the Great Sioux Reservation of North and South Dakota into six smaller reservations: Pine Ridge, Rosebud, Cheyenne River, Standing Rock, Lower Brule, and Crow Creek. In 1851, at Fort Laramie, the Dakota Sioux had signed a treaty defining the boundaries of their domain. In 1868, a new Fort Laramie treaty reduced the reservation to give U.S. miners access to Montana's gold. After Custer's defeat in 1876, the Sioux were punished by having the

western part of their land, which includes the Black Hills, sliced off the reservation. In 1889, another eleven million acres were lost.

Another large group of Indians who had to accept the same allotment treatment in 1889 were the Chippewa of Minnesota. Through the years, the Chippewa of the Lake Superior region had been forced to cede huge areas: in 1837, a large section of west-central Wisconsin and east-central Minnesota; in 1842, most of northern Wisconsin; in 1854, the northeastern portion of Minnesota. Civil War era treaties limited the Chippewa of Minnesota to a number of large reservations where the land was to be allotted. In 1889, a half-dozen Chippewa reservations had to cede land to the government, which in turn sold the land to non-Indians with the proceeds held in trust for the tribe. The individual Chippewa were given the choice of either accepting allotments on the original reservation or relocating to the White Earth Reservation and taking allotments there.

A similar rapid disappearance of land can be seen in the history of the Comanche, another Plains tribe. The Treaty of the Little Arkansas (1865) allowed these non-Apache Plains nomads to retain thirty million acres. Then just two years later, in the Medicine Lodge Treaty, the U.S. bowed to Texan objections by cutting Comanche land back to three million acres. By 1901, other cessions had reduced the Comanche tribal estate to one percent of the 1865 area.

One Plains tribe landed on its feet, despite land cessions, frequent forced relocations, and allotment. Challenged by both eastern immigrant and Plains tribes, the once-powerful Osage had little ability to resist American pressure. In a series of treaties in 1808, 1818, 1825, and 1870, the Osage had seen the ground disappear from under them. In 1872, they had to leave Kansas for Oklahoma, a removal so traumatic that nearly 50 percent of the tribe died between 1877 and 1884. Then it was discovered that the bluestem grass covering their new acres provided excellent grazing, and the ground below contained oil! Just as important, Osage intransigence had allowed them to reserve all mineral rights for the tribe as a whole, and this communal factor protected a great deal of the wealth flowing in. In forty years, the Osage received about $300 million in royalties. Finally, they were able to acquire individually 658 acres of land because they won the right to allot all their lands to the tribe. There was no Sooner-type or open run land grab.

It should be noted, also, that one large group of Indians neither were moved nor suffered a large amount of land loss. Possessing a relatively secure niche in Spanish New Mexican colonial society, the Pueblo Indians were divided into the Eastern Pueblo along the Rio Grande in New Mexico, and the Western Pueblo in western New Mexico and northeastern Arizona. A liberal interpretation by the Spanish governor of an 1812 Spanish constitution allowed the Pueblo by the late 1820s full citizenship and legal equality. In addition, the Pueblo Indian population not only stabilized but was steadily increasing. On the other hand, during the short-lived period of Mexican rule, the Pueblo received a great deal less protection from rapacious neighbors than they had been able to wring from Spanish officialdom. The later violent history of Indians in Mexico centered on the Mexican policy (particularly after 1857) of breaking up corporate Indian holdings of land and placing land tenure on a completely individual basis. Fortunately for the Pueblo Indians in the territory newly acquired by the Americans after the Treaty of Guadalupe Hidalgo in 1848, Congress confirmed thirty-five Spanish grants to the Pueblo, totaling 700,000 acres. This enlightened Indian land-ownership policy compares radically with the governmental philosophy in California and Texas after the Mexicans were ejected. Greedy settlers, of course, began to move in on much of the choice irrigable land. Since the Pueblo are not a single entity, their autonomous villages often lacked the funds and leadership to oppose interlopers on their lands. Only in 1924 did Congress assure the Pueblo their right to their prime agricultural land.

For the general history of American Indians, the Osage and Pueblo success stories represent exceptions proving the rule. More generally, American Indians were clobbered during the nineteenth century by having most of their communally owned and individually allotted lands taken away, their people reduced by some forty percent, and being forced to move anytime their homelands looked attractive to non-Indians. Understandably then, even among the over 50 percent of Indians who were American citizens by 1900, there remained an abhorrence of the American way of life. Even without a land base, the Native American was not Americanized.

Leroy Eid
University of Dayton (Ohio)

Union Pacific Railroad construction. Cheyenne Indians hunting buffalo near the newly laid tracks and telegraph lines.

♦ INDIAN LAND TENURE IN THE TWENTIETH CENTURY

Two major trends have affected the way Indians live in the twentieth century. In the first third of the century, Indians were confined to reservations and lost considerable land through the process of allotment, whereby reservation lands were divided into individual and privately owned tracts and the surplus lands were sold to non-Indians. This era led to a considerable loss of Indian land. A second major trend, especially after World War II, has been the migration of Indians to urban areas. By the latter quarter of the twentieth century, more than 75 percent of the Indian population were living in urban settings rather than on reservations.

Reservations and Land Allotment

A few reservations are located in the eastern United States, but most are in the Great Plains and in the West. Unlike the vast territories Indians held in pre-contact times, Indian reservations today represent only remnants of original lands. For example, the Zuni Reservation in New Mexico comprises nearly 500,000 acres of an original 15,000,000. As a result of treaty negotiations, most Indian nations lost their original lands and were moved to reservations. On reservations, Indians could no longer pursue their traditional hunting and gathering activities, which required large expanses of uninhabited lands. Often lacking in arable land and resources, reservations also offer few economic opportunities, especially in the dry West. The Indians' confinement on reservations forced them to live in poverty, under direct U.S. government rule.

By the last quarter of the nineteenth century, the Bureau of Indian Affairs (BIA) gained administration over Indian reservation economic and government matters. U.S. policy makers believed that reservations—where the BIA protected Indian land rights—would pacify the Indians and stabilize land relations with settlers. Over the decades, the BIA has promoted economic development and tribal self-government; it has assisted Indians in the development of irrigation systems and ranching economies; and it has promoted tribal management of reservation resources.

As early as 1887, the government implemented policies to assimilate Indians into U.S. society. Part of the assimilation plan involved a major readjustment of Indian land tenure by allotting reservation lands. These policies lead to the breakup of countless reservations and to the fragmentation of holdings within reservations.

Proponents of land allotment held that the ideal policy was to separate individual Indians from their tribe. They asserted that if Indians were granted private land—or an allotment, analogous to a homestead on the reservation—they would soon become productive yeoman farmers. Thus, Congress passed the General Allotment Act of 1887 (sometimes referred to as the Dawes Act), which authorized the BIA to survey reservation lands and to lay out individual farms. Under the Act, farmer/teachers would work with Indians during an apprenticeship period. After twenty-five years, Indians would receive a fee title or a deed to their allotments; once obtained, this deed "liberated" an Indian from his trustee, that is, the government. So long as Indian land remained in trust, no property taxes could be collected. This tax-free status has provided considerable security for individual Indians, although other aspects of allotment have diminished this trust security.

Many Indians, whom BIA officials judged as "competent," received fee title well before the twenty-five year period. These Indians tended to sell or lease their lands and often ended up destitute. Many Indians abandoned their land and moved to cities, or worked on non-Indian lands in or out of reservation borders. Others were forced to live with more prudent relatives or to live on tribal land that had not been allotted to individuals. Congress, in amending the Allotment Act in 1906, required that if Indians did not exploit their lands in a manner acceptable to policy, the government could lease their lands. In the early twentieth century, at least 25 percent of allotted lands were so leased; today, that percentage is much greater.

Once the government surveyed and distributed allotted lands among living tribal members—even over their protests—it opened the remaining Indian lands to settlement by non-Indian homesteaders. In addition, many Indians, unable to make a living farming, sold their allotments, usually well below market prices. Nearly a half-century later, by 1934, Indians had lost ownership of about 90 million acres through allotment. Moreover, since many Indian allottees left no wills that designated the inheritance of land, this land became subject to state inheritance laws. Thousands of allotments became encumbered by multiple joint heirs. Over time, the joint shares resulted in plots of land much too small to farm profitably.

Indian Reorganization Act

Land allotment disrupted tribal culture and fragmented reservation land and resources. In *Red Man's Land/White Man's Law* (1971), historian Wilcomb Washburn noted that Indians had been "forced to limit their life and their vision to an incomprehensible individual plot of 160 or so acres in a checkerboard of neighbors, hostile and friendly, rich and poor, white and red" (p. 75). In the 1920s, even conservative officials sought to modify what had become a destructive process. In 1934, as part of the New Deal administration, Congress stopped the process of land allotment by creating the Indian Reorganization Act (IRA). The IRA restored some surplus lands to tribal ownership, added some new lands, and authorized tribal restoration of allotted lands by purchase, provided it was fiscally possible. The IRA also encouraged tribal self government and economic enterprises. Prior to the IRA, many religious groups and national leaders had believed that holding land in private property would lead to the acculturation and assimilation of Indians. Speculative interests in Indian cropland, range, minerals, and timber urged Congress to sustain and even step up the pace of granting title to Indians, because it often meant either the sale or lease of Indian land. Ultimately, many Indians were dispossessed of their land and became dependent on government social services.

Many Indian reservation governments did not fully support the IRA; of 258 tribal communities at the time only 77 accepted the measure. Many tribes voted against the IRA out of fear that treaties would be annulled. Despite the intent of the IRA, tribal governments did not gain appreciable authority over the expenditure of their monies or over signing leases, for the BIA continued to overrule tribal council decisions. In effect, the IRA allowed some tribal governments to form new constitutions but in the end did not grant them any new or considerable powers.

Termination

Despite the efforts of Commissioner John Collier (1933–45) to make the Indian Reorganization Act work, Congress in the post-World War II era elected to discontinue the trusteeship of Indian tribes. By House Resolution 108 (1953), Indians became subject to the same laws, privileges, and responsibilities of all U.S. citizens. The resolution aimed to end Indian wardship to the U.S. government. Under this policy, which became known as termination, the U.S. government intended to sever all special legal ties and social service relations with Indian communities. In 1954, Congress terminated the Klamath Indians of southern Oregon; four Paiute bands, the Uintah and Ouray of Utah; and the Alabama and Coushatta of Texas. Other terminations followed over the next few years. Most tribes affected by this policy could not survive outside the legal protections of trusteeship. The Menominee of Wisconsin, terminated despite their appeals and their fears of additional taxes, sold valuable lakefront property to non-Indians. The former Menominee Reservation became a county under Wisconsin law. The Menominee struggled to sustain their lumber operations, the tribe's major source of income. As a terminated tribe, the Menominee lost valuable land and many people became impoverished. Because of their economic plight, the Menominee wanted to restore their rights as an Indian nation, and they appealed to Congress for restoration of their federal recognition as an Indian nation. By the mid-1970s, the Menominee became the first Indian nation to be restored to federal recognition after termination. Several terminated Indian groups— the Siletz of Oregon and more than half a dozen rancheria groups in California—later regained trust status.

Land Restoration and Claims

At various times, Congress has enacted legislation returning some former "surplus" lands or adding acreage to reservations. Congress has also restored some lands as a result of land claims litigation, when courts ruled in favor of the restoration of Indian land. The Havasupai, whose ancestral home was reduced to a small parcel within the Grand Canyon, received a 185,000-acre restoration. The Yakima in Washington and the Taos and Zuni Pueblo in New Mexico sought and regained limited sacred acreage. The restation of sacred places has resulted, in part, from the application of the American Indian Religious Freedom Act, provided that tribes convincingly demonstrate exclusive use for religious worship. Not all tribes have succeeded in this quest. Navajo and Hopi sued to stop the development of a ski resort located on the slopes of the San Francisco Peaks north of Flagstaff, Arizona, arguing that the mountains, as part of a sacred place, should in part be restored to them. The tribes, however, did not convince the court that they made exclusive use of the sacred places.

Tribal expectations fell dramatically when land claims litigation did not result in land restoration. In 1946, Congress created the Indian Claims Commission (ICC) so that one tribunal would hear all land claims from Indian tribes. Congress empowered the ICC to establish ground rules and procedures for the research and adjudication of hundreds of tribal claims over wrongful taking of land. It is possible that Congress intended to retire outstanding claims by tribes that clouded title to properties long held by non-Indians. Moreover, the claims process coincided in time with federal sentiments toward selective termination of trust responsibilities. Many tribes expected the ICC to award land, the title to which had passed out of Indian hands primarily in the nineteenth century. Unfortunately, the ICC chose early on to interpret its authority as having the power to award money rather than land. Many tribes, even those accepting money, have been disappointed or angered by this "day in court."

The claims process focused on the geographic extent of aboriginal territory as the basis for ascertaining the amount of money that tribes would net for their loss of land. Researchers for the plaintiff tribes and for the defendant U.S. government examined the historic/documentary record and explored the ethnographic past. While the tribes hoped for the largest geographic adju dication, the defendant sought a much reduced acreage figure. The process based monetary awards on the market value of an acre at the time of taking, which was often not more than $1.25. Many Indians openly rejected the process, condemning it as a judicial means to "get rid" of Indian land claims. The noted legal scholar, Vine Deloria, Jr. (Standing Rock Sioux), observed that many Indians who accepted monetary awards have suffered an irrevocable loss of land. Rejecting the process was a painful decision that few Indians made willingly. This, in part, explains why the Oglala Sioux continue to reject an award of more than $100 million for the loss of the Black Hills in South Dakota.

Congress has funded a few eastern tribes to help them purchase lands; both the Penobscot and Passamaquoddy in Maine will ultimately acquire about 300,000 acres of forest lands. Even though the ICC retired in 1978, the U.S. Claims Court has continued to hear claims cases. In 1991, the Zuni won a $25 million award for the loss of 15 million acres.

Reservation Life

Today, government programs seek to encourage individual and family farming or ranching and small business enterprises, in addition to the tribal operation of agriculture, ranching, lumbering, and tourism. Many Indians hope that the economic development of their reservations will sustain tribal lifeways, improve Indian income, and minimize interaction and confrontation with non-Indians. With BIA assistance, the Apache, Arapaho, Blackfeet, Navajo, and other nations have developed grazing programs. Many Indians manage housing projects for resident families, and they have entered into short- and long-term contracts for lease developments of timber, minerals, and other resources; they have also established various forms of manufacturing in conjunction with the private sector. Past BIA management of tribal timber resources has been scandalous, benefiting non-Indian interests more than Indian interests. Yet, in the past decade, the White Moun-

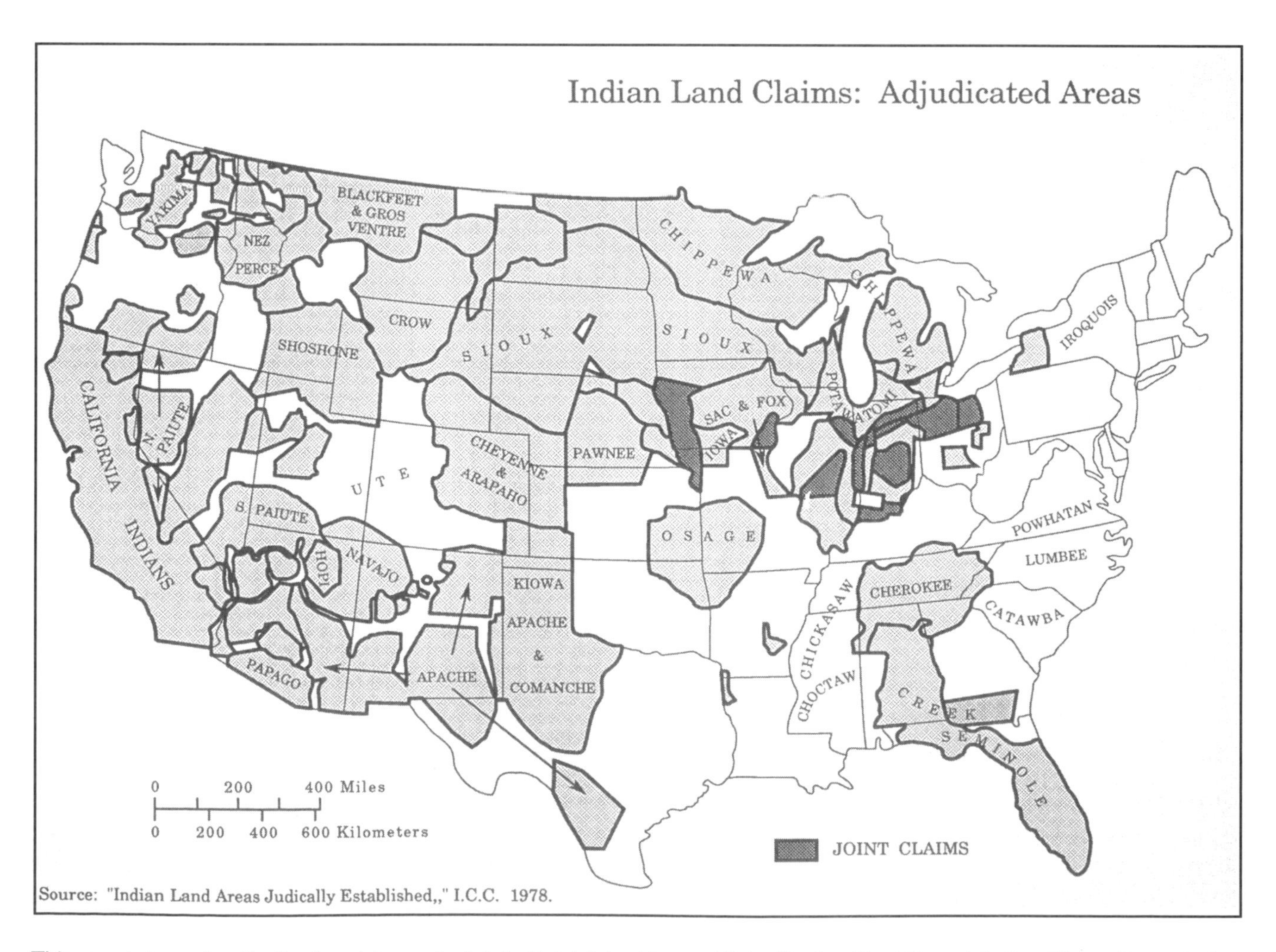

This map is based on "Indian Land Areas Judicially Established," as published in the *Final Report,* Indian Claims Commission, 1978, and published by permission of the University of New Mexico Press (Sutton, 1985). This map does not show the geographic areas of cases adjudicated by the U.S. Claims Court.

tain Apache in Arizona borrowed and repaid funds to develop a lumber industry to harvest pine and Douglas fir on the reservation and have employed more than three hundred Indians. The Blackfeet in Montana have established a pen-and-pencil factory, employing mostly Indians. Crow Indians in Montana have entered into leases for the exploitation of coal and oil. Many Indians have established visitor centers, museums, and craft stores, as well as tribally-run gas stations and other commercial ventures.

Only a small percentage of Indians benefit from many economic developments on reservations. A significant number of resident families receive welfare support and live at or below the poverty level. Indians are usually reported at the bottom of national income statistics and high unemployment characterizes most reservations. Tribal enterprises such as resort developments—Warm Springs, for example—as well as lumber operations—such as Menominee, Warm Springs, and White Mountain Apache—have successfully employed a number of Indians on a regular basis. However, Indian enterprises are not immune to general market downturns, there are inadequate numbers of enterprises on reservations, and reservation lands do not yield sufficient resource diversity to support more than a handful of resident Indians.

Today, some Indians enjoy a measure of employment in administrative and supervisory roles in tribal government. They may work in the administration directly, as elected or appointed officials, or they may work in tribal planning, in housing, health services, and the like. Some work for the BIA. An increasing number of young Indians have successfully completed high school, and some have attended, if not completed, college. In general, better educated Indians are more likely to work off the reservation. Only a few reservation communities have a sufficient number of college-educated Indians who might assume positions demanding professional skills. In response to this fact, the University of Oklahoma has recently established a graduate program in American Indian Natural Resource Management, which is, to date, the nation's sole academic program aimed at educating professionals to manage or co-manage tribal resources.

Reservation economies, in order to succeed, have followed the general trend toward increased mechanization and have put larger land units into production. Mechanization on the reservation precludes the need for a large work force and necessitates the employment of skilled and professional Indians. Many tribal leaders recognize that reservation land is far too limited and lacking in resources in order to support reservation populations. Aside from some limited high quality farm or ranch lands and notable timber and mineral resources, most reservations offer few long-term economic options. Many Indians, however, do not willingly choose to be farmers and do not care to engage in rural economic enterprises. Some Indians have done reasonably well in ranching, despite the overgrazed status of much of the tribal range.

Limitations on Economic Options

The absence of investment capital and business experience limits the economic options on reservations. Non-Indian enterprise and income tend to outweigh Indian enterprises on reservations. Consequently, leasing offers a way out for many Indians. In fact, in recent decades, 60 percent of irrigated lands and 75 percent of dry farmed acreage have been leased. While approximately fourteen reservations receive the bulk of the lease income from timber sales, most of the saw-timber cut on reservations in the Pacific Northwest is milled outside the area by non-Indian companies. In 1975, some twenty-two tribes formed the Council of Energy Resource Tribes (CERT), which has since expanded to forty-nine tribes. The CERT members collectively hold about 60 percent of all Indian lands and represent about half of all reservation Indians. CERT has emphasized the prudent development of tribal energy resources and improved tribal managerial skills, and it advises tribes about leasing in order to avoid contracts that return too little. The Blackfeet, Navajo, Osage, and Uintah and Ouray earn substantial income from natural resource sales.

The BIA's administrative control over reservation resources is another obstacle to successful economic development on reservations. The government's shifting policies—which range from sustaining tribes under trusteeship to terminating them—contribute to Indian skepticism over the purpose of government programs. The legacy of land allotment has undermined economic success by creating a checkerboard pattern of ownership which makes it difficult to exploit reservation resources. Due to the checkerboarding, the BIA leases the lands of many allottees. Leasing income, however, is usually six to nine times lower than market value.

The Administration for Native Americans (ANA), housed in the Department of Health and Human Services (HHS), has offered solutions to overcoming the obstacles to development on reservations. ANA, for example, has worked closely with CERT tribes, and has provided grant funds for priority projects encouraging economic growth and tribal governance. ANA thus identifies itself with the movement for tribal self determination, the recent policy granting tribal governments much greater control over their land, resources, and governments. Since its establishment in 1974, ANA has directly aided such tribal enterprises as the 110-unit Best Western Hotel on the Tulalip Indian Reservation in Washington. On the Yakima Indian Reservation, ANA helped fund a major wildlife resource management program that enhanced a public hunting program. The tribe

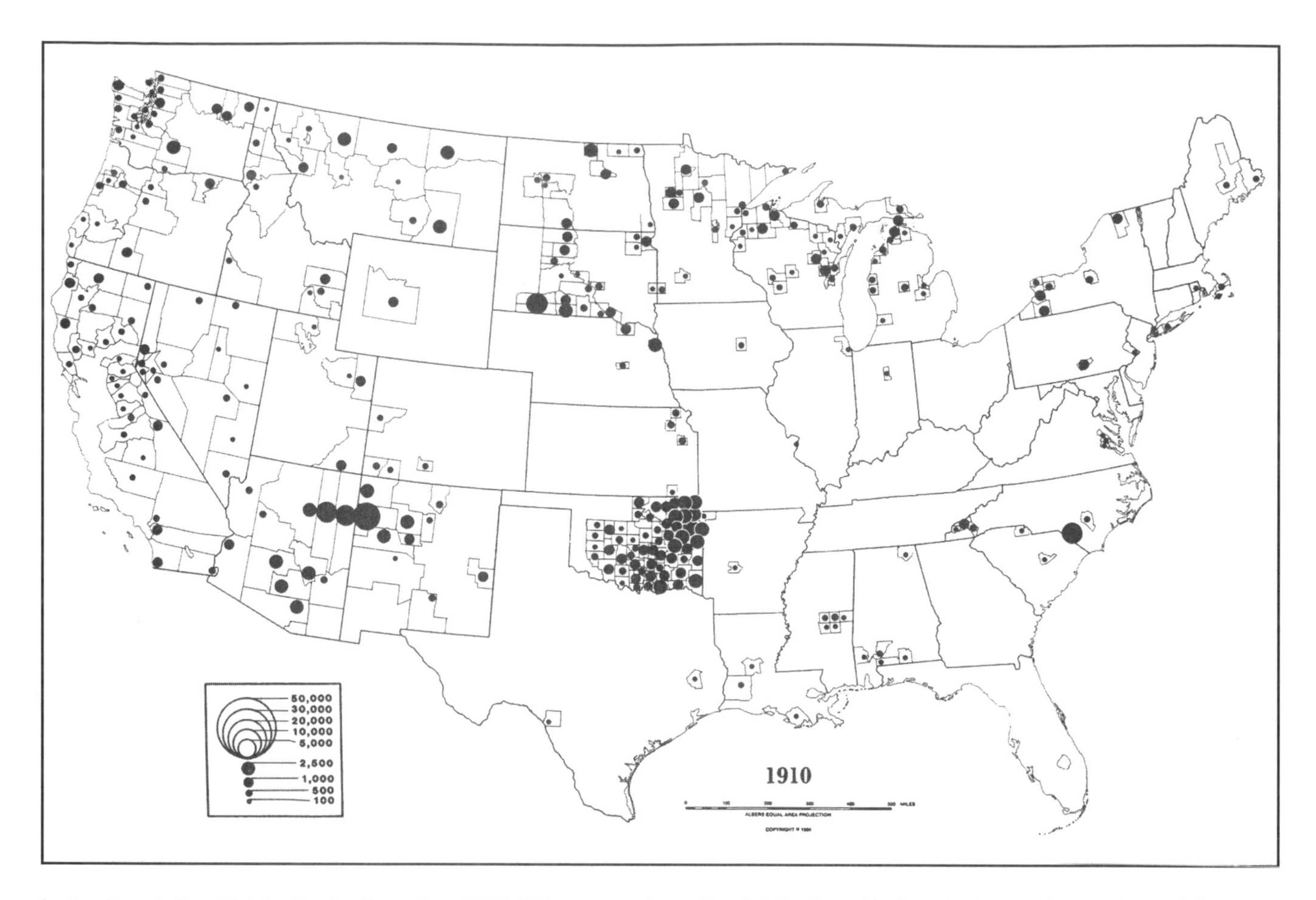

Indian Population Distribution by Counties: 1910. This map portrays the distribution of Indians in the contiguous forty-eight states for both reservations and urban centers but relies on countywide data. Used with permission of the University of Nebraska Press and Francis Prucha (1990). Base map by Department of Geography, University of Maryland, Baltimore County, 5401 Wilkens Avenue, Baltimore, Maryland 21228.

markets its own hunting licenses and anticipates a multi-million dollar revenues in the coming decades.

Residence, Mobility, and Relocation

In recent years, on many reservations, non-Indians have come to outnumber Indians living on the reservation. The large non-Indian population, which is sometimes a majority, makes it increasingly difficult for Indians to manage their own government and to control their economic institutions. Largely a result of the allotment process and of the opening of reservations, Indian populations on many reservations average less than 50 percent. On reservations in Arizona, the Dakotas, and New Mexico, Indians represent more than 90 percent of the population, whereas in California, in some Great Lakes states, and in Washington, Indians represent less than 30 percent of the reservation population. Policy makers once envisioned that the "mix" of Indian and non-Indian neighbors on reservation lands would hasten the assimilation of the tribes. Nevertheless, recent history demonstrates that simply mixing populations does not dissolve Indian identity and community.

Policies other than land allotment have also affected the mobility and residence of Indians. In the 1950s, the BIA instituted the Voluntary Relocation Program that sought to encourage Indians, especially younger ones, to leave reservations in order to live and work in larger urban centers such as Chicago, Denver, Los Angeles, Oklahoma City, and Seattle. Motivated by the expectation that Indians would find gainful employment in the cities, the BIA also sought alternative means to enable Indians to assimilate more readily. Despite financial and social assistance, many Indians have had considerable difficulty securing employment and adjusting to urban life, and often seek out other Indians in a perceived hostile environment.

Although the urbanization of Indians began well before the second World War, only 25 percent of all Indians were urbanized by 1960. According to the 1990 Census, 62 percent of all Indians live in towns and cities. More than 20,000 Indians live in metropolitan areas such as Los Angeles, Oklahoma City, Phoenix, and Tulsa, and at least 10,000 reside in some dozen other urban centers. Unfortunately, the living circumstances of urban Indians mirror those of most reservation Indians. Urbanizing Indians often exchange rural poverty for urban poverty. Problems of housing, unemployment, and discrimination in the city—as well as the stressful relationship between urban Indians and reservation Indians—have not been as closely studied as conditions on reservations have been.

Many urban Indians are enrolled tribal members and still retain legal and cultural ties to a tribe. As tribal members, urban Indians may occasionally benefit from per capita monetary distributions, such as have occurred with land claims awards. Even though they live in urban areas, many tribally affiliated Indians continue to own land and are affected by the BIA management of Indian trust lands.

Many urban Indians frequently return to reservations to visit relatives, to attend powwows and council meetings, and to vote in elections. They often hunt and fish on the reservation, and some are buried on tribal land. Conversely, reservation residents also frequent nearby towns and cities. They, too, may be visiting relatives, but usually they hold temporary jobs off the reservation and utilize local commercial and public services. Many reservation Indian students attend schools in nearby non-Indian communities, while some non-Indian students living on or adjacent to reservations attend reservation community colleges, and sometimes high schools and grade schools. (See Chapter 9 for more information on urbanization and nonreservation populations.)

Indian Country and Tribal Sovereignty

An Indian reservation is a special kind of property and a unique political place. What is called "Indian Country" embraces not only reservations and scattered Indian homesteads, but often includes areas adjacent to the reservation. This understanding of Indian Country evolved through the interaction of Indians and non-Indians on and off the reservation. Most people view reservations as property, but identify them less as political communities. According to current legal thought, Indian tribes retain inherent sovereign power unless it is abrogated by Congressional acts. The existence of such sovereign power is unknown to most non-Indians, who know very little about the relationship of tribal govern-

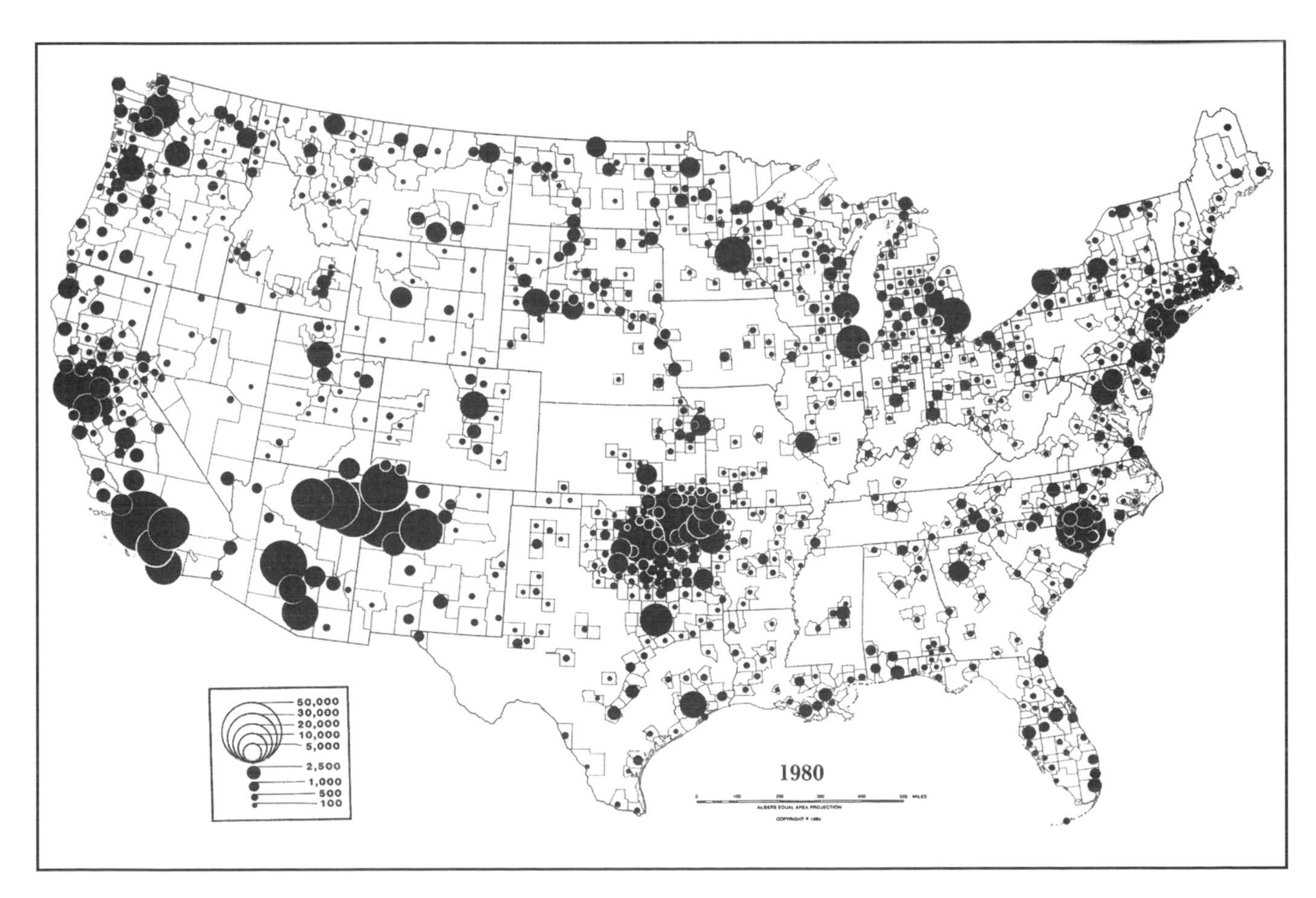

Indian Population by Counties and Standard Metropolitan Statistical Areas: 1980. This map portrays distributions of Indians as in the 1910 edition but includes Standard Metropolitan Statistical Areas (SMSAs). Used with permission of the University of Nebraska Press and Francis Prucha (1990). Base map by Department of Geography, University of Maryland.

ments to state and federal governments. In most states, state laws do not prevail over tribal governments on reservations and tribal governments have a direct relationship to the federal government.

Historically, Congress generally established federal law-and-order jurisdiction on reservations and in Indian Country while retaining exclusive authority to enforce the law. At various times, Congress has granted some measure of authority to the states; for example, in 1952, limited criminal and civil authority was transferred to several states: Iowa, Kansas, New York, and North Dakota. The following year, Congress, in Public Law 280, expanded this law-and-order authority on reservations in California, Nebraska, Minnesota, Oregon, and Wisconsin, and offered other states the option to adopt similar laws. This jurisdiction, which excluded the authority to tax or "encumber" Indian lands, was misinterpreted and become the vehicle for state intervention onto reservation jurisdiction. Congress amended this policy in the Indian Civil Rights Act (1964) so that states could not assume law and-order jurisdiction without tribal consent, and tribes could seek retrocession of any existing state law-and-order authority. This new legislation did not necessarily curtail state intervention, nor did it clear up the confusion over state and tribal jurisdiction.

Tribal assertions of sovereignty or autonomy resurfaced during the termination era. By 1968, the American Indian Movement (AIM) was organized and spread across the nation, drawing its membership from both reservation and urban Indians. Litigation and a new spirit of militancy overshadowed the efforts of older, Indian advocacy organizations dominated by non-Indian supporters (for example, the Indian Rights Association and the Association on American Indian Affairs). The takeover of Alcatraz Island in northern California in 1969 and the caravan of protesters who marched on Washington in the fall of 1972 in the so-called "Trail of Broken Treaties" contributed to Indian agitation. The confrontation in 1973 between tribal members and local law enforcement at Wounded Knee on the Pine Ridge reservation in South Dakota demonstrated that Indians were increasingly demanding greater autonomy within Indian Country. Resolution of the controversial Native land claims in Alaska finally came about through the passage of the Native Alaska Land Settlement Act in 1971. Indians in the 1970s and since have been demanding that the government fully honor all treaties. Federal funding created the Legal Services Corporation and the Native American Rights Fund which, together with other organizations, have helped to defend Indians and to mount successful lawsuits against non-Indians. (See also Chapter 7 on Activism.)

Self-Determination

As the core concept of a redirected Indian policy, self-determination ideally recognizes tribal sovereignty. This policy has not always been translated into a working reality. In 1975, Congress passed the Indian Self-Determination and Education Assistance Act, granting tribes greater negotiating authority to "plan, conduct and administer programs" independent of the BIA but still dependent on federal funding. Under this act, tribes would assume fuller responsibility for the management of their funds and for reservation programs such as housing and water development. The provisions of this act have both strengthened tribal government and have encouraged tribes to take on functions of taxation, planning, and the regulation of reservation activities. Nonetheless, few tribes have moved rapidly toward self-determination, fearing that a show of too much independence or an assertion of inherent sovereignty might lead to the reinstatement of the dreaded termination policies of the 1950s. As early as 1980, however, 370 tribal communities contracted for millions of dollars of federal services, most often coming from Housing and Urban Development (HUD) and Health and Human services (HHS).

The Zuni provide a good example of what is possible under the policy: they wrested control of federal programs such as housing, decentralized authority to the community level, replaced many officials with tribal officers and staff, and even required other BIA personnel to move into the Indian community to foster closer interaction. The tribe, not Washington, supervised BIA staff. On an even grander scale, the Navajo expanded their functions, and even established a Washington office. Education is crucial to self-determination; many tribes assumed supervision of reservation schools and, following the Navajo lead, established community colleges. Health programs and tribally-run health centers increased. Many tribes quickly learned how to manipulate the federal system in order to achieve their goals and to gain the services they required.

Critics of the policy of self-determination note that the BIA and other agencies still make basic decisions, and the policy, as Philip Deloria (Standing Rock Sioux), a law professor at the University of New Mexico, noted, is a "tactical shift in the fundamental commitment of society to bring Indians into the mainstream, not a movement toward true recognition of permanent rights to exist." While self-determination is attended by a number of gains—for example, law training scholarships have brought many Indians into the legal profession—progress has been slow and intermittent.

Federal and BIA bureaucracy has also expanded, overwhelming many tribes with massive paperwork that has interfered with the real growth of programs. And, as is the case with criminal justice planning, federal supervision and preexisting institutions have dominated efforts at self-determination. Indeed, the BIA has expanded its operations and its budget, in spite of the explicit directive of the Self Determination and Education Assistance Act to contract BIA services to tribal governments and Indian organizations. Historian Francis Prucha suggests that Indians' drive for self-determination and sovereignty is contradicted by the "seeds of dependency." More than one critic contends that tribes cannot have political self-determination without economic self determination, yet most tribes continue to depend upon federal funds.

The American Indian Policy Review Commission, also established in 1975, strongly endorsed tribal sovereignty and self-determination, yet demonstrated that almost all of the demands of tribes included the request for federal funds. Policy makers and their critics often seem ambivalent about the role of self-determination: at one extreme it maintains dependence, while at the other extreme it implies independence, which is seen as one step closer to termination of the trust relationship.

Retrospect and Prospect

A century of experimentation in Indian affairs has most often directly or indirectly focused on policy changes affecting trust lands. The treatment of tribes as nations and later as self-governing entities, and the treatment of Indians as wards and then later as citizens, reflect efforts to modify the trust relationship that has been the focus of Indian lands. Somewhat ambivalently, policy makers have urged tribes to take control of reservation economic affairs and to assert tribal property rights. Some critics feel that the BIA lacks accountability in terms of abetting Indian economic growth, and that tribes need grass root entrepreneurial capital and employers. Lawmakers, administrators, and scholars alike recognize the need for multiple approaches in Indian affairs. Not all tribes are equally ready to "go independent." Yet some Indians, such as the Navajo and White Mountain Apache, are moving toward levels of autonomy that provide them with greater opportunities to pursue their own goals.

More Indians will move to cities and more Indians will likely separate themselves from the land, which will reduce some of the pressure on limited reservation resources. Urban life, however, has not yet proven to be a satisfactory alternative for many Indians. Despite the urbanizing trend, Indian residence on the land will continue to reflect a desire to sustain a way of life, a protected place, and a territorial link to the past. For many Indians, reservation lands may become more important as havens against political and legal intrusion than as means for creating economic solvency.

Imre Sutton
California State University, Fullerton

♦ CANADIAN NATIVE DISTRIBUTION, HABITAT, AND DEMOGRAPHY

Introduction to Canada's First Nations

Canada's constitution (Canada Act, 1982) specifies three categories of "aboriginal peoples": Indians, Inuit, and Métis. The preferred collective term today is "First Nations," with its implication of many separate, formerly sovereign, entities.

"Indians" form by far the largest and most diverse of these categories. On contact with Europeans, Indian people occupied all but the northernmost reaches of Canada. Great differences in language, culture, and history separate Indian groups in Canada today, impeding common political action. Land claims and similar issues tend to be negotiated at the local level, often involving "tribal councils" of neighboring and related groups. At the national level, the Assembly of First Nations, a national Native organization, acts as the political voice for Canadian Indians. At the end of 1991, 511,791 people were legally recognized by the Canadian government as "Indians."

The Inuit, once known as the Eskimo (a term that has now almost totally disappeared in Canada), are the aboriginal occupants of the Arctic. Culturally and biologically distinct from other aboriginal Canadians, they, along with their relatives in Alaska and Greenland, are more closely related to native Siberian populations. They form a much more homogeneous population in Canada than Indian groups, speaking a single language (Inuktitut) from the Mackenzie River delta in the west near the Alaska border to Labrador in the east on the Atlantic Ocean. They fall under several political jurisdictions, but are united in a national political body, the Inuit Tapirisat of Canada. Unlike Indians, individual Inuit are not registered by the federal government, so population figures are less exact, but there are believed to be about 30,000 Inuit in Canada.

The Métis, unlike the previous two groups, emerged in Canada only in the historic period. They are a product of the unions between male fur traders, most commonly of French-Canadian origin, and Native women, particularly Cree. The resultant population of mixed ancestry forged a common identity on the Canadian Plains during the nineteenth century. Aspirations for a "Métis Nation" in the Canadian West were ended with their suppression by military forces in Saskatchewan in 1885. After this time they were expected to blend in with the dominant population, and the federal government took no administrative responsibility for them. Only in recent years have the Métis re-emerged in public consciousness. Despite being recognized as one of the "aboriginal peoples of Canada" when the constitution was written in 1982, it is still not clear how "Métis" should be defined today or how many people could be considered under this category.

Aboriginal peoples in Canada can be divided into eleven language families, with approximately fifty different languages. Algonkian is by far the largest and most widespread of the language families. Cree and Ojibwa, the two largest Algonkian languages, are spoken by Native people from Alberta to northern Quebec. The other large language family is Athapascan, with many closely related languages, spread across the northwestern portion of the country. Siouan, spoken by several groups on the Plains, and Iroquoian, around the eastern Great Lakes, are other important language families. Inuktitut, the language of the Canadian Inuit, belongs to the Eskimoan family. Six more families, some consisting of a single language, are restricted to the western portion of the country, in British Columbia.

The great majority of the aboriginal languages of Canada, however, are endangered. Only three—Cree, Ojibwa, and Inuktitut—are spoken over large areas today and are considered to have excellent chances of survival. Many aboriginal communities are making determined efforts to halt or reverse the gradual erosion of their languages. Language and cultural programs have been established in many schools, and a substantial percentage of aboriginal children now receive some form of Native language instruction.

The Algonkian of Eastern Canada

Members of the far-flung Algonkian-speaking family occupy a vast area of eastern and central Canada. They include the Ojibway and their relatives around the western Great Lakes, the Cree of northern Ontario and Quebec, the closely related Naskapi and Montagnais (now frequently known as Innu) of Labrador and adjacent Quebec, and the Micmac and Maliseet of the Maritime Provinces of the east coast. All are in the woodlands and northern forests; the Algonkian of the Plains will be covered in a later section.

The first aboriginal Canadians to come into continuous contact with Europeans were the Beothuk, the occupants of the island of Newfoundland. Their early extinction has left us too little evidence even to know if their language belongs to the Algonkian family. These were the original "Red Indians," a term that referred to their fondness for painting the body with red ochre and grease that was later commonly but erroneously applied to other North American Indians. They were pri-

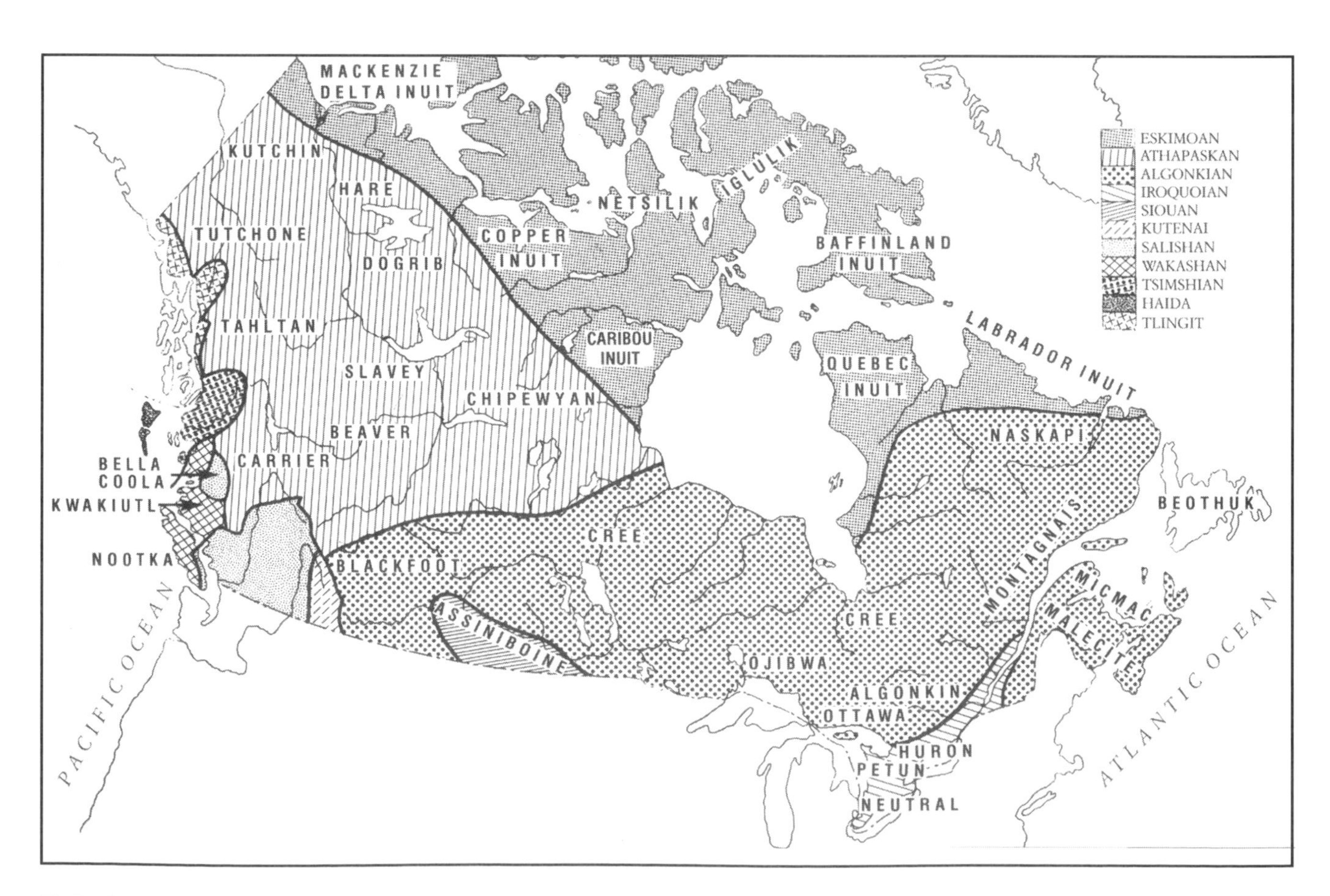

Native language families of Canada, showing approximate locations at time of European contact. Maps by Brian McMillan from *Native Peoples and Cultures of Canada* by Alan D. McMillan, 1988, published by Douglas & McIntyre. Reprinted by permission.

marily a coastal people, collecting shellfish and hunting both land and sea mammals. Bark-covered canoes allowed them to travel out into the stormy north Atlantic to harpoon seals and collect bird eggs from offshore islands. During the late autumn and winter the Beothuk moved into the interior forests where they constructed long wooden barriers to channel the caribou herds to where the hunters waited with spears or bows and arrows. Enough meat had to be taken and preserved from these hunts to last through the severe winters.

The historic extinction of the Beothuk is one of the tragic chapters in Canada's history. Increasing European settlement along the coastline forced the Beothuk into the interior of the island. Introduced diseases and hostile encounters with the newcomers greatly reduced their population. By the early nineteenth century, they were reduced to a small group, plagued by tuberculosis and malnutrition, living near the center of the island. In bungling attempts to establish communications, English colonists took several Beothuk captives. Tuberculosis, however, soon claimed these individuals, and with the 1829 death of Shanawdithit, the last survivor, the Beothuk passed into extinction.

The Micmac (sometimes written Mi'kmaq today) occupied the east coast of the Canadian mainland, including all three Maritime Provinces (Nova Scotia, New Brunswick, and Prince Edward Island) and Atlantic Quebec. Historically, they also settled in southern Newfoundland. The closely related Maliseet were more inland, along the St. John River valley in western New Brunswick.

Like the Beothuk, the Micmac moved with the seasons between coast and interior. Fish played a major role in their diet, along with shellfish, other seafoods such as lobster, sea birds and their eggs, and seals. Land mammals such as beaver and moose were hunted inland. They carried out this seasonal round with the use of bark-covered canoes along the coast and with snowshoes, sleds, and toboggans (the latter taking its English name directly from the Micmac) for the deep snow of the interior.

The numerous groups collectively known today as Ojibway (or Ojibwa, or, particularly in the United States, Chippewa) were originally centered on the western Great Lakes area. During the fur trade they expanded rapidly, east as far as Saskatchewan, north into northern Ontario, and south into southern Ontario and such American states as Michigan and Wisconsin. No collective identity was held across this vast area; they consisted of numerous small independent bands speaking a continuum of mutually intelligible dialects. Numerous separate groups, known in the historic records as Saulteaux, Ottawa, Nipissing, Mississauga, and others, are considered to be Ojibwa, based on a common language and shared traditions.

Ojibway subsistence was based on an annual round of hunting, fishing, and plant collecting. Sizable populations congregated seasonally at particularly good fishing locales, such as the rapids at Sault Sainte Marie located on Lake Superior. The shallow lakes of the area provided wild rice, which was an important part of the diet for many Ojibwa. Maple sugar was prepared from the sweet sap of the maple tree and used as a seasoning for a wide range of foods. Some of the southern groups, in contact with the Iroquoian-speaking Huron, practiced marginal agriculture or traded fish and furs for agricultural produce.

To the north were the Cree, who occupied the northern forests from Alberta to Quebec, along with the closely related Naskapi and Montagnais of Labrador and northeastern Quebec (the Labrador Algonkian now refer to themselves as Innu). As their environment provided fewer wild plant resources, and even good fishing locations were relatively rare, the northern groups relied more heavily on hunting. Moose, caribou, bear, and beaver were the major game species. This was a precarious life-style, particularly in winter when few resources were available, and winter starvation was an ever-present threat.

Numerous shared features characterize the woodlands Algonkian. Social organization usually took the form of small, highly mobile bands, although southern groups were able to gather seasonally in larger numbers. Societies were essentially egalitarian, although some status distinctions seem to have developed among groups such as the Micmac. To meet the needs of a mobile population, housing had to be simple and portable. Birchbark provided the ideal cover, although moose or caribou hide was used in the north. These could be rolled up and carried between camps, then quickly stretched over a framework of poles to form the dome-shaped structure known throughout eastern North America by the Algonkian term "wigwam." Birchbark also provided lightweight cover for the canoes that were so important to summer travel throughout the region. Snowshoes were essential in winter.

A fundamental part of Algonkian religious belief was respect for the animals they hunted. The hunter's skill was not enough alone; the animal had to offer itself to the hunter. Only through proper ceremonial acts could humans wrest from nature what they needed to survive. Feasts were held after the kill of larger game, to celebrate and to honor the animal. Particular care had to be taken with the bones, so that the animals would not be offended and avoid the hunters on future occasions. Animal skulls were hung from trees, and special platforms were built to keep the bones out of reach of the camp dogs. Divination rituals were also practiced to determine the location of the animals or to predict the outcome of the hunt. All the Algonkian groups had

Ojibway camp on Lake Huron, 1845. Painting by Paul Kane from his travels in the 1840s.

shamans, who used their ties to the supernatural world to cure diseases or to foretell the future. A widespread ritual was the "shaking tent," where the violent movements of a small shelter announced the arrival of spirit visitors to assist the shaman in such endeavors.

European arrival and the subsequent fur trade caused major changes in Algonkian life. Trade relations may have begun even prior to the earliest recorded contact. When Jacques Cartier first encountered the Micmac off the east coast in 1534, they were waving furs and hailing the ship, signaling their desire to trade. Iron knives and hatchets, copper kettles, blankets, and other European goods soon replaced many objects of aboriginal manufacture. A French writer in the 1630s noted that the Indians of the St. Lawrence River, the major trade artery of the early historic period, had already forsaken their traditional garb for European clothing, and that copper kettles had completely replaced traditional vessels of bark. Establishment of trading posts throughout Algonkian territory further tied Native groups to the fur trade. Many shifted their activities from hunting for food to trapping for furs, requiring a shift in diet to European foodstuffs and further dependence on the trading posts. Alcohol was widely used in trade, with devastating effects on many Natives. Diseases also arrived with the traders, causing great loss of Native life.

Many Cree and Ojibway tied their fortunes to the fur trade and became active participants. Some spread rapidly to the north and west, seeking new trapping lands for beaver and other fur-bearers. Their far-flung distribution today is largely a result of new opportunities offered by the historic fur trade. Others settled around the fur trade posts to get better access to European goods. Their interaction with the traders was to result in the emergence of a new people based on racial mixture—the Métis.

Today the Algonkian are scattered in small reserves across a large part of the country. Hunting, fishing and trapping are still important activities for many groups, particularly in the north. Environmental degradation, however, poses major problems. Massive hydroelectric projects in northern Quebec are flooding large areas and threatening the Cree way of life. In northwestern Ontario, industrial wastes have resulted in mercury pollution of the waterways, making fish, the mainstay of the Ojibway economy, unsafe to eat. In Labrador, the Innu maintain that low-level military training flights over their hunting grounds have scattered the caribou and destroyed their traditional way of life.

Although many Algonkian groups signed historic treaties, no such land surrenders took place in Quebec and Labrador. The Cree and Naskapi of northern Quebec signed the first land claims agreements in modern Canadian history in the 1970s. Other groups are still pressing for resolution of their claims.

The Iroquoian of the Eastern Great Lakes

The Iroquoian were part of a large linguistic stock centered on the area around the eastern Great Lakes. The Iroquoian, whose roots in Canada extend back into prehistory, consist of the Huron, Petun, and Neutral in Ontario, and the poorly known Iroquoian of the St. Lawrence River. Most in Canada today, however, are Iroquois proper or Six Nations, whose arrival in Canada stems from the tumultuous events of the historic period.

An agricultural economy distinguished the Iroquoian from all other aboriginal Canadians. They grew corn, beans, and squash, supplementing this agricultural diet by fishing and hunting. The everyday meal was a thick corn soup, to which pieces of fish, meat, or squash might be added for variety. Tobacco was also grown in their fields (the Jesuits referred to the Petun as "the Tobacco Nation").

Villages were large collections of longhouses, some containing several thousand individuals. The bark-covered longhouses sheltered multiple families, and could easily be extended in length if populations grew. Raised benches or sleeping platforms ran the length of each side, leaving a central corridor for the cooking fires. Fish and corn, as well as personal belongings, hung from the roof of the house or were buried in covered pits. Many villages were surrounded with palisades of poles twisted into the ground, often in several rows. Exhaustion of nearby soils and firewood supplies meant that villages had to be moved every ten to fifteen years.

The first to be encountered by Europeans were the Iroquoian of the St. Lawrence River. Jacques Cartier sailed up the St. Lawrence in 1535 and wintered over near the village of Stadacona (where modern Quebec City now stands). Cartier provides few details on the appearance of Stadacona but has left a fuller account of his brief visit to Hochelaga, a larger village upriver at the location of modern Montreal. Typical of Iroquoian villages, it was situated well back from the river for defensive reasons, requiring a walk through extensive fields of corn. Cartier describes about fifty bark-covered longhouses surrounded by a triple row of palisades, with ladders leading to platforms where defenders could stand during an attack.

The St. Lawrence Iroquoian were also the first casualties in a series of extinctions that were to overtake the northeastern groups early in the historic period. After Cartier's departure, no further historic records exist until the arrival on the St. Lawrence of Samuel de Champlain in 1603. By this time the Stadaconans and Hochelagans had vanished, leaving only war parties of Algonkian and Mohawk locked in bitter conflict over control of this vital trade waterway.

The Ontario Iroquoian, consisting of the Huron, Petun, and Neutral, survived into the mid-seventeenth century. The closely related Huron and Petun had coalesced by the early historic period around Georgian Bay, at the eastern end of Lake Huron. The Huron had particularly close ties with the French, who were drawn into this area by a combination of colonial policy, a lucrative fur trade, and missionary zeal. The most important source of information on traditional Huron culture is the voluminous writings of the Jesuits, chronicling their missionizing activities among the Huron from 1634 to 1650. The Neutral were to the south, concentrated around the western end of Lake Ontario. Their rejection of the Jesuits' proselytizing efforts means that details of their traditional culture are less well known.

All three groups were confederacies of separate tribes, linked in a common council. Village affairs were conducted by local councils, one concerned with feasts, ceremonies, and other peaceful pursuits, and another dedicated to matters of war. Councils attempted to reach a consensus, and all present were able to express their views.

Feasts, dances, and games brought together the social groups making up these confederacies. Lacrosse, often played between teams from different villages, was a popular sport, although often so roughly played that it could result in injuries. The most important ceremony, although only held every decade or so, was the Feast of the Dead. At this time the remains of all who had died since the last such ceremony were removed from their temporary graves and reburied in a common pit, known as an ossuary, with feasting and rituals to honor the dead.

Warfare shaped much of Iroquoian life. Prior to the disruptions of the early historic period, it seems to have been primarily motivated by a desire to avenge previous deaths and acquire personal prestige. Later the Iroquoian became embroiled in bitter warfare over access to furs and fur trade routes. Trophies of enemies killed were taken back to their villages, along with captives, some of whom were adopted and incorporated into the society. This seems to have been an important historic method of replacing individuals lost in warfare. Other captives were tortured to death in public spectacles.

Infectious diseases brought by Europeans greatly weakened the Ontario Iroquoian, but it was warfare that destroyed them as distinct political entities. Between 1648 and 1651 the Huron, Petun, and Neutral were overwhelmed by the military force of the League of the Iroquois, particularly the Seneca and Mohawk. Many perished at the hands of the Iroquois, others were driven out of their homelands to form refugee populations and eventually lose their distinct identity, while others were taken as captives and incorporated into Iroquois groups. When the Jesuits abandoned their base among the Huron and fled to Quebec City in 1650, they took with them several hundred Huron survivors. Known as the Huron of Lorette, or more recently as the Nation Huronne Wendat, this French-speaking community of several thousand people in Quebec today is the only recognized vestige of Huron culture in Canada.

The great majority of Iroquoian people in Canada today are Iroquois proper, members of the famed League of the Iroquois, whose homeland was in New York State. From west to east these were the Seneca, Cayuga, Onondaga, Oneida, and Mohawk. Early in the eighteenth century, an additional Iroquoian group, the Tuscarora, joined the league. The term Six Nations is commonly applied to the league members after this time.

The first of the League Iroquois to move into Canada came as a result of the missionizing efforts of the Jesuits. Large numbers of converts to Catholicism, primarily Mohawk, settled on the St. Lawrence during the late seventeenth century. Eventually these settlements became the modern Mohawk communities of Kahnawake and Kanesatake, near Montreal, and Akwesasne, straddling the international border with portions in Ontario, Quebec, and New York.

The largest wave of Iroquois arrival in Canada came after the American Revolution. The Mohawk had been staunch British loyalists, and most of the Iroquois fought on the British side during the war. After the war, they were granted lands in Canada for their loyalty. One group of Mohawk moved to the Bay of Quinte, on northern Lake Ontario. A larger group, under the famed Mohawk war leader Joseph Brant, settled along the Grand River in southern Ontario near modern Brantford. The several thousand individuals who arrived with Brant included members of all six Iroquois nations, plus a considerable number of Delaware, an Algonkian-speaking people originally living in present-day New York and New Jersey, and others who had lost their homelands and sought refuge in the league. Each established separate tribal villages along the Grand River. Today this land grant, although greatly reduced in size, is home to the largest Native community in Canada, the Six Nations of the Grand River.

A final arrival came with several hundred Oneida in the 1840s. Loss of their traditional lands and a desire to reunite with other members of the league led to their movement into southern Ontario. Today they are a large community known as the Oneidas of the Thames. The Canadian Iroquois today outnumber those who remain in their American homeland. Three of the four largest reserve communities in Canada are Iroquois. The Mohawk predominate, and it is the Mohawk language that has the best chance of survival. Mohawk insistence on controlling their own educational programs, particularly at Kahnawake, helps safeguard the language.

The Iroquois are in a unique situation in Canada. They consider themselves to be a sovereign people, entering Canada as loyal allies, and have rejected the policies of the Canadian government, which treats them as dependents. For many traditionalists, the only valid government structures are the hereditary councils within the League of the Iroquois. This position has led them into numerous clashes with the Canadian and U.S. governments.

This tension erupted in violence during the summer of 1990. The flashpoint was at Kanesatake, the Mohawk community at Oka, just west of Montreal. Expansion of a municipal golf course onto lands the Mohawk considered theirs led to resistance. When armed provincial police stormed the Mohawk barricades, the Mohawk responded with armed force. Mohawk from other communities rushed to join the defenders at the Oka barricades, and the people of Kahnawake forcefully closed the bridge that runs through their reserve, cutting off one of the major traffic arteries into Montreal. The Canadian government sent the army into what became a seventy-eight-day military standoff. While the situation was eventually defused, the underlying issues have not been resolved. It did, however, focus the attention of the Canadian government and people on Native grievances across the country.

Indians of the Plains

The environment of the Canadian Plains is the flat, semi-arid grasslands extending across the southern portions of Alberta, Saskatchewan, and Manitoba. Vast herds of bison once roamed across this open land, providing the economic basis for all Plains Natives. Not only did the Plains hunters rely on the bison for meat but also for the hides, which provided shelter and clothing. The stereotyped image of "Indian" in the public imagination is the Plains bison hunter and warrior, on horseback and clad in buckskin and feathers. Despite the common image of the warrior on horseback, horses were not always part of Plains culture. Throughout the millennia prior to European contact, Plains people traveled and hunted on foot, using dogs to help carry their goods. Horses arrived with the Spanish and were in common use among the southern Plains tribes by the mid-seventeenth century. It was a century later, however, before they were a significant feature in the lives of the Canadian Plains groups. Once horses were available in considerable numbers they transformed Plains societies, fostering greater mobility, increased trade and warfare, larger social groupings, and more elaborate material culture.

Speakers of Algonkian languages dominated the northern Plains. In the west were the members of the powerful Blackfoot Confederacy, composed of the Blackfoot, Blood, and Peigan. Their bitter foes throughout much of the historic period were the Plains Cree and Plains Ojibwa, recent arrivals from the woodlands to the east. Allied with them in their battles with the Blackfoot were the Assiniboine, members of the Siouan language family. Finally, a small Athapascan-speaking group, the Sarcee, arrived on the Plains early in the historic period and became part of the Blackfoot Confederacy.

All Plains groups based their lives on the vast herds of bison. With the arrival of the horse, hunters could ride along with the stampeding herd, selecting the animal with care and dispatching it with the bow and arrow. In addition, however, techniques that had been used for millennia continued throughout the historic period. Communal hunting methods, where large numbers of bison could be taken, include jumps, where bison were driven over a cliff edge, and pounds, where they were driven into a corral or natural trap. Both required considerable preparation, including construction of long drive lines to funnel the animals to the desired location. The cliffs at Head-Smashed-In in southern Alberta, perhaps the most famous of such sites, were used repeatedly for nearly 6,000 years, most recently by the historic Blackfoot.

Essential to the nomadic life-style were the tipi and travois. A cover of sewn bison hides was supported on a framework of poles to form the conical tipi. Flaps at the top helped control smoke from the central fire. An inside liner protected the occupants from drafts. Sleeping robes laid around the walls served as couches during the day. When the camp was set to move, the tipi could be taken down quickly and the cover packed with other possessions on a travois, a framework of poles which was dragged behind the horse.

Warfare was a pervasive part of the culture and provided the major route to prestige for young men. Military excursions ranged from a few individuals setting out to steal horses to large parties of allied groups engaged in full-scale war against traditional enemies. Warrior societies kept order in camp and on the hunt and provided a common bond linking the various bands into larger political organizations.

Religion permeated everyday life. Supernatural power could reside in any unusual object or feature of the landscape. Young people sought supernatural assistance by fasting and praying in secluded locations, hoping for a vision. Medicine bundles, the most important ritual possessions, contained sacred objects, often those indicated through supernatural encounters. Opening the bundle required elaborate ceremonies, as did its transfer to a new owner, each object being reverently displayed while prayers and songs invoked its spiritual

Assiniboine Indians hunting bison. Painting by Paul Kane from his travels in the 1840s.

power. Important religious events, such as the Sun Dance, brought together large numbers of people to participate in the ceremonies.

Introduced diseases and destruction of the bison herds struck at the heart of Plains cultures. Smallpox epidemics swept the Plains at intervals during the eighteenth and nineteenth centuries, taking great tolls of Native life. Wanton slaughter of the bison and opening of the prairies for European agricultural settlement meant disappearance of the herds by the early 1880s.

The Natives of the Plains, with their populations reduced and the bison largely gone, were in no position to resist government offers of assistance in exchange for signing treaties. Between 1871 and 1877, the Canadian Plains tribes ceded by treaty all claims to their lands. The treaties allocated reserves and provided small payments of money and farm equipment. Instructors were sent to the reserves to supervise the transition to farming, which was frequently a failure. Hunger and disease were widespread, while traditional customs and beliefs, such as the Sun Dance, were suppressed.

Refugees from American battles also moved into Canada during this time. The Dakota (also known as the Sioux) arrived in two waves. The first were eastern (Santee) Dakota from Minnesota, fleeing their homeland after a disastrous uprising and defeat in 1862. Initially settling near Fort Garry in southern Manitoba, many followed the declining bison herds west and north. The second arrival involved the western (Teton) Dakota and their famed chief Sitting Bull, seeking sanctuary after their annihilation of Colonel George Custer's army at the Battle of the Little Big Horn. Thousands of Dakota, including Sitting Bull, arrived in Saskatchewan during 1876 and 1877. By this time, however, the bison were nearly gone and the other Plains Natives were being confined to reserves. The Teton were denied land and rations, forcing most eventually to leave. Today the Dakota in Canada are primarily Santee, although one Teton community remains. All were eventually assigned reserves and are administered as Canadian Indians, although without treaty.

Despite miserable living conditions, outbreaks of violence were few. The only exception occurred in 1885, with the Métis rebellion under Louis Riel in Saskatchewan (see Riel's biography). Several groups of Plains Cree and Assiniboine, under chiefs Big Bear and Poundmaker (see their biographies), took up arms in sympathy, but the Blackfoot refused to be drawn into the conflict. The rebellion was short-lived and failed to win any consideration of Native grievances. Today many reserve communities, particularly in Manitoba and Saskatchewan, lack any real economic base. Movement to the cities is a common response, with Regina and Winnipeg having among the highest percentages of Native residents in the country. In Alberta, oil and gas revenues for some bands and ranching for others have offered higher levels of economic security.

The Plateau

The high, generally arid Plateau lies between the Rocky Mountains on the east and the Coast Mountains on the west. The environment varies from sagebrush near-desert in the rainshadow of the Coast Mountains to heavily forested mountain slopes on the edge of the Rockies. Only the northern half of the Plateau is in Canada, in southern British Columbia.

Three Native language families can be found in this area. Interior Salish is by far the largest family, with four languages: Lillooet, Thompson, Okanagan, and Shuswap. The Kutenai, who speak a linguistic isolate, are in the mountainous southeast of British Columbia. The Plateau Athapascan consist of the now-extinct Nicola in the central Canadian Plateau and the Chilcotin and several groups of southern Carrier in the north.

The Interior Salish, along with neighboring Athapascan, had a way of life based on hunting, fishing, and gathering plant foods, moving with the seasons as resources became available. Salmon played the major role in the economies of most groups, and much of the late summer and fall was spent intercepting the spawning runs. Canyons provided particularly good fishing locations, where masses of fish teemed in the eddies and could be easily scooped out of the water in large dip-nets or could be harpooned or taken in traps. Large numbers of people congregated around such locations, resulting in very high population densities in favored parts of the Plateau, such as the territory of the Thompson and Upper Lillooet. Large quantities of salmon were cut into thin strips and dried in the warm canyon breezes, providing an assured supply of food for the long winter months and a valued trading commodity to groups lacking adequate supplies of this vital resource.

The dominant type of winter dwelling in the Plateau was the semi-subterranean pit house. A log superstructure over a circular pit was covered with bark and earth, providing effective insulation against the cold. Winter villages consisted of a small cluster of pit houses, each sheltering several families. A few groups did not use the pit house, instead banking earth and snow against their mat-covered lodges. In the warmer months people dispersed to their fishing, hunting, root-digging, or berry-picking camps, living in simple structures of bark or mats over a framework of poles.

Each winter village was politically autonomous. Each had several leaders, or "chiefs," who were men respected for their oratory or skill in the hunt or battle. Shamans were individuals with supernatural powers capable of curing illness. Everyone was expected to obtain spirit power, setting out at puberty to seek a guardian spirit through the vision quest.

The Kutenai (also written Kootenay), on the mountainous eastern edge of the Plateau, differed considerably from other Plateau groups. They are a distinct people, confounding linguists with the unique nature of their language. Many of their culture traits resemble those of the Plains. In fact, their first historic encounters with European explorers took place on the Plains of southern Alberta, from which they were pushed by the Blackfoot.

The Kutenai are divided into Upper and Lower divisions. The Upper Kutenai, higher into the Rockies and closest to the Plains, had the strongest Plains cast to their culture. They hunted big game such as elk, deer, caribou, and mountain goats and sheep, but also crossed the mountains several times a year to hunt bison on the Plains. Such excursions brought them into conflict with the Blackfoot, requiring the full military organization of Plains warriors. The Lower Kutenai, further down the Kootenay River and along Kootenay Lake, relied on more typical Plateau resources such as deer, ducks, and fish, and displayed fewer Plains traits.

Among the Upper Kutenai, the Plains-style bison-hide-covered tipi was the year-round dwelling. The Lower Kutenai resided in mat-covered tipis, with elongated mat-covered lodges as winter dwellings. Both groups wore the typical tanned hide clothing of the Plains and Plateau. Plains-style feather headdresses were common among the Kutenai in relatively late times.

Initial contacts with Europeans came with Alexander Mackenzie's travel through Shuswap and Chilcotin lands to the Pacific in 1793 and with Simon Fraser's epic journey down the Fraser River in 1808. Fraser noticed copper kettles and other European goods traded in from the coast among the Plateau Salish. Extensive disruption of Native cultures, however, did not occur until 1858, with the gold rush in the Fraser Canyon. The sudden influx of thousands of gold-seekers resulted in Natives being displaced from their traditional lands. Smallpox and other diseases greatly diminished their numbers. During the 1870s and 1880s, they were assigned to small, scattered reserves.

The Plateau groups never ceded their land through treaties. Today land claims are among the most contentious issues, along with such other grievances as legal restrictions on Native fisheries. The Plateau people have formed political bodies to fight for resolution of these issues, and several have been prominent in Native affairs at the provincial and federal levels.

The Northwest Coast

Rainforest blankets the rugged Pacific coastline of British Columbia. The mountainous terrain, with its myriad islands, bays, and inlets, provided a bountiful environment for cultures adapted to a maritime way of life. Large dugout cedar canoes once traversed these waterways, providing the only means of transportation along the coast. Villages of cedar-plank houses were nestled in locations sheltered from the winter storms. Coastal culture extended far up the major rivers—the Nass, the Skeena, and the Fraser—so that even groups lacking direct access to salt water shared the coastal life-style.

This was by far the most linguistically diverse area of aboriginal Canada. Eighteen mutually unintelligible languages, clustered into five separate language families, were spoken. In the north are the Haida of the Queen Charlotte Islands and the Tsimshian on the mainland, along with the Tlingit, who occupied southeastern Alaska and extended a short distance into Canada. Haida and Tlingit are linguistic isolates, but Tsimshian has three languages—Coast Tsimshian, Nisga'a (Nass River), and Gitksan (Skeena River). To the south are members of the large Wakashan stock, divided into Kwakiutl and Nootka. Kwakiutl languages, from north to south, are Haisla (Kitamaat), Heiltsuk (Bella Bella), Oowekyala (Rivers Inlet), and Kwakwala (known as the Southern Kwakiutl or Kwakwaka'wakw). The two Nootkan languages are Nootka and Nitinat, although the people are known today as the Nuu-chah-nulth. The large Salish family includes Bella Coola (who now call themselves the Nuxalk) on the central coast, and Comox, Sechelt, Pentlatch (now extinct), Squamish, Halkomelem, and Straits on the southern coast. Four of these five language families occur only on the Northwest Coast, and all five are unique in Canada to British Columbia.

Everywhere along the coast, people relied on the bounty of the sea, beach, and rivers. Salmon was the fundamental resource for almost all groups. Huge quantities were taken by hook and line, nets, traps, and harpoons. While it was highly prized fresh, most was dried and stored for winter use. Halibut, cod, and other fish were also important. Herring were valued for the spawn, and eulachon, a small greasy smelt, was rendered down for its oil, providing a sauce to enliven the taste of dried foods. Seals and sea lions were hunted by all groups, although only the Nuu-chah-nulth went out onto the open sea to harpoon whales. Digging clams, prying mussels off the rocks, and collecting other such "beach foods" was primarily a female task, as was collecting various plant foods such as berries, shoots, and roots. Effective exploitation of various resources frequently required shifting residence in a seasonal pattern of movement. Important resource locations, such as salmon streams or productive berry patches, were jealously guarded private property. The abundance and security of the food supply supported the densest aboriginal population levels in Canada.

The western red cedar provided the basis for the technology of all Northwest Coast groups. The wood's long, straight grain allowed large planks to be split from a cedar log, using wedges of antler or hardwood tapped with a stone hammer. Most of the material culture items, from houses to canoes to storage and cooking boxes, were made of cedar. While woodworking was a male task, responsibility for weaving fell to the women, who used the bark and roots of the cedar to craft beautiful basketry, matting, and clothing.

Architectural styles varied from north to south, but all shared a basic pattern. Massive cedar posts supported huge roof beams and a series of rafters, forming a framework covered with split-cedar planks. These were large structures, meant to shelter a number of related families. Inside support posts could be carved with crest animals, and at the front of the house might stand a number of carved cedar monuments, the famous totem poles of the Northwest Coast. These were primarily heraldic in function, as important chiefs commissioned artists to depict family-owned crest images. Regional art styles differed considerably, and not all groups carved free-standing poles, but all had some tradition of monumental artwork in wood.

Most everyday clothing on the coast was woven from strips of cedar bark, pounded until soft and supple. Men wrapped cedar-bark blankets around their bodies, often fastening them with a pin at the front. Women wore skirts of shredded cedar bark and blankets or capes. In colder weather fur robes were added. Wide-brimmed woven hats protected both sexes from the sun and rain. Most people went barefoot year-round; only the upriver and most northerly groups used footgear. The hide moccasins and tailored clothing worn across the rest of aboriginal Canada were poorly suited to the wet maritime conditions of the Northwest Coast.

Ceremonial apparel, particularly on the northern coast, was much more elaborate. A high-ranking chief would be wrapped in a Chilkat blanket, woven of mountain goat wool with intricate crest designs. An elaborate headdress had a finely carved wooden frontlet inlaid with abalone shell and numerous ermine skins hanging down the sides and back.

The primary social unit all along the coast was a group of kin who shared a name and a tradition of descent from a common ancestor. Among the northern groups, membership in this kin group was matrilineal (traced through the mother). Elsewhere on the coast, membership could be claimed through either the male or female lines. These kin groups held ownership to all important resource locations, as well as such intangibles as names, ritual dances, and rights to depict certain crest figures such as Ravens or Killer-Whales.

Northwest Coast people placed great emphasis on inherited rank and privileges. Chiefs and nobles held high-ranking names and controlled access to group-owned territories and rights. Management of the group's resources allowed chiefs to accumulate wealth, which could be publicly distributed at feasts and potlatches to enhance their status. High-ranking individuals sought marriage partners of equivalent rank in other social groups, providing an opportunity for political alliance and the transfer of wealth, including names and ceremonial prerogatives. Commoners, who lacked important inherited rights, were essential to provide the labor necessary to accumulate food and wealth. Slaves, obtained through purchase or warfare, performed the most menial tasks.

Raiding and warfare were relatively commonplace. Motives were to avenge past injuries or to acquire important resource areas, such as salmon rivers. Raiding for slaves was also a major source of inter-group hostilities.

Intermarriage and shared ceremonial life linked villages, often at considerable distances. The major ceremony was the potlatch, which played an essential role in the ranking system. Any change in status required a chief and his kin to invite others to witness their claim. A high-status marriage, birth of an heir, the assumption of an inherited name, or the raising of a totem pole were all such occasions. An essential feature of the potlatch was the distribution of large quantities of gifts to all present. In case of a dispute, the potlatch provided a public forum for the resolution of conflicting claims.

Potlatches were enlivened by performances of masked dancers. These were primarily winter events, when supernatural forces were believed to dwell nearby and economic activities were greatly reduced. More theater than dance, the performances re-enacted ancestral encounters with supernatural beings, when important rights were transferred to the human world. Some of the finest examples of Northwest Coast art are the masks, rattles, and other items used in these performances.

Contact with Europeans did not occur until the 1770s. Fleeting contact with several Spanish expeditions preceded the arrival of Captain James Cook among the Nuu-chah-nulth in 1778. These early expeditions set the stage for the period of intensive trade that followed. Vessels from several nations descended on the coast beginning in the mid-1780s in a quest for valuable furs, particularly those of the sea otter. In return the coastal people received metal tools and other European goods, which sparked new heights in potlatching and artistic production. Introduced diseases also arrived with the traders' ships. Destruction of the sea otter stocks brought this period to a close early in the nineteenth century.

The land-based fur trade period soon followed. Hudson's Bay Company trading posts were established at key locations along the coast. Many Native groups resettled around the posts, requiring extensive changes in their economic and social systems. Readily available European goods, such as the Hudson's Bay Company blanket, replaced many items of aboriginal manufacture. Firearms from the traders made inter-tribal warfare more deadly, and alcohol brought social problems and demoralization to many groups. The more settled conditions around the posts also fostered the spread of epidemic diseases, taking great tolls of Native life.

A few small colonial treaties were signed with Native groups on Vancouver Island in the 1850s. These remain the only legal land settlements in British Columbia. After British Columbia entered the Canadian confederation in 1871, responsibility for Indian administration shifted to the federal government. Numerous small reserves were laid out throughout the province, but no resolution of the Native claim to the land was reached. Native customs were attacked by government agents and missionaries, leading to the outlawing of the potlatch in 1884.

The First Nations of British Columbia are active politically, with the land issue the paramount concern. Tribal councils have been formed along the coast to pursue their claims. Two north coast councils, the Nisga'a and the Gitksan-Wet'suwet'en, have taken their cases through the Canadian court system. None, however, has yet been resolved.

A cultural revival has occurred in recent decades. Northwest Coast art has been recognized as one of the world's great artforms, and a number of artists have achieved national and international acclaim (see the sections on art). Dances and ceremonies are continuing or being re-established in many Native communities. Local councils are taking control of their own educational programs, ensuring that their languages and histories are being taught to their children.

The Athapascan of the Western Subarctic

Members of the large Athapascan language family occupied much of northwestern North America, from the west side of Hudson Bay to interior Alaska. More than twenty Athapascan languages, including those in Alaska, have been defined for the Subarctic. All are closely related and tend to grade into one another through a series of intermediate dialects. Athapascan languages in the Canadian Subarctic, in rough order of number of speakers today, are: Chipewyan, Carrier, Slavey, Gwich'in (formerly written Kutchin), Tutchone, Tahltan, Dogrib, Hare, Beaver, Kaska, Sekani, Han, and Tagish. The last two hang on the brink of extinction. Many Athapascan, particularly those in the north, refer to themselves collectively as the Dene.

Northern boreal forest covers the land, which is crossed by numerous rivers and dotted with lakes. The region is physiographically diverse, with three broad divisions. In the east is the rocky country of the Canadian Shield. In the center are the Mackenzie Lowlands, sloping gradually to the Mackenzie River Delta. In the west are the mountains and valleys of the Cordillera, extending from the Yukon to central British Columbia.

Caribou and moose were the among the most important game animals for the Athapascan hunters. Bison herds were also available to some of the more southerly groups, and in the Cordillera mountain goats and sheep were hunted. Smaller mammals, especially the snowshoe hare, played an important role in the diet. Great numbers of migratory waterfowl could be taken for brief periods each year, and the lakes and rivers provided whitefish, lake trout, grayling, and other fish. Groups on the western edge of the Subarctic, where rivers flow to the Pacific, had access to bountiful runs of salmon.

Athapascan societies were small and highly mobile, following game across a large area. Group size and economic cycle varied with available resources, but throughout the Subarctic population density was low. Groups lacked formal chiefs, but individuals could take leadership roles for specific tasks, such as hunting, trade, or war. The social organization was flexible, and personal autonomy was valued.

Athapascan cultures differed with the environment. Three examples of local adaptations can be seen in the Chipewyan, the Beaver, and the Tahltan.

In the east are the Chipewyan, the most numerous and widespread of the Subarctic Athapascan. These were an "edge-of-the-forest" people, wintering in the northern forest and following the caribou herds far out onto the tundra or barrenlands during the summer. Caribou were taken along their migration routes, often by driving the herds into large circular brush enclosures where they could be more easily killed. The meat was dried for winter use; the hides were made into clothing and lodge covers, as well as cut into strips for snares, nets, and snowshoe lacings; the antlers and bones were important raw materials for tools, and the sinew was essential for sewing clothing. Fishing was second only to caribou hunting among the Chipewyan.

Further south are the Beaver, occupants of the Peace River region of northern Alberta and British Columbia. The Beaver life-style was based on hunting big game, such as moose and woods bison, along with smaller animals such as beaver. Bison herds were occasionally driven into pounds in much the same manner as the Plains tribes. Fishing was unimportant and was resorted to only when the search for game failed.

In the mountains of the Cordillera to the west are the Tahltan of northwestern British Columbia. The Stikine River provided the salmon runs that formed the basis of their economy. Contact with the Tlingit downriver resulted in the adoption of many Northwest Coast traits, such as potlatching and matrilineal clans. Their location allowed the Tahltan to become middlemen in trade between the Tlingit on the coast and the Athapascan further inland.

Snowshoes and sleds or toboggans were essential to winter transportation throughout the area. In summer, people traveled along the lakes and rivers in bark-covered canoes. Housing differed considerably among the Athapascan, but most used simple hide-covered conical or domed structures. More substantial winter houses were constructed in a few areas. In the Yukon, for example, the Han built rectangular pit houses that were heavily banked with turf to withstand the cold.

The historic fur trade brought major changes to the Western Subarctic. Posts were established on western Hudson Bay as early as 1682, although initially the trade was dominated by the Cree. Access to firearms and other goods gave the Cree an advantage in warfare, causing losses in lives and land among the Chipewyan. To bring the Chipewyan into direct trade, the Hudson's Bay Company constructed Fort Churchill in 1717, after negotiating a peace with the Cree. The Chipewyan failed to embrace the fur-trade life-style as fully as the Cree had done, but some groups moved further south to get better access to fur-bearing animals, abandoning their northern caribou hunts.

Following the epic travels of Alexander Mackenzie to the mouth of the Mackenzie River in 1789 and to the Pacific in 1793, the North West Company established fur trade posts throughout Athapascan territory, forcing the Hudson's Bay Company to move inland and do likewise. This period of competition ended with the merger of the two companies in 1821. Throughout the nineteenth century, many Athapascan groups became dependent on the trading posts, focusing their economies on trapping animals for furs. Metal tools and European clothing replaced aboriginal counterparts, and firearms and ammunition became essential trade items.

Discovery of gold brought massive cultural disruptions to the Cordilleran Athapascan. The Caribou gold rush, which reached its height in 1862, brought large numbers of gold-seekers into Carrier territory. The 1898 Klondike gold rush profoundly affected the Yukon Athapascan, nearly destroying the Han whose lands were at the center.

Increased non-Indian settlement in the northwest led the Canadian government to negotiate treaties with the Athapascan. Two large federal treaties cover much of traditional Athapascan land. Only the western groups in the Yukon and the Cordillera of British Columbia remain outside of treaty.

Athapascan communities in northern Canada today rely on some combination of trapping, government assistance, and wage labor. Continued encroachment of resource industries and non-Native settlement threatens local trapping and subsistence hunting. Native political organizations, such as the Dene Nation in the Northwest Territories, are fighting for recognition of Native land claims and right to self-determination.

The Inuit

The Inuit are the aboriginal occupants of the Arctic, the lands lying north of the tree line. The Arctic is physiographically varied, ranging from the rugged mountains and fjords of the eastern islands, to the rocky rolling terrain of the interior barrenlands, to the flat plain of the Mackenzie Delta. Winters are long and extremely cold, with a midwinter period in the northern regions where sunlight is entirely absent. Summers are short and moderate in temperature, with long daylight hours.

Inuktitut, the Inuit language, was spoken across the entire Canadian Arctic, with only minor differences in dialect. Population density across this vast area was low. Social groups were generally small, although certain seasonal tasks, such as winter sealing among the Central Inuit and whaling among the Mackenzie Delta Inuit, brought together larger numbers. Leadership was informal, with the opinion of the most experienced and respected elder carrying greatest weight.

All groups relied on some combination of hunting land and sea mammals, along with fishing. Caribou were by far the most important of the land mammals. Seals were the vital sea mammals, although walrus and whales were taken by some groups. Gathering played a minimal role in the Arctic economy, consisting only of such seasonal delicacies as berries and birds' eggs.

Caribou were also essential for their hides, taken in fall when they were in best condition and used to make winter clothing. Winter apparel consisted of two layers of coats, trousers, stockings, and boots, with the inner one having the hair next to the body. Summer clothing was a single layer, and could be of sealskin. Sealskin boots were also essential for wetter conditions. Women's clothing was often more elaborate than men's, with extra space at the back of the coat to carry babies against the mother's skin. Regional differences in clothing style and decoration were evident.

The successful food quest also required strict observation of taboos. One of the most widespread was the belief that products of land and sea must not be mixed. As a result, seal and caribou meat could never be cooked together, and all sewing of caribou skins for winter clothing had to be completed before the people moved to their sealing camps on the sea ice. Shamans held supernatural power, which enabled them to cure the sick, prophesy the future, and locate the game animals.

In the west were the Inuit of the Mackenzie Delta region, who were closely related to Inuit groups in northern Alaska. Whaling was an important part of their economy. The large bowhead whale was hunted on the Beaufort Sea from umiaks (large, hide-covered open boats), and the small beluga whales were hunted in the shallows of the delta from kayaks. This economy allowed the densest concentration of Inuit people in Canada, living in large villages of semi-subterranean driftwood log houses along the delta. Infectious diseases nearly wiped out these people by the end of the nineteenth century, and the population has been replaced in subsequent years by more recent arrivals from Alaska. These people consider themselves distinct from other Canadian Inuit today, referring to themselves as the Inuvialuit.

In the central Arctic are the Copper, Netsilik, Iglulik, and Baffinland Inuit. In the winter most groups moved far out onto the sea ice, hunting seals through their breathing holes in the ice. During this time they lived in dome-shaped snow houses (igloos), which were lit and heated by blubber lamps made of soapstone. In summer and fall people lived inland, fishing and hunting caribou while living in sealskin tents.

Closely related are the Caribou Inuit, dwelling on the interior barrenlands west of Hudson Bay. Theirs was a specialized way of life, relying almost totally on hunting caribou. Such reliance on a single resource is perilous, and periods of starvation did occur.

In the east were the various Inuit groups of northern Quebec and Labrador. They relied heavily on hunting sea mammals, including walrus and several species of seals and whales. These were harpooned from kayaks or umiaks in summer and from the ice edge in winter. Caribou and fish were also important.

Initial contact between Inuit and Europeans goes back to the Norse settlement of Greenland in the tenth century. The Inuit of the eastern Canadian Arctic were also in at least fleeting contact with the Norse. Shortly after 1500, fishermen and whalers of several European nations were in the waters off the Labrador coast and undoubtedly encountered Natives. The voyages of Martin Frobisher, beginning in 1576, began a new period of European exploration in the Arctic.

Moravian missionaries were active among the Inuit of Labrador by the 1770s. For the rest of the Canadian Arctic, however, sustained contact did not begin until the whalers arrived in the late nineteenth century. European whalers began to winter over in northern Hudson Bay, while U.S. whalers established a base on the northern Yukon coast. European goods became commonplace, while diseases drastically reduced Inuit populations. The Sadlermiut of Southampton Island in Hudson Bay went extinct, and the Inuit of the Mackenzie Delta were reduced to a small remnant population.

After the collapse of the whaling industry around 1910, European presence was limited to a relatively small number of trading posts, police posts, and mission stations. This lasted until World War II brought large numbers of military personnel into the Arctic. Following the war, the Canadian government took a much more active role in Inuit administration. Schools and medical stations were built, and housing programs were established. The Inuit were encouraged to move out of their hunting camps and relocate in settlements.

The Inuit Tapirisat of Canada is the national political organization formed to promote Inuit culture and identity and to provide a common front on political and economic issues. Canadian Inuit also participate in the Inuit Circumpolar Conference, an international organization bringing together Inuit from Greenland, Canada, Alaska, and Siberia to strengthen pan-Inuit communication and cultural activities, as well as to provide international cooperation in protecting the Arctic environment.

Land claims have been a major part of modern Inuit political struggles. Settlements were finalized with the Inuit of northern Quebec in 1975 and the Inuvialuit of the western Arctic in 1984. For the rest of the Northwest Territories the Inuit have sought to establish a self-governing homeland, to be known as Nunavut ("Our Land," in Inuktitut). This political unit, with an Inuit majority and a status similar to a province, is to be created by dividing the Northwest Territories into two parts. Various details are still under debate, but a tentative agreement has been reached, and Nunavut is expected to become a political reality in the not-too-distant future.

The Métis

The Métis (from an old French word meaning "mixed") emerged during the historic fur trade, the product of unions between the European male traders and Native women. Racial mixture by itself, however, does not determine a person's social or political identity. The numerous offspring from casual encounters during the early years of contact on Canada's east coast were simply raised as Indians, without a separate social group developing. The term *Métis* is best applied to those who, during the nineteenth century, forged a common identity on the eastern Plains and their descendants.

As the fur trade moved westward, many French-speaking men followed, establishing stable unions with Cree and Ojibway women. Kinship ties from such unions provided alliances that facilitated trade. Native wives served as interpreters and performed such skilled tasks as making snowshoes, drying meat, and dressing furs. Male children frequently also became traders, and a distinct group of mixed heritage individuals began to emerge.

To the north, the English and Scottish employees of the Hudson's Bay Company established unions with the surrounding Cree, despite company restrictions on racial mixture. In the early years of contact, such traders usually returned to Britain at the end of their service, leaving their "country-born" offspring at the forts. Only

Métis bison hunt near Fort Garry in 1846. Painting by Paul Kane from his travels in the 1840s.

a few high-ranking officers sent their mixed-race sons to be educated in England.

By the mid-eighteenth century, a large "mixed-blood" population had settled around the Great Lakes. Substantial communities of log cabins emerged at such strategic locations as Sault Sainte Marie. Intermarriages contributed to a common identity, merging the separate elements of their heritage. Depleted fur stocks and increased settlement from the east, however, led many to move westward to the Plains, where the distinctive Métis culture finally emerged.

The Métis heartland was at the confluence of the Red and Assiniboine rivers (modern Winnipeg, Manitoba). There they established themselves as buffalo hunters and provisioners for the North West Company, serving as an essential link in the long trade chain from Montreal to the northwestern posts. Geographic and social isolation, as well as a shared life-style, promoted a group identity, although differences still remained between the predominant French-speaking Métis, who were Catholics, and the Protestants of partial English and Scottish descent. Years of bitter confrontation between the two great fur trade companies helped forge the concept of a Métis Nation in the Canadian West.

The Métis life-style was threatened when the Hudson's Bay Company granted lands along the Red River for an agricultural colony in 1811. The North West Company, along whose main trade route the new colony lay, fueled the sparks of emerging Métis nationalism. Their concerns seemed justified when the new colony attempted to ban aspects of the Métis bison hunt and sale of pemmican, which is dried meat, usually buffalo or dear meat. The Métis organized under Cuthbert Grant, and the subsequent clash in 1816, known as the Battle of Seven Oaks, left the colony's governor and twenty settlers dead, forcefully establishing Métis rights in the area. After merger of the two fur trade companies in 1821 the Métis community at Red River grew rapidly and flourished in virtual isolation for nearly half a century.

The communal bison hunt was crucial to the Métis economy and central to their self-identity. Large parties set out on the hunt in their two-wheeled Red River carts pulled by horses or oxen. Once the herds were located, the bison were killed from horseback. The meat was cut into strips, dried, pounded into coarse powder, mixed with melted fat, and sewn into hide bags. This pemmican was a vital part of the fur trade economy, meant as provisions to the trading posts of the distant northwest. By the 1850s, however, the bison herds were disappearing, forcing the hunters to move further and further afield. Many began to winter out on the Plains, shortly followed by more permanent Métis settlements.

A serious threat to the Métis of the Red River area came with the transfer of Hudson's Bay Company lands to the Canadian government in 1869. Government surveyors began laying out lots without regard to local residents' holdings. Métis resistance was led by Louis Riel. They seized Fort Garry, the center of the Red River settlement, and established a provisional government. Their demands led to the Manitoba Act of 1870, by which Manitoba became a province of Canada. Despite provision for Métis land grants in the act, the new settlers and troops usurped most Métis lands, and their open hostility led the majority of the Manitoba Métis to move west, establishing new communities in Saskatchewan. Despite his election to the Canadian Parliament, Louis Riel was forced into exile and was never able to take his seat.

The Métis communities in Saskatchewan soon faced encroachment from the east. Government failure to deal with Métis claims to the land led to the Northwest Rebellion of 1885. Led again by Louis Riel, along with Gabriel Dumont as military commander (see Dumont's biography), the Métis declared a provisional government at their capital of Batoche. Several groups of Cree and Assiniboine joined the uprising. The Canadian military eventually overran the Métis at Batoche, and Riel was hanged in Regina, Alberta, for his role in the rebellion.

The defeat at Batoche brought the end of aspirations for a Métis Nation. Some Métis drifted south to Montana, while others moved north into the boreal forest, reaching as far as the Mackenzie River, where they could live by hunting and trapping. Those who remained found themselves largely excluded from the new economic order. As the Métis were expected to disappear, they were ignored by the Canadian government. Sir John A. Macdonald, the prime minister, denied their existence as a people, stating: "If they are Indians, they go with the tribe; if they are half-breeds they are whites." Excluded from reserves and federal programs for Indians, many Métis existed in poverty.

In the 1930s, several prominent Métis leaders emerged, and the Métis Association of Alberta was formed. Political pressure on the Alberta government led to the passage of the Métis Betterment Act in 1938, which set aside lands for Métis settlements. The only communal Métis lands in Canada today are the eight settlements that remain in Alberta.

After nearly a century as Canada's "forgotten people," the Métis are experiencing a cultural and political awakening. Part of the stimulus comes from the 1982 constitutional recognition of the Métis as one of the "aboriginal peoples of Canada," although it is uncertain what benefits have been obtained and who is entitled to share in them. The Native Council of Canada has represented Métis and non-status Indians at the national level since 1970. In 1983, the Métis National Council was established to present the distinct concerns of the Plains Métis.

Early Indian Administration

At confederation, the British North America Act (now known as the Constitution Act of 1867) assigned the federal government responsibility for "Indians and Lands reserved for Indians." Ever since, Indians have been treated differently than all other Canadians, who receive most services (such as education, health, and welfare) from the provincial governments.

In order to administer its charges, the federal government passed the first Indian Act in 1876. This again isolated Indian people, putting them under different legislation than other Canadians. The act provided government control over all aspects of Indian life, and served as a vehicle of assimilation by legally suppressing such Native ceremonies as the Sun Dance on the Plains and the potlatch on the Pacific coast. Although the act was extensively rewritten in 1951 and prohibitions on Native traditions were dropped, the act remains essentially a nineteenth-century colonial document.

Indian status comes from being registered on a list held by the federal government, which had the power to decide who was an Indian. Decisions were only partially based on race. Enfranchisement, the voluntary or involuntary loss of Indian status, was a peculiar provision of the Indian Act. It reflects the initial belief that Indian status was a transitional measure, providing protection only until a certain level of acculturation had occurred. The most infamous example is the provision that took away Indian status from all Indian women who married non-Indian men. As all dependent children also lost status, a large population of non-status Indians emerged. The sexist nature of this provision is clear from the fact that Indian males did not lose status when they married non-Indians; instead their wives became Indians under the Indian Act, regardless of their racial origins. This remained in place, despite several court challenges, until 1985. A revision in that year removed enfranchisement; status can now be neither gained nor lost. People who had been enfranchised, plus their first generation descendants, can now reclaim status, a process that is swelling the numbers of legally recognized Indians.

Indian reserves were set aside for the "use and benefit" of specific Indian bands, the administrative units recognized by the federal government. The earliest reserves appear to have been established in New France by the Catholic church. Later, reserves were determined through treaties in many areas; in others, such as Quebec and most of British Columbia, reserves were allocated without treaties. The process remains incomplete, as few reserves have been established in the Yukon and Northwest Territories. Title to reserve land is held by the Crown, making the reserves pockets of federal jurisdiction within the provinces. Under the terms of the Indian Act, a band cannot sell or otherwise dispose of reserve lands without surrendering them to the Crown. As reserves are set apart physically and legally, they have served to isolate Indian communities but have also helped maintain distinct ethnic identities. Many bands are now moving toward self-government, and federal control of reserve lands is increasingly being challenged.

Responsibility for education of Indian children was initially taken by Catholic religious orders in New France. Later, Protestant churches also became active in Indian education. By the nineteenth century, government policy involved the establishment of church-run residential schools. Such facilities supported government goals of acculturation by removing Indian children from their families, prohibiting their languages, and promoting a Christian Euro-Canadian life-style. The federal government continued to use the residential schools to meet their responsibilities for Indian education into the mid-twentieth century.

The Inuit are also considered a federal responsibility, although they are not subject to the provisions of the Indian Act and do not have reserves. Non-status Indians and Métis are not administered by the federal government. They fall under the jurisdiction of the provinces, as do all other Canadians, and receive no benefits or government recognition of Native status.

Canada's Treaties with First Nations

The earliest treaties between the British government and Indians were the "peace and friendship" treaties on the east coast, signed in the late seventeenth and eighteenth centuries. The British sought to forge alliances with Indian groups and gain their assistance in wars with the French. These early treaties do not include purchase or surrender of the land. After defeat of the French and with increased European settlement, the focus of the treaties shifted to land surrenders. Between about 1780 and 1850, small land conveyance treaties were negotiated with the Indians of what was to become southern Ontario. These treaties varied greatly but often involved only small, one-time payments for land.

In 1850, treaties with the Indians of the upper Great Lakes were negotiated by Commissioner W.B. Robinson. Known as the Robinson-Superior and Robinson-Huron treaties, they involved the surrender of large areas of land in exchange for reserves, lump-sum cash payments, annual payments to each member of the band, and promises of hunting and fishing rights over unoccupied Crown lands. These provided a model for later federal treaties.

The final pre-confederation treaties were negotiated on the Pacific coast between 1850 and 1854. Fourteen small treaties were signed on Vancouver Island, at that time a separate crown colony, with individual groups around European settlements such as Victoria. In return for surrendering their land, the Indians were confirmed in possession of their village sites, assured that they would be "at liberty to hunt over the unoccupied lands, and to carry on fisheries as formerly," and given small payments.

After confederation, Canada sought to extinguish Native claims in the west, in order to open the land for settlement. The federal "numbered treaties" began in 1871 with Treaty Number 1, affecting the Ojibway and Cree of southern Manitoba. By the time Treaty Number 7 was signed with the Indians of southern Alberta only six years later, the lands from western Lake Superior to the Rocky Mountains had been covered. Except for a northward addition to Treaty Number 6, treaty-making came to a halt for twenty-two years, until gold and oil discoveries in the north brought about new negotiations. Between Treaty Number 8 in 1899 and Treaty Number 11 in 1921, Native title was extinguished across much of northern Canada, from northern Ontario to the Mackenzie River in the Northwest Territories. Finally, the Williams treaties of 1923, which extinguished Native title to the last unsurrendered lands in southern Ontario, brought treaty-making in Canada to a close. (See the map of Canadian treaties in the Canadian Chronology in Chapter 1.)

Only minor differences exist in the terms of the federal treaties. Indians agreed to "cede, release, surrender, and yield up" their rights to the land in exchange for reserves, small cash payments, ammunition, uniforms and medals for the chiefs, small annual payments to each band member, and promises of continued hunting and fishing rights. Lasting benefits have been few. Gifts such as flags and medals were meant to enhance the illusion that these were pacts of friendship, when they were primarily deeds of sale. Not all reserve lands or other benefits promised under treaty were allocated, leading to a number of modern specific land claims. Hunting and fishing rights have been eroded by subsequent legislation. The 1982 constitution guarantees protection of existing treaty rights but cannot restore rights lost prior to that time.

Land Claims

Two types of land claims are recognized in government negotiations. Comprehensive claims are those based on aboriginal title, while specific claims are based on breach of lawful obligation.

Specific claims frequently involve unfulfilled treaty promises. These include reserve lands which were never allocated or resources, such as cattle, which were never provided. Other specific claims allege mismanagement of Indian lands or assets. Numerous claims of this type have been made in recent years, and a considerable number have been settled.

Comprehensive claims apply to areas where aboriginal title has never been extinguished through treaty or other legal process. Aboriginal title derives from Native ownership of the land prior to European colonization. An important part of the legal argument is the Royal Proclamation of 1763. This decree by King George III states that any lands not ceded to the crown are reserved for Indians. Thus, it has been argued, treaties are legally mandatory to extinguish Native title, and any land not ceded by treaty is still Native land. The colonial and dominion practice of signing treaties with Indians clearly indicates some recognition of aboriginal rights to the land.

In the 1970s, federal government policy changed to allow recognition of Native land claims. In part this was a response to the legal claim of the Nisga'a of northern British Columbia and the failure of the Supreme Court of Canada to come to a conclusive decision in 1973. The Office of Native Claims was established in Ottawa in 1974 to receive proposals for negotiation.

The first modern Native land claim settlement, the James Bay Agreement, was reached with the Cree and Inuit of northern Quebec in 1975. This was in response to provincial plans for massive hydroelectric development in the area. In 1978, the agreement was extended to include the Naskapi of northeastern Quebec. Then in 1984, the Inuvialuit of the western Arctic reached an agreement. All three settlements extinguished Native claim to the land in exchange for monetary compensation, ownership of some lands, hunting and trapping rights, and control of social programs such as education and health.

Other groups in the Canadian north are seeking greater self-determination through their claims and reject the extinguishment of aboriginal rights. Broad tentative agreements reached with the Dene and Métis of the Yukon and Northwest Territories broke down over such concerns. Instead negotiations are now taking place at the regional level, and agreements have recently been signed with the Gwich'in of the northern Yukon and the Sahtu-Dene of Great Bear Lake in the Northwest Territories. A tentative agreement has also been reached with the Inuit of the eastern Arctic, which would require division of the Northwest Territories to create a separate Inuit homeland known as Nunavut. These agreements also include monetary compensation and ownership of some lands within the traditional territories.

Groups in other non-treaty areas of Canada, such as Labrador and most of British Columbia, are also pursuing comprehensive claims. In British Columbia this is taking place at the level of individual bands or regional tribal councils. No agreements have yet been reached.

Land claims represent one of the major areas of "unfinished business" between Canadian Natives and government. They are seen by many as a validation of their aboriginal rights and as a mechanism by which economic independence can be achieved. As many aboriginal groups move toward their goal of self-government, land claims are seen as vital to provide an economic base.

Other Modern Issues

Economic problems plague many modern reserve communities. Inadequate housing, often overcrowded and lacking running water, is a common feature of reserve life, particularly for those in remote locations. Poor economic conditions also affect Native health; despite progress in recent decades, Native life expectancy is still about ten years less than the national average. The majority of Canadian reserves are in rural or remote areas, and many of these are inaccessible by road. The isolated nature of these reserves hinders the provision of better facilities.

A major concern for many band councils today is to initiate developments that will provide employment on their reserves. Native businesses, many aided by federal funding, have sprung up on reserves across Canada. Some fortunate bands hold valuable real estate near modern urban centers or have natural resources such as oil and gas on their land. For bands with small isolated reserves and few resources, opportunities for economic development are minimal, and conditions of poverty are widespread.

The search for employment and better economic conditions has led many Indians to relocate to the cities. Rates of urbanization have increased greatly over the last few decades. About 40 percent of Canadian Indians now normally reside off-reserve, mainly in urban centers. Métis and non-status Indians also swell the numbers of urban Natives.

Indian bands in Canada are increasingly taking control of administering their own lands and finances. A government committee on Indian self-government released its findings in 1983, dismissing the Indian Act and the present system of administration as unacceptable for the future. The committee report supported the right of Indian people to self-government and recommended that this be explicitly stated and entrenched in the Constitution of Canada. Indian First Nations governments would then be recognized as a distinct order of government within Canada. However, constitutional conferences with federal, provincial, and First Nations leaders collapsed in failure, largely due to provincial concerns over the undefined terms and costs of aboriginal self-government. The attempt to recognize self-government in the constitution has been abandoned, at least temporarily.

Larry Pierre of the Okanagan on the occasion of the First Nations Constitutional Conference, 1980, demanding Native participation in constitutional tasks.

There are other routes to aboriginal self-government. The Cree and Naskapi of northern Quebec have essentially achieved self-government through the terms of their land claims settlement, later set out in federal legislation as the Cree-Naskapi (of Quebec) Act in 1984. Another option is through direct negotiation. The Sechelt of coastal British Columbia, through terms of a negotiated agreement in 1986, have received title to their reserve lands, the right to draft their own constitution and laws, and are no longer bound by the terms of the Indian Act. This type of agreement, which refers only to reserve lands, is rejected by groups who tie their self-government aspirations to settlement of land claims over their traditional territory.

Education plays a key role in Native plans for the future, both for the preservation of Native culture and languages and in providing modern skills needed for self-government. Most Canadian Indian bands now administer all or part of their educational programs. Three aboriginal groups, the Nisga'a of British Columbia and the Cree and Inuit of northern Quebec, operate their own school boards. At the post-secondary level, federal funding for Indian and Inuit students to attend colleges and universities is resulting in the appearance of many young, articulate, educated Native leaders.

The First Nations of Canada have rejected the assimilationist policies of the Canadian government since confederation. Despite government assumptions, evident in some of the provisions of the Indian Act, First Nations were not doomed to disappear as distinct cultures. Today populations of Indian, Inuit, and Métis peoples are rapidly growing, and determined steps are being taken to preserve their languages and cultures. Self-government is seen as an opportunity for First Nations to take control over their own lives and ensure the survival of their cultures.

Alan D. McMillan
Simon Fraser University

References

Before 1699

Borah, Woodrow W. and Sherburne F. Cook. *The Aboriginal Population of Central Mexico on the Eve of the Spanish Conquest.* Ibero-Americana, 45. Berkeley: University of California Press, 1963.

Cook, Noble D. and W. George Lovell, eds. *Secret Judgements of God: Old World Disease in Colonial Spanish America.* Norman: University of Oklahoma Press, 1991.

Cook, Sherburne F. and Woodrow Borah. *Essays in Population History: Mexico and the Caribbean.* Berkeley: University of California Press, vol. 1, 1971; vol. 2, 1974.

____. *Essays in Population History: Mexico and California.* Berkeley: University of California Press, vol. 3, 1979.

____. *The Indian Population of Central Mexico, 1531–1610.* Ibero-Americana, 44. Berkeley: University of California Press, 1960.

Crosby, Alfred W., Jr. *The Columbian Exchange: Biological and Cultural Consequences of 1492.* Westport, CT: Greenwood Pub. Co., 1972.

____. *Ecological Imperialism: The Biological Expansion of Europe,* 900–1900. Cambridge: Cambridge University Press, 1986.

Daniels, John D. "The Indian Population of North America in 1492." *William and Mary Quarterly* 3rd ser. 49:2 (April 1992): 298–320.

Denevan, William M., ed. *The Native Population of the Americas in 1492.* Madison: University of Wisconsin Press, 1976.

Dobyns, Henry F. "Estimating Aboriginal American Population: An Appraisal of Techniques with a New Hemispheric Estimate." *Current Anthropology* 7 (October 1966): 395–416.

____. *Native American Historical Demography: A Critical Bibliography.* Bloomington: Published for the Newberry Library Center for the History of the American Indian by Indiana University Press, 1976.

____. *Their Number Become Thinned: Native American Population Dynamics in Eastern North America.* Knoxville: Published by the University of Tennessee Press in cooperation with the Newberry Library Center for the History of the American Indian, 1983.

Stearn, E. Wagner and Allen E. Stearn. *The Effect of Smallpox on the Destiny of the Amerindian.* Boston: B. Humphries, 1945.

Stiffarm, Lenore A. and Phil Lane, Jr. "The Demography of Native North America: A Question of American Indian Survival." In *The State of Native America: Genocide, Colonization, and Resistance,* edited by M. Annette Jaimes, 23–53. Boston: South End Press, 1992.

Thornton, Russell. *American Indian Holocaust and Survival: A Population History Since 1492.* Norman: University of Oklahoma Press, 1987.

Henry Dobyns

Eighteenth Century

Anderson, Gary C. *Kinsmen of Another Kind: Dakota-White Relations in the Upper Mississippi Valley, 1650–1862.* Lincoln: University of Nebraska Press, 1984.

Cook, Sherburne F. *The Conflict Between the California Indian and White Civilization.* Berkeley: University of California Press, 1976.

Edmunds, R. David. *The Potawatomis: Keepers of the Fire.* Norman: University of Oklahoma Press, 1978.

Gutierrez, Ramón A. *When Jesus Came, the Corn Mothers Went Away: Marriage, Sexuality, and Power in New Mexico, 1500–1846.* Stanford: Stanford University Press, 1991.

Jennings, Francis. *Empire of Fortune: Crowns, Colonies, and Tribes in the Seven Years War in America.* New York: Norton, 1988.

McConnell, Michael N. *A Country Between: The Upper Ohio Valley and Its Peoples, 1724–1774.* Lincoln: University of Nebraska Press, 1992.

Merrell, James H. *The Indians' New World: Catawbas and Their Neighbors from European Contact through the Era of Removal.* Chapel Hill: Published for the Institute of Early American History and Culture, Williamsburg, Virginia, by the University of North Carolina Press, 1989.

Ray, Arthur J. *Indians in the Fur Trade: Their Role as Trappers, Hunters, and Middlemen in the Lands Southwest of Hudson Bay, 1660–1870.* Toronto: University of Toronto Press, 1974.

Richter, Daniel K. *The Ordeal of the Longhouse: The Peoples of the Iroquois League in the Era of European Colonization.* Chapel Hill: Published for the Institute of Early American History and Culture, Williamsburg, Virginia, by the University of North Carolina Press, 1992.

Usner, Daniel H., Jr., *Indians, Settlers, and Slaves in a Frontier Exchange Economy: The Lower Mississippi Valley before 1783.* Chapel Hill: Published for the Institute of Early American History and Culture, Williamsburg, Virginia, by the University of North Carolina Press, 1992.

White, Richard. *The Middle Ground: Indians, Empires, and Republics in the Great Lakes Region, 1650–1815.* New York: Cambridge University Press, 1991.

Dan Usner

Nineteenth Century

Bee, Robert L. *The Yuma.* New York: Chelsea House, 1989.

Calloway, Colin G. *The Abenaki.* New York: Chelsea House, 1989.

Carlson, Leonard A. *Indians, Bureaucrats, and Land: The Dawes Act and the Decline of Indian Farming.* Westport, CT: Greenwood Press, 1981.

Dobyns, Henry F. *The Pima-Maricopa.* New York: Chelsea House, 1989.

Gibson, Arrell M. *The American Indian: Prehistory to Present.* Lexington, MA: D. C. Heath, 1980.

Maxwell, James A., ed. *America's Fascinating Indian Heritage.* Pleasantville, NY: Reader's Digest Association, 1978.

Merrell, James H. *The Catawbas.* New York: Chelsea House, 1989.

Olson, James S. and Raymond Wilson. *Native Americans in the Twentieth Century.* Provo, UT: Brigham Young University Press, 1984.

Simmons, William S. *The Narragansett.* New York: Chelsea House, 1989.

Spicer, Edward H. *The American Indians.* Cambridge, MA: Belnap Press of Harvard University Press, 1980.

Tanner, Helen H., ed. *Atlas of Great Lakes Indian History.* Norman: Published for the Newberry Library by the University of Oklahoma Press, 1987.

Trigger, Bruce, ed. *Northeast.* Vol. 15 of *Handbook of North American Indians.* Washington, DC: Smithsonian Institution, 1978.

Washburn, Wilcomb, ed. *History of Indian-White Relations.* Vol. 4 of *Handbook of North American Indians.* Washington, DC: Smithsonian Institution, 1988.

Wright, Muriel H. *A Guide to the Indian Tribes of Oklahoma.* Norman: University of Oklahoma Press, 1986.

Leroy Eid

Twentieth Century

Burt, Larry W. *Tribalism in Crisis: Federal Indian Policy, 1953–1961.* Albuquerque: University of New Mexico Press, 1982.

Carlson, Leonard A. *Indians, Bureaucrats, and Land: The Dawes Act and the Decline of Indian Farming.* Westport, CT: Greenwood Press, 1981.

Castile, George P. and Robert L. Bee. *State and Reservation: New Perspectives on Federal Indian Policy.* Tucson: University of Arizona Press, 1992.

Champagne, Duane. *American Indian Societies: Strategies and Conditions of Political and Cultural Survival.* Cultural Survival Report 32. Cambridge, MA: Cultural Survival, 1989.

Cohen, Fay G. *Treaties on Trial: The Continuing Controversy over Northwest Indian Fishing Rights.* Seattle: University of Washington Press, 1986.

Deloria, Vine, Jr. *Behind the Trail of Broken Treaties: An Indian Declaration of Independence.* New York: Delacorte, 1974.

____, ed. *American Indian Policy in the TwentiethCentury.* Norman: University of Oklahoma Press, 1985.

____ and Clifford Lytle. *American Indians, American Justice.* Austin: University of Texas Press, 1983.

Lopach, James J., Margery H. Brown, and Richmond L. Clow. *Tribal Government Today: Politics on Montana Indian Reservations.* Boulder, CO: Westview Press, 1990.

McCool, Daniel. *Command of the Waters: Iron Triangles, Federal Water Development, and Indian Water.* Berkeley: University of California Press, 1987.

McDonnell, Janet A. *The Dispossession of the American Indian, 1887–1934.* Bloomington: Indiana University Press, 1991.

Momaday, N. Scott. *House Made of Dawn.* New York: Harper & Row, 1968.

Philp, Kenneth R., ed. *Indian Self-Rule: First Hand Accounts of Indian-White Relations From Roosevelt to Reagan.* Salt Lake City: Howe Bros., 1986.

Prucha, Francis P. *Atlas of American Indian Affairs.* Lincoln: University of Nebraska Press, 1990.

____. *The Great Father: The United States Government and the American Indians.* 2 vols. Lincoln: University of Nebraska Press, 1984.

____. *The Indians in American Society: From the Revolutionary War to the Present.* Berkeley: University of California Press, 1985.

Shipek, Florence C. *Pushed into the Rocks: Southern California Indian Land Tenure, 1769–1986.* Lincoln: University of Nebraska Press, 1988.

Snipp, C. Matthew, ed. *Public Policy Impacts on American Indian Economic Development.* Albuquerque: Native American Studies, Institute for Native American Development, University of New Mexico, 1988.

Sutton, Imre. *Indian Land Tenure: Bibliographical Essays and a Guide to the Literature.* New York: Clearwater, 1975.

____, ed. *Irredeemable America: The Indians' Estate and Land Claims.* Albuquerque: University of New Mexico Press, 1985.

Vecsey, Christopher and William A. Starna, eds. *Iroquois Land Claims.* Syracuse, NY: Syracuse University Press, 1988.

Vogel, Virgil J. *This Country Was Ours: A Documentary History of the American Indian.* New York: Harper & Row, 1972.

Warner, Linda Sue. "The Emergence of American Indian Higher Education." *Thought & Action: The NEA Higher Education Journal* 8:1 (1992): 61–72.

Washburn, Wilcomb E. *Red Man's Land/White Man's Law: A Study of the Past and Present Status of the American Indian.* New York: Scribner, 1971.

____, ed. *History of Indian-White Relations.* Vol. 4 of *Handbook of North American Indians.* Washington, DC: Smithsonian Institution, 1988.

Wilkinson, Charles F. *American Indians, Time and the Law: Native Societies in a Modern Constitutional Democracy.* New Haven: Yale University Press, 1987.

Imre Sutton

Canadian Native Demography

Cox, Bruce A., ed. *Native People, Native Lands: Canadian Indians, Inuit and Metis.* Ottawa: Carlton University Press, 1988.

Damas, David, ed. *Arctic.* Vol. 5 of *Handbook of North American Indians.* Washington, DC: Smithsonian Institution, 1984.

Dickason, Olive P. *Canada's First Nations: A History of Founding Peoples from Earliest Times.* Toronto: McClelland and Stewart, 1992.

Fisher, Robin and Kenneth Coates, eds. *Out of the Background: Readings On Canadian Native History.* Toronto: Copp Clarke Pitman, 1988.

Frideres, James S. *Native Peoples in Canada: Contemporary Conflicts.* 3d ed. Scarborough, ON: Prentice-Hall Canada, 1988.

Helm, June, ed. *Subarctic.* Vol. 6 of *Handbook of North American Indians.* Washington, DC: Smithsonian Institution, 1981.

McMillan, Alan D. *Native Peoples and Cultures of Canada: An Anthropological Overview.* Vancouver: Douglas & McIntyre, 1988.

Miller, J. R. *Skyscrapers Hide the Heavens: A History of Indian-White Relations in Canada.* Toronto: University of Toronto Press, 1989.

Morrison, R. Bruce and C. Roderick Wilson, eds. *Native Peoples: The Canadian Experience.* Toronto: McClelland and Stewart, 1986.

Ponting, J. Rick, ed. *Arduous Journey: Canadian Indians and Decolonization.* Toronto: McClelland and Stewart, 1986.

Richardson, Boyce, ed. *Drum Beat: Anger and Renewal in Indian Country.* Toronto: Summerhill Press, 1989.

Suttles, Wayne, ed. *Northwest Coast.* Vol. 7 of *Handbook of North American Indians.* Washington, DC: Smithsonian Institution, 1990.

Trigger, Bruce G. *Natives and Newcomers: Canada's "Heroic Age" Reconsidered.* Kingston: McGill-Queen's University Press, 1985.

____, ed. *Northeast.* Vol. 15 of *Handbook of North American Indians.* Washington, DC: Smithsonian Institution, 1978.

Alan Macmillan

3

Major Culture Areas

♦ Northeastern Indians ♦ Southeastern Indians ♦ Southwestern Indians ♦ Northern Plains Indians ♦ Northwest Coast Indians ♦ Alaska Natives ♦ Oklahoma Indians ♦ Indians of the Plateau, Great Basin, and Rocky Mountains ♦ California Indians ♦ Aboriginal Peoples of Canada

Culture areas, such as Southwestern or Northeastern Woodlands, are used to describe geographical areas in which several Native American nations lived and shared a similar ecological environment, and hence similar methods of food production, such as hunting and gathering or horticulture. Nevertheless, within a specific culture area, there may be several very different cultures and a multiplicity of languages and dialects, such as the Southeast, where the Cherokee speak an Iroquoian language, while the Choctaw speak a Muskogean language. Anthropologists have used culture areas extensively, and they have been primarily interested in reconstructing how Indian peoples lived prior to extensive Western contact after 1500. This chapter presents a series of culture areas, however, that differs from the usual culture areas used by anthropologists, since our primary concern is for presenting contemporary Native North American life. The way that Native North Americans live today is more determined by political and economic relations with U.S. or Canadian society than by the ecological environments of the precontact period. For example, Oklahoma is a culture area on our list, and not on the traditional anthropologist lists, because during the nineteenth century, many Indian nations from the East, Plains, and other places, such as the Delaware, Shawnee, Cherokee, Choctaw, Modoc, and many others, were moved by the U.S. government to Indian Territory (present-day Oklahoma). While in Oklahoma, these nations were relegated to similar relations with the state of Oklahoma and the federal government, and were greatly affected by the changing national market economy, as were all U.S. citizens. These many immigrant tribes are now known as Oklahoman Indians, and they themselves identify as Oklahoman Indians. Similarly, we have used Canada as a culture area, rather than Arctic and sub-Arctic, and list Alaska and California as culture areas, because of their unique histories and relations with non-Indians.

Consequently, the ecological models of the anthropologists do not suit the purposes of portraying contemporary Native life. The following list of culture areas draws on the basic culture areas of anthropology, but our concerns are focused on providing an overview of the peoples who live in the culture area, their cultural, social, and political history, and major contemporary issues. Most culture areas have far too many tribes to discuss individually, so a regional map for each culture area is provided for the reader to note the range of contemporary Native peoples living in the culture area. The reader is also invited to see the map of non-recognized Indian communities in Chapter 9 and the directory of Indian communities at the end of this chapter. Since there are too many communities to describe within the space allowed, the authors selected specific Indian communities for short descriptions, and gave general overviews of the history and significant contemporary issues of the culture areas.

♦ NORTHEASTERN INDIANS

It is often asserted that the Northeast is not a single culture area but is a region that has significant ecological diversity while maintaining a nominal degree of cultural cohesiveness. During the period from 1000 B.C. to A.D. 200, the Adena Culture, a variety of mound building sites and cultures, was spread across the present-day Ohio Valley and extended east to sites in present-day western New York and western Pennsylvania. The Hopewell Culture, another mound building culture stretching across the southern Great Lakes and the Mississippi and Ohio Valleys, followed from A.D. 300 to A.D. 700. Both the Hopewell and Adena people lived in villages, and corn was a staple part of their diet. The mounds of this period, often built as burial memorials, were cone-shaped. The Mississippian Culture, A.D. 800 to A.D. 1600, had influence only in the southern portion of the northeast coast, and here the mounds became temples for an aristocratic priesthood. When the earliest Europeans visited the northeast area in the early 1500s they did not find stratified societies with temples built on mounds, but found fortified sedentary towns, with houses organized according to clan and lineage groups, as were found among the Iroquois along the St. Lawrence River. In the early 1500s, the peoples of the northeast had hunting cultures, horticulture (farming with hand implements) increased in the south. During the latter part of the sixteenth century, Algonkian speaking hunting nations, like the Ottawa and Ojibway, were migrating into the northeast area and started pushing sedentary Iroquoian people further west and south. Many Algonkian speaking nations, such as the Lenape (or Delaware) and Wampanoag, occupied the coastal regions of present-day New England, and they lived by hunting, fishing and planting corn, beans, pumpkins and other vegetables. Iroquoian peoples occupied present-day upstate New York and sites along the lower Great Lakes. It appears that during the 1500s, the Iroquoian peoples were already subject to Algonkian invasion, and the arrival of the Europeans tended to intensify the struggle. By the 1700s, these invasions induced many Algonkian nations to move further west into the Great Lakes region, where they often displaced the Natives of the region. Riding the wave of colonial expansion, the Ojibway, Potawatomi, and Ottawa all migrated into the upper Great Lakes area, and displaced the peoples of the Illinois Confederacy, who moved from Wisconsin into present-day Illinois. During the 1700s, the Ojibway moved into the Minnesota region and began to contest hunting, trapping, and wild rice resources.

American Indians in the Northeast region sustained almost continual contact with European explorers from about 1497 onward. Native American contact with Europeans was particularly prolonged and intense along the eastern seaboard of the Atlantic Ocean. Many coastal American Indian groups in the Northeast consequently did not have the liberty or the time to bounce back from

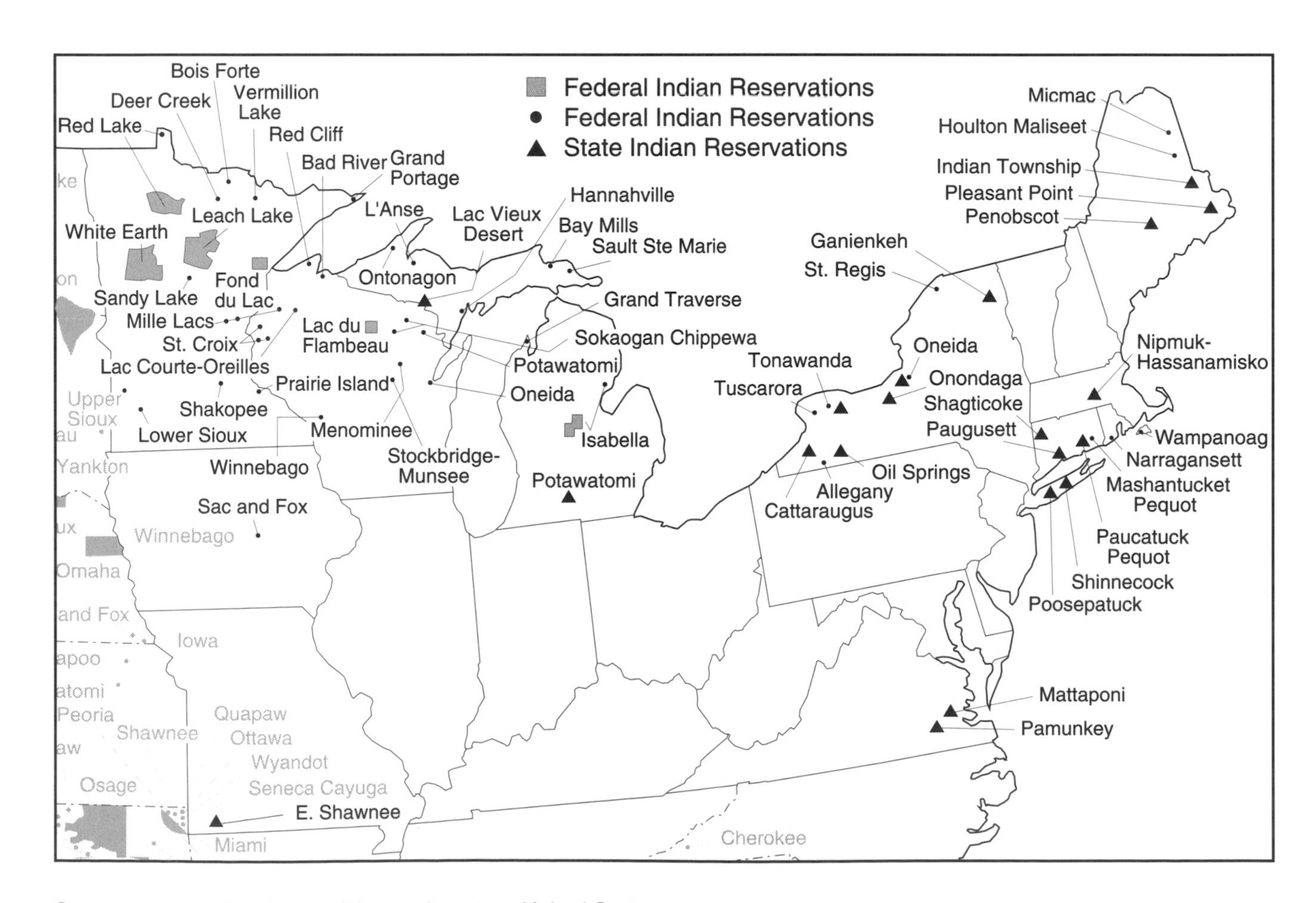

Contemporary Indian tribes of the northeastern United States.

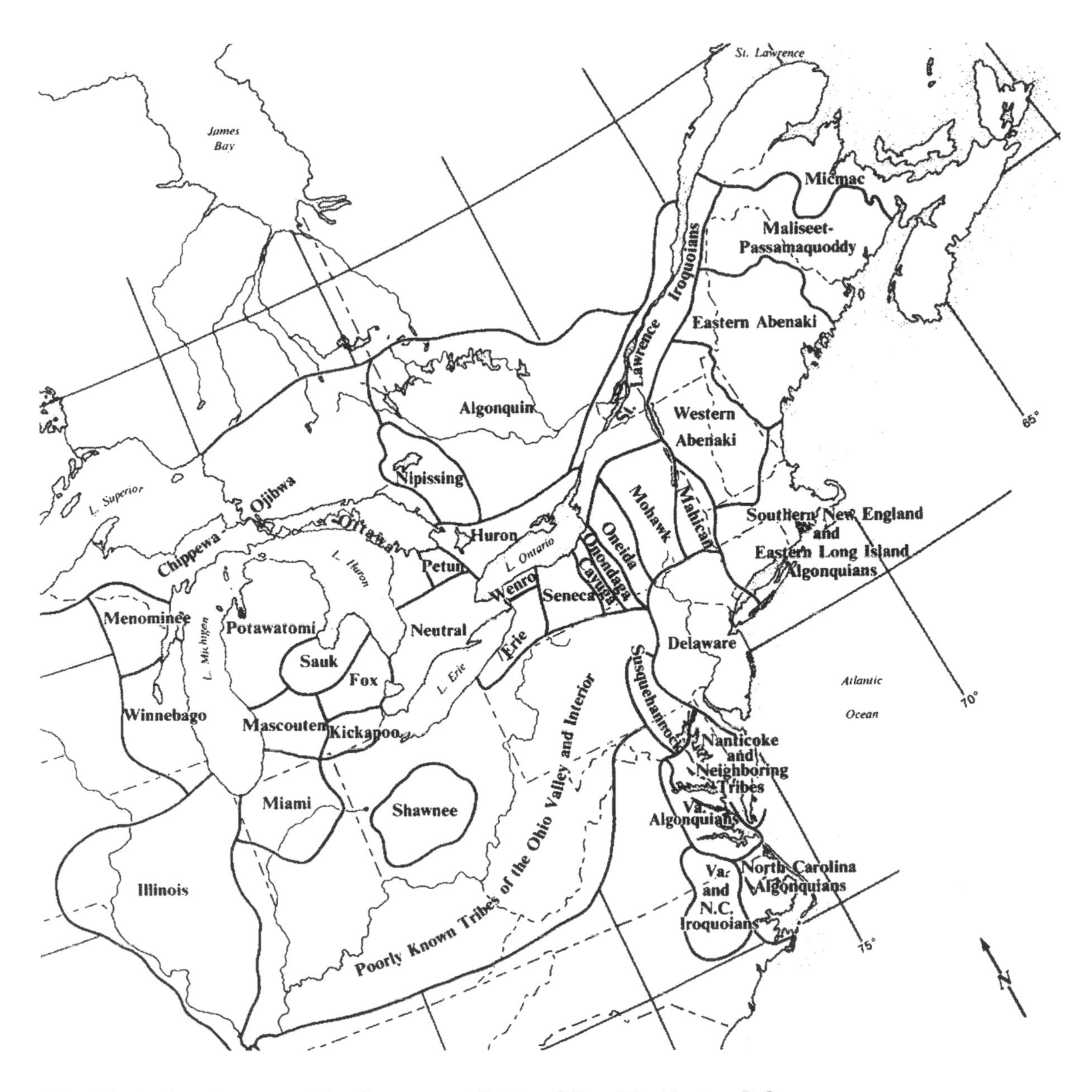

Key to Tribal Territories. Courtesy of the Government Printing Office, Washington, D.C.

the onslaught of European diseases, military aggression, land cessions, and political demands. Thus, these coastal groups were often dispersed into other tribes or decimated, often before Europeans were able to record information about them.

The coastal peoples of present-day New England were rapidly brought under colonial law by the end of King Philip's War (1675–76), and most Indians who stayed in the English New England colony were left to small towns, and adopted Christian religion and town government. Many of the New England Indians, most of whom were Algonkian speakers, lived on the margins of New England society and became "praying Indians." A similar fate awaited the Indians of Virginia: by 1675 the Powhatan Confederacy was demolished by Virginia settlers, and the Indians were forced to live under Virginia law and custom. As in New England, these Indians lived in obscurity until this century.

However, a surprising amount of their culture survives in coastal northeastern Indian oral traditions. The Penobscot and Passamaquoddy of Maine and several other groups (mostly of the Algonkian linguistic group) survive in their original homeland largely because white settler pressure was less severe in the northern coastal part of the region. The Algonkian speaking peoples of the southern coastal part of the region (the Powhatan, Nanticoke, Delaware, Pequot, Abenaki, and others) bore the full brunt of European settler pressure and thus had a great deal more difficulty maintaining their land base and traditions.

In the end, the Indian nations of the Great Lakes did not fare much better than the coastal peoples did. The Great Lakes region was inhabited by Central Algonkian and Siouan speaking groups (such as the Shawnee, Fox, Sauk, Kickapoo, Winnebago, Menominee, Potawatomi, Chippewa, Ottawa and others) who engaged in horticulture and hunting. Except for a few isolated examples, these groups did not come in contact with French traders until the latter part of the seventeenth century. Until well into the eighteenth century, the French used the Iroquois as middlemen in the fur trade, or they had to use devious routes to overcome the economic and military control of the Iroquois. In 1763, Pontiac, an Ottawa chief, and in 1805–12, Tecumseh, a Shawnee warrior,organized alliances of tribal groups and made political and military efforts to slow down European encroachment in the Great Lakes region. These efforts demonstrated the resolve of the Great Lakes Native peoples to resist European domination.

By the late 1790s, however, the once powerful Iroquois nations were scattered and living on small reservations of land in present-day New York and southern Canada. By the 1860s, the Algonkian speakers of the Great Lakes regions were also relegated to small reservations. These Indians suffered the fate of most northern Indian nations following the decline of the fur trade market: many Indians no longer had the means to trade for the manufactured goods—such as guns, metal tools, and textiles—that had become necessities during the 1700 and 1800s. Consequently, the impoverished Indians sold land, and in return lived on small reservations. However, in some cases, such as the Chippewa (Ojibway), the Indians retained treaty rights to hunt and fish in their accustomed places. These treaty rights to land and hunting and fishing places negotiated in the 1850s, later became major points of controversy in the 1970s and 1980s.

While some important groups in the Great Lakes—such as the Shawnee, Delaware, Potawatomi, and others—yielded to settler pressure and were dispersed to Oklahoma and other areas, many of today's indigenous groups along the Great Lakes live on reservations. Throughout much of this century most Indians of the Great Lakes region lived in poverty and in social and political marginality. Only after the 1960s were there greater efforts at community organization to assert treaty rights, land claims, and tribal and cultural identities.

The Iroquoian Peoples

Iroquoian is a term used to identify several indigenous nations that shared a similar language and culture. The major Iroquoian nations included the Mohawk, Seneca, Cayuga, Onondaga, Oneida, Susquehannock, Erie, Huron, and others. The Iroquoian peoples shared a similar way of life, usually based on intensive horticulture, fishing, and hunting. Their villages were often palisaded and organized according to clans, which were kinship groups reckoned through mothers.

At the time of European contact in the early 1500s, the Iroquoian peoples lived along the St. Lawrence River (in upper New York State), along the lower Great Lakes, and in the Susquehanna River Valley (in present-day Pennsylvania). Because of their inland location, they were relatively unaffected, compared to Native coastal peoples, by early European trade and settler expansion. Thus, we know more about the pre-colonial life-styles of the Iroquoian nations than we know about cultures and histories of the indigenous coastal nations.

One of the most well-known Iroquoian groups was the Five Nations of the Haudenosaunee, which means *People of the Longhouse.* Sometime between A.D.1000 and 1350, the Mohawk, Oneida, Onondaga, Cayuga, and Seneca formed a confederation consisting of their five nations, with chiefs drawn from forty-nine families, who were present at the origin of the confederacy. The origin story of the Iroquois confederacy holds that a Peacemaker, Deganawidah and his spokesman Hiawatha, planted a Great Tree of Peace at the Onondaga Nation (near Syracuse, New York) to resolve the blood feuds that had been dividing the Haudenosaunee people. Through the symbolic tree planting, the Haudenosaunee Peacemaker instituted peace, unity, and clear thinking among the Haudenosaunee people. Deganawidah passed on the Great Law, which is the constitution of the Iroquois Confederacy.

During the colonial period, this structure enabled them to take advantage of their political, economic, and geographic position in the northeast. By adopting members of other Iroquoian groups, such as the Huron and Tuscarora, the Haudenosaunee maintained their historically strategic position in the Northeast, between the colonies of New France and New York, in the fur trade, and during the diplomatic rivalries between England and France in the seventeenth and eighteenth centuries. At the height of their influence, from about 1650–1777, the Haudenosaunee heartland extended from Albany, New York to Niagara Falls, with its outermost borders stretching to southeastern Ontario, New England, northern Pennsylvania, and northeastern Ohio.

The Iroquois played an important role in the birth of the United States. Even before the advent of the American Revolution, the Haudenosaunee had counseled American leaders on the virtues of Iroquois-style unity, democracy, and liberty. From the writing of the Albany Plan of Union, a 1755 plan to unite the colonies, to the creation of the United States Constitution, the Iroquois were present in body and/or spirit as Americans sought to create a democratic alternative to the British monarchy. At the request of the founding fathers, Iroquois chiefs were present at the debates on the Declaration of Independence in Philadelphia in May and June of 1776. Over the course of several weeks, the Iroquois observed the new American nation emerging and gave the President, John Hancock, an Iroquois name, "Karanduawn," which means "the Great Tree." Indeed, some Americans, such as Thomas Jefferson, believed that American governments were very similar to American Indian governments like that of the Iroquois; Jefferson stated in 1787 that the "only condition on earth to be compared to [our government] . . . is that of the Indians, where they still have less government than we." On the eve of the Constitutional Convention, John Adams admonished the delegates to the Constitutional Convention to conduct "an accurate investigation of the form of government of the . . . Indians" since the separation of powers in American Indian governments [like the Iroquois] is "marked with a precision that excludes all controversy." During the Constitutional Convention, delegates such as James Wilson of Pennsylvania clearly stated that the "British government cannot be our model." In 1790, Thomas Jefferson and others toasted the U.S. Constitution as an [Iroquois] "tree of peace" that sheltered the Americans "with its branches of union." Thus, American Indian ideas associated with groups like the Iroquois of the Northeast had a decided impact on the development of American democracy.

Even though the Founding Fathers respected the Iroquois for their wisdom in governmental organization, between 1777 and 1800, the U.S. government allowed various land companies to buy virtually all Iroquois lands. By 1880, the Iroquois either left to live in Canada or were relegated to several small reservations in upper New York State. The remaining Iroquois lands and disputed territories were guaranteed by contract with the land companies and by treaties with the United States and New York State.

"[W]e know that
the Great Spirit is pleased that
we follow the traditions and
customs of our forefathers,
for in so doing
we receive his blessing;
we have received strength
and vigor for the chase....
No luxuries, no vices, no disputed titles,
no avaricious desires,
shake the foundations of our society,
or disturb our
peace and happiness."

– Seneca chief Red Jacket

Contemporary Haudenosaunee Cultural Restoration

The Haudenosaunee of the twentieth century saw the traditionalist Longhouse religion of the prophet, Handsome Lake, revived on the Caughnawaga and St. Regis Mohawk Reservations. Handsome Lake was a Seneca prophet whose ministry extended from 1799 to 1815. His message urged accommodation to the presence of the white people while maintaining many of the important traditional ways of the Haudenosaunee. In the 1830s, Iroquois traditionalists and the followers of Handsome Lake formed a church and resurrected the traditional Iroquois chief system in opposition to the "elected" chief system that currently asserts power on their reservations. Today, the Iroquois traditional chieftainship system is present on three reservations in New York (Onondaga, Tuscarora and Tonawanda Seneca). There, the clan mothers still nominate the chiefs of their clans, and the chiefs are brought into office through an ancient condolence ceremony.

The Iroquois have survived and they have struggled to maintain their ancient traditions. Various Iroquois languages are still spoken and they are being taught to Indian and non-Indian students alike. But the Iroquois culture has also changed, as it must if the people are to endure. Today, the Iroquois work in many of the same professions as the dominant society. They are ironworkers, steel workers, teachers, businessmen, and artists. However, many still maintain the traditional culture in the modern setting. At the Onondaga Reservation, the Great Law is still recited as it was in precolonial times, and such meetings are well attended by reservation and urban Iroquois. The great festivals and thanksgivings continue as a part of their lives. They are forging a life-style that includes the wisdom of their ancestors and the benefits of modern technology, to create a culture in which they can live comfortably and in peace.

Contemporary Iroquois are insisting on their treaty rights. For example, since the 1920s, Iroquois stage annual "border crossings" into Canada in the summer to assert their right, through the Jay's Treaty (1794), to uninhibited passage across the U.S. and Canadian border. The Iroquois have also filed claims against the U.S. government relating to fraudulent loss of land. The results of these claims have been uneven; many Iroquois believe that the only real settlement of land claims can come through some form of land restoration.

Recently, after a generation of struggle, the Iroquois were also able to repatriate, or reclaim, wampum belts that had been held in the New York State Museum. Wampum belts are diplomatic and ceremonial records made from shells and fastened into a string or chain of several rows. Symbols were embroidered into the belts as documents and historical records of diplomatic agreements, treaties, records of important historical events, and records of sacred and ceremonial law. The Iroquois wanted the wampum belts returned so that they could be used and cared for by people who can read and interpret these important documents. Today, as in the past, the Haudenosaunee use the wampum belts as a record of their laws, treaties, and other important events of the past. Wampum belts are analogous in importance to U.S. government documents, such as the Declaration of Independence and the United States Constitution.

Recently, Iroquois leaders have also been active in numerous international treaty forums relating to indigenous people's rights. Since the early 1900s, the Iroquois Confederacy has issued its own passports, which are recognized for travel purposes by many nations.

The Iroquois continue to have a strong affinity for their homeland. Their reservations are parcels of land that they have held on to for hundreds of years of settler pressure. Maintaining and preserving contemporary landholdings is crucial to the continuance of their communities, culture, and identity. The reservation is a place where the Iroquois practice their customs and rituals. Many urban Iroquois return to these homelands to be culturally and spiritually refreshed among their friends and kin. The Iroquois strive to retain their sovereignty, independence, and culture on their reservation communities.

Chippewa Fishing and Treaty Rights in Michigan, Wisconsin, and Minnesota

Many tribes in the northeast continue to struggle to gain national recognition, to maintain cultural communities, and to assert treaty rights. One of the most prominent examples of Native assertion of treaty rights involves the retention of fishing and hunting privileges among the Chippewa (Anishnabe) of Wisconsin and Minnesota.

The Chippewa in the upper Great Lakes region retained the right to hunt, fish, and gather on lands they sold through treaties to the United States government in the mid-1800s. The United States Constitution states that "treaties are the supreme law of the land"; states may not interfere with such treaties since they are based on the notion that Indian nations are sovereign and thus have rights to self-determination and self-government. In the early 1980s, the Chippewa began to reassert their aboriginal rights to hunt, fish, and gather in areas specified in treaties that were negotiated in the nineteenth century. This reassertion of treaty rights resulted in legal disputes. On January 25, 1983, a federal court agreed with the Lake Superior Chippewa that hunting, fishing and gathering rights still were reserved and protected in Chippewa treaties. This decision is known as the Voight Decision. Later, the U.S. Supreme Court refused to hear an appeal of the Voight Decision. Subsequently, federal judges returned the case to district court to "determine the scope of state regulation." Recent court decisions have defined the scope of Chippewa hunting, fishing, and gathering rights in Wisconsin so that they have a right:

> (1) to harvest and sell hunting, fishing, and gathering products,
> (2) to exercise these rights on private land if necessary to produce a modest living, and
> (3) to harvest a quantity sufficient to produce a modest living.

In addition, portions of the game and forest products (excluding commercial timber) available to the Chippewa through their treaty rights have been quantified in court rulings since the Voight decision. In 1991, the rulings in the Federal District Court implementing the Voight decision were allowed to stand since neither the Chippewa nor the State of Wisconsin appealed them by the deadline of May 1991. On May 20, 1991, the Chippewa announced their decision not to appeal with the following message:

> The . . . Lake Superior Chippewa . . . have preserved . . . [their hunting, fishing and gathering] rights for generations to come, [and they] . . . have this day foregone their right to further appeal . . . . They do this as a gesture of peace and friendship towards the people of Wisconsin, in a spirit they hope may be reciprocated on the part of the general citizenry and officials of this state.

The path to resolving Chippewa fishing rights was littered with racial conflict. During the Indian

Anishnabe man and woman gather wild rice from canoe in Minnesota. Courtesy of the Minnesota Historical Society.

spearfishing seasons in the late 1980s, Chippewa were subjected to violent harassment by non-Indians while attempting to exercise their treaty rights. They were also subject to numerous racial slurs by non-Indians. Anti-spearfishing slogans included: "Save a Walleye; spear a squaw" and "Custer had the right idea." A suit filed by the American Civil Liberties Union on behalf of the Chippewa served to deter some of the more ardent anti-Indian violent protests by the 1990 fishing season. Recently, the Chippewa have exercised their sovereignty by establishing gambling halls on their reservations.

Termination and the Menominee Nation of Wisconsin

In the 1950s, the U.S. government embarked on a policy to terminate the treaties and reservations of American Indian nations. The Menominee, a northeast Indian nation, was the first to be stripped of treaty rights under this policy. Although they were one of the most self-sufficient Indian nations, the Menominee were not prepared to cope with the withdrawal of federal services and trust responsibilities by the time their termination became final in 1961. Although criticism of the termination policy was rapidly mounting in Congress from 1958–60, the Menominee were unsuccessful in having their termination decision reevaluated.

Menominee Enterprises, Inc. (MEI) was set up to manage the tribe's forests, lumber mill, land, and other assets after termination, but it gave too much power to non-Menominee individuals over Menominee affairs. While the Menominee were made shareholders in the new corporation, a Milwaukee trust company controlled a block vote of minors and incompetents (almost 50 percent of the shareholder votes). When the Menominee reservation became Menominee county, taxes became unrealistically high, unemployment rose, medical care deteriorated and a large part of the housing stock became substandard. In 1967, MEI contracted with a land developer to subdivide lakefront property for sale to vacationers so that the tax base could be broadened. This decision outraged almost every Menominee, leading to the creation of DRUMS (Determination of Rights and Unity for Menominee Shareholders), which filed suit against MEI. The group also protested land sales to outsiders and advocated the restoration of federal jurisdiction on the Menominee reservation. In 1975, Congressional legislation was finally passed to restore the Menominee treaty rights and federal trust status.

Maine Indian Claims

Other Northeastern Indian groups have struggled to keep their land base and identity as the Iroquois have. In 1777, the U.S. government negotiated a treaty with the Maine Indians. In exchange for their assistance in the American Revolution, the government promised to protect the Maine Indians (this treaty, however, was never ratified and the U.S. government did not provide protection). In 1791, the Passamaquoddy Nation of Maine ceded all but 23,000 of its acres to the Commonwealth of Massachusetts (at this time, Massachusetts had jurisdiction over what is now the State of Maine). Another Maine Indian nation, the Penobscot, ceded almost all of its land through treaties in 1796 and 1818 and a land sale in 1833. The validity of these agreements was not questioned until 1972, when the Passamaquoddy Tribe asked the United States government to sue the State of Maine, arguing that the treaties and agreements had never been approved by the U.S. government. The attorney for the Passamaquoddy stated that the lack of approval of the agreements by the federal government rendered Massachusetts, and later Maine, in violation of the Indian Trade and Intercourse Act of 1790, which required the approval of the U.S. government for any transfer of lands from Indian ownership. The Secretary of the Interior, however, did not agree with the Maine Indians (the Interior Department held that the Maine Indians were not a federally recognized tribe) and did not sue; the Maine Indians went to court to claim approximately two thirds of the state of Maine. Basically, the following were the legal issues involved:

> (1) ascertaining the legality of applying the Indian Trade and Intercourse Act to the Passamaquoddy Indians;
> (2) resolving whether the Act instituted a trust relationship between the United States and the tribe;
> (3) determining whether the U.S. could deny the tribe's request to sue on the basis that there was no trust relationship.

Subsequently, the federal district court held in favor of the tribe on all points, stating that the language of the Act protected the lands of "any . . . tribe of Indians," and that the Passamaquoddy were, indeed, a tribe. The case was appealed to the circuit court and it reaffirmed the rulings of the lower court. However, its ruling narrowly defined the case, holding that the U.S. government had never sufficiently severed the trust relationship with the Maine Indians. The court also stated that it did not foreclose later consideration of whether Congress or the tribe should be deemed in some manner to have acquiesced in, or Congress to have ratified, the tribe's land transactions with Maine.

The state of Maine argued in this case that (1) the Intercourse Acts were never intended to apply to the thirteen original colonies after they became states; (2) the Indians transferred the lands before the Intercourse Act of 1790; and (3) in ratifying the process by which Maine was separated from Massachusetts and admitted as a state in 1820, Congress approved implicitly "all treaties concluded by Massachusetts up to that time."

This decision forced the federal government to act since the president, the Congress, the state, and the tribe all wanted a speedy and less costly solution to the case than continued adjudication. Negotiations began in earnest in 1977 when a report to President Jimmy Carter recommended: (1) the appropriation of $25 million for the Passamaquoddy and Penobscot tribes; (2) requiring the state of Maine to convey a 100,000-acre tract of land to the U.S. government,which would act as a trustee for the tribes; (3) giving assurances to the tribes that U. S. Bureau of Indian Affairs benefits would be accorded them in the future; (4) asking the state of Maine to continue state benefits to the tribes at current fiscal levels; (5) requiring the secretary of the interior to obtain 400,000 additional acres in the claims area for Maine Indians to purchase at fair market value, if so desired by them; (6) that, having received the consent of the state of Maine that it will accomplish the items in points 2 and 4 above, Congress, with tribal consent, shall extinguish all remaining aboriginal title to all lands in Maine; (7) that if tribal consent cannot be obtained, Congress will extinguish all aboriginal title, and the tribes' cases would then proceed through the judicial system to recover or not recover state owned land; (8) that if the consent of the state of Maine cannot be obtained, Congress will appropriate 25 million dollars for the use and benefit of the tribes and will extinguish all aboriginal title whereupon tribes' cases would proceed through the courts against the state-owned land in Maine.

In 1980, after protracted negotiation, the Maine Indians finally reached a settlement that implemented many of the above points while avoiding the pitfalls of numbers 7 and 8. At the signing of the Maine Indian Claims Settlement Act of 1980, President Carter asserted:

> This should be a proud day for . . . the tribes who placed their trust in the system that has not always treated them fairly, the leaders of the state of Maine who came openly to the bargaining table, the landowners who helped to make the settlement a reality by offering land for sale that they might not otherwise have wanted to sell, the members of Congress who realize the necessity of acting and all the citizens of Maine who have worked together to resolve this problem of land title.

If the President had not taken the lead in seeking a consensus, a long and costly court process or unilateral act by Congress might have resulted. But Carter seized the initiative by developing a reasonable set of recommendations and appointing a team to represent the U.S. government in negotiations with the Indians and Maine. In effect, Carter forced both the state of Maine and the Indians to negotiate an equitable solution to the Maine Indians' Claims case.

Contemporary Connecticut Indian Land Claims

Other cases involving the land claims of Indians of the Northeast have been working their way through the courts, but Congress and the courts have been slow to act on such suits in the 1980s. In the late 1970s, suits—filed in Connecticut by the Schaghticoke tribe, the Western Pequot tribe, and the Mohegan tribe—seeking lands allegedly alienated in violation of the Indian Trade and Intercourse Act of 1790, met with varying results. The Western Pequot obtained a settlement of their claims during the Reagan administration. A federal district court also held that the Mohegan were a tribe and thus had been violated under the Intercourse Act; the Supreme Court upheld this decision by refusing to review the lower court's decision. The Schaghticoke case remains unresolved, but the Schaghticoke Reservation of 400 acres of allotted land in Connecticut remains secure as a basis for rebuilding the Schaghticoke Nation.

Claims by Massachusetts Indians in the Last Generation

In 1974, the Wampanoag tribe of Gay Head sought recovery of 5,000 acres of land, and in 1976, the town of Gay Head, Massachusetts, voted to deed certain lands to the Indians. While some Indians have agreed to this proposal, others opposed, and final action had to be approved by the state of Massachusetts. The Wampanoag claims were further clouded in 1976, when the Mashpee tribe (Wampanoag) filed suit in federal court to recover 17,000 acres allegedly alienated in violation of the Intercourse Act by the state of Massachusetts. The federal courts subsequently held that the Mashpee were not a tribe and were therefore not subject to the act. The defense questioned the Mashpee's identity as Native Americans, alleging that the Mashpee had American Indian, Caucasian, and African-American blood. It is significant that Native Americans are the only American ethnic group that must legally "prove" their identity by blood quantum and that such exclusive and unequal standards were entertained in the U.S. court system. Contradictions in the court's decisions in these claims matters awaited further clarification. Finally, in 1987, the U.S. government formally recognized the Wampanoag Council of Gay Head, Massachusetts.

Recent New York Indian Land Claims

In New York, the Oneida, Cayuga, and St. Regis Mohawk also filed claims under the Intercourse Act. In 1970, the Oneida (New York, Wisconsin, and the Thomas Band Council of Ontario) filed suit for damages for the use of 100,000 acres obtained by New York without the approval of the U.S. government. Although the court ruled that the lands were illegally taken and that damages are in order, there has been little progress in finalizing an agreement. In 1979, the Oneida filed another claim for five million acres, but to date there has been no final resolution of this case.

The Cayuga laid claim to 64,000 acres in New York and got a negotiated settlement that included a $4 million trust fund and a 5,481 acre reservation in return for the extinguishment of the 64,000 acre claim. The land for the settlement was to come from a national forest land and a state park. However, the House of Representatives in 1980 failed to pass legislation to implement the negotiated settlement, and the Cayuga sought the return of the 64,000 acres and damages. The final resolution of this suit is still pending.

The St. Regis Mohawk filed land claims in upper New York State. A proposed settlement in 1980 would have granted them a $7.5 million federal trust fund and 9,750 acres of state land. The case is still under negotiation.

The land claims of the Oneida, Cayuga and Mohawk nations are among the most difficult claims cases of the twentieth century, and it will take years to settle and fully implement the negotiated agreements. However, these cases received a boost in 1985 when the Supreme Court held in *County of Oneida v. Oneida Indian Nation* that Oneida lands transferred over 175 years earlier had violated the Indian Intercourse Act. In a landmark decision in American Indian law, the court's opinion found no applicable statute of limitations and no legal basis to deny the Oneida's land claim. The *Oneida* case established important legal principles that apply to all pending and future Eastern Indian land claims.

Current Narragansett Indian Claims

In Rhode Island, the Narragansett Indians negotiated a claim with private landholders, the state of Rhode Island, representatives from the Carter Administration, and the town of Charlestown, where the claim was located. The agreement hammered out by the above parties provided the basis for state legislation and a federal statute that provided for the extinguishment of all Narragansett land claims in exchange for 900 acres from the state and another 900 acres to be purchased at federal expense. Subsequently, the Narragansett chartered a state corporation to manage the 1,800 acres of land. To implement the act, the U.S. government established a $3.5 million settlement fund.

Analysis of Intercourse Act Claims in the Northeast

The court decision that resulted in the Maine Indians obtaining resources and a larger land base clearly makes it easier for them to maintain their communities in the contemporary world. Other Indian groups in the Northeast that filed subsequent claims have had some successes and some failures. The most successful solutions to these claims issues come when tribal governments, Indian interest groups, Indian individuals and the federal and state governments are involved in the formulation and implementation of claims settlements. The most important case to date has been *County of Oneida v. Oneida Indian Nation*, since it upheld the American Indian argument that there is no applicable statute of limitations on the claims of Eastern Indians based on the Indian Intercourse Act. In 1985, another important administrative decision made by the Federal Internal Revenue Service helped the cause of American Indian recognition among Eastern Indians. When the IRS recognized the Pamunkey tribe of Virginia as a state (a *bona fide* governmental entity within the United States) for purposes of the Tribal Government Tax Status Act, the IRS, and by implication the U.S. government, asserted that the Pamunkey Nation of Virginia could exercise government functions under existing American Indian legislation. Eastern American Indian tribes have struggled to maintain their identity and land base in spite of overwhelming demographic pressures, obstacles, and land disputes; the legal ambiguities relating to the recognition or non-recognition of the Mashpee Indians of Massachusetts and other groups in the East also demonstrated the devastating results of non-recognition. (See also the subsection on nonrecognized tribes in Chapter 9.)

Ultimately, responsibility for changing American Indian policies rests with all of American society since the limits of such settlements are determined by the parameters of public opinion. If there is to be an equitable settlement of American Indians claims and issues in the Northeast, the general public and the Indian participants must both have a concept of the larger American Indian policy that squarely recognizes Native American and U.S. sovereignty and seeks to develop a plan of action that appreciates the complex forces, existing governmental entities, and special interests.

Conclusion

While Indian groups in the Northeast have won important precedent-setting cases in the last generation, it is important to note that the Iroquois and others have also been active in the international arena in presenting their claims over the taking of Indian lands, unfair leases, and restrictions on tribal religious practices. There is a growing body of international human rights law that recognizes that Native Americans are entitled to political and economic self-determination as well as religious freedom. Although the early European colonists who came to the Northeast did not appreciate the sovereignty of American Indians, contemporary federal and international law is paving the way for American Indians of the Northeast and elsewhere to survive as distinct communities with well-defined sovereign rights and powers.

Donald A. Grinde, Jr.
California Polytechnic State University,
San Luis Obispo

♦ SOUTHEASTERN INDIANS

When Europeans reached the southeastern United States, they encountered Native peoples who were the predecessors of tribes known today as the Catawba, the Cherokee, the Creek, the Chickasaw, the Choctaw, and the Seminole. Some of these peoples were emerging from the decline of the once widespread culture identified as Mississippian, a term referring to practices associated with the construction of ceremonial mounds central to a village and its cultivated fields of corn, beans, and squash. Although the earthen mounds were passing into disuse, the lives of the succeeding Native peoples still were town centered. In the sixteenth century the villages of the southeastern peoples were distributed across a territory bounded by the Atlantic Ocean, the Gulf of Mexico, the Trinity River in present Texas, and the Ohio River.

Central to the ritual life of these peoples was the Green Corn ceremony, an elaborate thanksgiving and renewal festival usually observed in mid-summer. The occasion was significant because the maturation of new corn promised food for winter and seeds for spring; crop failures threatened immediate hunger and long-term famine. The anthropologist Charles Hudson believes "we would have something approaching the Green Corn Ceremony if we combined Thanksgiving, New Year's festivities, Yom Kippur, Lent, and Mardi Gras."

The successful farming reflected in the Green Corn celebration was only part of the economy of the Southeastern Indians. Hunting also provided important dietary ingredients. Like farming, hunting was interconnected with spiritual beliefs. Hunters prayed to the spirits of the game before they went hunting, lest offending the animal spirits mean no game for the next hunt. Likewise, once on the hunt the hunter killed no more than needed, since useless slaughter also might anger the spirits of the game.

Even as the Southeastern peoples shared common practices in farming, hunting, and spiritual belief, they also shared games. One of the most widely played was

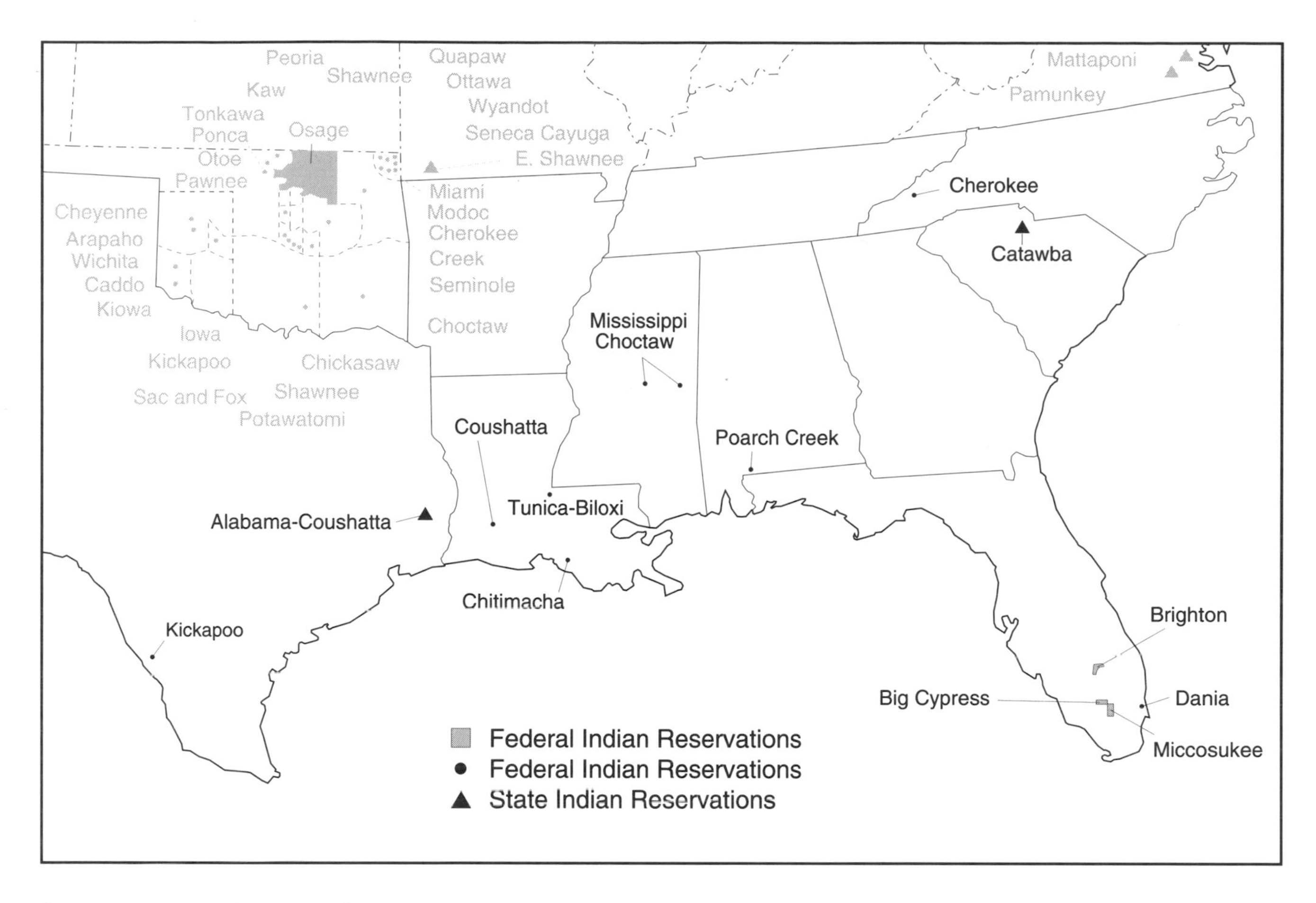

Contemporary southeastern tribes.

the ball game, vividly captured by the American painter George Catlin in his 1834 portrayals of a Choctaw ball play in Oklahoma. So great was Catlin's fascination that he depicted not only two scenes from a match, one with the ball in the air and the other with it on the ground, but also left a portrait of the Choctaw ball player named He-Who-Drinks-the-Juice-of-Stone. The contest was played by teams from competing villages on a level field perhaps 200 yards long. The object was for a team to throw a deerskin ball (stuffed with deer or squirrel hair) past the opposition's goal post at the other end of the field. In the southeastern versions of the game, the players carried two ball play sticks, which could be used to scoop up the ball and forward it.

Two other rituals common to the Southeastern cultures were the use of sacred tobacco and the black drink. The black drink, as the Europeans called it, was a tea brewed from the roasted leaves of the yaupon holly, a shrub which contained caffeine like coffee. Because the black drink ceremony was often a preliminary to any major decision or celebration, the participants were left highly stimulated. So important was this shrub to ceremonial life that it was cultivated in small patches far outside its normal range.

A second plant-oriented ritual involved the use of tobacco in a pipe, a ceremony associated with welcome and with diplomacy. The sacred or so-called white tobacco was put in a pipe and passed around the circle of participants, a practice which nauseated English Lieutenant Henry Timberlake on his visit to the Cherokee villages in 1760s.

Another similarity for these southeastern peoples was their life in villages, often bound together by common practices and language into a tribe. Most villages were governed by a council of elders and warriors presided over by a chief, who usually came to power through a combination of talent, accomplishment, and membership in an influential family or clan. In most southeastern societies, descent was traced through the mother's line.

Beyond the family, clan membership was extremely important, since clans transcended village boundaries, thus affording the individual a social and political connection throughout the tribe. The mixed-blood Creek leader Alexander McGillivray, for example, had the advantages of bilinguality, basic education, service as a British trading agent, and opportunity through the death of the Upper Creek principal warrior in 1782, but it was his mother's influential Wind clan that provided him a Creek political power base from 1783 to 1793, when he was a primary Creek leader.

Tribes were loose associations of villages bound together by language, heritage, custom, and proximity of location. None were tightly structured by modern standards; the Creek, for example, more appropriately might be called a confederation, since they were formed as much by outside pressure as by powerful cultural bonds. Certain villages in a tribal grouping sometimes were more influential or sacred than others, such as the Cherokee beloved town of Chota on the Little Tennessee River in present-day Tennessee; yet even the leader of a prominent town really had no more power than persuasion could provide. Efforts by European colonial powers to designate emperors for particular tribes were largely empty gestures. In most instances, if all the tribal villages or a percentage of them voted for war or approved a treaty, that decision prevailed only while those villages continued their support. Withdrawal of any village's support freed its people from obligations, a practice that frustrated Europeans, who professed to operate in terms of permanent treaties, boundaries, and alliances. Native peoples, however, were more attuned to political flexibility, social harmony, and spiritual significance than to contractual agreements.

Indeed the religious values of the southeastern peoples might be expressed best in terms of balance or harmony of human beings with one another as well as with the natural and spiritual worlds in which they saw themselves. All things had spirits, either good or evil; success in life depended on the careful cultivation of these spirits by the proper behaviors or the appropriate remedy if you were guilty of an act of disharmony. Even so grave an act as murder might be compensated for if the proper remedies were taken.

The old harmonies were shattered forever when the Europeans arrived. The first visitation for which there is substantial historical evidence was led by the Spanish adventurer Hernando de Soto. During 1540–41, de Soto led his expedition from Tampa Bay into Georgia and then to the Mississippi River. From these newcomers the Southeastern peoples learned of a foreign culture, and, unfortunately, of fatal European diseases, against which the Native peoples carried no inherited resistance; they died by the thousands. Continued Spanish exploration brought settlements along the Gulf and Atlantic borders from St. Augustine to Pensacola in present-day Florida.

Ultimately, European imperial rivalry brought French and English adventurers to the southeastern region. By the early seventeenth century, Spain, England, and France expanded their global territories by establishing outposts, subjugating Native peoples, and developing an economic exchange. Although all three promoted conversion of the Native peoples to Christianity, only the Spanish achieved limited and temporary success.

For the Native peoples, the exchange of furs and skins for European manufactures created a major alteration in the balance of their lives. Previously hunters had pursued the white-tailed deer only as need dictated. Because deer range only a five square mile area during their lifetimes, only careful avoidance of overhunting and controlled burning of forest underbrush (which renewed the vegetation) had maintained the deer herds. The new trade changed the balance, as European market demands for leather enticed the hunters to kill more than they needed. By the 1730s, there was a noticeable decline in the Southeastern deerskin trade.

At the same time, the trade goods impacted cultural patterns. The attraction of finished cloth and clothing items persuaded villagers that bartering was far easier than tanning deerskins. Desirable luxury items also could be obtained in the trade, which provided mirrors, knives, awls, scissors, and jew's harps. As a result, certain handicrafts disappeared, displaced by European weapons, tools, cloth, and decorative goods. Other dramatic trade-induced changes also altered Native societies as alcohol was introduced, gender roles were realigned, and towns became more non-Indian. Beverage alcohol quickly became a curse, as alcoholism and excessive drinking undermined village stability. Alcohol was used by unscrupulous colonials to influence the Native peoples into disadvantageous agreements.

Gender roles, too, were modified by the trade. Formerly these matrilineal, agricultural societies defined roles for males and females in relatively clear, yet balanced terms. Females were important because they bore the children, provided food from the fields, and transformed raw materials into usable products. The trade, however, gave a place of greater importance to the hunters, since commercial hunting brought both staples and luxury goods to the villages. Trading activities also ignored women, since the male-oriented Europeans sought to bargain with the hunters.

Still further social changes took place as traders took up residence in the villages. The households that they developed were patterned after the male-dominated European families. The children of these unions adopted their fathers' entrepreneurial life-styles, thus diluting traditional social practices and increasing the number of mixed bloods. As a result many tribes became economically dominated by mixed blood trader families toward the end of the eighteenth century.

The emergence of these trader-originated families also helped intensify tribal divisions. The mixed blood peoples often were among the first to adopt life-styles similar to their neighbors who were U.S. citizens. Among the Cherokee, the Choctaw, the Chickasaw, and the Creek, the new European cultural orientations were reflected in economic terms, as the mixed bloods used their linguistic, educational, and political advantages to prosper. Ferries, inns, trading posts, and farms most often were owned or controlled by those of mixed ancestry. In the 1830s, when the U.S. government sought to relocate the Southeastern peoples west of the Mississippi River, antagonism between conservatives and mixed blood entrepreneurs heightened arguments over whether or not the tribes should move. After removal, even though they may have lost more both in quality and quantity of life, the mixed bloods were better equipped to start again. Once relocated, they contended for political leadership and held economic control of mills, ferries, inns, stores, and ranching operations.

In the three centuries before their forced move westward, Southeastern tribal governments underwent evolution and transformation. From the earliest contacts, European sought to impose their own governmental views on their new neighbors by designating Indian nations, kings, princesses, and emperors. Such titles had little meaning for the Native peoples, who continued their tribal associations until early in the nineteenth century. Only as their populations became more and more mixed blood and as their U.S. neighbors greedily eyed their lands and pressured for removal did the villages and tribal councils seek more formally structured governments, modeled for practical diplomatic purposes after the government of the United States. In the decades just before the tribes were forced westward, they adopted constitutions and created governing bodies that were then transferred west. The Cherokee adopted a constitutional government in 1828, while the Choctaw constitution of 1826–30 proved unstable but was revived again in 1834. The more conservative Creek and Chickasaw retained their traditional government with little change until after removal to Indian Territory, where they adopted constitutional governments in the 1850s and 1860s. Originally they hoped such nation building would help them resist pressure from the United States. However, both before removal and during the period of so-called detribalization in the years between 1880 and 1934, much of this structure was destroyed. In the last fifty years, however, some of tribes have reconstituted their governments into the leadership that serves them today.

During the era of removal, because of the continued focus of basic power at the village level, not every individual tribal member, family, or village participated in the move west. The Native peoples living east of the Mississippi River today testify powerfully to the persistence and cultural tenacity of these peoples against overwhelming odds. Today's descendants of the Southeastern tribal peoples proudly continue to claim the heritage of their ancestors, in most cases virtually undistinguishable from their non-Indian neighbors. In 1990 there were 211,000 persons of Native American descent living in the ten states (North Carolina, South Carolina, Georgia, Florida, Kentucky, Tennessee, Alabama, Mississippi, Arkansas, and Louisiana) considered within the southeastern United States. In addition, Oklahoma has a Native American population of 252,000, many descended from Southeastern peoples. A century and a half after most of the Southeastern peoples were forced to move west, the Catawba, the Cherokee, the Creek, the Seminole, and the Choctaw continue to live in South Carolina, Mississippi, Alabama, North Carolina, and Florida.

The Catawba

Today most Catawba live in the vicinity of Rock Hill, South Carolina, either on a small state-owned reservation or in nearby communities; unlike many Native peoples, all live relatively close to their eighteenth century homelands. Because they are few in number and lack a large land base or potentially profitable natural resource, they are not well known. Their mere existence testifies powerfully to their persistence, resilience, and flexibility. Time after time observers predicted the end of the Catawba, yet they still survive.

As the British colonies emerged in the late seventeenth century, Indians settled along the upper Wateree River in South Carolina were identified as the Catawba nation. From the outset of Catawba-South Carolina relations, the Catawba followed a policy of friendly cooperation. During the American Revolution they served as scouts for the South Carolinians. They paid dearly for this when a British raiding force destroyed their settlements. In the years after the revolution, however, the Catawba wrapped themselves in the flag of patriotism shared with other revolutionary veterans, thus making it difficult for South Carolina to ignore them. Because they could claim no ancestral homeland for time immemorial, and because of colonial South Carolina's rapid expansion, the Catawba had sought and received a 144,000 acre reservation in 1763. For the next forty years they persisted by leasing their land, selling pottery and skins, practicing subsistence farming, and serving as slave catchers for tidewater slave owners. After 1800, the equation changed, when slavery and upland cotton marched into the Piedmont, the region of rolling hills between the level coastal plain of the Atlantic ocean and the rugged mountains of the southern Appalachians. At that point Catawba land became more valuable than tribal slave catching. Reduced in population to no more than thirty families and under unrelenting pressure to sell their land, the Catawba signed a treaty with South Carolina in 1840 exchanging their 144,000 acres for $5,000 and promises of assistance in relocation. Many moved to North Carolina in a fruitless attempt to live with the Cherokee. Within twelve years they returned to South Carolina, where they were given 630 acres of their old land.

After the Civil War, their survival faced another threat in the rise of Jim Crow legislation; in 1879 South Carolina law forbade interracial marriage. Freedom to move back and forth socially and economically became further restricted. Consequently the Catawba either had to cling to the security of Indianness or face an insurmountable color barrier that placed them in the "black" category. The Catawba responded by asserting their Indianness through speaking Catawba and expanding the production and sale of Indian crafts. Then, in a departure from their traditional resistance toward converting to Christianity, they welcomed Mormon missionaries in 1883. Over time the Mormons assisted the Catawba in building community cohesion and gaining education through the establishment of Catawba schools, a necessity in South Carolina, where the only schools for non-whites were for blacks. In the last fifty years, however, a modified racial climate has eliminated the need for separate Catawba schools; there are none listed in the 1990 report of the National Advisory Council on Indian Education.

In 1943, they became legal citizens of South Carolina and federally recognized Indians, which means they were acknowledged as a tribe and eligible for the governmental benefits available to existing tribes. The next year an additional 3,400 acres of land were purchased for them. Although this step was intended to allow the Catawba to become small farmers, that option proved unprofitable. By 1959, consequently, they voted to terminate their tribal status and sell most of their lands. Under the plan, any tribal member could choose land from the reservation tract or a cash settlement from the sale of unclaimed portions of the reservation. On July 2, 1960, the final tribal roll listed 631 Catawba; termination came on July 1, 1962.

Despite their vote to terminate and to sell the reservation, the Catawba persist, which is an astonishing testimony to their survival in the face of adversity. Some still have ties to the existing Old Reservation, others make and sell Catawba pottery, and a few have participated in the Indian awareness movements. In these modern Catawba still survive the spirits of ancestral heroes many decades after the predicted demise of the tribe.

The Cherokee

The Cherokee Indians who once inhabited the southern Appalachian mountains live today in widely separated areas. Those of the Eastern Band live in western North Carolina on or near the Qualla Boundary, as the Eastern Reservation is called; those who claim membership in the Western Band live in Oklahoma. There are many from both bands who live and work as Cherokee Americans throughout the United States. Those who keep their language alive speak an Iroquoian language with some regional variations.

According to archaeological evidence, the Cherokee and their ancestors lived in the southern Appalachians for several hundred years before the Europeans arrived. Seventeenth-century visitors to the Cherokee villages found them located in mountain river valleys where there was adequate space for dwellings, council houses, and agricultural fields. Because the Cherokee were a matrilineal society, their fields were controlled by the Cherokee women. Women of great influence became known as Beloved Women, often working behind the scenes in shaping decisions. A woman who had taken her husband's place in war might be awarded the title War Woman. That the role of women still has a powerful effect today is reflected in Wilma Mankiller's elections as tribal chair of the Western Cherokee (1987 and 1991).

In the late seventeenth century, there were approximately 30,000 Cherokee living in about sixty settlements. Within one hundred years, smallpox, other epidemics, and warfare had reduced their population to only 7,500.

From the early seventeenth through twentieth centuries, the major point of contention between the Cherokee and the Europeans was land. As the venerable chief Old Tassel bluntly put it in 1777: "Brothers . . . the issue is about our land." From 1783 to 1835 the Cherokee fought a losing battle in defense of their lands. After the revolution, land-hungry settlers crossed the mountains in search of homesteads; then came eager planters seeking new soil for upland cotton cultivation. By 1825, some Cherokee had relocated voluntarily to Arkansas and Texas, hoping to escape the encroaching Americans. Those still in the east were divided between the highly acculturated mixed bloods and the more conservative, traditionalist full bloods.

In 1835, a minority of the tribal leaders, primarily mixed bloods, signed the controversial Treaty of New Echota, which led to the eviction of those Cherokee living in South Carolina, Georgia, Tennessee, and Alabama. In North Carolina, however, about 1,000 Cherokee managed to escape removal with the cooperation of sympathetic state officials. According to their understanding of the treaties in 1817, 1819, and 1835, the Cherokee claimed North Carolina citizenship. One North Carolinian, William H. Thomas (or Wil-Usdi, as the Cherokee called him) bought land in his name for the Cherokee, went to court in their defense, and visited Washington on behalf of the Eastern Band's share in any general settlement with all Cherokee.

When the majority of the Cherokee moved to the Indian Territory (present-day Oklahoma), the tribe's internal problems were not solved. Hatred deepened after the political murders on June 22, 1839, of John

Ridge, Major Ridge, and Elias Boudinot, three Cherokee leaders who had signed the despised removal agreement.

During the early years west of the Mississippi, the Cherokee sought to survive economically, establish a workable government acceptable to all, reduce tribal factionalism, avoid rivalries with traditional tribal enemies, and maintain relations with the federal bureaucracy. Even in the west the Cherokee could not escape demands on their land base. Ranchers desired the Cherokee Outlet, a sixty-mile-wide strip running west from the 96th to the 100th meridians. After the Civil War, the federal government demanded land as compensation because the Cherokee Nation officially joined the South; this action ignored the loyal Union service of several hundred non-slaveowners. Then promoters of all stripes began eyeing the unused or unassigned Cherokee lands. Even after the Cherokee ceded their unassigned lands to the federal government in 1891, speculators schemed to divide the tribal land into individual allotments. Land interests ultimately prevailed with the passage of the Dawes Act (1887) and the Curtis Act (1898); the first divided the lands and the second eliminated tribal governments. The Curtis Act, however, led to wholesale fraud. After Oklahoma statehood in 1907 almost every species of trickery imaginable was practiced; the Cherokee were bribed, threatened, cajoled, bought out, and generally manipulated. With few exceptions all the mineral rich or arable lands fell into the hands of non-Cherokee.

Today, the Western Cherokee number more than 175,000, many of whom live in northeastern Oklahoma. Despite the frequent assertions of some non-Indians that there are fewer Indians, the opposite is true. There are more numerically, and, of those, an increasing number are proud to identify themselves so.

During the 1980s and 1990s, the Western Cherokee have reasserted themselves under the leadership of Principal Chief Wilma Mankiller. An inspirational leader who empowers people to independence, Mankiller was re-elected with more than 83 percent of the vote. Community re-building and building since the early 1980s has resulted in tribally owned businesses, including defense subcontracting plants and horticultural operations. The annual budget for the tribe is $54 million. Whether the accomplishment is as basic as the men, women, and children of the tiny village of Bell laying sixteen miles of pipe for running water, or as venturesome as the construction of a hydroelectric facility worth millions, power is returning to these Western Cherokee peoples at every level. The key to their success, says Mankiller, is that Cherokee never give up.

During the first three decades of the twentieth century, the Eastern Band wrestled with the related difficulties of tribal membership, enrollment, and allotment. When a tribal roll was opened, more than 12,000 people applied to be included; tribal leaders protested that no more than 2,000 could possibly be eligible. The long disagreement over this matter delayed any action of dividing the land until the Indian Reorganization Act of 1934 ended allotment of Indian land. There was a further economic decline in the 1930s when a chestnut blight destroyed more than 60 percent of the timber on the tribal lands. After World War II some economic recovery came to the Eastern Cherokee in the form of highways, a national park, and a historical drama. The roads needed for modern automobile travel were developed by those seeking creation of the Great Smoky Mountains National Park, whose lands lay adjacent to the Cherokee homeland. If visitors who came to the park in search of natural splendor could be tempted to stay overnight, an income-producing tourist industry might develop. By the early 1950s the Cherokee Historical Association had commissioned and then produced "Unto These Hills," an emotional drama based on the Cherokee experience. Regardless of its historical accuracy, it attracts many visitors, as do Oconoluftee Village and the Museum of the Cherokee Indian. All are aimed at affording a glimpse of Cherokee culture, distinct from the trinket businesses, where a few Cherokee pose for tourists in Plains Indian costumes. Even this prosperity, however, has had its problems, since much of the money and influence tends to be controlled by a relatively few Cherokee.

A cross section of Eastern Cherokee society includes tribal members with relatively stable incomes as well as many living near or below the poverty level. The relative isolation of many tribal members plus the seasonal nature of the tourist industry continues to work to the economic disadvantage of many Cherokee. One unusual bright spot on the economic horizon has been the development of an enormous bingo parlor, where almost 4,000 people can play for prizes worth thousands of dollars.

Today, there are more than 9,500 Eastern Cherokee who share an abiding sense of place and kinship, as well as an egalitarianism that makes tribal politics both interesting and fractious. Most of those who live on the Qualla Boundary, as the reservation for the Eastern Band of Cherokee is known, work in Waynesville or Sylva, North Carolina, while those from the outlying conservative Cherokee village known as Snowbird work for the National Forest Service, the Tennessee Valley Authority, or the Stanley Furniture plant in nearby Robbinsville, North Carolina. In an attempt to guarantee employment for their children, the Eastern Cherokee paid $28.8 million for the Carolina Mirror Company in 1986; as the tribal council leader has indicated, there is no future without jobs. Jobs will mean the Cherokee can continue their tradition of mixed dependency on both non-Indian economic culture and personal self-reliance that has allowed them to face the twenty-first century as both Cherokee and Americans.

The Creek

At the end of the twentieth century, the Creek, like their former adversaries the Cherokee, live in widely separated areas. Before the Civil War, the majority of the Creek moved to Indian Territory, but a remnant remained in Alabama. Today their descendants live in Alabama, Oklahoma, and across the United States.

After the arrival of the Europeans, the Muskogee peoples moved inland away from the expanding newcomers. Clustering on Ochese Creek as well as on the Chattahoochee River, the villagers were labeled Creek by British traders from Charleston, South Carolina. Those nearest to Charleston were called the Lower Creek, those farther away the Upper Creek. Expansion of Georgia after 1733 pushed these peoples deeper into the interior, eventually into present Alabama. From their towns they attempted to play off the European powers seeking dominance in eastern North America.

Wherever they located, Creek lands lay in the path of the westward expanding United States. Creek defensive actions brought repeated invasions until 1814, when forces under General Andrew Jackson defeated them at the Battle of Horseshoe Bend. In the minds of Jackson and his fellow expansionists, Creek resistance legitimized removal beyond the Mississippi River. Although the Creek ceded 20 million acres of southern Georgia and central Alabama lands at the Treaty of Fort Jackson, the Jacksonians would not be satisfied until all Native Americans east of the Mississippi had been relocated. The Creek War provided a convenient excuse for Tennessee to demand the removal of the Creek, the Cherokee, and the Chickasaw. Georgia politicians, moreover, were eager to manipulate the Creek agency for purposes of profit and land speculation. When Georgia succeeded in expelling the Creek, her neighbor Alabama acted to keep the refugees moving west. First, Alabama extended her laws over all the Indian lands in the state. Then, under the Treaty of 1832, the Creek Nation in the east was no longer recognized by the federal or state governments. Creeks who wished to claim allotments and stay in the east were soon subjected to constant harassment, as their white neighbors sought to drive them away. From 1820 to 1840, by one means or another, the Creek were forced to move to Indian Territory. They were exposed to a foreign climate, often without the barest of necessities, despite promised aid from the U.S. government. Dispossessed and abandoned, many died, yet others survived, intent on rebuilding the Creek Nation in the west. Those who remained behind in Alabama eked out a marginal existence, while resisting pressure to move. They insisted that according to the Treaty of Fort Jackson (1814) they could claim a section of land. Despite the pressures against them, a few held on; land belonging to the McGhee family was reaffirmed in 1836. Lynn McGhee's 240 acre claim at the headwaters of Perdido Creek became the center for three nearby settlements that came to be known as the Poarch Band of Creek. In 1975 the Poarch Band of Creek petitioned the U.S. Government for recognition and were acknowledged as a federally recognized tribe in 1984. Today these Poarch Creek peoples number more than 400; in 1990 their tribal chairman was Eddie L. Tullis, who was also chairperson of the National Advisory Council on Indian Education.

Christy Godwin O'Barr, Poarch Creek Indian Princess in 1987, sings at a 1987 Thanksgiving powwow.

The Seminole

During the years of Creek withdrawal westward, a number of Lower Creek migrated intro present Florida. In order to distinguish them from their kinsmen, British officials called these separatists the Seminole Creek, or Seminole, a corruption of the Spanish *cimarrone*. Quickly adapting to their new environment, they became skillful herders, raising sleek ponies and fat cattle on the grassy savannas. So complete was their cultural adjustment that one of their leading chiefs was named Cowkeeper, who was vividly described in the prose of William Bartram, a Philadelphia botanist who visited the Seminole in the 1770s.

When Georgia frontiersmen expanded farther south, the Seminole retreated again. They continued their adaptation, adopting lighter dress and modifying the Creek cabin so that it became an open-sided dwelling, called a *chiki*, with raised floor and thatched roof. Changes in agricultural patterns followed, since Florida soils differed from those to the north. Ultimately the pressure of expanding plantations and farms pushed the Seminole so far south they had little land.

During the period that these former Creek were becoming Seminole, they attracted the attention of both the neighboring states and the national government. Officials in Georgia, Alabama, and Florida became unhappy because the Seminole would not agree to join the exodus westward by southeastern tribes. Their presence threatened Florida's claim to all the state's lands. At the same time, the Seminole were regarded as dangerous to peace and stability, because they harbored runaway slaves. As long as the Seminole camps remained in Florida, their camps a refuge for runaways, no slave-owning planter could feel secure. For the slaves captured by the Seminole, however, slavery was a much less rigorous institution. Several former slaves rose to positions of influence through their ability as interpreters and their familiarity with plantation lifeways. In the 1830s the increasingly racist and xenophobic society in the southern United States denounced Seminole toleration of African-Americans. Outside the south, ironically, courageous Seminole resistance attracted some public sympathy.

No amount of sympathy, however, changed the federal government's demand that the Seminole move. By force and by forced treaty, the Seminole were transported west. By 1842, there were 2,833 Seminole survivors in Oklahoma. The Oklahoma Seminole of today are the descendants of these refugee peoples.

While many Seminole moved west, small bands in Florida remained hidden deep in Big Cypress Swamp, in the Everglades, and in other isolated areas. During the second half of the nineteenth century and the first decade of the next, these survivors existed by hunting, trapping, and fishing. The fashion industry's demand for bird feathers and animal skins offered them a means to trade for the basic necessities unavailable in nature. Most of their food came from subsistence farming of small patches.

Their fragile lifesystem began to collapse, however, early in the twentieth century. In 1906, Florida began to drain the Everglades in hope of producing more agricultural land for commercial purposes; more people began coming to Florida via the ever expanding railroad system; and both federal and state laws outlawed the use of bird plumes.

In the 1890s, however, Florida officials began buying land as a place for the Seminole to locate. The greatest difficulty arose in trying to persuade these fiercely independent people that they should live on these reservations. By 1932, less than 20 percent of the 562 Florida Seminole had relocated. The spirit of resistance and self-reliance built from years of avoiding the federal government was unlikely to disappear overnight. Living in remote, self-sufficient camps, they supplied their basic needs, but needed cash to buy coffee, salt, sugar, rifles, ammunition, and the seemingly ever-present sewing machine. With the decline of the trade in plumes and hides, seasonal agricultural labor became a source of cash. A few families became part of the growing tourist industry by establishing "commercial villages" where they put on public displays of "Seminole life."

During the 1930s, however, in response both to federal Indian policy and activities by tribal leaders and pro-tribal Florida interest groups, Seminole life patterns began to change. Tracts of land were obtained through purchase and exchange that resulted in the creation of several reservations, two of which were developed into cattle-raising operations. The success of the cattle ranches attracted some Seminole to abandon isolated settlements and relocate on the reservations. A new and more dependable economic base likewise meant an improved quality of life for the Seminole. At the same time the creation of federal agencies for the Seminole increased the tribe's exposure to and cooperation with federal officials. Also during the 1930s and 1940s came the first major success in converting the Seminole to Christianity. All of these changes went a long way toward forming the lives of the twentieth-century Seminole. Indeed the adaptability they have displayed since the seventeenth century has assisted them over and over again. Thereby they were able to deal with the termination policies of the 1950s as well as the creation and federal recognition in 1957 of the Seminole Tribe of Florida, Inc., followed in 1962 by the separation of a group who wished to be recognized as the Miccosukee Tribe of Indians.

Today, both the Seminole and the Miccosukee survive in heavily populated, non-Indian Florida. Beginning in 1979, the Seminole began operating a bingo parlor offering 1,700 seats and $10,000 jackpots. Since that time, more parlors have been opened, generating enough revenue to endow tribal scholarships, establish a credit union, and expand the tribal cattle herds. Despite this success, the tribe must be aware that they receive only 50 percent of the income and that organized crime is always ready to move in. On the environmental front, too, some difficulties may arise, as developers seek far and wide for new sources of natural resources, such as those in the Big Cypress area.

The Choctaw

Before the majority of the Choctaw were forced west in the nineteenth century, their settlements were located in present day central and southern Mississippi, as well as southwestern Alabama. During the seventeenth and eighteenth centuries, their lives were impacted by European newcomers. Although the French (and the Spanish after 1763) at New Orleans were the closest in proximity, enterprising English traders also reached their villages; the trade introduced cloth, firearms, tools, and alcohol. During the late seventeenth and early eighteenth centuries there was also traffic in Indian slaves, an exchange that intensified rivalries with the Chickasaw, the Creek, and other nearby peoples. Trade generated rivalries, as some villages supported the most generous provider of quality goods at the lowest prices, whether France, Spain or Great Britain. Included in the trade-induced stress were the resident traders, whose mixed-blood families later rose to positions of prominence in the tribe.

After the emergence of the United States, Choctaw lands became the stumbling block in Choctaw relations with the new country. Eager land developers paid little attention to Choctaw claims as they laid off lines across maps of the Mississippi Territory. So great was the demand for new acreage that the federal government pressured for rights of way to allow the construction of roads through the Choctaw homeland. Nothing seemed an obstacle to the settlers. From the time the Mississippi Territory was organized in 1798 until removal, politicians repeated their demands for the relocation of the tribes and the distribution of their lands. The cooperation of some Choctaw leaders was bought with cash and other gifts. Choctaw tribal integrity also was undermined by the efforts of missionaries to convert them into Christian farmers, who could practice a market agriculture.

In 1801, the Choctaw signed the Treaty of Fort Adams, hoping a definition of tribal boundaries would satisfy the demands of the United States. No treaty was ever enough, not even the combined results of Fort Adams, Mount Dexter (1805), and Doak's Stand (1820), the latter of which exchanged 9 million acres of Choctaw

Evajean Felihkatubbee, Choctaw Indian woman, cleaning a basket.

homelands for 13 million unfamiliar western acres. Although a few moved voluntarily, most wished to stay. Yet even loyal service as allies during the Creek War of 1813–14 did not protect them, for the determined state of Mississippi moved to terminate all their rights in 1830. By the notorious Dancing Rabbit Creek Treaty in September 1830, the Choctaw signed over their homelands and agreed to emigrate; this was accomplished through a combination of threatened force and the bribery of certain chiefs.

The Choctaw movement west was as painful as those of their southeastern neighbors. Fraud, mismanagement, and corruption marked those in charge of the move, while disease and death stalked the Choctaw each mile. The combined deaths from the journey's difficulties plus subsequent cholera and smallpox outbreaks reduced the tribal population from 18,963 in 1830 to 13,666 by 1860.

Once in the West, the Choctaw tended to follow divisional lines between mixed bloods and full bloods, with the former following the market agricultural economy they had practiced in Mississippi and the latter retreating to subsistence agriculture. Despite privation, drought, and floods, the Choctaw rebuilt their government, their towns, and their farms. By the 1850s their economy had recovered sufficiently to allow them to market cotton, cattle, and timber.

When they moved west, the Choctaw took along their slaves. Because of their close proximity to the Confederate states of Arkansas and Texas, the tribe almost unanimously sided with the Confederacy in 1861. At war's end, however, the Choctaw were forced to abolish slavery and to cede the western portion of their territory, for which they were compensated $300,000.

Yet even as they tried to rebuild once more , the U.S. Government pressured the Choctaw to abandon tribal control in favor of private land ownership. Railroad expansionists clamored for rights-of-way and land grants, while coal developers pressured for mineral rights and access. The end of the Choctaw Nationwas assured by the Curtis Act of 1898, under which the remaining tribal lands in Indian Territory were divided into individual private allotments. The process required the creation of a tribal roll listing 18,981 Oklahoma Choctaw, 5,994 freedmen and their descendants, and 1,639 Choctaw who had moved west from Mississippi after the Civil War. Approximately 1,000 Choctaw still lived in the east. After 1906 there was no tribal government, a status in effect until 1934 when the Indian Reorganization Act allowed a return toward tribal governments; the Choctaw first formed an Advisory Council, but did not elect a tribal chief until 1948.

In Oklahoma today, the tribal government promotes programs aimed at improving the quality of life among the Choctaw people. There is a Choctaw Housing Authority in Hugo, an Indian Hospital in Tallahina, three Indian health clinics, five community centers, and ten Headstart centers. Several businesses also are operated by the Choctaw, including a bingo parlor, a resort complex, and a travel center. Profits from these along with federal funds then can be directed toward projects needed by the tribe.

Those who remained behind in Mississippi were driven into the depths of poverty by the new landowners. Yet the Mississippi Choctaw persisted. After the passage of the Indian Reorganization Act, they moved slowly toward recognition as a separate entity; their cause was helped in 1944 by the creation of a land base, a 16,000 acre reservation. The federal government also sanctioned the Mississippi Choctaw Agency, which assists the seven Choctaw settlements with education and general welfare. With their tribal headquarters at Philadelphia, Mississippi, they have established a development company and created an industrial park, which houses plants producing not only greeting cards but also wiring harnesses and radio speakers for automobiles.

Despite some economic progress, the Mississippi Choctaw lag behind their neighbors in income, employment, education, health care, and housing. Nevertheless, more than 6,000 Choctaw live in Mississippi today, with approximately 4,400 living on the reservation itself. The majority speak both Choctaw and English, but there are continuing adult education efforts aimed at improving language skills and educational attainment. According to the revised tribal constitution of 1975, the Mississippi Choctaw govern themselves under the protection of the federal government. Together with their Oklahoma kin and those living elsewhere, the Choctaw number more than 45,000. Many travel each year to the Choctaw Indian Fair at Pearl River, Mississippi, or to the Tuskahoma, Oklahoma, Labor Day festival to celebrate and preserve their Choctaw heritage.

The Chickasaw

The Chickasaw, kinsmen of the Choctaw with whom they share the Muskogean language and a migration story, lived in present extreme northwestern Alabama, northern Mississippi, western Tennessee, and western Kentucky. Although relatively few in number, the 3,500 to 4,500 Chickasaw gained wide respect for courageously defending their homelands. Their success in defeating French invaders on three different occasions attracted the attention of the British, who won the Chickasaw as allies through exploiting their trade advantage. However, this involved the Chickasaw in an almost unending series of wars against France and her Indian allies. As a result many Chickasaw lives were lost; some losses were replaced, however, by the

Chickasaw practice of adoption and absorption of remnant tribes.

After the defeat of France in 1763, the Chickasaw lived in relative peace for more than twenty years under the leadership of Payamataha and Piomingo. Both these leaders tried to stem the tide of European influences, but pressure to accommodate came from increasing numbers of mixed-blood families, whose success in trade, agriculture, and slavery created a life-style different from the traditional Chickasaw way. During the Revolution, Chickasaw service as British allies brought more outsiders when Loyalists sought refuge in the Chickasaw towns. After the Revolution, the Chickasaw signed a treaty with the United States at Hopewell, South Carolina, in January 1786. The treaty guaranteed the Chickasaw their lands, territories, and the right to manage their own affairs.

Initial U.S. relations with the Chickasaw were ineffective, because the Spanish at New Orleans wooed the Chickasaw. Consequently Chickasaw politics were complicated by rivalries among a Spanish allied party, an American allied party, those who vacillated, and the self-serving mixed bloods. Pressure from the pro-Spanish Creek under Alexander McGillivray added to Chickasaw woes. McGillivray's death in 1793 and the signing of the Treaty of San Lorenzo (1798) reduced Chickasaw difficulties slightly.

Despite internal political rivalries, the Chickasaw became increasingly tied to the United States. After 1802 a government trading post operated at Chickasaw Bluffs (present-day Memphis) to trade for the skins and furs brought in by the still successful Chickasaw hunters. The tribe supported the United States by rejecting Tecumseh's appeals in 1811 and aiding Jackson's forces against the Redstick Creek at Horseshoe Bend in 1814. Their loyalty, however, did not protect them when U.S. commissioners stripped them in 1818 of their Tennessee and Kentucky lands, leaving only their territory in northern Mississippi and northwestern Alabama.

Although political rivalries prevailed within the nation, all agreed in their opposition to removal. Under constant pressure from both federal and state governments, a few Chickasaw leaders were persuaded to look at a proposed western territory in 1828, but they returned to report they found nothing suitable. Despite their persistence, their resistance was undermined by the passage of the Indian Removal Act (1830) in 1830 and the impact of Mississippi and Alabama state laws, especially the statutes that abolished tribal law and forbade the functioning of tribal government.

In 1830, at Franklin, Tennessee, the Chickasaw finally agreed to exchange their eastern territory for suitable western lands. The new stumbling block was suitability, which delayed migration for another seven years. When no acceptable land was found, the treaty of Pontotoc Creek (1832) was forced on them to increase the pressure. By then most Chickasaw regarded removal as inevitable. Ultimately, the Chickasaw were permitted to buy land in Indian Territory from their former neighbors the Choctaw. This arrangement was to be temporary, but after their migrations began in 1837, many Chickasaw preferred the security of Choctaw lands. They were persuaded to relocate only after the federal government had built Forts Washita and Arbuckle to protect them from the plains peoples.

By the 1850s, the beginnings of Chickasaw recovery were apparent in the farms, ferries, mills, gins, and mercantile establishments appearing in the Chickasaw District. Prosperity especially was obvious among the mixed bloods; a Colbert family member operated a Red River ferry at an annual profit of $1,000. One promising development was in stock raising, a natural step for the well-known breeders of the Chickasaw horse. During the 1850s a tribal constitution and government were put in place and efforts undertaken to establish schools.

Much of their recovery was undermined, however, by the Civil War. Although the Chickasaw had little affection for the South, their location near the southern states of Arkansas and Texas prompted them to join the Confederacy. Tragedy came in the destruction and dislocation caused by the war, as once again they underwent economic decline and loss of land. A particularly thorny problem was the place of the Chickasaw freedmen, the former slaves of the Chickasaw who became free at the end of the Civil War. From 1866 to 1906, the Chickasaw resisted pressure to incorporate the freedmen into the tribe. Final settlement of the matter came only when the names of 4,670 Chickasaw freedmen were listed on the tribal rolls in 1906. Pressure for more land cessions after the war disturbed the Chickasaw even as it did their neighbors. Some Chickasaw favored allotment as a means of ending the ongoing disputes with the federal and state governments and to satisfy individuals and businesses clamoring for land. Under the stipulations of the Dawes Commission, the Chickasaw began enrollment and allotment. The Chickasaw list included the names of 1,538 full bloods, 4,146 mixed bloods, 635 intermarried whites, and 4,670 Chickasaw freedmen. The result of this procedure ultimately was the loss of most Chickasaw lands and mineral developments. Even the tribal leadership became a shadow.

Within the last three decades, there has been an attempt to re-establish a Chickasaw presence in Oklahoma. One of the obstacles in the path is the fractional number of those who can claim to be Chickasaw. Practically speaking the Chickasaw, never numerous to begin with, are perhaps the most intermarried of those who once lived in the southeast. Nevertheless there are more than 8,000 persons today who identify themselves as Chickasaw. In recent years the governor and council of the Chickasaw Nation have worked to reawaken a sense of pride. Several local councils have been organized in Oklahoma counties and an annual gathering called at Byng, Oklahoma. A Chickasaw Housing Authority worked tirelessly in the 1970s to improve the quality of housing, especially those living at the poverty level. Arts and crafts outlets, a motel owned by the tribe, and several educational programs have been pushed, all of which offer economic opportunities and encouragement to the people who proudly carry their Chickasaw heritage into the twenty-first century.

Conclusion

For many of the Native peoples living in the Southeast today, the past twenty years have been a period of marked population growth. Those who reported their Indian heritage to the census questions in 1970 numbered nearly 70,000, while in 1990 the total had risen to more than 211,000. Included in this total are persons living as independent citizens in urban centers as well as those living as members of organized groups on or near reservations, such as the Eastern Cherokee, the Mississippi Choctaw, the Poarch Creek, the Seminole, and the Miccosukee. There are others closely attached to tribal remnants, some of whom wish federal recognition, and others of whom have abandoned it, such as the Catawba.

Attempts to retain identity through practicing culture and language are difficult as well as painstakingly slow. For those who speak no Cherokee, the learning process is a difficult one. Attending tribal gatherings, participating in attempts at intertribal cooperation, and taking steps toward recognition are all steps that may be taken. Many Southeastern peoples, however, face the twenty-first century with pride and expectation. The Seminole, the Eastern Cherokee, the Miccosukee, the Mississippi Choctaw, and the Poarch Creek enjoy the benefits of tribal organization and federal status. They anticipate continued economic opportunity and improvement. Their success, moreover, may encourage some of the smaller groups to press for federal recognition in hope of improving their situation.

James O'Donnell III
Marietta College

Dedication of new Poarch Creek Tribal Center, April 1987. Poarch Creek elder gives an opening blessing at the ceremony.

♦ SOUTHWESTERN INDIANS

Before European colonization, the area of the world that now comprises the U.S. Southwest and northern Mexican states was called Aztlán by the Aztecs, who built a powerful empire in central Mexico. Aztlán remained a coherent cultural and geopolitical region under Spanish rule until 1820 and under independent Mexican rule until 1848, when the United States annexed the northern part of Aztlán after the Mexican-American War, 1846–48. Mostly a desert and alpine arid and semi-arid region, the Southwest has a fragile land base. Water is a scarce commodity, and drought easily brings starvation to the inhabitants.

The pre-colonized Southwest, saw the gradual development of many agricultural communities, which by A.D. 900 consisted of multistory buildings and large ceremonial centers. These buildings very much resemble the round underground kiva ceremonial rooms found among the present-day Hopi in northern Arizona and the Pueblo villages in eastern New Mexico. First on the Colorado Plateau (Mesa Verde) in present-day Colorado, were the Anasazi, or "Ancient Ones," who lived in multistoried cliff dwellings. Between A.D. 900 and 1200, many major trade and ceremonial towns emerged at places known today as Canyon de Chelly and Chaco Canyon, where archeologists have been studying the ruins of these relatively large prehistoric towns. Some 100 to 200 towns developed and were interconnected by walkways and trade relations. The large cities of Central America appear to have carried on trade with towns to the north as far as the U.S. Southwest, and objects have been found to indicate that significant trade also took place with the Indian peoples living as far west as the Pacific Coast.

An extreme drought between 1275 and 1300 caused the Southwestern peoples to abandon their towns and move closer to fresh water sources. The Hopi moved to live in villages along the Colorado River, while most others moved to present-day eastern New Mexico and constructed villages along the Rio Grande River and its tributaries. In 1540, on the eve of Spanish exploration of northern Mexico, the village-dwelling agriculturalists numbered around 200,000. Other peoples, including many Hohokam speakers such as the Tohono O'Odham, were previously living by irrigation and farming but were forced to rely more and more on hunting and gathering in the harsh desert area of the Southwest, and

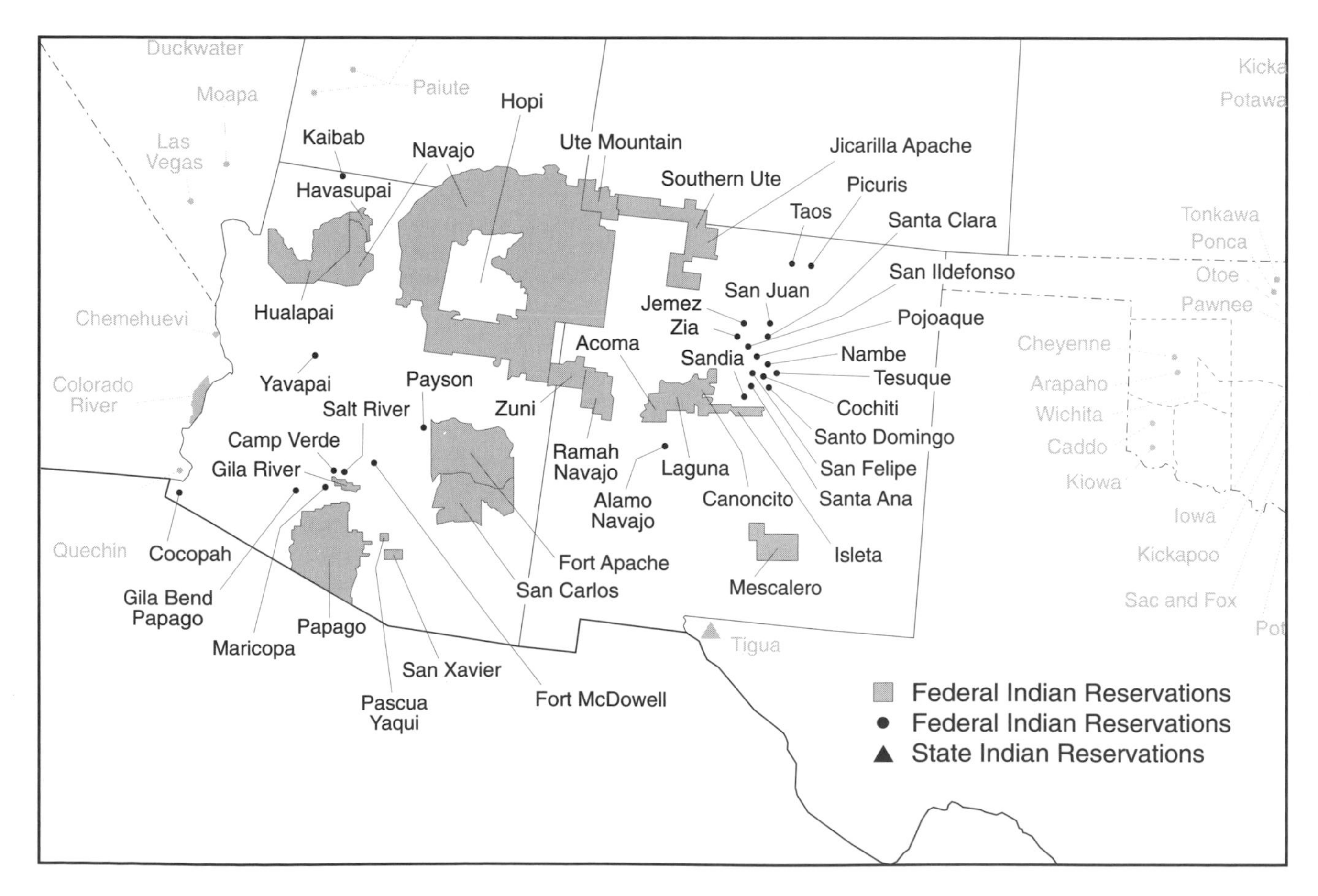

Contemporary southwestern tribes.

to live near major water sources such as the Colorado River.

Besides the Pueblo, the other major people in the Southwest were the Athapascan-speaking Navajo and Apache, who migrated south from the sub-Arctic around the thirteenth century. A hunting and gathering people, the Athapascan traded and intermarried with the village peoples and also became involved in the intervillage conflicts and wars engendered by disputes over water usage and territory. Navajo and Apache groups allied with one or another of the villages. Both the Navajo and western Apache bands absorbed significant aspects of Pueblo culture and world view. The Navajo creation history of early prehuman beings struggling to gain greater moral balance by moving from three dark worlds beneath the earth to the present fourth world parallels Hopi and other Pueblo creation stories. Similarly, some Apache groups adopted the ceremonies and dance costumes of the village farming peoples in the form of kachina dancers, which for the Pueblo were ancestral spirit beings who if properly placated, granted sufficient rain for the growing of crops. While the Navajo and Apache borrowed some elements of Pueblo culture and world view, the Athapascan combined the new elements with their own cultural themes and created complex and powerful creation histories and pantheons of spirit beings (see the Navajo creation history in the section on traditional Indian religions).

Hopi child clown.

When Spanish colonization began in the early 1600s, the village peoples were controlled strictly and their ceremonies and rituals suppressed. The Spanish authorities gave land grants to military officers for past service, and also granted the officers the right to command Indian labor. Many Pueblos were annually forced to perform work on the ranches and farms of the Spanish officers and upper class. Furthermore, by 1628, Spanish missionaries were establishing churches among the Pueblos and increasingly demanding conversion to Christianity and abandonment of traditional Indian religious views. Young Pueblos were forced into the Spanish military, which existed principally to make slave raids into areas peripheral to the New Mexico colony. For two centuries, the Navajo, the Apache, and the Ute, a hunting and gathering people who lived in present-day southern Colorado, defended themselves ferociously from these raids.

In 1682, the Pueblo spiritual leader, Popc, led a rebellion that forced the Spanish and allied Indians to retreat to present-day El Paso (Texas). Spanish military forces again regained control of the Pueblo villages in the Rio Grande Valley, by 1696, and many Pueblos left their villages to join the Navajo bands, which were hunting and migrating in the north. Thereafter many Navajo bands raided Spanish farms and the Pueblos for horses, manufactured goods, cattle, and sheep. Eventually, during the 1700s, many Navajo relied less on hunting and adopted the pastoral life of herding sheep. Eating mutton and sheep herding became the preferred way of life for many Navajo, and a large number of conservative Navajo continue to this day to herd sheep and cattle primarily for subsistence, while small numbers are sold and traded.

During the early eighteenth century, the Comanche, who emigrated from their Shoshoni homeland in present-day Wyoming, moved into the northern Spanish colony of New Mexico. The Comanche set out to control the horse trade on the southern Plains. By the mid-eighteenth century, the Comanche were the dominant bison-hunting people of the southern Plains and the Southwest. Their trade dominance grew to the point that they controlled the horse and gun trade, selling even to the Spanish themselves. By the late 1700s, there were 2,000 Comanche living east of the Rio Grande River and 4,000 living on the west side. Using war and bribery, the Spanish reached peace and trade agreements with a large number of Comanche, who with many Ute and Pueblos, fought as allies in Spanish campaigns against the Apache and the Navajo, who often raided the Spanish and Pueblo towns for horses, sheep, and trade goods. The raids and antagonism between the Athapascan Southwestern Indians and the Mexicans did not entirely diminish during the period of rule by the Mexican Republic (1820–48).

The U.S. military and traders entered the Southwest in full force in 1848 after the Mexican-American War. They met strong opposition from the Indian people, particularly the Apache.

The Apache

The Apache migrated into the Southwest to around the eleventh century. They formed a small part of a large migration of Athapascan peoples from the north and are closely related to the Navajo. They divided into small bands that spread over a 700 square mile territory, *Gran Apacheria*, as the Spaniards called it, including all of present-day New Mexico and Arizona. According to differences in language or dialect, the Apache formed into two major groups: the Jicarilla, Lipan, and Kiowa (Apache) living on the southern Plains and the Chiricahua, Mescalero, and Western Apache, who in the 1800s, were migrating westward into present-day New Mexico and Arizona.

The Apache lived by hunting big game and gathering wild plants and some farming. Their main shelter was a circular brush lodge with a fire in the center. Each Apachean group was composed of clans; basic social, economic, and political units, based on female inherited leadership. From their entrance into the Southwest, the Apache groups were in conflict with the Plains peoples in the East and with the Pima, Papago (now called the Tohono O'Odham), and the Pueblo, then living in what is now known as eastern New Mexico. They did not enjoy a close relationship with the agricultural peoples, the Pueblos, as did their relatives the Navajo, and less is known about the Apache in early times.

After the Apache were hunted down and captured by the U.S. military in the 1870s and 1880s, Apache survivors were herded into desolate reservations in present-day Arizona and New Mexico. Geronimo, a Chiricahua Apache medicine man, is best known among the Apache leaders who resisted settlement onto reservations. Their resistance assured Apache survival and reservation land bases in Arizona and New Mexico (see the biographies of Geronimo, Cochise, Natchez, and other Apache leaders).

Some of the contemporary Apache reservations have been leaders in economic development of reservation resources. The White Mountain Apache in Arizona manage with considerable success Sunrise Park Ski Resort and Fort Apache Timber Company. The lumber company employs about 300 Apache residents, and grosses about $20 million in annual income. The ski resort is also a major contributor to Fort Apache Reservation economy and is one of the most successful resort ventures in Indian Country. Other Apache reservations have also invested in tourism by opening cultural centers, and annual festivals to the public, and some reservation lands and lakes are open for public fishing and outdoor recreation. The Apache people retain strong ties to their culture, language, dances, and other traditions. Powwows are held each year, and often many Indian people from other reservations attend.

The Navajo Nation

The Navajo Nation is the largest Native nation, not only in the Southwest but in the United States, both in territory and population. With 17 million acres, the Navajo Reservation in Arizona and New Mexico is approximately the size of the state of West Virginia or the independent country of Belize in Central America. The population is at least 160,000, and some estimates project a quarter million Navajo by the year 2000. The present-day Navajo territory is located in the Four Corners region of Arizona, New Mexico, Utah, and Colorado, with land in all but the latter. Between 1820 and 1848, the Navajo land was claimed by the Mexican Republic although the Navajo never submitted to Mexican authority. The United States annexed Navajo territory under the 1848 Treaty of Guadalupe Hidalgo, which ended the Mexican-American War.

Unlike the Mexican government, however, the United States was willing to adopt extreme military measures to subdue the Indians and control their land base. The Navajo successfully resisted U.S. control for seventeen years, until the U.S. Civil War (1861–65), when the U.S. army and irregulars launched expeditions to search out the Navajo and destroy their economic livelihood. Many Navajo cornfields were burned, communities pillaged, fruit trees destroyed, and many sheep slaughtered, until the Navajo, facing starvation during 1863 and 1864, finally surrendered. The New Mexico trader Kit Carson was commissioned into the army with the rank of colonel and led irregular troops to capture and pacify numerous Navajo bands.

Eight thousand Navajo were rounded up and driven to a military-administered camp in the barren area of Bosque Redondo in eastern New Mexico, far from their high desert and alpine homeland. While there, a quarter of the Navajo died from starvation and exposure. In 1868, a treaty was negotiated with Navajo headmen, and the Navajo were allowed to settle on the present-day Navajo Reservation (see the biographies of Ganada Mucho, Manuelito, Barboncito, and other Navajo leaders).

From 1868 to 1922, when oil was discovered in Navajo territory, the Navajo were virtually ignored by the federal government. The land itself had been judged to be worthless, even for Texas longhorn cattle production. The presence of oil, however, led to intense intervention into Navajo affairs. In 1922, the Navajo Business Council was created by the U.S. agent, who needed a centralized authority to grant oil and mineral leases in the name of the entire Navajo Nation. Most Navajo were led by local headmen, who generally did not recognize a central Navajo government and often ignored the Navajo Business Council until its demise in 1936.

The Navajo firmly rejected the Indian Reorganization Act of 1934, federal legislation which sought to structure official tribal governments with constitutions. Instead the federal government allowed the Navajo to hold a constitutional convention, which proposed a government independent from the bureaucratic power of the Office of Indians Affairs (the Bureau of Indian Affairs, BIA, in the 1940s). The secretary of the interior rejected the Navajo constitution, which was a bold plan for greater Navajo political freedom. Instead, in 1938 the Department of the Interior created a new Navajo Business Council, composed of 74 elected Navajo members and generally elected chairman and vice-chairman. This government, known as the "Rules of 1938," provide the basis for the present Navajo Tribal Council.

During the late 1930s and 1940s, the Navajo became embroiled in a political and bureaucratic conflict with the BIA and U.S. government over the issues of grazing sheep and cattle on the Navajo Reservation. Most Navajo made their living from livestock, mainly sheep herding, but Navajo herds were generally small, a few hundred, and designed mainly for supplying family food, while some mutton and wool was traded at local stores for necessary manufactured goods. During the 1930s dust bowl period, government officials decided that the Navajo were raising too many sheep for the amount of grasslands and that the overgrazing would lead to ecological ruin of Navajo lands through erosion. Beginning with a massive stock reduction program, agents of the Agricultural Department slaughtered tens of thousands of Navajo sheep to prevent overgrazing and desertification. This conflict soured Navajo and government relations for several decades.

Although the Navajo Nation possesses water rights sufficient to irrigate and farm 5 million acres of their land, fewer than 100,000 acres are under cultivation. Most of the land is used for grazing 500,000 sheep, 50,000 cattle, and 30,000 goats. Much of the agricultural production is animal food grain. There exists a potential basis for a successful agricultural and pastoral economy, something much desired by Navajo traditionalists struggling to maintain their subsistence economy, as well as by some economic experts.

Nevertheless the Navajo pastoral economy often is eschewed by Navajo modernizers, who favor development of Navajo natural resources such as oil, gas, coal, and uranium. Much Navajo land was leased by the federal government during the 1920s and 1930s, so that the main income generated from the land is from mineral and mining leases and royalties. The territory is rich in reserve subsurface minerals and resources: 100 million barrels of oil; 25 billion cubic feet of natural gas; 5 billion tons of surface coal; and 80 million pounds of uranium. The major companies operating in the Navajo Nation are AMOCO, Exxon, Kerr-McGee, Gulf, and Texaco. There are 500,000 acres of commercial forest on Navajo territory, which yield millions of dollars in annual stumpage payments. The forest enterprise is controlled by the Navajo government under its Navajo Forest Products Industry.

There is a wide gap between the wealth of Navajo territory and the overwhelming poverty of its residents. Unemployment hovers around 50 percent. Most of those who are unemployed are unskilled and lacking in formal American education, many speaking little English. Few are familiar with the modern market economy. Support services, such as day care centers, are few. Early education is poor. The majority, some 75 percent, of employed Navajo work in the public sector, made possible by U.S. government funding amounting to hundreds of millions of dollars annually. The remaining workers on the reservation are employed in commercial agriculture, mining, forestry, wholesale and retail trade, and construction. Around 5 percent are employed in transportation, communications and utilities, all of which are Navajo-owned and -operated.

About 20 percent of the Navajo people live off the Navajo Reservation, and many have migrated to southwestern cities as well as to San Francisco and Los Angeles for jobs. Under the federal government's Indian Relocation Program of the 1950s, most Navajo who relocated chose California, since a large number were already living there, many having been rail workers for the Santa Fe Railroad since the 1920s. Due mainly to economic necessity, migration to and from the Navajo homeland is constant.

The influx of federal funds has not increased Navajo incomes even to national poverty levels. Navajo per capita income is around $1,000 a year. Federal funds are generally earmarked to relieve symptoms of poverty, not for capital development. The chief beneficiaries are the thousands of Navajo employees running the federal bureaucracy on the reservation; they make up a privileged group with a vested interest in maintaining and enlarging the tribal government bureaucracy.

The 1970s saw a rise in industrial activity, with the Navajo Nation taking remarkable initiatives. During the construction of the off-reservation Salt River power plant project at Page, Arizona, Navajo workers experi-

A middle-aged Navajo woman stands next to her traditional earthen hogan in Tuba City, Arizona.

enced blatant racial discrimination in pay and duties. They organized and pressed the Navajo Nation to support their demands, and newly elected Navajo chairman, Peter MacDonald, took up the challenge (see the biography of Peter MacDonald). Trade unions, until then banned on the reservation, were legalized and supported. The actions taken by Navajo workers and the Navajo Nation awakened workers throughout the Southwest, where the combined Mexican and Indian labor force had long been oppressed by ruling Anglo-Americans. Both New Mexico and Arizona were traditionally antiunion, with less than 5 percent of their work forces organized into trade unions. The Office of Navajo Labor Relations was established to mandate standards for Navajo workers' wages for jobs in or near the reservation. These standards required major construction projects to hire Navajo on a percentage or quota basis in specific numbers of skilled positions.

Trade unions are now an accepted part of the Navajo social structure, but are a far more democratic than their typical U.S. counterparts. The Office of Navajo Labor Relations supports local workers' associations within the reservation, based in the communities where the workers live. By the late 1970s, practically all Navajo workers in the private sector were members of labor unions.

Some observers have expressed concern at the successful unionization of Navajo workers, who receive nationally mandated union wages. They fear that the high income of Navajo industrial workers will encourage unbridled industrialization as well as an economic elite. However, traditional practices of Navajo family and clan sharing and generosity actually tend to equalize incomes in the reservation, through redistribution by means of gifts of money and goods from the high-paid workers to their less fortunate relatives and neighbors. It also appears that high-paid Navajo workers tend to invest surplus funds in the traditional pastoral economy by purchasing stock, fee, equipment, and trucks.

In 1971, the Navajo Nation supported the formation of Navajo Community College (NCC) at Tsaile, Arizona, on the Navajo Reservation. The locally controlled Indian community college was the first of its kind, and many Navajo, who otherwise did not want to leave the reservation to take college credit courses, enrolled at NCC. The college was so successful that within a few years other reservations were starting colleges and were gaining considerable success training reservation people, where U.S. college institutions were showing extremely poor results retaining and graduating Indian college students. Indian-controlled community colleges have been built on about thirty Indian reservations, and many more Indian reservations are contemplating building community colleges for their people and for surrounding non-Indian students. The community college movement has become one of the most significant events on many Indian reservations during the 1970s and 1980s. The movement to build Indian-controlled community colleges was greatly inspired by the ground-breaking work of the Navajo community and the pioneers who built Navajo Community College (see the section on Indian higher education).

In November 1982, young activist lawyer Peterson Zah won election as Navajo chairman. He was defeated four years later by MacDonald, but won again in 1990. About 35,000 Navajo vote in the Navajo tribal government elections, and over the years the Navajo government has evolved by borrowing both Western and traditional Navajo government institutions. The Navajo adopted a court system modeled after the U.S. legal system in 1959 in order to prevent the states of Arizona and New Mexico from extending their courts onto the Navajo Reservation. The Navajo prefer to manage their own courts and use their own ideas of justice, rather than submit to the U.S. court system. During the 1970s, the Navajo court system gained in power and respect, and many local courts manage disputes in the traditional manner of trying reconcile contentious parties, according to Navajo cultural views of resolving conflict more so than U.S. legal views. Until the 1950s, the Navajo government suffered from lack of local support, but since then it has tried directly to incorporate local political communities, often called chapters, into the government and electoral process, and in this way gain the support of the Navajo communities, which still tend toward local groupings and local leaders. The Navajo government has made considerable strides in attempting to provide a truly representative government, based

Navajo medicine man Albert Yazzie chats with Navajo Education Center staff after performing a Navajo Protection Way ceremony for Navajo servicemen and women who were involved in the Persian Gulf war with Iraq.

to some extent on traditional principles, and has developed the largest tribal government organization in Native North America.

The Hopi

The Hopi are descendants of the earliest inhabitants of the Southwest and for centuries occupied a large part of present-day northern Arizona. In their oral history they recount the arrival of the Paiute and the Ute, the Navajo, the Spanish, and then the Americans.

The Hopi elders tell of a time a long time ago before people were really human beings, when they lived underground; this was the period of the Third World. Before the early beings lived in the Third World, the early beings had to flee two other worlds farther underground, because of their immoral behavior and disruption of the social harmony of the First and Second Worlds. For some time these early people lived in peace with all the animals and there were no problems. But then, the people began to have disputes. A council was held, with animal representatives participating in the discussions. They agreed that the Third World had become morally corrupted and out of balance, and they had to seek peace by migrating from the underworld to a Fourth World above. The Hopi arrived in the Fourth World and encountered a frightening yet attractive spirit being, Masau-u, who asked them what they sought. Masau-u told the Hopi that they could live on the land of the Fourth World provided that they followed sacred rules. The Hopi would have to perform rituals to provide water for the desert land, and they would have to accept Masau-u's teachings, abiding by his/her social and religious rules. The Hopi agreed and made a covenant to obey Masau-u and serve as caretakers of the land. The Hopi attempt to keep this sacred covenant to this day.

Each Hopi clan retells a variation of the creation story, but they all share the same emergence story and consider the land they occupy as sacred. The Hopi believe they must fulfill particular sacred and ceremonial responsibilities. Creating rain for the dry land is essential and is accomplished through prayers and ceremonies held annually in the Hopi villages.

The Hopi live in northeastern Arizona, where their reservation is entirely surrounded by the large Navajo Reservation. Hopi society is divided into twelve phratries, or collections of clans, with numerous clans within each phratry. Children always belong to the clan of their mother. Like other Pueblo, Hopi honor kachinas, or rain spirits, and clan ancestors. Clans are extremely important for social and religious relations, and each clan has its own special sacred objects and ceremonies. Clan and ceremonial leaders continue to play major roles in Hopi ceremonial and social life. Many Hopi as well as Pueblo ceremonies are concerned with creating community harmony and appeasing the kachina spirits to bring rain for the Hopi crops. The Hopi were a horticultural people, who grew several varieties of corn, beans, squash, and other plants. Men hunted animals such as deer and elk, and the women gathered nuts, fruits, and roots.

In the middle and late 1500s, there may have been as many as a dozen Hopi villages along the Colorado River, but they were quickly decimated by early diseases, and by 1600, most Hopi retreated to their present villages in northern Arizona. There they were found by the Spanish, and starting in 1628 Spanish Catholic missions were established in several Hopi villages. The Hopi helped the Pueblos in the 1680 rebellion, and even after Spanish reconquest, the Hopi strongly resisted Spanish rule and Catholic religion.

The Hopi occupy about a dozen villages on the Hopi reservation. They still maintain many of their ceremonies, beliefs, and many still live in multistoried buildings that the Spanish called pueblos. Many within the Hopi community continue to uphold the traditional ways and

"Lynn," a Hopi woman.

actively resist U.S. cultural influences in religion, education, and government. During the 1930s, a small number of Hopi voted for adopting a constitutional government under the provisions of the Indian Reorganization Act (IRA) of 1934. The IRA was designed by the U.S. government to give Indian communities more control over their own affairs, by organizing Western-style governments among them. Many Indian nations, especially among the religiously conservative Pueblo and Hopi, rejected the IRA constitutional governments, because they more modeled after secular Western views of political organization and had little precedent or congruence with Indian political traditions and political governments. The Hopi community became divided between those willing to live under the IRA government and those who wanted to retain Hopi political institutions, which incorporated a considerable degree of traditional Hopi customs and religious orientation.

The conservative Hopi have been some of the most active nationalist Indian groups in the United States. Together with the conservative and nationalist Iroquois people of New York and southern Canada, conservative Hopi leaders have appealed to international forums such as the United Nations in order to gain redress for broken treaty agreements and for recognition of Indian national independence. Not all Hopi share the view that the Hopi reservation should be recognized as an independent nation within the international community. But the conservative Hopi reflect the active conservatism inherent within tightly interrelated Hopi clan and religious relations, which fosters strong attachment to tradition and motivates many Hopi to actively seek preservation of Hopi community and religious institutions.

The Pueblo Villages of New Mexico

When the Spanish arrived in the 1500s, there were ninety-eight villages, called pueblos by the Spanish, along the northern Rio Grande and its tributaries; within a few decades, there were only nineteen, all of which exist today. Although all Pueblo peoples have similar economic, governmental, and religious structures, they speak four distinct languages: Zuni, Keres, Tiwa, and Tewa. The languages remain strong, although most Pueblo Indians also speak English.

Each pueblo is autonomous and fiercely independent; however, all the pueblos participate in a loose federation, the All Indian Pueblo Council, which traces its origins to the successful 1680 Pueblo Revolt against the Spanish. The leader of the rebellion was Pope, a religious leader from San Juan Pueblo. The revolt started at Taos Pueblo and moved steadily to the southern pueblos, driving the Spanish and some Pueblo allies to El Paso in present-day Texas. For about a dozen years, the Pueblo enjoyed liberty (see the biography of Pope). The Spanish, however, reconquered the Pueblo by 1695 but thereafter refrained from tampering directly with Pueblo internal affairs, particularly religious ceremonies. Many Pueblo, especially those from Jemez Pueblo, did not want to live under Spanish rule and escaped to live among the Navajo and Apache bands, many of which were constantly raiding the Spanish and Pueblo villages for livestock and trade goods. The Pueblo had a profound effect on Navajo and Apache traditions and ceremonies, which were enriched with ideas borrowed from the Pueblo refugees. The remainder of the Pueblo lived under harsh Spanish rule, which demanded Catholic Christian conversion, and forced labor on the ranches of Spanish officers and political land grantees.

Under the rule of independent Mexico from 1821 to 1848, only the Pueblo among the Southwest Indians held full Mexican citizenship. Therefore, when the United States annexed the region, Pueblo people automatically became U.S. citizens, as did the other residents of the area. Not only was citizenship of little use to the Pueblo, but their territories did not fall under the federal government's developing reservation system, which normally put Indian lands under federal protection. Encroachment on Pueblo land, the finest farm land in the Southwest, accelerated rapidly. The Pueblo petitioned and then sued for Indian status, which they finally gained in 1916 through a U.S. Supreme Court decision. Meanwhile, they had lost some of their best lands as well as important religious sites.

A congressional investigation during the 1920s revealed that 12,000 non-Pueblo claimants were living on Pueblo lands. The All Indian Pueblo Council organized delegates from all the pueblos to regain their lands, which resulted in the 1924 Pueblo Lands Act. Assisting the Pueblo in their fight was John Collier, a young Indian rights activist on the staff of the General Federation of Women's Clubs. President Franklin D.Roosevelt later named Collier Indian commissioner, a position he held from 1933 to 1945. The Pueblo successfully mounted a campaign among non-Indians for a Native issue and set an important example for other Native peoples across the country.

Pueblo lands are secure, but land in that semi-arid region is of no use without water. The most important contemporary Pueblo Indian struggle is to maintain and to acquire water rights. Water law falls under common law in the Anglo-American legal system, and under federal law devolves to state jurisdiction. Indians fought for and won exemption to state control in the early twentieth century. The Winters Doctrine, arising from a 1909 Supreme Court case, defines Indian water rights, and is based on the theory

Christmas Day Matachine dancers at San Juan Pueblo.

that the federal government reserves power over federal lands, which includes the necessary water supply. The Winters Doctrine implies that Indian treaty rights include the right to adequate supplies of water necessary for the Indian reservations to carry on irrigation for agriculture and to meet their population and economic development needs. However, in a court decision in 1973, the Winters Doctrine was declared to be inapplicable to the Pueblo Indians of New Mexico, since the Pueblo were not officially Indians at the time the Winters case was adjudicated.

One the most significant events in recent Pueblo history is the return of the sacred Blue Lake and about 55,000 surrounding acres to the Taos Pueblo in 1975. Taos Pueblo had lost the land to the federal government, but after a thirty-year court and political struggle, the Taos Pueblo regained ownership of Blue Lake, a sacred site in Taos creation history, since it is considered the navel of the universe and the place where the Creator first created people. The people of Taos Pueblo held annual ceremonies at Blue Lake, many of which were crucial to the Taos Pueblo religious cycle, which, the Taos people believed, ensured the well-being and prosperity of the Taos community. The return of Blue Lake marked one of the few times that the federal government returned a major sacred site and surrounding lands to Indian control. It gave hope that in the future other Indian communities may successfully regain or protect their sacred sites, often unknown to the general public.

During the 1960s and 1970s, Zuni Pueblo became a model for the present-day U.S. government self-determination policy in Indian affairs. Like other Pueblo peoples, the Zuni have a strong tradition of religious community and strong attachments to their social and political freedom. During the 1960s, when federal funds became available through antipoverty programs like the Community Action Programs (CAP), many Indian communities, for the first time, gained access to significant funds and personnel, because of direct federal grants to local tribal governments within the CAP programs (see the chronology for the 1965 to 1970s period on antipoverty grants and tribal government revitalization). The Zuni, in the late 1960s, seized this opportunity and, armed with a little-used law that required the Bureau of Indian Affairs (BIA) to contract services to tribal governments, the Zuni tried to gain control over all BIA programs in the Zuni community. The Zuni were able to contract many BIA programs and ran most of them much more effectively and with greater community commitment and participation. The Zuni embarked on this plan as a means to exclude unwanted BIA interference into their government and community affairs. The Zuni came to the attention of President Richard Nixon, and in 1970, he made a speech in which he announced the beginning of the Indian self-determination policy, designed to allow tribal governments and reservation communities greater local control over BIA and federal programs and over local institutions such as schools. President Nixon held up the Zuni as an example to all Indian communities who wished to take a greater role in managing their local affairs.

The nineteen New Mexico pueblos remain strongly traditional communities that continue to practice and perform the major dances and rituals of their religions. They have consistently rejected U.S. efforts to significantly alter their religious, social, and cultural orders, since they continue to live by many of the religious views and customs of their forefathers. The Pueblo have generated many well-known artists, novelists, poets, scholars, and painters among their people (see the biographies of Paula Gunn Allen, Alfonso Ortiz, Leslie Marmon Silko, and other Pueblo).

The Future

The languages and cultures of the Native peoples of the Southwest endure, and their preservation most likely is ensured. For the Native peoples of the Southwest—the Paiute and the Ute, the Walapai and the Yavapai, the Mojave and the Tohono O'Odham, the Pima and Apache, the Navajo and the Hopi, and the Pueblo of New Mexico—the Southwest is their ancient homeland. Others have come and gone for over three centuries, and those who have stayed have had to learn the lessons of the ancients in order to survive in the vast, harsh land.

Roxanne Dunbar Ortiz
California State University, Hayward

San Ildefonso Pueblo feast day.

♦ NORTHERN PLAINS INDIANS

All contemporary tribal communities in the Plains north of Oklahoma possess their own distinctive qualities. Tribalism—loyalty to the group—endured despite a long history of economic and political forces designed to destroy Plains cultures. Despite U.S. attempts to end tribalism, the Indians' desire to preserve their cultural integrity, fostered changes that resulted in preservation of cultural life and heritage among contemporary northern Plains communities.

Most Indian nations identified with the High Plains Culture of horses and buffalo hunting did not live on the Plains until after 1750. Before European contact, all horses in North America died out about 8,000 to 10,000 years before the present. The horses that became part of the wild horses, or the American mustangs, were horses that escaped from early Spanish explorer expeditions. Some Indian nations lived on the Plains, but they lived in small huts and hunted the buffalo on foot. Most Indian nations, which are commonly regarded as Plains tribes, lived farther east. Most so-called Plains Indian nations migrated onto the Plains only during the colonial period, and mainly after 1650 when European expansion forced many Indians westward. Before moving onto the Plains, many so-called Plains Indian nations, such as the Sioux and Blackfeet, lived by hunting, growing corn, and gathering wild foods. During the 1650s and early 1700s the Iroquois, an upstate New York nation, started an expansionist trade and military campaign to control and maintain access to lands with fur bearing animals, which were necessary for trade with the Europeans. The Iroquois expansion pushed many Algonkian-speaking nations, such as the Chippewa and Ottawa, who migrated farther west into the upper Great Lakes area. The Chippewa, for example, during the 1700s and 1800s moved into present-day Minnesota, and, armed with guns from their European trade allies, began pushing the Sioux Indians onto the Plains by the latter half of the 1700s. By the early 1800s many Sioux bands moved onto the Plains from their original woodland homes in Minnesota and adopted the horse, buffalo hunting, the sacred ceremony of the Sun Dance, and began raiding the more sedentary farming peoples, such as the Mandan, Arikara, and Hidatsa, who were living along the Missouri River and eventually settled in present-day central North Dakota.

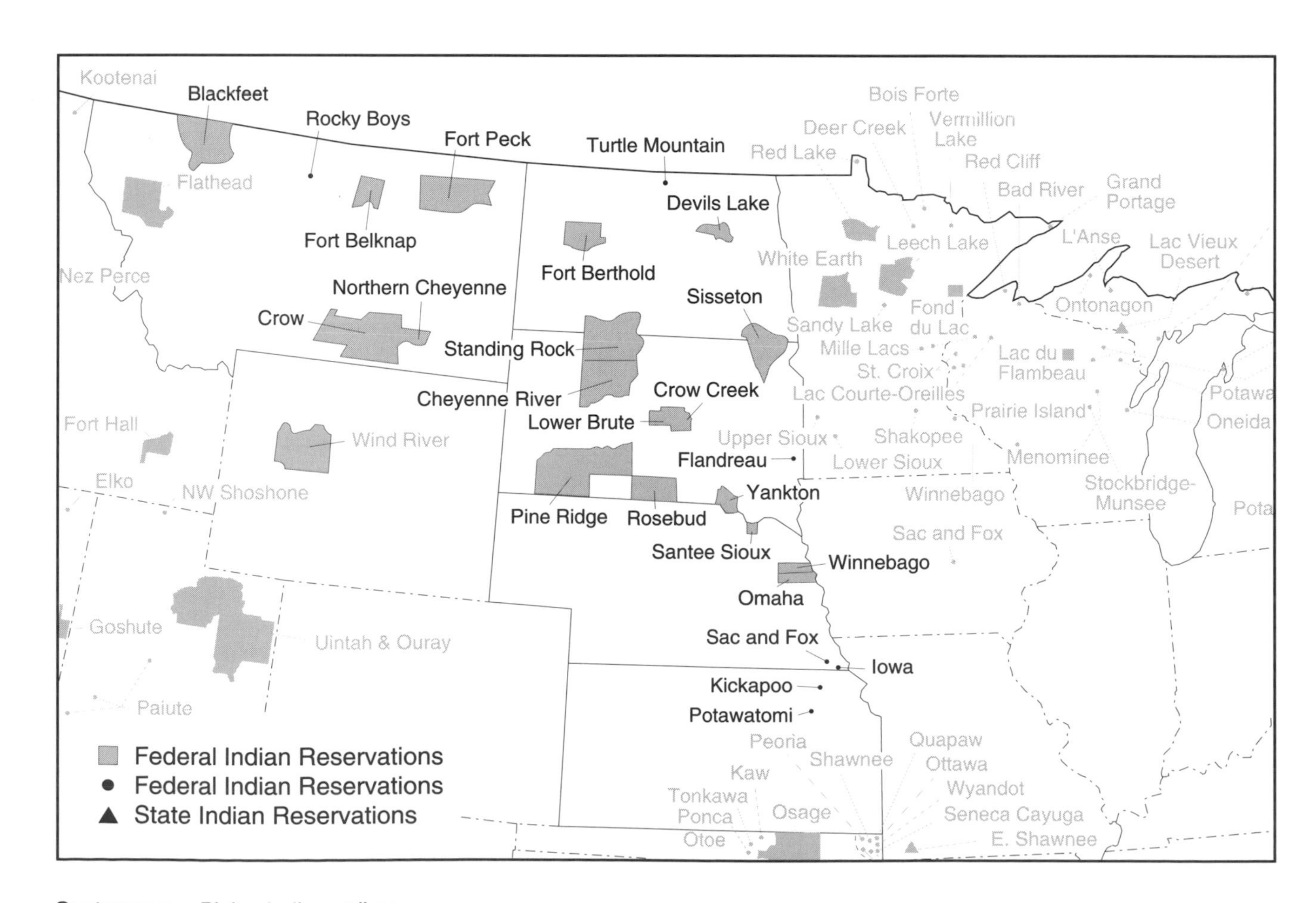

Contemporary Plains Indians tribes.

The experience of Cheyenne, an Algonkian-speaking nation, is typical for the peoples who migrated onto the Plains. In the early 1600s, the Cheyenne were located in present-day southern Canada and made their livelihood by hunting, farming, and gathering wild plants. The Iroquois expansion after 1650 pushed the Cheyenne farther west and, in the 1700s, early French explorers report that the Cheyenne people were living in present-day Minnesota. By the late 1700s, the Cheyenne were living in eastern North Dakota, and while still growing corn, were increasingly adopting the use of the horse and the hunting of buffalo. The Sheyenne River in eastern North Dakota is named after them. By the middle 1800s, the Cheyenne had moved to the western plains and had fully adopted Plains culture, including the Sun Dance—an annual renewal ceremony, military societies of young men, portable teepees, annual gatherings in the summer for religious ceremonies, and collective buffalo hunting. In the winter, the Cheyenne, as other Plains nations like the Sioux, Blackfeet, and Crow, broke into small bands and endured the cold winter months in separate locations.

The most common image non-Indians have of Indian people is that of the Plains culture, with fierce warriors, sacred Sun Dance ceremonies, and buffalo hunting. Nonetheless the Plains culture was a relatively new mode of life for Indians and was an adaptation to the rapid expansion of colonial settlements and the extension of the colonial sphere of political influence. The Plains culture lasted only about two centuries and does not characterize the way Indians lived for centuries before its emergence in the late 1700s. Before then, most Indians in the East were farmers and lived without horses, and many of the Plains nations such as the Sioux belonged to cultures that were related to the farming and mound-building communities of the Mississippi Culture (A.D..800 to 1500). Nevertheless, the Plains cultures flourished during the 1700s and during much of the 1800s and lasted until U.S. authorities pacified the Plains Indians and placed them on reservations. By the late 1870s, U.S. hunters had virtually slaughtered the large herds of buffalo, and, without adequate buffalo supplies as a major food source, the Indian Plains culture was no longer possible.

Historical Precedents

Two centuries ago, French, Scot, English, and Spanish traders moved onto the northern Plains, and their continual presence altered the demography and material culture of many Plains tribes. Traders, who were looking to exchange buffalo hides for guns, pots and pans, cloth, and other goods, preceded the more intensive settlements in the late 1880s. Diseases preceded and accompanied the European newcomers and caused many epidemics among the Plains nations. Smallpox, cholera, and whooping cough epidemics were responsible for dramatic declines in Plains Indian populations during the nineteenth and twentieth centuries. In 1837 a major smallpox epidemic dramatically reduced Mandan, Arikara, and Hidatsa numbers and forced them to combine clans and mix family lines; ultimately the three tribes coalesced and moved to a location near present-day Fort Berthold Reservation in North Dakota. Other Indian nations living on the Plains, such as the Sioux and Pawnee, suffered similar catastrophic population losses, though their exact numbers are hard to document.

The United States further displaced Plains Indian peoples by moving eastern Indian tribes to lands west of the Mississippi River. Starting in 1830, U.S. government policy authorized movement of most Indian nations east to the Mississippi River to new homelands west of the river. Most eastern Indian nations were moved to present-day Kansas and Oklahoma (See the Oklahoma section of this chapter, and see the Nineteenth Century section in Chapter 2). In the 1830s, groups from the Iowa, Kickapoo, Potawatomi, Chippewa, and Munsee Delaware, all eastern nations, migrated to Indian Territory in present-day Kansas. After agreeing to treaties with the U.S. government in 1865 and 1874, part of the Winnebago Nation, formerly located in Wisconsin, settled on a reservation in Nebraska. Frequently the indigenous Indian peoples considered the Indian newcomers as hostile intruders onto their lands and hunting territories. Warfare ensued as the eastern Indians tried to recreate their communities in the west, and the Plains Indians, like the Pawnee and the Ponca of present-day Kansas, tried to defend their hunting territories. In the 1880s and 1890s, the United States relocated the Pawnee and Ponca to Indian Territory in present-day Oklahoma.

Hostility on the Plains was escalated when the U.S. government assigned territorial boundaries for the Plains peoples in the 1851 Fort Laramie Treaty. Over the next thirty years, the United States redefined reservation boundaries by creating smaller reservations, sometimes forcing several tribes to live on the same reservation. The Shoshoni and Arapaho, once enemy nations, now cohabitate on the Wind River Reservation in Wyoming. A band of Assiniboine and a branch of the Yankton, both Siouan-speaking peoples, inhabit the Fort Peck Reservation in Montana. The Assiniboine and Gros Ventre, an Algonkian-speaking people, occupy the Fort Belknap Reservation in Montana.

Many Plains nations, however, resented U.S. restrictions on their freedom to move about the Plains, which had been their former tradition. The Lakota (the name some Sioux have for themselves), the Cheyenne, and the Blackfeet fought the United States and tried to keep U. S. settlers and miners from staying permanently in the area. Symbolizing their resistance to U.S. encroachments are such battles as the 1864 Sand Creek Battle in present-day Colorado, the 1866–68 Bozeman Trail War in Wyoming, and the defeat of U.S. troops led by Colonel George Custer at the 1876 Battle of the Little Big Horn in eastern Montana (see the biographies of Gall, Sitting Bull, Black Kettle, Crazy Horse, Lone Wolf, and other Plains Indian leaders).

By 1880, settlement on a reservation became the only political and economic option available, and the Plains Indians reluctantly moved to U.S. government controlled reservations. After resisting removal to Oklahoma in the late 1870s, by the early 1880s the Northern Cheyenne settled onto the Tongue River Reservation in eastern Montana. In 1916, a group of Plains Chippewa and Cree, both Algonkian-speaking peoples, found refugee on the Rocky Boy Reservation in Montana. However, in 1892, Chippewa leader Little Shell and his followers left the Turtle Mountain Reservation in northern North Dakota and joined the Cree and Métis (mixed-blood people) in a non-federally recognized community that survives at Great Falls, Montana.

Eventually, the U.S. government settled most Plains Indians on reservations. The people often gathered to live near relatives, and these hamlets became the present-day reservation communities. Indian agents had near total control over reservation Indian communities, and between 1887 and 1934, official U.S. policies discouraged the exercise of traditional Indian government, many ceremonies were banned and forced underground, and Indian cultural expression was generally discouraged in favor of Christianity and U.S. social life-styles. During this period Native languages were discouraged, and Native spiritual leaders continued their ceremonies out of the sight of U.S. officials. As a result, on many Plains reservations, traditional ceremonies like the Sun Dance were not actively revived for public consumption until the 1970s. Schools and mission churches were often constructed near reservation villages and missionaries, and school teachers and farmers introduced U.S. modes of life. Many Plains Indians continued to challenge U.S. control, however, by keeping children from attending schools. Despite initial hostility and resistance to settlement onto reservations, most contemporary Plains Indians consider their reservations home.

After 1880, reservation poverty forced many Plains Indians to seek clothing from mission charities and from government distributions. The clothes gotten in this way were altered by tribal artisans to suit Plains Indian tastes. The ribbon shirt is one example of tribal modification, in which colored ribbons are sewn on a "cowboy" shirt in order to make a distinct article of Indian clothing. Quilts followed a similar pattern, and northern Plainswomen are famous for their star quilts, which are richly designed blankets that many non-Indians buy as art pieces. Missionaries instructed women to quilt and introduced the eight point star pattern found on many quilt patterns. Today the star quilt has become a distinctive Plains design. Used as gifts, the quilts help perpetuate the Plains tradition of giveaways at pow-wows and at some ceremonial occasions, such as funerals among the Northern Cheyenne.

Early Reservation Economic Pursuits

U.S. reservation policy limited trade and forced reservation Plains Indians to pursue a narrower range of economic activities. The upper Missouri River Fort Berthold Reservation, where the Mandan, Hidatsa, and Arikara settled, continued pre-reservation farming by planting crops. Downstream on the Missouri River, the Omaha and Winnebago also maintained farming pursuits. Other Plains peoples adopted farming. In North and South Dakota, the Sioux on the Sisseton Reservation, the Fort Totten Reservation, and the Yankton Reservation developed subsistence agricultural economies but were unable to purchase equipment necessary to farm large operations, because they lacked access to credit. On the other hand, in the western Plains reservations in Montana, many reservation Indians attempted to farm but were unable to harvest enough crops for subsistence purposes. The absence of fertile reservation land for adequate farming forced many reservation Indians to subsist on government rations or to sell reservation lands and use the money to purchase cattle.

Limited farming success on the semi-arid prairie encouraged the Office of Indians Affairs (later the Bureau of Indian Affairs, or BIA) to plan reservation irrigation projects, which began in the 1890s on the Blackfeet, the Crow, the Fort Belknap, and the Fort Peck reservations in Montana. The tribes paid the costs of the irrigation projects, which changed the reservation landscape as canals crisscrossed reservation farmland.

U.S. government agents encouraged cattle ranching as an alternative to irrigation agriculture. Ranching required less capital than farming, but even after reservation Indians began stockraising, their ranches remained small. Size, however, did not dictate success. By the turn of the century, Blackfeet ranchers registered over 400 cattle brands. Both the Blackfeet and the Northern Cheyenne ranchers produced quality stock, and cattle buyers from Chicago purchased animals from these reservations.

The Sioux Indians on the Standing Rock Reservation in North Dakota and the Cheyenne River, Pine Ridge, Lower Brulé, Crow Creek, and Rosebud reservations in South Dakota had less success. Unable to stock their ranges with cattle, the Standing Rock, the Cheyenne River, and the Rosebud Sioux leased portions of their reservations to cattle companies at the turn of the century. A disadvantage to leasing was that the tribes lost short-term control over the land; however, they did retain ownership.

Pine Ridge and Rosebud cattle operations declined further during World War I (1914–18), when government officials encouraged Indian cattlemen to liquidate their small herds. This forced them either to lease or to sell land. Despite obstacles and hardships, many Plains Indians considered the early twentieth century cattle operations as the zenith of their reservation economic experience, because stock provided stable subsistence. More important, many western Plains reservations never recovered from the loss of their cattle operations, and today only a small percentage of reservation residents manage profitable stock operations. On the Northern Cheyenne reservation, for example, only 10 percent of the families make a living by cattle ranching.

Land Allotment

Beginning with the 1854 Omaha Treaty, land allotment—dividing tribal common lands into small individual tracts—became standard provision in Plains treaties and agreements. The General Allotment Act of 1887 applied the land allotment policy to all Plains reservations and also provided a mechanism for granting citizenship to the allotees. The legislation authorized the president to order the division of reservation lands into individual tracts. Allotting agents issued 40 acre to 640 acre tracts to individual tribal members. After twenty-five years, the allotted land converted to fee simple title (meaning the owner could sell whenever they wished), and U.S. citizenship was granted with the change in land status. Congressmen hoped that division and privatization of the Indian land base would eliminate Indian reservations and give individual Indians' full status as citizens, which would protect their rights.

Allotment failed for many reasons. Dividing semiarid lands was ecologically unsound. Economically, reservation Indians lack access to credit, which is an economic barrier to farming profitably. Land allotment citizenship provisions failed politically because local communities refused to accept reservation Indians as social or political equals.

Irrigation projects also hastened the loss of allotted land. Congress authorized allottees to take a small irrigable allotment on a project and a larger non-irrigable tract of grazing land. Many reservation Plains Indians sold their irrigated properties, because they were unable to build improvements necessary to farm. The United States also encouraged tribes to sell non-allotted tribal lands to repay the costs of constructing the irrigation projects. This further reduced the reservation resource base. Last of all, irrigation projects never recovered operation and maintenance costs and forced tribes to operate projects for non-Indians who purchased irrigable allotted lands.

After allotment, entire sections of unallotted reservation lands were sold. U.S. homesteaders purchased these non-allotted surveyed tracts and lived in the midst of the reservation. Portions of reservations never opened to homesteading were called "closed" lands. Many individual Indians sold allotments when leasing became unprofitable, and the Office of Indian Affairs sold land when the agency declared an Indian allottee incompetent.

Allotment also created heirship lands, when an allottee died without a will. In such cases, the United States granted the estate jointly to all heirs. In many cases when there was a relatively large number of heirs, shares in the deceased's allotted land were very small. Continuing the joint heirship practice beyond the first generation usually rendered the jointly owned allotments too small for economic purposes and forced the heirs either to sell or to lease the land. Today, if heirs lease the land, all receive smaller and smaller rent receipts as new heirs are added; and if they sell, the land is lost. Administering heirship lands remains a common problem on all Plains reservations and makes resource management decisions difficult.

Allotting land on Plains reservations increased the federal government's role in reservation affairs, since more staff were employed to handle additional work loads. For example, the Indian Service established a government banking system known as the Individual Indian Monies (IIM), where the reservation superintendent deposited monies gained from rent and sale of allotted lands. Consequently allotees had to trust the BIA to properly manage their money.

The Reservation New Deal

Allotment reduced the ability of reservation communities to participate in the prairie agricultural markets and made any downturn in the economy particularly hard-felt on the reservations. After World War I, Plains communities experienced an agricultural depression that drove lessees off the land and deprived many reservations of income. By 1930, private relief organizations were dispensing assistance to several reservation communities, because many were unable to provide for themselves.

Seeking to relieve suffering throughout the nation, Congress created a direct work relief program in 1933 known as the Civilian Conservation Corps (CCC) to employ the jobless in conservation projects. Initially reservations were excluded from this program, but Department of the Interior officials transferred the CCC concept to reservations, where unemployment was higher than among non-tribal populations. To direct this effort, Interior officials created the Indian Emergency Conservation Work (IECW), more commonly known as the Civilian Conservation Corps-Indian Division (CCC-

ID), which provided employment for reservation irrigation, forestry, and grazing projects.

For many reservation Indians, this was the first time they had ever worked for wages, and the program provided relief income. Collectively, all New Deal reservation programs were crucial to reduce suffering. For example, nearly 95 percent of the Rosebud Reservation's working population found employment in New Deal direct relief reservation programs during the Depression.

Coinciding with reservation work programs, Commissioner of Indian Affairs John Collier advocated the creation of tribal economic corporations to manage tribal resources. Collier's plan became partially embodied in the Indian Reorganization Act (IRA) of 1934, which allowed reservation communities to vote to reorganize their governments along the U.S. democratic model and to create tribal economic corporations. Although Collier's proposal focused on reservation economic self-sufficiency, his proposition spawned bitter partisan battles as reservation residents discussed the strengths and weaknesses of the IRA.

These disputes contributed to the evolution of contemporary reservation political culture. Despite compelling reasons to support the IRA, many conservative Plains reservation communities would not support this legislation. The Yankton, the Standing Rock, the Crow, the Wind River, and the Fort Peck reservation communities rejected the IRA at tribal elections. Other reservations, such as Pine Ridge, approved the IRA by voting to accept the Act, then drafting new constitutions, and last of all, but more infrequently approving corporate tribal charters. Out of a total of over 500 recognized U.S. Indian tribes, only ninety-two accepted the IRA, and only about half that number went on to create tribal economic corporations. Nevertheless, while most reservation communities did not adopt the IRA, the BIA required that all tribal governments draft bylaws that in practical effect operated much like constitutional governments.

Tribal support for the IRA decreased by the end of the decade because the act failed to increase reservation self-rule. One reason for this dwindling support was that the BIA increased the number of Indian Service employees to administer Indian New Deal programs, instead of reducing government employees and turning reservation operations over to tribal governments. This trend was especially aggravating to Indians, who witnessed funding increases for the BIA. On the other hand, the passage of the Social Security Act in 1935 enabled many reservation Indians to obtain relief assistance from federal agencies.

World War II

America's entrance into World War II (1939–45) ended congressional appropriations for direct work relief programs. Jobless workers either entered the armed services or found employment in war-related industries. Plains climatic conditions also improved in the early 1940s, advancing agricultural prospects, but most reservation Indians did not participate in this prosperity. With a diminishing land base and an increasing population that had limited access to credit, most reservation Indians only marginally participated in the rural recovery either as field hands in labor intensive production or as sellers and lessors of land.

Since there were few reservation alternatives for employment, military service became an opportunity for many young Indian people, and as a result, many enlisted in the U.S. armed services. Many Indian soldiers sent money home to relatives who remained on reservations. For others, some found limited work opportunities in war-related industries such as urban munitions plants, and, some Sioux found work closer to home at the ammunition ordnance storage facility at Igloo, South Dakota, near the Pine Ridge Reservation.

The Post-War Experience

World War II changed Plains reservation life. Men and women left the reservations and either went to war or found work at war industries located in urban areas. After the war, many returned to their respective reservations, determined to improve their communities' economic, health, and housing conditions.

Wartime experiences made the post-war Plains reservation leaders more vocal and more aggressive than their predecessors. These pacesetters wanted greater self-rule to control reservation resources and institutions. Post-World War II Indian reservation leaders asserted that economic development was a tribal right and prepared reservation economic planning documents urging greater exploitation of tribal resources and labor to improve reservation economic welfare. These leaders also demanded equal rights with other citizens, and to achieve equality, they demanded that Congress repeal discriminatory legislation, especially the restrictive liquor laws, which prohibited sale of alcohol to Indians. In 1952, the Indian alcohol prohibition was lifted, and now reservation governments have the right to decide whether or not to allow sale of alcohol on their reservations.

To improve economic conditions, tribal leaders needed to build infrastructures, such as roads, economic development parks, and telephone services that would facilitate economic commerce. Building economic infrastructure, however, was an imposing task, because most Plains reservations had few resources and little capital to pay for such improvements. Economically disadvantaged, the Plains peoples were distant from markets and possessed neither investment income nor access to credit, which made economic improvement difficult.

Reservation people wanted to end that pattern of economic dependency and develop their own ranching operations. They wanted to remain on the reservations, but many factors worked against them. The inability to find credit and an inadequate land base prohibited individuals from beginning ranching operations. In addition, the technological evolution decreased the demand for manual labor, reducing such employment opportunities as temporary agricultural laborers during the annual fall harvest. After World War II, new mechanized combines and other harvesting equipment rapidly spread throughout the Plains, and, for crops like wheat, oats, and other grains, the new equipment was more efficient and cheaper than traditional harvesting by seasonal labor. Consequently, in the postwar period, mechanization took away a major source of seasonal farm labor income from many Plains Indian communities, causing them to slide further into poverty.

Unable to increase their participation in the local economy, many reservation residents turned to wage work. Ideally, tribal leaders wanted labor intensive industries to locate either on or near reservations. A benefit to potential employers was that reservations contained a skilled or semiskilled work force trained during military service or at defense plants. For Indian community members, reservation-based industries would minimize family disruptions and the necessity of leaving their cultural communities, with its social and ceremonial events, for the oftentimes alien environments of cities or nearby towns.

However, industrial leaders were reluctant to establish plants near or on northern Plains reservations because of the distance from both suppliers and distributors. An alternative was to encourage Indian families to resettle in urban centers where jobs could be found. In the early 1950s, the U.S. government sponsored a program to assist rural reservation people to migrate to cities and to find jobs. Many Blackfeet moved to Seattle and New Hampshire, while many Oglala and Brule relocated to Chicago, Dallas, and Oakland. After obtaining employment, often in construction, many lost their jobs during the 1957 recession, and many returned jobless to their reservations. Others, however, remained in urban areas such as Los Angeles, Chicago, and Minne-

Blackfeet residence with sweat lodge and canvas lodge in foreground, Blackfeet Reservation, Montana.

apolis, where significant urban Indian communities are present today.

Relocation pulled many Indian people away from the reservation's cultural environment and family activities. In order to maintain reservation ties, many tribal people preferred to work at jobs that were near the reservation. Others preferred only to work seasonally in urban areas, usually in the winter, and then return to the reservation during the summers, in time to participate in tribal ceremonies and powwows. The automobile encouraged migration from reservations and enabled many reservation people to work greater distances from their homes, while maintaining contact with their rural tribal communities.

Nearby reservation communities often provided temporary employment, usually seasonal construction work. That forced individuals to rely on local and state social services during periods of unemployment. Under these conditions the emigrants' economic livelihood did not improve, especially when an entire family depended on intermittent income. Even more important, the limited opportunities available in off-reservation communities made the plight of most reservation Indians more visible and encouraged discrimination.

Some Omaha and Winnebago left their reservations and assumed residence in Omaha, Nebraska, and Sioux City, Iowa. Many Crow moved to Billings, Montana, and a few Blackfeet found limited employment in Great Falls, Montana. Kansas City, due to its proximity to several reservations, became a common location for Kansas Indians who were looking for work. Rapid City and Sioux Falls, South Dakota, and Bismarck, North Dakota, became favorite Lakota destinations.

Many times, Indians seeking off-reservation work selected locales because of their proximity to reservation and familiarity with the city, or because friends and relatives were already there. The cities, with associated pressures and distractions, strained the ability of many Indians to preserve tribal identity, because of the need to adjust to the urban environment. Regardless of destination, relocation changed Plains demography and scattered tribal populations across the country. These migrations made it more difficult to maintain family relations and ceremonial ties. The reservations remained important cultural homelands for those living off the reservation.

The departure for urban environments did not improve reservation conditions for those who remained. Throughout the upper Missouri drainage, the U.S. Army Corps of Engineers completed one dam after another in the 1950s and 1960s and changed the living and subsistence patterns of several reservation communities. Tribal communities along the Missouri River lost to flooding valuable land that provided many reservation residents with fuel and food. The Fort Berthold, Cheyenne River, Standing Rock, Yankton, Lower Brule, Crow Creek, and Fort Peck reservations lost entire communities, as rising water forced reservation residents either to relocate in new communities (New Town, North Dakota, in the case of the Fort Berthold Reservation) or move to existing communities (Eagle Butte, South Dakota, in the case of the Cheyenne River Sioux Reservation). Damming prairie rivers did not stop with the Missouri River but expanded as tributaries were dammed, including the Big Horn River on the Crow Reservation. This hydraulic destruction continued the pattern of reservations supplying resources to non-tribal consumers and increased reservation poverty.

Plains reservations did not experience postwar prosperity, but instead reservation poverty increased. Plains Indian poverty excluded them from the 1950s termination legislation, was designed to turn over tribal affairs to local state governments. Eventually, however, the Plains state governments refused to assume responsibilities over terminated Indian people, since the gains in tax revenues would have been far outweighed by the social welfare costs of supporting the impoverished Indian Plains communities.

The nation's war on poverty, initiated in the early 1960s, provided the rural Plains reservations with hope for economic progress. In 1964, Congress extended the Office of Economic Opportunity (OEO) programs to reservations and enabled tribal governments and tribal communities to write and administer Indian Community Action Program (ICAP) development grants. This provided tribal organizations an opportunity to improve reservation standards of living by building homes, constructing sanitary systems, and enhancing education. Like previous New Deal direct relief programs of the late 1930s, the 1960s enterprises provided short term employment but did not build reservations infrastructures, and government dollars continued to pass from the reservation to non-tribal communities.

OEO and associated programs encouraged reservation communities to take control of reservation programs extending beyond economic projects. The Crow tribe initiated a language program for young children in the Head Start Program, thereby providing a language foundation that strengthened cultural bonds. Even more important, the 1960s political climate, which favored civil rights and greater cultural awareness, increased tribal activism. The Plains reservations served as focal points for the American Indian Movement (AIM), an Indian Red Power organization, resulting in a seventy-three-day siege at Wounded Knee, South Dakota, in early 1973. In 1890, Wounded Knee was the site of Seventh Cavalry massacre of over two hundred Sioux men, women, and children.

Self determination—permitting tribes to manage tribal operations—became U.S. policy in 1971 after a

Kicking Women Singers at the North American Indian Days, Browning, Montana.

speech by President Richard Nixon (1969–74). Nevertheless over the next two decades, the U.S. government, through the BIA, maintained control over tribal government budgets and law-making, thus making the trend toward tribal government self-determination a hollow victory.

Neither political activism nor government programs addressed major economic problems when government funds declined during the administrations of presidents Ronald Reagan and George Bush (1981–93). In order to generate income, some resource-rich tribes began to investigate the selling of coal and oil. As energy resources increased in value in the 1970s, companies pursued coal and oil contracts with several Plains reservations. The international energy crisis became a blessing and a curse to the several reservations. Tribal leaders hoped energy leases would provide jobs and would increase tribal government budgets. On the other hand, there was not universal support in the reservations on the issue of coal sales, because of the long-range environmental and cultural effects. In the late 1970s, the Northern Cheyenne voted to reject massive coal sales and potentially millions of dollars of royalty income, because strip mining threatened to destroy nearly half of the Northern Cheyenne's Tongue River Reservation land base.

Different energy programs characterized each reservation, but the desire to control individual reservation energy development remained a common theme. The Crow entered into coal-mining contracts, the Blackfeet entered into oil exploration contracts, and the Fort Peck leadership opened the reservation to oil exploration, but oil companies paid Fort Peck prices.

Erratic energy markets encouraged tribes to pursue more stable economic projects. The Fort Peck (Montana) and Fort Totten (North Dakota) reservations built manufacturing plants that relied on government defense contracts. The Turtle Mountain Reservation, North Dakota, also sought contract work with the U.S. Defense Department for manufacturing trailers to haul heavy military equipment. These were successful reservation industries, but they employed only a small percentage of the people and forced most residents either to seek employment off the reservation or to remain unemployed or underemployed on the reservation.

Nevertheless, after decades of economic development effort, Plains reservations are still some of the most impoverished places in the United States. Regardless of the standard applied, Plains Indians are among the poorest of the poor (for example, real unemployment reached 80 percent on the Northern Cheyenne Reservation). High unemployment creates low reservation standards of living and results in malnutrition, poor health, and sub-standard housing.

Many Indian reservation communities adopted and modified U.S. institutions as a means to maintain their identity and traditions. Initially, tribal contact with U.S. schools produced negative experiences, as teachers tried to remove children from their culture, family, and heritage. Instead of fighting the schools, tribal leaders demanded change and assumed greater control over their children's education. Reservation parents and leaders insisted that school curricula become more relevant to reservation needs and values. Now many elementary and secondary reservation schools emphasize study of Indian cultures and help prepare children to participate in the reservation cultural community.

This concept has been carried into higher education. On the Plains, tribes have been leaders in community education, establishing a large number of tribally controlled community colleges. These institutions satisfy local needs to educate individuals, providing a mechanism for high school dropouts to complete graduation requirements, and providing college students with skills essential for employment (see the section on Indian Higher Education).

Improving each reservation's education system is essential, because residents need specific skills before they can even work for their own tribal governments. For example, tribal governments today administer multimillion dollar budgets, providing funds for a wide array of services from education to economic development. To accomplish these services, tribal leaders require that employees have expertise in accounting, administration, and environmental issues.

Contemporary reservation life is the result of change and continuity reflecting the ability of Plains Indians to accommodate outsiders without surrendering their cultural heritage. As a result, Plains cultures endure, because many tribal members continue to attend powwows, tribal fairs, Sun Dances, sweat ceremonies, and naming ceremonies. Powwows are held annually in most Plains reservations, and many powwows still retain sacred dances as well as more social and public dances. Since the 1970s, many Plains tribes have revived public enactment of the traditional Sun Dance or adopted new versions of the Sun Dance, as with the Crow, who in the 1940s accepted a Sun Dance ceremony from the Shoshoni on the Wind River Reservation in Wyoming.

Mosquito Run, Milk River Indian Days, August 1986, Fort Belknap Agency, Montana.

On the Northern Cheyenne reservation, each of the four major reservation communities holds a powwow, during which a major Sun Dance is held in early July at Lame Deer, Montana, where the tribal government buildings are located. Traditional giveaway ceremonies are carried out at many Plains powwows. The purpose of the giveaways is to cement ties of friendship with members of other tribal communities. The peyote religion, or Native American Church, finds many converts among the Plains peoples (see the sections on Indian religions). Urban Indians maintain their cultural ties by either returning to their reservations to take part in the annual ceremonies and powwows or by participating in tribal social activities at urban Indian centers. Many sacred ceremonies and significant aspects of Plains culture remain strongly supported by Plains reservation communities. Despite poverty and isolation, Plains Indian culture is alive and well.

Richmond Clow
University of Montana, Missoula

♦ NORTHWEST COAST INDIANS

The cultures of the Northwest Coast have long fascinated scholars because of the region's unique life-styles, sophisticated art, and flamboyant ceremonies. These cultures underwent dramatic changes beginning in the late eighteenth century when Europeans came into the area. Nevertheless, Northwest Coast Indians persist today as distinct cultures within the ever expanding Canadian and American societies, largely because of their tenacity, but also because of the leading role they have taken in exerting their aboriginal rights to land and resources. A reliance on two Northwest Coast resources, salmon and cedar, was a characteristic of almost all of the diverse peoples of the area at the time of European contact, and to a certain extent, today.

To discuss the nature of the Northwest Coast culture prior to European contact, we have to be largely speculative. By basing our discussion on archaeological, historical, and ethnographic information, we can satisfactorily reconstruct the traditional lifeways of the Northwest Coast people. As today, aboriginally a great deal of variation was evident along the coast. The Indians spoke a variety of languages and represented an assortment of cultural adaptations to the coastal environment. Some groups relied more heavily on salmon than others. Some were whalers or deep-sea fishers. Some lived inland and relied more heavily on the fruits of the forest and on big game. Some traded extensively, while others stayed close to home and let traders come to them. Some warred on their neighbors, while others were the prey. Despite these differences, the Northwest Coast culture area can be discussed in general terms, as a way of laying a foundation upon which to explore the post-contact history of the various tribes.

Tribal Distribution

The Northwest Coast culture area is generally considered to be the part of North America that lies along the Pacific Ocean from roughly 42 north latitude (the California-Oregon border) to 60 north latitude. This includes southeast Alaska and western portions of British Columbia, Washington, and Oregon. To introduce the various Northwest Coast tribes, we will begin at the north end of the culture area and work southward. Present-day place names are used in this discussion.

The Tlingit inhabited the area that is now southeast Alaska, from Yakutat Bay to Portland Canal. The Tlingit fished salmon in kin-owned areas and also depended upon other resources of the sea, especially halibut and seal. Clinging to the mountainous shores and rugged offshore islands, Tlingit villages were usually large in comparison to other Northwest Coast tribes. The total Tlingit population at the time of European contact is estimated to have been 15,000.

Immediately to the south of the Tlingit, the Haida inhabited the southern portion of Prince of Wales Island in southeast Alaska and the Queen Charlotte Islands in British Columbia. Well known along the coast for their woodworking skills, especially large totem poles and huge seaworthy canoes, the several bands of Haida probably numbered about 14,000 when first contacted in the late 1700s.

The Tlingit, the Haida, and a third group, the Tsimshian, are sometimes collectively known as the "northern matrilineal tribes" because of their distinctive form of social organization. The Tsimshian, who resided on the north-central coast of British Columbia, and inland in the Nass and Skeena River valleys, numbered approximately 14,500 at the time of first contact.

Various bands of Kwakwala speakers lived along the south-central British Columbia coast and adjacent eastern shores of Vancouver Island. These bands can be broadly divided into the northern groups and the southern groups. The northern groups include the Haisla, Haihais, Bella Bella, and Owekeeno; the southern groups are known collectively as the Kwakiutl, or Kwakwaka'wakw. The Kwakiutl are famous in anthropological literature for their extravagant ceremonies known as "potlatches" (discussed later in this entry) and also for the other types of religious and secular ceremonies that permeated every aspect of their lives. At the time of contact, these groups numbered approximately 7,500 for the northern groups and 19,000 for the southern.

Facing the Pacific Ocean, the west coast of Vancouver Island was home to the Nuu-Chah-Nulth (formerly known as Nootka). They and the Makah (a closely related group

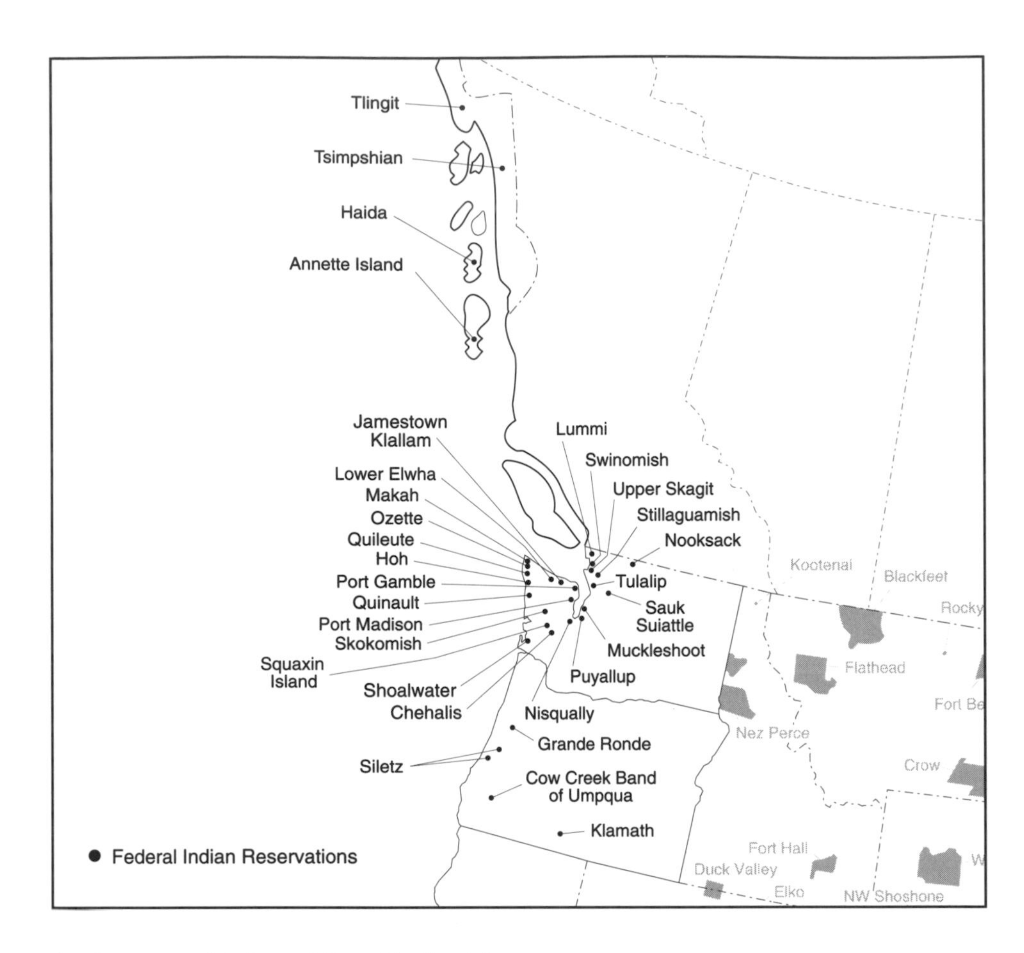

Contemporary Northwest Coast Indian tribes.

who lived across the Strait of Juan de Fuca in present-day Washington State) were famous for their skills as whalers and deep-sea navigators. One of the Nuu-Chah-Nulth bands was host to the first European settlement on the Northwest Coast. The bands totaled about 10,000 at the time of contact.

The Coast Salish, consisting of more than three dozen distinct tribes and bands, resided in southwest mainland British Columbia, southeast Vancouver Island, and much of western Washington. Two linguistically related groups, the Bella Coola of the central coast of British Columbia and the Tillamook of the north-central Oregon coast, make up the largest number of Salish speakers in the Northwest Coast culture area. The Bella Coola numbered about 3,000; the Tillamook about 4,000. The rest of the Coast Salish, which for linguistic and cultural reasons are perhaps better broken down into four groupings, numbered 4,000 for the Northern Coast Salish, 20,000 for the Central Coast Salish, 12,500 for the Southern Coast Salish, and 12,000 for the Southwestern Coast Salish.

The Chinook inhabited the lower Columbia River from the Cascade Mountains to the Pacific Ocean. The Chinook are, perhaps, the Native group most written about in Northwest Coast history—they are renowned in history and legend as traders extraordinaire. Because they controlled the waterways into the interior, the Chinook were masters over trade north and south along the coast and inland to the Columbia Plateau and beyond. In addition to their prowess as traders, the Chinook also realized the potential of the enormous Columbia River salmon runs. Numbering perhaps 10,500 in the mid-1700s, by 1850, the Chinook population had dwindled to just a few hundred.

Numerous bands of linguistically diverse tribes resided along the Oregon Coast and inland in the Willamette River Valley. These groups spoke a number of languages from unrelated linguistic stocks such as Athapascan and Penutian. Culturally, these tribes were transitional between the Northwest Coast and California culture areas and shared many traits in common with both. In all, they numbered as many as 30,000 people when first contacted by Europeans.

The Annual Cycle of Economic Subsistence

While the most striking thing about the Northwest Coast culture area may be the linguistic and cultural diversity evident from north to south, we nevertheless can identify some general characteristics. Let us explore a "yearly round" of social and economic activities as a means of identifying some of the culture traits common to the Northwest Coast.

Housing

The typical habitation of the Northwest Coast Indians was the longhouse. The structure was large, capable of sheltering several families. Generally, the families who inhabited a longhouse were related to one another in some way: among the northern matrilineal groups, they were related through the female lineage; among the other tribes, the relation was through either the house owner or his spouse.

Inside the longhouse, each family had its own area, usually partitioned off. Central fires burned for heat and light, but each family cooked its own meals and ate separately. Families could change houses if they wished, or the house might break up in the summer months while individual families pursued subsistence activities. In the winter, the longhouse served as a ceremonial center; the partitions were taken down to make room for dances and for guests.

Food Resources

Certainly the most prolific and dependable resource throughout the Northwest Coast was the abundant runs of salmon. Five species of salmon inhabit the Pacific Coast, spending their adult life in the offshore waters and traveling up freshwater streams to spawn. Native people caught some salmon by trolling in the saltwater, but large numbers of fish taken for preservation were captured in or near the freshwater streams with traps, weirs, and nets. Typically, salmon enter freshwater in the spring; subsequent runs may occur throughout the summer and into the fall. Because not every stream supports all five species nor successive runs, some Northwest Coast groups focused their attention on specific runs of fish to take in abundance for drying or smoking as a means of preservation. Preserved salmon provided a dietary staple which was supplemented with other locally available food resources, such as shellfish, plant foods, marine mammals, land mammals, and waterfowl.

Although some salmon fishing took place throughout the year, the bulk of the fish were taken in the spring and fall at specific locations where the family groups tended to resort year after year. Probably the most widely employed fishing device at such locations was the weir, a barricade placed across a stream to divert the runs of fish into a trap. While the men worked the traps, the women cut the fish along the back, removing the bone and internal organs. The filleted fish were then hung on a rack to be preserved by drying winds, or in the rafters

The inside of a house at Nootka Sound, from the Cook Expedition, 1778. Courtesy of Special Collections Division, University of Washington Libraries.

of the longhouse where the slow-burning fires would dry them. Some groups preserved as much as five hundred pounds of fish per person through the year and, indeed, even to this day, many Native people feel a meal is incomplete without at least a little salmon.

Not all of the summer was spent salmon fishing. For many groups shellfish—especially clams, mussels, and oysters—provided important food. Shellfish could be taken anytime of year, although in some areas the flesh might be poisonous in the summer months. Usually the "spring tides," when the lowest tides of the year occurred during the daylight hours, were the important shellfish gathering times. As with salmon, shellfish were also dried in abundance, providing not only sustenance, but also an important trade item with groups farther inland.

In late spring, many other types of fish were utilized, depending upon local availability. For example, the Tsimshian harvested tons of a small fish known as oolichan, which was rendered into oil. Oolichan was an important addition to the diet, as well as a trade item. Other Northwest Coast groups harvested herring (both the fish and the spawn), halibut, rockfish, and other deep sea fish. Marine mammals—seals, porpoise, and whales—were also harvested. Whales, especially gray whales, were taken during their migratory pass in the spring. The Nuu-Chah-Nulth, Makah, and Quileute, who were all expert whalers, hunted these large animals from dugout canoes, using hand-thrown spears. Other Northwest Coast tribes might have used a whale that had beached or drifted ashore, but the Nuu-Chah-Nulth, Makah, and Quileute pursued the migrating whales far out at sea. Many miles from shore, for days on end, these Native whalers would pursue their quarry in hopes of not only obtaining an important source of food, but also the prestige that came with being a successful whaler.

The land mammals most frequently hunted by the Northwest Coast Indians were deer, elk, bear, and mountain goat. Either solitary hunters would hunt the animals, or groups would drive them into nets or ambushes. Typically, the inland groups were more involved in hunting land mammals. Mountain goats were most particularly hunted for their horns, which could be fashioned into implements, usually spoons, and for their wool, which was spun into yarn and then woven into blankets for ceremonial garb and day-to-day use. In addition to mountain goats, some women kept a type of small dog which could be shorn like a sheep; its woolly fur was then spun into yarn.

The time of gathering plant foods began in the spring, but was more intensive in the late summer and early fall. Starchy tubers, such as camas and wapato, and broken fern roots were taken in abundance, in some cases from kin-controlled plots. Berries and other fruits were also abundant; they were dried as well as eaten fresh.

Culture

Of course, the Northwest Coast people did not simply spend their time in the pursuit of food. Artisans, such as weavers, basket makers, wood carvers, and stone workers spent many hours crafting their handiwork. Winter months were busy with ceremonial activities such as spirit dances, ceremonial performances, the demonstration of inherited privileges like masked dances, and the most famous ceremony of all, the potlatch. Potlatches, the ceremonial distribution of wealth goods, could actually take place any time of year, to commemorate a naming, wedding, or funeral. Potlatching was a way for an individual to express his social standing in the community, and to reinforce that position through the giving away of wealth and feasting with the guests. Numerous other ceremonies also were held, but certainly the potlatch is the most widely known. Some evidence suggests that potlatching may have increased in the 1800s because of the influx of wealth items through the fur trade and subsequent interactions with Europeans, but that was only one of the dramatic changes to occur during the contact period.

European Contact

Many of the earliest explorers of northern North America, such as John Cabot, who sailed from England in 1497, were searching for a direct passage from Europe to China by way of an open sea passage across North America. Such an ocean route would have allowed Europeans an efficient means of carrying on trade with the Far Eastern empires. In the end, no such passage existed, but considerable European effort was expended before the twentieth century in search of the fabled Northwest Passage. In their continuing search for wealth and for the Northwest Passage, Europeans eventually reached the Northwest Coast during the latter part of the eighteenth century. Initially, the Spanish explored northward from their settlements in Mexico. Shortly afterward, the Russians reached southeast Alaska from Siberia. At first, the Europeans found little to compel them to stay. Some shipboard trade took place, but the Northwest Coast was not particularly rich in furs, and the Natives were hard bargainers. Soon, however, sea otter pelts began to bring in phenomenal prices in China, and a lively trade quickly developed.

In 1789, the Spanish established a post at Nootka Sound on Vancouver Island and the struggle for control of trade began. The trade eventually included the Russians, Spanish, British, and Americans. The Native people were unconcerned with European political struggles so long as they gained access to manufactured goods. Such items greatly increased the Natives' efficiency and economic well-being. The initial changes brought by the fur trade were primarily in material goods; little change was evident in social or religious life.

In 1795, the Spanish relinquished claim to the area north of 42 latitude, the Russians held southeast Alaska, and in 1818, the British and Americans agreed to joint occupation of the area in between. In 1811, the establishment of land-based trading operations began with the building of the American Fur Company's post at the mouth of the Columbia River. Lost during the War of 1812, the post eventually fell into the hands of the Hudson's Bay Company which came to dominate the fur trade of the Northwest. The Hudson's Bay Company expanded operations to Fort Vancouver in 1824, Fort Langley in 1827, Fort Nisqually and Fort McLoughlin in 1833, Cowlitz Station in 1838, Fort Victoria in 1843, and by agreement with the Russians, Fort Stikine and Fort Taku in 1840. The economic control of the Northwest Coast was in the hands of the Hudson's Bay Company until the 1840s, when American settlers began moving into the joint-occupied area. In 1846, the British and Americans negotiated the Treaty of Oregon, establishing the boundary at the 49th parallel between the United States and Canada.

Through the late 1800s, non-Native settlement of the Northwest Coast progressed at a staggering rate. The settlement period was marked by the negotiation of treaties in the United States, by the establishment of reservation communities in British Columbia, and by the contraction of villages into a few Native communities in Alaska. During the same time, the Native population rapidly declined because of European diseases for which the Indians had no resistance. By 1900, non-Natives outnumbered Natives in most areas and the Native societies were quickly engulfed by the growing dominant society.

New religious expressions among the Indians became evident early in the settlement period. Considerable evidence shows that syncretic movements occurred as well as strong efforts to continue the practice of traditional religious expression of shamanism and spirit quests. Christianity attracted many converts as well, especially among those communities in close proximity to non-Native communities. Today in any given Native community, there are a number of Christians, as well as followers of Shakerism, a religious movement stemming from the experience of a Coast Salish prophet in

Cedar house, Dundas Island, British Columbia.

the 1880s. Still other Northwest Coast Indians are practitioners of the traditional forms of spiritualism.

As the non-Native population became more dominant, the Northwest Coast people found it increasingly difficult to continue to fish, hunt, and gather as they had before. Fishing, logging, and farming became the area's principle economic activities. Conflicts over non-Native and Native uses of the land and resources were inevitable. As Native societies became more restricted in their traditional activities, they sought wage labor in nearby non-Native communities, or became entangled in the growing poverty and political domination of the reservation communities. Many Native people chose to leave the reservations during this time, an act encouraged by government policy.

Contemporary Life

The Northwest Coast culture of the twentieth century is a complex combination of traditional values and of political-economic factors that emerged from interaction with the dominant society. Modern Northwest Coast Natives—now minorities in their own land—are citizens of either Canada or the United States. They also have the rights and privileges that go with being a member of a tribe or band.

While the multi-family longhouses were abandoned in most areas by 1900, the strong kin ties that were a part of the longhouse living situation have endured. Extended family groups depend upon one another in times of need, for assistance in sponsoring feasts or potlatches, and to support one another in the attempt to gain political power. Many Native communities may at first appear indistinguishable from their non-Native neighbors, but behind the familiar housing, clothing, and jobs is an undercurrent of Native life that has persisted and adapted to the modern context.

To understand the changes that have occurred over the past 100 years, we must look at some important political events that have had lasting impacts on the Northwest Coast people. Because the Native people have lived under different polities, their situations have all been different. Historical changes in the Northwest Coast can best be studied by looking individually at three main areas within the region: Alaska, British Columbia, and Western Washington and Oregon.

Alaska Until 1867, the Tlingit and some of the Haida lived in an area of North America claimed by Russia. While southeast Alaska was part of Russian America, the impact on the Native people was minimal. Even after the United States acquired Alaska, its isolation meant the Native people were left to themselves. In the 1890s, however, the situation began to change rapidly. With the Alaskan gold rush, followed by the influx of settlers, the Native people rapidly found themselves part of a larger political reality. They participated in the growing economy as fishers, loggers, and in other occupations. Many adopted Christianity in the late 1800s and early 1900s. Formal education became a priority for many Tlingit and Haida families.

As interest in Alaska's resources grew, and especially when oil was discovered in the North Slope, soon after Alaska's statehood in 1959, it became clear that some settlement had to be reached between the United States government and the Native people. In 1971, the Alaska Native Claims Settlement Act terminated Native title to land in Alaska. In return, Alaska Natives were to select certain lands that they would retain. They received federal funds to establish Native-controlled share holding corporations to be operated as profit-making operations. The Native people of southeast Alaska were formed into one of thirteen corporations that have since become the primary political bodies of the Native people. Although the Native villages have elected their own political bodies and other forms of Native political expression are available, the Native corporations wield the most power and influence.

Since its inception, the Alaska Native Claims Settlement Act has been the primary political influence in Native Alaska. Unencumbered by a reservation system, the Tlingit and Haida have prospered. As they begin to exert their Native rights over land and resources, they will likely continue to be a dominant force in the state of Alaska.

British Columbia The Native people of British Columbia have had a somewhat different experience. Many of the Native people live in remote areas and have participated in the principle economic activities of the province, especially logging and commercial fishing. Unlike most Native people of Canada, the Natives of British Columbia never signed treaties with the federal government (although the Hudson's Bay Company negotiated a few legally valid treaties with Native people on Vancouver Island). Instead of treaties, British Columbia instituted a system of reserves, setting aside Natives' lands until they became assimilated into the dominant society.

Native policy in Canada primarily stems from the "Indian Act," an all-encompassing piece of legislation first passed in 1884 and revised several times since (the last in 1985). With special attention to the Northwest Coast, the Indian Act specifically outlawed the potlatch. British Columbia officials were incapable of enforcing this policy until the 1920s when concerted efforts were made to abolish the ceremony. While potlatching never completely disappeared, it did go underground for many years. When the potlatch law was abolished in 1951, potlatching was publicly revived.

Beginning in the 1880s, Native leaders in British Columbia sought to affirm Native rights to land and resources. Forming a province-wide organization in 1916, the tribes have actively pursued recognition of their claims. Although seeking reprieve in the courts as early as the 1920s, it was not until the 1970s that the tribes began to make some important progress. With the provision in the Canadian Constitution of 1982 that "existing aboriginal and treaty rights of the aboriginal peoples of Canada are . . . recognized and affirmed," the British Columbia Natives finally had a firm commitment on the part of the federal government to support their claims. Nevertheless, the outcomes of land and resource claims have been varied. Perhaps the most famous case was one in which the Gitskan (Tsimshian) were involved. This claim attempted to assert Native sovereignty over a large portion of west-central British Columbia. Dragging through the courts for several years, the case was decided against the Gitskan in 1991. The case is currently under appeal. Simultaneously, a case involving Coast Salish fishing on the Fraser River was decided in favor of the Native claim to aboriginal rights to the resources. Since there is no clear agenda in the recognition of Native rights in British Columbia, their future prospects remain unclear.

Western Washington and Oregon The Native people of western Washington and Oregon represent the third set of circumstances of historical change in the Northwest Coast. In the mid-1850s, these tribes entered into treaties with the United States government, forming the basis of interaction for the last 135 years. Most important among the treaty provisions was the establishment of reservations and the protection of certain aboriginal rights, especially fishing. From the treaty era to the present, various federal policies have been enacted which have had lasting impacts on the Native people of the northwest United States. Beginning with "assimilationist" policy in the late 1800s and continuing into the present era of "self-determination," the federal policies that have marked the relationship between Native people and the federal government can be used as a means of discussing social changes in this region.

Assimilation refers to the social, cultural, and political incorporation of a person or group into the mainstream national culture and society. From the 1880s to 1934, the U.S. government actively sought to convince Indians to abandon their traditional cultures and join U.S. society and culture. Perhaps the most influential policy of the assimilationist period was the General

Native fashion show, Prince George, British Columbia.

Allotment Act of 1887. This policy allowed for the allotment of reservation lands. Allotting parcels of land to individuals had two dramatic impacts on the Native people. First, it was designed to instill a Western notion of private property in the form of alienable land. Second, it served to break up the multi-family units and encouraged individual activities, especially farming. The long-lasting effect of allotment was that since the land was individually owned, the tribe had no means to keep reservation land in the control of the tribe. Consequently, much land was sold to non-tribal members. From the implementation of the General Allotment Act, to the 1930s, the design of federal policy was to break up the tribal units and encourage the assimilation of Native people into the dominant society. This was reinforced by the schooling of children in off-reservation boarding schools that taught them trades and required that they speak English. A famous saying of boarding school administrators succinctly sums up their educational philosophy: "Kill the Indian but save the person." Children from the Northwest Coast went to many different boarding schools, but the most common was Chemawa, near Salem, Oregon.

In 1924, all Native people of the United States were granted citizenship. Instead of marking the desired results of forced assimilation, it marked the end of an era of policy. In the 1930s, Congress passed a series of new legislative acts that were designed to strengthen the tribal units and encourage independent tribal economic development. Under the Indian Reorganization Act of 1934, tribes in the Northwest were assisted in developing tribal governments based on a constitution and governed by elected bodies of officials. Rather than encouraging independent development, however, the Indian Reorganization Act actually strengthened the power that the Bureau of Indian Affairs had over the Native people's lives. For example, now the Bureau of Indian Affairs has the power to override decisions made by tribal governments even though tribes are considered sovereigns within the United States. The bold new plans of the federal government during the 1930s were to be short-lived after World War II when the United States began a series of policies designed to terminate the special relationship Native people had with the federal government. Many powers, such as law enforcement, were turned over to the states; individual Indians were encouraged to leave the reservations for urban areas; some tribes were actually terminated—formal ties with the federal government ended and tribal resources divided among the individuals, who collectively ceased being a federally recognized Indian tribe with legal protections for land and tribal rights.

Termination policies were enacted in two important ways. First, the relocation policies, described as "termination by attrition," encouraged reservation residents to move to urban areas where they were to find jobs. However, since the reservation populations were generally undereducated and unskilled, the types of jobs they found were usually menial. Making minimum wage, they were forced to live in the least desirable parts of the cities and as a result urban Indian ghettos were created in cities like Portland and Seattle. Some reservations estimate that as many as one-third of their entire populations were relocated during the 1950s, an action which not only created a drain on the reservation community, but also created an intertribal urban population. Today, approximately 20,000 Native people live in Seattle where they are represented by such groups as the United Indians of All Tribes Foundation.

The second action was the actual termination of some tribes. While many tribes throughout the United States were scheduled for termination, in actuality most were not. Three Oregon tribes were terminated: the Klamath of southeast Oregon and the Siletz and Grande Ronde of the Oregon coast. Siletz and Grande Ronde were the reservation homes of the Oregon coast tribes, and because of their economic success, they were considered likely candidates of termination of their relationship with the federal government. It soon became clear that without their special status as a federally recognized tribe, the Siletz and Grand Ronde had little power to hold their lands together and continue to promote economic well-being. Almost as soon as they were terminated, both tribes sought to be reinstated as federally recognized tribes, an act that was finally granted after nearly thirty years.

The prospects for the future are promising. As Native communities in Alaska, British Columbia, Washington, and Oregon begin to assert their sovereignty as a means to develop economically and politically, they will continue to bring about positive change in a culturally sensitive manner. The present era of "self-determination" is marked by Indian tribes successfully exerting their legal rights to land and resources and the strengthening of tribal self-governance to promote development. The self-determination policy recognizes tribal interests in regaining greater control over reservation institutions, such as education and local administration, and over tribal economic resources such as land, minerals, and hunting and fishing. Perhaps the most well-known example of this is the 1974 "Boldt Decision," the court case *United States v. Washington* brought by the treaty tribes of western Washington. This case determined that Native people retained certain rights to fisheries and other resource gathering activities that included the right to commercial use of the salmon resource. Consequently, the Native people now harvest 50 percent of the commercial salmon resource as well as significant numbers of other fisheries such as herring, halibut, and crab. This treaty-assured right has formed a base upon which other

Chief Shake's house at Wrangell, about the turn of the twentieth century.

economic activities, such as processing and marketing, have been built. Additionally, Native people operate hatcheries that release millions of salmon fry into the public waters every year.

Although Natives participate in American and Canadian society, this does not mean that they have "assimilated" or "acculturated" or any of the other terms that suggest they are no longer Indian. Speaking English, fishing with modern power boats and synthetic nets, or even carving a dug-out canoe with a chain saw does not mean that the Northwest Coast Natives are any less Indian. White Americans, after all, are not expected to cook in the fireplace or support themselves by hitching the horse to the plow. Being a Northwest Coast Indian today means participating in the modern political and economic structures of North American society while maintaining a distinct ethnic identity. It is this identity that will strengthen the efforts toward tribal development—a development that will not only lead to the persistence of Native people into the twenty-first century, but will also lead to their prosperity.

Daniel Boxberger
Western Washington University

♦ ALASKA NATIVES

Traditional Life

There are four major indigenous groups in Alaska: the Aleut, the Eskimo (Yupik and Inuit), the coastal Tlingit and Haida, and the Athapascan. While all have been traced to the people who crossed the Bering Land Bridge (Berengia) 25,000 to 40,000 years ago each has occupied a different territory, spoken a distinctive language, and built a unique heritage.

The Aleut occupy the 1,400-mile-long Aleutian Chain, part of the Alaskan peninsula and the Pribilof Islands in the Bering Sea. An area rich in resources, it supported the densest aboriginal population in Alaska. At the time of the first Russian voyages in the seventeenth century, there were approximately 16,000 Aleut, most residing in the eastern region. The rich marine environment provided the Aleut with a wide variety of sea life, including sea urchins, clams, octopus, fish, sea otters, seals, and whales, which were used for food, clothing, and homes. Birds and their eggs, berries, wild rice and celery, and plant stalks were also part of their diet. The men were skilled open sea hunters and relied on two-person skin boats (*baidarka*) for hunting seals and whales.

Aleutian villages were situated along the coast, allowing easy access to the sea. They were small, usually supporting 100 to 200 inhabitants. Two to five families lived in semi-subterranean houses called *barabaras*. A person's lineage followed the mother's line, and children were disciplined and trained by the mother's family. Men were responsible for hunting and the care of implements and boats. Women cared for the home and gathered food along the beaches and shallow intertidal zones. Traditional society was divided between a small group of nobles, commoners, and slaves captured in wars with other villages. Aleut chiefs were the most respected hunters with long experience and exceptional abilities. Chiefs had little power, and decisions required common agreement. Internal conflict was reduced by making war on others for retribution, the taking of slaves, or trading through intermediaries. The family served as the basis of village organization, economic exchange, warfare, and occasionally political authority.

The Eskimo reside in an extensive and diverse environment from the deep fjords and mountain ranges of the south to the windswept mountains of the Alaskan peninsula, to the tundra and relative flat coasts and lowlands of the Arctic province. Yupik Eskimo is spoken in southwestern Alaska and Inuit to the north stretching across northern Canada to Greenland. Subsistence patterns varied from the caribou hunters of interior Alaska, to the Arctic whalers along the coasts, and the fishermen of southwestern Alaska.

Yupik and Inuit societies were geared toward the continual search for food. They are classified by anthropologists as "central-based wanderers" who spent part of the year on the move and some time at a settlement, or "central base." From a dozen to fifty people would travel together. Extended families composed of three to four generations were basic to an individual's life. Families were relatively equal and autonomous; they would often share with others, intermarry, and hunt together. There was considerable conflict, though, between different groups; strangers with no specific reasons for being in an area were in great danger.

Within each family, people were divided by age and gender. At the head was the boss, or *umialik*. Leaders were usually those who displayed exceptional skill or courage and those who were able to anticipate future

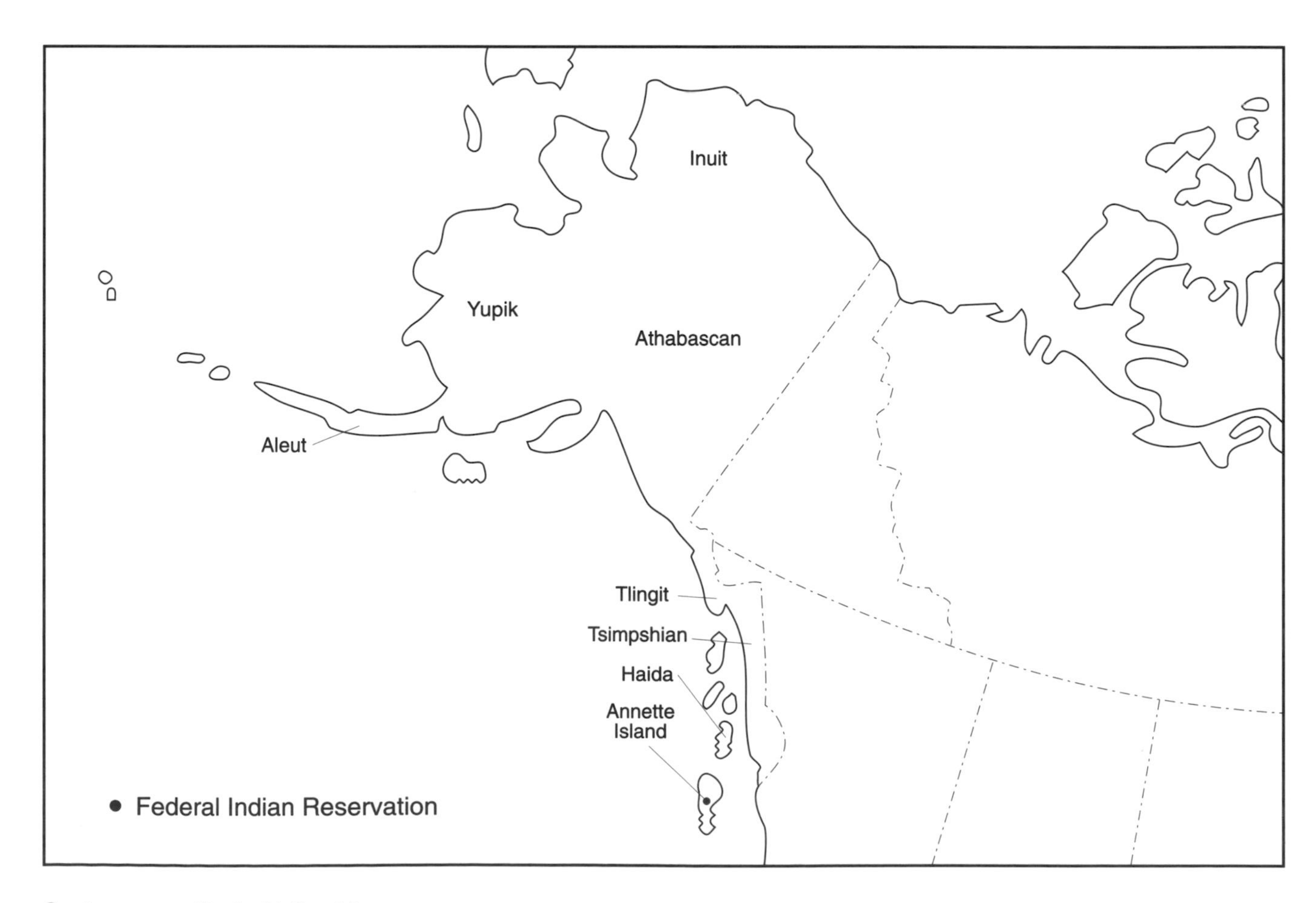

Contemporary Alaska Native tribes.

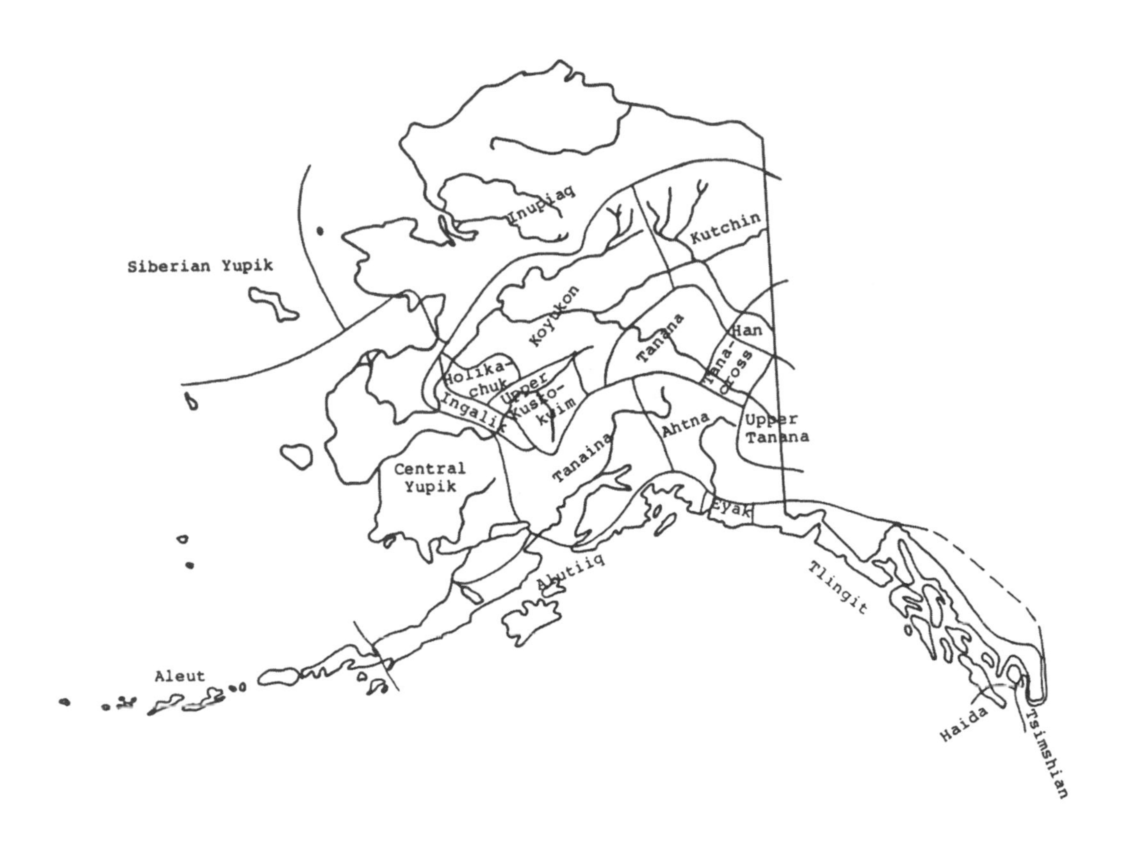

Major languages of Alaska Natives.

problems. Shamans, or spiritual leaders, were also influential because of their familiarity with the spiritual world, their curative powers, and their prescience. Every settlement had a gathering place, or *qargi*, where men, boys, and families would meet for conversation and ritual.

Three major groups occupied southeastern Alaska: the Tlingit, the Haida, and the Tsimshian. Geographically the area is distinct. It is isolated, with high mountains and dense forest to the east and the Pacific Ocean to the west; it is interlaced by fjords and valleys on the mainland and a string of islands off the coast. It is a bountiful environment, which nurtured a formal and complex social system.

Society was divided between two major *moieties*, the Eagle and the Raven, which had their own rules and corporate functions. Within each moiety were numerous clans. The clan was the fundamental political unit; each had its own territory, history, and particular traits. The clan was responsible for settling feuds, property, and subsistence activities. The most basic unit was the house, which was run by a "master of the house," a maternal or great uncle. Houses had their own plots, name, and crest, which displayed major cultural figures in the history of the clan and house. Clans and houses had rights to specific areas for fishing, berry picking, and hunting. In practice anyone could use the sites provided they asked for permission. Areas between each territory were open for travel for everyone.

Rank and status, built on the accumulation of wealth, underlay the system of clans and houses. Possession of material goods, including slaves, crests, blankets, totems, a generous disposition, oratorical skill, and past accomplishments, determined the position of individuals, clans, and houses. The potlatch was an integral part of southeastern cultures. It involved a feast, performances, and the distribution of valuable goods. Potlatches were given to honor an individual and they served to strengthen kin relations, to display one's generosity, and to honor the memory of those who had passed away.

The northern Athapascan occupied a vast territory that extended through most of interior Alaska, bordered by the Arctic to the north and the temperate forests to the south. Included in this area were six subgroups: the Ingalik, the Koyukon, Tanana, Tanaina, Ahtna, and the Upper Tanana. While each group lacked a formal tribal system, they did occupy exclusive territory. Within each territory were smaller bands, which followed the seasonal migration of game, and families, who would, for part of the year, live separately in order to fish and hunt. Composed of people related by blood and marriage, bands were responsible for subsistence activities, territorial boundaries, and the settlement of disputes between families.

Men formed hunting partnerships; one killed the animal and the other distributed it. Resources were always shared. Because food was sometimes scarce, mobility and flexibility were imperative. There was little need to accumulate possessions. The Athapascan practiced what is termed "strategic hunting," in which fish were directed into weirs, caribou were corralled, and waterfowl were taken in their breeding grounds.

Neither primitive nor simple, traditional Native communities in Alaska were extremely well-adapted to the physical environment in which they lived, from the Arctic regions of northern Alaska to the rain forests of the southeast, to the cool and windy climates of the Aleutian chain. The Alaska Natives were also bounded by an intricate kinship system that usually specified who could marry and where the couple would live, as well as ownership of fishing and hunting places and leadership. Social and economic relations allowed for popular understanding and local initiative, equity, and community and kinship reciprocity of material goods and services. These relations also delineated the performance of social and religious obligations, such as potlatch exchanges, and other ritual reciprocities, such as performing funeral services for in-laws, as among the Tlingit. There was a precarious balance between the physical environment and the subsistence needs of each community. Natural disasters, population growth, or outside intrusion could easily upset the balance of human and natural environmental relations.

Russian Colonialism

With the advent of European expansion in the eighteenth century, circumstances in Alaska began to change dramatically. The Russians were first. The voyages of Alexei Chirikof and Vitus Bering in 1741 led to awareness of potential profit from sea otter and seal skins. Siberian fur hunters, the *promishleniki*, soon launched hunting expeditions in the area. An imperial decree was issued in 1766, claiming Russian dominion over the Aleutians, but there was little government regulation of Russian traders and hunters. In response to this anarchy and the competition with other Europeans, the Russian American Company was organized in 1799. The company's charter anticipated the conversion of Natives to Christianity and claimed that the "Islanders" (Aleut) would be treated amicably.

However, the relationship between Russians and Aleut was anything but amicable. Although the exact numbers are not known, it is estimated that 90 percent of the indigenous population was lost to disease or murder. The survivors were in a state of virtual servitude. The Russians used the men as pelagic (open sea) hunters and, as they moved into eastern Alaska, as warriors. Despite its brutality Russian commercial expansion in Alaska was limited to the coast. There were occasional forays to the interior, but they were infrequent because of hostile tribes, impassable terrain, and severe temperatures. By 1867, when the United States acquired control of the territory, Russia ruled only a small portion of it.

American Colonialism

U.S. expansion into Alaska was propelled by an interest in fur and, more importantly, gold. In 1867, the Treaty of Cession was signed which transferred jurisdiction over Alaska to the United States. Article III was particularly important for Alaska Natives: "The Uncivilized tribes will be subject to such laws and regulations as the United States may, from time to time, adopt in regard to aboriginal tribes in that country." Congress recognized this obligation in 1884 when it passed first Organic Act, which extended the civil and criminal laws of Oregon to Alaska: "Indians or other persons in said district shall not be disturbed in the possession of any lands actually in their use or occupation or now claimed by them but the terms under which such persons may acquire title to such lands is reserved for future legislation by Congress."

Despite this disclaimer in the Organic Act, land was usually available for the U.S. economic interests who needed it. The first fish canneries were built in 1878, and within six years they were spread along the entire southern coast of Alaska. In 1878, the first gold mining camp was constructed. Gold prospecting and disputes between miners resulted in the territory's first civil government. Legislation in 1891, 1898, and 1900 permitted trade and manufacturing sites, townsites, homesteading, rights of way for a railroad, and the harvesting of timber.

During World War II, national leaders became more aware of the strategic importance of Alaska. This realization, coupled with the influx of money and people, produced a viable effort to achieve admittance into the Union. In his State of the Union message in 1946, President Truman recommended statehood. Owing to partisan opposition and doubts about the financial capability of the territory, recognition was delayed. Finally a compromise was reached, and Alaska and Hawaii were admitted simultaneously. On January 3, 1959, President Eisenhower proclaimed Alaska the forty-ninth state.

The Land Claims Movement

The Alaska Statehood Act granted the state 104 million acres of land. As public officials began selecting land, imposing rules, and applying laws, Native opposition arose. For example, the Bureau of Land Management, the agency in the Department of the Interior responsible for federal lands, issued a license to the Atomic Energy Commission (AEC), which regulates the use of nuclear materials in the United States, to use 1,600 square miles around Point Hope, an Inuit village on the northwestern coast of Alaska, for an experimental nuclear explosion to create a deep water port. However no one consulted the residents of nearby villages. Another issue was the enforcement of the Migratory Bird Treaty Act between Canada and the United States. The treaty prohibits the hunting of migratory birds between March 10 and September 1. In 1961, the Inuit staged a "duck-in" to protest the restrictions. Many were arrested.

In March 1961, the president of the Point Hope Village Council wrote to the Association of American Indian Affairs (AAIA), which was founded in 1923 to provide legal and technical assistance to Indian tribes, and asked for help. The AAIA and the Indian Rights Association, established in 1882 to protect the rights of American Indians, provided funds for intervillage meetings, at which experiences were shared, rights explained, and common solutions proposed. Within six years, twelve regional associations were formed to pursue their respective land claims. Early in 1967 regional leaders formed the Alaska Federation of Natives (AFN) to secure their rights, enlighten the public about their position, preserve their cultural values, and gain an equitable settlement (see the biography of Howard Rock).

The first major bill to settle the claims of Alaska Natives was introduced in June 1967. The key to a congressional decision was oil. In the late 1960s, large quantities of oil were discovered in Prudhoe Bay on the north coast of Alaska. Several large oil companies worked to extract and transport the crude oil to refineries and markets in the lower forty-eight states. Indian land claims, however, prevented construction of the pipeline from Prudhoe Bay to the port at Valdez in southern Alaska. Native villages, in particular Stevens Village, an Athapascan village in the interior, claimed land over the pipeline route, and gained a court injunction against construction until Indian title to the land was clarified. Thereafter the oil companies actively lobbied Congress and President Richard Nixon in order to gain a quick settlement to Native land claims issues in Alaska. By late 1971, an unusual coalition of oil companies, the Alaska Native lobbying organization (AFN), the state of Alaska, and the federal government moved to settle Alaska Native claims through congressional legislation. President Nixon and the U.S. Senate wanted a domestic source of oil that would counter the increase in prices in 1970 and the shortage of fuel and heating oil. The state of Alaska needed the revenue that private development would generate. The oil industry and the House of Representatives wanted a permit to build the Alaska pipeline. Conservationists wanted more park and wilderness area, and Alaska Natives wanted their land. The Alaska Native Claims Settlement Act (ANCSA) was signed into law on December 18, 1971.

Under terms of the settlement Alaska Natives received $962 million and 44 million acres of land. In exchange, claims over the remaining 335 million acres were extinguished. ANCSA cleared the path for the construction of the Alaska pipeline. It also led to the withdrawal of millions of acres of public lands for national parks and forests, scenic rivers, and wilderness areas. State officials were also permitted to select the remainder of their land under provisions of the statehood act. In the end, 12 percent of Alaska will be privately owned by Alaska Natives, 28 percent by the state, and 59 percent by the federal government.

There are two important assumptions of the Settlement Act. First is the expectation that Natives will be assimilated into the American mainstream and away from a communal life-style to an economy based on private ownership, individualism, and free enterprise. Twelve regional profit-making corporations were es-

Inuit children, Barrow, Alaska.

tablished and given significant responsibilities, including the distribution of money to village corporations and individuals, the control of subsurface resources, the economic development of each region, the promotion of village interests, and the facilitation of intervillage cooperation. Village corporations were also created to use and manage the land and control local development. A second assumption of ANCSA was that the profit corporations and the market system would lead to more employment and educational opportunities, healthier communities, and increasing economic independence for Alaska Natives.

Social and Economic Profile of Alaska Natives

There are over 100,000 Alaska Natives in the United States. Of the 85,603 who live in Alaska, 44,000 are Yupik or Inuit, 31,000 are Athapascan, Tlingit, Haida, or Tsimshian, and 10,000 are Aleut. The majority (56 percent) live in small villages ranging in size from 50 to 900 people. The total number of Alaska Natives is growing rapidly. During the decade of the 1980s, the Inuit and Yupik population grew by 30 percent, Indian peoples by 43 percent, and Aleut by 24 percent. However, the Native proportion of the total population of the state is dropping steadily from 26 percent in 1950, to 17 percent in 1980, to 15.6 percent in 1990. Natives, though, are the majority in five ANCSA defined regions: the Arctic Slope, Bering Straits, Bristol Bay, Calista, and the Northwest Arctic.

Alaska Natives are younger than the general population: 61 percent are under 29 years of age. Their median age is 23. The dependency of Native children on family employment is almost twice that of non-Natives. The average Native family has four children. Increasingly, Alaska Natives are moving to urban areas; 12 percent lived in cities in 1960, 31 percent in 1980, and 44 percent in 1990. Anchorage now has more Alaska Natives than any other area in the state. The populations of regional service centers such as Dillingham, Bethel, Nome, Barrow, and Fort Yukon, as well as small villages, have grown as well.

In the last twenty years, there have been improvements in the lives of Alaska Natives. Through contracts with the Alaska Area Native Health Service and other state and federal agencies, Native associations now administer most health programs. The results have been largely positive. Alaska Natives now live longer and with less fear of epidemic diseases like tuberculosis. Similar changes have occurred in Native education, housing, and employment. Secondary schools now dot the rural landscape, where none existed in the 1960s. The number of high school graduates and those enrolled in college or vocational training has increased. Through the creation of district and regional school boards, Native communities have gained some control over school curriculum and class scheduling. The majority of houses now have indoor plumbing, phones, and sewer and water outlets. Each region has a non-profit housing agency which, through funds from the Department of Housing and Urban Development (HUD), provides low income housing assistance, builds new houses, and collects rents and mortgage payments. Unemployment has also been reduced in some areas because of the growth of local governments, private construction and organization, and expanding industries in fishing, oil, and gas. The major employer in rural Alaska is government. More than 60 percent of the labor force is employed by either federal, state, or local governments. Most jobs are related to public service and administration.

While the ANCSA and subsequent efforts have resulted in a few improvements, fundamental problems remain. The incidence of poverty among Alaska Natives is much higher than for non-Natives. From 2,500 to 3,500 Native families receive food stamps, Aid to Families With Dependent Children payments, and Adult Public Assistance. More than 18,000 rural households rely on low-income energy subsidies. More than 25 percent of the Native population live below the official poverty level. Unemployment among Natives is twice that of non-Native Alaskans. In the western region of the state, half the Native workforce is without a job. Native family incomes are less then half of the average family income in Alaska. Further, the costs of living in rural areas are much higher than in the cities. An average family in Nome or Kotzebue will spend 62 percent more per week on food or 165 percent more for electricity than a family in Anchorage, the largest city in Alaska.

The lack of access to quality health services and preventive care and poor living conditions have led to higher death rates among Alaska Natives from preventable causes, such as infectious and respiratory diseases, congenital problems, and infant mortality. There are other statistics that indicate many Natives have difficult lives, since Alaska Natives die from violent causes, accidents, homicides, suicides, and alcoholism at a much higher rate than in the general population. The Native suicide and homicide rates are four times the U.S. average. Among young males 20 to 24 years of age, the suicides are twenty times the national average. Death from accidents is five times higher; infant mortality and sudden infant death syndrome is two times higher; infant spinal disorders are thirty-six times the national rate, and so on.

Alaska Natives have addressed these and other problems in three major ways: through the protection of their subsistence life-style, through the economic development of their villages and regions, and the strengthening of their tribal governments.

Subsistence

Traditional subsistence economies in Alaska were small, self-sufficient, and practical household economies. People used what they produced. Alliances for trade did exist. Coastal communities would exchange seal oil for caribou skins for example; but trading relationships were limited. Food and clothing were locally produced and shared among kin and within local camps. The sharing of resources was common. People were united through blood and marriage. Kinship was a way of organizing labor, establishing rights, forming groups, and distributing wealth. Aboriginal life was cyclic and inseparable from the patterns and turns of nature. Inuit whalers, for example, hunted caribou in the summer for clothing and bedding and snared small animals for food. In the fall they returned to the coast for trade and the gathering of food on the beaches. Later men hunted seals on the open sea, until the ice returned. In midwinter, seals, fish, and bears were hunted on the ice. By April, when the ice melted enough, boat crews were in pursuit of bowhead whales. Near the end of June, when the whales had migrated south, birds and seals were the primary sources of food.

The subsistence economy is central to the lives of most Alaska Natives. It is estimated that each person in rural Alaska consumes 354 pounds of traditional food per year. More than 50 percent of rural food comes from subsistence activities. These resources are also used for clothing, transportation (fish are given to dog teams), heating, housing, and arts and crafts. Traditional values of sharing, cooperation, and reciprocity also continue. Large extended families still live together. Customary rules guide distribution and consumption of subsistence resources. Many Natives consider themselves first and foremost hunters and fishermen. There is evidence too that subsistence economies are not only resilient but growing in certain villages.

Efforts to protect and nourish subsistence have borne some fruit and much rancor. In 1978, the state of Alaska passed legislation recognizing a priority to subsistence use in the event of a shortage of fish or game. Native rights to hunt and fish were extinguished by ANCSA but were partially restored when Congress included a rural subsistence preference in the Alaska National Lands Conservation Act (ANILCA) in 1980, which classified all federal lands in Alaska. The national government permitted the state to regulate fish and game as long as federal and state law were in agreement, i.e., contained a rural subsistence priority.

The Alaska law was then challenged in court because it excluded city residents who depend on subsistence and included people in rural areas who do not. In 1989 the Alaska Supreme Court agreed and ruled that residency as a criterion for subsistence violates constitutional prohibitions against exclusive or special privileges to hunt and fish and was a denial of equal rights. Since state law was no longer consistent with the subsistence preference in ANILCA, the federal government assumed the responsibility for the management of fish and game. Alaska's governor then initiated a suit against the Federal Subsistence Board for overstepping its regulatory authority.

In response to the conflict over subsistence, Native leaders have made three recommendations: the adoption of a constitutional amendment that would enable the state to comply with federal law; the passage of state legislation that would protect the subsistence rights of individuals in cities; and the provision that tribal members be accorded a subsistence priority on traditional lands. At a summit meeting on subsistence in March 1992, Alaska Natives reaffirmed their opposition to any changes in the legal protection of subsistence and existing state policies with regard to the management of fish and game resources.

Economic Development

An important assumption of the Alaska Native Claims Settlement Act was that money and the profit orientation of village and regional corporations would lead to more employment and educational opportunities, healthier communities, and increasing economic independence for Alaska Natives. Regional corporations were given significant responsibilities, including the distribution of money to villages and individual Natives, the control of subsurface resources, and the economic development of their region. The corporations received over $440 million between 1972 and 1981.

The performance of these corporations in the last twenty years has been mixed. Few have achieved financial stability. Four of the corporations reported cumulative losses between 1973 and 1990, and eight increased their assets. But six of these achieved a positive balance only through the sale of their net operating losses to large outside companies for tax write-offs. Profitable corporations have relied on the development of their natural resources or investments in securities or the oil and gas industry. Of the nearly $1.4 billion worth of assets held by the twelve corporations, half consists of buildings, equipment, and real estate; 18 percent is invested in securities; 20 percent is held in escrow by the Internal Revenue Service; and the rest consists of parcels of land, insurance policies, and miscellaneous payments.

The impact of these business ventures on the day-to-day lives of Alaska Natives has been, with a few exceptions, minimal. At-large stockholders (those not affiliated with a village corporation) have received about $6,500 from the settlement of land claims; village stockholders were paid $1,500. Only two corporations, the Arctic Slope Regional Corporation and the Northwest

Arctic Native Association, employ a significant number of their shareholders. Of the 7,500 employees of the twelve corporations, only 33 percent are Native. Cook Inlet Region, Inc., is the only company to pay substantial dividends. There are over 25,000 younger Alaska Natives who are not members of a regional corporation, because they were born after December 18, 1971, and hence are not eligible to enroll as shareholders.

There are also 172 village corporations organized under the Alaska Native Claims Settlement Act. They own the surface estate to 22 million acres of land, and they received almost half of the compensation payments from Congress. The amount of money and land held by each corporation varies with the number of stockholders. These corporations are expected to manage their lands and guide the economic development of their communities. With the exception of a few of the larger villages or those with valuable resources, their impact on local economies has been limited. Most have been hampered by insufficient funds, bad advice, and litigation. For many village corporations, the minimum state requirements of incorporation have imposed intolerable costs.

Tribal Sovereignty

Many Alaska Natives are convinced that the solutions to many of their problems lies in the development of strong and effective tribal governments. Villages have claimed to have an inherent right to self-rule and may therefore form their own governments, regulate their own affairs, manage their own assets, impose taxes, and so on (see the discussion of tribal sovereignty in the law sections).

Federal recognition of tribal governments has been uneven. Congress has passed legislation recognizing tribes in Alaska. After years of delay, the Department of the Interior approved a tribal constitution for an interior village in 1990. In 1991 the Secretary of the Interior, in a speech before the annual meeting of the Alaska Federation of Natives, expressed his support for strong tribal governments and self-determination.

Judicial decisions though have been more confusing. Two recent cases are particularly important. In 1987 two Native villages sued the state of Alaska for the money they were supposed to have received under a revenue-sharing program. State officials had withheld the funds, because they felt such payments would favor a racial class. The federal district court dismissed the suit arguing that states are immune from suits. The Ninth Circuit Court of Appeals reversed this decision on three grounds: each village had a governing council organized under the Indian Reorganization Act, a 1934 Act granting greater self-government to tribal governments; the village's legal suit was constitutional because federal power is supreme, something the state agreed to when it was admitted to the Union; and, finally, the state was guilty of racial discrimination by not distributing the money. Revenue-sharing was for political entities, such as village councils, a local form of government, but not for ethnic organizations. However, in 1991, the U.S. Supreme Court partially reversed this

Native Regional Corporations and Their Shareholders

Regional corporation	Total shareholders	Cumulative dividends	Equity per share	Native employees
Ahtna	1,100	$2,402	$23,336	55
Aleut	3,249	501	3,243	5
ASRC	3,738	1,857	12,850	827
Bering Straits	6,200	102	4,001	9
Bristol Bay	5,200	1,606	8,708	7
Calistal	3,306	59	482	n/a
Chugach	2,109	761	21,284	39
Cook Inlet	6,553	10,456	54,493	l20
Doyon	9,061	1,062	14,591	69
Koniag	3,731	0	4,958	4
NANA	5,000	2,489	10,579	978
Sealaska	15,700	1,348	9,731	33

Source: *Adapted from Steve Colt, "Financial Performance of Native Regional Corporations,"* Alaska Review of Social and Economic Conditions *Volume 28, no. 2 (December l99l).*

decision when it ruled that a tribe or a village may not sue a state, since neither tribes nor state have mutually surrendered their immunity.

A second case involving the village of Tyonek, a small Athapascan village near Anchorage, recognized lands received under ANCSA as "Indian Country" and upheld the power of the council to exclude non-Natives from their community. The state of Alaska has vigorously blocked most Alaska Native efforts to gain greater tribal self-government. In 1987 the Alaska Supreme Court ruled in a dispute over a declaration of tribal sovereignty by a village government against an aggrieved contractor, that the village "does not have sovereign immunity because it, like most Native groups in Alaska, is not self-governing in any meaningful sense." Confident of their reasoning the justices applied their interpretation to all villages in Alaska. In 1991 the governor reversed an earlier administrative order and proclaimed his opposition to "the expansion of tribal government powers and the creation of Indian country in Alaska."

Despite these obstacles, Alaska Natives realize that powers not exercised are powers not recognized. Therefore village councils have established tribal courts, dissolved city governments, passed restrictive ordnances, formed regional associations, claimed jurisdiction over their land and resources, and controlled entry into their communities. In the end most are confident that their efforts will lead to better solutions for their problems and more control over their future.

David Maas
University of Alaska, Anchorage

♦ OKLAHOMA INDIANS

The land that is now encompassed within the state of Oklahoma appears on nineteenth century maps as "Indian Territory." Even today, Oklahoma is the home of the largest number of Indian tribes and peoples within the United States. In the late twentieth century thirty-eight federally recognized Indian Nations continue to exercise their sovereign tribal status within Oklahoma on the lands once known as "Indian Territory." Ironically, only a few of these tribes occupied any part of the state prior to European contact.

The vast majority of Oklahoma Indian tribes were "resettled" in Oklahoma, most involuntarily, under the nineteenth-century federal Indian removal policy. In the formative years of American Indian policy, settlers and local communities pressured tribal communities to give up their large tribal land holdings. In response, the federal government adopted a policy to compel tribes to exchange their historic homelands for new "permanent" lands on unorganized federal domain in the West, where, theoretically, no conflicts would arise with non-Indians. Under treaty guarantees this new land was to remain forever in the hands of Indian tribes who were promised that non-Indians would not be allowed to settle in their midst. At the beginning of the twentieth century, in violation of these agreements, Oklahoma was admitted to the Union as the forty-sixth state (1907).

In the late 1820s and throughout the 1830s, the earliest and most dramatic of the Eastern Indian removals to what is now Oklahoma were those of the Five Civilized Tribes (the Choctaw, Chickasaw, Creek, Cherokee, and Seminole). These tribes were called civilized because they adopted constitutional governments, some of their people adopted Christianity, and they formed tribal school systems. Driven out of the South on what historians know as "The Trail of Tears," tens of thousands of their numbers perished on forced marches that were often conducted in the dead of winter. As many as one-third of their tribal members, especially the very young and the very old, died before they reached the new Indian territory. Prior to the American Civil War other tribes, including the Quapaw, Seneca, and Shawnee, were also removed to what is now Oklahoma. Ultimately, at least sixty-five Indian Nations came to be listed historically as having been at one time or another Oklahoma tribes. These included

> Alabama, Anadarko, Apache, Apalachicola, Arapaho, Caddo, Cahakia, Catawba, Cayuga, Cherokee, Cheyenne, Chickasaw, Chippewa, Choctaw, Comanche, Conestoga, Creek, Delaware, Eel River, Erie, Hainai, Hitchiti, Illinois, Iowa, Kaskashia, Kansa, Kichai, Kickapoo, Kiowa, Kiowa-Apache, Koasati, Lipan, Miami, Michigomea, Modoc, Mohawk, Moingwena, Munsee, Natchez, Nez Percé, Osage, Oto and Missouri, Ottawa, Pawnee, Peoria, Piankashaw, Ponca, Potawatomi, Quapaw, Sauk and Fox, Seminole, Seneca, Shawnee, Skidi, Stockbridge, Tamaroa, Tawakoni, Tonkawa, Tuscarora, Tuskegee, Waco, Wea, Wichita, Wyandot, Yuchi.

During the Andrew Jackson Administration (1830–38), a companion policy to removal was the proposed establishment of an Indian commonwealth or territory in the removal area (now Oklahoma), to be governed by a confederation of tribes. The Western Territory bill of 1834 proposed an "Indian Territory" that was to be composed of Kansas, Oklahoma, parts of Nebraska, Colorado, and Wyoming. None of these proposals of the 1830s was enacted and the territory set aside for Indians gradually shrank to what is now the state of Oklahoma. Unorganized Indian Territory west of the Mississippi disappeared as one after another of the new territorial governments were established and states were admit-

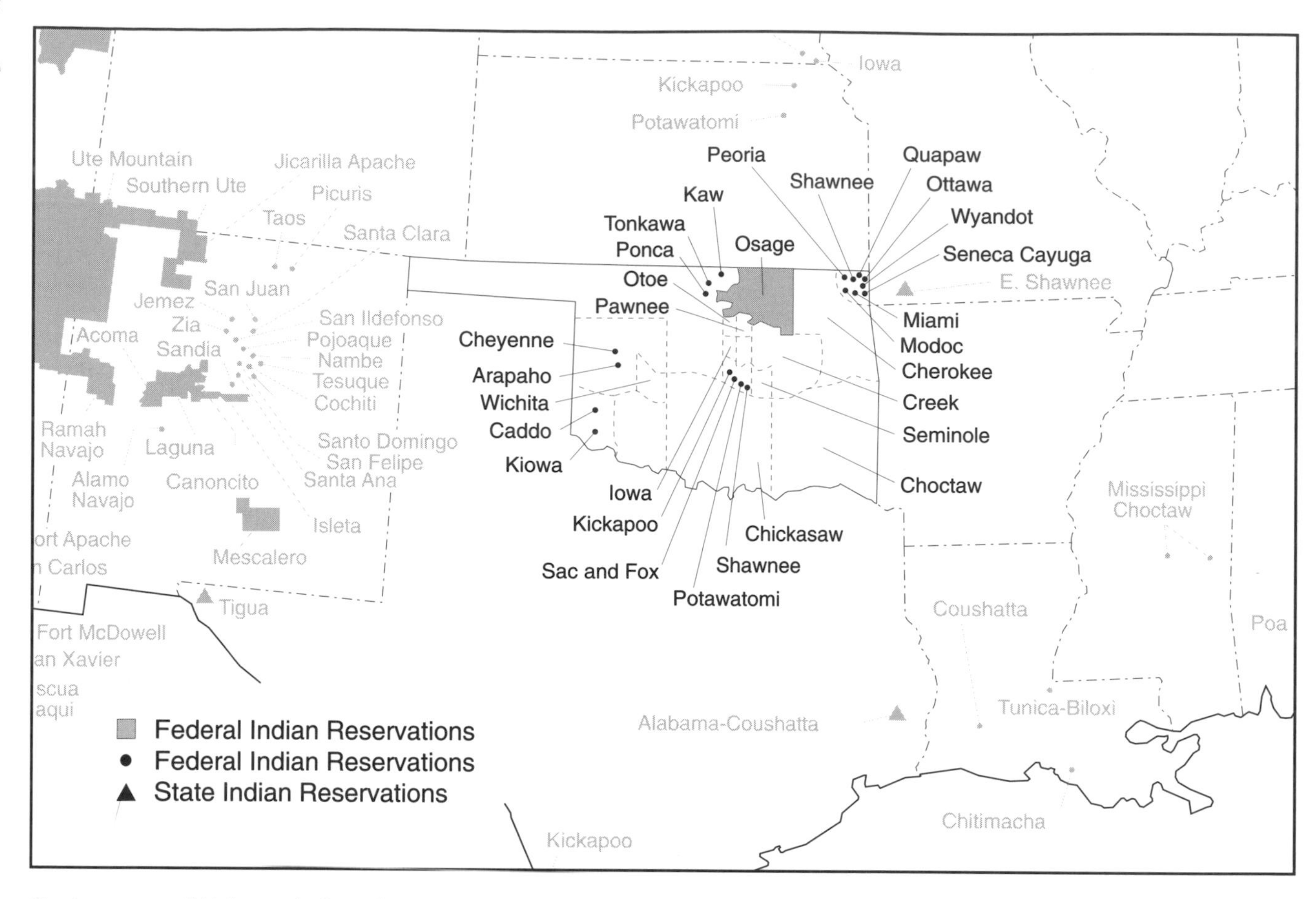

Contemporary Oklahoma Indian tribes.

ted to the Union. When Kansas Territory was organized in 1854, the remaining unorganized area reserved for Indian tribes had boundaries almost identical to present-day Oklahoma. By 1868, the land that would later become Oklahoma was the only unorganized territory left in the lower forty-eight states. It was to this land that the federal government forced many remaining Indian nations. Although no territorial Indian government was ever established, the name *Indian Territory* gradually came into common use as the collective term for the lands of the Five Tribes and other Indian tribes settled amongst them. From 1865 until Oklahoma's admission to the Union in 1907, Congress frequently used the term in statutes and defined the boundaries of Indian Territory in laws passed in 1889 and 1890.

Indian tribes in Oklahoma have continuously operated their own sovereign governments from pre-contact times through forced removal and statehood up to the present. After the end of the bloody Trail of Tears, the Five Tribes established comprehensive governments in Indian Territory and exercised self-rule relatively free of federal interference. The Five Tribes achieved a level of literacy and economic prosperity that exceeded many of the neighboring states. Before the American Civil War, these Indian tribes enjoyed a "golden age" in which tribal Indian traditions and the economic richness of this new land merged to produce a culturally diverse and prosperous Native civilization.

The Civil War had a dramatic impact on the Five Tribes. A number of tribal members owned slaves and supported the Confederacy. The Choctaw and Chickasaw Nations, whose lands adjoined Confederate Arkansas and Texas, sided with the Confederacy. The three most northerly tribes (Creek, Cherokee, and Seminole) were politically divided but nonetheless made treaties with the South. Loyalist factions continued to favor the North, and many tribal citizens fought on both sides. The Cherokee, Creek, and Seminole each lost as much as 20 to 25 percent of their population. In 1866 and 1867, the Five Tribes were compelled to accept new treaties and agreements that ceded western portions of their tribal territories, abolished slavery, granted railroad rights-of-way, and provided for the settlement of other tribes on their former lands and for the eventual allotment of tribal lands.

After the Civil War, other Indians—including many of the powerful Plains tribes such as the Comanche, Kiowa, and Cheyenne—were removed to the western Indian Territory lands yielded by the Five Tribes along with other strong tribal groups such as the Apache. Thousands of U.S. settlers illegally moved into Indian Territory, and many lawless and violent drifters made Indian Territory a notorious haven for bandits and killers. In an effort to maintain law and order for non-Indians in Indian Territory, Congress established a special federal court for Indian Territory over which Isaac C. Parker, known as "the Hanging Judge," presided. In 1889, the famous Oklahoma land run opened the so-called "unassigned lands" in central Indian Territory to U.S. settlers, and in 1890 the Oklahoma Organic Act reduced Indian Territory to its eastern portion, the lands of the Five Tribes and the Quapaw Agency Tribes. During this time an Organic Act created Oklahoma Territory in the western part of Indian Territory and established a U.S. territorial government. The Act expressly preserved tribal authority and federal jurisdiction in both Oklahoma and Indian territories. The status of Indian tribes in Oklahoma Territory was thus similar to that of tribes in other organized territories.

During the 1890s, the land of many Oklahoma tribes were allotted or divided pursuant to the General Allotment Act of 1887. In 1893 the Dawes Commission was established to seek allotment of the lands of the Five Tribes, which were exempted from the General Allotment Act. In 1898 Congress passed the Curtis Act to speed up the allotment process. The Act provided for allotment of Five Tribes lands, and other allotment agreements and statutes followed. The Five Tribes Act of 1906 preserved tribal governments and comprehensively addressed allotment and other Indian issues. Shortly thereafter, the Oklahoma Enabling Act provided for the admission of Indian Territory and Oklahoma Territory as the state of Oklahoma. Oklahoma proclaimed statehood in 1907.

Statehood was the bitter culmination of decades of conflict and of self-righteous programs to transform Indian Territory into a U.S. commonwealth and to make the American Indian into a red farmer. Few non-Indians ever understood the depth of the Indians' agony at the passing of their nationhood. In the *Chronicles of Oklahoma* 26 (Winter 1948–49), Edward E. Dale, the dean of Oklahoma's historians, wrote with some surprise of the sadness an Indian woman still felt when she remembered the 1907 festivities to celebrate Oklahoma statehood. This Cherokee woman, married to a non-Indian,

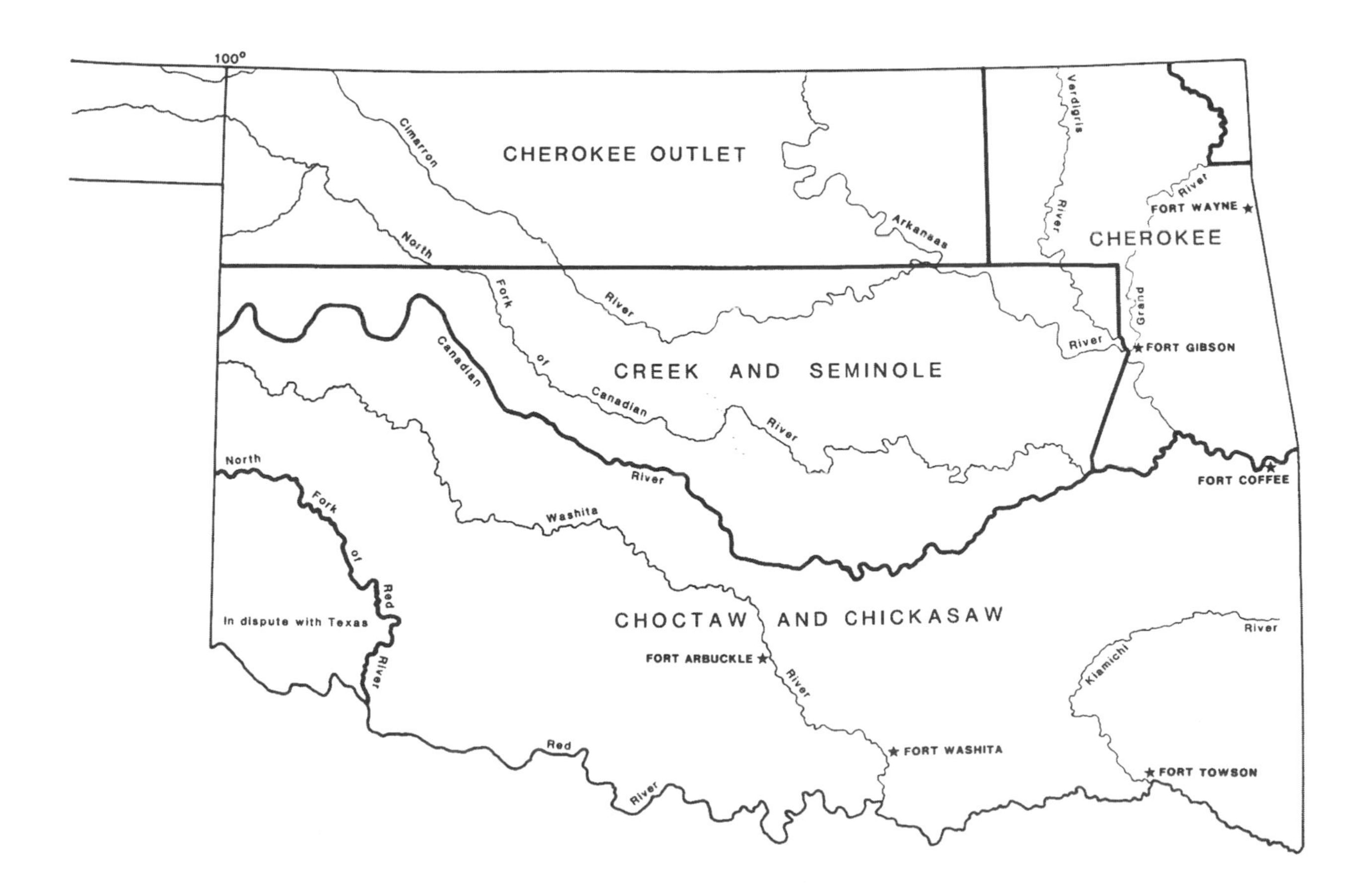

Indian Territory, removal to 1855. Reprinted from *Atlas of American Indian Affairs,* by Francis Paul Prucha, by permission of the University of Nebraska Press. Copyright 1990 by the University of Nebraska Press.

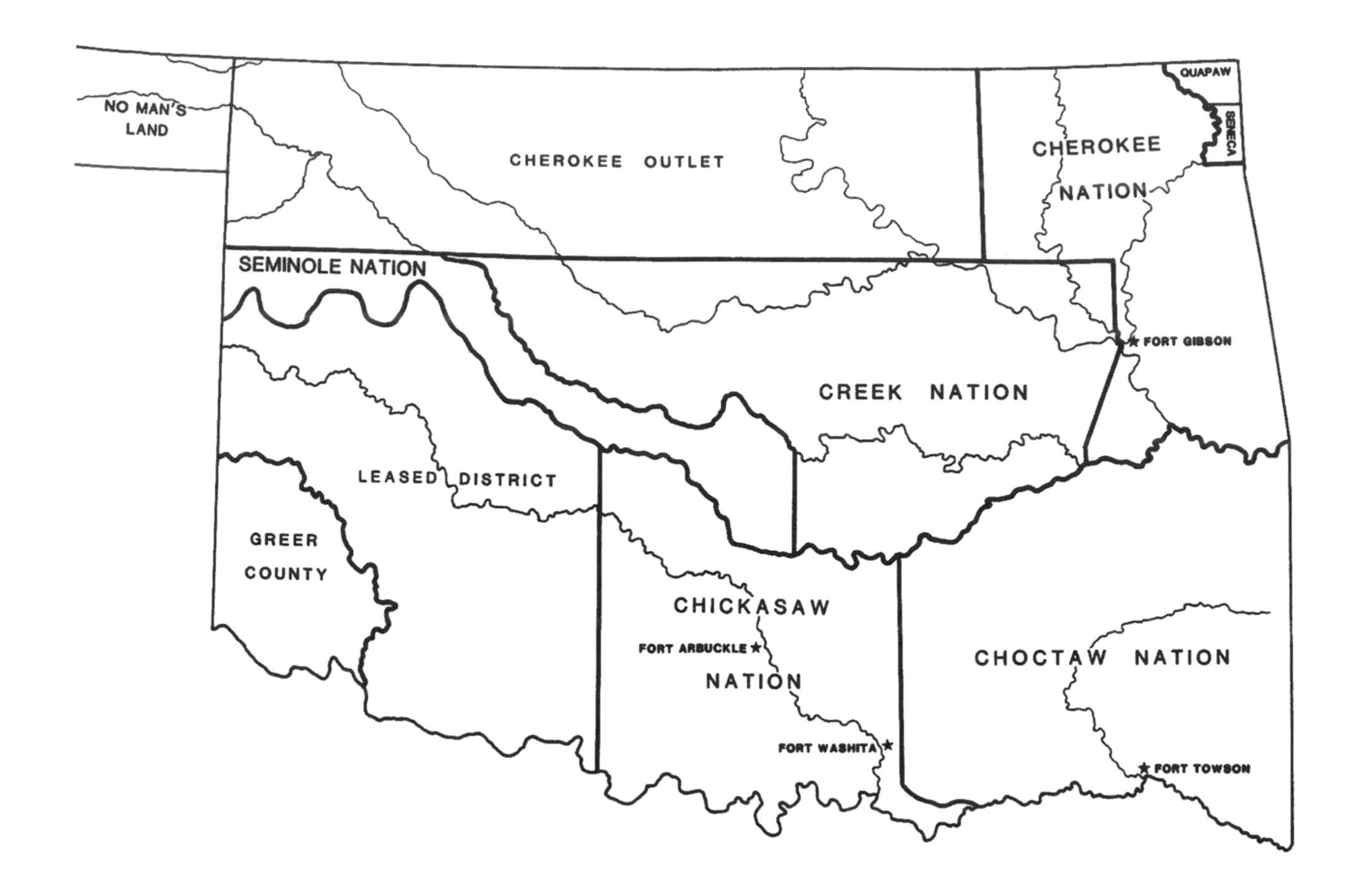

Indian Territory 1855–66. Reprinted from *Atlas of American Indian Affairs,* by Francis Paul Prucha, by permission of the University of Nebraska Press. Copyright 1990 by the University of Nebraska Press.

refused to attend the statehood ceremonies with her husband. He returned and said to her: "Well, Mary, we no longer live in the Cherokee Nation. All of us are now citizens of the state of Oklahoma." Tears came to her eyes thirty years later as she recalled that day. "It broke my heart. I went to bed and cried all night long. It seemed more than I could bear that the Cherokee Nation, my country and my people's country, was no more" (p. 382).

Since Oklahoma's statehood, the status of Indian tribes in Oklahoma has been similar to that of tribes in other states. The popularly held view that Oklahoma Indians are subject to special regulations generally applies only to narrowly defined property interests of individual members of the Five Tribes and the Osage Tribe. When Congress passed the Indian Reorganization Act of 1934, Oklahoma tribes were excepted from many of its important provisions. Two years later Congress passed the Oklahoma Indian Welfare Act that authorizes tribal organization in a manner similar to the Indian Reorganization Act and extends "any other rights or privileges served to an organized Indian tribe . . . ." Like all other Indian tribes, tribes in Oklahoma retain powers of self-government and sovereignty except to the extent that their powers have been limited by treaties, agreements, or federal legislation. Although the land base of Oklahoma tribes has been substantially reduced by the allotment process, their inherent powers of self-government are undiminished.

The time before the American Civil War is remembered as the Golden Age of the Oklahoma Indian. For many Indians this age followed the brutal, nearly genocidal expulsion from their original homelands. Such irony pervades much of Oklahoma's Indian life. The present Indian nature of the state results not from aboriginal Indian choice but from U.S. policy. Most Oklahoma Indians opposed coming to the state. Oklahoma's Indian people are largely descendants of nineteenth century emigrants who had been driven by the U.S. government from almost every other section of the country. More bitterly ironic, Indians found in Oklahoma a quiet haven. Eventually, they came to love this land, and in the end it, too, was taken from them.

Generalizing about the coming of the Indian to Oklahoma is not easy. Tribes came at different times and for different purposes. Divisions of the same tribe were often split by migration. Oklahoma was historically a great and open hunting ground through which many Native peoples passed. State boundaries and formal tribal borders were unknown prior to U.S. occupation. Even the rigid recognition of formal tribal units was a political concept borrowed from the European legal tradition. Certainly fee-simple land ownership with its feudal property implications was foreign to the mind of the aboriginal American. Furthermore, in a society where splinter factions were free to move away from the main body of a tribe, portions of groups as large as the Seneca or the Osage or the Cherokee might be settled in several states as well as in Indian Territory. Still other tribes never settled anywhere, in the traditional European sense, but rather ranged from the plains of Texas into the Rocky Mountains and beyond.

Fewer than half a dozen of Oklahoma's tribes are indigenous. Only a few of the currently identifiable Oklahoma tribes were within the state when the Europeans arrived. Very early ancestors of the Oklahoma Indians, such as Plainview, Clovis, and Folsom man, as well as more immediate paleolithic ancestors, had disappeared. The great prehistoric Indian civilizations with their mounds and their monumental art, such as those unearthed at Spiro in the 1930s, were gone when the first European explorers came to Oklahoma. Quapaw and Caddoan ancestors of the Wichita and Caddo by that time had settled on this land with their village farming culture. Tribes like the Osage hunted in these domains, and nomadic bands such as the Plains Apache and the Comanche followed the migratory herds across the state. To appreciate the nature of Indian settlement in the state, we must distinguish among hunting, migration, and permanent residence. Further, we must appreciate the concept of a home base to which roving tribes might return with some regularity.

The major thrust of Indian settlement in Oklahoma resulted from U.S. policy, which consisted of formal negotiations; informal counsel, bribery, and threats; and military force. As early as 1803, Thomas Jefferson had spoken of a permanent Indian area or territory beyond the boundaries of U.S. society. Since before the founding of the nation, Indian tribes had been driven westward by both warfare and treaty negotiations. By

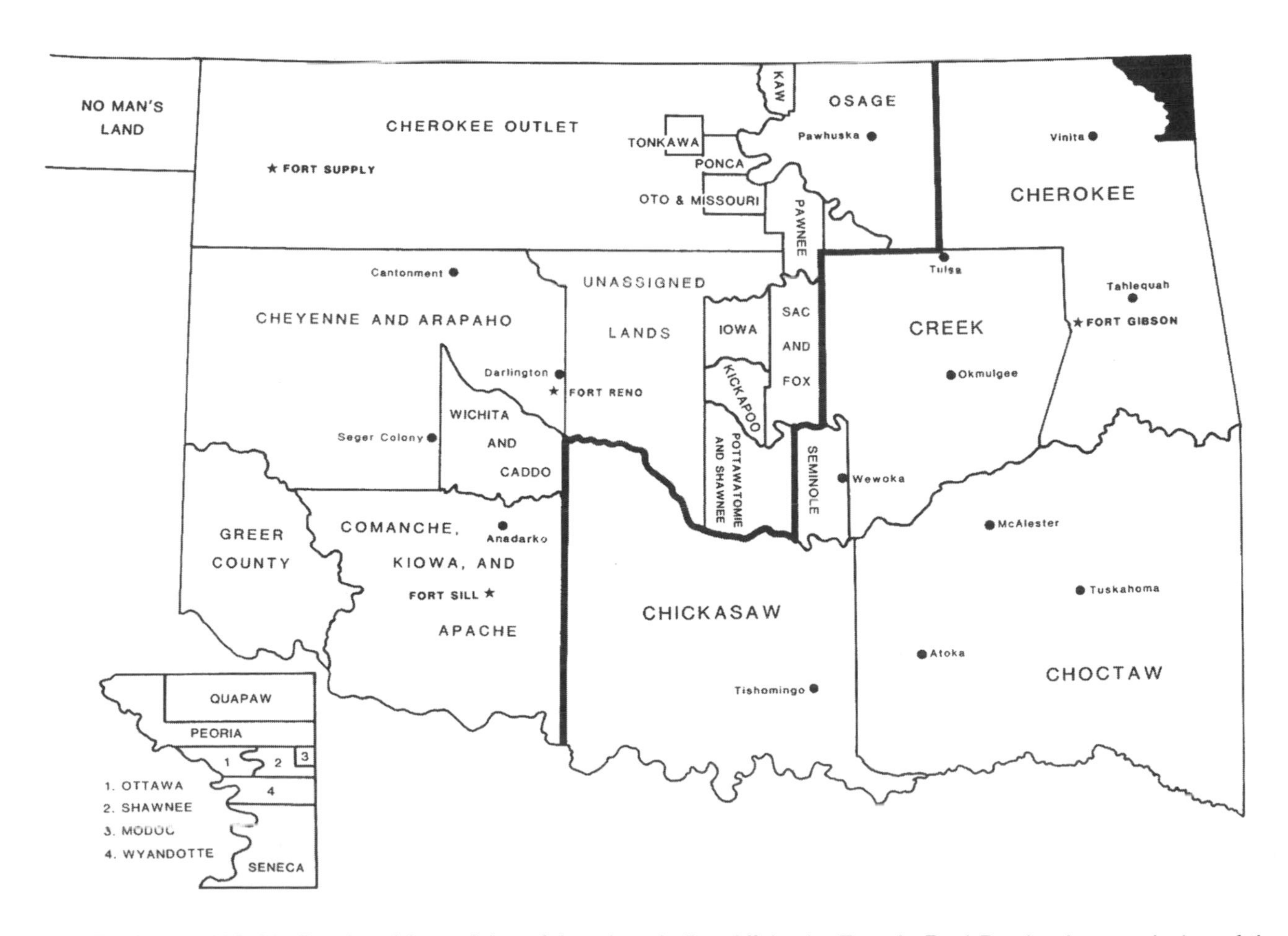

Indian Territory, 1866–89. Reprinted from *Atlas of American Indian Affairs,* by Francis Paul Prucha, by permission of the University of Nebraska Press. Copyright 1990 by the University of Nebraska Press.

various inducements and by the application of brute force more than sixty Indian tribes originally from other states were ultimately removed to and resettled in Oklahoma. One contemporary observer noted that this process "conformed in no phase or degree to any pattern," for "there was an infinite variety of methods, experiences, and details." Tribes were removed—particularly at the turn of the century for the northern Indians of Ohio, Indiana, Illinois, and New York—without plan or experience. Many once powerful tribes—such as the Shawnee, Sac and Fox, and Potawatomi—were fragmented, lost, or reduced in station before they arrived in the Indian Territory.

Voluntary migrations and inducements by treaty settled portions of such tribes as the Seneca, Quapaw, Osage, Shawnee, Choctaw, Creek, and Cherokee in Oklahoma before Andrew Jackson's Indian Removal Act was fully implemented in the 1830s. In these earlier removals there seemed to be no system or order. Some tribes were moved several times before they reached Oklahoma. Many tribal groups, sensing the futility of resistance to removal, sought a negotiated compromise that avoided the brutality of a forced military march to their new country. By the early 1830s, there were established tribal governments in Oklahoma of "old settler" or "western" factions of the Choctaw, Creek, and Cherokee, as well as separate political subdivisions of groups like the Osage, whose greatest numbers would not come to Oklahoma until much later. For example, in 1831, the Seneca exchanged land in Ohio's Sandusky Valley for 67,000 acres north of the western Cherokee, while a short time later another group of Seneca and Shawnee received a similar Indian Territory tract. In 1833, a band of Quapaw moved from the Red River to lands north and east of the Cherokee.

The tragedy of the brutal forced migration of almost sixty thousand members of the great southern nations—the Creek, Cherokee, Choctaw, Chickasaw, and Seminole—is known as the "Trail of Tears"; as many as one-fourth of the Indians died from exposure and exhaustion. The agony of this experience is etched in the consciousness of the Five Civilized Tribes and of non-Indian Oklahomans as well. In turn, other tribes joined these southern tribes in Oklahoma, particularly northern woodland peoples, whose experiences were often as disastrous.

Between the end of the Civil War and the opening of Oklahoma's Unassigned Lands in 1889, the number of Indian tribes permanently living in Oklahoma changed. The many Plains and woodland tribes who joined the earlier inhabitants brought a diversity of Indian culture not present in any other state. In the northeast corner of the state, the Peoria, Modoc, Ottawa, Shawnee, and Wyandot joined the Seneca and the Quapaw. In the northeastern and central portions of the state were the Osage, the Kaw, the Pawnee, the Tonkawa, the Ponca, the Oto and Missouri, the Sac and Fox, the Iowa, the Kickapoo, the Potawatomi, and the Shawnee. Dominating the eastern half of the state and spilling into the west were Cherokee, Creek, Choctaw, Chickasaw, and Seminole. In the western part of the state, around the military outposts of Fort Reno and Fort Sill, the great tribes of the plains were ultimately located. The Comanche, Kiowa, and Apache lands bordered on Texas. The Wichita and Caddo tribes nestled between this reservation and the reservation lands of the Cheyenne and Arapaho.

Ironically, more has been written and less is known about the history and culture of these Oklahoma tribes than about any other group of Native Americans. As many as 600,000 present-day Oklahomans identify themselves as Indians. Yet within the state of Oklahoma, there remains a widespread perception that the Indian and the Indian's culture is vanishing. "Non-Indians . . . are more ignorant of the Indian than the Indian is of them," according to a recent study of the population of Oklahoma City. "This is so because the majority of whites and blacks have had little personal contact with individual Indians and [even] that has been extremely superficial."

The contemporary facts are unmistakable. Oklahoma has more Indians from more varied tribes than any other state in the Union. It has more separate tribal groups historically associated with the state and more currently recognized tribes than any other state. A higher percentage of its population is Indian, and that population is more widely distributed among the state's counties than in Arizona, New Mexico, or the Dakotas. Indians once owned all the land in the state but now have a greatly reduced land base, the lowest income level, and the highest unemployment rate of any group in the state. Today more Oklahoma Indians are participating in more Indian-sponsored activities than in any period since statehood. The number of Oklahoma Indians is increasing. Indian tribes are again functioning as political and economic units, electing officials, administering programs, and dispensing justice.

The state is truly what Chief Allen Wright's Choctaw name for it, Okla Homma, conveys in a free translation: "Home of the Red People." More than sixty-seven tribes and bands have been located within the state and twenty-nine of them continue to be recognized. A population breakdown suggests that there are 100,000 sociocultural Indians, 220,000 persons recognized by the Bureau of Indian Affairs as legal Indians, and 600,000 Oklahomans of Indian descent. Tulsa and Oklahoma City rank second and third behind Los Angeles in Indian population within city boundaries. The sixty-five-mile trade radius of Tulsa constitutes the highest non-reservation concentration of Indians anywhere in the world.

The great diversity of Oklahoma's Indian population is lost in these statistics. Not only the Plains tribes and the Five Civilized Tribes reside in Oklahoma. Among the state's larger tribal groups are peoples as varied as the Ponca, the Apache, the Comanche, and the Choctaw. With urban migration Indians from at least fifty other non-Oklahoma tribes have recently moved to the state. More and more of Oklahoma's Indians have ancestors from two to four or more tribes. An Osage-Cherokee, a Kiowa-Miami, and a Creek-Omaha are not unusual. The current generation is producing children who are such combinations as Choctaw-Ponca-Cheyenne-Delaware or Cherokee-Osage-Omaha-Creek-Apache.

Even among members of the same tribe there are great cultural and personal differences. Today as many as 10,000 Cherokee speak their native tongue in a tribe that began adopting European cultural variants in the eighteenth century. While the Oklahoma U.S. Senator, Robert L. Owen (1907–25), an enrolled Cherokee, co-authored the Federal Reserve Act of 1913, the Cherokee Kee-Too-Wah, an ancient religious society, were reading the ancient wampum belts and feeding the sacred fire with the blood of a white rooster.

Oklahoma has historically been a land of great contrasts between and among Indian people. Contemporary distinctions within the same or among different tribal groups are reflective of similar differences among Indians even in the age before widespread settlement of non-Indians within the state. Nineteenth century accounts of travelers, Indian tribal documents, missionary diaries, government negotiations, military reports, and trader journals clearly establish that there has never been a single, unified Oklahoma Indian culture. It is as rich and diverse as all of Indian America.

For convenience, Oklahoma's Indian tribes are often grouped into broad categories, such as the Five Civilized Tribes and the Plains Indians, or into semi-geographic, quasi-cultural divisions, such as Hunters of the Plains, Plains Farmers, Woodland Peoples, or Northern and Southern Woodland, Prairie, Plains, and High Plains Indians. Such artificial subdivisions are meaningful only when we remember the broad cross-cultural similarities and the genuinely unique aspects of each tribe. The Choctaw and Seminole, two "civilized" tribes, are in major respects culturally distinct, just as are the plains groups, such as the Kiowa and the Arapaho. To appreciate these varied cultures and what the Oklahoma Indian lost after the coming of white immigrants, one must understand the nature of Indian life on the prairie and in the woodland before the Civil War and the Treaty of Medicine Lodge. It is the culture of this golden age to which Oklahoma's modern Indians look with nostalgia.

The traditional Indian culture of Plains tribes such as the Cheyenne, Arapaho, Kiowa, and Comanche is familiar to most Americans. Their seemingly free and independent life has come to symbolize Oklahoma's Native peoples. These were hunter cultures, uniquely varied in many respects. Each depended on the existence of open lands that could be freely roamed and an abundant supply of wild game. Plains Indian thought, culture, and organization were complex. A civil, military, and religious structure preserved law and order, provided security, and assured economic and social well-being. It was a life intimately tied to the earth and to the natural cycles of life.

In absolute numbers, the Five Civilized Tribes and the Plains Indians historically constituted the largest blocs of Oklahoma Indians, but there were and still are other important and colorful Oklahoma tribes, such as the Sac and Fox, the Osage, the Potawatomi, the Quapaw, the Delaware, the Kickapoo, the Seneca, and the Shawnee. In addition, surviving portions of such tribes as the Catawba, the Natchez, and the Biloxi and groups such as the Yuchi and the Hitchiti were integrated into Oklahoma Indian governments, particularly those of the Choctaw, the Creek, and the Cherokee. During his tour of Indian Territory in the 1840s, Major Ethan Allen Hitchcock concluded that "fragments of Indian tribes are scattered in every direction."

The Oklahoma Indian tribes' viewpoints and problems are often lost in their cultural diversity and amidst their internal dissension. Yet even before the opening of Indian lands to non-Indian settlement, these tribes reacted to similar challenges and faced many of the same dangers from their common non-Indian and Indian enemies. As early as 1824, the tribes faced an invasion of commercial hunters and an assault on Native game. General Matthew Arbuckle reported two thousand hunters systematically killing fur-bearing animals in order to sell their peltries.

The U.S. challenge to the Indian way of thinking and living was a challenge to all Indian people. The unity among the Plains, woodland, and prairie tribes is not so readily apparent in material life and culture but emerges clearly at a philosophical and spiritual level. The great oneness of Oklahoma Indian tribes is spiritual. Peoples as seemingly diverse as the Cheyenne and the Cherokee reflect Indian attitudes in their perception of the earth, the supernatural, and the association of man's spirit and the spirits of animals.

For example, the Cheyenne Wolf Soldiers, the last of the seven great Cheyenne soldier societies to be organized, served as a defensive and protective association. The Cheyenne soldier-society warrior, draped in the skin of a wolf, sought protective power and acquired strength from the animal. Richard West, the Cheyenne artist, has captured this animal warrior as lawman in his paintings and sculptures of the Wolf Soldier. The Cherokee, too, had many customs and legends about the wolf, which included wolf songs and medicine formulas. Even after the Cherokee had adopted their highly acclaimed constitutional government (1828–1907) and established peace officers or light-horsemen modeled after frontier sheriffs, they turned to the animal powers of the spirit world.

The close of the American Civil War and the 1867 Indian Treaty gathering at Medicine Lodge in Kansas signaled the beginning of the end of the old, free Indian nationhood. New treaties forced upon the Five Civilized Tribes at Fort Smith in 1866 contained provisions that ultimately opened the way for railroads to cross their domains and for the U.S. settler onslaught that followed. The signing of the Treaty of Medicine Lodge with leaders of Plains tribes—including the Kiowa, the Cheyenne, the Arapaho, and the Comanche—foreshadowed the federal government's effort to confine the tribes to reservations and to compel them to follow the "white man's road."

The Oklahoma Indian was caught on the crest of one of those great cycles that recur throughout American history. Westward expansion was itself an old story. Many of the Indians removed to Oklahoma, including the Shawnee, the Cherokee, the Seneca, and the Creek, had been caught in earlier stages of the cycle. But this expansion was somehow different. It was more determined, better organized, and much faster, more efficient, and more difficult to resist. Powered by technological marvels such as railroads, the steam engine, and the mechanical harvester, the new expansion was also propelled by the "go-getter" spirit that infused the nation after the war. The military energy of the Union victory survived on the frontier. Congress, boardrooms, taverns, and churches shared a determination to thrust the nation westward. Landless Americans from older sections and newer emigrants who had temporarily settled elsewhere demanded Indian lands. There was no place left to remove the Indian, and there was little sympathy for the preservation of a way of life that left farmlands unturned, coal unmined, and timber uncut.

By 1889, the life of the Oklahoma Indian was changing. The military balance of power rested with the white man. The great romantic, free, nomadic-hunter civilization of the Plains was past or, at least, passing. The Plains Indian wars were coming to an end, with many Oklahoma tribal leaders held captive in distant jails. The brutal massacre known as the Battle of the Washita (1868), in which George Armstrong Custer attacked Black Kettle's peaceful Cheyenne village, demonstrated the growing rift between the Indian "Spartans of the Plains" and U.S. soldiers. The "blue coats" appear more frequently and grow larger and larger in the Indians' ledger-book drawings. Even the golden days of intense tribal creativity were ending for the Five Civilized Tribes, who were now left fiercely struggling to preserve whatever steps toward acculturation they had earlier made.

The year 1889 might appear on an Oklahoma Indian calendar as "the time when white farmers came with wives." Oklahoma Indian tribes were, in a real sense, still sovereign; they were "domestic dependent nations," in the words of former U.S. Supreme Court Chief Justice John Marshall. Until that fateful year, although they were subject to many federal regulations, Indians owned all the lands that were to become Oklahoma. Non-Indians within their domain were either government or military officials, who relied on Indian sufferance. Illegal intruders were subject to expulsion under existing treaties. These sovereign Indian nations were the only groups in Oklahoma whose political power and landed estate would diminish with the establishment of territorial government that had begun in 1889 and culminated in the admission of Oklahoma to statehood in 1907.

A great drama opened Oklahoma's Indian lands and ended the exclusive Indian possession of these domains. Fifty thousand potential homesteaders vied to stake out claims to the ten thousand farms of 160 acres each. It was an epic if condensed enactment of the entire frontier-settlement process. The Oklahoma land rush of April 22, 1889, has been recreated in song and story, in novel and in film, but how the Oklahoma Indian came to that year of 1889 and what happened subsequently has been largely ignored.

Before 1889, when the United States acquired the disputed Unassigned Lands from the Creek and Seminole, Oklahoma was exclusively Indian country in a legal, political, and social sense. Not so after that eventful year 1889, when the first of a series of runs opened these tribal lands to U.S. settlers. By 1975 the Bureau of Indian Affairs reported that Oklahoma Indian tribal lands encompassed only 65,000 acres and that Indians as private citizens owned only a million acres. The size of tribal acreage grows slowly from year to year but is still a fraction of the once great Indian territories.

The long-range result of federal policy was that by the time of statehood in 1907, many Oklahoma Indians were handed land with a negotiable title. In many cases, this title was a fee simple absolute title and was subject only to a limitation or restriction by supervision for a term of years in other cases. Most Oklahoma Indians were destined to become landless, because Indian tribes no longer held the land, and title soon passed to non-Indians. Indian land was thus lost, allotted to individuals despite the protests of the vast majority of Indians who wished to retain tribal ownership.

Among the Five Civilized Tribes tribal lands were shifted to individual members with remarkable speed. The Dawes Commission's preparation of the rolls began with the Curtis Act in June 1898 and continued through March 1907, with a few additional names being added in 1914. In all, the commission placed 101,526 persons on the final rolls of the Five Civilized Tribes. Of this number, full bloods constituted 26,794; another 3,534 were enrolled as having three-fourths or more Indian blood; 6,859 were listed as one-half to three-fourths Indian; 40,934 were listed as having less than one-half Indian blood. The commission also prepared a separate roll of 23,405 blacks, known as freedmen. Enrollments and land figures from the Dawes enrollment and allotment follow:

The total Five Tribe's tribal land base was 19,525,966 acres, 15,794,400 acres of which were allotted. The balance of 4 million acres included 309 townsites, which were sold, and segregated coal and timber, as well as other unallotted lands, sold at public auction.

Tribe	Enrolled	Acres	Allotted
Cherokee	40,193	4,420,068	4,420,068
Creek	18,712	3,079,095	2,993,920
Seminole	3,119	365,852	359,697
Choctaw	26,730	6,953,048	8,091,386
Chickasaw	10,955	4,707,904	(jointly with Choctaw and Chickasaw)

Today, Oklahoma Indians, especially full-blood descendants, suffer from these earlier federal programs to enroll Indians in tribes and to allot to individual Indians their tribally owned domains. When the Dawes Commission rolls were drawn at the turn of the century, many traditionalist Indians like the Crazy Snake Creek refused to enroll because they believed that the United States was violating its treaty promises. Many were enrolled against their will, but others escaped the roving enrollment parties. Thus Oklahoma's mixed-blood Indians are often federally recognized, while many full-bloods and their descendants are treated as non-Indian. Other full-bloods enrolled themselves as quarter-bloods or eighth-bloods so that they would not have restrictions on their lands and the need for guardians. As a result, in tribes such as the Choctaw, Seminole, Cherokee, Creek, and Chickasaw, whose rolls have been closed by act of Congress, enrollees' descendants are denied educational and other Indian benefits to which, by their correct blood quantum, they are entitled.

But the Indian and Indian attitudes were not so easily lost even in the statehood movement. Oklahoma may be the only state in which the Indian had a significant and long-lasting impact on the form of state government and on the nature of the constitutional legal system. Many important Oklahoma constitutional provisions, such as prohibition of alien ownership of land and limitation on corporate buying or dealing in real estate, were products of the unique Oklahoma Indian experience. The Five Civilized Tribes and the non-Indians who allied with them to control the Oklahoma Constitutional Convention dominated the attitudes and the development of the new Oklahoma government. Among the reasons for this influence was the experience gained in 1905 at the Sequoyah Constitutional Convention, a meeting called to prepare for the single statehood of the Indian Territory. William H. Murray held correctly that "some of the most important provisions of the [Oklahoma] Constitution derived their inspiration from the Sequoyah Constitution."

Oklahoma Indians have scattered throughout the world. Thousands of Oklahoma Indians living outside the state plan their vacations to come home for their tribal celebrations. Whether Comanche, Cheyenne, Kiowa, Shawnee, Ponca, Delaware, Quapaw, Creek, or Seminole, there is a time and a place for renewal, a need to call for strength from the arrows or the wampum. And there is also a time that brings together Indians from many tribes for powwows and gourd dances, rodeos and competitions, visits and quarrels, rekindled romances and revitalized disputes. Oklahoma's Red Earth celebration in June is now the largest Indian celebration in the world.

The summer and the summer dances bring scholars and tourists to see the Indians. But Oklahoma Indianness is hidden and confusing. Much of the Oklahoma Indian way is lost to the outsider because the Indian-world has both a public and a private aspect and may, on the same occasion, involve both. An Indian legend shared by many Oklahoma tribes says that certain Indians can become transparent, turn into leaves on trees, or become small enough to ride on a bird's wing. Oklahoma Indians have been remarkably successful in doing just that. Indians have succeeded in hiding many aspects of their culture or camouflaging things Indian so that the Indianness is kept from the eye of the tourist or even the scholar. The outsider looking for a buffalo misses the deer, the raven, or the bright summer sun itself, which are all very Indian.

Much of the Indianness of Oklahoma is hidden because the Oklahoma Indian does not conform to non-Indian understandings of what is and is not Indian. A Boy Scout hobbyist in feathers and headdress is by definition Indian to students of the frontier myths, while a full-blood worshiper who wears blue jeans, a white shirt, and a Stetson hat and holds up the corporate seal of the Kee-Too-Wah is not Indian in the eyes of most U.S. moviegoers.

Furthermore, Oklahoma has few of the great geographic mountain and desert movie-set vistas that proclaim Indianness. There is no Oklahoma Monument Valley. No Oklahoma tribes have, like the Pueblo, drawn a whole school of painters and poets to record and romanticize their cultural ceremonies, crafts, and majestic landscapes. There are no Indian entrepreneurs

Ponca Indian powwow near Ponca City, Oklahoma.

who merchandise Oklahoma's Indian arts and crafts around a natural attraction such as the Grand Canyon. For this most Oklahoma Indians are grateful.

Non-Indians imagine warbonnets and buffalo when they think of the Indian, but many of Oklahoma's Indian people have woodland or prairie heritages. They are the descendants of the front-line Indian soldiers of the seventeenth, eighteenth, and early nineteenth centuries. Their brave leaders were the Tecumsehs, the Osceolas, and the Little Turtles (see their biographies), the great warriors of the Seneca, the Shawnee, the Miami, the Creek, the Delaware, and the Seminole. These tribes fought the bloody pitched colonial and national battles of the eastern forests and the upland rivers. These tribes learned early the lessons of adaptation and acculturation that allowed them to adopt some U.S. cultural forms while retaining Indian substance. That these tribes survived is a testimony to their ingenuity. They saw, that change was, paradoxically, their only hope of survival as an Indian people. Their lifeways, the summer rituals and the reunions are no less Indian because they celebrate the fire or the green corn and not the buffalo.

Oklahoma Indians have historically loved to perform, to play and dance for themselves or crowds, to "play Indian" or just to play. Colonial Indians traveling to Europe, Geronimo at the St. Louis World's Fair, the professional Indian dance troupe, the Osage ballerinas, Indians in Pawnee Bill's and the 101 Ranch shows all share the same tradition. Modern Indian teams and professional athletes reflect and continue the legacy of the great Indian professional football teams, Oklahoma's long list of Indian athletes, the successful Plains Indian baseball teams, and the most famous of all twentieth century sports figures, Jim Thorpe (see his biography). No competitive sport in the world can be as exciting as a Sunday afternoon stickball game back in the Oklahoma hills. Nor can any group of actors be as proud or arrogant as a group of Oklahoma Indians dressed by a Hollywood director in make-believe Indian costumes. If one sees only the outward performance of the dances and the dancers and of the Indians at play, one misses the spirit of the real world of Oklahoma's Indian people.

To Oklahoma Indians, the seasons still matter. To a people who are a part of the cycles of life of this planet, who live outside the artificial atmosphere of central heating and cooling and beyond the control of packaged good and preplanned public entertainment, the seasons are a measure of life. To the Oklahoma Indian, the summer celebrations bring more than oppressive heat and fresh tomatoes; they bring to life a world of family, tribe, politics, tradition, and ceremony. In its way this world is as Indian, as real for this modern Oklahoma Indian, as the world of his ancestors ever could be. As one young Indian explained, "Being an Indian doesn't depend upon how you dress or whether you have an old Ford or a young pony. Indians in bright cars and neat suits are still of the eagle race and as the people of the eagle race we are still a proud people who have kept alive a great spirit" (Jack Gregory and Rennard Strickland *Adventures of an Indian Boy*, 1974, page 29).

The crucible of Oklahoma, the sharing of similar historical experiences and government policies, has helped produce this spirit and to contribute to the uniqueness of Oklahoma Indian culture. A great many factors have contributed to the evolution of this modern Oklahoma Indianness. For example, since most Oklahoma Indian tribes, as immigrant Indians, were separated from their historic homelands, the strong and ancient geographic-cultural ties that non-literate as well as literate peoples associate with landmarks do not exist within the state. For a relatively long period of time prior to the Civil War, many Oklahoma Indian tribes adapted themselves and their culture to their new location with neither the pressure of geographic-cultural ties nor the presence of many external non-Indian pressures. Dating from the first half of the nineteenth century, there is a history of tribal cooperation and intertribal meetings among the Indian groups in Oklahoma. Stimulated in part by the federal government's decisions to treat removed and reservation peoples alike and in part by a sense of common problems, these conferences reduced tribal hostility and stimulated united action.

The opening of Indian Territory to U.S. settlers and the general policy to end common ownership of Indian lands by allotting tribally held lands to individual Indians came at approximately the same time in Oklahoma history. They created a varied series of clashes and conflicts. The present-day absence of a large body of tribally owned land and the earlier federal failure to retain traditional reservations no doubt created a vastly different Oklahoma Indian community, as did the aggressive manner in which the Dawes Commission distributed Indian farmlands and township lots which were subsequently sold with government approval. Towns with sizable non-Indian population pockets therefore existed amidst Indian lands almost from the moment of settlement. The percentage of land in Indian hands was quickly reduced.

Yet another crucial factor was the fact that a number of Indian tribes, as well as by the state of Oklahoma, shared the assumption that statehood in 1907 changed forever the nature and purpose of tribal government. Following statehood the nation tended to legislate for the Indians of Oklahoma, particularly the Five Civilized Tribes, as separate legislative units not to be treated as the Indian tribes of other states. Added to this was the presence of a great body of mixed blood Indian leaders who moved easily into the process of creating state governmental structures and who represented the interests of the entire state from positions of national or state leadership. Further, full blood tribal leaders chose not to move into Oklahoma state government, retreating and withdrawing from the state political arena.

Much of Oklahoma Indian life has been culturally bifurcated. Since statehood, tribes have treated their recognized civil and traditional religious groups as separate tribal bodies, creating uniquely Indian religious and cultural pockets that are hidden within seemingly acculturated Native populations. Other issues, divisive in many non-Oklahoma tribes, such as the role of women, have had little disruptive effect in Oklahoma, perhaps because those issues have few historic roots in this population. Oklahoma Indian women, many of whom are from matrilineal groups, exert a major and even dominant influence in many tribes and in most Indian families. Furthermore, Oklahoma Indian tribes have never developed a rigidly defined concept of "Indianness" and have encouraged the development of divergent cultural strains. There is a little historical evidence of tribal division based on degree of Indian blood, which indicates a strong degree of cultural confidence, a kind of Native sureness that Oklahoma tribes define as Indian pride and some non-Oklahoma Indians regard as arrogance. Voluntary separation and cultural segregation that is geographically intensified by traditional Indian settlement patterns combine to eliminate factional conflict. Finally, the size of the Indian population that is not physically identifiable as Indian but is of Indian descent in proportion to the size of the non-Indian population of the state creates a kind of "Indian culturality" that exists in no other state and that, at least in the abstract, defines "being Indian" as socially desirable.

This particular set of cultural and historical circumstances occurred nowhere else in the Indian country of the West. None of these factors, alone, produced Oklahoma's unique Indian culture. Other factors, no doubt, contributed significantly to the development of Oklahoma Indian culture and values. Taken together, these attitudes and events helped shape the diverse tribal cultures of the immigrant Native American groups who are Oklahoma's Indians.

Today Oklahoma tribes seem to be undergoing a revived interest in the old ways and an increased pride in Indianness. As Wayne Wallace, of the Indian Job

Corps, explains: "Indians have pride in who they are and where they come from. . . . The values of Indian people are just as good and important as the values of non-Indians." Yet numbers of modern Indians from all tribes choose to deny, to ignore, or to forget all that appears to be Native. Others retreat completely into the distant Indian hills, into an Indian world of the mind, to hide from the threat of the non-Indian world. The late Pam Chibitty, a Comanche-Shawnee-Delaware who worked with Indian people at the Native American Coalition of Tulsa, noted that for many Indians adjustment is not easy. "Some withdraw into an all-Indian world shunning non-Indians and modern society, others 'sell out' and go on to the modern white man's world and forget their backgrounds."

Within the individual Indian's life; there are many distinctly personal values and attitudes that are influenced by an Indian heritage. Among Indians of the same generation and of the same tribe, there is no static view of Indianness. The world of the Oklahoma Indian is dynamic, varied, and diverse. And yet in some ways, Indian culture is becoming increasingly pan-Indian in the sense that many tribes share such events as powwows, gourd dances, and urban planning seminars. Oklahoma Indian life remains family-oriented, and the tribe is still important. The life of the Indian is more than dances at Anadarko, more than church-sponsored wild-onion dinners or public ceremonials. Events such as the birthday of Grandmother Anquoe or Mrs. Adair are at the heart of the real Indian world. Much of this personal Indian world remains hidden from non-Indian Oklahomans.

That the contemporary Indian lives in two worlds has generated the misperception of a kind of Native American cultural schizophrenia. Oklahoma Indians, like Oklahoma non-Indians, live in a world that balances elements of diverse cultural traditions. The Indian brings a unique perspective to problem resolution. Two or more cultural currents may coexist so that the Indian must play many roles. Some of these roles are entirely consistent; others are hopelessly discordant. "Indian life does not fall into rigid categories," as one Oklahoma anthropologist, Carol Rachlin, notes. "It is, rather, a complex of interlocking circles, each exerting pressures and controls upon the others. An individual functions in different capacities in these circles or groups" (*The American Indian Today*, 1968, page 107).

The varied life of the real Oklahoma Indian exposes the bankruptcy of the stereotypic image of the Indian. The Indian lawyer in a three-piece suit can easily transform himself into a feathered championship fancy dancer. An elected county law-enforcement official returns to his office the morning after attending a peyote meeting. A nurse leaves the hospital and goes to have tobacco "treated." The computer worker has her house smoked with cedar. A man of 1/256 Indian blood sits in a French restaurant in Tulsa expounding on tribal genealogy, while the almost full-blood descendant of a great chieftain of the same tribe tells her high school history teacher not to tell her classmates that she is Indian. A gentle, hard-working full-blood is pulled from his job and charged with harboring an Indian felon because, as a religious leader, he has followed the traditional Indian legal ways of his people. A nationally honored scholar-author consults his medicine doctor when a witch is haunting him. An internationally famous Indian artist tours China and Russia to renew her art. Such is the world of the Oklahoma Indian.

The spirit of a civilization conveys more about the meaning of people's lives than do artifacts or documents. To understand cultural spirit is difficult, especially if one was not born into that culture. Attempting to capture the spirit of Christianity, an old Kiowa man went to a missionary service, contributed when the collection plate was passed, and settled down for the sermon. This Kiowa, Old Mokeen, who had already given what he thought to be generous, rose when the request for more funds came, squared his shoulders, and spoke to the missionary in broken English: "Whatza matter this Jesus—why he all time broke?"

The corn road, the buffalo road, and the peyote road are different from one another, but the spirit with which one follows the road, not the road itself, is the essence of Indianness. This Indian spirit, an Indian way of seeing and of being, makes a quarter-blood Chickasaw or an eighth-blood Comanche perceive as an Indian. "I believe that there is such a thing as Indian sensibility," T.C. Cannon, a Caddo-Kiowa, once explained. "This has to do with the idea of a collective history. It's reflected in your upbringing and the remarks that you hear every day from birth and the kind of behavior and emotion you see around you."

Rennard Strickland
University of Oklahoma

♦ INDIANS OF THE PLATEAU, GREAT BASIN, AND ROCKY MOUNTAINS

Numerous American Indian communities continue to live today in their ancestral homes on the Columbia Plateau of eastern Oregon and Washington State; in the Great Basin, largely Nevada, western Colorado, southeastern Idaho, and parts of eastern California; and in the Rocky Mountains, largely northeastern Colorado, Wyoming, and western Montana. The plateau Indians once enjoyed a rich environment oriented toward the region's rivers, where they traditionally fished for salmon. The lands on which they lived were lush with many varieties

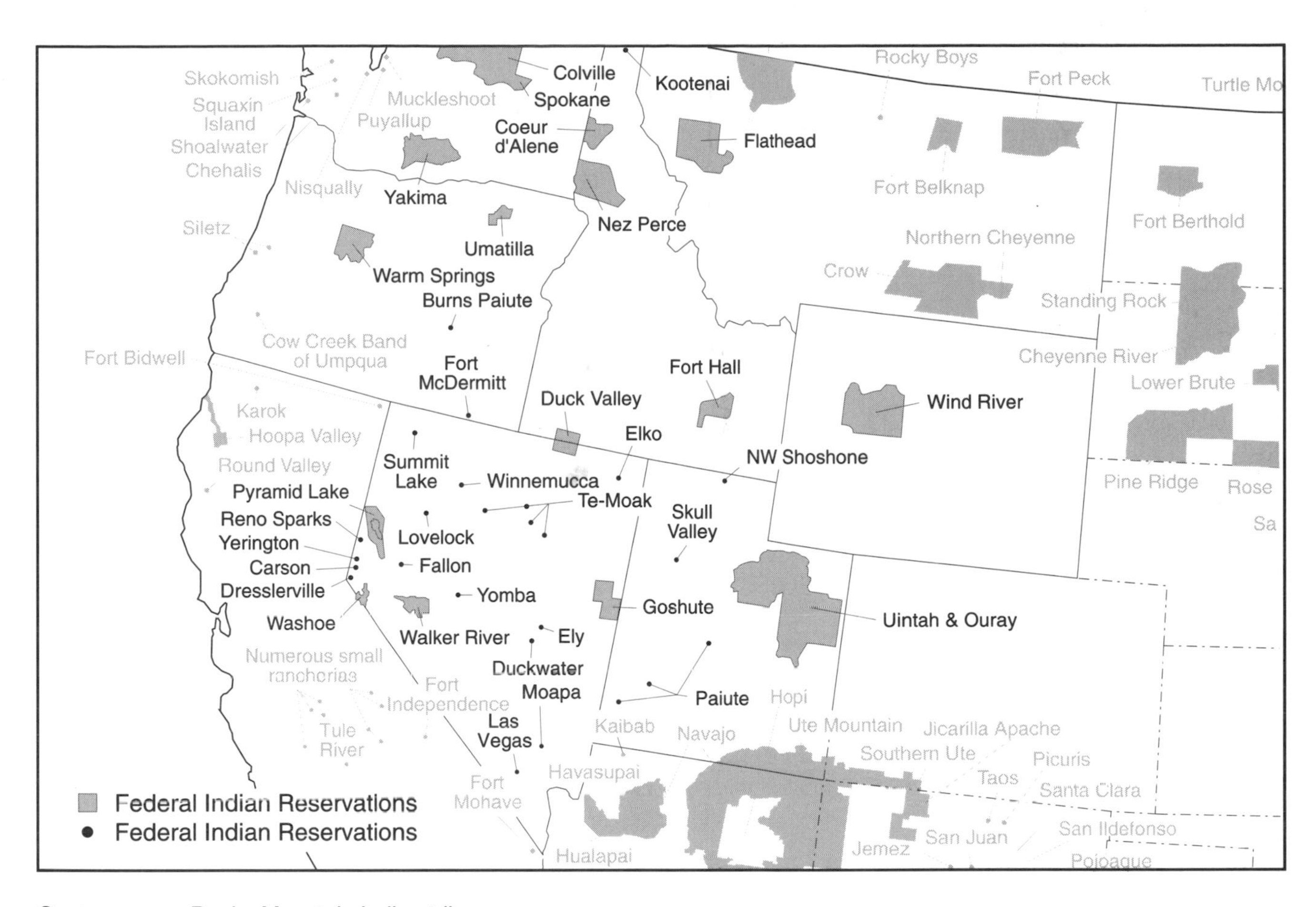

Contemporary Rocky Mountain Indian tribes.

of roots, berries, and game. The plateau and mountain tribes lived on the edge of evergreen forests and high prairies, where they learned a deep respect for the earth. The Great Basin peoples, largely Paiute, Bannock, and Shoshoni, lived in the high deserts and intermountain regions. East of the Plateau tribes, the Bitterroot and Rocky Mountains rise majestically, separating them from the mountain Indians. Large portions of Washington, Oregon, Montana, and Idaho contain high deserts and plateaus, where a host of Native Americans lived by gathering an abundance of roots and berries as well as by fishing and hunting. Similarly, the Paiute and Shoshoni of the Great Basin lived in small bands that hunted for food and gathered roots and berries.

In the plateau and mountain regions, the Indian nations shared may similar cultural traditions. Indian elders among the Flathead, Spokane, Wishram, Yakima, Nez Percé, Cayuse, Okanogan, and others say that the Creator placed them on the plateau and in the mountains at the beginning of time. Moreover, they argue that their history began when the earth was young, when plant and animal people interacted closely with the first humans. All of the tribes enjoy a rich oral tradition about their origins, and tribal elders consider the stories to be both literature and history. Many stories emerged from that time so long ago, but these stories form the basis of Native American cultural history.

One story recalls a time when five North Wind Brothers moved into the region and locked the plateau and mountain region in freezing cold. Coyote—the ever-present culture hero of many western Native peoples—whose actions often were the cause of both positive and negative events, became a follower of the North Wind. Many of the plants and animals chose sides, as either followers of the North Wind Brothers or antagonists against them. In particular, the North Wind Brothers encountered the Salmon people, who are large, edible fish that lay their eggs upstream of rivers that run to the ocean. In the stories of the Native peoples, animals often can communicate with humans, animals, and other beings. The Salmon Chief and his tribe lived in the Pacific Ocean, but in the spring of the year, they traveled up the rivers flowing into the Pacific. When the Salmon Chief led his people up one of the rivers, they were met by thick sheets of ice that prevented their traveling to their spawning grounds. The North Wind Brothers stood fast against the Salmon Chief, so the leader challenged the five brothers to a wrestling match on the ice. The

Salmon Chief beat three of the brothers, but he lost to the fourth. The North Wind Brothers and their followers fell upon Salmon Chief and all of his people, killing them in an attempt to destroy the entire tribe. They even cut open the wife of Salmon Chief, who carried numerous eggs. The North Wind Brothers smashed every egg, except one that fell between two deep and tightly wedged rocks. Believing that the egg would dry up, the North Wind Brothers left the area.

The Creator had watched the struggle between the Wind and the Salmon, and he took pity on the Salmon people. He sent a strong rain to wash the blood from the earth, and from the bosom of the rocks he washed the tiny salmon egg into the river. The Creator fertilized and nurtured the egg until a small salmon was born. The salmon returned to the ocean, where his grandmother cared for him and trained him to meet the future challenge of the North Wind Brothers. When Young Chinook Salmon was of age, he traveled upriver to meet the forces that had killed his mother and father. He met the five North Wind Brothers on the ice, and one by one he defeated them. However, Young Chinook Salmon did not kill the younger sister of the North Wind Brothers, and every winter she returns to bring a mild version of the cold once known when her five brothers ruled the region.

Like the battle between the salmon and the wind, the Indians of the plateau and mountains have long been engaged in a struggle for survival against European traders and settlers, who moved into the region and nearly destroyed the original inhabitants. In the nineteenth century, many Indian communities suffered a near-death experience, but like the small egg that survived, so did these Native people.

In the first decade of the 1800s, Indians living in present-day Oregon, Washington, Idaho, and Montana met Meriwether Lewis and William Clark, who led a U.S. expedition (1806–1809) to explore the Louisiana Purchase, land west of the Mississippi bought from France in 1803. Indians from the plateau and mountains probably met European traders visiting the Chinook and Clatsop Indians living along the Columbia River and the coasts of Oregon and Washington. However, the interior tribes share a common experience through their relations with Lewis and Clark.

When the explorers reached the Great Falls (near present-day Great Falls, Montana) of the Missouri River, they needed horses and information in order to cross the Rocky Mountains. With a small party, Lewis set out on foot to find the Shoshoni Indians. After some time, the men met several Shoshoni women, to whom they gave gifts. The women belonged to the Lemhi band of Shoshoni people, and their leader was Chief Kameawaite. After much effort, Lewis convinced Kameawaite to supply horses and guides to lead the U.S. exploring party over the Rocky Mountains. When the Shoshoni and explorers returned to Great Falls, Kameawaite willingly helped Lewis and Clark, because they had returned his long-lost sister, Sacajewea. Sacajewea and her husband, Touissant Charbonneau, served as guides to the Lewis and Clark expedition to Great Falls from a Hidatsa village in present-day central North Dakota. Some years earlier, enemies of the Shoshoni had stolen Kameawaite's sister, Sacajewea, who was sold into slavery and eventually bought by Charbonneau. Kameawaite contributed significantly to the safe journey of the famous explorers. The Shoshoni chief led the expedition through most of present-day Montana and showed them the way into the country of the Flathead Indians, in present-day western Montana. In like fashion, the Flathead guided Lewis and Clark westward across the panhandle of present-day Idaho.

In October 1805, the Lewis and Clark expedition entered the lands of the Nez Percé, who provided the explorers with kindness, food, and canoes to take them to the Pacific Ocean. With the aid of Nez Percé scouts, the explorers traveled quickly by canoe to the homelands of the Palouse Indians, safely reaching the Palouse village of Quosispah. Several Indians greeted Lewis and Clark at this village, and they celebrated the arrival of the *Suyapo*, "Crowned Heads" or "Crowned Hats," by singing long into the night. Palouse, Yakima, Wanapum, Wishram, Walla Walla, Cayuse, and a host of other tribes sent representatives to meet the U.S. explorers. The Indians and explorers traded goods, and Lewis and Clark honored some of the chiefs with special medals bearing the words *Peace and Friendship*. Relations between the two peoples were friendly, and the explorers soon continued their trip down the Columbia River, in present-day Oregon State, past the villages of the Skin, Wishram, Tenino, Wasco, Clackamus, Cathlapotle, Wahkiakum, and Cathlamet.

The explorers spent a rainy winter among the Clatsop Indians living south of the Columbia River before returning to the United States. The United States claimed the entire Northwest—including the plateau and mountains—for their country, and they encouraged others to relocate to the region. Lewis and Clark reported the many wondrous things they had seen, including the vast numbers of fur-bearing animals. By 1810, in less than a year after their journey, British traders traveled through the Northwest in quest of a river route from the interior of Canada to the Pacific Ocean. Soon three major fur trading companies, the Northwest Company, the American Fur Company, and the Hudson's Bay Company, set up trading posts or factories in the Northwest.

Fort Astoria in Oregon along the Columbia River served as a key trading center for the Americans, but the British purchased the post in 1813 and renamed it Fort George. In 1824, the Hudson's Bay Company opened

Fort Vancouver in present-day Washington, and they operated factories or posts on the plateau. While the company worked with Shoshoni, Paiute, and Bannock to procure furs, they depended on the plateau tribes for horses. Fort Nez Percé, Fort Okanogan, Fort Colville, and Fort Spokane, all named after plateau tribes, traded with Indians and supplied the Hudson's Bay Company with some furs and many horses. The British company enjoyed a prosperous Indian trade on the plateau and intermountain areas until the 1850s, when they had depleted the number of fur-bearing animals and when the United States took firm control of the region.

The traders and trappers became the first to occupy Indian lands in the region. A few of them tried to convert the Indians to Christianity, but the major thrust of the mission system on the plateau began in the 1830s. The Presbyterian missionary couples Marcus and Narcissa Whitman and Henry and Eliza Spalding established the first missions in the Northwest among the Cayuse and the Nez Percé. Catholic missionaries followed these early Presbyterian ministers, establishing missions among the Flathead, Sanpoil, Nespelem, Colville, Yakima, Umatilla, and others. Some Indians gravitated to Christianity, while others retreated into their own traditional religions. Controversy over whether to adopt Christianity split many plateau and mountain Indian communities into pro- and anti-Christians.

Between 1836 and 1843, the Presbyterian Whitmans and Spaldings worked diligently among the Indians with mixed results. In 1843, a significant event altered the course of events: Joe Meek, William Craig, and other former fur trappers opened a wagon road, later called the Oregon Trail, from Idaho across the Blue Mountains of Oregon, along the Columbia River, and into the Grande Ronde River Valley of Oregon. Soon many settlers and travelers used the Oregon Trail to travel to the Pacific northwest coast. The newcomers established territorial governments in the present-day states of Oregon and Washington, asserting political power over the indigenous peoples. Tensions mounted as disease, introduced by the newcomers, spread among the Indians, threatening their physical survival. In the interior, measles ravaged the Cayuse, and they blamed Dr. Whitman for the epidemic. A few Cayuse murdered the doctor, his wife, and eleven others. Oregon Volunteers marched to engage the Cayuse but eventually fought the Palouse, after the Volunteers tried stealing about 400 Indian horses. The conflict was settled after a few Cayuse surrendered and were later hanged.

Of equal importance, after Maidu Indians discovered gold in 1848 along the American River in northern California, miners invaded California, killing Indians with guns and viruses. The California mining frontier moved northward into the lands of the Modoc, Klamath, and Chetco. Gold was soon discovered on the plateau and in the mountains, where Indians resisted the invasion of their homelands by miners who had little or no regard for Indians or their rights. The miners extended their diggings north into Oregon and Washington and east into Idaho and Montana. The United States soon gave more attention to the area, and in 1853, it created two separate territories there. Oregon Territory included lands in present-day Oregon, Idaho, and Wyoming. Washington Territory included lands in present-day Washington, Idaho, and Montana. With the new government came American Indian policy bent on liquidating Indian title to the land, concentration of Indians onto smaller parcels of land called reservations, and the establishment of military and civil power over the tribes.

In 1854, Governor Isaac I. Stevens made a whirlwind tour of the coastal tribes of Washington Territory, coercing some of them into ceding their lands to the government. He made treaties at Medicine Creek, Point Elliott, and Point No Point. The Indians of Puget Sound secured for themselves only a small portion of their lands and fell victim to the power of the Bureau of Indian Affairs. Stevens had a more difficult time with the plateau Indians. In May 1855, Stevens made three treaties with the inland tribes, creating the Yakima, Nez Percé, and Umatilla reservations. Although he did not negotiate treaties with the Salish-speaking Indians of the plateau, he concluded a treaty with some Flathead, which forced the Kutenai, Kalispel, and Flathead to move onto a reservation. Oregon superintendent of Indian affairs Joel Palmer helped Stevens with the Walla Walla Council before concluding treaties with the Tenino, Wasco, Wishram, and other people living along the Columbia River. He created the Warm Springs Reservation of Oregon south of the Columbia River, where he expected the tribes to live in peace with the Paiute of Oregon. Palmer negotiated treaties with several different tribes in Oregon, but over time, the U.S. government took nearly all Indian land in the territory, leaving Native Americans with virtually no land base. As a result of territorial government, the United States and its citizens took control of the plateau and mountain Indians but not without a fight.

Shortly after the Walla Walla Council of 1855, white miners discovered gold north of the Spokane River in Oregon Territory. Miners invaded the inland Northwest, and some stole and murdered a few Indians, which led to retaliation by Yakima warriors, who executed several miners. War resulted after two Yakima murdered Indian agent Andrew Jackson Bolon. Between 1855 and 1858, the Indians of the Columbia Plateau fought a series of fights with volunteer and U. S Army troops. After some initial successes, the Yakima retreated north. Volunteer troops from Oregon and Washington invaded the lands of Walla Walla, Umatilla, Cayuse, and Palouse Indians living near the Snake River in present-day Oregon. Few of these people had been involved in the conflict in the Yakima country, but the volunteer soldiers sought to punish all Indians. The Plateau Indian War concluded at the Battle of Four Lake and Spokane Plain when the combined forces of Yakima, Palouse, Spokane, Flathead, Okanogan, and others suffered a loss at the hands of the U.S. military led by Colonel George Wright. Several tribes chose not to enter a war with the United States, but all of them felt the power of the federal government and the settlers who had taken their land.

Contact with settlers came relatively late for the Great Basin peoples, such as the numerous local bands of Paiute. But in the 1850s, many Great Basin Indians, who primarily lived by hunting animals and gathering roots and plants, relatively quickly went to work for U.S. ranchers and farmers. Many worked for wages as cowboys driving cattle, and others performed a variety of wage-labor jobs such as planting, cultivating, and harvesting grains and taking care of livestock. The ranchers and farmers were willing to hire the Indian workers, since farm and ranch hands were quite scarce in the Great Basin region.

The rapidly changing political and economic situation of the Great Basin region helped spark two social movements, which are often called the 1870 Ghost Dance and the 1890 Ghost Dance. The 1870 movement was started by the Paiute mystic Wodziwob, whose teachings spread primarily among the northern and western California Indians. The California Indians, at this time, were under great distress from disease, poverty, political subordination (see the California entry), and aggressive miners, who wanted the Indians out of the mining fields. Many California Indians adopted the Ghost Dance-associated hand game, a gambling game with ritual singing and betting while one team tries to hide bones and the other tries to guess who has the bones. The second, or 1890, Ghost Dance is more well known and was initiated by Wovoka, the son of a Paiute shaman. This Ghost Dance drew upon the early teachings of Wodziwob and emphasized the return of game and relatives who had died over the past several decades. Many Indians had died of diseases, and game, especially buffalo on the Plains, was noticeably declining. Many Indian nations in the West were gravely

The prophet Wovoka (seated) in his later years.

concerned that changing conditions threatened their entire way of life. The Ghost Dance incorporated many Paiute traditions, such as a Round Dance. Performed to gain communication with or honor dead ancestors, the Round Dance became a central feature of the Ghost Dance, which in 1888 to 1890 spread rapidly among many western Indian tribes, especially among the Plains nations. The dance was performed to achieve successful transition to the next world after death, and in some versions the dance was to help facilitate a great worldly change in which many dead ancestors would return to live on earth and the game would be replenished. These events would restore the Indian nations to their former, more prosperous condition, before the intrusion of U.S. settlers and government. The Ghost Dance movement declined rapidly after the 1890 massacre of Sioux at Wounded Knee in South Dakota. Units of the Seventh Cavalry killed at least two hundred Sioux, many of whom were women and children. After the Wounded Knee incident, the U.S. government officially discouraged the Ghost Dance, and because the Ghost Dance predictions of a cataclysmic worldly reorganization did not come to pass, within a few years the movement declined to only a few tribes, and occasional Ghost Dance spiritual leaders sprinkled among some of the Plains nations. Wovoka encouraged the Great Basin and other Indian people to keep the moral teachings he received in a vision from the Great Spirit by loving one another and living in peace with every one, teachings that he most likely adapted from Christian thought, with which he was familiar. As late as the 1920s, Wovoka told other Indians—usually avoiding discussions with non-Indians—that he had visited with God and a new world was coming for the Indians.

The Nez Percé of present-day Idaho lived peacefully with the United States until 1860, when "traders" found gold on their lands. Gold miners quickly moved into the Nez Percé country, and the Bureau of Indian Affairs responded by shrinking the Nez Percé Reservation to one-tenth its original size. All the Nez Percé chiefs refused to sign the treaty of 1863, except Chief Lawyer who had no authority to sell Nez Percé lands. Still, he signed the "Thief Treaty," and the ultimate result was war. In 1876, General Oliver O. Howard demanded that the non-treaty Nez Percé move onto the reservation in present-day eastern Idaho. When the people had no other choice than to either accept peace or go to war, they chose to move to the reservation. Nevertheless, war erupted when three young men killed several settlers. In fear of U.S. retaliation, Chief Looking Glass led the Nez Percé out of Idaho into Montana and south toward the Crow Indians. When the Crow refused to help, the Nez Percé turned north toward Canada. U.S. forces led by Colonel Nelson A. Miles intercepted the Nez Percé near the Bear Paw Mountains of Montana, and he accepted the surrender of Chief Joseph, a central Nez Percé leader. Rather than returning the Nez Percé to Idaho in accordance with the surrender agreement, U.S. General William Tecumseh Sherman transported the men, women, and children to Fort Leavenworth, Kansas, and to Indian Territory, present-day Oklahoma. The Nez Percé remained in Indian Territory until 1885, when the government permitted them to return to the Northwest. Some Nez Percé returned to Idaho, but others, like Joseph, were forced to live on the Colville Reservation in central Washington.

The Shoshoni, Bannock, and Paiute people also made a stand against the United States. Originally, the United States established the Fort Hall Reservation in present-day eastern Idaho for the Boise-Bruneau band of Shoshoni, but soon the government forced the Bannock to accept reservation life at Fort Hall. Many of Bannock decided to go to the reservation and receive rations. The government, however, did not make goods its promises of food, and many Shoshoni and Bannock faced starvation. When the Bannock, Paiute, and Shoshoni living on the Fort Hall Reservation tried to continue their seasonal economic migrations for buffalo hunting and the gathering of roots and berries, it was.only a short time before they began to feel pressure from the Bureau of Indian Affairs (BIA) and Christian missionaries to stop. Discontent spread at Fort Hall, and on May 30, 1878, a few Indians stole some cattle and killed two cowboys, which started a series of battles. By June 1878, it had escalated into a significant military conflict. Numbering only 700 people, the Bannock and Paiute joined forces in southeastern Oregon, where they fought the Battle of Camp Curry. After the battle, the Bannock and Paiute moved north toward the Umatilla Reservation in present-day Oregon. U.S. forces subdued the Shoshoni and Bannock and returned them to the Fort Hall Reservation.

During the 1880s, reformers of American Indian policies determined that the trouble with Indians was that they held reservations communally and not individually. In an attempt to help Indians, liberal reformers decided to break up reservations into individual lots so that Indians would have private plots and want to productively work their ranch or farm. U.S. policymakers reasoned that this land policy would enable Indians to become "civilized," because they would have a direct stake in their own economic livelihood. Most reformers, however, knew little about Indian cultures or economic practices, such as their methods of hunting, fishing, and gathering. Few if any Indians in the plateau, mountain, or Great Basin regions farmed, and it would take years for them to alter their cultures to accommodate U.S. reformers. Many Indians refused to give up their traditional economic practices in order to adopt farming. Life on the reservations was hard, the people became dependent on U.S. government rations, and most reservations could not adequately support the small Indian populations that lived on the reservation.

In 1887, Congress passed the General Allotment Act, which called for the division of reservations into individual parcels of 160, 80, or 40 acres. Each Indian received an allotment, and the excess land was sold to non-Indian settlers. After twenty-five years, Indian allotees could sell their individual allotments.

The government began allotting the Yakima Reservation in Washington State in the 1890s and continued the process until 1914. Conservative Indians, particularly elders and worshipers of the Washani religion, a newly emergent religion that taught preservation of Indian land and many traditions, opposed allotment. Some Yakima agreed to take allotments, although many felt it contrary to tribal tradition. Between 1890 and 1914, the United States made 4,506 allotments on the Yakima Reservation, totaling 440,000 acres. Because many conservative Yakima resisted taking allotments, 798,000 acres of reservation land was not allotted and remained in tribal hands. The government also allotted land on the Spokane Reservation in Washington. On June 19, 1902, Congress passed a resolution directing the secretary of the interior to allot Spokane tribal lands. The Indians had little choice in the matter, because the United States forced 651 members of the tribe to accept allotments totaling 64,750 acres. The government sold the remainder of the Spokane Reservation to non-Indian timber, agricultural, and ranching interests.

Like many Indians, the Coeur d'Alene people of Idaho lost a huge portion of their original domain. On November 8, 1873, the president created the Coeur d'Alene Reservation with 598,500 acres. However, in agreeing to the executive order creating the reservation, the Coeur d'Alene lost 184,960 acres of their homeland in eastern Washington and western Idaho. When the government allotted reservation lands from 1905 to 1909 over the objections of Coeur d'Alene chief Peter Moctelme, the Coeur d'Alene and Spokane were left with only 51,040 acres of lands they traditionally had lived on.

A similar situation to that of the Coeur d'Alene occurred on the Flathead Reservation of Montana, where the Pend d'Oreille (also known as Upper Kalispel), Kutenai and Flathead lived. Originally, these Indians controlled 1,242,969 acres of land. Between 1904 and 1908, the government allotted 80 acres to individuals interested in farm lands and 160 acres to Indians wishing to ranch. A total of 2,378 Indians received allotments on the Flathead Reservation. At the same time, the U.S. government sold 404,047 acres of former Indian lands to U.S. settlers, and the state of Montana took another 60,843 acres for school purposes. The United States kept 1,757 acres of the Indian lands for itself, thus assuming control over most of the original lands of the Flathead people. On May 2, 1910, the government opened the remainder of the reservation land for settlement and development by non-Indians.

During the late nineteenth and early twentieth centuries, Native Americans lost more than their estates. They also lost elements of their culture, language, and families through the efforts of the Bureau of Indian Affairs to "civilize" them. Indian reformers often wanted Indians to leave their Native cultures, which the reformers considered backward. U.S. policymakers believed that the best road for Indians to travel was to adopt U.S. culture and that education was the most effective way to civilize Native Americans. Indian schools emerged on several reservations, where U.S. teachers tried to discourage Indian students from practicing Indian languages, cultures, traditions, and religions. Churches established mission schools on some reservations, but, by the late nineteenth century, the Bureau of Indian Affairs controlled most reservation educational institutions.

Through the Indian agents and the superintendents of the Indian schools, the Bureau of Indian Affairs operated most of the reservation schools. Although boys and girls both attended these schools, the administrators and teachers focused their attention primarily on boys, mirroring the gender bias prevalent in U.S. society. Teachers taught Indian children to speak, read, and write English, and they punished the children when they spoke Indian languages. Indian students learned the subjects that were taught in most U.S. elementary schools of the time, but the major emphasis was on vocational education. Teachers trained girls to be waitresses, maids, and housekeepers, and Indian boys studied printing, masonry, and carpentry. Many Indian boys and girls were sent to work in nearby towns and homes, where they learned from on-the-job training but earned little or no money. Most reservations had elementary schools, but the Bureau of Indian Affairs sent older children—Shoshoni, Bannock, Nez Percé, Nespelem, Paiute, Okanogan, and others—to Carlisle in Pennsylvania, Haskell in Oklahoma, Sherman in California, or one of the other boarding schools. Some Indian boarding schools continue to function today, although the attitudes and curriculum of the boarding schools no longer directly discourage the expression of Indian cultures as they did in the early twentieth century.

While forced education dramatically altered Indian cultures of the Columbia Plateau, the Great Basin, and Rocky Mountains, other factors, such as disease, also influenced the lives of these Indians. While smallpox, measles, and venereal diseases ravaged the tribes in the nineteenth century, tuberculosis, pneumonia, and influenza killed thousands of Indians in the twentieth century. Between 1888 and 1930, among the Indians of the Confederated Yakima Nation, more deaths occurred between the time of birth and age one than any other age category. Infant mortality most often resulted from the above-mentioned diseases. Each tribe had its traditional Native doctors, men and women who knew the healing herbs, medical techniques, prayers, and songs, but they were too often unable to fight the newly introduced diseases. Some Indians were treated by government doctors, but too many were not. The Native American population in the region suffered severely from disease until the 1930s, when the Indian Health Service received more funds for combating infectious diseases.

During the 1930s, Congress passed the Indian Reorganization Act, which allowed tribes to reassert themselves legally in a new way. Indians who accepted the Indian Reorganization Act could place their allotments in a trust so the lands could not be sold. The tribes could also reorganize into new political entities with tribal laws and constitutions. Some of the tribes of the plateau and mountains accepted the Indian Reorganization Act, while others did not. The Confederated Salish and Kutenai Tribes of the Flathead Reservation, the Confederated Tribes of the Umatilla Indian Reservation, the Confederated Tribes of the Warm Springs Reservation, and others voted to accept the Indian Reorganization Act. Regardless, all of the plateau and mountain tribes and many of the Great Basin tribes created tribal governments that helped guide them during the twentieth century. Certainly all of the tribes took advantage of the Indian Claims Commission established in 1946.

Prior to establishment of the Indian Claims Commission, the United States forced Indian tribes to take their cases directly to Congress, a branch of government not known for moving quickly to settle Indian land claims. For years the tribes had taken their problems involving land, water, and resources to Congress, without result. The Indian Claims Commission offered tribes a mechanism through which they could sue the federal government for treaty violations involving a host of issues. In every case settled by the Indian Claims Commission, the tribes received a monetary compensation rather than any land returned. Some Native Americans objected to this arrangement, but it was the only one used by the commission. For example, in settling claims of the numerous bands of Shoshoni and Bannock people, the Claims Commission separated the 1957 Shoshoni-Bannock claim into several parts, a part of which dealt with the Northern, Northwestern, and Western bands of Shoshoni. The case took so long that the U.S. Court of Claims made the determination of the case after the Claims Commission expired in 1978. On October 8, 1982, one section of the Shoshoni claim, which dealt with federal mismanagement of timber and grazing resources, was settled in favor of the Shoshoni bands, who were awarded $1.6 million.

In July 1951, the Nez Percé tribe of Idaho and the Nez Percé living on the Colville Reservation filed petitions with the Indian Claims Commission regarding compensation for the theft of their original homelands, particularly those in northeastern Oregon and western Idaho. The Claims Commission combined the petitions of the two groups into one claim on February 27, 1953. Finally in 1971, the commission awarded the Nez Percé $3.5 million.

During the 1950s, the federal government sought to dissolve, or terminate, the reservation system and end its treaty and legal relationship with various tribes in the United States. Most notable was the government's attempt to terminate the Confederated Tribes of the Colville Reservation in Washington State. Colville tribal members living off the the reservation generally favored termination because it would bring them a cash settlement. However, tribal members living on the reservation generally opposed termination, because it abrogated treaty rights and threatened to disperse Indian cultures and communities. The leaders of the Confederated Tribes struggled over the issue of termination during the 1950s and 1960s. The most vocal opponent of termination was Lucy Covington, a member of a prominent political family on the reservation. Covington stood nearly single-handedly against proponents of termination, and she never surrendered her position. As a result of her efforts, the tribe never agreed to termination, and it has been solidly opposed to the concept ever since.

Since the threat of termination receded in the 1960s, many tribes have made significant strides in health, education, and economic development. Each year the Colville Tribe sponsors workshops on cultural revitalization, and they encourage their young people to participate in their annual Powwow and Circle Celebration held in Nespelem, Washington. The tribe owns a sawmill, a package log cabin sales business, and a trading post. Several young people attend colleges and universities in the region, and several students have returned to their reservation to contribute their expertise to developing the reservation economy and community. A similar situation has occurred on the Flathead Reservation, where the Kutenai, Kalispel, and Flathead have initiated a cultural heritage project to preserve their languages, oral histories, and songs. The Flathead tribe maintains a business relationship with Montana Power Company, which operates Kerr Dam on the reservation and also operates a resort at Blue Bay along the shores of Flathead Lake.

The Shoshoni and Bannock tribal members from the Fort Hall Reservation are often employed in ranching, farming, and small businesses. The tribe owns its own agricultural enterprise as well as a construction business. Most important is the 20,000-acre irrigation project that the tribe operates, bringing water to Indians and non-Indians alike. The tribe enjoys its own health center, adult education program, and youth recreation pro-

Nii'eihii No'eiihi', or the Eagle Drum, is the official ceremonial and social drum group of the Arapaho tribe. Their presence is required at any large gathering. Seated front left is Helen Cedartree, a noted elder of the tribe. Her Arapaho name is, appropriately, Tei'betebii, or Strong Old Woman. Taken at the annual Ethete (Wyoming) Celebration Powwow.

gram. The same is true at the Wind River Reservation, in Wyoming, where suicide has plagued young people at a rate much higher than the national average. The Cayuse, Umatilla, and Walla Walla Indians living on the Umatilla Reservation in Oregon face similar problems, and they are responding by emphasizing both traditional culture and modern education. The tribe established a scholarship fund for college-age students, a day care center, and health education programs for young people. The emphasis on education and the encouragement of young people to seek post-secondary education is a common element of reservation life among the Indians of the plateau and mountains.

Two of the most active tribes in the region in terms of educational and economic self-determination are the Warm Springs of Oregon and Yakima people in Washington. Indians of the Warms Springs Reservation have carefully logged the western edge of their reservation, and they have their own Warm Springs Forest Products Industries which include a sawmill and plywood plant. The also built their own resort and convention center called *Kah-Nee-Ta*, which has generated considerable money for programs in health and education. The elders encourage their young people to complete degrees in higher education, and some have returned to their homes to contribute to the well-being of their people. The Indians at Warm Springs have herds of wild horses, which they sell, and they manage a salmon hatchery through their own laws of fish and game. In 1982 the tribe became the first in the United States to open its own hydroelectric plant, the Pelton Reregulating Dam, providing energy that is sold to the Pacific Power and Light Company. While the people of the Warm Springs Reservation have been successful in terms of education, health, and economic development, they have maintained a good deal of their traditional religion through the Washani religion—a spiritual faith they share with many Indians living on the Yakima Reservation.

Of all the tribes of the plateau and mountain region, the Yakima have been the most successful in maintaining their spiritual beliefs and promoting their own economic self-determination. The tribe manages its own forest products industry, annually cutting about 150 million board feet of lumber. They have their own furniture manufacturing plant, and they manage 2.7 million acres of rangeland and 150,000 acres of farmland. The Yakima control their own water through the Wapato Project, and they have been highly successful in overseeing small businesses, banking, and fishing enterprises. With the funds the tribe has generated, it has initiated a major housing project, the Yakima Tribal Housing Authority. In addition, in 1980 the Yakima opened an extensive tribal cultural center, the largest of its kind in the country. Beautifully designed, shaped largely like a longhouse, the cultural center contains a library, museum, gift shop, theater, restaurant, and office space. The Yakima emphasize education, offering tribal scholarships to young people and a summer educational program that prepares students for college study. Each year, the Yakima people support numerous powwows and festivals to celebrate their heritage.

Programs for teaching Indian languages on the Colville, Umatilla, Nez Percé, Coeur d'Alene, Spokane, and Yakima reservations began in the 1970s and continue in the 1990s with even greater awareness of the need for language preservation. While the tribes themselves are responsible for the maintenance of language, university scholars have joined hands with some of the tribes to write and teach the language. Native Americans of the region consider language retention one of their most important projects.

Perhaps the most significant issue facing the Indians of the plateau and eastern mountain region is fishing rights. Native Americans in Washington, Oregon, and Idaho protested the destruction of the salmon, and they stood firm in their resolve to assert their treaty rights, which guaranteed them the right to fish, hunt, graze, and gather in all usual and accustomed areas on and off the reservations. The fight for fishing rights continued throughout the twentieth century, and in 1974, they won the Boldt Decision, which acknowledged the right of Indians to fish in common with non-Indians, with Indians having the right to half of the harvestable fish catch. The Supreme Court has upheld the Boldt Decision, but opposition from state officials and recreational fishing organizations has not ended. The Nez Percé, Yakima, Palouse, Wanapum, and other tribes have continued to fight for their fishing rights and have stood against the

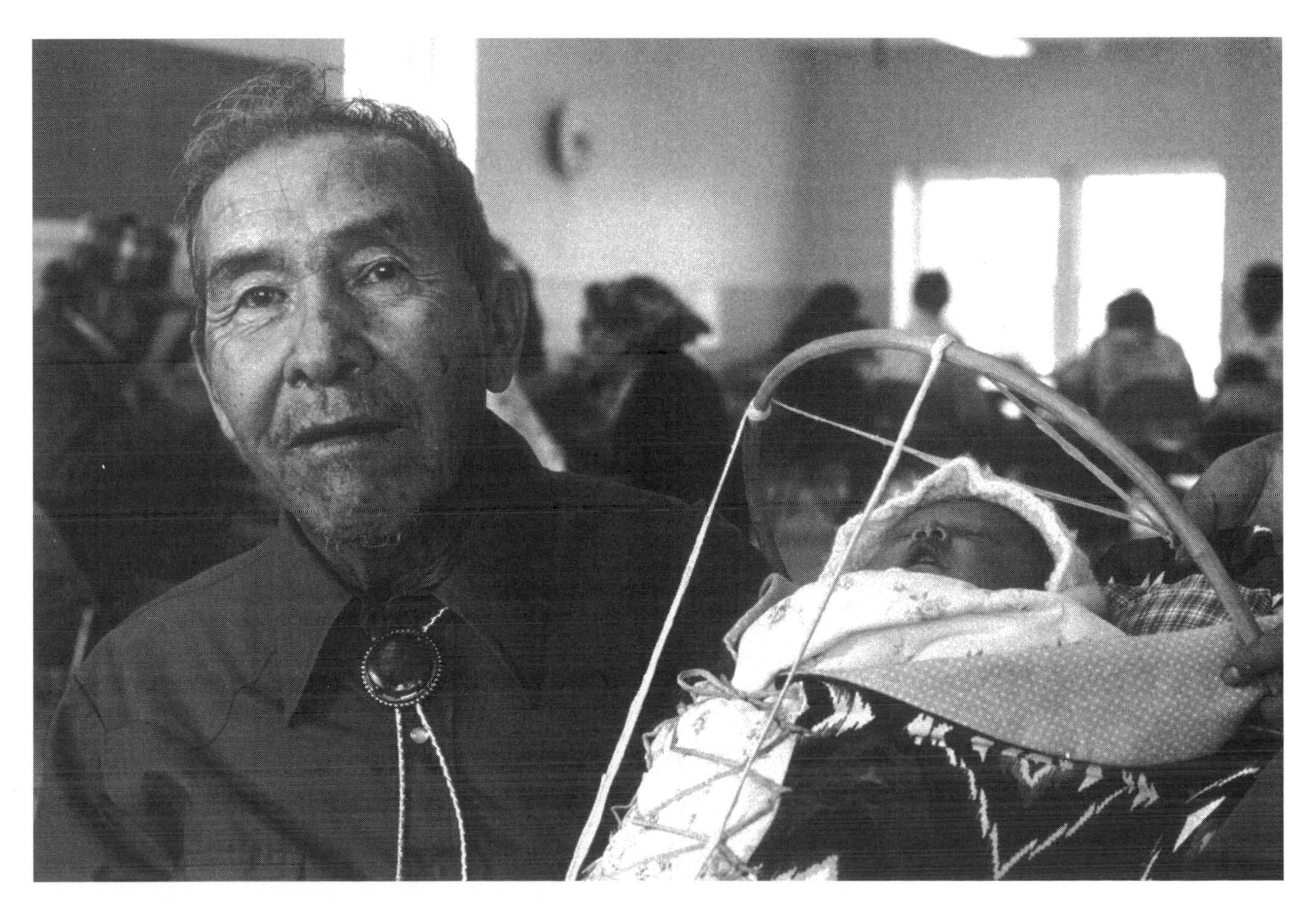

Ben Goggles was in his 70s when he died in 1978. He was the father of ten daughters and the head of the Arapaho Sun Dance for many years. His Arapaho name was Hoonino', or Quill.

discrimination they have suffered from state law enforcement agents, who refuse to recognize the federal treaty rights of the tribes.

The Boldt Decision, upheld by the Supreme Court, has not ended the fishing rights struggle throughout the inland Northwest. During the 1980s, a case involving David Sohappy, an Indian elder of mixed Yakima and Wenatchi blood, illuminated the continual struggle of Native Americans to protect and defend their fishing rights. Sohappy represented the feelings of many Northwestern Indians when he argued that his right to fish did not hinge merely on the articles of the Yakima Treaty of 1855. He insisted that the right to use the salmon had first come to the people as a result of Coyote—the trickster, changer—who, according to tradition, broke a dam, guarded by monsters, at the mouth of the Columbia River and led the salmon into the inland rivers.

As a result of exerting his traditional fishing rights, Sohappy was arrested by state and federal game and fish authorities. He was tried in a federal court and sentenced to prison in Spokane. He was later transferred to California to a federal jail. Ultimately, he was released from prison, but he continued to fight for fishing rights until his death. The fishing rights issue in the Northwest is an ongoing battle for Native Americans and those who support their rights. The fishing rights issue is such a major concern that it became a campaign issue during the race for Washington State governor in 1992. Times had changed, and many Washington State citizens supported Native people in their traditional and treaty rights to fish in their accustomed places. The state of Washington elected a governor in November 1992 who supported Indian treaty and fishing rights.

The Indians of the plateau, Great Basin, and mountains are a diverse people. All of them enjoyed a long history of growth and development before the arrival of Lewis and Clark. Yet all of them have been forced to contend with the United States as well as the state governments near their homes. They have lost most of their native estates and elements of their rich cultural heritages. They have all fought for their lives, sovereignty, and rights. They have all weathered many storms, and they all continue to exist today. Since the 1960s, the tribes have asserted themselves with greater vigor, offering tribally managed educational, health, and economic development programs. The tribes have attempted to preserve their languages and culture through diverse programs, projects, and institutions. The people of this region have a spirit about them tying their past traditions to life today. This spirit has sustained them since the time of creation, and this spirit will propel them into the twenty-first century.

Clifford E. Trafzer
University of California, Riverside

Cleone Thunder was born in April 1903. She lived most of her life in the Ethete (Wyoming) area, except for a few years in Oklahoma. She has four children and has not yet counted all of her great-great-grandchildren. Her Arapaho name, Hiisei Nouuceh, or Woman Running out of the Lodge, was given to her by her father when she was a baby. It commemorated a brave Crow woman who ran from her tipi holding a baby and faced attacking Arapaho warriors. The woman shouted, "You can do anything with me, I have just given birth."

♦ CALIFORNIA INDIANS

Without exception, the Native peoples of California believe they originated in North America. Despite unproven theories of a Siberian origin and migration favored by the non-Indian academics, traditional origin stories tell of a creator or creators whose wondrous powers brought forth the physical universe and all plant and animal life. The members of each group saw themselves as the center of that creation and viewed their neighbors as less favored. This cultural centrism created the precedent that tribal territories were sacred and intimately connected the divine intentions of the Creator. Consequently, land, place, and sacred sites all had a tie to the Creator and to traditional events that were the major events and symbols in Indian histories.

At the time of first contact with Europeans (1540), the population of the California Indians was approximately 310,000 to 340,000 people. These astounding numbers made it the most densely populated area in what is now the United States. The mild climate and abundance of wild foods proved more than adequate sustenance for such a population (see map below). Social organization among this population varied. The San Joaquin Valley Yokut and the Yuman along the Colorado River are examples of large tribes sharing a common language and possessing a well-defined territory and a degree of political unity. More common was the organization of populations that were essentially village centered, sometimes called tribelets. These groups, too, possessed well-defined territories. Villages ranged in size from 100 to 500 persons, with several villages displaying allegiance to a large central village where the headman or chief resided. Although neither type of social organization permitted chiefs more than limited ceremonial authority, they were most often wise and influential individuals who could galvanize community action, if supported by various types of councils made up of lineage elders. While female chiefs were not unknown, the majority were men whose succession to office was hereditary. Other authority figures included a shaman, a combination physician, psychologist, herbalist, and spiritual leader; and family lineage heads. Social and economic stratification existed to a varying degree throughout aboriginal California, but it was most pronounced in northwestern California, which in many ways resembled the hierarchical and ordered societies of the Pacific Northwest area.

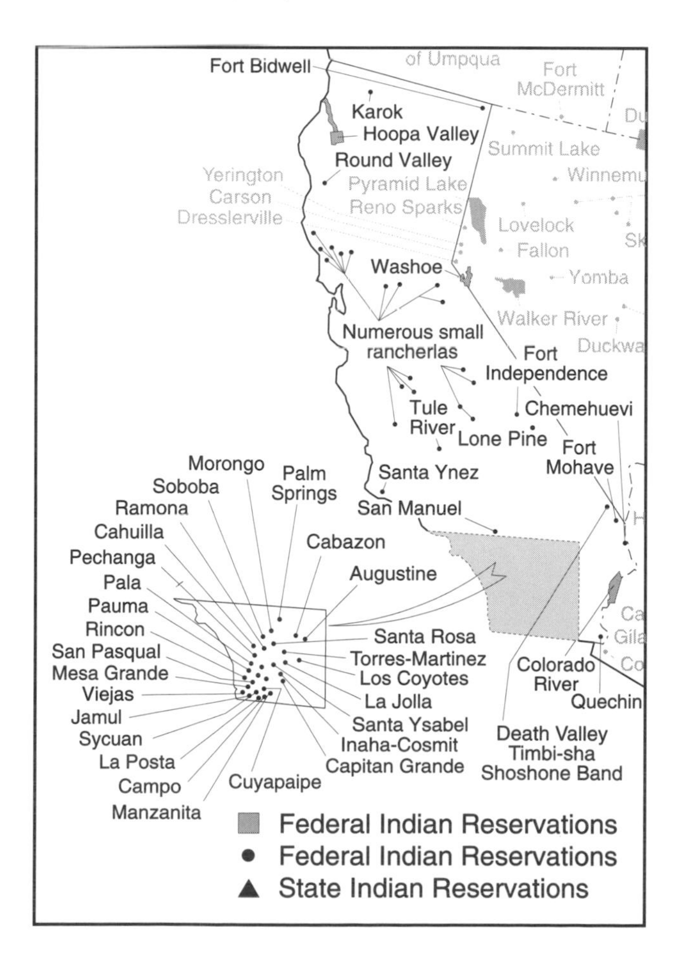

Contemporary California Indian tribes.

Because of the varied ecological zones found throughout the state, several regional economic adaptive strategies shaped the economy and food quest. Northern coastal tribes fished, hunted sea mammals, and collected tidelands resources. Riverine and lakeshore dwelling groups hunted, trapped, and fished. Central valley, Plains, and foothill tribes hunted and gathered wild foodstuffs. The greatest variety of regional lifeways and economic activities were found in southern California. The Channel Islands, near present-day Los Angeles, and adjacent coast were rich in sea-associated resources. Inland groups hunted and collected, while tribes living along the Colorado River and a few neighboring groups practiced the only agriculture found in aboriginal California.

Native Californian world view centered typically around seeking a balance between physical and spiritual well-being of the extended family and tribe. Such balance in both spheres is best understood in terms of reciprocity. For instance, individuals and villages made offerings to the creator and earth spirits and in return expected a favorable relationship between themselves and the natural elements, such as access to game animals, wild foods, favorable winds, sufficient rain, fertility, and the like. Similarly, reciprocity formed the basis for economic relationships between individuals, extended families, and neighboring villages. Each group's territory and its resources were jealously guarded. Trespassing and poaching were serious offenses and were the principal causes of intergroup conflicts that periodically erupted.

European Contact

The arrival of Europeans in California illustrates the profoundly different world views that clashed as various European empires scrambled to exploit the resources and peoples of the Americas. The story of one of the earliest European encounters illustrates this point well. In 1579, the English explorer Francis Drake anchored somewhere off the Sonoma County coast, in present-day northern California. The astounded Coast Miwok peoples exhibited behavior that seemed both incredible and incomprehensible to the English sailors.

English understandings of that encounter included a number of erroneous assumptions. Records of the Drake expedition refer to the headman of the local Indians as a "king," implying a European-like, highly centralized office of authority that could control both subjects' land

and lives. In fact, no such offices of authority existed anywhere in Native California societies. The English also claim this "king" gladly surrendered all of "his" territory and sovereignty to an unknown ruler half a world away. Finally, the English concluded the Coast Miwok regarded them as "gods."

The Coast Miwok, on the other hand, viewed all material objects of the pale strangers who arrived on their shores with fear and refused to accept the newcomers' gifts. At the same time, they offered gifts of baskets, food, and other ritual objects. While the men showed considerable awe and reverence towards the strangers, the Native women's behavior bewildered the sailors. Females tore at their cheeks and upper chests, crying and shrieking and throwing themselves on the rocky landscape while walking among the young En-

The traditional tribal areas of the Indians of California.

glishmen. Following a five-week stay, the newcomers departed, still baffled by the odd reception offered them by the otherwise hospitable Natives.

The mystery of the Indians' peculiar behavior was solved when anthropological data provided by Native traditionalists revealed elements of Coast Miwok culture that provided a reasonable explanation. The Coast Miwok Indians believed the land of the dead lay to the west; in fact, the path to that place passed directly beyond Drake's encampment. The women were exhibiting mourning behavior. The young English sailors had sparse beards (like Native men) and were furthermore deeply tanned from years of open ocean sailing. The English gifts were refused because of strict sanctions about bringing back anything from the land of the dead. Clearly, the Coast Miwok believed they had been visited by their departed ancestors.

Spanish Colonization

Permanent colonization created a catastrophe of indescribable proportions for the Indians of California. Spanish colonization began in earnest in 1769 with the establishment of a mission in the Native village of Cosoy, later called San Diego by the newcomers. The Spanish institutions of colonization were the military presidios (or forts) to protect the Franciscan missionaries and later the Hispanic colonists who established pueblos (civilian towns). It was the missions, however, that had the greatest impact on the Native population. The Spanish empire's plan was to reduce the numerous free and independent Native hunting and collecting villages and societies into a mass of peon laborers. To accomplish this goal, the padres created a chain of twenty-three missions, with two missions on the Colorado River in the extreme southeastern tip of the state and a string along the coast from San Diego to Sonoma in the north. These institutions were much more than churches. When fully functional, they resembled Caribbean plantations. Under Spanish law, once baptized, the neophytes, as the Indians were called, would be compelled to move from their Native villages into designated areas adjacent to the mission. Between 1769 and 1836, about 80,000 California Indians were baptized and subjected to the mission labor and evangelization programs of the Spanish Empire.

At the missions, the Indians could be more closely controlled. At the age of five or six, the neophyte children were removed from their families and locked in dorm-like barracks under the vigilance of colonists, which served the dual purpose of indoctrinating the children and ensuring that their parents would not attempt to oppose colonial authority. Indian girls were locked up when not laboring or attending religious services, were freed only after marriage, and, if widowed, were again confined in the female barracks until remarriage or death. Adults were compelled to labor without pay. The soldiers and padres instituted floggings, incarceration, and various labor punishments to compel Native acquiescence to Spanish authority. Neither women nor children were exempt from beatings and other forms of compulsion. One Costanoan Indian neophyte named Lorenzo Asisara reported, "We were always trembling with fear of the lash."

The missions were only supposed to exist for ten years, a time limit the Spanish Crown deemed sufficient to convert the Indians into a disciplined and subservient labor force for a small elite of Spanish males. The sincerity of "religious conversions" under such circumstances is doubtful. Despite these harsh measures, considerable resistance erupted among the "converts." As Spanish borderlands historian David Weber observed, "Oppressed in body and spirit, many mission Indians sought ways to extricate themselves from the loving embrace of the sons of St. Francis."

Three types of resistance developed to the nightmare that Native groups found themselves caught up in. The first and most prevalent form of resistance was passive. Many mission Indians either refused to learn Spanish or feigned ignorance of commands given in that language. Slow and poorly performed labor was widely reported and can be seen today in the construction and work of the old missions. Native laborers covertly drew traditional Indian symbols on fired floor tiles and other surfaces throughout the mission's buildings. Both infanticide and abortions were practiced by Native women unwilling to give birth to children conceived through sexual assaults by the soldiers or to supply a new generation of laborers for the colonists. A fascinating aspect of passive resistance was the periodic outbreak of covert Native religious activities to reverse baptisms or offer solace to the terrified masses of neophytes.

Fugitivism or simply running away from the Franciscan labor mills seemed to be the simplest solution, once the unsavory and oppressive nature of mission life was revealed. But Spanish law and Franciscan practice permitted the soldiers to pursue runaway Indians. The padres kept detailed records of baptized Indians for each village, and squads of soldiers stationed at each mission routinely patrolled the surrounding territories. Furthermore, Native traditions forbade anyone not belonging to a village from demanding refuge there. Non-Christian villages soon learned that if they did offer refuge to runaways, they risked military assaults and hostage-taking. Worse still, the fugitives infected non-Christian village populations with the new diseases contracted at the missions. Murderous waves of epidemic diseases and the general poor health of the neophyte population kept many from even attempting the physical rigors of flight. Nevertheless, widespread fugitivism was reported. Thousands of Indian neophytes fled. However, only about 10 percent, or about 8,000, escaped the missions.

Overt resistance to Spanish domination took several forms. A type of guerrilla warfare became prevalent before 1820. Charismatic and talented ex-neophytes like the Coast Miwok Pomponio and the Northern Valley Yokut Estanislao organized stock-raiding attacks against mission, presidio, and civilian herds of cattle, horses, and sheep.

Individuals and groups of mission Indians sometimes poisoned the padres. Four padres were poisoned at Mission San Miguel, one of whom died in 1801. In 1811, a San Diego neophyte killed a padre with poison. The next year, Indians at Mission Santa Cruz smothered and castrated a padre there for making an especially terrifying new torture instrument and being unwise enough to announce he would employ it the next Sunday. In 1836, southern California Cahuilla Indians kidnapped the padre at Mission San Gabriel and horsewhipped him, as so many of their tribesmen had been whipped.

Mission Indian insurrections were spectacular, and several occurred. The earliest revolt occurred at Mission San Diego in October 1775, when 1,000 Kumeyaay warriors sacked and burned the mission and killed the padre. In 1781, the Quechan Indians living along the banks of the Colorado River utterly destroyed two missions established in their territory just the previous year. In that rebellion, they killed fifty-five colonists, including four padres, thirty-one soldiers, and twenty civilians. That military action denied access to the only known overland route to California from Mexico for the remainder of the Spanish era.

In 1785, San Gabriel Mission neophytes, organized by a female shaman called Toypurina, were thwarted in their attempt to destroy the mission and kill the padres. At her trial, the defiant holy woman declared, "I hate the padres and all of you for living here on my native soil . . . for trespassing upon the lands of my forefathers and despoiling our tribal domains."

That sentiment provoked the last large-scale revolt by mission Indians. The Chumash Indians of the Santa Barbara coast had endured nearly three decades of colonization when, in 1824, neophytes from missions Santa Barbara, San Ynez, and La Purisima rose en masse to protect their lives and regain their lost freedom and sovereignty. A pitched battle ensued at Mission Santa Barbara, and then the Indians fled. Santa Ynez neophytes also abandoned their mission and joined the others from Santa Barbara at Mission La Purisima, which they took over for longer than a month. Although most were eventually persuaded to surrender after a siege and full-scale assault by presidio troops using cannons, a significant number of them absolutely refused to return to the missions and instead sought refuge in the interior, where they issued this defiant message to colonial authorities who pleaded with them to return: "We shall maintain ourselves with what God will provide for us in the open country. Moreover, we are soldiers, stone-masons, carpenters, etc., and we will provide for ourselves by our work."

Despite their defiant sentiments, it was the introduced diseases that ultimately destroyed the majority of Native peoples in contact with the colonists. Native Americans had no immunities to even the most common European childhood diseases. A series of murderous epidemics swept through the mission Indian populations from 1777 to 1833. Thousands of Indian men, women, and children succumbed to the previously unknown diseases. When the missions finally collapsed in 1836, about 100,000 Indians had died.

The independence movement that created the Mexican Republic (1820) forbade the Franciscan padres from compelling labor from the Indians. The Mexican government allowed Indians to leave the missions, but corrupt officials conspired to prevent a distribution of developed lands to surviving ex-mission Indians. Those tribesmen whose native territories now included missions, presidios, and pueblos were nearly universally deprived of their lands and forced deeply into debt peonage, which resulted in further powerlessness. Many ex-neophytes fled into the interior or to their former tribal domains. But the landscape had changed profoundly. The horses, mules, sheep, pigs, and goats introduced into the California biosphere ravaged the delicate Native grasses and continued to multiply in alarming numbers. Mission agricultural practices began to systematically squeeze out Native vegetation. The California Indians were less able to live off the land than before Spanish colonization.

Some tribes and village populations had virtually disappeared from the face of the earth. So many lineages had been destroyed that the previous forms of aboriginal leadership no longer existed. Out of this political vacuum evolved new leaders, who assumed much more authority than had been previously allowed any single individual in aboriginal society. Some assumed the Spanish title of alcalde, or captain, and adapted aboriginal life to include the hunting and capturing of half-wild horses and mules, which provided food and valued trade items. Patterning their tactics on the mission Indian stock raiders of the recent past, a widespread and lucrative stock-raiding complex emerged in post-mission California. Among these new leaders was an ex-neophyte Plains Miwok called Yozcolo, who terrorized the Hispanic military and civilian populations around southern San Francisco Bay, until he was killed in battle near Los Gatos in 1839.

In southern California, Cahuilla, Mohave, and Gabrielino tribesmen joined forces with New Mexico mountain men in a decade-long series of raids that devastated the Californios' livestock. One spectacular raid in 1840 involved the theft of more than 3,000 horses from ranches as far north as San Luis Obispo to San Juan Capistrano in the south. The Californios pursuing the stolen horses suffered the indignity of having their mounts stolen while resting. Having no choice, they walked across the desert till they were picked up by another group of Californios.

The Swiss immigrant Johann August Sutter established a fortress deep in the interior of the Sacramento Valley after promising Mexican authorities to stem the tide of stock-raiding that seriously threatened Mexican authority. Like other colonists of the period, he established a private army of Indians to protect his fort and enslave free Indians.

Despite a steady decline in the Native population throughout this period, the constant onslaught of stock raids began to push back interior Mexican outposts. After 1840, numerous interior ranches were abandoned under threat from the now well-mounted and armed groups of "horse thief Indians." Even Sutter began futile efforts to sell his fortress to the Mexican government after costly campaigns with interior Miwok warriors. But the Mexican government had, by 1845, lost control of the actions of its own citizens. The authority of the Mexican Republic was about to collapse. Meanwhile, both disease and violence had taken grim toll of Native lives. By 1845, little over 100,000 California Indians survived the Mexican Republic's occupation of their territories.

The Bear Flag Revolt and the Mexican War (1846–48) brought momentous changes for the Native peoples of California. The majority of Indians who were involved in that conflict allied themselves with the Americans. Company H of the California Battalion was made up of central Valley Miwok and Yokut warriors. In Southern California loyalties were split. Some, like the mountain Cahuilla chief Juan Antonio, fought for the Mexican Republic, while others participated on the U.S. side in the Battle for Los Angeles in 1847. However the new U.S. occupation brought yet more death and labor exploitation to Native groups whatever their loyalties.

Shortly after the Treaty of Guadalupe Hidalgo ended the Mexican-American War in 1848, a flood of gold miners descended upon California. Most of the Sierra Nevada and foothill tribesmen had been only indirectly affected by Hispanic colonization efforts , which were concentrated along the coast, but now they would bear the brunt of an incredibly violent horde of immigrants. Early in the Gold Rush, a few Indians were employed by miners or mined gold on their own. Soon Indians found themselves hunted like wild game.

Worse still was a series of state laws passed in the mid-1850s that virtually enslaved Indians and institutionalized the legal kidnapping of Indian children for labor and sexual exploitation, despite the fact that California entered the Union as a "free state" in 1851. At the same time, the federal government was negotiating treaties with California Indians (1851–52). These treaties promised California Indians 7.5 million acres of land in exchange for surrendering the remainder of the state. A deluge of protests from non-Indian Californians fearing that the treaty lands might contain gold was sufficient to assure the treaties' defeat in the U.S. Senate, which must ratify all treaties. Afterwards, the bewildered and now hunted Indians were subjected to the earliest form of reservation life. The federal government began establishing reservations in the state in 1851. They were located on military reserves, where supposedly the Native population might be protected by the army from U.S. citizens.

The government reserves in reality served fewer than 2,000 Indians at any given time. The vast majority of California Indians survived the best they could, withdrawing into remote and marginal areas and attempting to avoid contact with U.S. settlers, but violence against them continued, ranging from casual homicide of individuals to vigilante raids and the occasional army massacre.

Protesting the taxation of their small cattle herd, the Kupa Indians of southern California fought a war against the citizens of San Diego in 1851. The Hupa Indians of northern California successfully fought vigilante and militia campaigns until 1864, when they were granted a reservation of their own, now the largest in the state. The last and largest war against California Indians was fought against the Modoc Indians of northeastern California. Under the leadership of Captain Jack (see his biography), fifty Modoc warriors and their families held off an army of over 3,000 for nearly a year. In the end, Jack and three others surrendered and were hanged by orders of a paramilitary court. Captain Jack and Schochin John were decapitated following their deaths, and their heads were sent to Washington, D.C. and eventually wound up in the Smithsonian Institution.

By 1870, a new religious movement, called the Ghost Dance, swept west from Nevada, predicting the end of the world and promising the return of dead relatives and the game animals. Desperate Natives who had experienced first-hand the appalling widespread death, violence, and now real starvation, found the doctrines especially appealing. The movement lasted about two years and revitalized the Kuksu and Hesi ceremonies among the Pomo, Patwin, and neighboring groups. It also developed a new class of spiritual leaders called dreamer doctors. Finally, the Ghost Dance prophesy of the end of the world proved true, for the Indian world was gone.

It is no coincidence that the Ghost Dance swept through California when it did. Just prior to that event,

Spring Rancheria (Cahuilla), c. 1886.

the federal government had inaugurated a new policy to reform the widespread corruption in the Office of Indian Affairs (renamed the Bureau of Indian Affairs, or BIA, in the late 1940s). Part of that plan, called President Ulysses S. Grant's Peace Policy of 1869, called for the introduction of educational programs for Indian children. However, that policy once more unleashed hordes of missionaries upon the Indians to "save" them. Native ceremonies were outlawed on many reservations in a misguided effort to make Indians adopt U.S. culture and lifeways.

The federal campaign to educate Indian children was launched aggressively in 1879. Off-reservation boarding schools took Indian children to schools thousands of miles from their homes and subjected them to military-type discipline. Native languages were forbidden, corporal punishment was used freely, and starchy foods dominated their diets. The dormitories echoed with children's homesick and lonely cries. The legacy of these social engineering policies was the creation of several generations of Indians who, abducted from their tribes, returned home virtually strangers, unable to communicate with their elders and ignorant of the skills and knowledge to continue practicing their culture. Even more sinister was the lack of parenting skills in the generations of Indian mothers and fathers. Preventing such practical skills from developing is an effective element in the plan to destroy a people.

The next approach was to divide the corporate tribally owned lands on reservations into tiny private parcels. This federal program, called the Dawes Allotment Act of 1887, was intended to introduce the Indians to private ownership of property. If an Indian moved onto his allotment, cut his hair, surrendered his children to the boarding schools, severed his tribal ties, and did exactly as told by the Indian agent for twenty years, he could receive title to his allotment, pay taxes on his land, and become a citizen of the United States. However, like other tribal peoples, California Indians considered this act as yet another attack on their religious beliefs about the earth and the tribe's relationship to it. In practice, it proved to be a tool to deprive Indians of their remaining lands, and, almost everywhere, Indians opposed the Dawes Act. Nevertheless, the Office of Indian Affairs missionaries and so-called reformers were unrelenting in these efforts and countless others to make the Indians into what they considered acceptable people.

By 1900, fewer than 18,000 California Indians survived after 130 years of colonization and foreign domination. This staggering population decline left the Indians dazed, reeling, and deeply demoralized. Hunger, destitution, homelessness, unemployment, and discrimination were widespread, yet a number of Native leaders worked diligently for their communities.

Following in the path of the activist Indian Rights Association of Philadelphia, a group of southern California citizens organized the Sequoya League. They assisted the Kupa Indians, who had lost a bid in the Supreme Court to keep their ancestral home, now called Warner's Hot Springs in the mountainous interior of San Diego County. Through their efforts, Kupa leaders reluctantly selected a new home nearby at a place called Pala. Similar groups in northern California helped secure small homesite reservations, called rancherias, for homeless Pomo Indians at Manchester near Point Arena in Mendocino County and another at Chico for Wintun Indians.

One of the choice ironies of the boarding school experience was the unexpected development of a pantribal consciousness that emerged among Indian youth, which gave birth to pan-Indian reform groups. The first reform group to actually include California Indians was the Mission Indian Federation (MIF), founded in 1919. The MIF relentlessly attacked incompetent Indian administration officials and policies. Even urban Indians in Los Angeles had an active chapter. The group worked for more autonomy for tribal governments, full civil rights for Indians, protection of Indian water rights, opposition to the Dawes Act, and the elimination of the Bureau of Indian Affairs. In 1921, fifty-seven MIF leaders were arrested for conspiracy against the government for their opposition to allotment. Eventually all charges were dropped.

The first all-Indian reform group formed in Northern California by Stephen Knight and other Pomo Indians, was the California Indian Brotherhood. That group sought rancherias for homeless Indians and integration of Indian children into public schools with free lunches and clothing assistance. This far-sighted group even sought opportunities for college education for Indian youth.

The problems confronting twentieth-century California Indian survivors had many similarities, with some variation from community to community. One issue united them, however, like no other—the enduring sense of injustice regarding the broken federal treaties of 1851–52. There was little incentive for the treaties to be

Sensioni Cibimoat, basket maker from Warner's Ranch, 1903.

Gabrielino traditional homes, Mission San Gabriel.

honored, since Indians had no voting rights and no way to pressure elected officials. But Native peoples never forgot those solemn promises and were determined to seek redress. Virtually all reform groups as well as individual tribes sought some kind of solution for more that a half a century. Eventually, two settlements were reached. The first in 1944 eventually paid $150.00 to every California Indian who could prove biological legacy to an Indian alive in 1850. A second effort through the Indian Claims Commission (a federal entity established on the basis of the pioneering claims of the California Indians) resulted in payment of only $.47 an acre in compensation for lands outside treaty areas. Despite protests, the government per capita payments to individual resulted in less than $800.00 per person paid in 1968. Few desperately poor Indians could turn down even that meager amount. However, a small number of Indians refused to cash those checks in hopes of yet a new settlement.

Another important contemporary issue remains education. Federal off-reservation boarding schools were supplemented by reservation boarding schools and day schools before 1900. These schools at least allowed families to remain in contact, but chronic illness and lack of clothing, food, and even shoes caused considerable absenteeism, which eventually closed many of them. By 1917, the public schools began to experience increased enrollment of Indian children. When Congress gave U.S. citizenship to all Indians in 1924, a gradual transfer of Indian students to public schools followed. But academic success did not. Racial and cultural prejudices in textbooks and among teachers led to isolation, shame, and feelings of low self-esteem for Indian children and set them up for failure. The classrooms became battlegrounds where Indian children had to endure the negative experience or fight back. The latter course ensured a perpetual cycle of academic failure, condemning generations of Indian children to economic failure and unemployment.

One important focus of reform efforts was health access. While seven Indian hospitals had been established at boarding schools and other sites by 1930, local hospitals often refused to treat the Native population, claiming that was the federal government's responsibility. A growing chorus of criticism prompted the establishment of a separate division of health within the Bureau of Indian Affairs in 1924. Public health nurses were then allowed to provide services to Indians. However, services were still denied to unrecognized and homeless Indians, leaving as many as one-third of the Indian population without medical care. A new wave of indignation was forcefully expressed in a federal hearing conducted in 1929, but ironically these hearings only confirmed a 1912 survey that the health of the Indian population was dismal. Ultimately, the loss of their land base and food resources crippled their ability to rebound.

Approximately thirty reservations had been established by 1900. The critical needs of northern California Indians for lands were addressed in a series of congressional acts to provide homesites for landless Indians. By 1930, an additional thirty-six parcels of federal trust properties called rancherias were established. They had the same status as reservations but were substantially smaller, and they lacked developed water sources. Indians have been critical of the Bureau of Indian Affairs for failing to protect water rights, a problem that has plagued reservation leaders to this day. Allotment, or forced division of Indian trust lands into individual parcels, was pursued by the BIA despite that fact that these parcels were often of very small size. Considerable evidence points to the common practice of manipulating tribal leaders through assignment of choice reservation lands to Indians willing to cooperate with government interests. Numerous abuses and a national scandal concerning loss of millions of acres of allotted lands finally prompted Congress to act. The new Roosevelt administration's Indian Reorganization Act of 1934 ended allotment and permitted formation of tribal governments. Despite this progress, however, tribal governments effectively remained under economic control of the Bureau of Indian Affairs.

Termination

The end of the Second World War (1945) heralded an era of anti-communist xenophobia that ultimately stalled the slow but steady reform in the Bureau of Indian Affairs. The Hoover Commission study of 1948 recommended severing all federal relations with Indian tribes and peoples, including federal assistance to Indian peoples, whose poverty the government had engineered in the first place. That policy would be called Termination. The program called for an end to all health, education, and welfare assistance provided by the federal government and envisioned a division of tribal lands to individuals. In reality, it was a resurrection of the discredited Dawes Allotment Act of 1887.

Ramona Lugu, Cahuilla, at her home.

California Indians were an early target; after allotment Indian land would eventually be subject to state property taxation. Until then, immunity from state taxation allowed poverty-stricken Indians to retain their lands. Taxing them would bring about the final dispossession of the land through tax defaults. Furthermore, dispossession would bring disintegration to Native California's tribes, communities, and cultures—and the so-called Indian problem would finally be solved, at least as far as the government was concerned. By 1952, Congress had enthusiastically embraced termination. The BIA sold over 1,200 allotments. In the following year, California came under Public Law 280, an act that would further termination goals by turning over civil and criminal jurisdiction from federal authorities to state and local authorities. At first, state and local governments were enthusiastic, envisioning an expanded tax base. However, after several years of study, it became apparent that the burden of services it would have to assume would far outweigh any tax revenues. Consequently, their enthusiasm began to cool rapidly, though not before Congress passed the Rancheria Act of 1958. This act provided for reservation and rancheria members to decide whether to accept or reject termination. Federal authorities descended upon the isolated and powerless rancheria residents with exaggerated promises of new housing, road and domestic water system improvements, and even college scholarships for Native children. Oblivious to the looming threat of tax defaults, the BIA eventually convinced thirty-six of the most isolated and least sophisticated California Indian groups into committing tribal and cultural suicide by accepting termination. Sure enough, by 1970, 5,000 acres of tribal lands were lost to tax defaults and forced sales. The stunned and reeling tribesmen lost their recognition as Indians, and cultural and social decay of Indian community institutions accelerated.

Cultural Revitalization

The modern era of California Indian affairs can be divided into civil rights and cultural survival. The national sweep of the civil rights era from the mid-1960s to the present afforded new opportunities for national attention to the cause of the American Indians. On college campuses, racial minorities and their supporters demanded the hiring of minority faculty and staff, along with aggressive recruiting of minority students. The first college to establish a Native American studies program was San Francisco State University. The program's faculty, staff, and students were largely made up of non-California Indians relocated to the San Francisco Bay Area from other states, under part of a national termination program. Followed shortly by the University of California, Berkeley, and the University of California, Los Angeles (UCLA), these programs provided a multidisciplinary approach to the study of American Indian in the past and present.

Most importantly, the new Native studies programs addressed the future of American Indians and tribalism. The idea of actually controlling the future and shaping federal Indian policy made for an intoxicating euphoria that provided a kind of self-assurance not witnessed among Native leaders since the Indian wars of the last century. It furthermore produced a new generation of leaders, pressing legal and other avenues toward creating self-sufficient and responsible Native communities, new scholars contributing to the academic study of the American Indians, and numerous public school teachers in classrooms throughout the state. Both UCLA and UC Berkeley have developed important scholarly journals, the *American Indian Quarterly* and the *American Indian Culture and Research Journal.*

More access to health and legal services also emerged during this period. The California Rural Indian Health Board was established in 1968 to fund several demonstrations projects in fifteen rural and reservation communities, restoring services that in many cases had been denied California Indians since 1956. Legal assistance on issues of land, water, and civil rights became available as part of the U.S. government's War on Poverty programs of the 1970s. California Indian Legal Services strengthened tribal ability to oppose still-archaic BIA policies. They continue to provide important leverage in fighting for civil rights of Indian individuals and tribes.

This era also gave rise to a succession of land occupations by Native peoples in California, setting a national trend. In fall 1969, fewer than 100 Indian college students from UCLA, UC Berkeley, and San Francisco State landed on Alcatraz Island to reclaim that abandoned federal prison as Indian land, causing a media sensation around the world. The Native Americans cleverly pointed out the island was just like reservations: no water, no electricity, no jobs! They also pointed out that it was isolated from the wealth that surrounds it. At last, Native peoples had discovered a vehicle that would focus attention on the current conditions of America's aboriginal people. Following the Alcatraz occupation, other land occupations occurred, such as the protest attempted by the Pit River Indians at a public utility campground in Shasta County in 1971. The Pomo Indian occupation of an abandoned national defense radio listening station in rural Sonoma County resulted in the establishment of Ya-Ka-Ama (our land), an educational and Native plant center. A similar occupation near the University of California at Davis resulted in the establishment of a fully accredited American Indian junior college called Deganaweda-Quetzelquatl University.

Unprecedented population growth in California during the 1970s and 1980s resulted in the construction of millions of new homes and businesses, unearthing thou-

Indian protesters in prison courtyard on Alcatraz Island.

sands of California Indian burials and occupation sites. Traditionalists were dismayed that archaeologists intended to add the findings to existing inventories of skeletons and objects found in Indian burials, long neglected and seldom studied, gathering dust in warehouses, archaeology labs, and campus basements. Anthropologists' standard defense was that they were the Indians' best friends and so much valuable information could be gained from the "data," as they euphemistically referred to the remains of Native ancestors. The Indians demanded to know why these human remains continue to be removed from the ground and why it only happens to Indians.

About this time, it was discovered that the skull of nationally known Modoc war leader (1872) Captain Jack was part of the physical anthropology collection of the Smithsonian Institution in Washington, D.C. Outrage over this case and thousands of other lesser known Indian skeletons and burial goods led to a national program of repatriation of the thousands and thousands of Indian skeletons to their tribes of origin. In 1978, Governor Edmund G. Brown, Jr. created the Native American Heritage Commission (NAHC), which had the responsibility of mitigating human remains issues associated with construction. The NAHC attempted to compel universities and other state agencies holding human remains to submit plans for the ultimate disposition of the remains and associated burial goods. The NAHC has become an effective clearing house for these matters. Recent federal laws of 1990 mandate that federally funded museums inventory their American Indian human skeleton collections and develop a plan for repatriation to appropriate tribes. While a few archaeologists have argued against this policy, most agree that little new scientific information has been developed from collections that have already been in their possession for as long as a century. Native peoples often counter, if these human remains indeed possess such valuable data, why, then, are they not being systematically studied? For traditional peoples, it is a simple matter of dignity and the respect all citizens expect of their government and its laws.

Sign pointing to Pit River Nation, 1973.

Tribal Recognition

In retrospect, it seems miraculous that Native cultures in California survived at all, yet they have not only survived but have actually undergone a renaissance. Indian education centers throughout the state have developed Native language, culture, and dance classes. The first tribally controlled museum was established by Cahuilla traditionalists on the Morongo Indian Reservation in 1964. The Malki Museum also developed an impressive publication program, including the scholarly quarterly *The Journal of California Anthropology*. Several other reservation communities have followed suit.

In 1987, an entirely unique publication, called *News From Native California*, began publication. The widely read quarterly covers history, ethnography, current events, legislation, and the arts. Another event unique to California is the annual California Indian Conference, established in 1984. This event brings together scholars, Native traditionalists, and experts at state and federal levels to share their research and interests in the past, present, and future of California Indians. Usually, it is hosted at a major college; in 1992, it was held at Sonoma State University.

Recently, California Indian artists, both traditional and contemporary, have established a national reputation in the larger Indian art world. While late nineteenth- and early twentieth-century California Indian basketmakers have long been acknowledged as the finest in the world, a well-documented decline in the number of practitioners occurred over the last sixty years. With recent new interest in that important Native art form, a new generation of Native basketmakers now holds annual gatherings, notably at Ya-Ka-Ama, and promises to preserve and extend the artistic boundaries of their art. More contemporary California Indian artists such as Jean LaMarr, Frank La Pena, Harry Fonseca, L. Frank Manriquez, James Luna, and Kathleen Smith, among others are considered on the cutting edge of the modern Indian art world.

Despite the declaration by anthropologists, historians, and other writers that several California Indian tribes and cultures are extinct, it is well known among Native peoples that many of these groups are not in fact gone. Some have never been recognized by the government, like the Gabrielino and Juaneño of southern California. Others, like the Guidiville band of Pomo Indians, were terminated in 1966 and are seeking reinstatement or recognition. These disenfranchised groups have organized themselves and are currently aggressively pursuing their cause in the U.S. Congress.

In 1993, about 200,000 California Indians live in the state. Perhaps as many as 60,000 live on reservations and rancherias. The remainder live in nearby towns and cities. And while about two-thirds have some degree of non-Indian blood in their racial make-up, most today proudly claim their heritage.

Edward Castillo
Sonoma (California) State University

♦ ABORIGINAL PEOPLES IN CANADA

Although the aboriginal peoples of Canada are a small segment of the total population, they have always played a significant role in Canadian history. Their historic and contemporary importance is now acknowledged in Section 35, Parts 1 and 2, of the Canadian *Constitution Act, 1982*, which states,

> 35(1) The existing aboriginal and treaty rights of the aboriginal peoples of Canada are hereby recognized and affirmed.
> 35(2) In this Act, 'aboriginal peoples of Canada' includes the Indian, Inuit and Métis peoples of Canada.

The constitutional recognition of aboriginal peoples and their rights, however, occurred only after a protracted struggle on the part of aboriginal leaders to convince federal and provincial government officials of the legitimacy of their claims. While constitutional recognition signifies a landmark achievement for Canadian Indians, Inuit, and Métis, it is only one step in their quest for an enlarged political and legal status within the Canadian confederation that will give them a greater degree of control over their future. Moreover, significant strides must be taken in the social and economic development of aboriginal peoples. The legacies of past government policies have left aboriginal peoples as the most disadvantaged group in Canadian society. The rates of social pathology among aboriginal peoples as evidenced by the degree of alcohol abuse, crime, incarceration, and suicide, among other indicators, are well over the levels of non-aboriginals. In addition, unemployment rates for aboriginal peoples far exceed those for the remainder of the Canadian population. Increasingly, aboriginal leaders see self-government for their peoples as the only way to escape these deplorable conditions. The mounting pressure by aboriginal leaders for the constitutional recognition of their right to self-government, coupled with an increased awareness by other Canadians of the plight of aboriginal peoples, continues to maintain aboriginal issues at a prominent place on the Canadian political agenda.

Aboriginal Peoples: A Profile

Although Indians, Métis, and Inuit are now collectively recognized as aboriginal peoples, their cultural, legal, and political differences remain very important as the Canadian state attempts to accommodate their respective demands. Indians in Canada have traditionally been subdivided into three groups: status, treaty, and non-status Indians. A status Indian is a person registered or entitled to be registered as an Indian for purposes of the Indian Act, which was first passed in 1876 and which sets forth a policy of assimilating Natives into Canadian society. Status Indians are members of the 633 bands across Canada; "bands" are legal-administrative bodies established under the Indian Act that correspond generally to traditional tribal and kinship group affinities. Unlike the practice in the United States, in the establishment of the Canadian reserve system different tribes were not placed together on the same reserve; nor were groups of Indians relocated to reservations far from their ancestral homelands. Most bands are located south of the sixtieth parallel on reserves, numbering 2,281, within the provinces. The Indian "register" (1990) estimates that there are 500,000 status Indians in Canada. (See map of Canadian Native areas in front pages.)

Treaty Indians are those persons who are registered members of, or can prove descent from, a band that signed a treaty. Most status Indians are treaty Indians, except those living in areas not covered by treaties, such as most of the province of British Columbia.

Non-status Indians are those persons of Indian ancestry and cultural affiliation who have lost their right to be registered under the Indian Act. The most common reason for loss of status was marriage of a registered Indian woman to a non-Indian. Loss of status has also occurred in other ways, such as voluntary renunciation, compulsory enfranchisement to non-Indian status, and failure of government officials to include some Indian families in the registry. Indians who served in the military during the world wars, for example, usually became enfranchised, losing their status as Indians. Non-status Indians do not have a distinct constitutional standing but are grouped with the Métis for jurisdictional and public policy purposes. The situation for many non-status Indians changed in 1985, when the federal government amended the Indian Act with Bill C-31 to restore registered Indian status to those women and their children who had lost it through marriage. Aboriginal women's groups welcomed this change. However, the response of Indian communities to Bill C-31 was not uniformly favorable; many Indian bands saw the bill as an unwarranted intrusion on their right to control band membership. The reinstatement process was largely completed by 1991, adding approximately 92,000 Indians to the registry.

The Inuit are those aboriginal people who inhabit Canada's northernmost regions, including the Mackenzie Delta, the Northwest Territories, the northern coasts of Hudson Bay, the Arctic Islands, Labrador, and parts of northern Quebec. The Inuit were classified with registered Indians for program and jurisdictional purposes in 1939, by a decision of the Supreme Court of Canada. They are the smallest group of Canadian aboriginal people, numbering around 35,000 (1990).

The Métis are people of mixed Indian and non-Indian ancestry. The term *Métis* originally referred to people of mixed ancestry living on the prairies. This is the definition now generally endorsed by the Métis National Council, which considers the contemporary Métis to be the descendants of the Métis community that developed on the prairies in the 1800s, and of individuals who received land grants and/or scrip under the Manitoba Act, 1870, or the Dominion Lands Act, 1879. Statistics Canada now includes in the category of Métis all people living in any part of Canada who claim mixed Indian and non-Indian ancestry. This classification corresponds to the definition of the Native Council of Canada, an umbrella group representing Métis and non-status Indians and now also identifying itself as the voice of urban Indians. The 1986 census set Canada's Métis and non-status Indian population at 400,000. Métis spokesmen themselves dispute the census figure and suggest the combined population of Métis and non-status Indians is close to one million. Approximately two-thirds of the Métis live in the provinces of Manitoba, Saskatchewan, and Alberta and in the Northwest Territories; the remainder are scattered throughout the rest of the country.

Finally, although aboriginal peoples remain widely distributed throughout rural Canada, recent decades have witnessed a growing migration of aboriginal peoples to urban areas. In western urban centers such as Vancouver, Edmonton, Calgary, Regina, Saskatoon, and Winnipeg, aboriginal peoples comprise a substantial portion of the population. The Department of Indian Affairs and Northern Development (DIAND) estimates that approximately one-third of status Indians now live off their reserves. (See map of Canadian Native languages in Canadian section of Chapter 2 and see maps in Chapter 4.)

The Indians

When Europeans first reached the Canadian east coast, every part of Canada was occupied by diverse Indian societies well established in their respective territories. Although European colonizers may have stereotyped all Indians as nomadic hunters, in Canada at the time of contact there were Indians living in villages in coastal British Columbia, southern Ontario, and western Quebec. Furthermore, Indians in central Canada were already engaged in agricultural activities. The Europeans "discovered" an inhabited land, and many historians believe that during the 1500s a catastrophic population decline resulting from the introduction of new diseases was what made possible European settlement of the continent.

The diverse Indian cultures encountered by the Europeans can be categorized according to the regions they occupied and the languages they spoke. On the Atlantic coast were the Beothuk, Micmac, and Malecite, whose economy centered on tidal and river fishing. Around the Great Lakes were Indian farmers—including the Huron and Iroquois—who lived in villages and grew crops such as corn and tobacco. The prairie Indians—the Assiniboine, Plains Cree, Blackfoot, Sarcee, Saulteaux, and Gros Ventre—followed the buffalo. In the coastal mountains, seashore and islands of British Columbia, salmon was the main source of food for the many different peoples who lived there. Stretching across the country throughout the northern forests were the Montagnais, Naskapi, Abenaki, Ottawa, Algonquin, Ojibwa, and Cree, nomadic peoples who hunted and fished. North of the treeline were the seafaring Inuit. Some of the regions were populated by linguistically homogeneous cultures; in others, such as British Columbia, a wide variety of languages were spoken within a small geographic area.

Today these diverse cultures are represented by a national Native organization, the Assembly of First Nations (AFN), formerly the National Indian Brotherhood. Twentieth-century Indian political activity in Canada began at the local and regional level, national organizing of Indians being forbidden by the 1927 Indian Act. Even today, regional influences and differences are apparent in the operation of the AFN. Composed of the 633 (1992) band chiefs from across the country, the assembly regularly faces internal political splits. One of the most important issues dividing AFN constituents is the difference between "treaty" and "non-treaty" groups whose roads to self-government are not always parallel. Complicating the matter is the fact that Canadian Indian bands vary considerably in their degree of political militancy—from outright nationalist to much more accommodationist positions. Moreover, as demographic shifts have seen increasing numbers of Indian migrating into Canadian cities, the assembly's position as the voice of reserve Indians has been challenged by more urban-based associations, such as the Native Council of Canada. Still, a national event such as the 1990 confrontation over land between the Mohawk and the Canadian Government at Oka, Quebec, can galvanize widespread support and solidarity among Canada's Indian peoples.

Indian-Government Relationships: Federal Modern-day Canada was established by the British North America Act of 1867. Prior to that point, relationships between Indians and Europeans had involved the French and British Crowns, who began negotiating Indian treaties as early as the 1600s. These early agreements were usually "peace and friendship" treaties; the issues involved were military and political, and Indian nations often played a crucial role as ally or enemy of the European powers. Later treaties, however, involved the surrender by Indians of large tracts of land—a policy of the British Colonial Office. The policy was articulated in the Royal Proclamation of 1763, which was issued by King George III after the end of the war between England and France over their New World acquisitions. The main purpose of the proclamation was to establish governments for the territories that England acquired from France; however, the last five paragraphs made reference to Indians, reserving certain areas of the continent for them, and providing an elaborate mechanism by which other lands could be surrendered to the Crown.

The Robinson-Huron and Robinson-Superior treaties, concluded in 1850 in Ontario, established the model for the later land surrender treaties numbered One to Eleven. The final treaty, Number 11, was signed in 1921. Upon the surrender of land, Indian reserves were established according to a formula which, since Treaty Three, has been one "section" (640 acres) of land for every family of five. The numbered treaties also typically contained a guarantee of Indian hunting rights on surrendered, unoccupied Crown land; made provisions for education and agricultural development on the reserves; and included a system of annuities. What the various signatories to the treaties understood themselves to be agreeing to at the time has since become a matter for debate. Areas of conflict cover a great deal of ground, including the contemporary implications of certain treaty provisions. For example, a university education is now claimed by Indian groups as a treaty right; Indians also argue that the "medicine chest" provision in many treaties now obligates the government to provide universal health care for them. Some Indian leaders argue that Indian people were duped and cheated during the treaty-making process and that more lands, rights, and benefits are due; from this perspective the renegotiation or "renovation" of treaties is in order. (See the map of Canadian and Native treaties in the Canadian Chronology in Chapter 1.)

The treaty relationship between Indian peoples and the Canadian state has been paralleled by another legal relationship. Section 91(24) of the Constitution Act, 1867 established the federal government's responsibility for Indian peoples and lands. A major effect of this grant of authority was to continue a trust relationship between Indians and the federal government established by the Royal Proclamation. Put simply, the trust relationship involves an obligation on the part of the crown to ensure that the best interests of Indians are served where the management and protection of Indian proprietary interests are involved. The obligations created by this trust relationship have experienced an uneven history of compliance on the part of the federal government. This checkered attitude has also marked the judiciary's approach to interpreting the federal government's trust obligations to Indians.

A recent decision of the Supreme Court in *Guerin v. Regina* (1986), however, involving the Musqueam band near Vancouver, suggests that the courts may be more willing to provide judicial sanction for what Indian peoples have always considered a cornerstone of their relationship with the Canadian state. In this case the court held that DIAND breached its fiduciary obligation to the Musqueam band by renting out part of the reserve for a golf course at a rate far below what the commercial rental value of the land actually should be. The depth of feeling by Indians toward the trust relationship approaches the status of an article of faith and is consistently utilized by Indian leaders as a barrier against provincial encroachment against their lands.

To fulfill its responsibilities to Indians under Section 91(24), the federal government created a separate legal regime for them by passing the Indian Act, 1876. This act was revised in 1951 and 1985. Basically, the Indian Act had two major objectives: to establish a regime for administering the affairs of Indians and to create the conditions for their assimilation into the dominant Euro-Canadian society. For administering Indian affairs, the Indian Act established a reserve system, which included a system of Indian governments. Importantly, the Indian Act did not, and still does not, recognize Canadian Indians as retaining any right to self-government—inherent, constitutional, or otherwise. In setting up the reserve system, the Indian Act did several things: first, it defined legally who is entitled to be a status Indian; second, it established a system for the management of Indian lands and monies; third, it created legal units known as band governments to administer reserve communities and endowed band governments with a number of powers that would ordinarily be exercised by municipal governments; and fourth, it created a national administrative structure that has functioned as a microcosm of other Canadian governments for reserve Indians. Through the reserve system, the Department of Indian Affairs and Northern Development has traditionally provided a complex of services that other Canadians receive from provincial governments, such as health care, education, and law enforcement.

A significant effect of the Indian Act was the imposition on Indian bands of a council elective system that, in structure as well as underlying principles, resembles a non-Indian municipal government. The band council elective system represented a major attempt by the federal government to "civilize," that is, to assimilate Indian peoples. Within the broad objective of assimilation, the band council system was intended to accomplish two goals: first, to indoctrinate Indians into the Euro-Canadian system of political beliefs, thus preparing them ultimately to live within non-Indian municipal government systems; and second, to eliminate traditional Indian belief systems and governing processes. With the exception of a few Indian bands across Canada—most notably the Mohawk—who have fought vigorously to retain their traditional governing methods, the band council elective system is now widely established within Indian communities across Canada.

The colonial administrative nature of the Indian Act remains essentially unchanged today, even though the federal government appears to recognize a genuine need for changing it. The government is, moreover, attempting to accomplish this objective through several legislative and administrative initiatives for devolution of authority to band governments. However, ultimate authority over the management of Indian lands and finances still remains largely with the minister of Indian and northern affairs, should his or her office choose to exercise it. Moreover, the bylaw making authority of band governments is subject to ministerial disallowance, and money bylaws are subject to ministerial approval. The straitjacket of the Indian Act remains a thorn in the side of Indian bands that seek greater control over their own social, economic, and political development.

Indian-Government Relationships: The Provinces The jurisdiction of the provinces over Indians is tied to Section 91(24) of the Canadian Constitution and the Indian Act's Section 88, which subjects Indians to all provincially enacted laws that generally apply to provincial citizens. Indians are therefore considered provincial citizens for purposes of these laws. Only in instances where such laws conflict with provisions of the Indian Act, or if they touch rights under treaty, or if they are discriminatory in respect to treatment of Indians, are such laws of general application considered not to apply. However, historically the interpretation of Section 88 by Canadian courts reveals an incremental pattern wherein the "declaratory" authority of the provinces over Indians has been expanded. Under this judicial doctrine, provincial laws apply by virtue of the provinces' general constitutional authority, without requiring the authority of Section 88 for validity. The courts have supported the view that unless there is clear evidence of a conflict with federal legislation, etc., that could interfere with federal activity or the application of federal laws, provincial laws of general application may apply to Indians even on reserves, unless they impair "Indianess," as defined by law, custom, or tradition. In cases where legislative vacuums have raised federal-provincial jurisdictional questions in regard to Indians, the courts have tended to expand provincial jurisdiction over Indians. In some instances, the courts have created overlapping federal and provincial jurisdictions. As a consequence, under some circumstances the exercise of authority by Indian bands is subject to both federal and provincial jurisdiction.

Since the 1950s, provincial jurisdiction over Indians and Indian lands has also been expanded by a number of tripartite administrative agreements. In several provinces, for example, the federal and provincial governments have negotiated tripartite agreements that extend provincial power over the administration of justice to Indian reserves, thus allowing the creation of reserve police forces under provisions of provincial police acts.

Federal responsibility for social and other services to Indians is also based in Section 91(24) of the Canadian Constitution. Even though this grant of authority is permissive and not mandatory with respect to providing services to Indians, the federal government has traditionally assumed responsibility for Indians living on reserves. On the other hand, it has taken the position that Indians living off the reserves fall under the general social responsibility mandate of the province. For the most part, provinces have accepted social responsibility for Indians living off-reserve. Provinces, however, have consistently refused to extend their social responsibility mandate to Indians living on reserves, despite the fact that no prohibitive constitutional barrier exists as long as the restrictions included in Section 88 of the Indian Act arc observed.

Indians demonstrating in the early 1960s.

Jurisdiction over Land A final aspect of Indian-government relationships involves jurisdiction over land. Outside of the Yukon and Northwest territories, the federal government owns very little land in Canada. Section 109 of the Constitution Act, 1867, as well as a number of federal-provincial agreements such as the Natural Resources Transfer Act, 1930 (pertaining to the prairie provinces of Alberta, Saskatchewan and Manitoba) gives the provinces control over nearly all Crown lands within their borders. While these federal and provincial agreements have established a patchwork of provincial obligations to surrender land for purposes established in treaties between the Crown and Indian nations where such treaties exist, provinces must concur in the way those obligations are defined and implemented. Consequently, all treaty claims by Indian bands located within provinces for lands outside of existing reserves or claims for land based on aboriginal title (that is, traditional occupancy) are laid against the provinces.

The historical record of the provinces in accommodating Indian land claims has been a dismal one. In some instances, land transfer has taken place only after major confrontations. The Lubicon Lake Cree began to make progress on a forty-eight year old land claim in northern Alberta only after they blockaded access to nearly 10,000 square kilometers of oil- and timber-rich land, threatening the resource extraction industry in the area. However, negotiations between the Lubicon band and the federal government were stalemated from 1989 to 1993. The Lubicon and their American adviser blame government intransigence. Meanwhile, 125 Lubicon members joined with other Alberta Indians and formed the 450 member Woodland Cree Band, which received a settlement including a 143 square kilometer reserve and $19 million for economic development. In 1991, in a vote organized and monitored by DIAND, the Woodland Cree Band concluded an agreement amidst irregularities such as on-the-spot cash payments and a promise of $1,000 a head for a positive outcome.

Another contentious land claim is that of the Kanesatake Mohawk, who in 1990 were able to force action on a land claim at Oka, in southern Quebec, by setting up blockades to prevent the development of a golf course on land that the Kanesatake have traditionally claimed as their own. After the failure of Quebec provincial police to remove the barricades, during which one provincial police officer was killed, the government of Quebec received authorization to use the Canadian Armed Forces to remove the barricades. In order to defuse the situation, the federal government purchased the disputed land at Oka and offered it to the Kanesatake as a part of a negotiated settlement package that includes economic development and other benefits. The relationship between the Mohawk, the federal government, and the government of Quebec in particular, however, remains tense and problematic.

Socio-Economic Development Political confrontations such as took place between the federal government and the Lubicon Cree or the Kanesatake Mohawk must be viewed against the background of the often desperate situations in which many Canadian Indians find themselves. The socioeconomic conditions on Indian reserves have been described as more typical of Third World countries than of a northern industrialized democracy. The statistical indicators (DIAND, 1990) are bleak. Indian life expectancy is ten years below the national average. The suicide rate is double that of the general population, and the rate of violent death is triple. Nearly a third of Indian families are headed by a single parent. Twenty percent of status Indians live in overcrowded dwellings, and 25 percent live in unheated houses. Government transfer payments are the major source of income for close to half of Canadian Indians. Over the last decade a number of these indicators have been improving, but Indians nevertheless remain one of the most disadvantaged segments of the population.

One area in which there have been some hopeful developments is education. As Indian populations have grown, there has been an influx of Indian students into all levels of the education system, which has caught the system off-guard. Indian children are staying in school longer and pursuing their education to higher levels, partly as a result of the increased number of band-operated schools—of which in 1993 there are more than 300. In 1969, only 10 percent of Indian children remained in school until the last year of high school; in 1989, the number was over 40 percent. During these two decades, the number of federally sponsored students pursuing post-secondary education rose from 60 to 22,000. This has recently led to a "funding crunch" for Indian college and university students, most of whom rely on financial sponsorship from DIAND and/or their bands. Increasingly, Indian students are pursuing not just their individual aspirations but also community goals through post-secondary education, posing challenges both for funders and for the institutions, which have to face accusations about the irrelevance or ethnocentrism of their curricula. University education broadens the employment prospects available for Indian students and

Dene school children, Northwest Territory.

improves the human resource base available to their communities. Yet the new generation of educated Indians are sometimes perceived as a threat to established power structures on their reserves, and, moreover, there are community concerns about the degree to which a "white" education may cause the students to become separated from their cultural roots.

The history of "Indian education" in Canada is a topic that has recently come in for much discussion, focusing on the system of residential boarding schools that engulfed multiple generations of Indian children. The schools, usually Catholic or Anglican, were a front-line tool in the project of assimilating Indians into the dominant Canadian society. Indian children were removed from their homes and families and placed in institutions, where they were indoctrinated with the tenets of Euro-Christianity, steeped in the practices of European culture, taught that their Native ways were heretical and uncivilized, and punished for any attachment to indigenous language and culture. Contemporaneous photographs taken at the residential schools are evocative of the children's experience—rows of tidy Indian schoolchildren, dressed in white pinafores and buttoned up shirts, hair scraped back, faces unsmiling. But the process of "civilizing" Indian children was an abusive one, and the residential schools are retrospectively being viewed with horror by many. Boarding school continues to be a necessity today for some Indian students—especially those at the high school level—who live in communities too small and remote to sustain secondary schools; but the prospect of having to leave home for a high school education bars many from completing it.

This massive attempt at assimilation of Indian peoples was on the surface a failure—Indian languages and cultures, however fragile, survive in contemporary Canada. Yet the multigenerational experience of the residential school system has left scars that have been concealed for many years. But now, former students are speaking out to their own peoples and to the Canadian public at large. The artistic community in Canada was one of the first mainstream participants to tackle the subject of abuse of Indian children at residential schools; a television drama about a young Blackfoot girl's experience received critical acclaim and the support of many aboriginal communities, despite a controversy over the fact that the script authors were not Natives. Another catalyst for discussion was the personal testimony of a prominent Indian leader from Manitoba that as a child he had been the victim of both physical and sexual abuse at a Catholic boarding school. As the evidence from various quarters has mounted about the abuse of Indian schoolchildren, there have been calls from the Indian community for apologies and reparations. Few voices have been raised in defense of the missionary educators. In any event, the legacy of the residential school system, so recently brought to public consciousness, is likely to reverberate for some time in the relationship between Indian peoples and wider Canadian society.

The Inuit

The Inuit of Canada live in the far north of the country above the treeline, in small communities on the Mackenzie Delta, along the coasts of the Northwest Territories, on the shores of Hudson Bay, in Labrador, northern Quebec, and scattered across the Arctic Islands. They are thought to have been among the last of aboriginal peoples to migrate across the Bering land bridge from Siberia to Alaska, their ancestors arriving in Canada around 10,000 B.C. The Inuit were formerly known as "Eskimos," which comes from a Cree word meaning "raw meat eaters." Today they call themselves Inuit, which is the Inuktitut word for "the people."

The Inuit of Canada share one culture and one language, although there are different dialects of Inuktitut. Their settlement pattern along coastlines reflects a historical life-style tied to marine harvesting. They hunted seal, whale, and walrus in the waters of the north but would also travel inland for caribou, fish and waterfowl. Most Inuit lived in small groups of related families, sometimes coming together at fishing or sealing camps. Sharing the results of their hunt was a key aspect of Inuit culture; some communities had formal distribution systems for sharing out the catch. Life in the Arctic was difficult—starvation was always a possibility—but for centuries the ancestors of today's Inuit survived in this region.

Although Inuit in the eastern Arctic may have encountered the Norse explorers who reached Canada in the tenth century, sustained contact between Inuit and Europeans did not take place until the nineteenth century. American and Scottish whalers sailed north in pursuit of the bowhead whale, which they hunted to near extinction. The whalers hired Inuit to act as guides and crew, and some of them took Inuit wives. The trading posts established by the Hudson's Bay Company were another means of contact between Inuit and Europeans, and over the next century many Inuit forsook their traditional hunting pursuits in favor of fur trapping. They came to rely on European trade goods for survival, and when the fur trade collapsed in the 1940s, the effect on the Inuit was devastating. Hunger and disease afflicted many communities.

The Canadian government did not turn its attention to the plight of the Inuit until the 1950s. Relief supplies were sent to the starving communities, and the Inuit were encouraged to settle permanently around the Hudson Bay trading posts. The federal government undertook to provide the kinds of services for the Inuit that it did for Canadian Indians, and nearly all of the Inuit gave up their traditional way of life to settle in small

Inuit hunting seals on the ice. The Inuit and their way of life, as observed by Frobisher's men on Baffin Island in 1576–78. Engravings, after drawings made by Captain G. F. Lyon on Melville Peninsula in 1822, published in W. E. Parry, *Journal of a second voyage for the discovery of a North-west Passage*, London, 1824.

northern villages. During this decade, the federal government also relocated a group of Inuit from northern Quebec to two different locations in the High Arctic as, among other motives, an assertion of territorial sovereignty in the north; four decades later the Inuit Tapirisat of Canada, the national political organization of the Inuit, called on the government for an apology and compensatory payments to the Inuit whose lives had been disrupted.

Because of the remoteness of Canada's Inuit from centers of government, their legal status was ambiguous for a number of years. The Inuit were brought into a direct relationship with the federal government in 1939. In that year, the Supreme Court of Canada decided in *Re Eskimos* that the Inuit come within the term *Indians* in Section 91(24) of the British North American Act. The Indian Act itself excludes Inuit from the operations of the Department of Indians Affairs, but as a result of *Re Eskimos*, the federal government's power to make laws affecting Indians and their lands also includes the Inuit. Today the Inuit are involved with several levels of government. In the Northwest Territories, Inuit and other Canadians are governed by the territorial government, which was moved from Ottawa to Yellowknife in 1967. In northern Quebec, the signing of the James Bay and Northern Quebec Agreement in 1975 established a regional government for Inuit in that area. And the province of Newfoundland and the federal government have negotiated a cost-sharing arrangement for provision of government services to the Inuit of Labrador, in which the provincial government retains primary administrative responsibility.

Like Canadian Indians and Métis, contemporary Inuit are seeking a greater degree of self-determination for their people. The Inuit live in the only part of Canada where aboriginal inhabitants are in the majority, and they have sought a public, regional government in the north rather than an ethnically based one. A variety of organizations represent Inuit interests. The Inuit Tapirisat (Brotherhood) of Canada (ITC) was formed in 1971 as the "voice of the north." The impetus that gave birth to the ITC was the Inuit desire to negotiate a land claim with the federal government, a responsibility which has since been assumed by the Tungavik Federation of Nunavut (TFN). In 1979, the Tapirisat created the Inuit Committee on National Issues (ICNI), whose main role is to coordinate and present Inuit views on constitutional reform.

Inuit political aspirations are intimately tied to their pursuit of land claims. Unlike Indian groups who entered into treaties, the Inuit's claims to aboriginal rights were not dealt with (and were not made) before the modern era. In 1973, the federal government agreed to enter land claims negotiations with the Inuit, and the ITC submitted its claim on behalf of the Inuit of Nunavut (the eastern Arctic) to the federal government in 1976. Since 1982, the TFN has been responsible for land claims negotiations. The nine-member negotiating team has its head office in Ottawa, and there are regional offices in Coppermine, Rankin Inlet, Frobisher Bay, and Igloolik.

The Inuit were involved in the first modern land claims agreement to be reached in Canada, with the James Bay Cree and the Inuit of northern Quebec. The agreement, signed in 1975, guaranteed the aboriginal signatories exclusive hunting and fishing rights over parts of northern Quebec, "ownership" of other parcels similar to Indian "ownership" of reserve lands, the Kativik regional government for the Inuit of the area, education and language rights in Inuktitut, and a cash and royalties settlement, which for the Inuit amounted to $90 million. In return, the Inuit and Cree relinquished any further claim to lands covered by the agreement. A second land claim was settled in 1984 with the 2,500 Inuvialuit of the western Arctic, who obtained 242,000 square kilometers of land and a cash settlement of $45 million. The largest Inuit land claim involves the proposed division of the Northwest Territories into Denedah, Athapascan land in the west, and Nunavut, Inuit land, in the east. In 1976, the ITC submitted a land claim for the eastern Arctic and a proposal for the creation of a new territory called "Nunavut," to include all areas north of the treeline. The claim to Nunavut, which was settled late in 1991, involves a vast area of the Arctic. The settlement involved a payment of $580 million and 350,00 square kilometers of land. Community ratification of the land claim settlement was expected to take place in 1992. In the process, the Inuit agreed to the "extinguishment" of their aboriginal rights claim to the rest of their traditional lands (1.6 million square kilometers).

But other groups besides the Inuit have an interest in the development of Nunavut, and their viewpoints have been far from uniform. In a 1992 territorial plebiscite, 54 percent of the Northwest Territories approved the western boundary for the new territory, an overwhelming endorsement on the part of the Inuit. However, there has been opposition to the creation of Nunavut from the Dene Indians, with whom the Inuit have had longstanding border disputes. The Assembly of First Nations criticized the deal for giving up too much in the way of aboriginal rights. Non-Native northerners, who have traditionally formed political coalitions with the Inuit and the Inuvialuit, are concerned about the makeup of future governments in the remainder of the Northwest Territory. While non-Natives are a slight majority in the west, the Dene are likely to be the dominant group after territorial division. A suggestion has already been made that non-Natives should be excluded from the cabinet of the new western territory. The development of Nunavut, however, is proceeding. It is expected that the new territory will be created by the end of this century. The federal government has given support to the Nunavut deal, which does not involve constitutionally entrenched self-government or the recognition of Inuit sovereignty. As a public government, rather than an ethnically based one, Nunavut would nevertheless give *de facto* self-government to the Inuit, who make up about 85 percent of the eastern Arctic population.

The Inuit economy has undergone an enormous change in the last forty years, from a hunting and trapping base to diversification involving tourism, arts and crafts, and development of both renewable and nonrenewable resources. Government, however, is still the biggest employer in the North, accounting for 30 percent to 40 percent of the total. The outlook for mining and oil and gas exploration is not bright at present, and the tourism sector is poorly developed. The unemployment rate among the Inuit is very high, the population is young, and educational attainment is low. All the statistics point to an impending crisis. Many Inuit communities still rely on traditional hunting, fishing, and sealing activities both for a food supply and as a source of cash income. However, the recent outgrowth of environmental activism known as the "animal rights" movement has posed a serious threat to survival of northern aboriginal communities. In the late 1960s, a highly emotional campaign was organized against a non-Inuit commercial industrial kill of newly born harp seals in the waters of Atlantic Canada. The campaign developed into an attack on seal hunting in general, and it had a devastating effect on the Arctic Inuit and their traditional hunt for mature ringed seals. By 1982, the European Community had boycotted all seal product imports, a serious blow to the Inuit economy. Many Inuit were forced to leave the land for an uncertain future in communities with little wage employment; loss of economic self-sufficiency and social alienation have resulted in an escalation of health and social problems.

Canada's small Inuit population faces challenges on many fronts. Protection of Inuit culture is a priority for many, and there have been positive developments, notably in education. Inuktitut instruction has been introduced into elementary schools, and textbooks have been written in both Inuktitut and English, especially for the North. A Native press has developed, which prints newsletters and magazines in both languages, and the Inuit Broadcasting Corporation was established in 1981 to provide programming in Inuktitut. Canadian Inuit also participate in the Inuit Circumpolar Conference (ICC), which represents 115,000 Canadian, Alaska, Soviet, and Greenland Inuit on international issues affecting the Arctic. The ICC, a non-governmental member of the United Nations, meets every three years; the current president of the conference is Mary Simon, a Canadian Inuit from Kuujjuaq, Quebec.

The Métis

Canada's Métis have been called "the forgotten people," and it was considered a major victory for them to have been included in the definition of "aboriginal people" in Canada's 1982 Constitution. The word *Métis*, "mixed," describes someone of mixed Indian and European ancestry. Originally, it referred to the children of marriages between Indian women and the European men who participated in the Canadian fur trade. On the prairies, French fur traders often took Cree wives; in the north, English and Scottish traders married Dene women, and the offspring of both sets of relationships were the original Métis. In contemporary times, the term is used more broadly to refer to people of mixed Indian-European ancestry anywhere in Canada, regardless of where their ancestors lived. Two-thirds of the self-identified Métis are still concentrated in the prairie provinces of Alberta, Saskatchewan, and Manitoba. Another significant group of Métis live in the Northwest Territories and ally themselves with the Dene Nation for the purposes of pursuing land claims.

The Métis have also been called "the children of the fur trade." European fur traders derived many benefits from association with Indian women and their families—their familiarity with the forests and waterways, their Native technological skills, their social and political "connections," which facilitated commercial trade. The children of these unions, in turn, were often incorporated into the business—acting as interpreters and middlemen in the trade. The Métis participated in the plains economy as hunters, trappers, traders, carters, and small farmers, developing a distinctive culture combining European and Indian traditions. But over time, the European influence over the Métis homeland continued to grow; the traditional Métis way of life was threatened, and a sense of Métis nationalism began to

Inuit meeting to discuss hamlet business, Cape Dorset, Northwest Territory.

develop in response. In 1811, the Hudson's Bay Company made a large land grant in the Red River Valley of Manitoba for the purpose of establishing a new colony with an agricultural economy. Over the next half-century, homesteaders from eastern Canada settled along the Red and Assiniboine rivers, arousing Métis antipathy.

In 1869, the Hudson's Bay Company sold the Métis homeland to Canada, a union which was opposed by the Métis. A challenge to the new governor of the territory, "the Red River Resistance," was led by Louis Riel, Jr., the son of a prominent Métis. Riel and his followers established a provisional government, asserting their right to do so under the Law of Nations. They arrested several men for resisting Métis law and executed one of them—an easterner named Thomas Scott—causing an uproar. Negotiations with the government of Canada ensued, and in the Manitoba Act of 1870, many of the Métis demands were met, including allotments of land to individual Métis and their children. But in the following years, conflict continued between the Métis and the incoming settlers. The plains economy was shifting further to the west along with the buffalo herds, and many Métis chose to follow. But Canadian settlers were not far behind, with their continued disruption of the Métis way of life. In 1884, the Métis of Saskatchewan, finding the government of Canada unresponsive to their complaints, sent for Louis Riel, then living in the state of Montana. Riel returned to petition Ottawa for, among other things, land title for the Métis and provincial status for Saskatchewan, Assiniboine, and Alberta. The response was unsatisfactory, and Riel again set up a defiant provisional government. A series of armed conflicts followed, after which Riel was captured, put on trial, and hanged for treason in November 1885.

In the years following the "Riel Rebellion," referred to by the Métis as "The War of Resistance at Batoche," the Canadian government made some efforts to deal with the grievances that had led to conflict. Manitoba Métis were given 1.4 million acres of land to extinguish their "Indian title" in that province. Both land parcels and "scrip" (a certificate for the value of a parcel of land) were distributed to the Métis. Many chose to sell both land and scrip—rather than change their traditional lifestyle and engage in cash-cropping—and followed the dwindling plains economy west. However, by the twentieth century, large numbers of Métis had become impoverished and marginalized.

There is much contemporary debate about Canada's treatment of Louis Riel in particular and of the Métis in general. To some, Riel is a martyr; as the centenary of his death approached, a call was made for his posthumous pardon. To others, he is a more ambivalent figure, whose mental illness and religious mysticism are more interesting than his political activism. In any event, the life and person of Riel continue to fascinate Canadians—a favored subject for artists and writers as well as historians.

The demands that Riel made upon Canada have not been forgotten in the century since his death. Prior to 1982, the Métis had argued for many years that they were entitled to aboriginal rights, and today Métis spokesmen continue the battle for "equal recognition" with Inuit and Indians as one of Canada's three aboriginal peoples. Various political organizations—at the provincial, territorial and federal levels—carry on the struggle for Métis rights and jostle with other aboriginal groups for position and resources in Canadian society. The first Métis political organization was established in Saskatchewan in 1937, but it was not until the 1960s that provincial Métis organizations sprang up in Manitoba, Alberta, and British Columbia. In 1970 the Western Métis formed a new organization, the Native Council of Canada (NCC), to represent both Métis and non-status Indians and promote their social, economic, and political aspirations. The NCC has taken a "pan-Canadian" approach, defining a Métis as anyone of mixed European and Indian blood. However, in the 1980s, it faced a challenge from the prairie Métis, who define "the Métis" as a particular national group that arose in the historical Métis homeland during the development of the fur trade. The Métis National Council (MNC) was established in 1983 by those prairie Métis who felt the NCC was not adequately pressing for establishment of a Métis land base.

Métis politics are also carried on vigorously at the provincial level, and relations between the Métis and different levels of government vary considerably across the country. Alberta was the first province to recognize formally a distinct responsibility to its Métis population. The Métis Betterment Act was passed in 1938 after an investigation into the socioeconomic problems of the Métis. In 1938 and 1939, Alberta established twelve Métis colonies or "Settlements" in the northern part of the province; however, some of these communities were displaced when oil and gas were discovered, and real devolution of responsibility to the Métis has been a long, drawn-out process. By 1960, there were only eight communities left. In the following two decades, the Métis sought not only protection for these remaining lands but also compensation for oil and gas taken from their territory. An agreement was eventually reached in 1990 which saw 500,000 hectares and $310 million transferred to 5,000 of Alberta's Métis. Today the settlements, eight in number, are governed by elected councils with quasi-municipal powers over such areas as policing, housing, and land use; Métis who live outside the settlements are considered ordinary citizens by the government of Alberta.

Alberta's relationship with the Métis is an exception, however. In Saskatchewan, Métis "farms" have been established (with very small land bases), but special recognition of the Métis has been unusual elsewhere. In some cases, the Métis are pursuing their aspirations through the courts. The most important lawsuit is in Manitoba, where in 1992 the provincial Métis Association is seeking compensation for the 1.4 million acres granted to individual Métis by the 1870 Manitoba Act but largely lost to their descendants. The issues in this case involve detailed historical research into Métis disposition of land and scrip from 1870 until the early twentieth century, with accusations of governmental deception and fraud being common (although unproven).

Apart from the prairies, the largest Métis population is located in the Northwest Territories. There many Métis adopted the life-style of their Indian neighbors; today the NWT Métis have both a higher educational level and a higher employment level than the Dene and Inuit of the area. The Métis Association of the NWT and the Dene Nation agreed in 1981 to negotiate a land claim jointly against the federal government. An agreement in principle was reached in 1988, but the deal fell apart in 1991 when some of the Dene chiefs balked at the principle that some of their aboriginal rights would be "extinguished" upon signing of the agreement. There is an internal split within the Dene Nation between the Dene of the northern Mackenzie Delta and the Dene of the south. The northern Dene are faced with the immediate prospect of oil and gas development; without a signed land claim in their possession they may have little influence over the course of development and few opportunities to ensure that it accrues to the benefit of local communities. For the southern Dene, resource development is a less pressing concern; their leaders have the luxury of time in which to argue for more philosophical points in land claims negotiations. When the overall Dene-Métis claim broke apart, Ottawa agreed to negotiate separate regional claims—one of which has already been signed with the Gwich'in Tribal Council. But the Métis, without the bargaining power afforded by a united front, seem once again likely to suffer in the now divided claims negotiations process.

The Métis elsewhere in Canada continue to experience the marginalization and impoverishment of many Native peoples. Despite their constitutional recognition as an aboriginal people in 1982, individual Métis continue to "fall through the cracks" of the Canadian social welfare structure. The relationship between national Métis organizations and other aboriginal groups has also been problematic. The Métis continue to point out that governments do not treat the Métis the same way they do the Indians and Inuit and insist that this is unjust: "equality for aboriginal peoples" is a Métis battle cry. The Métis national agenda is largely driven by a desire for a concrete land base, rather than for further constitutional amendment; this occasionally puts them at odds with Indian and Inuit organizations, whose assets and aspirations are different. Unlike the Inuit and Indians, the Métis have always been under provincial rather than federal jurisdiction; the "constitutionalization" of their status has not changed that fact. For program purposes, such as subsidized housing, the federal government deals with the Métis as "disadvantaged" people rather than as "aboriginal" ones. With one notable exception, Canadian Métis have been treated like other Canadian citizens; the exception is the Métis of Alberta. However, that province maintains that its special treatment of Métis was spurred by the social and economic needs of individual Métis, not by recognition of Métis aboriginal rights. Legally, and despite the Constitution Act of 1982, the Métis' claim for aboriginal status has not gone very far.

The Changing Status of Canada's Aboriginal Peoples

The modern era of aboriginal politics can be dated from the release of the 1969 White Paper on Indian Policy by the federal government. The main thrust of the White Paper was a proposal to eliminate the special legal status of Canadian Indians and Inuit, who would then be provided government services through mainstream institutions, primarily provincial ones. Canadian Indians took immediate exception to this proposal and countered with their own Red Paper arguing in favor of special legal status on the grounds of aboriginal and treaty rights. However, the White Paper was more than a policy vehicle. It was also a statement of philosophy expressing the liberal individualistic vision of the state, in which the legal equality of individuals takes precedence over special benefits and status for groups. Specific questions of aboriginal rights in Canada have been entangled with a broader conflict: the vision of Canada as a liberal individualistic state versus the vision of Canada as a collection of historical communities. The Trudeau government, which produced the White Paper, was strongly committed to the former, and the only grounds it acknowledged as justifying special treatment for Indians were social and economic disadvantage. The "liberal" ideology of the White Paper had very little appeal for aboriginal Canadians, however. The White Paper had also echoed the expectation dating from colonial times that aboriginal peoples would eventually be assimilated into larger Canadian society, but since 1969 Canada's aboriginal peoples have consistently, publicly, and forcefully resisted assimilation.

The White Paper initiative of the federal government had some important consequences for Indian peoples. First, it accelerated a trend started earlier to bring Indians into a consultative role where Indian policy is involved. A significant outcome of this was the establishment of a program under the jurisdiction of the secretary of state to provide core funding to political associations representing aboriginal groups. This funding was originally intended to help aboriginal political organizations participate in the consultative process. During the 1970s and 1980s, however, the number of government departments involved in the funding of aboriginal political associations increased as well as the mandated purposes for which the funding could be used. Aboriginal peoples were given federal money to research land and treaty claims, to prepare constitutional proposals, and to provide limited delivery of social services.

In the second place, the White Paper heightened Indian, and subsequently other aboriginal people's, awareness and appreciation of their cultural and political heritage. It provided a focal point around which Indian peoples across Canada could unite and rally in opposition to what they believed to be detrimental government policies. Consequently, the 1970s and the decades that followed have become periods of Indian political activism in Canada, and the National Indian Brotherhood (NIB; after 1981 renamed the Assembly of First Nations) assumed a position of leadership among aboriginal peoples that it maintained for much of the decade. Aboriginal organizations demonstrated in the streets, lobbied in the Cabinet, and sued in the law courts—seeking to shake off the bureaucratic yoke of Indian Affairs and acquire greater control over their own communities.

Aboriginal Peoples in the Constitutional Forum

Near the end of the decade, aboriginal aspirations became entangled with Canadian constitutional politics. In the face of a growing separatist movement in Quebec, the Liberal government of Prime Minister Pierre Trudeau, the top official of Canada, took control of the national agenda with a project for renovating federalism, adopting the Constitution and entrenching a Charter of Rights much like the U.S. Bill of Rights. During the national debate, the leaders of the NIB came to realize that Canadian constitutional renewal was both a potential threat to their exclusive relationship with the federal government and an opportunity for wider assertion of their claims. The NIB leadership sought to participate with the prime minister and the provincial premiers in the "First Ministers' Conferences" on constitutional reform; when they were offered only observer status, they boycotted the meetings and carried out a success-

Chipewyan Indian houses, Smith Landing, Fort Smith.

ful lobbying effort in Great Britain to force their demands to be taken more seriously. In the end, when the Constitution was adopted in 1982, the "existing aboriginal and treaty rights of the aboriginal peoples of Canada" were recognized and affirmed, and a series of First Ministers' Conferences were scheduled to work towards definition of those rights.

The conferences were held in 1983, 1984, 1985, and 1987, attended by the eleven "First Ministers," representatives of the four main aboriginal organizations and government leaders from the Yukon and Northwest Territories. The agenda for discussion was extensive: aboriginal title over land; hunting, fishing, and trapping rights; preservation of aboriginal languages and cultures; delivery of government services; aboriginal sovereignty; equality of aboriginal women and men; and constitutional entrenchment of a Charter of Aboriginal Rights. Over the five-year period, however, discussion came to focus on one main issue: aboriginal self-government.

By the third conference in 1985, the item at the top of the aboriginal agenda was constitutional entrenchment of a right to self-government. Such an amendment was met with considerable resistance by Canadian governments, especially by provincial premiers in provinces with large numbers of aboriginal communities. British Columbia, for example, accounts for 1,629 of Canada's 2,281 Indian reserves. Would the province be forced to negotiate a self-government agreement with every one of them? The legal issue for debate was whether aboriginal self-government had to be clearly defined before it was entrenched in the Constitution (as most premiers insisted), or whether the principle should first be entrenched and then defined later through a process of negotiation (as aboriginal peoples demanded). Another way of looking at the question is whether the right to self-government is something to be delegated to aboriginal peoples by "higher" levels of government or whether (as aboriginal peoples insist) their right to self-government is "inherent," a right which they have never surrendered and which continues sovereign today. At the constitutional conferences, the former position prevailed and the conference process ended—in considerable bitterness—without any agreement on a self-government amendment of the Canadian Constitution.

The reluctance of the federal and provincial governments in Canada to legitimize claims of Native Indian peoples to self-government and to recognize their status as distinct societies was additionally illustrated by the 1987 Constitutional Accord, more commonly known as the Meech Lake Accord (signed at Meech Lake, Quebec). The accord, which excluded participation by aboriginal peoples, was drawn up in June 1987, just four months after the last constitutional conference on aboriginal rights ended in failure. The date of June 23, 1990, was set as the deadline for ratification of the accord by all provincial legislatures and the federal parliament, a condition necessary to give the accord the status of a constitutional amendment. The fundamental objective of the accord was to bring the province of Quebec into the constitutional fold through a form of renewed federalism. While the accord formally recognized Quebec as "a distinct society" with unique linguistic and cultural rights, aboriginal peoples were given only token recognition in a clause stating that their "rights" would not be affected. Aboriginal leaders reacted quickly to the accord, arguing that the sole recognition of Quebec as a "distinct society" denied that aboriginal peoples also comprise "distinct societies" within Canada.

Despite vociferous opposition to the accord by aboriginal leaders, only three provinces—Manitoba, New Brunswick, and Newfoundland—responded to their concerns that they be given greater recognition in the accord. None of the provincial proposals, however, came close to what aboriginal peoples were demanding as their proper place in the Canadian federal system. Moreover, the three provinces allowed their proposals to be watered down during a June 1990 First Ministers' meeting, called by Prime Minister Mulroney to break the impasse that had arisen among the provinces over the accord. Rather than include a new provision in the accord to deal directly with aboriginal rights and the unique nature of aboriginal societies, the First Ministers only agreed during this meeting to resurrect the former mechanism for dealing with aboriginal self-government by adding another amendment to the Constitution Act, 1982 that would provide for future constitutional conferences devoted to matters of concern to aboriginal peoples. First Ministers also agreed to establish a parliamentary committee to study a so-called "Canada clause" as a basis for a future constitutional amendment, in which aboriginal peoples would be recognized as part of the distinctive fabric of Canadian society.

In effect, the constitutional agreement that arose from the 1990 First Ministers' meeting did two things to aboriginal peoples. First, it returned them to the constitutional position they occupied in 1982, prior to the original conferences on aboriginal rights. Second, it required aboriginal peoples to defend their arguments that they constitute a fundamental characteristic of Canadian society, even though their ancestors were the original inhabitants of Canada. Not surprisingly, aboriginal leaders reacted negatively to this new agreement, arguing that it perpetuated the myth that there are only two founding nations in Canada—English and French. Moreover, they felt that the second agreement continued the hierarchy of recognition established by the original agreement, which denied them the same status within Canada as provinces, a situation which many Indian leaders, for example, have been seeking.

Arguing that "we must put an end to the lie that there are two founding nations in Canada," Indian leaders in Manitoba supported Elijah Harper, the lone Indian member of the Manitoba Legislative Assembly, in his efforts to prevent the Manitoba legislature from ratifying the Meech Lake Accord and the 1990 agreement before the June 23 deadline. Manitoba, along with Newfoundland and New Brunswick, had not yet ratified the Meech Lake Accord. By utilizing the special procedural rules of the Manitoba legislature for considering constitutional amendments, Harper was able to prevent the agreements from being approved before the deadline. The success of aboriginal leaders in blocking the constitutional entrenchment of the Meech Lake Accord forced the federal and provincial governments finally to recognize the growing political acumen and strength of aboriginal peoples. Moreover, during this process aboriginal leaders were able to create allies among those other groups in Canada that are reluctant to support a privileged status for Quebec in Canadian society or that wish to see their own interests protected in the constitution, such as women and other visible minorities.

During fall 1991, the federal government once again initiated a process for resolving Canada's constitutional difficulties. Entitled "Shaping Canada's Future Together," the process began with the establishment of a parliamentary Special Joint Committee on a Renewed Canada. The mandate of the committee was to receive recommendations from all levels of governments, interested groups, and individuals across Canada, after which the committee would enter recommendations about a renewed federalism into the grist of the constitutional mill. Perhaps as a result of the effective political maneuvering of aboriginal leaders and the growing public support for the demands of aboriginal peoples as evidenced in public opinion polls, the federal government decided to approach the participation of aboriginal peoples in a much different way than that used in the Meech Lake negotiations. Each national aboriginal organization was given a large federal grant to conduct a "parallel process" among their own constituents. The objective of this strategy was to allow the leadership of each national aboriginal organization to come up with a constitutional proposal dealing with the place of their peoples in a renewed federal system that would be rooted in the expressed needs of members. These proposals were then to be submitted to the Special Joint Parliamentary Committee for incorporation into its recommendations to parliament as well as in future constitutional negotiations.

On September 25, 1991, the federal government tabled a number of constitutional proposals dealing with aboriginal peoples, particularly aboriginal self-government, before the joint committee. Despite the caveat by the federal government that these proposals were not the final word on the subject, it was apparent that whatever ideas aboriginal leaders generate, the federal proposals were the baseline for future constitutional discussions.

In brief, the federal constitutional proposals affecting aboriginal peoples were divided into several groups. First, aboriginal peoples would be included in a "Canada clause" defining what it means to be Canadian. Essentially, the Canada clause would refer to the fact that aboriginal peoples have been historically self-governing and that aboriginal rights are recognized in Canada. Second, the right to self-government would be constitutionally entrenched. Negotiations could begin immediately on the forms and jurisdictions of aboriginal governments. Any agreement concluded would be constitutionally entrenched. After ten years, the right to self-government would be legally enforceable in the courts, meaning in effect that aboriginal peoples could ask the courts to define their right to self-government if negotiations did not succeed. Third, and unlike the Meech Lake process, aboriginal political organizations were to be allowed to participate in future constitutional discussions. Fourth, a continuing process to involve aboriginal peoples in constitutional matters that affect them was to be established. Fifth, aboriginal peoples would be given guaranteed representation in a reformed Canadian Senate. And last, the Charter of Rights and Freedoms would apply to aboriginal governments.

The Special Joint Committee on a Renewed Canada, however, turned out to be only a preliminary stage in the constitutional saga that occurred during 1992. Between January and March, a series of nationally televised "Renewal of Canada" conferences, consisting of constitutional experts, advocacy groups, and concerned citizens, took place in Canada's major cities. Following these conferences, a series of multilateral meetings were scheduled between the federal minister of constitutional affairs, governmental representatives from the provinces and territories, and the heads of Canada's major aboriginal political associations. On July 7, this group issued a status report of negotiations, which formed the basis of discussions for several First Ministers' meetings in late August. The result of these meetings was a consensus report on the Constitution, commonly known as the Charlottetown Accord, because of the location of the First Minister's meetings in Charlottetown, Prince Edward Island.

The Charlottetown Accord, after some legal fine-tuning, became the position on renewed federalism that Canadians were asked to either support or reject during an August 26 national referendum. The Charlottetown Accord incorporated in modified form a number of the constitutional positions on aboriginal peoples put forth previously by the federal government. It also included a number of the arguments advanced by aboriginal leaders during the 1992 constitutional discussions.

First, the Charlottetown Accord proposed that a new Canada clause be included as Section 2 of the Constitution Act of 1867. As it applies to aboriginal peoples, the suggested Canada clause held that the Constitution, including the Charter of Rights and Freedoms, should be interpreted in light of the fact that aboriginal peoples "have the right to promote their languages, cultures and traditions and to ensure the integrity of their societies, and their governments constitute one of three orders of government in Canada."

Second, the accord held that the Constitution should be amended to recognize that aboriginal peoples have the inherent right of self-government within Canada. The exercise of the right of self-government included authority to "(a) safeguard and develop their language, culture, economies, identities, institutions and traditions; and (b) develop, maintain and strengthen their relationships with their lands, waters and environment so as to determine and control their development as peoples according to their own values and priorities and ensure the integrity of their societies."

In contrast to the earlier federal proposal, however, the validity of the inherent right to self-government in the courts was only to be delayed for a five-year period, rather then ten years, in order to give aboriginal peoples time to work out the forms and jurisdictions of aboriginal governments with federal and provincial officials. The addition of the word *inherent* to the right of self-government marked a significant departure from the previous federal position. The differences between "a right to self-government" and "an inherent right to self-government" is far more than a question of semantics. In their insistence on inherency, aboriginal leaders claim that aboriginal peoples have always had a right to self-government, a right that precedes European colonization and the formation of the Canadian state. Furthermore, that right continues to exist today as the foundation for aboriginal self-government. In contrast, the federal government's historic position arguing for a non-inherent right to self-government implies that self-government for aboriginal peoples derives from the authority of the Canadian state. Underlying the federal proposal have been two important, interrelated positions. First, the federal government rejects any claim of sovereignty in the international sense on the part of aboriginal peoples. This has been a consistent position. The federal government's treatment of the Mohawk claim to independence, for example, has been based on this principle. Second, federal officials were fearful that the word "inherent" coul imply that no federal or provincial laws would apply to aboriginal peoples, except with their consent. Such a situation would represent a radical departure from traditional Canadian constitutional, legislative, and judicial doctrines.

The acceptance of the inherent right to self-government by federal and provincial governments was in part due to the pressure asserted by aboriginal leaders in particular and also due to public pressure on leaders to "get a constitutional deal" and move on the economy. Federal and provincial acceptance of the inherent right to self-government within Canada, however, was not left unqualified. The accord also stated that a constitutional provision should be added to ensure that laws passed by aboriginal governments would not be inconsistent with the preservation of peace, order, and good government in Canada. In essence this means that on the surface, any aboriginal law that is inconsistent with a fundamental principle of Canadian constitutional democracy could be nullified by the courts.

Third, the accord held that the Charter of Rights and Freedoms should apply to aboriginal governments. In contrast to the earlier federal position, however, the accord held that aboriginal governments should have access to Section 33 of Constitution Act, 1982, which allows parliament and the provincial legislatures to opt out charter provisions for a five-year period, if they desire. This represented a major concession to aboriginal participants in the constitutional discussions. Aboriginal leaders have consistently argued that the charter, which is based upon the individualistic values of Western liberalism, runs counter to the communal-based non-Western values of aboriginal peoples. In applying the charter to aboriginal governments, the federal government has traditionally desired to accomplish two objectives. One is to protect individual aboriginal persons from possible arbitrary actions on the part of their own governments. Another is the desire to extend the protection of the charter to aboriginal persons as Canadian citizens. The application of Section 33 to aboriginal governments stands a as partial reconciliation with the aboriginal position.

Fourth, the Charlottetown Accord continued to argue that some form of guaranteed aboriginal representation in any reformed Senate be put in the constitution and also suggested that aboriginal representation be considered for the House of Commons, Parliament's lower house.

Fifth, the accord recommended that the Constitution be amended to provide for four First Ministers' Conferences on aboriginal matters beginning no later that 1996 and following every two years thereafter.

Finally, in a radical departure from the current constitutional division of powers between the federal government and the provinces in Canada, the accord proposed that all aboriginal peoples be brought under Section 91(24), which has given the federal government constitutional authority over status Indians and by judicial incorporation authority over the Inuit. This provision implied access for the Métis to programs and funding available to status Indians under the Indian Act, an astonishing reversal of the federal government's position for over a century. Equally astonishing was the fact that Indian and Inuit leaders participating in the constitutional discussions also agreed. The financial implications of Section 91(24) recognition of the Métis were addressed only obliquely and deferred into a future political accord. Also deferred into a political accord was a provision committing five provinces and the federal government to negotiate an arrangement with the "Métis Nation" covering self-government, land and resources, and the financing of Métis institutions, programs and services.

On October 26, 1992, the Charlottetown Accord was decisively rejected by the Canadian electorate, and because the accord was voted on as a total package, the aboriginal right to self-government once again failed to achieve constitutional status, even though both pre-referendum and post-referendum analyses suggested the presence of a strong pro-aboriginal sentiment among the Canadian population. Reaction to the defeat of the accord by Indian and Métis leadership was characterized by anger and frustration, while that of the Inuit reflected moderate disappointment, probably owing to the fact that significant progress toward a non-constitutional based form of self-government had already occurred for this group. But while the feelings of the leadership toward the failure of the accord seemed to reflect the attitude of the Métis population in general, the reaction of a large number of status Indians, particularly treaty Indians, departed from that of the leadership. Many Indians felt that the provisions in the accord dealing with self-government did not go far enough, and they were especially fearful of the "peace, order, and good government" restrictions on Indian government authority. Others felt strongly that the constitutional proposals would weaken traditional treaty relationships by destroying the nation-to-nation basis upon which treaties had been originally negotiated. In fact, treaty areas number six and seven publicly disassociated themselves from the elected leadership of the Assembly of First Nations position on the accord. And there appeared to be a generalized concern over the future effects on financial support for Indians if Métis were to be brought under Section 91(24) of the Constitution. Ironically, Elijah Harper, a key figure in the death of the Meech Lake Accord, had publicly expressed disapproval of the Charlottetown Accord. In the end, it appeared that the Assembly of First Nations leadership was unable to convince rank and file Indians of the merits of the accord since it failed to achieve the support of a majority of voters on Indian reserves.

The failure of the Charlottetown Accord has effectively placed constitutional recognition of aboriginal self-government in limbo for some time, although it will undoubtably return to the constitutional arena in the future. In the meantime, aboriginal peoples will continue to strive for incremental gains to eventually acquire greater control over their own communities.

Aboriginal Peoples in the Legislative, Administrative, and Judicial Arenas

During the 1980s, the federal government introduced a number of initiatives dealing with aboriginal self-government and land claims. Federal policy in the area of aboriginal self-government is designed to allow a greater degree of aboriginal self- administration of their own communities in order that they can begin their own process of political, social, and economic development. These policy initiatives involved a recognition on the part of the federal government that, given the stalled constitutional negotiations on aboriginal rights, something must be done to accommodate the increasing demands of aboriginal leaders for self-government. The government's actions also responded to a 1983 report of a Special Committee on Indian Self-Government of the Canadian Parliament that delivered a scathing indictment of the restrictive nature of the present Indian Act as well as other governmental policies toward Indians. In all cases the federal government has insisted its policies will not prejudice any constitutional negotiations regarding aboriginal self-government or other negotiations involving land-claims and treaty rights.

Community-Based Self-Government In the case of status Indians, the most significant of the federal policies is the "community-based self-government negotiations approach," which allows for a limited degree of structural change to band or tribal political institutions and a greater degree of self-administration of programs in the areas of education, health, child welfare, social services, and environment, among others. Since some of the matters involved in this approach touch upon provincial jurisdiction, the provinces must be involved in negotiations between the federal government and bands or tribal groups where provincial interests are involved. Once negotiations have been finalized, Parliament passes a special act removing the band or tribal group from the Indian Act regarding the negotiated points of agreement.

The major precedent for community-based self-government involves the Sechelt Band in lower mainland British Columbia. The Sechelt Act (1986) is an individualized piece of legislation designed to meet the specific needs of the Sechelt Indians in the areas of taxation and control over lands and resources. An earlier precedent the Cree-Naskapi Agreement (the James Bay Agreement) is, as discussed before, a much broader piece of legislation tied to a land claim settlement with Quebec. The form of government established is regional in nature, providing for a number of regional governments and authorities to deal with political, economic, social, and cultural matters affecting the signatories.

Despite their disappointment over the failure of the constitutional process, a large number of bands and tribal groups are now involved at some stage in the community self-government negotiations process. Several Indian bands and groups, including the Gitksan and Wet'suwet'en in British Columbia, the Alexander and Sawridge Bands in Alberta, the Kahnawake Mohawk in Quebec, and the United Indian Councils of the Mississauga and Chippewa Indians in Ontario, have signed framework agreements, the final step in negotiations before the agreements go before Parliament.

The interest expressed by many Indian communities in community based self-government appears to be in part a pragmatic recognition that this approach presents them not only with an opportunity to acquire a degree of autonomy not possible under the Indian Act but also a limited chance to restore some of their traditional governing practices. Moreover, given the uncertainty about the future of constitutionally based Indian government, many Indian leaders believe that it is better to move ahead on a modest scale than wait for something that may never be realized. Indian leaders understand that this approach basically involves self-administration and not self-government in the political sense. While this approach does provide them with a broader scope for action when compared to authority given to Indian governments under the Indian Act, it still involves devolution of authority from other levels of Canadian government and therefore does not alter the basic positions of the federal government and the provinces in Canada with respect to jurisdiction and responsibility over Indians. This approach certainly fits the present mode of Canadian federalism. It remains a long way, however, from meeting the aspirations of Indian peoples for recognition of their inherent right to self-government.

Non-constitutional initiatives to bring about a greater degree of self-determination for the Métis have been complicated by the fact that, with the exception of those living in the territories, they remain under provincial jurisdiction and, apart from some of the Métis living in Alberta, lack a coherent land base. In 1985, however, the federal government signaled its willingness to participate in a tripartite negotiations process that would allow the Métis greater decision-making in areas such as housing, health care, economic development, social services, language use, and cultural development. De-

Cree woman sewing.

spite the willingness of the federal government to assume some financial responsibility for Métis peoples, progress in this area has been relatively slow, since these discussions must be initiated by the provincial governments. It also remains to be seen whether the federal government follow up on its apparent commitment to become more involved with the Métis as manifested in the failed Charlottetown Accord.

The Inuit quest for self-government as discussed previously is linked to two principles: land claims settlements and public government. The Nunavut government that will emerge from the Inuit land claims settlement in the Northwest Territories will be a public government and have powers similar to those of the existing Northwest Territories government. Also, the Labrador Inuit have expressed their intention to negotiate a self-government arrangement within context of their comprehensive land claim. Unlike the bilateral nature of the process to develop a Nunavut government in the Northwest Territories, the province of Newfoundland will be involved in any self-government agreement reached with the Labrador Inuit.

Land Claims In addition to self-government, land claims have held a dominant position on the political agenda of aboriginal peoples for the last several decades. Land, of course, not only holds a unique status within aboriginal culture; in the eyes of aboriginal people, it is also the key to their social and economic development. Land is the basis of their survival as distinct peoples. As pointed out earlier, land claims in Canada have been divided into two general types—comprehensive and specific—and governments have formulated policies for both types of claims.

Comprehensive claims policy acknowledges that aboriginal peoples have inherent interests in certain lands based upon traditional occupation and that claims can be made when it can be shown that aboriginal interests have not been extinguished. Modern comprehensive claims policy emerged from a decision of the Canadian Supreme Court in the Calder case (1973), which involved a land claim based upon aboriginal title by the Nisga'a Indians of British Columbia. Although the Nisga'a claim was dismissed on a technicality, the Court was divided as to whether aboriginal title based upon traditional occupancy still existed, and therefore did not reject the concept of aboriginal title. Fearing that future court decisions might provide judicial sanction to aboriginal title, the federal government established a Native Claims Office in the Department of Indian Affairs and instituted a claims process for both aboriginal and specific claims, the latter involving disputes over treaty land entitlement matters.

Despite the fact that both structures and processes have existed since 1974 for dealing with aboriginal land claims, and despite the millions of dollars given to aboriginal political associations for land claim research, the record to the present in satisfying land claims for Indians and Métis has been poor. This record is a product of a number of factors. First, non-Indian stakeholders, including the provinces, have been reluctant to recognize aboriginal claims where land and other proprietary interests are involved. For example, in the case of natural resources, revenue from royalties can comprise a substantial proportion of government income. It is not surprising that the most progress toward comprehensive land claim settlements are involved has occurred in the Territories. Second, the federal government itself, due to a lack of both financial and administrative resources, has limited the number of claims it can handle at any one point in time, creating a backlog in the claims process. Third, there have been a number of disagreements between aboriginal peoples themselves over particular claims. Examples include disagreement between the Inuit and Dene over the appropriate boundaries for territorial divisions, disputes between Métis and Indians where land claims cover mixed communities, divisions between regional and national political associations about the acceptability of proposed claim settlement packages, and disputes over proposed settlements with specific tribal groups themselves, such as the Lubicon band mentioned earlier. And finally, judicial doctrine regarding the existence of aboriginal title has been inconsistent. A prominent example of this situation is the land claim of the Gitksan-Wet'suwet'en Indians of British Columbia. This case, initiated in 1984, involved a claim of aboriginal title over 57,000 square kilometers of land in northwestern British Columbia. In a decision handed down on March 8, 1991, in the British Columbia Supreme Court, Chief Justice Allan McEachern argued that "the aboriginal rights of Natives were lawfully extinguished by the Crown in the colonial period." In the face of this decision the Gitksan-Wet'suwet'en tribal leaders appealed to the Canadian Supreme Court, while the federal government vowed to pursue an equitable negotiated land settlement.

Toward the Future

The decade of the 1990s may become a watershed in the history of Canada's aboriginal peoples. The 1990s could witness Canada's historical policy of assimilation transformed to one of respect for the cultural and political diversity of aboriginal peoples. This decade could also see the marginal social and economic status of aboriginal peoples improved to bring them more in line with the rest of Canadian society.

Despite the failure of the Charlottetown Accord, the positive attitudes of both governmental leaders and public at large towards aboriginal peoples favors a just resolution of the concerns of aboriginal peoples. Constitutional entrenchment of the right to self-government that also preserves the integrity of treaties, even though it may take some years to achieve, would appear to be the most desirable solution in the long run, since it could provide aboriginal peoples with an identifiable constitutional footing for dealing with the federal and provincial governments as well as the courts. However, even if constitutionalization of aboriginal self-government does not take place, both the federal and provincial governments seem to be willing to develop new legislative, financial, and administrative initiatives, as well as continue present policies to redress aboriginal grievances. Governments, however, may confront the reality of fiscal pressures. Aboriginal Canadians, whatever their rights are determined to be, must compete with other Canadians for financial and other resources.

Even so, progress toward self-governing status will remain uneven among the three aboriginal groups. The Inuit will probably make the most rapid progress, because their massive land claims negotiations have been settled and the type of government they seek is of the inclusive, public kind. Status Indians will continue to face a number of impediments. The continued presence of intransigent non-Indian stakeholders at both the federal and provincial levels, plus the lack of progress by Indian leaders themselves in developing operational concepts of self-government, will remain significant stumbling blocks. Progress by the Métis toward self-government will continue to be the slowest among the three aboriginal groups. The lack of identifiable land bases, except for the Alberta Settlements, means that most Métis must seek some off-reserve organizational structure for self-government. This situation, when coupled with the ambivalent jurisdictional status of the Métis, indicates that progress toward Métis self-government will probably proceed at a snail-like pace.

Hopeful signs are also emerging that the land claims process, in both the comprehensive and specific land claims areas, will be accelerated in the 1990s. Reversing more than one hundred years of land claims policy, the British Columbia government has recently recognized the concept of aboriginal land title and the implications for aboriginal self-government that go along with it. British Columbia is now participating in a tripartite land claims process involving federal officials, provincial officials, and Indian leaders in an attempt to settle some of the decades old land claims in the province. In the Yukon, the federal government has, after two decades, finally reached an agreement with both status and non-status Indians, which provides for ownership over 41,000 square kilometers of land, self-government arrangements, and involvement in wildlife management, among other things. Finally, the federal government has established a new Indian Claims Commission to hear appeals from Indians dissatisfied with federal offers to settle specific land claims arising from treaty violations or other misdeeds by the government.

Sally Karatak at museum in traditional Inuit beaded dress, Yellowknife, Northwest Territory.

In the administration of justice, there appears to be a growing recognition that something must be done to ensure that Canada's legal system provides fair and just treatment of aboriginal peoples. During the past several years, three provinces—Nova Scotia, Alberta, and Manitoba—created commissions of inquiry to examine how aboriginal peoples are treated within their respective justice systems. In a broad indictment of the courts, law enforcement agencies, and the correctional system, all three commissions reported that aboriginal peoples have been subject to systemic discrimination by the legal system. In fact, the Manitoba justice inquiry stated bluntly that "Canada's treatment of its first citizens has been an international disgrace." Arguing that poverty, social inequality, and a lack of understanding of Native culture and beliefs underpin the inability of the justice system to treat aboriginal peoples fairly, the commissioners in each province recommended that serious attention be given to the establishment of aboriginal controlled police, correctional, and judicial systems. The recommendations of the justice inquiries have been echoed by the Law Reform Commission, an agency created to advise the federal Minister of Justice on matters requiring legal reform.

And last, after years of lobbying by aboriginal leaders, the federal government has established a Royal Commission on Aboriginal Peoples. Co-chaired by Georges Erasmus, former grand chief of the Assembly of First Nations, the commission is charged with conducting a broad inquiry into the economic, social, legal, and political issues that affect the lives of aboriginal peoples. After extensive background studies, hearings, and deliberations, sometime in the mid-1990s the commission is expected to report back to the federal government with its findings and recommendations.

In the final analysis, however, the future of Canada's aboriginal peoples is integrally tied to the fate of Canada as a nation. The rejection of the Charlottetown Accord seems to have given renewed vigor to the leaders of the separatist movements in Quebec. If the province of Quebec establishes a quasi-independent political relationship with the rest of Canada, then new arrangements must be developed for the Indian, Métis, and Inuit peoples living within her borders. Developing these new arrangements will not be an easy or necessarily peaceful process. Moreover, what happens to the aboriginal peoples in Quebec, should that province withdraw from confederation, has significant implications for the recognition of aboriginal self-government, land claims, and culture in the rest of Canada. Within this context, the future of aboriginal peoples in Canada is dependent not only on the willingness of Canadian governments and citizens to understand and meet their needs, but also on the strength of aboriginal peoples themselves to survive as distinct cultures and continue their struggle for justice.

J. Anthony Long and Katherine Beaty Chiste
University of Lethbridge (Alberta)
Canada

Glossary

A

aboriginal The first people or native people of an area. The Native Americans are the aboriginal people of North America. Under the Canadian Constitution Act of 1982, an aboriginal person is defined as being an Indian, Inuit, or Métis. Aboriginal is often used interchangeably with the terms *native* and *indigenous*.

aboriginal rights Rights enjoyed by a people by virtue of the fact that their ancestors inhabited an area from time immemorial before the first Europeans came. These rights include ownership of land and resources, cultural rights, and political self-determination. There are widely divergent views on the validity of these rights. On one end of the spectrum, some deny the existence of aboriginal rights; on the other end, some claim that aboriginal rights give natives the inherent right to govern themselves and their lands.

aboriginal title The earliest discussion of aboriginal title in Canada came in a nineteenth-century lawsuit involving Indian lands in Ontario. At that point, aboriginal (then "Indian") title was understood to be of a usufructuary nature, that is, to give Indians a temporary right to use their lands for subsistence purposes. Indian title was not understood to equal "fee simple" ownership. A century later, however, the doctrine of aboriginal title has been expanded to include in practical terms much broader rights. *See* fee-simple ownership *and* usufructuary.

abrogation The termination of an international agreement or treaty, for example, when Congress enacts a law completely abolishing a treaty and breaking all the U.S. promises to an Indian nation.

acculturation The transference of culture from one group to another, usually from a more dominant group to a less dominant one, which thereby loses its previous culture.

agriculturalists Indian peoples who depended to a significant extent on crops which they planted themselves.

Alaska Native Claims Settlement Act (ANCSA) A 1971 congressional act that extinguished Alaska Natives' claims to land. In compensation, the Alaska Natives retained 44 million acres and received $962.5 million.

Algonkians A group of Indian peoples who speak an Algonkian language. This is the largest language group in Canada. It includes many peoples with very different cultures, from the Atlantic coast to the western prairies.

alienate Transfer of an ownership interest, for example, when tribal land is sold to nontribal members.

alkaloid Any of a number of colorless, crystalline, bitter organic substances, such as caffeine, morphine, quinine, and strychnine, having alkaline properties and containing nitrogen. Alkaloids are found in plants and, sometimes, in animals and can have a strong toxic effect on the human or animal system.

allotment The policy, peaking in the 1880s and 1890s, of subdividing Indian reservations into individual, privately owned ("patented" or "fee patent") parcels of land. The division of communally held lands on many Indian reservations into individually owned parcels, thereby nearly eliminating communal ownership of land and resources, which was a defining element of tribal life. The allotment policy was ended in 1934, but it left a legacy of "checkerboard" land ownership on reservations, where often, the tribe, non-Indians, and Indian allottees own small and scattered segments of land. *See* General Allotment Act of 1887.

Amargosa complex A series of artifacts linked to the ancient hunting and gathering peoples of the Mohave Desert in the southwest, dated from 1600 B.C. to A.D. 1000.

American Indian Movement (AIM) An Indian activist organization originating in Minneapolis, Minnesota, in the 1960s. AIM was originally organized to protect urban Indians from police harassment and to assist Indian children to obtain culturally sensitive education. In the 1970s, AIM expanded its activities to include more traditional issues, such as assertion of treaty rights, tribal sovereignty, and international recognition of Indian nations.

Anasazi An early pueblo culture that flourished between A.D. 900 and 1200. The present-day Hopi Indians are believed to be descendants of the Anasazi, which in Hopi means *ancient ones*.

annuities (1) In the United States, annuities are annual payments for land in accordance with Indian treaties. Instead of paying for Indian land in one large sum, the U.S. government usually spread the expense over many years by smaller sums for a number of years. (2) In Canada, annuities were small annual payments made to bands, which surrendered lands to the Crown, or English monarch, who formally claimed public land in Canada.

archaeology The study of past cultures through an analysis of their physical remains, such as tools or pottery. From such remains, archaeologists piece together an idea of what ancient cultures may have been like.

Archaic period The time between eight thousand and two thousand years ago defined in most areas by cultures dependent on hunting and gathering.

Articles of Confederation The original agreement among the thirteen original U.S. colonies to form a new, independent country. The articles were adopted on November 15, 1777, ratified by the thirteen colonies in 1781, and remained in force until 1789, when the present constitution was ratified.

artifacts Any products of human cultural activity, such as tools, weapons, or artworks, found in archaeological contexts.

Assembly of First Nations (AFN) The successor organization to the National Indian Brotherhood (NIB) as the national political body representing first nations of Canada at the national political level, such as at the First Ministers' Conferences, where the Canadian prime minister and provincial leaders met to discuss provisions of a new Canadian constitution. The chiefs of each Indian first nation represent their bands at the national assemblies of chiefs, which constitutes the AFN.

assimilation The idea that one group of people, usually a minority, are becoming like another and are being absorbed by a majority society. For example, for many years it was believed that U.S. Indians were assimilating into the dominant culture, but that idea no longer holds much credence.

associated funerary objects Objects believed to have been placed with individual human remains at the time of death or later as a part of the death rite or ceremony of a culture and which, along with the human remains, are currently in the possession or control of a federal agency or museum. Items exclusively made for burial purposes or to contain human remains are also considered associated funerary objects.

Athapaskan A group of Indian peoples who speak an Athapaskan language. These languages dominate in northwestern Canada south of the treeline.

B

band (1) A small, loosely organized social group composed of several families. (2) In Canada, originally a social and economic unit of nomadic hunting peoples, but since confederation, a community of Indians registered under the Indian Act. Registered Indians are called "status Indians." *See* status Indians.

band council In Canada, the local form of native government consisting of a chief and councillors, who are elected for two- or three-year terms to carry on band business. The actual duties and responsibilities of band councils are specified in the Indian Act. *See* Indian Act.

band council resolution The method by which Canadian band councils pass motions or record decisions. Band council resolutions are statements outlining a decision of the band council. The minister of Indian Affairs, or senior officials of that department, must approve band council resolutions whenever they involve band lands or monies.

Berengia During the last glacial age, before fifteen thousand years ago, a land mass between Asia and Alaska in the Bering Sea that served as a land bridge for the first migrations to the continents of the western hemisphere.

bicultural/bilingual education An education system that combines the languages, values, and beliefs of two cultures in its curriculum to give students the skills to live and function in both cultures.

Bill C-31 A 1985 act of the Canadian Parliament that restored legal status to aboriginal women and their children who had lost status through marriage to non-

Indians. The bill corrected a section of the Indian Act that revoked status for women married to non-Indians while permitting Indian men to confer Indian status upon non-Indian wives. While aboriginal women's groups welcomed this change, many Indian communities opposed the bill as an intrusion into their jurisdiction over band membership.

bill of rights A statement of fundamental rights guaranteed to members of a nation. The U.S. Bill of Rights consists of the first ten amendments to the Constitution and were adopted in the late 1780s. Canada adopted its first bill of rights in 1960. The fundamental purpose of the Canadian Bill of Rights was to ensure equality of rights, and, as a consequence, Canada's native people were allowed to vote in Canadian federal elections.

boarding school A school run by the government or a religious or private organization, in which the children live. Boarding schools designed to educate native children took them away from the influence of their family and culture.

"booming" Forceful nineteenth-century advocacy of the desirability of seizing most of the remaining land of Native Americans.

Bosque Redondo The Navajo reservation in present-day eastern New Mexico where for four years (1864–68), the Navajo were forced to live after being rounded up and concentrated together.

branch In linguistics, a subdivision of a language grouping (either a phylum or a family of languages).

British North America Act (1867) The legislation passed by the British Parliament in 1867 that created the country of Canada. The British North America Act was renamed the Constitution Act, 1867. The act outlines in section 91 the areas of federal (Canadian national government) jurisdiction, and sub-section 24 of section 91 gives the Canadian Parliament exclusive powers to pass legislation concerning "Indians, and lands reserved for the Indians."

Bureau of Indian Affairs (BIA) A federal agency charged with the trust responsibility for tribal land, education, and water rights.

C

California missions The twenty-one individual Catholic missions founded between 1769 and 1823, containing a church, a dormitory for Native Americans, and successful farm and cattle operations based on forced Indian labor.

camas A plant (Camassia quamash), the bulbs of which were an important source of food for the native people of the Northwest Coast and the Columbia Plateau. The bulbs were gathered in the late summer and baked to prepare for eating or storage.

Campbell tradition Archaeological remains of a group of California cultures dated from 3000 B.C. to A.D. 1500 and later. The remains are believed to be ancestral to the present-day Chumash from the Santa Barbara area.

Canada Originally this designation referred only to part of France's possessions in Canada (roughly corresponding to today's southern Quebec). After 1791 it came to refer to the two Canadas, Lower Canada (southern Quebec) and Upper Canada (southern Ontario). With confederation by the North American Act in 1867, it came to refer to all the provinces and territories collectively.

Canadian Aboriginal Economic Development Strategy (CAEDS) Launched in 1989, a program that seeks to promote economic development among native people. The program coordinates funding services of several federal agencies to focus on aboriginal economic development problems. Participating federal agencies include the Department for Indian Affairs and Northern Development (DIAND), the Department of Employment and Immigration Canada (EIC), and the Department of Industry, Science and Technology. The program emphasizes long-term planning and is geared toward business ventures and entrepreneurship.

Canadian Charter of Rights and Freedoms This section of the Canadian Constitution Act, 1982 combines protection of individual rights, such as freedom of conscience and religion, with group rights involving issues such as language. Judicial decisions involving the charter are having a profound impact on Canadian society. In the 1982 Constitution, aboriginal and treaty rights were not included in the charter itself but in a separate part of the text. A provision of the Canadian charter that differentiates it from the U.S. Bill of Rights allows governments to "opt out" of charter requirements through legislative fiat.

Canadian test of basic skills A test of a student's reading, writing, and mathematical skills commonly used in Canada.

castor gras A French term meaning *greasy beaver*, which referred to beaver pelts that had been used as clothing long enough for the long guard hairs to fall out and for the shorter barbed hairs to absorb body oils and perspiration. Especially during the early fur trade, Europeans sought castor gras because of its value for making felt.

cautery The act of cauterizing, which is to burn with a hot iron or needle, or with a caustic substance, so as to destroy dead or unwanted tissue in order to prevent the spread of infection.

caveat "Caution." A legal action by which a person or party claims ownership of, or interest in, land registered in the name of another party.

cession Giving up of Indian land, often in exchange for a reservation or grant of land set aside for the Indians' permanent and exclusive use and occupancy.

Charlottetown Accord (1992) An attempt at constitutional reform in Canada, named after the Prince Edward Island city where it was reached. It would have entrenched the inherent right to aboriginal self-government in the Constitution, as well as decentralizing many aspects of Canadian government. In the process of drafting this accord, national aboriginal leaders were included as quasi-equal participants for the first time. However, in a national referendum in October 1992, both aboriginal and other Canadians rejected the Charlottetown Accord, and aboriginal political aspirations were again forced to seek out non-constitutional forums.

chiki A Seminole word for their open-sided, thatched-roof shelter, which evolved in Florida from the Creek cabin of their ancestors.

cimarrone A Spanish term for wild or `untamed. Cimarrone was applied to the Lower Creek Indians who migrated into Florida in the latter part of the eighteenth century and later became the Seminole Indians.

"citizens plus" In Canada, the concept that Indians are a distinct class of persons with special rights by virtue of their aboriginal title and treaty rights, which non-Indian citizens do not enjoy.

civil service reform Late nineteenth-century movement in the United States to reform government service. The policy separated politics from government office holding, which meant in the Indian Service that elected officials were prevented from directly appointing political friends to well-paying positions. Appointment to and retention of government administrative positions became based on competence and the possession of formal qualifications of individual applicants and job holders.

"civilization" or forced acculturation A major U.S. Indian policy from 1887 to 1934 that included pacification of Indians, their conversion to Christianity, and their adoption of a "civilized" occupation such as farming. *See* acculturation *and* assimilation.

clan The basic social and political organization of many, but not all, Indian societies, which consists of a number of related house groups and families. In some cases, persons who claimed to be related and shared a common symbol or totem, usually an animal such as the bear or the turtle.

Clovis points Ancient spearheads made in a style of polished, tapered, and cylindrical shape, which first appeared among North American peoples about 10,000 B.C. These peoples practiced a hunting and gathering way of life that depended on many now-extinct species such as woolly mammoth, dire wolf, and camels.

Cochise culture The name that refers to groups of hunters and gathers who lived in present-day southeastern Arizona and southwestern New Mexico from about 13,000 to 500 B.C. This cultural period is named in honor of the Apache leader, Cochise, who in the late 1800s gave resistance to U.S. troops in the same area.

Community Health Representatives (CHR) Program A Medical Services Branch (MSB) program to train Indian and Inuit people at the community level in elementary public health, so that they can provide a link between their community and the health facility in that community.

Compact of 1802 Agreement between the state of Georgia and the U.S. federal government in which the latter retained rights to negotiate land treaties with Indians in present-day Mississippi, Georgia, and Alabama, while Georgia was restricted to its present-day boundaries and given assurance that the federal government would peaceably remove any Indian nations from within Georgia's chartered limits.

comprehensive claim According to the Canadian government's land-claims policy, an aboriginal claim, based on aboriginal rights, to land not covered by treaty.

concentration A major U.S. government Indian policy of the mid-nineteenth century involving concentration of Indian tribes on reservations west of the Mississippi River. *See* Removal Act.

Concordat In Roman Catholic Church law ("canon law" or sacred law), a treaty made by the Vatican (or "Holy See" or the Pope).

confederacy An alliance of friendship among several tribes or bands in which they agree to regulate some of their activities under common rules and obligations. This could mean the obligation to give military aid if attacked or the right to seek redress for personal or group injuries suffered from other alliance members before the body of the confederacy. The latter was the case within the Iroquois Confederacy of upstate New York.

consensus Universal agreement. Indian political or social decisionmaking usually required that all interested groups agree to a proposition before it was binding. Majority rule was not sufficient for a decision, but rather all groups (bands, clans, lineages, villages, or triblets) had to agree, otherwise each group acted the way it thought proper or best.

conservatives Members of an Indian nation who followed traditional ways of living, often claiming the Native American way as preferred. Conservatives often represent a cultural and political segment of an Indian nation and usually live differently. They have political and cultural goals of preserving Indian culture and identity that other members of the nation might be willing to give up.

constituencies Groups of individuals, where each group forms a district for purposes of representation.

constitution The written form of a country's governing structure, which establishes the basic functions and division of powers between different levels of government, such as federal and provincial governments in Canada, or federal, state, and city governments in the United States. In the United States, the Constitution was adopted in 1789, but since then several amendments or changes have modified the original document. The Canadian constitution is set forth in the Constitution Act 1867, 1930, and 1982. In August 1992, further major constitutional additions and amendments were proposed, but before becoming law, the amendments must be ratified, or agreed to, by the Canadian provincial legislatures. *See* British North America Act.

Contract Health Service (CHS) The purchase of health care by the Indian Health Service (IHS) through contractual arrangements with hospitals, private physicians, and clinic groups, and dentists and providers of ancillary health services to supplement and complement other health care resources available to American Indians and Alaska Natives.

Council on Energy Resource Tribes (CERT) An organization formed by U.S. Indian tribes who have substantial marketable natural resources on their reservation lands. CERT provides its member tribes with expertise for marketing and managing their resources.

Crown The formal head of state, symbolized by the king or queen of England. In Canada, the Crown is divided between the federal government, "the Crown in right of Canada," and the provincial governments, "the Crown in right of (name of province)."

crown lands Land under the sovereign ownership or protection of the Canadian federal government or the provincial governments. The treaties recognized the Indian's right to hunt and fish on "unoccupied Crown lands," which has been greatly diminished by privatization of land, designation of national parks or wilderness parks, or reservation by legislation (i. e., "occupied") by any purpose.

culture The nonbiological and socially transmitted system of concepts, institutions, behavior, and materials by which a society adapts to its effective natural and human environment.

culture area A device anthropologists have used to discuss large numbers of people in a contiguous geographical area. Generally, it is assumed that the various peoples in a culture area are similar in lifeways.

cultural patrimony Refers to any object having ongoing historical, traditional, or cultural importance central to the Native American group or culture itself, rather than property owned by an individual Native American. It therefore cannot be alienated, appropriated, or conveyed by any individual regardless of whether the individual is a member of the tribe. Any such object is considered inalienable, not for sale, by such Native American group at the time the object was separated from the group.

D

demography The statistical study of populations, including migration, birth, death, health, and marriage data.

dependence (1) In nineteenth-century international law and federal Indian law, the relationship between a weak country and a strong country that agrees to protect it. In 1831, the Supreme Court labeled Indian tribes as "domestic nations," because the United States had agreed, by treaty, to protect them from others. (2) The situation by which Indians came to depend on trade of animal furs for European manufactured goods, especially metal goods like hoes, guns, and hatchets. Indians stopped producing their own stone tools and came to depend on trade to supply some necessary economic goods.

diminutive A grammatical construction conveying a meaning of smallness.

discouraged workers Unemployed workers who have abandoned their search for a new job.

diuretic An agent that increases the amount of urine.

domestic dependent nation The expression was used by U.S. Supreme Court Justice John Marshall in the case *Cherokee Nation v. Georgia* in 1831, which denied the Cherokee Nation, and all Indian nations, status as independent foreign nations. Instead, Justice Marshall described the relation of the Indian governments to the U.S. as more akin to "domestic dependent nations."

Dorset culture An Inuit (Eskimo) cultural tradition dated from 1000 B.C. to A.D. 1000. They were adapted to the harsh environments of the Canadian Arctic, relying heavily on fishing and hunting sea mammals.

E

Economic Opportunity Act of 1964 A congressional act that provided funding to local Community Action Programs (C.A.P.) and authorized Indian tribes to designate themselves as C.A.P. agencies for the purposes of the act.

economy The sphere of society in which individuals and the community organize to satisfy subsistence needs with production of food, clothing, shelter, and, in some societies, personal wealth.

edema An abnormal accumulation of fluid in cells, tissues, or cavities of the body, resulting in swelling.

egalitarianism The view that people are equal, especially politically or socially.

encomienda A practice by which the Spanish king rewarded public service with grants of land and rights to demand work from the local population. Encomiendas were granted in the Southwest and throughout Latin and South America. Local Indians were forced to work for the landlords, who in turn tried to convert the Indians to Christianity.

Encinitas tradition Archaeological remains of a group of cultures derived from Paleo-Indian ancestors. The Encinitas people depended heavily on fishing and collecting shellfish along the California coast. The Encinitas tradition dates from 5500 to 3000 B.C.

encroach The illegal and sometimes forcible entry of an individual or group on the land or property of another. For example, during much of the 1800s, Indian nations often complained that U.S. settlers established farms on Indian lands without permission and in violation of treaties with the U.S. government.

enema A liquid injected into the colon through the anus, as a purgative or for medicinal purposes.

enfranchisement In Canada's Indian Act, a process by which an aboriginal Canadian gives up his legal status as an Indian and assumes all the rights of a citizen of Canada. Until 1960, this was the only procedure for a Canadian Indian to gain the right to vote or to purchase alcohol. Few native people chose enfranchisement because they would lose their treaty rights, they would have to accept their share of band trust funds, and they would surrender all rights to reserve lands or participation in band elections or community affairs.

Equal Protection Clause Part of the Fourteenth Amendment to the U.S. Constitution, adopted in the wake of the Civil War, which requires the equal treatment of all citizens—except "Indians not taxed" (tribal Indians).

ergative A grammatical construction in which the subjects of some verb forms are treated similarly to the objects of other verb forms.

ethnography A descriptive account of a particular culture. Ethnographies generally discuss the economic, political, social, and religious life of a people.

ethnopoetics The study of traditional oral literature, concerned with how linguistic features are used for artistic effect.

etiology The causes of a specific disease.

evidential A construction indicating the source of validity of the information in a sentence.

exclusive Referring to a first person plural pronoun, which excludes the person spoken to, "I and someone else, but not you."

extinguished The act of giving up claims to land in exchange for compensation such as money, parcels of land, and goods and services.

extradition The process by which a person who has escaped from the country where he or she is accused of a crime is demanded by and then returned forcibly to that country to stand trial. Extradition is usually governed by treaties between the countries concerned. There is no general principle, in international law, that requires governments to return fugitives.

F

family In linguistics, a group of languages clearly descended from a single "parent" language.

Federal Acknowledgment Process (F.A.P.) Established in 1978 by an act of Congress, a Bureau of Indian Affairs program that established procedures to extend federal recognition to previously unrecognized Indian tribes and communities. About 150 Indian communities have applied to the U.S. government for certification as Indian tribes. *See* federal recognition.

federal agency Any department, agency, or instrumentality of the United States.

federal lands Any land, other than tribal lands, that are controlled or owned by the United States.

federal recognition Acknowledgment by the U.S. government of government-to-government relationships with certain Indian tribes. Federal recognition can be obtained by satisfying the criteria of the Federal Acknowledgment Process administered through the U.S. Department of the Interior, by federal statute enacted by Congress, or by court decree. *See* Federal Acknowledgment Project *and* federally recognized tribes.

federally recognized tribes Those Indian tribes with which the U.S. government maintains official relations, as established by treaty, executive order, or act of Congress.

Federation of Saskatchewan Indian Nations (FSIN) An association organized along with the Indian Association of Alberta in the 1940s, which has a mandate and objective to serve the political interest of the native bands with federal treaties within the province of Saskatchewan. *See* Indian Association of Alberta.

fee-simple ownership A form of individual ownership of property, usually land, where the owner has the sole right to sell the land to any buyers, and no other parties have significant claims to the land.

fiduciary A relationship founded in trust and responsibility for looking after the best interests of a group, organization, or committee.

Fifth Amendment Part of the Bill of Rights of the U.S. Constitution, which forbids any taking of "private property" without "due process of law" and compensation. Indian treaties and reservation lands are now recognized as being "property" within the meaning of this provision.

First Ministers' Conference (FMC) A recently developed Canadian political tradition, the FMC is a gathering of Canada's "first ministers"—the ten provincial premiers and the national prime minister. In the 1990s, leaders of the Canadian territories have been included on occasion along with aboriginal leaders. At first, FMCs were oriented toward specific issues and problems; however, increasingly the FMC is supplanting traditional parliamentary politics as the primary decision-making forum in Canada.

first nations A term that came into common usage in the 1970s to distinguish and give recognition to Canada's Indian nations as the original peoples on the North American continent.

Five Civilized Tribes A name given to the Cherokee, Choctaw, Chickasaw, Creek, and Seminole tribes during the second half of the 1900s because they adopted democratic constitutional governments and schools.

Folsom points Ancient flaked and grooved pieces of flint that were used as spearheads by paleo-Indians, or Stone Age Indians, before 10,000 B.C.

Formative period A term used to describe the period of early settlement of Indians into villages. In the Southwest, the settlement of villages, with some dependence on farming, occurred between A.D. 200 and 900.

freedmen Former slaves who were freed after the Civil War and by the Thirteenth Amendment to the U.S. Constitution. The Cherokee, Choctaw, Chickasaw, Creek, and Seminole all held slaves and, after the Civil War, in one way or another included their freedmen into their national institutions.

fricative A consonant produced by letting the air pass through the mouth with audible noise, as contrasted with a stop, when the air is abruptly held in the mouth.

G

General Allotment Act of 1887 A law that applied the principle of allotting in severalty tribal reservation lands to individual resident tribesmen. Generally, a tract of 160 acres for a head of household, 80 acres for single people, and 40 acres per child was received in trust status for a period of twenty-five years; thereafter, the allottee owned the land in fee simple. The General Allotment Act was designed to divide Indian reservations into small, privately owned plots and release the surplus lands to U.S. settlers. Under the General Allotment Act, between 1887 and 1934, over 90 million acres of Indian land were sold to U.S. citizens.

General Revenue Sharing Program (1972–86) A federal program to share federal tax revenues with state and local governments in the United States, including states, counties, cities, town, and Indian tribes and Alaska Native villages, "which perform substantial governmental functions."

genetic relationship In linguistics, the relationship between "sister" languages descended from a single parent language.

Ghost Dance Part of a largely religious movement in the 1870s and into the late 1880s and early 1890s. The movement hoped to restore the buffalo herds to the Plains and restore the old Indian Plains life. It was believed that many of the people lost in epidemics and warfare would be returned to life if certain ritual and religious precautions were observed. *See* the biography of Wovoka and information on the Great Basin and Plains in the 1870s to 1890s.

glottal stop In linguistics, a consonant produced by closing and opening the vocal cords, interrupting the flow of air.

glottalization In linguistics, a closure and re-opening of the vocal cords simultaneously with the production of a sound in the mouth.

government-to-government relationship The official relation between the U.S. federal government and the tribal governments of Indian tribes, which is defined by the mention of Indian tribes in the U.S. Constitution and through legal rulings. In this relation, the U.S. government recognizes inherent rights of Indian tribes to self-government and to the ownership of land.

Great Basin Elevated region covering a great deal of several western U.S. states (Nevada, eastern California, western Colorado, Utah, eastern Oregon, and western Wyoming), which contains no drainage for water outside the region. Consequently, water must drain toward the center, hence the name Great Basin.

Great Society Name given to domestic policy during the administration of President Lyndon B. Johnson (1963–69), especially anti-poverty and social welfare measures.

H

habeas corpus Literally, from Latin "you have the body." A claim presented to a court stating that a person is being held in custody or jail in violation of law. In Indian country, normally this writ of habeas corpus is available only to criminal defendants who have been convicted in tribal courts and who claim that their convictions were obtained without adherence to the Indian Civil Rights Act (for example, evidence was improperly seized or the criminal statute used as the basis for conviction violated rights of free speech).

Haudenosaunee The name of the people often called the Iroquois or Five Nations, or Six Nations after 1717. Literally, it means "The People of the Long House," referring to the extended multifamily houses in which the Iroquois lived.

Health and Welfare Canada The department of the Canadian federal government responsible for the health of all Canadians. It is divided into several branches; the Medical Services Branch serves the health needs of Inuit and Indians.

health status A measurement of the state of health of a given population, usually reported in numbers per 1,000 population and utilizing such indicators as morbidity, mortality, and infant death rates.

heathens Anyone of another religion with different fundamental views of religion. Indians were considered heathens by the early Catholic Spanish explorers and by the Puritans in New England. Indians considered Europeans also to have little understanding of religion or culture. For example, the Choctaw regarded early English traders as untutored and nonspiritual beings because they did not understand Choctaw religious views and did not practice correct religious rituals and social etiquette.

hierarchical Structured by class or rank.

Home Guard Indians In Canada, bands of Indians who lived near fur trade posts and had a relatively more intense trading relationship with traders than most Indian bands. Home Guard bands and traders exchanged various goods and services, and also tended to develop kinship ties.

hunters Indians who depended on hunting, fishing, or gathering, as opposed to farming, for their food. Most aboriginal groups in Canada were hunting peoples.

I

IHS Service population Those American Indians, Eskimos, and Aleuts (as identified by the census) who reside in the geographic areas in which the Indian Health Service (IHS) has responsibilities. These areas are the thirty-two reservation states (including California), and the geographic areas are defined as on or near reservations or within a contract health service delivery area (CHSDA).

in situ "In place." A term applied to archaeological remains found in their original, undisturbed location or position.

inalienable In linguistics, referring to a noun for which a possessor must always be specified, especially kin terms and body parts.

Immersion schools Canadian schools where the language used is different from the students' first language. For example, Indian children who spoke their native language were often sent to schools where only English was spoken. This was a method of getting them to speak English and learn Canadian culture.

inclusive In linguistics, referring to a first person plural pronoun that includes the person spoken to, "I and you."

Indian (1) In Canada, according to the Indian Act first passed in 1876 and revised in 1985, a person who is registered as an Indian or is entitled to be registered as an Indian. Such an Indian may also be called a registered Indian or status Indian. *See* status Indians. (2) In the U.S., any individual who self-identifies as an American Indian or Alaska Native and who is determined by his tribe to be a fully enrolled tribal member.

Indian Act In Canada, the overriding legislation that sets forth the policies of the federal government toward native people. This legislation passed by the Canadian government defines the legal status of Indians. First passed by the Canadian Parliament in 1876, the act was revised in 1951 and subsequently amended in 1985. Essentially, the Indian Act had four major objectives. First, it defined status Indians. Second, it established the reserve system. Third, it created legal entities known as bands with governments to administer reserve communities. And fourth, it created a national administrative structure, the Department of Indian Affairs, to administer the act. Under the Indian Act, the minister of Indian affairs and northern development holds ministerial and trust responsibility for "status Indians" recognized by the Canadian federal government. *See* band, band council, British North America Act, and status Indians.

Indian Association of Alberta (IAA). Officially incorporated in 1944, IAA serves as an organization representing the political interests of the treaty Indians of the province of Alberta. The IAA promotes unity and spiritual strength of Indian nations in the protection of their lands, rights, and cultures. The organization receives its mandates from the chiefs, councillors, and members of the Alberta first nations, the member native bands of Alberta.

Indian country Land where Indian government and custom rule. In more recent times, Indian country refers to Indian reservations where Indian tribal governments are regulated by federal law and the Bureau of Indian Affairs.

Indian Delegation Act of 1946 (Public Law 687) A congressional act that authorized substantial delegations of formal authority from the secretary of the interior to the commissioner of Indian affairs and from the commissioner to his subordinates, the twelve area directors who work on a day-to-day basis with local BIA agency offices and tribal governments on Indian reservations.

Indian Education Act (1972) A congressional act that provided education financial assistance to communities with Indian students in their schools.

Indian Health Care Improvement Act (Public Law 94-437) Through a program of increased funding levels in the Indian Health Service budget, the act was intended to improve the health status of American Indians and Alaska Natives up to a level equal to the general U.S. population. Funding was directed to urban populations and funds were used to expand health services, and build and renovate medical and sanitation facilities. It also established programs designed to increase the number of Indian health professionals and to improve care access for Indian people living in urban areas.

Indian Health Service (IHS) The seventh agency within the U.S. Public Health Service, this federal agency's mission is to upgrade the health status of American Indians to the highest level possible. The IHS is composed of eleven regional administrative units called area offices. Within these units, the IHS operates 45 hospitals, 65 health centers, 6 school health centers, and 201 other treatment programs. In 1987, the state of California was designated an area office, the latest addition to the IHS. There are no IHS facilities in California, only Indian-operated and -managed clinics.

Indian New Deal Legislation enacted in the 1930s during the Roosevelt administration promoting tribal government and economic recovery programs for reservations.

Indian Removal The United States government policy, beginning in the 1820s and lasting through the 1850s, of moving all Indian tribes west of the Mississippi River, to make room for U.S. settlement of the lands in the east. By 1860, this policy resulted in the removal of most eastern Indian nations to locations in present-day Kansas and Oklahoma.

Indian Reorganization Act of 1934 (IRA) A congressional act providing reservation communities the opportunity to re-organize their tribal governments and adopt a new tribal constitution and tribal charter, and organize tribal business corporations. It also provided a revolving loan fund and other support services to participating tribes.

Indian Self-Determination and Education Assistance Act of 1975 (Public Law 93-638) This act enabled tribes to contract, at their own option, to provide any service currently being provided by either the Bureau of Indian Affairs or the Indian Health Service. If the tribes change their policies about contracting government services, they have the right to return the administration of a contracted service to the relevant federal agency. The Self-Determination Act was designed to allow Indian tribes and organizations to have more direct control over federal programs that operated within reservation communities.

Indian Territory The area west of the Mississippi River, primarily present-day Kansas and Oklahoma, to which the United States once planned to move all of the eastern Indians. Indian Territory was the home of nearly one-third of all U.S. Indians in 1880. Parts of Indian Territory were opened to U.S. settlers, over Indian objections, in 1889. By 1907, the last remnants of Indian Territory were admitted to the Union as the state of Oklahoma, as non-Indians had become an overwhelming majority of the population.

Indian tribe Any tribe, band, nation, or other organized group or community of Indians recognized as being eligible for special programs and services provided by the United States because of its status. *See* federally recognized tribes.

indigenous Native to the area.

industry A classification system in which firms that produce similar goods or services are grouped together into distinct categories.

infant death rate A ratio of infant deaths within the first year of life to the total live births in a particular time period, usually five or ten years.

injunction A court order prohibiting a person or legal entity from carrying out a given action, or ordering a person or organization to carry out a specific task. For example, in 1832, the U.S. Supreme Court in the case *Worcester v. Georgia* ruled that the Georgia government had no legal right to abolish the Cherokee government, which had its capital in territory claimed by Georgia. The Court, however, did not issue an injunction to the state of Georgia to prohibit it from extending its laws over the Cherokee Nation.

inpatient A patient admitted to a bed in a hospital to have treatment and stay overnight at least one night.

intransitive In linguistics, characterizing verbs that have subjects but not direct objects, opposite of transitive.

Inuit Formerly known as Eskimos, Inuit are members of one of several peoples who traditionally inhabited areas north of the treeline, in northern Alaska, northern Canada, and Greenland. They all speak dialects of the same language. In Canada, Inuit have the same legal status as Indians. The word Inuit means *people*. Forming a majority in the new Canadian territory of Nunavut, they will in effect be self-governing by the turn of the twenty-first century.

Inuk The singular of Inuit.

Iroquoian Indian peoples who speak an Iroquoian language, such as the Huron, Mohawk, and Onondaga.

Iroquoian League The Iroquois Confederacy, an alliance of government and cultural and legal unity, which was formed before European colonization by the Mohawk, Cayuga, Onondaga, Oneida, and Seneca nations of present-day upstate New York. Also called the Five Nations and, after being joined by the Tuscarora in the early 1700s, the Six Nations.

isolate (language isolate) A language without close historical relationships to other languages.

J

Jim Crow legislation After 1890, laws passed by many southern states designed to segregate the U.S. population by race. Many native people were automatically classified as black.

Johnson-O'Malley Act of 1934 Permitted the Indian Office to contract with the states to provide education, health, and welfare services to Indians on reservations within their borders. For example, the act allowed Indian children to attend public schools at the expense of the Indian Office.

jurisdiction The empowerment of a governing body to oversee regulations and laws within an assigned area. The extent of legal power of a government, legislature, or of a court over its people and territory. Jurisdiction is defined in terms of persons, subject matter, and geography. For example, Alabama courts have jurisdiction in cases involving people, property, or activities only in the state of Alabama.

K

Kachina A deity or group of benevolent spirit beings among the Pueblo. *See* the book cover art, "Kachinas Emerging," by Hopi artist and poet Michael Kabotie.

kiva Among the Pueblo cultures, an underground ceremonial chamber formed in the shape of a circle. A cycle of often-secret annual rituals takes place the kivas. Leaders gather in the kivas to discuss religious and other important issues concerning the pueblo community.

L

labiovelar In linguistics, characterizing consonants produced with the rear part of the tongue, with simultaneous rounding of the lips.

labor force participation An individual who is working or looking for work is considered to be participating in the labor force. Anyone who does not have a job and is not looking for work is not in the labor force.

land cession treaty A treaty in which a group of people surrender certain rights to land in exchange for other rights, usually hunting rights or an annual payment.

land claim, comprehensive In the 1970s, the Canadian government agreed to negotiate comprehensive land claims with aboriginal groups whose ancestors had not ceded their land rights by signing a land surrender treaty. Claims negotiations involve a lengthy process, which, when successful, leads to cash settlements, land title, and devolution of authority. When settled, comprehensive claims agreements acquire the constitutional status of treaties.

land claim, specific Specific land claims are made against the Canadian state where it is argued that treaty commitments have not been met. The meaning of treaty rights themselves has expanded considerably over the years, allowing ever more specific claims to be made on treaty grounds. But usually specific land claims refer to as-yet unallocated lands.

language area A geographical region in which languages of different families have become similar because of borrowing.

law A measure or set of rules passed by a governing body to regulate the actions of the people in the interest of the majority of the nation.

legend A folktale that deals with the experiences of individuals or happenings of a distant past.

libertarian A person who places great value on individual consent and personal freedom.

life expectancy The average number of years remaining to a person at a particular age, based on a given set of age-specific death rates, generally the mortality (death rate) conditions existing in the period mentioned.

line A unit in the structure of a literary composition, defined in terms of its parallelism of structure with an adjacent line.

lingua franca (trade language) A mixed language used for communication between people of different native languages.

linguistics The study of language. Usually the sounds, structure, and meaning of a language are analyzed and compared with other languages.

litigation The use of courts or a legal process to achieve an end or contest an issue. For example, when in the early 1830s, the state of Georgia extended its laws over the Cherokee Nation, the Cherokee appealed to the U.S. Supreme Court to resolve their differences with the Georgians.

location ticket In Canada, the right granted by the government to an Indian to use part of reserve land as if it were private property. Location tickets were part of the Canadian government's attempts to encourage Indians to accept private property rather than hold land in common.

Long Walk The 300-mile forced walk in 1864 from the Navajo's home to an assigned reservation, Bosque Redondo, near Fort Sumner, 180 miles southeast of Santa Fe, New Mexico.

longhouse In the Northwest Coast, a longhouse is a dwelling in which several nuclear families share the structure. Usually, the families are related to one another. The Iroquois or Six Nations of upstate New York also had a similar tradition of living in longhouses with related extended families.

loyalists An expression used during the Revolutionary War (1775–83) for persons who chose the side of the British and attempted to help the British cause.

M

Magna Carta An agreement of fundamental rights, also known as the Great Charter of England, signed in 1215 A.D. by King John and his English noblemen. Many of our modern ideas on government and democracy have developed from this fundamental constitutional document, empowering freedom and justice. *See* Proclamation of 1763.

maize Also known as corn, an important crop plant, initially domesticated in Mexico over six thousand years ago.

Manifest Destiny During the 1900s, a broadly held belief among the U.S. population that it was inevitable that the U.S. nation would expand across the North American continent from the Atlantic to the Pacific Ocean. Belief in Manifest Destiny served as a rationalization for the seizure of Indian land, and, in 1846, to justify war with Mexico, which led to the annexation of Texas, New Mexico, Arizona, and California.

matrilineal A kinship system in which inheritance of names, wealth, or other property transfer through the mother's family and/or clan.

materialism The belief that economic well-being or wealth are of central human concern, while spiritual or cultural understandings or comforts are of secondary concern or relatively meaningless.

Medical Services Branch (MSB) The branch of the Department of National Health and Welfare of the Canadian federal government responsible for Indian and Inuit health.

Medicine Chest Clause A clause in Treaty No. 6 (1876) between the Canadian government and the Indian tribes in Northern Alberta on which is based the claim that Indian people in Canada have a perpetual right to free health care provided by the Canadian federal government.

mega-fauna The large animals, such as woolly mammoth, ground sloth, and saber-toothed tiger, which died off about 8000 B.C. after the last glacier receded far north.

Meriam Report of 1928 An exhaustive investigation of Indian administration and a major criticism of Indian policies and administration since passage of the General Allotment Act of 1887. The report had a major influence on Indian affairs during the administrations of Presidents Herbert Hoover (1929–33) and Franklin D. Roosevelt (1933-45). It helped formulate the policies of the Indian New Deal, which originated with passage of the Indian Reorganization Act of 1934, and allowed Indians greater self-government and the right to retain cultural ceremonies and events.

mescaline A white, crystalline alkaloid, psychedelic drug obtained from mescal buttons, and found in peyote buttons.

metate A stone with a slightly hollow center that is used for grinding corn.

Métis French for "mixed-blood." This term has been used in several different ways. Usually it refers to mixed-blood people in western Canada who are conscious of belonging to a distinct community. The Canadian Constitution recognizes Métis as aboriginal peoples. The term is also used to refer to any person of mixed Indian-European descent, and more specifically to a descendant of a native parent, usually Cree or Ojibway, and a non-native parent, usually French, but also some English, who settled in the Red River area of what is now the province of Manitoba during the days of the fur trade, which lasted from the 1700s to the late 1800s.

Mississippian period The period between A.D. 900 and 1500 when in the eastern United States there arose complex chiefdom societies and maize-farming communities. The Mississippian tradition is associated with the building of flat-topped earthen mounds, which were religious and political centers. Many of the Mississippian towns, sometimes holding as many as thirty thousand people, were fortified with palisades. One of the largest Mississippian societies was located at Cahokia, near present-day St. Louis, Missouri.

moiety A French expression which means divided into two halves. For anthropologists, the terms refers to a society divided into two major clusters of clans. For example, among the Tlingit, there are Eagle and Raven moieties, which divide the society into two groups of about twenty-five clans. Among the Tlingit, moiety relations govern marriage rules, since Raven moiety members must marry an Eagle and vice-versa.

morphology In linguistics, the formation of words by combinations of stems, prefixes, and suffixes, as contrasted with syntax.

mortality The proportion of deaths to population.

moxa A soft, downy material, burned on the skin as a cauterizing agent or counter-irritant.

Muskogean A family of related languages spoken by many Indian nations of the southeast including the Choctaw, Chickasaw, Creek, Seminole, and Natchez.

myth A narrative tale concerned with the Creator, spirits, and the nature and meaning of the universe and humans.

N

nation A community of people who share the right to political self-rule, and/or who share a common identity, and who usually share a similar culture, the same language, the same economy, and a mutually recognized territory.

National Indian Brotherhood (NIB) Founded in 1968, a Canadian national Indian political organization. The NIB now serves as the legal executive office for the Assembly of First Nations. *See* Assembly of First Nations.

Native American Of or relating to a tribe, people, or culture indigenous to the United States.

need An estimate of the amount of medical care required to provide adequate services to a population in terms of the amount of disease present or preventable, often contrasted to demand.

New Deal Name given to domestic policy during the administration of President Franklin D. Roosevelt (1933–45).

New Frontier Name given to domestic policy during the administration of President John F. Kennedy (1961–63).

non-IHS-service population Those Indians who do not reside in the geographic areas in which Indian Health Service has responsibility.

non-recognized tribe Indian communities that do not have official government-to-government relations with the U.S. government, because they did not sign a treaty with the U.S., lost their recognized status by termination, or have no executive orders or agreements that require the U.S. government to provide services or to protect their land and resources in a trust relationship.

non-status Indians People in Canada who consider themselves to be Indians but whom the Canadian government does not recognize as Indians under the Indian Act, because they have failed to establish or have lost or abandoned their Indian status rights.

non-treaty Indians Canadian Indian people whose relationship with the government is not affected by any treaties. Non-treaty Indians can be either status or non-status Indians.

Northwest Territories (NWT) Today this term refers to a large Canadian territory (capital city, Yellowknife) north of the 60th parallel. Natives compose a large percentage of the population. Originally (1870), the Northwest Territories referred to most of Canada west of Ontario except British Columbia, including present-day Alberta and Saskatchewan and most of Manitoba.

Northwest Passage As late as the 1790s, Europeans believed there was a short ocean passage in the northern latitudes connecting the Atlantic and Pacific Oceans. Many of the earliest European explorations in northern North America were prompted by this myth.

numeral classifier In linguistics, a grammatical element used in counting, indicating the form or shape of the objects counted.

Nunavut A proposed new territory (now part of the Northwest Territories), which would cover most of Canada north of the treeline. Inuit are the majority of the region's population. The proposal to establish Nunavut was part of an aboriginal land claim.

O

occupation A classification system in which jobs that require similar activities are grouped together into distinct categories.

Oklahoma "Runs" Spectacular one-day chances to legally acquire former Indian land in present-day Oklahoma. Most of the "runs" occurred in the 1890s.

"On or near" The federal regulation that Contract Health Service can be provided only to American Indians residing on a reservation or in a county that borders a reservation.

Oolichan (Eulachon) A small fish (Thaleichthys pacificus) captured in freshwater streams by the Northwest Coast people. Oolichan were especially important as a source of oil.

oral history A historical research method that investigates the past by speaking to people rather than relying on the written word.

outpatient A patient who receives diagnosis or treatment in a clinic or dispensary connected with a hospital but is not admitted as a bed patient. Sometimes used as a synonym for ambulatory.

P

Paleo-Arctic tradition A term used to describe the tools left behind by the first Native Americans, who lived in the arctic regions of Alaska and Canada. The Paleo-Arctic tradition began between 9000 and 8000 B.C. and continued as late as 5000 B.C.

paleo-Indians The ancestors of contemporary Native Americans and the first people to come to North America over fourteen thousand years ago.

Paleo-Plateau tradition A term used to describe the various Archaic period cultures of the Columbia-Fraser Plateau of Washington state and British Columbia. The Paleo-Plateau tradition lasted from 8000 to 3000 B.C.

Papal Bull A decree made by a Catholic Pope. Bulls used to have the force of law within the Roman Catholic Church, but today are considered to be statements of policy only.

patronage Providing jobs in exchange for political services. For example, before 1890 most jobs with the U.S. Indian administration were jobs gained through patronage relations with congressmen and other high government officials.

Penner Report A report prepared in 1983 by a special committee of the House of Commons on Indian self-government in Canada. The report is named after committee chairman, Keith Penner, a member of Parliament for the Liberal party.

peyote A bitter stimulant obtained from the button-like structures of the mescal cactus plant, which some Indian groups use as part of their religious practices. The peyote buttons are taken during ceremonies of the Native American Church, which was officially established in 1918, but began on the Plains as early as the 1860s.

phoneme One of the set of contrasting sound units in a language.

phylum Plural phyla. A group of language families hypothesized to be descended from a single parent language.

pictograph A simplified pictorial representation of a historical occurrence.

Piedmont A region in the southeast United States marked by rolling hills and open valleys located between the relatively flat coastal plain and the more rugged Appalachian Mountains.

Pinto Basin tradition A term describing a series of archaeological hunting and gathering cultures from the Great Basin, dating over the period of 5000 to 1500 B.C.

plenary power The exclusive authority of Congress (as opposed to the states of the Union) to make laws concerning Indian tribes. This special power can be traced to Article I, Section 8 (the "Indian Commerce Clause") of the Constitution. Plenary means full or complete.

policy A statement that outlines the means and philosophy by which a group or government will try to fulfill one or more of its major goals or interests.

polygamy Having more than one spouse at the same time.

potlatch A feast in recognition of important life events, e. g., birth, death, marriage. The giving of a potlatch conferred value, prestige, and honor to all those involved. During a potlatch, or "giveaway," the hosts gave food, clothes, songs, and culturally significant gifts, such as copper engraved valuables, to the guests. The potlatch ceremony was practiced by tribes in the Pacific Northwest. "Giveaways" are similar events held in other regions of North America.

poultice A hot, soft, moist mass, as of flour, herbs, mustard, etc., sometimes spread on cloth, applied to a sore or inflamed part of the body.

preemption The power of the federal government to override state law in fields such as Indian affairs. This power comes from Article VI, Section 2 of the U.S. Constitution (the "Supremacy Clause"), which says federal laws and treaties are "the supreme Law of the Land."

presidio Spanish military post in the American Southwest.

Privy Council (Judicial Committee of the Privy Council) In the British Empire, the Privy Council in London was the final court of appeal from the colonial governors and courts. It was a committee of Peers (titled noblemen) chosen by the Crown (the reigning King or Queen). Until 1949, the Privy Council, in London, England, was the highest court of appeal in Canada and was therefore somewhat analogous to the U.S. Supreme Court.

Proclamation of 1763 A declaration of policy by the British government that reserved the land west of the Appalachian Mountains for Indian use, and restricted English settlements to land east of the divide, or central ridge, of the Appalachians. In Canada, the proclamation provides the basis of English recognition of Indian rights to use and live on their territory, but only at the pleasure of the British Crown, which by this act claimed ownership of all Indian lands.

proto-language The prehistoric parent language from which several historical languages are descended.

Public Law 280 (1953) A congressional act that transferred criminal and civil jurisdiction in Indian country from the federal government to the states of California, Minnesota, Nebraska, Oregon, and Wisconsin (and after 1959 to Alaska). Other states were given the option to assume jurisdiction by legislation. In 1968, PL 280 was amended to require tribal consent to the transfer of jurisdiction.

pueblo A Spanish word for the multi-storied stone or adobe Indian villages of the American Southwest. Also a name used for the Indians who inhabited such communal buildings.

Q/R

radiocarbon dating A technique that measures the natural radioactive content of organic materials, such as charcoal, in order to measure the approximate age of the materials or objects found in archaeological sites.

rancheria A Spanish word applied to the numerous, small Indian reservations of California.

ratification The confirmation of a treaty by the national legislature—in the United States, by the Senate. In most countries, a treaty must be ratified before it becomes law.

red power A term applied to an Indian social movement and a series of protest activities during the 1960s and 1970s.

reduplication In linguistics, repetition of part of a stem, often used to indicate plurality or habitual action.

referenda Referring measures passed upon or proposed by the legislature to the voters for approval or rejection.

registered Indians *See* status Indians.

relocation In 1951, the federal government established the Direct Employment Assistance program to encourage reservation Indians to move to urban areas such as Los Angeles, Chicago, Minneapolis, and Denver. This and subsequent programs came to be known as "relocation" programs.

Removal Act A congressional act passed in 1830 which authorized and funded the peaceful exchange of lands and removal of Indians to Indian Territory, west of the Mississippi River.

repatriation Through court cases and legislative lobbying, tribes have demanded the return of museum- and university-held skeletal remains of Indians and funerary objects for reburial or other appropriate disposition.

reservation/rancheria Lands set aside by U.S. government authority for use and occupation by a group of Indians.

reservation state An area within which the Indian Health Service has responsibilities for providing health care to American Indians or Alaska Natives.

reserve In Canada, land set aside for specific Indian bands. "Indian reserve lands" as defined by the Indian Act. Essentially the same meaning as the U.S. term "reservation." In Canada, legal title is held in trust by the federal Crown in the right of Canada and may not be leased or sold until "surrendered" to the Crown by a referendum by band members.

reserved-rights doctrine A legal theory that Indian communities and governments maintain all rights to self-government, exercise of cultural rights, to religious freedom, rights to land, to water, and other resources, unless Congress expressly takes those rights away.

residual resource The final or remaining course of action for patients seeking medical care from a provider.

restitution Transfer of property or payment of money to prevent an unjust loss from the acts of another.

retrocession A bureaucratic procedure of the Bureau of Indian Affairs that allows Indian communities within PL 280 states (California, Alaska, Wisconsin, Oregon, Nebraska, and Minnesota) to petition the federal government to bar state government regulation of courts and law enforcement on the reservation.

revitalization A social management carried out by a group usually in response to major changes in its society, such as pressures to assimilate. Revitalization attempts to create new culture with beliefs, values, and attitudes that blend some aspects of the old culture with the new living conditions.

Robinson Superior Treaty of 1850 On September 7, 1850, at Sault Ste. Marie, Ontario, the Honorable William B. Robinson of Toronto, Ontario, acting on behalf of the British Crown, met with three chiefs and five principal men representing Michipicoten, Fort William, and Gull River bands of Ojibwa Indians to sign a document referred to as the Robinson Superior Treaty, the first modern Indian treaty in Canada .

According to the treaty, the Ojibwa people surrendered considerable land, and were paid two thousand pounds in English money and allotted three reserves. A similar agreement, referred to as the Robinson Huron Treaty of 1850, removed Indian land claims from the north shore of Lake Huron.

Rose Spring phase A term given by archaeologists to a time period (1500 B.C. to A.D. 500) when hunter and gatherer cultures occupied the region of the Owens Valley of present-day eastern California.

royal prerogative The rights and privileges of a sovereign over subjects independent of both statutes and the courts.

rural Indian An Indian residing in a non-urban area, generally on or near a reservation.

S

sacred objects Specific ceremonial objects needed by Native American religious leaders for the practice of traditional Native American religions.

San Dieguito tradition A distinctive artifact tradition known from present-day California and Nevada and dating to about 8000 to 6000 B.C. The tools of the San Dieguito people show a heavy reliance on hunting, but with some evidence of gathering of wild plants.

scrip A document given to Métis people during the late nineteenth century in order to extinguish aboriginal title. Scrip could be exchanged for money or land.

secular A word referring to the mundane or ordinary and nonreligious aspects or times of everyday life.

sedentary A term that refers to permanent settlement, where the people usually engage in farming for a livelihood and, for the most part, have abandoned hunting or nomadic herding as the mainstay of their economy.

self-determination Indians exercising their right to govern and make decisions affecting their own lives and affairs on their own land. In international law, the right of every "people" to choose its own form of government and control its own future. Since the 1970s, Congress has used this word to describe programs designed to give Indian tribes greater control over the schools, health facilities, and social services on reservations. *See* Indian Self-Determination and Education Assistance Act.

seminars Roman Catholic schools that teach religion and other subjects.

severance tax A tax assessed by a government on mining or petroleum companies when they remove minerals or natural resources from the ground.

Shaker Religion A religious movement that began with the prophet John Slocum, whose death and rebirth in the 1880s started a movement among the native people of Puget Sound. The movement combined many elements of traditional Coast Salish religion with Christianity. It soon spread through the northwest United States.

shaman/shamanism An individual versed in supernatural matters who performed in rituals and was expected to cure the sick, envision the future, and help with hunting and other economic activities. Often, a shaman is a healer who uses spiritual encounters or contacts to enact a cure on the patient. Many shamans deal with ailments that are spiritual rather than physical.

Siouan A large language family that includes Siouan-related languages such as Lakota, Nakota, Dakota, and Crow.

site In archaeology, a location of past cultural activity of defined space with more or less continuous archaeological evidence.

smallpox A highly contagious disease which left survivors with badly scarred skin. Native Americans often died by the thousands because their ancestors had not developed resistance to the infection, which was introduced to North America by Europeans.

smoke shop An Indian-owned store on a reservation that sells cigarettes at a relatively cheap price because state sales tax need not be included.

Snyder Act of 1921 Provided permanent funding authorization for "the general support and civilization of the Indians." To carry out these objectives, the act authorized the Indian Office to provide educational, health, and welfare services to Indian people, to irrigate and make other improvements on Indian lands, and to employ personnel to support these objectives. The Snyder Act signaled a change toward a permanent Indian-federal government relationship.

socialize A process by which an individual learns to adjust to the group by acquiring social behaviors of which the group approves.

Sooner Frontiersmen who illegally squatted on Indian land before the U.S. government had extinguished Indian land claims and title.

sovereignty Deriving from *sovereign*, which means a ruler or king. In international law, being completely independent and not subject to any other ruler or government. The inherent right of a nation to exercise complete and absolute governance over its people and its affairs. In U.S. federal Indian law, sovereignty means having a distinct, but not completely independent government.

specific claim According to Canadian government land claims policy since 1973, an aboriginal claim based on rights set out in treaties, Indian acts, or other legislation.

Spirit Dance In the Northwest Coast, a song and dance performed by an individual who has had a guardian spirit encounter. The Spirit Dances are held in the winter months.

Strait of Georgia tradition An archaeological cultural tradition from the western coastal area of Canada believed to be ancestral to the Coast Salish and other present-day Native American groups of the area. The Strait of Georgia tradition dated from 3000 to 200 B.C.

state-recognized tribes Those Indian communities whose governments and land are officially recognized by their surrounding state government, but are not usually recognized by the federal government as an Indian reservation.

status Indians In Canada, if a person meets the definitional requirements of the Indian Act, they are entitled to be registered on the Indian Register (or Band Membership List) kept by the Department of Indian Affairs in Ottawa. The guidelines for determining status are complex. The criteria are legal rather than based on racial characteristics or blood quantum. All treaty Indians are status Indians, but not all status Indians are treaty Indians. In 1985, Parliament passed an amendment to the Indian Act that allows each native band to adopt its own rules for determining band membership. Many of the new band codes for determining Indian status vary among themselves and with the old rules of the Indian Act.

statute A law enacted by the highest legislature in the nation or state.

statutory Refers to those provisions enacted by law by a legislative body.

stop In linguistics, a consonant produced by shutting off the flow of air momentarily.

subsistence A term that describes a small and localized economy oriented to the production of goods and services primarily for household use, and bound by rules of kinship, sharing, and reciprocity.

Sun Dance An annual world renewal and purification ceremony performed with some variation among many of the northern Plains Indian nations such as the Cheyenne and the Sioux. One striking aspect of the ceremony was the personal sacrifice that some men made by self-torture in order to gain a vision that might provide spiritual insight and knowledge beneficial to the community.

sweat lodge A sacred Indian ceremony involving construction of a lodge made of willow saplings bent to form a dome and covered with animals skins, blankets or canvas tarp. A hole is dug in the middle of the lodge in which hot rocks are placed and water poured over them, often by a medicine man, in a ceremonial way often accompanied by praying and singing. The ceremony can have many purposes including spiritual cleansing and healing.

sweetgrass ceremony A ceremony in which braided sweetgrass is burned and participants "smudge" themselves with the smoke, similar to incense in other religions.

syllabary A type of writing system in which the basic unit represents a sequence of consonant plus vowel, constituting a syllable. In comparison, alphabets have either a consonant, a letter, or a vowel (in English—a, e, i, o u), which compose the basic unit of the writing system, as in English or Latin. The famous Cherokee writing system invented by Sequoia is a syllabary and not an alphabet.

syncretic movements A religious belief system that combines symbols and beliefs from two or more religions. In native North America, there are many native religions that combine elements of traditional religion with Christianity. Some such Indian religious movements are the Delaware Prophet movement of the early 1760s, the Handsome Lake movement beginning in 1799, the Ghost Dances of the 1870s and early 1890s, the ongoing Shaker movement of the Pacific Northwest, and the Native American Church or Peyote cult.

syntax The combination of words into sentences, as contrasted with morphology, the formation of words by combinations of stems, prefixes, and suffixes.

T

termination The policy of Congress in the 1950s and 1960s to withdraw federal trust status from Indian bands, communities and tribes. Those tribes that were "terminated" by an act of Congress no longer functioned as governments that madc their own laws, but instead were placed under state laws.

theocracy A government or society led by religious leaders.

Thule tradition The archaeological culture, dated from A.D. 100 to 1500 and later, defined as the direct ancestral culture of the present-day Inuit throughout the Arctic. The Thule people were hunters skillful at exploiting sea mammals.

trade language (lingua franca) A mixed language used for communication between people of different native languages.

Trail of Tears In the 1830s, a series of forced emigrations by groups of Cherokee, Creek, Seminole, and perhaps some Choctaw, from the Southeast to Indian Territory, present-day Oklahoma, caused by the removal policy.

transitive In linguistics, a characterizing verb that has both subject and direct object, opposite of intransitive.

treaty (1) In Canada, an agreement between Indian peoples and the Canadian government. Some maintain that these treaties are comparable to treaties between independent nations, while others claim they are merely contracts between the government and some of its subjects. Between 1871 and 1923, the Canadian government made twelve numbered treaties with native bands. Since 1923, the Canadian government has stopped using this term in its agreements with aboriginal peoples. (2) A formal agreement between two or more sovereign nations on issues of war, peace, trade, and other relations. Before 1871, the U.S. government ratified about 270 treaties with Indian nations. After 1871, the U.S. government stopped making treaties with Indians. *See* treaties.

treaties Agreements negotiated between two parties, which set out the benefits both sides will receive as a result of one side giving up their title to a territory of land. In Canada, commonly referred to as Modern Treaties or Numbered Treaties. After Canada gained its own constitution under confederation in 1867, the new federal government of Canada signed a series of modern treaties numbered 1 through 11 between 1871 and 1921. Also included as "modern " treaties are the Robinson-Superior and Robinson-Huron treaties of 1850 with the Ojibway of Ontario occupying the north shores of Lake Huron and Lake Superior. The government negotiator, the Honorable William B. Robinson of Toronto is recognized for establishing the "treaty method" of obtaining Indian "title surrenders" to land in return for "treaty rights." The Chippewa and Missassauga Agreements of 1923 were the last formally negotiated Indian treaties in Canada. *See* treaty.

treaty Indian In Canada, descendants of Indians entitled to benefits under the treaties signed by the Crown and specific Indian bands between 1725 and 1921. Those who "took treaty" and surrendered their land rights for specific benefits.

tribal groups A term, especially in British Columbia, for various language and culture groups that reject centralized bureaucracies, whether attached to government or native organizations.

tribal sovereignty The powers of self-government held by Indian communities.

tribe A group of natives sharing a common ancestry, language, culture, and name.

trust Property that is protected from being taxed or sold by the federal government for a period of time and is held in benefit of a trustee. In U.S. Indian affairs, the government holds trust of Indian lands and resources.

trust responsibility The responsibility of the federal government to protect Indian lives and property; to compensate Indians for any loss due to government mismanagement; and, generally, to act in the best interests of Indians. Originally called "guardianship" and sometimes described by lawyers as a "fiduciary duty."

trust status A legal relationship of an Indian person or tribe with the United States, within which the U.S. government has final and broad authority over the actions of individual Indians or over tribal governments.

U

unemployment rate A statistic published by the federal Bureau of Labor Statistics. It is the percent of the labor force without employment. Unemployed persons who have given up their search for work are not counted in this statistic because they are not considered part of the labor force.

unilaterally "On its own," often referring to U.S. government policy when it abandoned a treaty promise without agreement or compensation to an Indian nation.

urban Indian An Indian residing in urban metropolitan areas or cities.

usufructuary (1) In Canada, the inherent right of using and enjoying the natural products of lands (e. g., game, fish, plants, fruits) of which the underlying title belongs to another, usually the Crown. (2) A way of using land, common among Indian farmers and hunters, where land belongs to an individual, clan, or village as long as that group has a history of continual usage of the land, hunting area, or fishing site. Usufruct rights are recognized by others and are lost whenever a group discontinues use.

V

values The generally agreed upon goals, purposes, and issues of importance in a community.

variety A local language variant, referring either to languages of the same family or to dialects of the same language.

velar In linguistics, characterizing consonants produced with the rear part of the tongue. *See* labiovelar.

vision quest A sacred Indian ceremony that involves an individual, often a teenage boy, going to a secluded place to fast (go without food or water) for a period of time (usually a few days) to learn about the spiritual side of himself and possibly have a vision of his spiritual helper, a spirit being who will give him guidance and strength.

voiced In linguistics, a sound pronounced with vibration of the vocal cords.

voiceless In linguistics, a sound pronounced without vibration of the vocal cords.

vowel harmony In linguistics, a process in which vowels change to resemble vowels in nearby grammatical environments.

W

wampum Small, cylindrical, blue and white beads cut from the shell of the quahog, a large Atlantic coast clam. Long strings of wampum were used as trade exchange, while broad, woven "belts" of wampum were used to record treaties among the tribes and, later, with Europeans.

Wapato A plant (Sagittaria latifolia) that grows in shallow lakes and marshy areas. The root was an important source of food for many groups in the Northwest Coast.

wardship According to some legal theory, the relationship between the U.S. government and Indians, where the government has trust responsibility over the affairs and resources of the Indians.

weir A fishing device that operates by blocking off a portion of a stream with a fence-like structure. Migrating fish are then forced to find openings in their weir where the people then capture them.

Westward movement Name given the displacement of Native American peoples by the movement of Americans from the eastern shoreline in the seventeenth century to the West Coast in the nineteenth century.

Woodland period A major time period usually dating from 500 B.C. to A.D. 900. During this period, Native American cultures developed complex ceremonial centers that included construction of large mounds. The Woodland period cultures were the first to practice farming in northeastern North America.

world view The unconscious philosophical outlook held by the members of a society.

General Bibliography

♦ General Studies ♦ Anthropology ♦ Architecture ♦ Art ♦ Atlases ♦ Autobiography ♦ Demography ♦ History ♦ Image/Stereotypes ♦ Land ♦ Legal Status/Laws ♦ Literature and Poetry ♦ Oral Tradition ♦ Policy ♦ Prehistory ♦ Religion ♦ Sociology ♦ Urbanization ♦ Women ♦ Canada

♦ GENERAL STUDIES

Armstrong, Virginia Irving. *I Have Spoken: American History Through the Voices of the Indians*. Athens, OH: Swallow Press, 1971.

Bierhorst, John. *The Mythology of North America*. New York: William Morrow, 1985.

Boas, Franz. *Race, Language, and Culture*. New York: Macmillan, 1940.

Bowden, Henry Warner. *American Indians and Christian Missions*. Chicago: University of Chicago Press, 1981.

Boxberger, Daniel L., ed. *Native North Americans: An Ethnohistorical Approach*. Dubuque, IA: Kendall/Hunt, 1990.

Champagne, Duane. *American Indian Societies: Strategies and Conditions of Political and Cultural Survival*. Cambridge, MA: Cultural Survival, Inc., 1989.

Edmunds, R. David, ed. *American Indian Leaders: Studies in Diversity*. Lincoln: University of Nebraska Press, 1981.

Feest, Christian F. *Indians and Europe: An Interdisciplinary Collection of Essays*. Aachen, Germany: Ed. Herodot, 1987.

Hamilton, Charles, ed. *Cry of the Thunderbird*. Norman: University of Oklahoma Press, 1972.

Leitch, Barbara. *A Concise Dictionary of Indian Tribes of North America*. Algonac, MI: Reference Publications, 1979.

♦ ANTHROPOLOGY

Biolsi, Thomas. *Organizing the Lakota: The Political Economy of the New Deal on the Pine Ridge and Rosebud Reservations*. Tucson: University of Arizona Press, 1992.

Deloria, Vine. *We Talk, You Listen: New Tribes, New Turf*. New York: Macmillan, 1970.

Fowler, Loretta. *Shared Symbols, Contested Meanings: Gros Ventre Culture & History, 1778–1984*. Ithaca, NY: Cornell University Press, 1987.

Lowie, Robert. *Indians of the Plains*. Garden City, NY: American Museum of Natural History, Natural History Press, 1963.

Nabokov, Peter, ed. *Native American Testimony: A Chronicle of Indian-White Relations from Prophecy to the Present, 1492–1992*. New York: Viking, 1991.

Ortiz, Alfonso. *The Tewa World: Space, Time, Being, and Becoming in a Pueblo Society*. Chicago: University of Chicago Press, 1969.

Parker, Arthur. *Parker on the Iroquois*. Syracuse, NY: Syracuse University Press, 1968.

Sando, Joe. *Nee Hemish: A History of Jemez Pueblo*. Albuquerque: University of New Mexico Press, 1982.

———. *Pueblo Nations: Eight Centuries of Pueblo Indian History*. Santa Fe, NM: Clearlight, 1992.

Stands in Timber, John. *Cheyenne Memories*. New Haven, CT: Yale University Press, 1967.

Swanton, John R. *The Indian Tribes of North America*. Washington, DC: Smithsonian Institution Press, 1968.

———. *Indians of the Southeastern United States*. Grosse Pointe, MI: Scholarly Press, 1969.

♦ ARCHITECTURE

Morgan, William N. *Prehistoric Architecture in the Eastern United States*. Cambridge, MA: MIT Press, 1980.

Nabokov, Peter. *Native American Architecture*. New York: Oxford University Press, 1989.

♦ ART

Berlo, Janet C. *The Early Years of Native American Art History*. Seattle: University of Washington Press, 1992.

Brody, J.J. *Anasazi & Pueblo Painting*. Albuquerque: University of New Mexico Press, 1991.

———. *Indian Painters & White Patrons*. Albuquerque: University of New Mexico Press, 1971.

Dockstader, Frederick. *Indian Art in America: The Arts and Crafts of the North American Indian*. Greenwich, CT: New York Graphic Society, 1966.

Feder, Norman. *Two Hundred Years of North American Indian Art*. New York: Praeger, 1971.

Feest, Christian. *Native Arts of North America: The Arts and Crafts of the North American Indian*. New York: Oxford University Press, 1980.

Grant, Campbell. *The Rock Art of the North American Indians: The Imprint of Man*. New York: Thomas Y. Crowell, 1967.

Mathews, Zena Pearlstone and Aldona Jonaitis. *Native North American Art History: Selected Readings*. Palo Alto, CA: Peck Publications, 1982.

Penney, David W. *Art of the American Indian Frontier: The Chandler-Pohrt Collection*. Detroit: Detroit Institute of Arts; Seattle: University of Washington Press, 1992.

Porter, Frank W. III. *The Art of Native American Basketry: A Living Legacy*. Westport, CT: Greenwood Press, 1990.

♦ ATLASES

Coe, Michael, E.P. Benson, and D.R. Snow, eds. *Atlas of Ancient America*. New York: Facts on File, 1986.

Ferguson, Thomas J. *A Zuni Atlas*. Norman: University of Oklahoma Press, 1985.

Goodman, James. *The Navajo Atlas: Environments, Resources, People and History of the Dine Bikeyah*. Norman: University of Oklahoma Press, 1982.

Prucha, Francis Paul. *Atlas of American Indian Affairs*. Lincoln: University of Nebraska Press, 1990.

Sturtevant, William C. *Early Indian Tribes, Culture Areas, & Linguistic Stocks*. Reston, VA: Dept. of Interior, U.S. Geological Survey, 1991.

Tanner, Helen Hornbeck, et al. *Atlas of Great Lakes Indian History*. Norman: University of Oklahoma Press, 1986.

Waldman, Carl. *Atlas of the North American Indian*. New York: Facts on File, 1985.

♦ AUTOBIOGRAPHY

Allen, Elsie. *Pomo Basketmaking: A Supreme Art for the Weaver*. Healdsburg, CA: Naturegraph, 1972.

Bennett, Kay. *Kaibah: Recollection of a Navajo Girlhood*. Los Angeles: Westernlore Press, 1964.

Blowsnake, Sam. *Crashing Thunder: The Autobiography of an American Indian*. Lincoln: University of Nebraska Press, 1983.

Brumble, H. David. *American Indian Autobiography*. Berkeley: University of California Press, 1988.

Campbell, Maria. *Halfbreed*. Toronto: McClelland and Stewart-Bantam, Ltd., 1973.

Cuero, Delfina. *The Autobiography of Delfina Cuero, a Diegueño Indian*. Banning, CA: Malki Museum Press, 1970.

Eastman, Charles Alexander. *From the Deep Woods to Civilization: Chapters in the Autobiography of an Indian*. Lincoln: University of Nebraska Press, 1977.

———. *Indian Boyhood.* Boston: Little, Brown and Co., 1922.

Fitzgerald, Michael Oren. *Yellowtail, Crow Medicine Man and Sun Dance Chief: An Autobiography.* Norman: University of Oklahoma Press, 1991.

Giago, Tim A., Jr. *The Aboriginal Sin: Reflections on the Holy Rosary Indian Mission School.* San Francisco: Indian Historian Press, 1978.

Johnson, Broderick H., ed. *Stories of Traditional Navajo Life and Culture, by Twenty-two Navajo Men and Women.* Tsaile, AZ: Navajo Community College Press, 1977.

Kakianak, Nathan. *Eskimo Boyhood: An Autobiography in Psychosocial Perspective.* Lexington: University Press of Kentucky, 1974.

Krupat, Arnold. *For Those Who Come After: A Study of Native American Autobiography.* Berkeley: University of California Press, 1985.

La Flesche, Francis. *The Middle Five: Indian Schoolboys of the Omaha Tribe.* Lincoln: University of Nebraska Press, 1978.

Lame Deer, John (Fire). *Lame Deer: Seeker of Visions.* New York: Simon and Schuster, 1972.

Left Handed. *Son of Old Man Hat: A Navaho Autobiography.* Lincoln: University of Nebraska Press, 1967.

Leighton, Alexander, and Dorothea Leighton. *Gregorio, the Hand-Trembler: A Psychobiological Personality Study of a Navaho Indian.* Cambridge, MA: Peabody Museum of American Archaeology and Ethnology, Harvard University, 1949.

Mitchell, Frank. *Navajo Blessingway Singer: The Autobiography of Frank Mitchell, 1881–1967.* Tucson: University of Arizona Press, 1978.

Modesto, Ruby. *Not for Innocent Ears: Spiritual Traditions of a Cahuilla Medicine Woman.* Angelus Oaks, CA: Sweetlight Books, 1980.

Scott, Lalla. *Karnee: A Paiute Narrative.* Reno: University of Nevada Press, 1966.

Underhill, Ruth. *Papago Woman.* New York: Holt, Rinehart and Winston, 1979.

Yava, Albert. *Big Falling Snow: A Tewa-Hopi Indian's Life and Times and the History and Traditions of His People.* New York: Crown Publishers, 1978.

♦ DEMOGRAPHY

Cook, Sherburne F. *The Conflict Between the California Indian and White Civilization.* Berkeley: University of California Press, 1976.

Crosby, Alfred W., Jr. *The Columbian Exchange: Biological and Cultural Consequences of 1492.* Westport, CT: Greenwood Press, 1972.

Dobyns, Henry F. *Their Number Become Thinned: Native American Population Dynamics in Eastern North America.* Knoxville, TN: University of Tennessee Press, Newberry Library Center for the History of the American Indian, 1983.

Duffy, John. *Epidemics in Colonial America.* Baton Rouge: Louisiana State University Press, 1953.

Snipp, C. Matthew. *American Indians: The First of this Land.* New York: Russell Sage Foundation, 1989.

Stearn, Esther W. and Allen E. Stearn. *The Effect of Smallpox on the Destiny of the Amerindian.* Boston: Bruce Humphries, Inc., 1945.

Stuart, Paul. *Nations Within a Nation: Historical Statistics of American Indians.* Westport, CT: Greenwood Press, 1987.

Thornton, Russell. *American Indian Holocaust and Survival: A Population History Since 1492.* Norman: University of Oklahoma Press, 1987.

Verano, John W. and Douglas Ubelaker. *Disease and Demography in the Americas.* Washington, DC: Smithsonian Institution Press, 1992.

♦ HISTORY

Calloway, Colin G., ed. *New Directions in American Indian History.* Norman: University of Oklahoma Press, 1988.

Costo, Rupert and Jeanette Henry Costo. *The Missions of California: A Legacy of Genocide.* San Francisco: Indian Historian Press, American Indian Historical Society, 1987.

Debo, Angie. *A History of the Indians of the United States*. Norman: University of Oklahoma Press, 1971.

Gibson, Arrell M. *The American Indian: Prehistory to Present*. Lexington, MA: D. C. Heath, 1980.

Hoxie, Frederick E., ed. *Indians in American History: An Introduction*. Arlington Heights, IL: Harlan Davidson, 1988.

Hurt, R. Douglas. *Indian Agriculture in America: Prehistory to the Present*. Lawrence: University Press of Kansas, 1987.

Josephy, Alvin M., Jr., ed. *America in 1492: The World of the Indian Peoples Before the Arrival of Columbus*. New York: Knopf, 1992.

Kehoe, Alice. *North American Indians: A Comparative Account*. Englewood, NJ: Prentice-Hall, 1981.

Leacock, Eleanore Burke and Nancy O. Lurie, eds. *North American Indians in Historical Perspective*. Prospect Heights, IL: Waveland Press, 1988.

McNickle, D'Arcy. *Native American Tribalism: Indian Survivals and Renewals*. New York: Oxford University Press, 1973.

———. *They Came Here First: The Epic of the American Indian*. New York: Farrar, Straus & Giroux, 1975.

Olson, James S. and Raymond Wilson. *Native Americans in the Twentieth Century*. Provo, UT: Brigham Young University Press, 1984.

Spicer, Edward H. *Cycles of Conquest: The Impact of Spain, Mexico, and the Untied States on the Indians of the Southwest, 1533–1960*. Tucson: University of Arizona Press, 1962.

Wallace, Anthony F. C. *Death and Rebirth of the Seneca*. New York: Knopf, 1969.

♦ IMAGE/STEREOTYPES

Bataille, Gretchen and Charles L.P. Silet, eds. *The Pretend Indians: Images of Native Americans in the Movies*. Ames: Iowa State University Press, 1980.

Berkhofer, Robert F. *The White Man's Indian: Images of the American Indian, from Columbus to the Present*. New York: Knopf, 1978.

Dippie, Brian. *The Vanishing American: White Attitudes and U.S. Indian Policy*. Middletown, CT: Wesleyan University Press, 1982.

Stedman, Raymond W. *Shadows of the Indian: Stereotypes in American Culture*. Norman: University of Oklahoma Press, 1982.

♦ LAND

Confederation of American Indians, comp. *Indian Reservations: A State and Federal Handbook*. Jefferson, NC: McFarland, 1986.

Kickingbird, Kirke and Karen Ducheneaux. *One Hundred Million Acres*. New York: Macmillan, 1973.

McPherson, Robert S. *Sacred Land, Sacred View*. Salt Lake City, UT: Signature Books, 1992.

Vecsey, Christopher and William S. Starna. *Iroquois Land Claims*. Syracuse, NY: Syracuse University Press, 1988.

White, Richard. *Land Use, Environment, and Social Change*. Seattle: University of Washington Press, 1992.

♦ LEGAL STATUS/LAWS

Burton, Lloyd. *American Indian Water Rights and the Limits of the Law*. Lawrence: University Press of Kansas, 1991.

Cohen, Felix. *Felix Cohen's Handbook of Federal Indian Law*. 2d ed. Charlottesville, VA: Michie/Bobbs-Merrill, 1982.

Falkowski, James E. *Indian Law/Race Law*. New York: Praeger, 1992.

Price, H. Marcus, III. *Disputing the Dead: U.S. Law on Aboriginal Remains and Grave Goods*. Columbia: University of Missouri Press, 1991.

Wilkinson, Charles F. *American Indians, Time and Law: Native Societies in a Modern Constitutional Democracy*. New Haven, CT: Yale University Press, 1987.

♦ LITERATURE AND POETRY

Alexie, Sherman. *The Business of Fancydancing: Stories and Poems*. Brooklyn, NY: Hanging Loose Press, 1992.

———. *Old Shirts and New Skins*. Los Angeles: American Indian Studies Center, University of California, 1993.

Allen, Paula Gunn. *Sacred Hoop: Recovering the Feminine in American Indian Traditions*. Boston: Beacon Press, 1986.

———. *Shadow Country*. Los Angeles: American Indian Studies Center, University of California, 1982.

———, ed. *Spider Woman's Granddaughters: Traditional Tales and Contemporary Writing by Native American Women*. New York: Fawcett Columbine, 1990.

———, ed. *Studies in American Indian Literature: Critical Essays and Course Designs*. New York: Modern Language Association of America, 1983.

Brant, Beth. *Food and Spirits: Stories*. Ithaca, NY: Firebrand Books, 1991.

———. *Mohawk Trail*. Ithaca, NY: Firebrand Books, 1985.

Bruchac, Joseph. *Survival This Way: Interviews with American Indian Poets*. Tucson: University of Arizona Press, 1987.

Bush, Barney. *Inherit the Blood: Poetry and Fiction*. New York: Thunder's Mouth Press, 1985.

———. *My Horse and a Jukebox*. Los Angeles: American Indian Studies Center, University of California, 1979.

Dorris, Michael. *A Yellow Raft in Blue Water*. New York: Henry Holt, 1987.

Erdrich, Louise. *Jacklight*. New York: Holt, Rinehart, and Winston, 1984.

———. *Love Medicine: A Novel*. New York: Holt, Rinehart, and Winston, 1984.

———. *Tracks: A Novel*. New York; Henry Holt, 1988.

Hale, Janet Campbell. *The Jailing of Cecelia Capture*. New York: Random House, 1985.

Harjo, Joy. *Secrets from the Center of the World*. Tucson: Sun Tracks, University of Arizona Press, 1989.

———. *She Had Some Horses*. New York: Thunder's Mouth Press, 1983.

Hogan, Linda. *Calling Myself Home*. Greenfield Center, NY: Greenfield Review Press, 1978.

———. *Mean Spirit*. New York: Atheneum, 1990.

Kabotie, Michael. *Migration Tears: Poems about Transitions*. Los Angeles: American Indian Studies Center, University of California, 1987.

Lesley, Craig, ed. *Talking Leaves: Contemporary Native American Short Stories*. New York: Dell, 1991.

Lincoln, Kenneth. *Native American Renaissance*. Berkeley: University of California Press, 1983.

Momaday, N. Scott. *House Made of Dawn*. New York: Harper & Row, 1968.

———. *The Way to Rainy Mountain*. Albuquerque: University of New Mexico Press, 1969.

Ortiz, Simon. *Fightin': New and Collected Stories*. New York: Thunder's Mouth Press, 1983.

———. *From Sand Creek: Rising in This Heart Which Is Our America*. New York: Thunder's Mouth Press, 1981.

———. *A Good Journey*. Tucson: Sun Tracks, University of Arizona Press, 1984.

Rose, Wendy. *The Halfbreed Chronicles and Other Poems*. Los Angeles: West End Press, 1985.

———. *Lost Copper: Poems*. Banning: Malki Museum Press, 1980.

Silko, Leslie Marmon. *Ceremony*. New York: Viking Press, 1977.

———. *Storyteller*. New York: Seaver Books, 1981.

TallMountain, Mary. *The Light on the Tent Wall: A Bridging*. Los Angeles: American Indian Studies Center, University of California, 1990.

Tedlock, Dennis. *The Spoken Word and the Work of Interpretation*. Philadelphia: University of Pennsylvania Press, 1983.

Vizenor, Gerald. *The Heirs of Columbus*. Middleton, CT: Wesleyan University Press, 1991.

———. *Wordarrows: Indians and Whites in the New Fur Trade*. Minneapolis: University of Minnesota Press, 1978.

Walters, Anna Lee. *Ghost Singer: A Novel.* Flagstaff, AZ: Northland Press, 1988.

———. *The Sun Is Not Merciful: Short Stories.* Ithaca, NY: Firebrand Books, 1985.

Welch, James. *The Death of Jim Loney.* New York: Harper & Row, 1979.

———. *Fools Crow.* New York: Viking, 1986.

———. *The Indian Lawyer.* New York: W.W. Norton, 1990.

♦ ORAL TRADITION

Bullchild, Percy. *The Sun Came Down.* San Francisco: Harper & Row, 1985.

Erdoes, Richard and Alfonso Ortiz, eds. *American Indian Myths and Legends.* New York: Pantheon Books, 1984.

Garter Snake. *The Seven Visions of Bull Lodge.* Ann Arbor, MI: Bear Claw Press, 1980.

Margolin, Malcolm, ed. *The Way We Lived: California Indian Reminiscences, Stories, and Songs.* Berkeley, CA: Heyday Books, 1981.

Norman, Howard A., trans. *Wishing Bone Cycle: Narrative Poems from the Swampy Cree Indians.* Santa Barbara, CA: Ross-Erikson, 1982.

Swann, Brian. *Smoothing the Ground: Essays in Native American Oral Literature.* Berkeley: University of California Press, 1983.

♦ POLICY

Castile, George Pierre, and Robert L. Bee. *State and Reservation: New Perspectives on Federal Indian Policy.* Tucson: University of Arizona Press, 1992.

Deloria, Vine, Jr. , ed. *American Indian Policy in the Twentieth Century.* Norman: University of Oklahoma Press, 1985.

Deloria, Vine, Jr. *Behind the Trail of Broken Treaties: An Indian Declaration of Independence.* Austin: University of Texas Press, 1985.

Green, Donald E. and Thomas V. Tonnesen, eds. *American Indians: Social Justice and Public Policy.* Milwaukee: University of Wisconsin System, 1991.

Horsman, Reginald. *Expansion and American Indian Policy, 1783–1812.* East Lansing: Michigan State University Press, 1967.

Joe, Jennie, ed. *American Indian Policy and Cultural Values: Conflict and Accommodation.* Los Angeles: American Indian Studies Center, University of California, 1986.

Josephy, Alvin M., Jr. *Red Power: The American Indians' Fight for Freedom.* New York: American Heritage Press, 1971.

Lyden, Fremont J. and Lyman H. Legters, eds. *Native Americans and Public Policy.* Pittsburgh, PA: University of Pittsburgh Press, 1992.

McNickle, D'Arcy. *Native American Tribalism: Indian Survivals and Renewals.* New York: Oxford University Press, 1973.

Philp, Kenneth R. *John Collier's Crusade for Indian Reform, 1920–1954.* Tucson: University of Arizona Press, 1977.

Prucha, Francis Paul. *Documents of United States Indian Policy.* 2d ed. Lincoln: University of Nebraska Press, 1990.

———. *The Great Father: The U.S. Government and the American Indians.* Abridged ed. Lincoln: University of Nebraska Press, 1986.

Satz, Ronald N. *American Indian Policy in the Jacksonian Era.* Lincoln: University of Nebraska Press, 1975.

Sheehan, Bernard W. *Seeds of Extinction: Jeffersonian Philanthropy and the American Indian.* Chapel Hill: University of North Carolina Press, 1973.

Snipp, Matthew. *Public Policy Impacts on American Indian Economic Development.* Albuquerque: Institute for Native American Development, University of New Mexico, 1988.

Trennert, Robert A., Jr. *Alternative to Extinction: Federal Indian Policy in the Beginnings of the Reservation System, 1846–51.* Philadelphia: Temple University Press, 1975.

Washburn, Wilcomb E. *Red Man's Land/White Man's Law: A Study of the Past and Present Status of the American Indian.* New York: Scribner, 1971.

♦ PREHISTORY

Aveni, Anthony F., ed. *Native American Astronomy.* Austin: University of Texas Press, 1977.

Fowler, Melvin L. *The Cahokia Atlas: A Historical Atlas of Cahokia Archaeology.* Springfield, IL: Illinois Historic Preservation Agency, 1989.

Jennings, Jesse D., ed. *Ancient Native Americans.* San Francisco: W. H. Freeman, 1978.

Jennings, Jesse D. *Prehistory of North America.* New York: McGraw-Hill, 1968.

Snow, Dean R. *The Archaeology of North America. New York: Viking, 1976.*

♦ RELIGION

Beck, Peggy V. and Anna Lcc Walters. *The Sacred: Ways of Knowledge, Sources of Life.* Tsaile, AZ: Navajo Community College Press; Flagstaff: Northland, 1990.

Black Elk. *Black Elk Speaks: Being the Life Story of a Holy Man of the Oglala Sioux.* Lincoln: University of Nebraska Press, 1979.

Coffer, William E. (Koi Hosh). *Spirits of the Sacred Mountains: Creation Stories of the American Indian.* New York: Van Nostrand Reinhold, 1978.

Dozier, Edward P. *Hano: A Tewa Indian Community in Arizona.* New York: Holt, Rinehart and Winston, 1966.

———. *The Hopi-Tewa of Arizona.* Berkeley: University of California Press, 1954.

Fire, John. *Lame Deer: Seeker of Visions.* New York: Simon and Schuster, 1972.

Fools Crow. *Fools Crow.* Garden City, NY: Doubleday, 1979.

Gill, Sam D. *Native American Religions: An Introduction.* Belmont, CA: Wadsworth, 1982.

Hittman, Michael, for the Yerington Paiute Tribe. *Wovoka and the Ghost Dance: A Sourcebook.* Carson City, NV: Grace Dangberg Foundation, 1990.

Hultkrantz, Ake. *Native Religions of North America: The Power of Visions and Fertility.* San Francisco: Harper & Row, 1987.

McLoughlin, William, Walter H. Conser, Jr., and Virginia Duffy McLoughlin. *The Cherokee Ghost Dance: Essays on the Southeastern Indians, 1789–1861.* Macon, GA: Mercer, 1984.

Mooney, James. *The Ghost-Dance Religion and the Sioux Outbreak of 1890.* Lincoln: University of Nebraska Press, 1991.

Powers, William K. *Oglala Religion.* Lincoln: University of Nebraska Press, 1977.

Sullivan, Lawrence E., ed. *Native American Religions: North America.* New York: Macmillan, 1987.

Vecsey, Christopher, ed. *Handbook of American Indian Religious Freedom.* New York: Crossroads, 1991.

Zolbrod, Paul, trans. *Dine Bahane':The Navajo Creation Story.* Albuquerque: University of New Mexico Press, 1984.

♦ SOCIOLOGY

Champagne, Duane. *Social Order and Political Change: Constitutional Governments Among the Cherokee, the Choctaw, the Chickasaw, and the Creek.* Stanford, CA: Stanford University Press, 1992.

Guillemin, Jeanne. *Urban Renegades: The Cultural Strategy of American Indians.* New York: Columbia University Press, 1975.

Thornton, Russell. *We Shall Live Again: The 1879 and 1890 Ghost Dance Movements as Demographic Revitalization.* Cambridge: Cambridge University Press, 1986.

Weibel-Orlando, Joan. *Indian Country, L.A.: Maintaining Ethnic Community in Complex Society.* Urbana: University of Illinois Press, 1991.

White, Richard. *Roots of Dependency: Subsistence, Environment, and Social Change among the Choctaws, Pawnees, and Navajos.* Lincoln: University of Nebraska Press, 1983.

♦ URBANIZATION

Cook, Sherburne F. *The Population of the California Indians, 1796–1970.* Berkeley: University of California Press, 1976.

Gunther, Erna *Indian Life on the Northwest Coast of North America, as Seen by the Early Explorers and Fur Traders During the Last Decades of the Eighteenth Century.* Chicago: University of Chicago Press, 1972.

♦ WOMEN

Albers, Patricia and Beatrice Medicine. *The Hidden Half: Studies of Plains Indian Women.* Washington, DC: University Press of America, 1983.

Bataille, Gretchen M. and Kathleen M. Sands. *American Indian Women, Telling Their Lives.* Lincoln: University of Nebraska Press, 1984.

Crow Dog, Mary and Richard Erdoes. *Lakota Woman.* New York: Grove Weidenfeld, 1990.

Green, Rayna, ed. *That's What She Said: Contemporary Poetry and Fiction by Native American Women.* Bloomington: Indiana University Press, 1984.

Landes, Ruth. *The Ojibwa Woman.* New York: Columbia University Press, 1938.

Spittal, W. G., ed. *Iroquois Women: An Anthology.* Ohswekan, ON: Iroqrafts, 1990.

♦ CANADA

Adams, Howard. *Prison of Grass: Canada from the Native Point of View.* Rev. ed. Saskatoon, SK: Fifth House, 1989.

Barron, F. Laurie and James B. Waldram, eds. *1885 and After: Native Society in Transition.* Regina, SK: University of Regina, Canadian Plains Research Center, 1986.

Boldt, Menno and J. Anthony Long, eds. *The Quest for Justice: Aboriginal Peoples and Aboriginal Rights.* Toronto: University of Toronto Press, 1985.

Brown, George and Ron Maguire. *Indian Treaties in Historical Perspective.* Ottawa, ON: Research Branch, Dept. of Indian and Northern Affairs, 1979.

Brown, Jennifer S.H. *Strangers in Blood: Fur Trade Company Families in Indian Country.* Vancouver: University of British Columbia Press, 1980.

Carter, Sarah. *Lost Harvests: Prairie Indian Reserve Farmers and Government Policy.* Montreal, PQ: McGill-Queen's University Press, 1990.

Darnell, Regna, and Michael Foster. *Native North American Interaction Patterns.* Quebec: Canadian Museum of Civilization, National Museums of Canada, 1988.

Dewdney, Selwyn H. *They Shared to Survive: the Native Peoples of Canada.* Toronto: Macmillan of Canada, 1975.

Dickason, Olive. *Canada's First Nations: A History of Founding Peoples from Earliest Times.* Norman: University of Oklahoma Press, 1992.

———. *The Myth of the Savage: And the Beginnings of French Colonialism in the Americas.* Edmonton: University of Alberta Press, 1984.

Getty, Ian A.L. and Antoine S. Lussier. *As Long as the Sun Shines and Water Flows: A Reader in Canadian Native Studies.* Vancouver: University of British Columbia Press, 1983.

Grant, John W. *Moon of Wintertime: Missionaries and the Indians of Canada in Encounter Since 1534.* Toronto: University of Toronto Press, 1984.

Grey Owl. *A Book of Grey Owl: Pages from the Writings of Wa-sha-quon-asin.* Toronto: Macmillan of Canada, 1964.

Harris, R. Cole, ed. *Historical Atlas of Canada: From the Beginning to 1800.* Toronto: University of Toronto Press, 1987.

Hodge, Frederick Webb. *Handbook of Indians of Canada.* New York: Kraus Reprint, 1969.

Jenness, Diamond. *The Indians of Canada.* 7th ed. Toronto: University of Toronto Press, 1977.

King, Thomas, ed. *All My Relations: An Anthology of Contemporary Canadian Native Fiction.* Norman: University of Oklahoma Press, 1992.

Little Bear, Leroy and Menno Boldt, eds. *Pathways to Self-Determination.* Toronto: University of Toronto Press, 1984.

Long, J. Anthony, Menno Boldt, and Leroy Little Bear, eds. *Governments in Conflict?: Provinces and Indian Nations in Canada.* Toronto: University of Toronto Press, 1988.

Lowes, Warren. *Indian Giver: A Legacy of North American Native Peoples.* Penticon, BC: Theytus Books, 1986.

McMillan, Allan D. *Native Peoples and Cultures of Canada.* Vancouver, BC: Douglas and McIntyre, 1988.

Miller, David R., et al. *The First Ones: Readings in Indian/Native Studies.* Craven, SK: Saskatchewan Indian Federated College, 1992.

Miller, James Rodger. *Skyscrapers Hide the Heavens: A History of Indian-White Relations in Canada.* Rev. ed. Toronto: University of Toronto Press, 1991.

Miller, J.R., ed. *Sweet Promises: A Reader on Indian-White Relations in Canada.* Toronto: University of Toronto Press, 1991.

Morrison, R. Bruce and C. Roderick Wilson. *Native Peoples: The Canadian Experience.* Toronto: McClelland and Stewart, 1986.

Morrisseau, Norval. *Legends of My People, the Great Ojibway.* Toronto: Ryerson Press, 1965.

Pelletier, Wilfred and Ted Poole. *No Foreign Land: The Biography of a Northern American Indian.* New York: Pantheon Books, 1974.

Perreault, Jeanne and Sylvia Vance, eds. *Writing the Circle: Native Women of Western Canada: An Anthology.* Norman: University of Oklahoma Press, 1993.

Peterson, Jacqueline and Jennifer S.H. Brown, eds. *The New Peoples: Being and Becoming Métis in North America.* Lincoln: University of Nebraska Press, 1985.

Petrone, Penny. *Native Literature in Canada: From the Oral Tradition to the Present.* Toronto: Oxford University Press, 1990.

Price, John A. *Indians of Canada: Cultural Dynamics.* Scarborough, ON: Prentice-Hall of Canada, 1979.

Ray, Arthur J. *Indians in the Fur Trade: Their Role as Trappers, Hunters, and Middlemen in the Lands Southwest of Hudson Bay, 1660–1870.* Toronto: University of Toronto Press, 1974.

Redbird, Duke. *We are Métis: A View of the Development of a Native Canadian People.* Willowdale, ON: Ontario Métis & Non Status Indian Association, 1980.

Smith, Donald B. *Sacred Feathers: the Reverend Peter Jones (Kahkewaquonaby) & the Mississauga Indians.* Lincoln: University of Nebraska Press, 1987.

Tennant, Paul. *Aboriginal Peoples and Politics: The Indian Land Question in B.C.* Vancouver: University of British Columbia Press, 1990.

Trigger, Bruce G. *Natives and Newcomers: Canada's "Heroic Age" Reconsidered.* Montreal: McGill-Queen's University Press, 1985.

Waldram, James B. and John D. O'Neil. *Native Studies Review: Native Health Research in Canada.* Saskatoon: Native Studies Dept., University of Saskatchewan, 1989.

Weaver, Sally M. *Making Canadian Indian Policy: The Hidden Agenda, 1968–70.* Toronto: University of Toronto Press, 1981.

Illustrations

Chronology: *p. 2:* Mesa Verde Cliff Palace (courtesy of Daniel Rogers); *p. 3:* North America Time Line; *p. 4:* A woolly mammoth, one of the late Pleistocene megafauna species hunted by Paleo-Indians (courtesy of Jesse D. Jennings); *p. 5:* Map of North America showing geographical regions and locations; *p. 6:* Dog pulling travois. Dogs were domesticated by Native people as far back as 10,000 B.C. Paleo Indians often trained dogs to pull loads during their seasonal migrations (courtesy of Lori Cooper); *p. 7:* A monolithic stone axe from Georgia engraved with Southeastern Ceremonial Complex iconography (catalogue number 317614, National Museum of Natural History, Department of Anthropology, Smithsonian Insititution); *p. 12:* An early Colonial drawing of an Indian town in the Southeast (courtesy of American Heritage Press); *p. 13:* The circular "beehive" house used by the ancestors of the modern-day Caddo and Wichita. Dwellings of this type, averaging thirty-five feet in diameter, were ideal for the sedentary Caddo, providing comfortable weatherproof living quarters, warm in the winter and cool in the summer (courtesy of Caddoans Mounds State Historic Site, Texas); *p. 15:* The town of Secota, in present-day Beaufort County, North Carolina, was engraved by De Bry in the seventeenth century to illustrate the village life of peoples he met. This drawing and those of other settlements visited by early English observers give a visual idea of the lifeways that developed eight hundred years earlier throughout the Southeast and Midwest at the beginning of the Mississippian period; *p. 16:* Pottery of the Casa Grandes people (catalogue number 323868, Department of Anthropology, Smithsonian Institution); *p. 17:* Pueblo Bonito at Chaco Canyon in the present-day Southwest (courtesy of Mark Nohl, NM Economics & Tourism, Dept., Joseph M. Montoya Building, 100 St. Francis Drive, Santa Fe, NM 87503); *p. 20:* "Proceedings of the Floridians in deliberating on important affairs." Drawing by Le Moyne, engraving from T. de Bry, *America*, Part II, 1591, plate XXIX (courtesy of American Heritage Publishing Co.); *p. 21:* "Pocahontas saving the life of Captain John Smith, from T. de Bry *America*, Part XIII, 1634, page *37* (courtesy of American Heritage Publishing Co.); *p. 22:* "Huron dancing ceremony to cure sickness" from Champlain, *Voyages et descouvertures*, Paris, 1620 (courtesy of American Heritage Publishing Co.); *p. 24:* Native Nations and Confederacies of New England (courtesy of Bruce Johansen and John Kahionhes Fadden); *p. 25:* Map of Virginia by Ralph Hall, 1636 (courtesy of American Heritage Publishing Co.); *p. 27:* Walpi, an ancient Hopi Pueblo village (courtesy of Owen Seumptewa); *p. 28:* The restored church at St. Ildefonso Pueblo (courtesy of Mark Nohl, NM Economics & Tourism, Dept., Joseph M. Montoya Building, 100 St. Francis Drive, Santa Fe, NM 87503; *p. 29:* Iroquois conference, 1753 (drawing by John Kahionhes Fadden); *p. 30:* Early colonists often observed Native societies (courtesy John Kahionhes Fadden); *p. 33:* Hendrick, Abraham, and Franklin at the Albany Conference, 1754 (courtesy of John Kahionhes Fadden); *p. 35:* On 11 June, 1776, an Onondaga sachem gave John Hancock an Iroquois name at Independence Hall (drawing by John Kahionhes Fadden); *p. 37:* On May 2, 1786, Cornplanter addressed

Congress in New York City (drawing by John Kahionhes Fadden); *p. 42:* California Paiute Indian family at campfire (courtesy of the Palmquist Collection); *p. 43:* California Mission Indians making basket and hair rope (courtesy of Frank Wood's Picture Bank, Alexandria, VA); *p. 45:* Reception of Indians at the White House (courtesy of Frank Wood's Picture Bank, Alexandria, VA); *p. 46:* Scene of Indians hunting buffalo, painted on buffalo skin (courtesy of the National Museum of the American Indian, Smithsonian Institution); *p. 47:* Sioux woman cutting buffalo meat in hunting camp (courtesy of the National Park Service); *p. 48:* Arapaho family cooking dinner (courtesy of Department of the Army, catalogue number P3042); *p. 49:* Scene shortly after Wounded Knee Massacre,1890 (courtesy of the National Museum of Natural History); *p. 50:* Cartoon criticizing mismanagement of Indian affairs by politically appointed Indian agents (courtesy of Media Projects); *p. 51:* Cartoon criticizing Department of Interior management of Indian affairs (courtesy of Media Projects); *p. 53:* Indian airmen performing a mock Indian dance for their fellow servicemen during World War II (courtesy of the Archives Trust Fund); *p. 55:* Myra Dorothy Brown (Arapaho) died July 11, 1991 at the age of 89. Her name as a young woman was Yeiy or Otter (courtesy of Sara Wiles); *p. 55:* Nooksack tribal gathering and salmon bake to discuss fishing rights, Deming, Wash., 1970 (courtesy of Stephen Lehmer); *p. 60:* Members of the Iroquois League protesting for their rights to cross U. S.-Canadian Border in accordance with the 1794 Jay Treaty, July 1969 (courtesy of the Buffalo and Erie County Historical Society.; *p. 61:* Desirae Caldwell writing on chalkboard (courtesy of Mike McClure); *p. 62:* Alcatraz Island declaration by Indians of All Tribes (courtesy of Stephen Lehmer); *p. 63:* Powwow singers, Alcatraz Island (courtesy of Stephen Lehmer); *p. 63:* Puyallup Indian arrested for protesting violation of treaty fishing rights (courtesy of Stephen Lehmer); *p. 64:* Indians protesting discrimination in hiring at the Bureau of Indian Affairs office in Denver, Colorado, 1970 (courtesy of the Denver Public Library, Western History Department); *p. 65:* Taos Pueblo (courtesy of Mark Nohl, New Mexico Economic & Tourism Department, Joseph M. Montoya Building, 100 St. Francis Drive, Santa Fe, NM 87503); *p. 66:* Title VII (Indian Education) Gifted and Talented program provides an electronic video microscope for 3–6 classes. Patricia C'Hair and Franklin Martel show how the TV monitor can display microscopic views to large groups (courtesy of Mike McClure); *p. 66:* Hopi elder with woman and child outside of Hopi pueblo (courtesy of Owen Seumptewa); *p. 68:* Inuit blanket toss, Barrow, Alaska (courtesy of Chris Wooley); *p. 69:* Umiaq frame, Point Hope, Alaska (courtesy of Chris Wooley); *p. 72:* Hopi Bureau of Indian Affairs police officers and a tribal Ranger placed an elderly Navajo man in custody for allegedly trespassing and interfering with the Hopi BIA fencing crew in the Hopi partitioned lands. The incident is about the ongoing Navajo and Hopi land dispute problems (courtesy of Paul Natonabah, *Navajo Times*); *p. 72:* Wyoming Indian High School students Marla Jimerson and Sonya Willow (courtesy of Mike McClure); *p. 74:* Albert Begay holds his daughter, 15-month-old Devona, after she was given a measle shot by nurse Ron Garnanez at the Shiprock (NM) Indian Hospital (courtesy of Paul Natonabah, *Navajo Times*); *p. 76:* Cutting maktak (whale blubber) for distribution. Barrow, Alaska. (courtesy of Chris Wooley); *p. 77:* Indians participate in The Longest Walk, a protest to bring attention to broken treaties and ill treatment of Indian people. 1978 (courtesy of Random House Inc.); *p. 79:* A Sun Dance at Pine Ridge, a Sioux reservation in southern South Dakota (courtesy of Stephen Lehmer); *p. 80:* The sacred pole is the center of all Sun Dances. Crow Sun Dancers are preparing to approach the sacred center (courtesy of Theresa Fiedor Mock); *p. 80:* Indian Maiden, Lame Deer, Montana. Northern Cheyenne Indian Reservation (courtesy of Lori Cooper); *p. 81:* Poster of Indian Child Welfare conference at the University of California, Los Angeles; *p. 85:* Crow Indians protesting state fish and game regulations (courtesy of Theresa Fiedor Mock); *p. 86:* Medals won by Jim Thorpe in 1912 Olympic Games returned to the Thorpe family in 1982 (courtesy of the Bettman Archive); *p. 87:* George Kelly, Sr. of Beclabito, New Mexico, was among hundreds of Navajo who converged at the Shiprock High School gymnasium to hear attorney Stewart Udall explain the recently approved U.S. Congress Radiation Exposure Compensation Act. Kelly, who uses an oxygen tank twenty-four hours a day to help with his breathing, was diagnosed as having a lung disease due to working in the unventilated uranium mines for thirty years (courtesy of Paul Natonabah, *Navajo Times*); *p. 89:* Coolidge Dam on San Carlos Apache Reservation, Arizona (courtesy of Stephen Lehmer); *p. 90:* A Cherokee woman puts the finishing touches on a basket at the Oconaluftee Living Village, where tourists may view traditional Cherokee life (courtesy of Thomas C. Donnelly); *p. 93:* Returning from seal hunt. Barrow, Alaska (courtesy of Chris Wooley); *p. 94:* Boy's Mother (played by Sherice Guina) sings to boy after Lord of the Sun sent a spark of life to earth (where the boy was conceived). Pueblo Indian tale, "Arrow to the Sun," is portrayed by Wyoming Indian Elementary School students in class play (courtesy of Mike McClure); *p. 98:* Martin Gutierrez, 12, looks on as Baudelio Gutierrez, 13, shows their grandfather Thomas Brown Sr., 78, some of the math textbooks during Grandparent's Day activities at Wyoming Indian Middle School (courtesy of Mike McClure); *p. 99:* Indian students march during "American Indian Heritage Month" (courtesy of

Mike McClure); *p. 100:* Daisy Hooee famous Hopi craftsperson passes on knowledge to the next generation (courtesy of Stephen Lehmer); *p. 101:* The Navajo Nation officially welcomed home all war veterans and the Navajo service men and women that served in the Persian Gulf War during Operation Desert Storm. Approximately 450 Navajo service personnel served in the Gulf (courtesy of Paul Natonabah, *Navajo Times*); *p. 102:* Window Rock Elementary students perform a Navajo Gourd Dance as part of their demonstration and skill in traditional and culture category during Native American Indian Day (courtesy of Paul Natonabah, *Navajo Times*); *p. 104:* In order to cement a trade alliance, Champlain joined Huron and Algonquin raids on the Iroquois in 1609. This was the most successful of several raids that Champlain joined (courtesy of the National Library of Canada, Rare Book Collection/ Bibliotheque Nationale du Canada, Collection des livres rares); *p. 105: Indian Trading Furs*, 1785, by C. W. Fefferys. In almost every region in Canada early Native Euro-Canadian interaction was based on the mutually beneficial fur trade. In this eighteenth-century engraving, an Indian examines a gun he is about to buy. Natives proved to be skillful traders throughout the fur trade era (courtesy of the National Archives of Canada; *p. 108:* Interior of Inuit house (courtesy of American Heritage Press); *p. 109:* Inuit man ice fishing (courtesy of Tessa Macintosh, NT government); *p. 112:* Louis Riel's execution in 1885 vaulted him to the status of martyr for the Métis cause. He remains one of the most controversial figures in Candadian history (courtesy of the National Archives of Canada, C18084); *p. 114:* Indian treaty area in Canada. Maps by Brian McMillan from *Native Peoples and Cultures of Canada* by Alan D. McMillan, 1988, published by Douglas & McIntyre. Reprinted by permission; *p. 116 :* Two Inuit fishing in a traditional manner (courtesy of Tessa Macintosh, NT government); *p. 118:* A women's sewing group in a village in the Northwest Territory (courtesy of Tessa Macintosh, NT government); *p. 119:* Coppermine kids, Northwest Territory, winter celebrations (courtesy of Tessa Macintosh, photo by Joanne Irons, NT government); *p. 125:* Indians gather at the home of Grace McCarthy, Human Resources Minister, to protest the British Columbia government's child welfare policies. During the 1980s, Indians fought to take control of a wide range of government services as part of their claim to their right to self-government (courtesy of *Vancouver Sun*-Ken Oakes, October 1980); *p. 127:* Indian chiefs open the first minister's conference on aboriginial issues, March 1983. This conference, guaranteed by the 1982 Constitution, marked the first time that aboriginals were given full participation at constitutional conferences (courtesy of Canadian Press, *Globe and Mail*, March 17,1983); *p. 131:* Dene girl at Blanchford Lake Lodge Springs Camp, Quinzee buildings and snowshoes (courtesy of Tessa Macintosh, NT government); *p. 133:* Charlie Ugyuk, an Inuit carver, carving soapstone, Northwest Territory (courtesy of Tessa Macintosh, NT government); *p. 133:* Inuit hunters in the Canadian North; *p. 134:* Repulse Bay, Inuit street scene (courtesy of Tessa Macintosh, NT government).

Demography: *p. 190:* Storing crops in the public granary. Many of the islands produce an abundance of fruits. These are gathered twice a year, carried home in canoes, and stored in low and roomy granaries, built of stones and earth and thickly roofed with palm branches and a kind of soft earth. Drawings by John White and Jacques Le Moyne and engraved by Theodore de Bry (courtesy of American Heritage Press); *p. 192:* Kiva at San Juan Pueblo (courtesy of Mark Nohl, NM Economics & Tourism, Dept., Joseph M. Montoya Building, 100 St. Francis Drive, Santa Fe, NM 87503); *p. 193:* Taos Pueblo (courtesy of Mark Nohl, NM Economics & Tourism, Dept., Joseph M. Montoya Building, 100 St. Francis Drive, Santa Fe, NM 87503); *p. 196:* Construction of fortified towns among the Floridians. Drawing by Le Moyne, engraving from Theodore de Bry, *America*, Part II, 1591, plate XXX (courtesy of the American Heritage Press); *p. 201:* Crow Tipis. In the eighteenth century, the Crow were migrating and living throughout the northern Plains area, where they followed the buffalo herds for their sustenance. They had divided into two major groups; the mountain and river Crow (courtesy of Theresa Fiedor Mock); *p. 202:* Mandan Earth Lodge (courtesy of Nebraska State Historical Society); *p. 205:* Homelands of Indians who were forced to migrate to Indian territory in present day Kansas and Oklahoma (courtesy of Duane Champagne); *p. 208:* Map of Indian Territory before 1854 (courtesy of D. C. Heath and Company); *p. 211:* Plains Indian Squaw Dance, 1893 (courtesy of the South Dakota Historical Society); *p. 214:* Fort Niabrara in Nebraska. Plains Indians performing grass dance (courtesy of the South Dakota Historical Society); *p. 215:* Union Pacific Railroad Construction. Cheyenne Indians hunting buffalo near the newly laid tracks and telegraph lines (courtesy of Utah State Historical Society); *p. 218:* Indian Land Claims: Adjudicated Areas. This map is based on "Indian Land Areas Judicially Established," as published in the *Final Report*, Indian Claims Commission, 1978, and published by permission of the University of New Mexico Press (Sutton, 1985). This map does not show the geographic areas of cases adjudicated by the U.S. Claims Court (courtesy of Imre Sutton); *p. 220:* Indian Population Distribution by Counties: 1910. This map portrays the distribution of Indians in the contiguous forty-eight states for both reservations and urban centers, but relies on countywide data. Used with permission of the University of Nebraska Press and Francis Prucha (1990).

Base map by Department of Geography, University of Maryland; *p. 221:* Indian Population by Counties and Standard Metropolitan Statistical Areas, 1980. This map portrays distributions of Indians as in the 1910 edition, but includes Standard Metropolitan Statistical Areas (SMSAs). Base map by Department of Geography, University of Maryland, 5401 Wilkens Ave. Baltimore, MD 21228 (Reprinted from the *Atlas of American Indian Affairs*, by Francis Paul Prucha, by permission of the University of Nebraska Press. Copyright 1990 by the University of Nebraska Press); *p. 224*; Native Language Families of Canada, showing approximate locations at time of European contact. Maps by Brian McMillan from *Native Peoples and Cultures of Canada* by Alan D. McMillan, 1988, published by Douglas & McIntyre. Reprinted by permission.; *p. 226:* Ojibwa camp on Lake Huron, 1845. Painting by Paul Kane from his travels in the 1840s (courtesy of Royal Ontario Museum, Toronto, Ontario, Canada); *p. 229:* Assiniboine Indians hunting bison. Painting by Paul Kane from his travels in the 1840s (courtesy of Royal Ontario Museum, Toronto, Ontario, Canada); *p. 236:* Métis bison hunt near Fort Garry in 1846. Painting by Paul Kane from his travels in 1840s (courtesy of Royal Ontario Museum, Toronto, Ontario, Canada); *p. 240:* Larry Pierre of the Okanagan on the occasion of the First Nations Constitutional Conference, 1980, demanding Native participation in constitutional tasks (courtesy of Canapress Photo Service, photo by Rod MacIvor).

Major Culture Areas: *p. 246:* Contemporary Indian tribes of the northeastern United States; *p. 247:* Key to Tribal Territories (courtesy of the Government Printing Office, Washington, DC); *p. 249:* Iroquois false face dancers performed healing ceremonies for members of the tribe (courtesy of National Museum of the American Indian); *p. 251:* Anishnabe man and woman gather wild rice from canoe in Minnesota (courtesy of the Minnesota Historical Society); *p. 255:* Contemporary southeastern tribes; *p. 260:* Christy Godwin O'Barr, Poarch Creek Indian Princess in 1987, sings at 1987 Thanksgiving powwow (courtesy of Elizabeth D. Purdum, used by permission from *Indians of the Southeastern United States in the Late 20th Century*, edited by J. Anthony Paredes, 1992, The University of Alabama); *p. 262:* Evajean Felihkatubbee, Choctaw Indian woman, cleaning basket; *p. 265:* Dedication of new Poarch Creek Tribal Center, April 1987. Poarch Creek elder gives opening blessing at the ceremony (courtesy of Elizabeth D. Purdum, used by permission from *Indians of the Southeastern United States in the Late 20th Century*, edited by J. Anthony Paredes, 1992, The University of Alabama); *p. 266:* Contemporary southwestern tribes; *p. 267:* Hopi child clown (courtesy of Owen Seumptewa); *p. 270:* A middle-aged Navajo woman stands next to her traditional earthen hogan in Tuba City, Arizona (courtesy of Paul Natonabah, *Navajo Times*); *p. 271:* Navajo medicine man Albert Yazzie chats with Navajo Education Center staff after performing a Navajo Protection Way ceremony for Navajo servicemen and women who were involved in the Persian Gulf war with Iraq (courtesy of Paul Natonabah, *Navajo Times*); *p. 272:* Matachine dancers at San Juan Pueblo (courtesy of Mark Nohl, NM Economics & Tourism Dept., Joseph M. Montoya Building, 100 St. Francis Drive, Santa Fe, NM 87503); *p. 275:* San Ildefonso Pueblo feast day (courtesy of Mark Nohl, NM Economics & Tourism, Dept., Joseph M. Montoya Building, 100 St. Francis Drive, Santa Fe, NM 87503); *p. 276:* Contemporary Plains Indian tribes; *p. 281:* Blackfeet residence with sweat lodge and canvas lodge in foreground, Blackfeet Reservation, Montana (courtesy of Ken Blackbird); *p. 283:* Kicking Women Singers at the North American Indian Days, Browning, Montana (courtesy of Ken Blackbird); *p. 284:* Mosquito Run, Milk River Indian Days, August 1986, Fort Belknap Agency, Montana (courtesy of Ken Blackbird); *p. 286:* Contemporary Northwest Coast Indian tribes; *p. 287:* The inside of a house at Nootka Sound, from the Cook Expedition, 1778 (courtesy of John Webber, artist. Special Collections Division, University of Washington Libraries, Negative N. NA 3918); *p. 289:* Cedar house, Dundas Island, British Columbia (courtesy of Chris Wooley); *p. 291:* Native fashion show, Prince George, British Columbia (courtesy of Chris Wooley); *p. 293:* Chief Shake's House at Wrangell, about the turn of the twentieth century; *p. 294:* Contemporary Alaska Native tribes; *p. 295:* Major languages of Alaska Natives (courtesy of Alaska Native Language Center); *p. 297:* Inuit children, Barrow, Alaska (courtesty of Tessa Macintosh); *p. 302:* Contemporary Oklahoma Indian tribes. (courtesy of Duane Champagne); *p.303:* Indian Territory, removal to 1855. Reprinted from *Atlas of American Indian Affairs*, by Francis Paul Prucha, by permission of the University of Nebraska Press. Copyright 1990 by the University of Nebraska Press); *p. 304:* Indian Territory, 1855–66 Reprinted from *Atlas of American Indian Affairs*, by Francis Paul Prucha, by permission of the University of Nebraska Press. Copyright 1990 by the University of Nebraska Press); *p. 305:* Indian Territory, 1866–89. Reprinted from *Atlas of American Indian Affairs*, by Francis Paul Prucha, by permission of the University of Nebraska Press. Copyright 1990 by the University of Nebraska Press); *p. 310:* Ponca Indian powwow near Ponca City, Oklahoma (courtesy of Stephen Lehmer); *p. 313:* Contemporary Rocky Mountain Indian tribes; *p. 316:* The prophet Wovoka (seated) in his later years (courtesy of the Nevada State Historical Society); *p. 320:* Nii'eihii No'eiihi', or the Eagle Drum, is the official ceremonial and social drum group of the Arapaho tribe. Their presence is required at any large gathering. Seated front left is Helen Cedartree, a noted elder of the Tribe. Her Arapaho name is appropriately Tei'betebii or Strong Old Woman. Taken at the annual Ethete (Wyoming) Celebration Powwow (courtesy of Sara Wiles); *p. 321:* Ben Goggles was in his 70s when he died in 1978. He was the father of ten daughters and the head of the Arapaho Sun Dance for many years. His Arapaho name was Hoonino' or Quill (courtesy of Sara Wiles); *p. 322:* Cleone Thunder was born in April 1903. She lived most of her life in the Ethete (Wyoming) Area, except for a few years in Oklahoma. She has four children and has not yet counted all of her great-great-grandchildren. Her Arapaho name, Hiisei Nouuceh or Woman Running out of the Lodge, was given to her by her father when she was a baby. It commemorated a brave Crow woman who ran from her tipi holding a baby and faced attacking Arapaho warriors. The woman shouted, "You can do anything with me, I have just given birth" (courtesy of Sara Wiles); *p. 323:* Contemporary California Indian tribes; *p. 324:* The traditional tribal areas of the Indians of California; *p. 328:* Spring Rancheria (Cahuilla), c. 1886 (courtesy of Historic Resource Department, Riverside, CA); *p. 329:* Sensioni Cibimoat, basket maker from Warner's Ranch, 1903 (courtesy of Los Angeles City Library); *p. 330:* Gabrielino, traditional homes, Mission San Gabriel (courtesy of Los Angeles City Library); *p. 331:* Ramona Lugu, Cahuilla, at her home (courtesy of Los Angeles City Library); *p. 333:* Indian protesters in prison courtyard on Alcatraz Island (courtesy of Leroy Seidel); *p. 333:* Sign pointing to Pit River Nation, 1973 (courtesy of Stephen Lehmer); *p. 338:* Indians demonstrating in the early 1960s; *p. 339:* Dene school children, Northwest Territory; *p. 341:* Inuit hunting seals on the ice. The Inuit and their way of life, as observed by Frobisher's men on Baffin Island in 1576–78. Engravings, after drawings made by Captain G. F. Lyon on Melville Peninsula in 1822, published in W. E. Parry, *Journal of a second voyage for the discovery of a North-west Passage*, London, 1824 (courtesy of the American Heritage Press); *p. 343:* Inuit meeting to discuss hamlet business, Cape Dorset, Northwest Territory (courtesy D. Mandin, NT government); *p. 346:* Chipewyan Indian houses. Smith Landing, Fort Smith; *p. 351:* Cree woman sewing; *p. 353:* Sally Karatak at Museum in traditional Inuit beaded dress. Yellowknife, Northwest Territory (courtesy Tessa Macintosh, NT government).

Native North American Languages: *p. 429:* Map of Native North American Language, Families, and Phyla. From *International Encyclopedia of Linguistics*, volume 3, edited by William Bright. Copyright 1992 by Oxford University Press, Inc. Reprinted by permission; *p. 431:* Map of Athabascan migrations from the sub-Arctic to the Southwest (courtesy of Oxford University Press); *p. 434:* Examples of Plains sign language; *p. 436:* Nootka text (courtesy of Yale University); *p.444:* Cherokee syllabary (mistakenly called "Alphabet") from *Beginning Cherokee*, by Ruth Bradley Holmes and Betty Sharp Smith, 2d ed. Norman: University of Oklahoma Press, 1977; *p. 445:* Example of Cherokee in Sequoyah's syllabary, in phonetic transcription, and in translation. From *Beginning Cherokee*, by Ruth Bradley Holmes and Betty Sharp Smith, 2d ed. Norman: University of Oklahoma Press, 1977; *p. 446.* The Inuit people of the Arctic try to preserve their language by providing reading material in Inuit for their young people (courtesy of Inuit Broadcasting Corporation).

Law and Legislation: *p. 451:* Cherokee delegation to Washington, D.C. in 1866. L. to R.: John Rollin Ridge, Saladin Watie, Richard Field, E. C. Boudinot & W. P. Adair (courtesy of the Archives & Manuscripts Division of the Oklahoma Historical Society); *p. 452:* Five Sauk and Fox and three Kansa flank the U.S. Commissioner of Indian Affairs; *p. 453:* Choctaw Council House, Tuskahoma, Oklahoma (photo by Oklahoma Tourism); *p. 457:* Shoshoni-Bannock Tribal Court on the Fort Hall Reservation, Idaho (courtesy of Bureau of Indian Affairs); *p. 461:* Acting Chief Justice Homer Bluehouse, left, swears in the new Navajo Nation Supreme Court chief Justice Robert Yazzie, at a ceremony held at Navajo Education Center (courtesy of Paul Natonabah, *Navajo Times*); *p.467:* Charles A. Bates, allotment officer on the Pine Ridge Reservation, with American Horse and an interpreter, about 1907. On many reservations, allotment violated treaty provisions made a generation earlier, but the Supreme Court upheld Congressional authority to allot Indian lands without tribal consent (courtesy of Denver Public Library, Western History Department); *p. 468:* The second Fort Laramie Treaty in 1868 brought an end to one Plains Indian war and set the stage for another. Here, Sioux leaders meet with the United States delegation, which includes Generals Harney, Sherman, and Terry, and, at the far right holding a ledger, Commissioner of Indian Affairs Taylor (courtesy of Anthropological Archives, Smithsonian); *p. 469:* Puyallup fishing rights protest covered by media,Tacoma, Washington, 1970 (courtesy of Stephen Lehmer); *p. 472:* "Wampum" in the collection of the Vatican, Rome, recording a 1610 agreement with the Mikmaq (Micmac), made in present-day Nova Scotia; *p. 473:* Title page of one of the first Indian treaties to be printed in English, the 1677 Articles of Peace with the Pamunkey and Nottoway of the eastern shore of Virginia; *p. 475:* Exchange of gifts, such as Indian furs and skins, and European medals, marked each stage of negotiations under Six Nations' diplomatic protocols, as depicted in this 1770 engraving. In the background are two symbols of unity: the Covenant Chain and Great Tree of Peace (courtesy of the John Carter Brown Library); *p. 481:* "Annuities" being paid to Lake Superior Chippewa in Wisconsin, about 1871. After the Civil War, payments for land under individual treaties were gradually converted into a centralized social-welfare program, through which Indians received services under federal supervision instead of cash (courtesy of Charles A. Zimmerman); *p. 484:* The 1960s and 1970s were a time of Indian protest and, as the courts began to restore tribal treaty rights, some communities challenged Native claims. For example, in the city of Tacoma, in Pierce County, Washington, pressure began to build, encouraging fish and game authorities to confiscate fishing nets, contesting acknowledgment of tribal lands (courtesy of Stephen Lehmer); *p.488:* Sergeants Red Tomahawk and Eagle Man, Standing Rock Agency Police (courtesy of Denver Public Library, Western History Department); *p. 490:* Navajo Tribal Court trial in process (courtesy of the Bureau of Indian Affairs, Public Affairs); *p. 491:* Navajo Nation Supreme Court associate justice Homer Bluehouse swears in new Navajo police officers during a police cadets graduation ceremony at the Law Enforcement Training and Academy facilities at Toyei, Arizona (courtesy of Paul Natonabah, *Navajo Times*); *p. 511:* Women mending birch bark canoe at North West Angle of Lake of the Woods, Ontario (circa 1872); *p. 513:* The high projecting bow and stern of the Pacific Coast Kwakiutl canoe were often elaborately painted and carved with figures representing legendary ancestors; *p. 516:* Inuit woman on a snowmobile; *p. 520:* Tabitha Bernard makes traditional Dene bannock at her tent camp, Fort McPherson, Northwest Territory, 1988 (courtesy of Tessa Macintosh, NT government); *p. 527:* Lillian Shamee and son Clifford in amonti (baby carrying parka) Eskimo Point. Northwest Territory, 1988 (courtesy of Tessa Macintosh, NT government); *p. 529:* Annie Kilabuk and Iga Ishulutak at "Qittaq Qamarq," women's sewing group, stretching sealskin in a village in Northwest Territory, 1990 (courtesy of Tessa Macintosh, NT government).

Administration: *p. 538:* "The Start NO 150," just after the signal, wagons west of the Chilocco School grounds beginning to roll, opening of the Cherokee Outlet, September 16, 1893 (courtesy Oklahoma Historical Society); *p. 539:* The boarding schools for Indians sought the complete transformation of the Indians to white ways. These scenes from the school at Genoa, Nebraska, circa1910, shows a school band; *p. 542:* Department of Interior Organization Chart; *p. 545:* Bureau of Indian Affairs organization chart; *p. 546:* Wayland Large works on spreadsheets at BIA office while on co-op work assignment (courtesy of Mike McClure); *p. 551:* Department of Indian and Northern Affairs organization chart.

Activism: *p. 566:* The Quaker City banquet of the Society of American Indians. Hotel Walton, February 14, 1914 ; *p. 568:* Tuscarora protest against the New York State Power Authority's condemnation of their lands for a reservoir 1958 (courtesy of the Buffalo and Erie County Historical Society); *p. 569:* Tuscarora protesting reservoir (courtesy of the Buffalo and Erie County Historical Society); *p. 570:* Indian children playing on Alcatraz Island during the 1969–71 occupation. Note burnt out structure (previously warden's house) (photographer unknown); *p. 571:* During the 1969–71 Indian occupation of Alcatraz Island, Indian men and women learned bead work and other cultural skills (photographer unknown); *p. 577:* Canadian Natives protesting before Parliament for land rights and aboriginal rights within the Canadian Constitution (courtesy of Canapress Photo Service).

Environment: *p.596:* Wyoming Indian Elementary School students show the radio collars they decorated. The collars were put on antelope that were released on the Wind River Indian Reservation. Students, from left, are Tyson Smith, Jude Hass, Kirsten Collins, Lawrence McCabe, Daisy Felter and Rosa Hungary (courtesy of Mike McClure); *p. 597:* Wyoming Indian Junior High School students tour National Weather Service facility at Lander, Wyoming (courtesy of Mike McClure).

Urbanization and Non-Reservation Populations: *p. 607:* Urban Indians drumming in downtown Los Angeles (courtesy of Glenda Ahhaitty); *p. 610:* Los Angeles urban Indian Center; *p. 611:* Indian college students from the American Indian Studies program University of California, Los Angeles sell fry bread on Bruin walk; *p. 612–13:* Non-recognized Indian communities (courtesy of Duane Champagne); *p. 617:* First annual Vancouver, British Columbia War Dance Ceremonies, 1970 (courtesy of Stephen Lehmer).

Religion: *p. 634:* Ceremonies at the death of a chief or of priests. Drawing by Le Moyne, engraving from T. de Bry, *America*, Part II, 1591, plate XL (courtesy of American Heritage Press); *p. 637:* Native leaders often consulted shamans on important issues. Drawing by Le Moyne, engraving from T. de Bry, *America*, Part II, 1591, plate XI (courtesy of American Heritage Press); *p. 642:* The humpback flute player Kokopelli, with horned serpent (Utah) (courtesy of Linda Connor); *p. 644:* Arapaho Ghost Dance (courtesy of Smithsonian Institution); *p. 647:* Dressing for ceremonies. Blackfoot (courtesy of National Museum of the American Indian, Smithsonian Institution); *p. 650:* In contemporary times many Indians continue to participate in traditional ceremonies (courtesy of Paul Natonabah, *Navajo Times*); *p. 652:*

Henry Crow Dog praying in a sweat lodge, 1969 (courtesy of Richard Erdoes); *p. 653:* Grey Squirrel, a medicine man, giving herbs to Rainbow Stevens, a patient, seated on sand painting, 1963 (courtesy of National Museum of the American Indian, Smithsonian Institution); *p. 656:* Hopi Anak'china Dance; clown antics, Oraibi, Arizona, 1912 (courtesy of National Museum of the American Indian, Smithsonian Institution); *p. 657:* Sun Dance piercing at Crow Dog's place, 1971 (courtesy of Richard Erdoes); *p. 659:* St. Joseph Roman Catholic Mission, Laguna Pueblo, founded 1699 (courtesy of Howard Meredith); *p. 660:* Good Shepherd Episcopal Mission, Fort Defiance, Navajo Nation (courtesy of Howard Meredith); *p. 665:* The Reverend Bob Pinezaddleby (Kiowa) minister of the Mount Scott United Methodist Comanche Mission (courtesy of Howard Meredith); *p. 666:* The Right Reverend Stephen Plummer (Navajo) bishop of the Episcopal Diocese of the Navajo Nation (courtesy of Howard Meredith); *p. 667:* Dick West (Cheyenne), long-time head of the Indian Art Department of Bacone College, an agency of the American Baptist Church (courtesy of Howard Meredith); *p. 669:* Apache Crown Dance, White Mountain Apache Reservation, Whiteriver, Arizona, 1971. This traditional puberty rite is performed to this day, blessing the participant with a prosperous future (courtesy of Stephen Lehmer); *p. 672:* Baptism of Paiute Indians (courtesy of Smithsonian Institution); *p. 673:* Native American revitalization movements; *p. 674:* John Wilson introduced many elements of Christianity into the peyote religion. His version is the generally recognized version of the religion today (courtesy of the Museum of the American Indian, Smithsonian Institution); *p. 675:* Quanah Parker, Comanche leader who greatly facilitated the spread of the peyote religion among the Plains Indians during the 1880s and 1890s ; *p. 678:* Revival of the Ghost Dance, May 1974 (courtesy of Richard Erdoes); *p. 682:* Blessing Way purification ceremony, 1964. The medicine man is Allie Brown (courtesy of National Museum of the American Indian, Smithsonian Insitution).

Arts: *p. 694:* Petroglyph, Galisteo, New Mexico, 1991 (courtesy of Linda Connor); *p 695:* New Mexico petroglyph (courtesy of Linda Connor); *p. 696:* Carving of Hopi Kachina (courtesy of Owen Seumptewa); *p. 697:* Decorative elements of Hopi architecture. Detail from photo by Owen Seumptewa; *p. 700:* Indian artist Norval Morrisseau at work; *p. 701:* Watercolor of Southwestern Indian children by Earl Sisto for 1992 UCLA Indian Child Welfare Conference; *p. 703:* Excerpt from Creek Gar Dance with leader-chorus response and alternation of words and vocables (courtesy of Charlotte Heth); *p. 704:* Plains rawhide drum, played by several men simultaneously (courtesy of Charlotte Heth); *p. 705:* Peter Garcia, drummer, at San Juan Pueblo Yellow Corn Dance (courtesy of Charlotte Heth); *p. 706:* Cloud Dance, San Juan Pueblo. Men are playing gourd rattles (courtesy of Charlotte Heth); *p. 707:* Northern Plains Traditional dancer at Red Earth, Oklahoma City, Oklahoma (courtesy of Charlotte Heth); *p. 708:* Cheyenne children playing hand games at Red Earth, Oklahoma City, Oklahoma (courtesy of Charlotte Heth); *p. 713:* Excerpt from Forty-nine Dance song, "One-Eyed Ford," with English words and vocables (courtesy of Charlotte Heth); *p. 714:* Kwakiutl totem poles at Alert Bay (circa 1910); *p. 715:* Crow beaded mirror with case, Montana, circa 1880 (courtesy of the Philbrook Art Center, Tulsa, Oklahoma); *p. 716:* Navajo sandpainting rug woven by Altnabah. Early twentieth century. Museum of Northern Arizona, Object Number E3716 (courtesy of Museum of Northern Arizona, Route 4, Box 720, Flagstaff, AZ 86001, photo by Anthony Richardson); *p. 717:* Masked dancers participating in a Kwakiutl winter ceremonial; *p. 718:* Maria Martinez, potter of San Ildefonso Puelo, New Mexico and her blackware designs, 1940s (courtesy of the Museum of New Mexico—Palace of the Governors); *p. 719: Agents of Oppression.* Diego Romero, contemporary artist/potter. This bowl combines a blend of traditional Membres (A.D. 500–1100) pottery and a concern for contemporary Native American issues. Romero is a graduate of the Institute of American Indian Arts, Santa Fe and received the Master of Fine Arts degree from University of California, Los Angeles (courtesy of Diego Romero); *p. 721:* Nora Naranjo-Morse *Pearlene Teaching Her Cousins Poker*, 1987. Mixed Media (courtesy of Nora Naranjo-Morse); *p. 722:* Jolen Rickard, *Self-Portrait–Three Sisters*, 1988 (courtesy of Jolene Rickard); *p. 723:* Arrowheads and flints; *p. 725:* Reconstructed Iroquois longhouse in Brantford, Ontario. A False Face Society mask grimaces in the foreground; *p. 726:* A turn-of-the century artist paints traditional Haida patterns on a hat of woven spruce root; *p. 727:* Modern-day British Columbia artist Vicor Mowatt works traditional Haida patterns into a cedar box; *p. 729: Coyote and the Disciples of Vine Deloria*, Diego Romero. Here the disciples of Vine Deloria are driving over the bones of their ancestors while Coyote (the trickster) is leading them astray. Romero was first introduced to Indian issues by reading Vine Deloria's books (courtesy of Diego Romero); *p. 730: Crow Summer Night Tipi*, from painting by Kevin Red Star (courtesy of Kevin Red Star), whose art is exclusively represented by Merida Gallery, Inc., Red Lodge, Montana.

Native American Literature: *p. 754:* Early American Indians often recorded histories and stories on rocks and cliffs at sacred sites. The above petroglyphs were found in San Gabriel Canyon in Southern California (courtesy of the Los Angeles Public Library); *p. 755:* Stories and legends were often re-enacted through dances. Here the American Indian Dance Theatre per forms an Eagle Dance (courtesy of Hanay Geiogamah); *p. 756:* Northwest Coast dancers embodied spiritual beings and reenacted creation histories and traditional stories (courtesy of Hanay Geiogamah).

Media: *p. 764:* Fancy Shawl Dance: A highlight of the American Indian Dance Theatre performance is the Women's Fancy Shawl Dance in which female members of the company exhibit their grace and virtuousity as they spin around the stage, displaying intricate dance steps while twirling colorful shawls to the beat of the drum (courtesy of Hanay Geiogamah); *p. 765:* Southern Men's Traditional Dance. Morgan Tosee, a member of the Comanche tribe of Oklahoma, is a champion Southern Men's Traditional dancer with the American Indian Dance Theatre (courtesy of Hanay Geiogamah); *p. 767* (Left to right) Chester Mahooty, an elder of the Zuni Tribe of New Mexico, Morgan Tosee, a member of the Comanche tribe of Oklahoma, and Ramona Roach, a Navajo tribe member from New Mexico, are part of the cast of all-Native American dancers and musicians with the American Indian Dance Theatre (courtesy of Hanay Geiogamah); *p. 769:* Plains Indians who played roles in Hollywood movies take a break on the rollercoaster ride, Long Beach, California, 1930s (courtesy of the Los Angeles Public Library); *p. 770:* Urban Indian picketing Warner Brothers in the making of the movie *They Died With Their Boots On* (courtesy of the Los Angeles Public Library); *p. 771:* Will Sampson (Creek) and Jack Nicholson starred in the hit movie *One Flew over the Cuckoo's Nest* (1975) Copyright 1975 The Saul Zaentz Company. All rights reserved; *p. 775:* A scene from the play *Dry Lips Oughta Move to Kapuskasing* (1989) by Tomson Highway. Native Earth Performing Arts, Inc., Toronto, Ontario, Canada.

Health: *p. 802: Mode of treating the sick.* Drawing by Le Moyne, engraving from T. de Bry, *America,* Part 2 (courtesy of American Heritage Press.; *p. 803 : Medicine Lodge.* The patient lies in a Plains tipi. The Indian at left shakes a gourd rattle. The central figure, apparently the medicine man, holds a pipe in his right hand and the patient's wrist in the other, as if taking the pulse. A drummer sits at right. From "Life of an Indian," *Harper's Illustrated Weekly,* June 20, 1868. From *American Indian Medicine,* by Virgil J. Vogel. Copyright 1970 by University of Oklahoma Press; *p. 805:* Medicine man ministering to a patient. Notice the bowl and pestle for mixing medicines. The medicine man is shaking a gourd rattle and may be singing a medicine song. From Schoolcraft's *History, Condition and Prospect of the Indian Tribes* . . . . From *American Indian Medicine,* by Virgil J. Vogel. Copyright 1970, University of Oklahoma Press; *p. 807:* May apple (Podophyllum peltatum L.) American Indian purgative. From *American Indian Medicine,* by Virgil J. Vogel. Copyright 1970, University of Oklahoma Press.; *p. 809:* Flowering dogwood (Cornus florida L.) American Indian febrifuge (fever reducing agent). From *American Indian Medicine,* by Virgil J. Vogel. Copyright 1970. University of Oklahoma Press; *p. 815:* Entrance to medical buildings at Crow Agency, Montana (courtesy of Theresa Friedor Mock); *p. 817:* Organizational chart for Indian Health Service; *p. 822:* Canadian and status Indian live birth rates; *p. 823:* Canadian and status Indian mortality rates, 1978–86; *p. 824:* Canadian and status Indian age-and sex-adjusted mortality rates; *p. 826:* National neonatal post-neonatal and infant mortality rates; *p. 834:* Indian Medicines.

Education: *p. 856:* Group of Omaha boys in cadet uniforms, Carlisle Indian School, Pennsylvania, 1880 (courtesy of the National Archives Trust Fund Board); *p. 859:* Morning Rae Ferris on "Respect" (courtesy of Mike McClure); *p. 861:* Sherice Guina, Lori Martel, Sami Dresser and Michaelyn Tillman are shown dissecting a heart while learning anatomy in Rick Henry-Ford's fourth grade classroom (courtesy of Mike McClure); *p. 862:* Indian student choosing to study fancy dance (courtesy of Mike McClure); *p. 864:* Andi LeBeau and Kirsten Martel enjoy a moment during graduation, 1990 (courtesy of Mike McClure); *p. 866:* American Indian/Alaska Native dropout rates from various studies; *p. 867:* National education goals for American Indians and Alaska Natives; *p. 868:* A Strategic Framework for Improving Schools; *p. 870:* Indian students dancing at annual Medicine Ways Conference held at University of California, Riverside (courtesy Clifford Trafzer); *p. 871:* Darryl Wilson, Indian author, lecturing to Indian students at the University of California, Davis (courtesy of Clifford Trafzer); *p. 872:* Indian student drum at annual UCLA American Indian Student Association powwow; *p. 873:* Indian students from UCLA American Indian Studies Center taking a break from their studies, relaxing on a California beach; *p. 875:* U.S. tribal colleges by state and year established; *p. 879:* UCLA American Indian students participated in the first annual Indian Child Welfare Conference, August 1990; *p. 881:* Inuit teacher's aide; *p. 885:* More than 75 percent of Canada's Native bands now administer all or parts of their education program; *p. 886:* Native child working on grammar; *p. 887:* Preserving Native languages is an essential part of Indian education today (public domain); *p. 888:* Archaeological diggings at sight in Ontario (photo by the Woodland Indian Cultural Educational Center); *p. 889:* Insarvik School, Repulse Bay (Inuit), 1992 (courtesy of Tessa Macintosh, NT government); *p. 891:* Dene jigging. Midway Lake Gwichin Music Festival. Fort McPherson, Northwest Territory, 1988 (courtesy of NT government and photo by B. Sekulich).

Economy: *p. 916:* Bringing in wild animals, fish, and other stores. Drawing by Le Moyne, engraving from T. de Bry, *America*, Part II, 1591, plate XXIII (courtesy of American Heritage Press); *p. 918:* How They Till the Soil and Plant. Drawing by Le Moyne, engraving from T. de Bry, *America*, Part II, 1591, plate XXIII (courtesy of American Heritage Press); *p. 922:* A young Navajo welder puts his skills and knowledge to the test at a Transwestern Pipeline Co. training session (courtesy of Paul Natonabah, *Navajo Times*); *p. 923:* Bernice Bigman, auditor, makes the final audit of the finished electrical harness before shipment to Parkard Electric Division of General Motor Corporation (courtesy of Paul Natonabah, *Navajo Times*); *p. 928:* School board members tour construction site at new high school building (courtesy of Mike McClure); *p. 931:* A logging truck hauls ponderosa pine into the logging yard for lumber process at Navajo Forest Products Industry at Navajo, New Mexico (courtesy Paul Natonabah, Navajo Times); *p. 934:* Overall view of electronic manufacturing on the electrical harness assembly line inside Chiih To Industrious Incorporated at Sanders, Arizona (courtesy of Paul Natonabah, *Navajo Times*); *p. 938:* Percentage in 1970 and 1980 of Unemployed Blacks, Whites, and American Indians and Alaska Natives Aged 16 and Over (reprinted from C. Matthew Snipp, *American Indians: The First of This Land*, Copyright 1989 Russell Sage Foundation. Used with permission of the Russell Sage Foundation); *p. 939:* Percentage in 1970 and 1980 of Blacks, Whites, and American Indians and Alaska Natives Aged 16 and Over Not in the Labor Force (reprinted from C. Matthew Snipp, *American Indians: The First of This Land*, Copyright 1989 Russell Sage Foundation. Used with permission of the Russell Sage Foundation); *p. 940:* Percent Distribution of Time at Work and Weeks of Unemployment in 1979 for American Indians and Alaska Natives Aged 16 and Over (reprinted from C. Matthew Snipp, *American Indians: The First of This Land*, Copyright 1989 Russell Sage Foundation. Used with permission of the Russell Sage Foundation); *p. 941:* Percent Distribution of the Civilian Labor Force Status of American Indians and Alaska Natives Aged 16 and Over, by Education and Sex, 1980 (reprinted from C. Matthew Snipp, *American Indians: The First of This Land*, Copyright 1989 Russell Sage Foundation. Used with permission of the Russell Sage Foundation); *p. 942:* Percent Distribution of the Labor Force Participation of American Indians Aged 16 and Over Residing on the 16 Largest Reservations in 1980 (reprinted from C. Matthew Snipp, *American Indians: The First of This Land*, Copyright 1989 Russell Sage Foundation. Used with permission of the Russell Sage Foundation); *p. 943:* Percent Distribution of Blacks, Whites, and American Indians Aged 16 and Over Employed in Manual and Nonmanual Occupations, 1970–80 (reprinted from C. Matthew Snipp, *American Indians: The First of This Land*, Copyright 1989 Russell Sage Foundation. Used with permission of the Russell Sage Foundation); *p. 944:* Percent Distribution of Employed Blacks, Whites, and American Indians and Alaska Natives in Selected Occupations, 1980 (reprinted from C. Matthew Snipp, *American Indians: The First of This Land*, Copyright 1989 Russell Sage Foundation. Used with permission of the Russell Sage Foundation); *p. 945* Percent Distribution of Class of Worker of Employed Blacks, Whites, and American Indians, 1970–80 (reprinted from C. Matthew Snipp, *American Indians: The First of This Land*, Copyright 1989 Russell Sage Foundation. Used with permission of the Russell Sage Foundation); *p. 951:* During the1970s many Native American social service center emerged in large cities such as the Los Angeles American Indian Center, one depicted here; *p. 955:* Open house at graphic arts training program, Southern California Indian Center, Los Angeles, California, 1986 (courtesy of Mike Burgess); *p. 956 :* Visiting dignitaries at dedication of new Poarch Creek Band Tribal Center, April 1987 (courtesy of Anthony Paredes); *p. 960* Madeline Providence (Dene) at cooking fire and smoking dry fish. Kakisa Lake, 1984 (courtesy of Tessa Macintosh, NT government); *p. 962:* Noel Nadli checking the fish nets. Point Providence, 1984 (courtesy of Tessa Macintosh, NT government); *p. 965:* Thebacha College Trades Complex, Fort Smith, 1988 (courtesy of Tessa Macintosh); *p. 966:* Special programs have been designed to build a modern education system around the values of traditional Indian culture; *p. 973:* The Nootka Indians of the Pacific coast used the two-pronged harpoon for hunting seals; *p. 974:* Fishing camp at Restigouche, New Brunswick (circa 1920); *p. 978:* Indian from Golden Lake Reserve, Ontario, building a canoe; *p. 981:* Cree fisherman mending a fishing net; *p. 982:* Indian artist Arthur Shilling at work.

Prominent Native North Americans: *p. 999:* Sherman Alexie; *p. 999:* Paula Gunn Allen (photo by Tama Rothchild); *p. 1001:* Will Antell; *p. 1002:* Paul Apadoca; *p. 1005:* Carolyn Attneave; *p. 1006:* Louis W. Ballard; *p. 1007:* Dennis Banks (photo by Alice Lambert); *p. 1010:* Patricia Benedict-Phillips; *p. 1011:* Robert L. Bennett; *p. 1013:* Black Kettle (courtesy of the Colorado Historical Society); *p. 1015:* George Blue Spruce, Jr.; *p. 1016:* Gertrude Bonnin (courtesy of Bruguier Collection); *p. 1021:* Joseph Bruchac (photo by Martin Benjamin); *p. 1022:* Leonard Bruguier; *p. 1025:* Captain Jack; *p. 1028:* Edward D. Castillo; *p. 1028:* John Castillo; *p. 1029:* Duane Champagne; *p. 1030:* Dean Chavers; *p. 1032:* Carter Blue Clark; *p. 1035:* Elizabeth Cook-Lynn (photo by Carolyn Forbes); *p. 1038:* Crowfoot; *p. 1041:* Ada Deer; *p. 1046:* Olive Patricia Dickason; *p. 1049:* Dull Knife; *p. 1051:* Walter

Echo-Hawk (photo by Thorny Lieberman); *p. 1052:* John Echohawk (photo by Thorny Lieberman); *p. 1054:* William R. Ernisse; *p. 1055:* Don Fixico; *p. 1057:* Jack Forbes (photo by Carolyn L. Forbes); *p. 1058:* Billy Frank, Jr.; *p. 1059:* Gall (courtesy of the Colorado Historical Society); *p. 1060:* Hanay Geiogamah; *p. 1062:* Forest J. Gerrard; *p. 1063:* Geronimo (courtesy of National Museum of the American Indian); *p. 1063:* Tim Giago; *p. 1068:* Joy Harjo (photo by Robyn Stoutenburg); *p. 1070:* Ira Hamilton Hayes; *p. 1071:* William L. Hensley; *p. 1072:* Charlotte W. Heth; *p. 1074:* Norbert S. Hill, Jr.; *p. 1075:* George P. Horse Capture; *p. 1079:* Ted Jojola; *p. 1080:* Joseph; *p. 1082:* William W. Keeler (courtesy of Corporate Archives, Phillips Petroleum); *p. 1084:* Keokuk (courtesy of Smithsonian Institution); *p. 1084:* K. Kirke Kickingbird; *p. 1085:* Clara Sue Kidwell; *p. 1089:* Stella Leach (courtesy of Stephen Lehmer); *p. 1091:* Little Crow (courtesy Nebraska State Historical Society); *p. 1096:* Lone Wolf (courtesy of Amon Carter Museum, Fort Worth, Texas); *p. 1099:* Wilma P. Mankiller (courtesy of Cherokee Nation Communications); *p. 1100:* Manuelito (courtesy of the Colorado Historical Society); *p. 1101:* Leonard Stephen Marchand; *p. 1108:* Cheryl Metoyer-Duran; *p. 1108:* Billy Mills; *p. 1112:* R. Carlos Nakai (photo by John Running); *p. 1114:* Natchez (courtesy of the Colorado Historical Society); *p. 1116:* Grayson Noley; *p. 1117:* Richard Oakes (courtesy of Stephen Lehmer); *p. 1119:* V. Paul Ojibway; *p. 1121:* Earl Old Person; *p. 1126:* Elizabeth Anne Parent; *p. 1126:* Ely S. Parker; *p. 1127:* Quanah Parker and his wife; *p. 1128:* William Lewis Paul, Sr. (courtesy of the Alaska Historical Library); *p. 1132:* F. Browning Pipestem; *p. 1136:* Poundmaker ; *p. 1140:* Red Cloud; *p. 1142:* Kevin Red Star; *p. 1144:* John Rollin Ridge; *p. 1145:* Gary Robinson; *p. 1148:* William Penn Adair Rogers; *p. 1148:* Roman Nose (courtesy of the Kansas State Historical Society); *p. 1150:* John Ross; *p. 1152:* Velma S. Salabiye; *p. 1153:* Will Sampson (courtesy of The Saul Zaentz Company. All Rights Reserved.) ; *p. 1154:* Joe S. Sando (photo by Marcie Keegan); *p. 1155:* Satank (courtesy of Amon Carter Museum, Fort Worth, Texas); *p. 1157:* Bert D. Seabourn; *p. 1162:* Allogan Slagle; *p. 1166:* Chris Spotted Eagle (photo by Allen Beaulieu); *p. 1166:* Spotted Tail (courtesy of the Nebraska Historical Society); *p. 1167:* Steven Stallings; *p. 1170:* Rennard James Strickland; *p. 1173:* Mary TallMountain; *p. 1176:* Russell Thornton; *p. 1177:* John W. Tippeconic II; *p. 1179:* Clifford Trafzer; *p. 1180:* John Trudell (courtesy of Stephen Lehmer); *p. 1184:* Washakie (courtesy of the Smithsonian Institution); *p. 1186:* Laura Weber; *p. 1188:* Susan Williams; *p. 1190:* Sarah Winnemucca (courtesy of the Nevada State Historical Society); *p. 1192:* Rosita Worl (photo by David Perry); *p. 1193:* Wovoka (courtesy of the Nevada State Historical Society); *p. 1194:* Peterson Zah (courtesy of Paul Natonabah, *Navajo Times*).

Index

A

B

C

D

E

F

G

H

I

J

K

L

M

N

O

P

Q

R

S

T

U

V

W

Y

Z

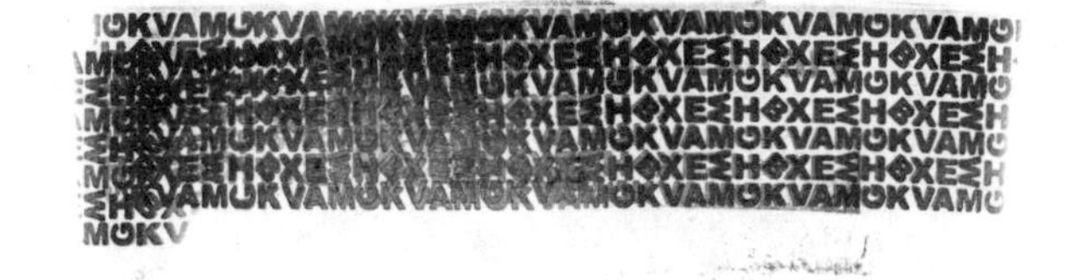